SPECIAL EDITION
USING
Macromedia
Studio 8

Sean Nicholson

Kristin Henry

800 East 96th Street
Indianapolis, Indiana 46240

CONTENTS AT A GLANCE

SPECIAL EDITION USING MACROMEDIA STUDIO 8

Copyright © 2006 by Que Publishing

International Standard Book Number: 0-789-73385-4

Library of Congress Catalog Card Number: 2004115842

Printed in the United States of America

First Printing: November 2005

08   07   06   05   4   3   2   1

Trademarks

Warning and Disclaimer

Bulk Sales

Que Publishing offers excellent discounts on this book when ordered in quantity for bulk purchases or special sales. For more information, please contact

U.S. Corporate and Government Sales
1-800-382-3419
corpsales@pearsontechgroup.com

For sales outside of the U.S., please contact

International Sales
international@pearsoned.com

Senior Acquisitions Editor
Linda Bump Harrison

Development Editors
Jon Steever
Ginny Bess

Managing Editor
Charlotte Clapp

Project Editor
Seth Kerney

Copy Editor
Margo Catts

Indexer
Heather McNeill

Proofreader
Jessica McCarty

Technical Editor
M.D. Dundon

Publishing Coordinator
Vanessa Evans

Multimedia Developer
Dan Scherf

Interior Designer
Anne Jones

Cover Designer
Anne Jones

Page Layout
Nonie Ratcliff
Julie Parks

CONTENTS

About the Author

Sean Nicholson is an intranet administrator for Williams Lea, a corporate information solutions provider to the legal and financial industry. Sean is currently designing and implementing intranet-based solutions for the largest law firm in Kansas City and is leading Williams Lea's Knowledge Management initiative for the firm. In addition, Sean owns a private consulting company and offers contract and consulting work on database and web development for organizations and individuals.

Prior to his move to Williams Lea, Sean served as the network administrator and web developer for the Career Services Center at the University of Missouri—Kansas City. At UMKC, he developed departmental websites and websites for nonprofit organizations, and led projects including the creation of UMKC's CareerExec Employment Database and their online Virtual Career Fair.

Sean has a juris doctorate from UMKC, but opted to follow a career path in technology rather than law. Sean has been working with computers since the day a shiny new Apple II computer showed up at his house when he was 12 (a long time ago). Sean began building web pages with simple text editors and has been developing sites in Dreamweaver since version 1.0 was released. In addition, he has used DrumBeat, UltraDev, and now Dreamweaver extensively in both web-based and intranet-based projects.

Sean's technical publications include *Discover Excel 97*, *Teach Yourself Outlook 98 in 24 Hours*, *Inside Dreamweaver UltraDev 4*, *Dreamweaver MX Magic*, and *Dreamweaver MX 2004 and Databases*. He has also written several legal articles ranging in topics from Canadian water rights to the protection of historic artifacts lost at sea.

During his free time, Sean can be found traveling with his family or riding his motorcycle to biker events nationwide.

About the Contributing Author

Kristin Henry is president and lead developer at GalaxyGoo (www.galaxygoo.org), a nonprofit organization dedicated to increasing science literacy. She specializes in developing educational applications and interactive visualizations of scientific data with Flash. Henry has presented at both industry and academic conferences including FlashForward and the Gordon Research Conference on Visualization in Science and Education.

DEDICATION

For Deborah—my best friend and soulmate. Words can't express how much I appreciate your love, encouragement, and patience.

—Sean

ACKNOWLEDGMENTS

Huge thanks go out to:

Kristin Henry for jumping feet first into her first writing project and surviving the craziness; M.D. Dundon for finding all the technical issues and going above and beyond to offer her expertise; Margo Catts, Ginny Bess, Jon Steever, Seth Kerney, Dan Knott, and David Fender for their editing talent and helpful suggestions. Thanks team!

A special thanks goes to my editor and friend, Linda Bump Harrison. This project was full of twists and turns and, at times, we both wanted to pull our hair out (or pull someone else's hair out <G>). Thanks for putting the team together, keeping us on track, and helping us create a great book. You're THE BEST!

WE WANT TO HEAR FROM YOU!

As the reader of this book, *you* are our most important critic and commentator. We value your opinion and want to know what we're doing right, what we could do better, what areas you'd like to see us publish in, and any other words of wisdom you're willing to pass our way.

You can email or write me directly to let me know what you did or didn't like about this book—as well as what we can do to make our books stronger.

Please note that I cannot help you with technical problems related to the topic of this book, and that due to the high volume of mail I receive, I might not be able to reply to every message.

When you write, please be sure to include this book's title and author as well as your name and phone or email address. I will carefully review your comments and share them with the author and editors who worked on the book.

Email: graphics@quepublishing.com

Mail: Mark Taber
Associate Publisher
Que Publishing
800 East 96th Street
Indianapolis, IN 46240 USA

READER SERVICES

For more information about this book or another Que title, visit our website at www.quepublishing.com. Type the ISBN (excluding hyphens) or the title of a book in the Search field to find the page you're looking for.

INTRODUCTION

In this introduction

Macromedia Studio 8 is the most recent version of a powerful product suite consisting of Fireworks 8, Flash 8, ColdFusion MX 7, Dreamweaver 8, and Contribute 3.

Fireworks 8 is the graphic-editing program that focuses primarily on creating content for the Web. Fireworks leads the industry in its capability to generate crisp, clean graphics that are compressed effectively for the Web.

Flash 8 is a powerful tool used to create rich media content and interactive web applications. When combined with the powerful Flash Player, developers can create entire websites and standalone rich media movies that can be viewed in any browser. Because the Flash Player already exists in the vast majority of web browsers installed today, developers can rest assured that their visitors will be able to view content without having to install additional plug-ins.

ColdFusion MX 7 is a web server application that enables you to connect your web pages to your database to display dynamically generated content.

Dreamweaver 8 is the leading web development application and can be used to create websites, intranet sites, extranet sites, and even CD-ROM–based interactive applications. In addition, using Dreamweaver's design and code views, you can easily develop the layout of your pages and code any server-side or client-side scripts.

Finally, Contribute 3 provides an easy-to-use authoring and editing tool that allows nearly anyone to manage website content without requiring any understanding of HTML.

Individually, these products are powerful tools that can be used to develop dynamic web applications, produce rich media content, and create colorful graphics. Together, however, the Macromedia Studio represents one of the most powerful web development tools on the market.

WHAT'S NEW IN STUDIO 8?

Some of the applications in Studio 8 have integrated new features. Although these are covered in more depth in the coming chapters, here is a brief overview of what new features to keep an eye out for:

Fireworks's new features include

- New Image Editing panel
- New Auto Shape Properties panel
- New Special Characters panel
- New symbol libraries
- Additional default styles
- CSS-based pop-up menus
- New blend modes
- Enhanced slicing capabilities

Flash's new features include

- Script Assist mode
- Object drawing model
- Improved panel management
- Higher-quality video codec
- Built-in filter effects
- FlashType font rendering engine
- Improved text tool
- Enhanced stroke properties
- Advanced gradient control

ColdFusion's new features include

- A brand new, Java-based engine and compiler
- Enhanced reporting tools
- Printer-friendly web content
- Improved charting and graphing features
- More powerful Verity search engine
- Mobile device communication via Event Gateways

Dreamweaver's new features include

- Enhanced support for Cascading Style Sheets
- Flash Video integration
- New Code View toolbar
- Improved site synchronization and WebDAV functionality
- File comparison integration
- Capability to save panel layouts
- The return of the Timelines panel

Contribute's new features include

- More than 200 sample web pages
- Image editing toolbar
- Enhanced video capability
- New approval system
- CSS style previews
- New Shared Assets panel
- FlashPaper 2.0

WHO SHOULD READ THIS BOOK?

If you're reading this section of the introduction, you may be sifting through the dozens of books available online or at your local bookstore, trying to determine which one will suit your needs. Let's look briefly at what this book focuses on, the instructional method used, and the results that can be expected, and this should give you an idea as to whether the book will meet your needs.

If you are a beginning developer who is interested in learning about each of the studio programs, then this book can help you gain a solid understanding of each application and its uses. Intermediate developers who have experience with applications similar to those included in the Studio suite will benefit as well from learning how the various suite programs can enhance their existing skill sets and reduce development time. Advanced developers will benefit from an understanding of how each of the applications integrates with the others. Although advanced Flash developers might understand the ins and outs of ActionScript, they might not know the best ways to integrate their Flash creations into a ColdFusion-based site or an intranet application developed in ASP.

With respect to the instructional method used, this book uses a writing style that is informal and relaxed. Learning how to use one new product, let alone five, can be a bit on the difficult side, so a little humor can go a long way in communicating the information. So, with respect to the various bad jokes and silly puns you'll find throughout the book, I apologize in advance <G>.

When you are finished reading the book, you should have a solid understanding of each of the applications and how to use their most common features. After you have completed the chapters and the exercises for each section, the book should also serve as an excellent reference tool for future projects.

HOW TO USE THIS BOOK

This book consists of six sections. The first section focuses on an introduction to the Studio suite as a whole and the other five are devoted to each of the five individual programs that make up the suite.

The first step toward using this book effectively is to read the chapters in Part I. These chapters familiarize you with the common elements that span the Studio applications and give details about additional software that might be helpful as you use the book.

After that, you can either read the book from front to back or choose the application you would like to focus on first. I would suggest the first approach because the flow of the book is similar to the workflow that is commonly encountered in projects where you are asked to diagram out a site, create the underlying graphics, develop rich media, and then pull it all together into a static or dynamic website. By reading the chapters in order, you get an understanding of not only what you can do with each individual program, but the workflow involved in developing a website from scratch and how each program can work with the others to accomplish the end result.

If, however, you choose to dive into a specific section, you'll be happy to know that you can complete each section and the accompanying exercise without having finished the prior sections. Any files that you need to complete a section exercise can be found on the companion website, so simply download the appropriate files and you're off to the races.

In addition, I will be maintaining additional reference information on the companion website for the book at website at http://www.xhorizon.com/retroscycles, so feel free to stop by and check those out.

CONVENTIONS USED IN THIS BOOK

Throughout the book, you are going to find text that is formatted in various ways to indicate code, new features, or information that you should pay special attention to.

Pay close attention to the use of italics throughout the text. Italicized words or phrases indicate the definition of a new phrase or term, so you might see a sentence such as "A *path* consists of one or more connected segments." Understanding the language of graphic, rich media, and web development is an important part of working with the Studio suite. Terms such as keyframes, server behaviors, slices, and snippets might not mean much to you now, but after you have completed the book they will have become part of your technical vocabulary.

Initial caps indicate words that appear in the user interface, such as menu items, dialog boxes, or commands. An example might be a sentence such as "Click the OK button to close the New CSS Style dialog box." Because New CSS Style is capitalized, you should be interacting with a box that is identified onscreen as "New CSS Style."

Any instances of code used in the book are formatted in a special font so they are easily identifiable. Instances of code in languages such as HTML, ColdFusion Markup Language (CFML), ActionScript, or JavaScript will look like this:

```
<p align="Right">Welcome To My Website</p>
```

Inside blocks of code, italicized words indicate actual code that you need to substitute with your own information. So, using the preceding example, you might see this:

```
<p align="Right">Welcome To Your Name's Site</p>
```

Throughout the book, specific naming conventions are used to clearly label specific objects. For instance, a text field might be labeled tfFirstName. If you are new to graphic, rich media, or web design and have not established programming conventions such as these, pay close attention to the way it is done in this book because it could help you understand the importance of following conventions.

In addition, when dealing with the code snippets provided in the book, it is very important the you pay *close* attention to the capitalization of your code. Certain languages such as JavaScript and VB.NET are case sensitive, so `varFirstName` and `VarFirstName` would reference totally different objects. Of all the requests for support with regard to the various books I have authored, capitalization is the most frequent issue.

Finally, be on the lookout for tips, cautions, notes, and cross-reference sections. Each one has a special indicator and can save you time and energy by helping you avoid pitfalls or pointing out additional resources. The sections can be identified as follows:

TIP

Tips contain insights and techniques that will help you use Studio MX more effectively.

NOTE

Notes contain extra information or alternative techniques for performing tasks that will enhance your current understanding of the topic.

CAUTION

Cautions warn you of potential "gotcha" issues.

GETTING STARTED WITH MACROMEDIA STUDIO 8

CHAPTER 1

GETTING READY TO ROLL—PLANNING AND CONFIGURING

In this chapter

PLANNING AND DESIGNING YOUR SITE

So, you have your first project in mind or maybe even a client or two lined up and you're ready to break out your new copy of Macromedia Studio and start building websites, right? But where do you start? Should you start creating tables, drawing images, or creating keyframes? If you want to set yourself up for success and avoid frustration and wasted time, the best place to start isn't necessarily with Studio, but with a good old-fashioned pencil and notepad.

When it comes to creating a website, a little preplanning can go a long way in determining the elements you need, the tools you'll require to create them, and the process involved to bring the project to completion. Rather than just tossing design ideas into the workspace, try answering a few questions that can guide you in the process, such as

- What kind of site am I looking to build?
- Who is my target audience? Is this for the Web or an intranet?
- What features and functionality will serve the audience?
- What type of content will be added to the pages? Static or dynamic?
- If dynamic, what database management system will be needed and what platform will be used?
- How many pages will the site require? What types of pages are they?
- Does a template for look and feel already exist?
- Is artwork already available for use? If not, do I know what layout would work best?
- Where will this site be hosted?
- Does the host offer the server functionality (such as databases, specific platforms, and so on) that I need?

CAUTION

> This is in no way an exhaustive list of questions that you should be discussing with your client, but a simple list of generic questions that can serve as a starting point for a conversation.

TIP

> Maintain a running list of questions and answers for each of your projects or clients. In addition, with each project that you complete, review the questions and answers and add any appropriate questions to a master question list that you use with each new client.

These questions, among many others, can be a starting point for putting together a project plan. This plan lays out the process of building the site and gets you started in thinking about the potential issues that might arise.

For instance, suppose that for the exercises in this book, you have been approached by a local motorcycle dealership who would like you to build a site that advertises their services, allows people to contact them, and also displays the various motorcycles that they have in stock. They have a logo that they use on their letterhead, but would like for you to create a new logo for use on the Web. After a little time talking with the client and planning, you have the following answers to your questions:

Q: What kind of site am I looking to build?

A: A small, 10–15 page site that is attractive, easy to navigate, and presents all the information the client has asked for.

Q: Who is my target audience? Is this for the Web or an intranet?

A: This is a website and the audience is potential customers in the client's local area who are researching motorcycles for purchase.

Q: What features and functionality will serve the audience?

A: The site should have a basic set of pages, including a home page, contact page, "about us" page with an employee slideshow, a page about services offered, and a list of motorcycles (and their details) for sale. Eventually, they would also like to add functionality for selling merchandise via eCommerce.

Q: What type of content will be added to the pages? Static or dynamic?

A: Because the client is asking for future capacity for eCommerce, it would be best to use pages that draw their content from a database. If the site is designed this way from the start, adding the appropriate tables and pages to accommodate eCommerce should be easier down the road. In addition, the information about the motorcycles in inventory can be stored in the database as well.

Q: If dynamic, what database management system (DBMS) will be needed and what platform will be used?

A: Because this will not begin as a high-traffic site and cost is an issue, Microsoft Access is suitable for the DBMS. If the site generates traffic beyond what Access is capable of handling, the site can then be upgraded to SQL Server.

Q: How many pages will the site require? What types of pages are they?

A: The site will require approximately 10 pages based on the ColdFusion platform.

Q: Does a template for look and feel already exist?

A: No. The client would like for you to provide the layout.

Q: Is artwork already available for use? If not, what layout would work best?

A: Artwork is not available, so the client would like you to create it for the site.

Q: Where will this site be hosted?

A: The client is a member of a local Chamber of Commerce and has arranged to have the site hosted there for a monthly fee.

Q: Does the host offer the server functionality (for example, databases, specific platforms, and so on) that I need?

A: Yes. After a discussion with the Chamber of Commerce, it was determined that the server is running ColdFusion Server on a Windows 2000 Server platform, so creating connections to an Access database poses no problems.

Armed with the answers to these questions, you are now ready to think about what tools you have at your disposal and what, if any, tools you need to acquire for the project.

CHOOSING YOUR TOOLS

Using the answers to the questions already outlined, the next step in the process is to determine what tools you need to produce the client's site.

From your conversation with the client, you know that they do not have a website already, so you need to plan the structure of the site and develop a layout. This process can be done with good old-fashioned pen and paper or by using some of the diagramming tools found in Fireworks 8.

After you have a basic layout developed, you need to create the underlying graphics that can be inserted into the pages. Using Fireworks, you can create the company's new logo and any navigation buttons that are needed for the site.

The client also mentioned that they would like to have an About Us page that has a slideshow of photos of the employees, facilities, and so forth. Using Flash, the slideshow can be created with an XML document that allows the client to easily update the slideshow if a new employee is hired, someone leaves the company, or a new facility is acquired.

Finally, because they hope to grow their inventory of motorcycles continually, the details about each motorcycle for sale will be stored in an Access database, which will be connected to their ColdFusion-based web pages. To accomplish this, we can use the Developer's edition of ColdFusion, along with Dreamweaver, to produce and test the dynamic pages.

You may have noticed that the project conveniently uses each of the programs included in the Macromedia Studio. As you progress through the chapters, you will get a better understanding of the role that each program plays in the project lifecycle and why the combination of the five programs makes the Studio suite so powerful.

STREAMLINING YOUR DEVELOPMENT

Now that you know what tools will be involved throughout the project, let's look at some elements you can design to streamline the development of the site and minimize the time it takes to complete the project.

The first reusable tool would be the site template. Developing a template for the page's layout not only decreases development time by allowing you to reuse the same template over and over, but it ensures that each page within the site uses the same basic elements and code.

As you will see later on, using a template makes it especially easy when you need to replace an image or object on every page within the site. Templates are covered in more depth in the Dreamweaver section of the book, but as you proceed, it's a good idea to have the concept of a reusable template on your mind.

Another reusable element that you can take advantage of is called a *snippet*. The term refers to a small "chunk" of code that you can conveniently store and reuse over and over. For each project that you create, it's a good idea to create snippets out of any code that you might find useful on other projects. This saves you time and energy re-creating code and ensures consistency across your various sites. As you proceed through the project, I'll point out areas where you might consider creating a code snippet for reuse later.

Cascading style sheets (CSS) also speed the development of your site. A single style sheet can contain all the various ways to format text and objects within your site. This single document is then linked to every document in your site, making those styles available in one central location. The nice thing about style sheets comes when you want to change a style. Instead of changing it on every single page in the site, you just change it in the style sheet and the change propagates out to every page that relies on the style sheet. Over the past few years, Dreamweaver has really integrated CSS into the development process, making it much easier to manage. With the latest release of Flash, Macromedia has continued focusing on CSS by improving the capability to use CSS to format Flash-based content.

One additional set of streamlining tools that I focus on are *library objects*. As you will see, library objects enable you to store and reuse objects such as images, sounds, movie files, and more by simply dragging and dropping them into your pages. Another nice feature of library objects is the fact that they are reusable in nearly every application in the Studio suite. For instance, graphics created in Fireworks can be used in Flash and Dreamweaver and can even be quickly edited in any of these applications through the round-trip features built in to Flash, Fireworks, and Dreamweaver. As I cover each application, I point out situations where round-trip functionality might apply.

With these reusable elements at your disposal, the last issue you need to consider before you start looking at the Studio tools themselves is that of supplemental software.

SUPPLEMENTAL SOFTWARE

Throughout the process of developing the site and all the necessary elements, there are a couple pieces of supplemental software that, although not absolutely necessary, assist in your understanding of how the site works.

INTERNET INFORMATION SERVICES (IIS) OR APACHE WEB SERVER

Although the ColdFusion server does include an internal web server, Macromedia has indicated that it is best suited for the development environment and not intended to replace more powerful web server applications, like IIS or Apache. Therefore, it's a good idea to install and configure a web server on your local machine so that you can test your site as you progress.

1

CAUTION

> If you are using a machine that has Windows XP Home Edition, it is not capable of using IIS unless you make significant modifications to operating system files. Therefore, if you are using the Home Edition, you can either upgrade to the Professional Edition or choose to run Apache Web Server.

Throughout this book, IIS is used because it's included in most versions of Windows, but if you are a Mac user or you prefer a server such as Apache or SunOne, you can use those as well. IIS can be installed with your Windows Operating System CD, the Apache web server can be downloaded from http://www.apache.org, and SunOne can be downloaded at http://www.sun.com/software/products/web_srvr/home_web_srvr.xml.

NOTE

> For additional information on configuring each of these web server applications for use with ColdFusion, check out this site:
>
> http://livedocs.macromedia.com/coldfusion/7/htmldocs/00000049.htm

MACROMEDIA FLASH PLAYER

As mentioned earlier, one of the elements you will be developing for the client is a Flash slideshow of their employees and facilities. Therefore, to fully test the Flash movie you are going to create, you need to have the latest version of the Flash Player installed on your local machine. When you install Macromedia Studio, the Flash Player should be installed as well, but you can test to ensure that the player is installed and configured correctly by going to Macromedia's website at http://www.macromedia.com. Their site is Flash based, so if you are able to view their site correctly, Flash is installed properly on your machine.

MICROSOFT ACCESS

The final piece of supplementary software that will be helpful in developing the site is Microsoft Access. Since you are going to create database-driven pages for the website, the content will be stored in Access and then rendered on the pages when they are accessed. Although it is not imperative that you have Access installed on your machine, it might be helpful to be able to open the Access database and view the table structure and field properties that have been created for the site.

TROUBLESHOOTING

How can I tell whether IIS is properly configured on my machine?

The first thing to do is check to see whether there is an `Inetpub` folder located in your `C:` drive. If there is, it is likely that IIS is installed. To check whether it is functioning correctly, choose Start, Programs, Accessories, Notepad, and type **Hello World** in the document. Save the document as `C:\Inetpub\wwwroot\hello.htm`. Finally, open Internet Explorer and type `http://localhost/hello.htm` in the address bar. If a page is returned that says `Hello World`, IIS is functioning correctly.

If you are not able to view the page, try reinstalling IIS or Apache and trying again.

I have installed ColdFusion and plan on using the web server included with ColdFusion, but every time I type `http://localhost`, *I get an error.*

The ColdFusion web server application works only on port 8500, so if you are planning on using the ColdFusion web server for development, type `http://localhost:8500` instead.

BEST PRACTICES—MAINTAINING SECURITY PATCHES ON YOUR WEB SERVER APPLICATIONS

Running a web server application on your local workstation can expose your computer to risks that previously did not exist. By enabling a web server, you can expose your files and databases to snooping eyes, so being aware of (and promptly testing and installing) all security patches is necessary to ensure that your data is protected. This advice is not limited to Windows systems running IIS, either. Apache and SunOne are often the target of attacks as well, so be sure to check the knowledge base of the company that provides your web server application and keep those patches up to date!

CHAPTER 2

GETTING COMFORTABLE WITH THE STUDIO 8 ENVIRONMENT

In this chapter

STUDIO 8: COMMON APPLICATION ELEMENTS

To provide continuity between the development applications within Studio (except ColdFusion), Macromedia has created a set of common user-interface elements that are shared across each application. Familiarizing yourself with how these tools work and their distinctions across the individual programs can help you work faster and smarter.

NOTE

> ColdFusion is not considered a development application, but rather a utility for managing the ColdFusion environment, so it does not share any common elements with the other programs in the Studio suite.

Studio's common elements include

- A central workspace for creating pages, movies, or images. In Flash, the workspace is called the *Stage*. In each of the other development applications, the workspace is called the *document window*.
- A main menu bar at the top of the screen, with File, Edit, View, Insert, Modify, Commands, Window, and Help menus.
- A secondary toolbar located below the main menu bar.
- Panels that provide access to specific functionality. The panels all work the same in the way they are opened, closed, minimized, maximized, docked, and undocked.
- A Property inspector that enables you to see and modify common attributes of the selected object.
- A Tools panel (in Fireworks and Flash) located, by default, on the left side of the workspace.

Figures 2.1–2.3 show the main interface features for Flash, Fireworks, and Dreamweaver, respectively.

In addition, many of the applications share common options within the various menus, common commands on the main toolbar, and common keyboard shortcut keys.

Figure 2.1
The Flash interface.

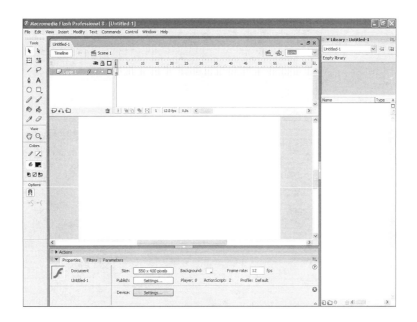

Figure 2.2
The Fireworks
interface.

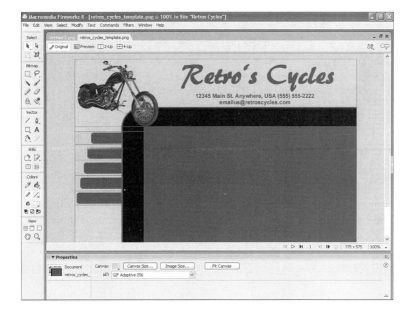

Figure 2.3
The Dreamweaver
interface.

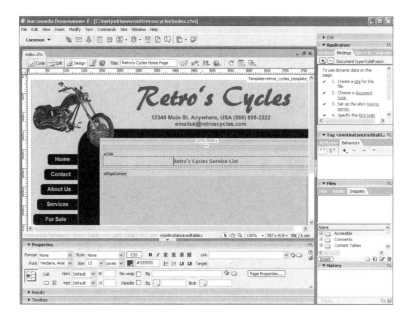

MAIN MENU AND TOOLBAR

At the very top of each of the development programs within Studio, you can find a typical menu bar that allows you to create, open, close, and save documents, as well as perform activities such as cutting and pasting, printing, and finding help.

The main menus also indicate what shortcut keys can be used to accomplish the same task. For instance, when clicking on the File menu in any application, you also see that the Cmd-N or Ctrl+N shortcut allows you to create a new document in the same way that the File, New menu command does.

> **NOTE**
>
> In Flash, the main toolbar is not displayed by default. Instead, you need to choose Window, Toolbars, Main to activate it.

PANELS

One of the unique elements within Studio is the use of panels to provide access to feature functionality. Each panel groups similar features together so they can be easily located. This also enables you to hide or display the panels at your convenience, which enables you to customize your workspace depending on your needs.

Any of the panels can also be docked and undocked, so you can arrange them any way you want or even allow them to float. As shown in Figure 2.4, undock a panel by positioning the cursor over the upper-left corner of the panel, and when the cursor has changed to a Move icon, drag the panel to the desired location.

Figure 2.4
To dock or undock a panel, grab it by the upper-left corner.

After a panel has been undocked, you can move it around by clicking and dragging on the gradient bar at the top of the panel. Keep in mind, however, that you have to grab it by the upper-left corner again to redock it.

You can also resize panels by positioning the cursor at any edge or corner. When the cursor turns into a two-headed arrow, as shown in Figure 2.5, the panel is resizable and you can simply click and drag to resize.

Figure 2.5
To resize a panel, grab it by an edge or corner. When the cursor turns into a two-headed arrow, you can drag to resize.

PROPERTY INSPECTOR

Each of Studio's development programs also includes a Property inspector that provides information regarding the attributes of any object that is selected. Using the Property inspector, you can examine and modify attributes such as size, location, and name.

Some objects also contain their own unique properties that can be adjusted with the Property inspector. In each of the programs, the Property inspector changes depending on the type of object that has been selected.

For instance, when a text object is selected, a wide variety of properties is visible including styles, alignment, font, size, and color. For the most part, the buttons that enable you to adjust these text properties look a lot like those found in today's popular word processors. This means that you can apply bold formatting to a text object by simply selecting it and clicking the B button in the Property inspector, shown in Figure 2.6.

Figure 2.6
Text attributes in the Property inspector are similar to those found in popular word processors.

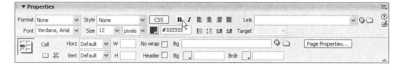

TOOLS PANEL

Flash and Fireworks share a common group of editing tools that are displayed in the Tools panel. By default, this panel is located to the left of the workspace and is divided into subsections. These subsections include a View section, a Colors section, and one or more sections for editing tools. Flash also has an Options section where you can select options associated with the currently selected editing tool, such as the Round Rectangle Radius option shown in Figure 2.7. Fireworks also includes a Web section, with tools for preparing graphics for use on the Web.

Figure 2.7
The Round Rectangle Radius option in Flash.

The View section contains tools to manipulate the view of the workspace, as opposed to objects in the workspace. The Hand tool and the Zoom tool are common to Flash and Fireworks.

With the Hand tool you can move the workspace view by clicking anywhere in the workspace and moving the mouse. The Zoom tool, on the other hand, enables you to zoom in and out on specific areas of the workspace. You can also drag out a selection box around any area to zoom in on that specific area and in Flash, the Options section enables you to select Zoom In or Zoom Out modes.

In Fireworks, the View section also enables you to easily customize the workspace by viewing the workspace full-screen, with or without menus.

TOOLS

The broadest and deepest areas of overlap relate to the editing tools found in the Tools panel. Selection, Subselection, Line, Lasso, Pen, Pencil, Text, Rectangle, Ellipse, Eyedropper, and Eraser tools are all found in Flash and Fireworks.

Many of the basic concepts and techniques for using these tools are the same in all three programs. Common elements include the basics of strokes, fills, and gradients, as well as the workings of tools such as Selection, Subselection, Line, Lasso, Pen, Text, Rectangle, Ellipse, and Eyedropper. The Eraser, though it has the same basic function in all Studio programs—deleting objects or portions of objects—differs enough among programs to deserve separate treatment for each. The same is true of the Brush tool, common only to Flash and Fireworks.

STROKES AND FILLS

With vector drawings, tools are used to create two elements: strokes and fills. *Strokes* consist of lines, whereas *fills* are areas (commonly found inside strokes). For instance, if you were to draw a circle in Flash, the outside line of the circle would be described as the stroke. The shaded, colored, or transparent area that fills the circle, on the other hand, would be the fill.

> **NOTE**
>
> Fills can be applied only to closed shapes such as circles or polygons.

In shapes that contain both strokes and fills, each is independent of the other, so you could modify the fill color of the circle without changing the stroke color in any way.

Be aware, however, that Flash treats overlapping shapes differently than Fireworks. For instance, if you draw an object, such as a simple circle, on the stage in Flash and then draw a second object that overlaps it, the area of the first object that has been overlapped is replaced by the second overlapping object. This is different from Fireworks, where the second object merely covers the portion of the original object that it overlaps.

SETTING STROKE AND FILL COLORS

In Flash and Fireworks, setting the stroke or fill color can be achieved by either

- Clicking in the Stroke or Fill box in the Colors section of the Tools panel.
- Selecting the object and then clicking the Stroke or Fill box in the Property inspector.

After the Stroke or Fill box has been clicked, the color selection panel is displayed, as shown in Figure 2.8.

Figure 2.8
The color selection panel in Fireworks.

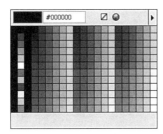

Within the color selection panel, there are several subpanels, the simplest of which is the web-safe color picker. This panel contains swatches for the 216 generic colors common to the two major operating systems, Macintosh and Windows. As shown in Figure 2.9, a color mixer enables you to go beyond the web-safe colors by mixing your own custom colors.

Figure 2.9
The color mixer enables you to create your own custom colors.

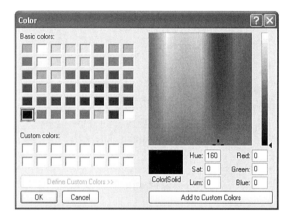

Although there are several options for mixing custom colors, all three programs support Red, Green, Blue (RGB), and Hue, Saturation, Brightness (HSB).

NOTE

RGB is the standard additive color model created for graphics viewed on computer monitors. Unless you are accustomed to using HSB color, stick to using RGB values.

In Flash and Fireworks, if you click on the upper-right corner of the colors mixer (as shown in Figure 2.10) you get a pop-up menu offering various color-related functions, including selecting a color mode (RGB or HSB) and saving a custom color as a swatch, which you can later retrieve from the swatches panel (see Figure 2.11).

Figure 2.10
Click on the upper-right corner of the colors mixer in Flash and Fireworks for a pop-up menu of color-related options.

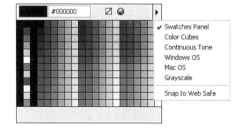

Dreamweaver, not being a graphics editor, does not work with strokes and fills, but it has a color picker that enables you to control the color attribute of HTML objects.

Figure 2.11
Fireworks swatches panel.

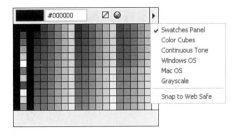

WORKING WITH FILLS

When working with shapes, remember that you can apply a fill to any shape that is enclosed. In addition, the fill can be solid, gradient, or (in Flash and Fireworks) bitmaps.

Solid fills consist of colors from the traditional color palette, where gradient fills blend from one color to the next. Bitmap fills are graphics that are imported into the fill as a repeating background for the object.

If you choose to work with a gradient fill, you can also select from different types of gradients. Linear gradients display colors in a striped pattern, whereas radial gradients display colors in a circular pattern from the center outward.

The programs do have a number of minor differences when it comes to working with fills. For instance:

- In all the programs, you select a gradient or solid fill by using a drop-down menu. In Flash, the drop-down menu and gradient definition bar are in the Color Mixer panel (see Figure 2.12) and you have to click on the Fill property to get to the drop-down. In Fireworks, they're in the Property inspector (see Figure 2.13).

- In Flash and Fireworks, shapes such as rectangles and circles are filled by default. In both applications you can also set the "no fill" option by clicking the white box with a diagonal red line through it.

- In Flash and Fireworks you can edit a fill without first selecting the object by clicking any enclosed area with the Paint Bucket tool.

Figure 2.12
The Flash Color Mixer panel.

Figure 2.13
The Fireworks
Property inspector.

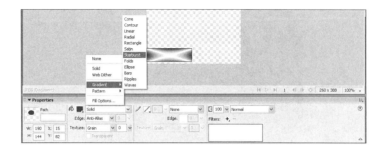

WORKING WITH GRADIENTS

All the Studio 8 programs except Dreamweaver can create gradient fills. You can also create custom gradients specifying how many and which colors are used by using a gradient definition bar and gradient pointers.

When you create a custom gradient, each pointer marks the spot where a particular color occurs in its nonblended form. To change the colors in the gradient, click on gradient pointers and assign new colors to them. To move a pointer, click and drag it.

Again, the programs show some minor differences in the interface. For instance, to create new gradient pointers in Flash and Fireworks, you click just below the definition bar, between the two original pointers.

To change a gradient color, click on a pointer. In Fireworks, the web-safe color picker pops up automatically. In Flash, access the color picker by clicking the color box at the top left of the Colors Mixer.

THE EYEDROPPER TOOL

The basic purpose of the Eyedropper tool is the same throughout all the Studio programs: It speeds up color selection by enabling you to copy colors from an existing object. Although the Eyedropper tools in Fireworks and Flash are limited to the stroke and fill of existing objects (including the toolbars themselves), Dreamweaver's Eyedropper can pick up colors from anywhere on the screen—even outside its own windows. If you click on a bitmap with the Eyedropper tool, it picks up the color of the individual pixel on which you click.

NOTE

> Although Dreamweaver's Eyedropper tool can be used to select colors outside of its own windows, it cannot span multiple monitors. Therefore, it is limited to colors being displayed on the same monitor as that on which Dreamweaver is being displayed.

The Eyedropper is temporarily activated whenever you click on a color box. (This is the only way to activate the Eyedropper in Dreamweaver.) So throughout Studio 8, you can sample a color from another object by selecting the object or objects whose stroke or fill color you want to change, clicking a Stroke or Fill color box, and then clicking on a swatch or on an object to select the color you want.

THE LINE TOOL

The Line tool is the most basic of the drawing tools in the fact that it draws only straight lines. To draw a line, select the Line tool and then click and drag to create lines. Holding the Shift key while you drag creates lines that are vertical, horizontal, or at a 45° angle.

You can, of course, use the Line tool to draw closed shapes such as squares or rectangles that can have fills applied to them. However, you must manually add a fill, using the Paint Bucket tool, after you have closed a shape.

THE PENCIL TOOL

The Pencil tool enables you to draw freeform lines and shapes. Select the Pencil tool and then click and drag to sketch lines with the mouse. As with the Line tool, holding the Shift key while you drag constrains the angle to vertical, horizontal, and 45°. In Flash and Fireworks, after creating a closed shape, you can fill it manually by using the Paint Bucket tool.

NOTE

> When I refer to a closed shape, I'm talking about a stroke that forms a shape such as a circle or polygon. A closed shape can be filled because Fireworks or Flash understand that they should fill only the area that is enclosed (for example, inside the circle).

Flash has a unique feature in the three pencil modes in the Options section of the Toolbox: Straighten, Smooth, and Ink (maintain rough shapes).

RECTANGLE AND ELLIPSE TOOLS

The Rectangle and Ellipse ("Oval" in Flash) tools enable you to draw these simple shapes by just clicking and dragging. Holding the Shift key while dragging results in drawing symmetric circles or squares.

In Fireworks, click and hold on the Rectangle to bring up a fly-out with the Ellipse tool, as well as a Polygon tool and a number of Auto Shapes such as a spiral, an arrow, a star, and a doughnut.

You can also draw rectangles with rounded corners. The interfaces are slightly different for each program, but the result is the same. In Flash, after selecting the Rectangle tool, select the Round Rectangle Radius modifier at the bottom of the Tools panel. Enter a number in the Corner Radius field; the higher the number, the rounder the corners. In Fireworks, click and hold on the Rectangle tool and select the Rounded Rectangle smart shape from the fly-out that appears (see Figure 2.14).

Figure 2.14
The Fireworks
Rounded Rectangle
feature.

THE PEN TOOL

The Pen tool is an extremely powerful drawing tool. If you haven't used an illustration program before, the Pen tool will take some getting used to, particularly the way it draws curves. After you have become comfortable with it, however, you will be rewarded with precisely drawn curves and irregular shapes that cannot be achieved with any other tool.

The Pen tool draws by connecting a series of anchor points. A straight line or curve connecting two anchor points is called a path. Your final shape is achieved by joining a series of anchor points and paths.

For instance, if you select the Pen tool and move your mouse pointer onto the workspace, a small x appears to the right of the pen, as shown in Figure 2.15, indicating where the first anchor point will be placed. When you click on that spot, the anchor point is created.

Figure 2.15
The Pen tool displays
a small x as you place
the first anchor point
of a shape.

DRAWING STRAIGHT LINE SEGMENTS

To draw a straight line segment, just click and release, move the mouse, and click again. As with the line tool, holding the Shift key while dragging draws vertical, horizontal, or diagonal lines. To end an open path, double-click the final anchor point or select a different tool.

You can also Cmd-click (Mac) or Ctrl+click (Windows) off the path. To end a closed path, hold the Pen over the first anchor point. A small dot appears to the right of the Pen, indicating that you can close the path, as shown in Figure 2.16. Then click just once.

Figure 2.16
The Pen tool displays a small circle if you are correctly positioned to close a path.

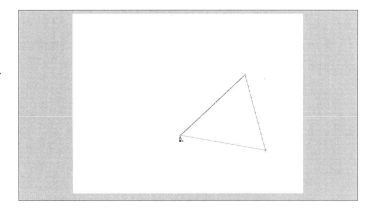

DRAWING CURVED SEGMENTS

The Pen tool creates Bezier curves, controlled by control handles, as shown in Figure 2.17. The length and angle of the control handles determine the shape of the curve.

The easiest way to create a curve segment is to click and release at the point where you want the segment to start, move to the point where you want it to end, and click and drag. Whichever way you drag, the curve is created in the opposite direction. To create another curve on the same path, move again, and click and drag again. Or you could make the next segment a straight line by just clicking, rather than clicking and dragging. Points created by clicking are corner points and do not have control handles. Points created by clicking and dragging are curve points and do have control handles. To end the path, move off the path and Cmd-click (Mac) or Ctrl+click (Windows).

Figure 2.17
The anatomy of a curve: two anchor points, each with two control handles.

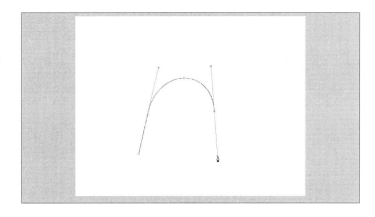

To convert a corner point to a curve point, and create curvature in the straight line segments, select the point with the Subselection tool and Option-click (Mac) or Alt+click (Windows) and drag. To convert a curve point to a corner point, click on the point with the Pen tool. Clicking on a corner point with the Pen tool deletes the point.

To close a curved path, just click on the initial anchor point, or else click on the initial anchor point and drag away from the curve, as shown in Figure 2.18.

Figure 2.18
Click on the initial anchor point and drag away from the curve to close a curved path.

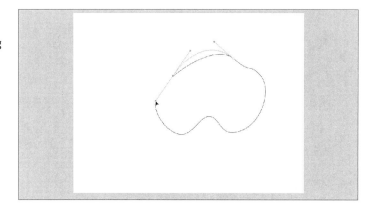

ADJUSTING ANCHOR POINTS AND HANDLES

The easiest way to work with the Pen tool is to complete a path and then move, add, and delete anchor points and adjust handles.

To adjust anchor points you must first select them. Use the Subselection tool and click on a path to reveal the anchor points, as shown in Figure 2.19.

Figure 2.19
Click on a path with the Subselection tool to reveal anchor points.

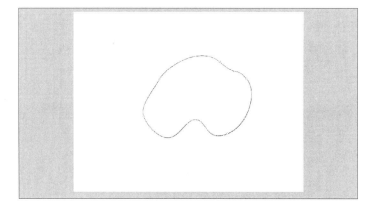

If you click directly on an anchor, you both select that point and reveal all others in the path. If you click on a path but not directly on an anchor point, you simply reveal the anchor points in the path and must then click directly on one to select it. Shift+click additional anchor points to add them to the selection. You can then click directly on an anchor to reveal any control handles. Click and drag anchor points to move them, as shown in Figure 2.20. You can also select an anchor point and use the arrow keys to nudge it.

Figure 2.20
Click and drag a control handle to alter a curve's shape.

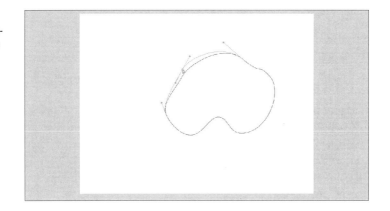

You can also add anchor points. Position the Pen tool on the path. A small plus sign appears next to the Pen tool. Click to create the anchor point.

You can delete anchor points by selecting them with the Subselection tool and pressing the Delete key.

ADJUSTING CURVED SEGMENTS

To adjust the size and angle of a curve without moving anchor points, use the Subselection tool to select the path, select the anchor point, and click and drag its control handles. Where two curved segments intersect, two control handles extend away from a common anchor point. Each handle controls a curve on either side of a common anchor point. Dragging one end of a double control handle changes the curves on both sides of the anchor point, which stays in place as shown in Figure 2.21.

To adjust only the curved segment on just one side, rather than both, Option-drag (Mac) or Alt+drag (Windows) only one end of a double control handle.

Figure 2.21
Dragging one end of a double control handle changes curves on both sides of the shared anchor point.

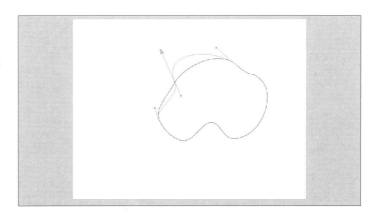

If a curve segment intersects a straight segment, you see a control handle just on the curve side of the anchor. Click and drag this handle with the Subselection tool to change the arc, or click and drag the anchor point to move the curve.

In Flash, you can also click and drag with the Selection tool to move segments. In Fireworks, clicking on a segment with the Selection tool selects the whole path, and dragging moves it.

OPTIMIZING CURVES

After you have created a curve, you can reduce the number of points that define it, keeping the same basic shape but smoothing it out. This is called optimizing the curve. To do this in Fireworks, use Modify, Alter Path, Simplify. In Flash, use Modify, Shape, Optimize. You can set a slider to maximize or minimize optimization. In Fireworks, you can also set the optimization amount numerically. Flash gives you the option of running several smoothing passes in one operation.

TIP

> If you want to smooth or straighten a segment of a shape in Flash, you can also select just that segment and then choose Modify, Smooth, or Straighten from the toolbar.

WORKING WITH TEXT

The Studio programs all share common methods of working with text, including basic functions such as adding, editing, and deleting text, as well as assigning character attributes such as bold and italic, and paragraph attributes such as indentation and justification. Many of these functions are also similar to those of widely used programs such as Microsoft Word.

Some functions, such as dynamic text (text loaded at runtime as opposed to authoring time) and user input fields (where the user can enter text), are restricted to Flash and Dreamweaver because only those programs have the means to control the runtime environment (that is, the Flash Player or the browser).

NOTE

> As you develop with the various Studio applications, you'll notice that for the most part, what you see in the development environment is exactly the same as the end result. There are times, however, when what you see at author-time (what you see when you're working with the development tool) is different from what you see at runtime (what you see when you actually display the end result in a browser or by viewing the final product).
>
> For example, in Dreamweaver, when you place a data binding in your web page, you don't see the actual data that is drawn from the database because that occurs only at runtime. To see the data, you need to view the page in a web browser.
>
> So be aware that although many of the applications are WYSIWYG (what you see is what you get), you may have to take a few extra steps in some cases to proof your work.

Fireworks offers special text effects, such as drop shadows, that make the text appear to stand out from the page.

In the Property inspector, Dreamweaver offers only text attributes that are supported in HTML, such as bold, italic, color, font, indentation, and justification. Other attributes, such as spacing between characters, are not supported in HTML or Dreamweaver.

Flash's support for a subset of Cascading Style Sheet (CSS) tags, used to format text, provides standard-based integration with Dreamweaver, which has become more CSS-centric over the last few versions.

ADDING TEXT

Adding text to Fireworks and Flash requires that you select the Text tool, click in the workspace where you want the text to be placed, and then type the text you want to display. Dreamweaver's Text tool, however, is similar to a word processor, so you can simply drop your cursor anywhere in the document where you want to display the text and type away.

NOTE

In Flash and Fireworks, you can also click and drag with the Text tool to create a fixed-width text block. Text entered into this text block wraps vertically after it reaches the width limitations of the text block.

RESIZING TEXT BLOCKS

After you have created a text block, both Flash and Fireworks enable you to resize it by clicking on the appropriate handle, as shown in Figure 2.22. As you drag the handle, the block changes size and the text reflows to fit the box. You can also use the Width and Height fields in the Property inspector to resize text blocks, but doing so distorts the text vertically or horizontally, depending on which field you alter

Figure 2.22
Drag a text box's handle to resize a text box.

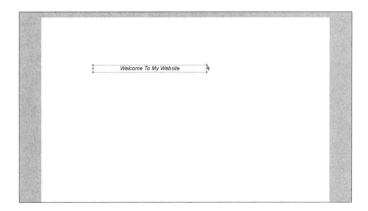

Welcome To My Website

CAUTION

> When working with text boxes, the only time you should ever use scaling tools to change the height or width of a text box is when you want to stretch the text to create a strange or funny effect. Using a scaling tool to change the height or width of a text box skews and stretches not only the box, but the text inside. If you need to change the size of your text box, be sure that you select the Text tool and then change the size by dragging on the text box handles. Using the Text tool maintains the integrity of your text and still allows you to make adjustments to the box.

TIP

> In Flash and Fireworks, handles appear only when the Text tool is selected and the cursor is in the text block.

As you drag a handle, the block changes size and the spacing between characters and lines also changes, whereas the line breaks stay the same.

CHANGING TEXT GLOBALLY

In Flash and Fireworks, you can set the default attributes of text by choosing the Text tool and making changes in the Property inspector. After these attributes are set, any instances of text that are placed on the page have those attributes until they are modified.

Some properties, such as text orientation (vertical, horizontal, left-to-right, right-to-left) in Flash and Fireworks, can be changed only globally. Such properties change for the whole text block, whether the Selection or Subselection tool has been used to select the text block as a whole, or whether the Text tool has been used to select particular characters or paragraphs.

CHARACTER AND PARAGRAPH ATTRIBUTES

Text attributes can be divided into those that affect paragraphs and those that affect individual characters. The most commonly used paragraph attribute is justification: aligned left, aligned right, centered, and justified (aligned left and right). Others include line spacing, first-line indent, and margins. Common character attributes, on the other hand, include font, point size, character position, character spacing, and kerning.

To make paragraph-level changes, select the Text tool. Then, to make changes to just one paragraph, click anywhere in that paragraph. Alternatively, you can select any part of one or more paragraphs. Any subsequent paragraph-level changes made in the Property inspector affect all the chosen paragraphs.

To make character-level changes, click and drag with the Text tool to select the text you want to change, as shown in Figure 2.23. Any subsequent character-level changes made in the Property inspector affect just the selected characters.

Figure 2.23
Click and drag with the Text tool to edit individual letters within text blocks.

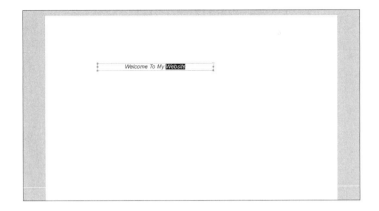

2

FONT, POINT SIZE, COLOR, AND STYLES

Different fonts can easily be selected from the drop-down menu in the Property inspector. In Flash and Dreamweaver, you can also type in the font name and it will be applied to the selected text.

Likewise, you can select a font size or you can type in a specific font size in each of the four programs. All four also offer alternative means to select the font size: a pop-up slider in Flash and Fireworks and a drop-down listing of just the most commonly used font sizes in Dreamweaver. Although typing the desired size is generally the quickest way to set the font size, using the sliders enables you to preview the text at many different sizes.

When working with text color, Flash and Fireworks assign the selected fill color to your text. Dreamweaver doesn't distinguish between stroke and fill, so there's just one color selection box.

You can also force font styles by using the Bold and Italic buttons. In Dreamweaver and Flash, consider creating and applying a CSS tag instead. That way, later on, you can make global changes to all bolded text just by changing the tag.

> **TIP**
>
> In Flash, when including the font in a movie, it may be preferable to use a bold or italic version of a font rather than the Bold and Italic buttons, because you can lose much of the subtlety of a typeface by forcing a bold or italic style that it wasn't designed for. When working with text in Dreamweaver, however, you're using system fonts (fonts provided by the user's computer) and can't be sure that the bold or italic versions will be available on all machines. Therefore, it's common to just stick with standard fonts and use the Bold and Italic buttons in Dreamweaver.

TEXT DIRECTION

Flash and Fireworks both enable you to control text direction: horizontal left-to-right, horizontal right-to-left (not available in Flash), vertical left-to-right, and vertical right-to-left. In Fireworks, you can also control text direction by attaching the text to a path.

KERNING AND CHARACTER SPACING

Kerning refers to the amount of space between two letters or characters, whereas *character spacing* applies to larger groups of characters or entire blocks of text. Both kerning and character spacing can be defined by positive or negative settings. Positive settings increase the amount of space between letters, and negative settings decrease space until letters eventually overlap, as shown in Figure 2.24. Zero is neutral.

Figure 2.24
Character spacing: +20 on the top, 0 in the middle, –5 at the bottom.

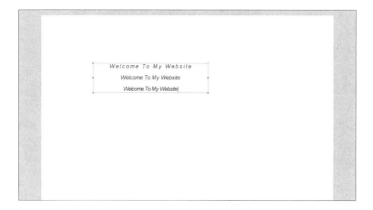

For general legibility in blocks of copy, it's best to work within a range of 0 to +5 or even less, depending on text size. The smaller the point size, the greater the effect of character spacing. Many fonts have desirable kerning built in. In Flash and Fireworks, you can use this kerning by selecting the Auto Kern option. As already mentioned, Dreamweaver does not support these options.

In Flash and Fireworks, select letters, words, or entire text blocks; then enter a positive or negative number in the character spacing field. In Flash and Fireworks, you can also drag a slider to select the amount of spacing. When used with vertical text, character spacing determines the amount of vertical space between characters. In Flash, you can also set a preference to turn off kerning of vertical text; then character spacing affects only horizontal text.

ALIGNMENT AND JUSTIFICATION

In all four programs, use Alignment buttons to specify left-aligned, centered, right-aligned, or full justification of paragraphs. Full justification creates newspaper-style paragraphs that are aligned on both the left and right sides. When using full justification, be sure to check the amount of space that is created by the justification so that large, distracting gaps do not appear between words. Do not use full justification with bitmap fonts, or they stretch and become blurry. These settings also apply to vertical text in the programs that support that.

TROUBLESHOOTING

One of my panels has disappeared. How do I turn it back on?

The easiest way to find a panel is to choose Window from the main menu. The Window menu contains all the panels and their subpanels. As you find yourself using specific panels more often than others, learn their shortcut keys so you can turn them on or off easily.

In Dreamweaver, can I turn off all the panels to maximize my space?

Sure, but there is a better way to keep the panels you find useful open but hidden. To do this, choose Window, Hide Panels from the main menu or simply press the F4 key. The panels located to the right of the workspace are now hidden. To restore them, choose Window, Show Panels or press F4 again. Note that when you restore the panels, they are arranged exactly as you left them.

BEST PRACTICES—FAMILIARIZING YOURSELF WITH PANEL FUNCTIONALITY AND CUSTOMIZING YOUR WORKSPACE

At first glance, any of the Studio programs can be a bit overwhelming. In addition to the typical menus, there are panels on the left, panels on the right, and buttons, drop-downs, and boxes on every panel. The good news is that all these options are what make the Studio applications some of the most powerful on the market. The bad news is that you have to learn about every feature to take full advantage of what the programs have to offer.

Don't worry, though. The panels really aren't as intimidating as they might appear at first glance and after you get used to them, I think you'll find them to be very intuitive. The best thing you can do to get started, however, is to open each panel and familiarize yourself with the functionality that exists. Make some notes and if you don't think you'll use the panel very often, minimize it or turn it off altogether. This enables you to customize your workspace to fit your needs, but still find features located in a hidden panel should you need them.

FIREWORKS 8

CHAPTER **3**

INTRODUCING FIREWORKS 8

In this chapter

WHAT'S NEW IN FIREWORKS 8

Several new features have been introduced in Fireworks 8, as well as enhancements of some existing features. New feature functionality includes

- **The new Image Editing panel**—Provides access to commonly used image editing tools, filters, and menu commands.
- **The new Auto Shape Properties panel**—Enables you to modify the properties of Auto Shapes.
- **The new Special Characters panel**—Using this panel you can insert special characters into text blocks.
- **The new Add Shadow command**—Enables you to add a shadow effect to vector objects and text blocks.
- **New symbol libraries**—Additional buttons, bullets, themes, and animations have been added to the Fireworks 8 libraries.
- **New default styles**—Additional styles have been added in Fireworks 8.
- **New default patterns and textures**—Patterns and textures for use in filling shapes have been updated.
- **CSS-based pop-up menus**—Pop-up menus created in Fireworks 8 are now CSS-based, rather than JavaScript.
- **New blend modes**—25 new blend modes have been added, including Negative, Hard Light, Soft Light, Freeze, and a host of others.
- **Additional import file formats**—Formats such as QuickTime, TGA, MacPaint, and others are now available for import into Fireworks 8.
- **Additional slicing capabilities**—Slices can now be polygons or rectangles.

Those existing features that have received updates include

- **The capability to save multiple selections**—Using the marquee tool, you can now save, restore, and name multiple selections within PNG files.
- **Shift-Click functionality in the Layers panel**—Enables you to make contiguous selections within the panel.
- **Stored Autosave preferences**—Fireworks preferences are autosaved by the application to ensure that your preferences remain consistent each time you run the application.
- **Enhanced vector compatibility**—Vector attributes of fills and strokes are preserved when objects are moved between Fireworks and Flash.
- **Improved JPEG compression**—JPEG files can be exported into smaller files with better quality.
- **Improvements to the Color Replace, Remove Red Eye, and Vector Path tools and Popup Previews**—Each of these tools has been improved to enhance functionality.
- **Export Preview renamed to Image Preview**—The functionality remains largely the same, but the navigation link has simply been renamed.

FIREWORKS 8 ENVIRONMENT

Now that you know what new and enhanced features to look out for, let's take some time to explore the Fireworks work environment as a whole. The Fireworks workspace comprises the Document window, Property inspector, menus, tools, and other panels. If you've used any of the other Macromedia Studio programs, there's a good chance the Fireworks environment will look familiar with its Document window, toolbar, and docked panel groups.

A QUICK LOOK AT THE FIREWORKS ENVIRONMENT

When you open Fireworks, you are greeted with the start page (see Figure 3.1), which is common to all development programs within the Studio. The start page enables you to open a recent file, create a new file, access Fireworks tutorials, as well as hop on the Web with Fireworks Exchange to add new capabilities to the program. If you don't care for the start page, simply check the Don't Show Again box located in the bottom-left corner of the page.

NOTE

> If you turn off the start page and later decide you want to reactivate it, you can do so by choosing Edit, Preferences and checking the Show Start Page check box.

Figure 3.1
The Fireworks 8 start page.

The first step in exploring Fireworks 8 is to use the start page to create a new file by selecting the Fireworks file under the Create New heading, or to choose File, New from the menu bar. The New Document dialog box (see Figure 3.2) appears, where you can select the dimension for your new document.

Figure 3.2
The New Document dialog box lets you control the canvas size and canvas color for each new document.

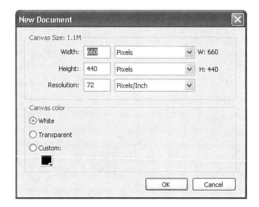

After you've set the canvas size and canvas color for the document, you see an interface that looks similar to most of the other programs in Studio (see Figure 3.3).

Figure 3.3
The Fireworks interface puts nearly everything you need at your fingertips.

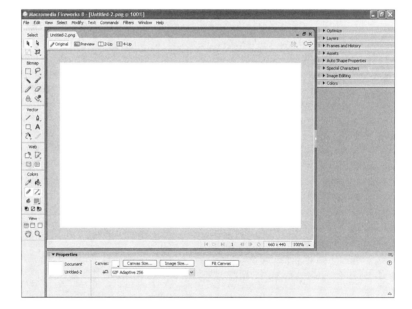

THE MAJOR INTERFACE ELEMENTS

The Fireworks 8 interface comprises five elements, each with its own features:

- **Document window**—The Document window contains the canvas and the additional work area surrounding the canvas. The canvas is the "live" area where your images appear and is where you create, edit, and delete objects that make up your images. Assets in the gray area are not exported unless you drag them back onto the canvas. At the top of the Document window are Original, Preview, 2-Up Preview, and 4-Up

Preview buttons (see Figure 3.4). The preview buttons display the graphic as it would appear in a browser based on optimization settings you can choose for each different view.

Figure 3.4
The Preview buttons let you see how your graphics will look with various optimization settings.

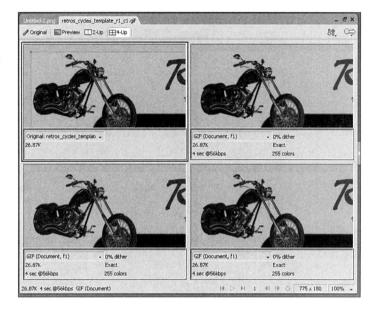

- **Tools**—Also referred to as the Toolbar, the Tools panel contains several tools that enable you to create and edit a variety of graphics, including text, vector objects, bitmaps, and web objects.
- **Property inspector**—The Property inspector is a panel that changes the tools and modifiers displayed based on the object selected.
- **Menu**—Common to nearly all graphical interfaces is a top row of menus and submenus to group common commands.
- **Panels**—Like other Studio programs, the panels in Fireworks are docked to the right of the screen. The default panels include Optimize, Layers, Assets, and Frames and History.

DOCUMENT WINDOW

The Document window contains the image or asset on which you are working, as well as a few other goodies. The most important part of the Document window is the canvas and the gray work area that surrounds it. As described earlier, the canvas represents the actual document as it would be exported. Graphics, or assets, in the gray area are not visible in the exported document. The work area is handy for storing graphics or to use for bleeds.

In the top-right corner of the Document window is the Quick Export menu (see Figure 3.5). This menu is used to quickly send your graphics to other Macromedia programs such as Dreamweaver, Flash, or Director, or even to enable you to preview them in a web browser.

Figure 3.5
The Quick Export menu sends assets to other Studio programs.

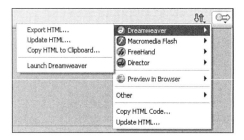

NOTE

The Quick Export menu was previously referred to as the Send To menu.

The bottom of the Document window contains animation controls that are activated if you are working with multiple frames.

The grayed-out X circle to the right of the animation controls is used to exit bitmap mode and is also activated only if you are working in bitmap mode.

Moving farther right is the page preview which, when clicked, shows a preview of the document's height and width as well as the image's pixel width, height, and resolution, as shown in Figure 3.6.

Figure 3.6
The Page Preview window gives you a snapshot of your document's width, height, and resolution.

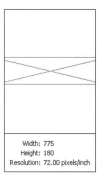

At the far right-lower corner is the magnification pop-up menu, where you can see and change the magnification at which you view your document. Click the down arrow to change the magnification to one of 14 preset magnifications (see Figure 3.7).

Figure 3.7
The page magnifica-
tion pop-up menu lets
you control the mag-
nification of your can-
vas from 6%–6400%.

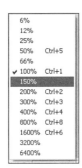

TOOLS UNIQUE TO FIREWORKS

Many of the tools used in Fireworks are similar to tools found in other Studio programs. For instance, there is little variation in how the selection and drawing tools work between the programs. There are, however, a few administrative tools specific to Fireworks, as well as some robust image modification tools we'll discuss in the following sections.

SELECT TOOLS GROUP

As the name indicates, the Select tools are used to select objects, as well as reposition and resize assets.

SELECT BEHIND

Unique to Fireworks is the Select Behind tool (see Figure 3.8), which enables you to select objects beneath or stacked behind other objects. You can access the tool by clicking and holding on the Pointer tool and then choosing Select Behind tool.

Figure 3.8
The Select Behind tool
enables you to select
objects placed behind
other objects.

DISTORT

The Distort tool enables the user to distort objects by arbitrarily resizing points and sides, as well as by rotating them. Select the object you want to modify; then use the Distort tool (see Figure 3.9) to move one of the object handles.

EXPORT AREA

The Export Area tool (see Figure 3.10) is used to define an area on the canvas for export. Select the tool and click and drag to define the export area. Release the mouse button and press the Enter key. The Export Preview dialog box appears, enabling you to control the export settings.

Figure 3.9
The Distort tool enables you to distort and rotate objects.

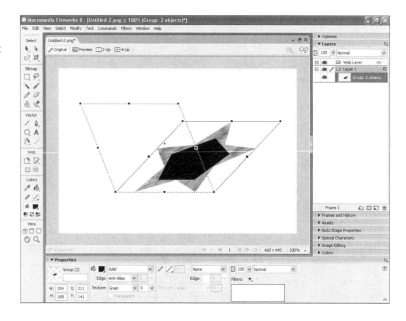

Figure 3.10
The Export Area tool enables you to define an area for export.

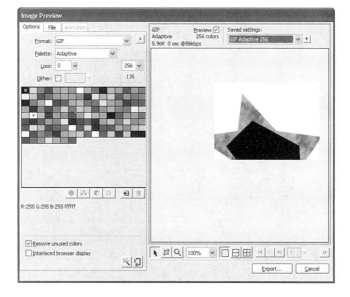

BITMAP TOOLS

The Bitmap group contains 19 tools that are used to modify bitmap images.

MARQUEE

The Marquee tool, or "marching ants," is used to define a rectangular area of pixels. Select the Marquee tool and click and drag to create a rectangular area that you can modify (see

Figure 3.11). To deselect the area choose Select, Deselect [Cmd-Shift-A] (Ctrl+D) from the upper menu bar or select any area outside the marquee.

When you use any of the Marquee or Lasso tools, as well as the Magic Wand tool, the Property inspector has an Edge menu that gives three Edge options for the tool when you copy and paste the selection:

- **Hard**—Creates a selection with a defined edge.
- **Anti-alias**—Reduces jagged edges in the selection.
- **Feather**—Softens the edge of the selection.

When you choose the Marquee or Oval Marquee tool, the Property inspector also shows a Style menu that gives three selection style options:

- **Normal**—Creates a marquee in which the height and width are independent of each other.
- **Fixed Ratio**—Sets the height and width to a defined ratio.
- **Fixed Size**—Constrains the height and width to a defined dimension.

Figure 3.11
The Marquee tool defines a bitmap area selection.

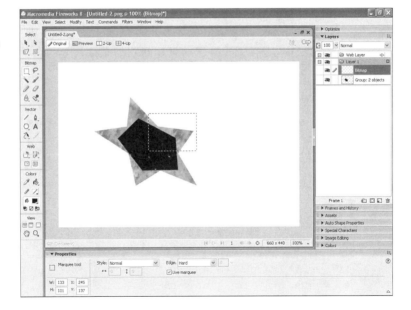

OVAL MARQUEE

The Oval Marquee tool is identical to the Marquee tool except that it defines an elliptical area of pixels.

LASSO

The Lasso tool enables you to draw a freeform selection area. This is handy if you are selecting pixels in complex shapes (see Figure 3.12).

Figure 3.12
The Lasso tool is used to select pixels often found in complex shapes.

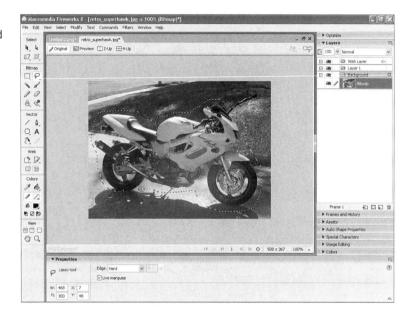

POLYGON LASSO

The Polygon Lasso tool enables you to draw a polygonal selection area with numerous points (see Figure 3.13). This is a smarter choice than the Lasso tool if you need to select areas with straight lines.

MAGIC WAND

The Magic Wand tool is probably one of the most used tools in image editing. Using this tool, you can select contiguous pixels of a similar color (see Figure 3.14). Using the Property inspector, you can control the Tolerance (0–255) and Edge (Hard, Anti-Alias, or Feather).

Adjusting the Tolerance setting controls the tonal range of colors that are selected when you click a pixel with the Magic Wand. If you enter 0 and click a pixel, only adjacent pixels of exactly the same tone are selected. Conversely, if you enter 255, all colors in the object are selected.

Figure 3.13
The Polygon Lasso tool is used to select a polygonal pixel area.

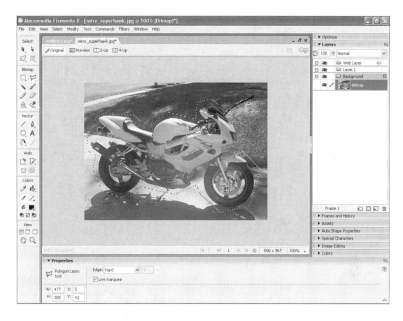

Figure 3.14
The Magic Wand tool is used to select pixels that are similar in color.

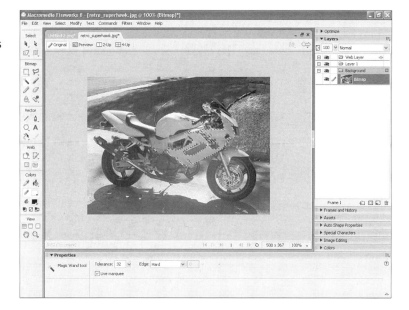

BRUSH

Like its real-world counterpart, the Brush tool (see Figure 3.15) is used to apply paint to a canvas. Rather than applying acrylic, oil, or watercolor paint, the Fireworks Brush tool applies pixels with a variety of settings.

Figure 3.15
The Brush tool is used like an artist's brush to apply colored pixels to your digital canvas.

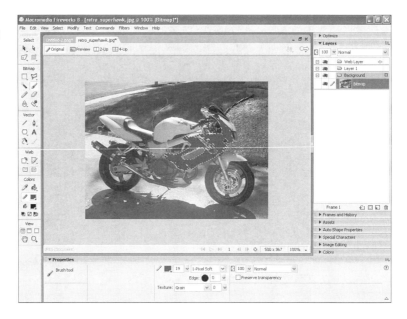

The power of the Brush tool can be utilized when you use the Property inspector (see Figure 3.16), the Stroke Options pop-up menu, and the Edit Stroke dialog box to add incredible control over every aspect of the brush. You adjust pixel color, brush size, edge effect, brush shape, texture, and transparency. In fact, you can use more than 50 types of brush strokes.

Figure 3.16
The Property inspector gives you incredible control over the Brush tool's properties.

PENCIL

The Pencil tool is basically a single-pixel version of the Brush tool. The Pencil tool is constrained to be a 1-pixel brush (see Figure 3.17). Using the Property inspector, you can control the Pencil tool's color, anti-alias, and transparency.

Figure 3.17
The Pencil tool is a
1-pixel brush.

ERASER

The Eraser tool (see Figure 3.18) is used to remove pixels from an image. Think of it as the anti-Brush tool. Using the Property inspector, you can control the Eraser tool's size, edge, shape, and transparency.

The Eraser tool, however, is not a universal eraser. Note that it is a bitmap tool and erases only pixels. It does not erase vector graphics such as shapes you create with the vector tools. This nuance has driven many to near insanity until they realized they were trying to use the wrong tool for the job.

BLUR

The Blur tool (see Figure 3.19) creates the effect of blurring pixels, giving a soft or out-of-focus effect. The Property inspector enables you to control the size, shape, edge, and intensity of the blur.

Figure 3.18
The Eraser tool removes pixels from an image.

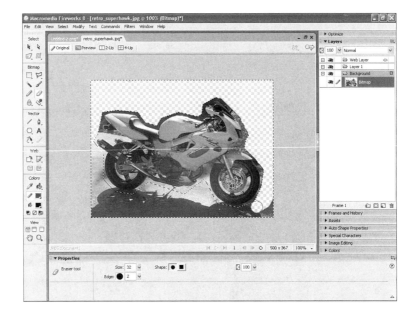

Figure 3.19
The Blur tool is used to blur sections of an image or the entire image.

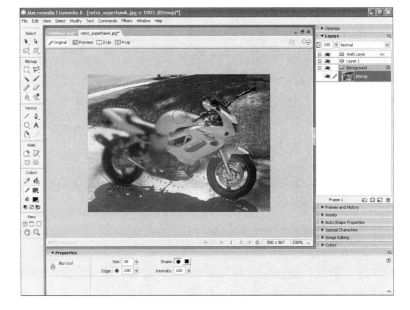

SHARPEN

The Sharpen tool (see Figure 3.20) increases the contrast between pixels and is useful for repairing out-of-focus images. The Property inspector enables you to control the size, shape, edge, and intensity of the effect.

Figure 3.20
The Sharpen tool increases contrast between pixels.

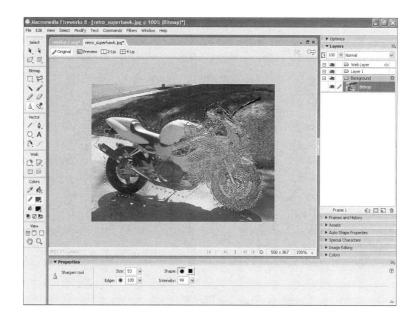

3

DODGE

A throwback to the darkroom days of photography, the Dodge tool is used to lighten pixels on the image (see Figure 3.21). Dodging areas of an image is useful to bring out more detail in darker pixels. The Property inspector enables you to control the size, edge, shape, range, and exposure of the dodge. You can apply the Dodge tool to three tonal ranges:

- **Shadows**—Change the dark portions of the image.
- **Highlights**—Change the light portions of the image.
- **Midtones**—Change the middle range of the image.

The exposure ranges from 0% to 100%. Specify a lower percentage value for a lessened effect, and a higher percentage for a stronger effect.

BURN

Another darkroom tool brought to the digital age is the Burn tool (see Figure 3.22). The Burn tool is used to darken pixels in the image. As with the Dodge tool, the Property inspector enables you to control the size, edge, shape, range, and exposure of the burn.

Hold down Alt (Windows) or Option (Macintosh) as you drag the tool to switch back and forth between the Burn tool and the Dodge tool.

Figure 3.21
The Dodge tool was used to turn the seat from black to white by lightening the pixels.

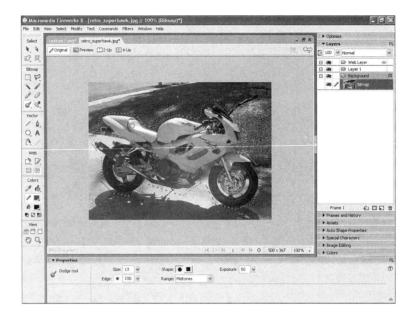

Figure 3.22
The paint was darkened from yellow to brown using the Burn tool.

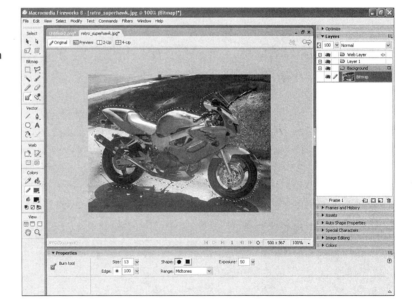

SMUDGE

The Smudge tool (see Figure 3.23) smears and displaces images. Visually, the effect is similar to that of the Blur tool. However, think of taking your finger and rubbing the wet ink on your freshly printed image. That's the Smudge tool. The Property inspector enables you to set the size, shape, edge, and pressure of the stroke. It also enables you to use a specified color at the beginning of each smudge stroke. If the smudge color is checked, the color under the tool pointer is used. If the Use Entire Document check box is selected, the tool uses color data from all objects on all layers to smudge the image.

Figure 3.23
The Smudge tool smears colors, allowing the motorcycle to look like it's already moving.

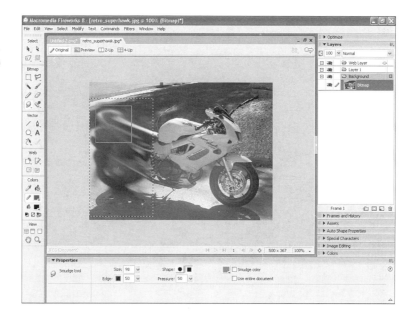

RUBBER STAMP

The Rubber Stamp tool takes pixels or objects from one area of your canvas and paints them in another. This replication process from one area to another is called "cloning." Select the Rubber Stamp tool and click the area you want to clone. The sampling pointer turns into crosshairs. Move to a different part of the image with the pointer. You will now see two pointers. The first one is the source and the second is the Rubber Stamp. As you drag the second pointer, pixels beneath the first pointer are copied and applied to the area beneath the second (see Figure 3.24).

Use the Property inspector to control the Rubber Stamp tool's size, edge, and transparency. When Source Aligned is selected, the sampling pointer moves vertically and horizontally in alignment with the second. When Source Aligned is deselected, the sample area is fixed, regardless of where the second pointer is moved. If the Use Entire Document check box is selected, the tool samples from all objects on all layers. When this option is deselected, the Rubber Stamp tool samples from the active object only.

REPLACE COLOR

The Replace Color tool (see Figure 3.25) lets you select one color and paint over it with a different color. To use the Replace Color tool, choose whether you want to select replacement colors from the swatches or from the image itself using the From drop-down. If you choose to select from the swatches, click the Change Color well in the Property inspector to select the color and choose a color from the pop-up menu. You can also click in the image to choose the color you want to replace.

Figure 3.24
The Rubber Stamp tool was used to clone the SuperHawk logo and place a duplicate below the bike.

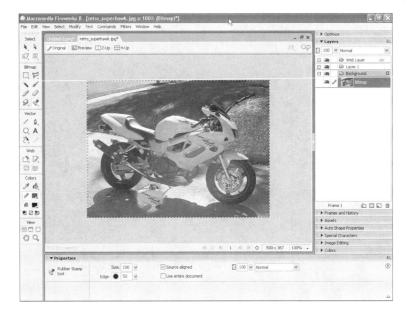

Figure 3.25
The Replace Color tool replaces the yellow in the gas tank with red.

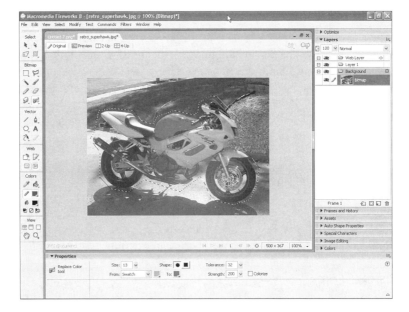

Next, click the To color well in the Property inspector to select the replacement color; then choose a color from the pop-up menu. You can also select a color from the image by dragging the tool over the color you want to replace.

The Property inspector enables you to control brush size and shape, as well as color tolerance and strength. Select Colorize to replace the Change color with the To color. Deselect Colorize to tint the Change color with the To color, leaving some of the Change color intact.

TIP

> Keep in mind that as you change the colors of your images or objects, you can always undo the effects if you don't like them by choosing Edit, Undo from the menu bar.

RED-EYE REMOVAL

The Red-Eye Removal tool is used to correct the red-eye effect in photographs. This tool is essentially a stripped-down version of the Replace Color tool in that it paints only red areas of an image and replaces the red pixels with grays and blacks (see Figure 3.26). The functionality of the Red-Eye Removal tool has been enhanced in Fireworks 8 to enable you to more accurately identify and remedy red-eye in your photographs.

Figure 3.26
Get the red out with the Red-Eye Removal tool.

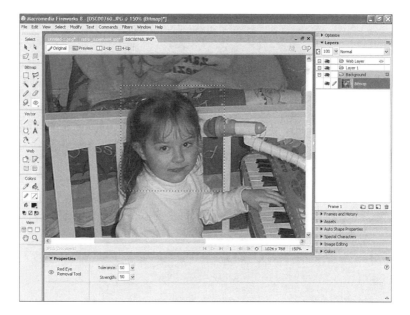

Select the Red-Eye Removal tool and drag a selection marquee across or click on the red pupils in the photograph to replace the red pixels. Use the Property inspector to set stroke attributes, brush tip size, brush tip shape, and tolerance (0 replaces only red; 255 replaces all hues that contain red). Strength sets the darkness of the grays used to replace reddish colors.

VECTOR TOOLS

Although working with photographs and imported images revolves around bitmaps, Fireworks also has some powerful vector tools that enable you to unleash the illustrator within. In addition, you can compress and export both photographs and vectors in formats that are optimized for the Web. This section looks at Fireworks's vector tools and what they can do.

LINE

The Line tool (see Figure 3.27) is used to draw straight lines. To draw a straight line, select the Line tool and then click on the canvas and drag to create the line. Hold down the Opt or Alt key while dragging to constrain the line to 45° increments. In the Property inspector you can adjust the stroke color, width, and line type, along with the selected line's transparency, overall size (width and height), and position (x and y fields).

Figure 3.27
A small sampling of some of the lines you can create with the Line tool.

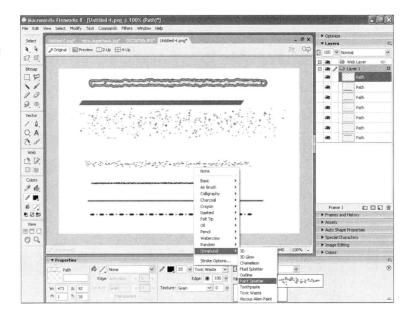

PEN TOOL

The Pen tool is used to draw complex shape and vector paths, similar in nature to the complex illustration tools offered by Macromedia's FreeHand illustration program. To draw straight lines, create plot points by clicking the pen tool anywhere on the canvas. It's as simple as playing connect-the-dots, as shown in Figure 3.28. Select the Pen tool and start clicking on the canvas. When you plot the next point, the previous line segment is deselected, as indicated by a hollow white center plot point. A straight line, representing the path, connects the two points.

TIP

When creating paths between plot points, holding the Shift key ensures that the lines are straight.

Figure 3.28
The Pen tool can draw lines after you plot a series of points.

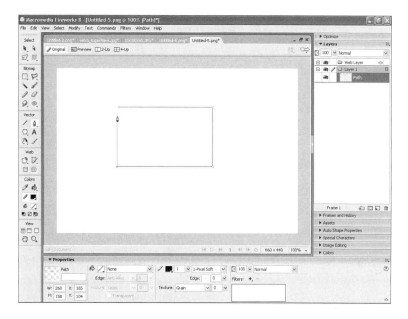

To draw an open path, plot the points until the path is complete and then double-click the final point or select any tool in the toolbar. To draw a closed path, create points until the shape is complete and return to click on the first point again. When you hover over the first point, a hollow circle appears to the right of the Pen tool cursor. Clicking on the first point closes the path.

To draw a curve, press and hold the mouse button down to position the control handles as you draw. While drawing curves is easy, drawing curves that actually represent what you had in your mind's eye is usually not (see Figure 3.29). Keep in mind that the farther you drag the mouse, the greater the effect on the curve. One way to practice drawing curves is by tracing existing images or other rounded objects to get the feeling for how curves are created.

After an object has been created with the Pen tool, you can easily remove the points that define its shape or add additional points to modify its shape. To remove a plot point, click on it and it is removed from the path. Remove curved points by clicking and dragging in the opposite direction of the curve. Add new plot points by clicking anywhere on the path where a plot point doesn't already exist. If you want to edit the location of existing plot points, choose the subselection tool and you can drag the plot point to a new location.

Figure 3.29
The Pen tool can be used to draw curved lines as well.

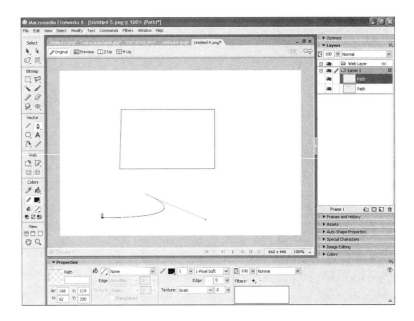

As you can see, the Pen tool offers many of the illustration features that are included in more complex illustration applications such as FreeHand or Illustrator. Although the Pen tool certainly can't compete with these applications for full-blown illustration, it does provide some of the basic functionality that enables you to illustrate within Fireworks without having to rely on one of these more complex applications.

VECTOR PATH

If you are interested in using Fireworks to create basic illustrations, the Vector Path tool (see Figure 3.30) is a great place to start. The Vector Path tool is the vector version of the Pencil tool, and it enables you to do freeform illustration. Points are automatically inserted as you draw. To use the Vector Path tool, select the tool from the Pen pop-up menu and start drawing. You can always come back and edit the shape later with the Sub-selection tool.

Use the Property inspector to control your line characteristics.

REDRAW PATH

The Redraw Path tool is another drawing tool that enables you to modify an existing path either by extending the path on either or both ends or by changing its existing structure. Using this tool enables you to extend or change any segment of the path while retaining the path's stroke, fill, and effect characteristics (see Figure 3.31). Basically, it gives you a quick, easy tool to make adjustments to any path on your canvas without having to redraw the path with the Pen tool.

Figure 3.30
The Vector Path tool is the freehand vector drawing tool.

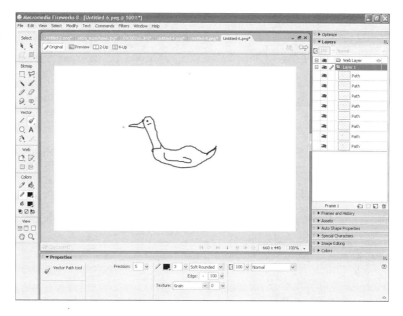

Figure 3.31
The Redraw Path tool is used to extend a previously drawn line segment.

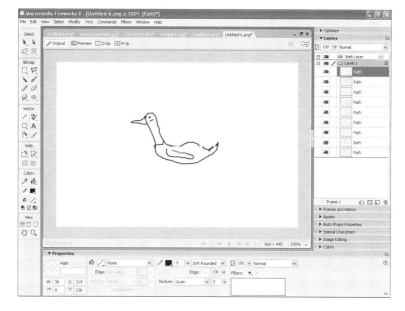

Select the Redraw Path tool, located in the Pen tool pop-up menu, and move the pointer directly over the path. The pointer changes to the Redraw Path pointer. Drag to extend the path segment and the new portion of the path is highlighted in red. Release the mouse button and you're good to go.

RECTANGLE

The Rectangle tool is used to draw rectangles and squares. To draw a rectangle, select the Rectangle tool and drag on the canvas to draw. Release the mouse button when you are finished and modify the rectangle's characteristics as needed in the Property inspector. To draw a perfect square, hold down the Shift key as you draw.

ELLIPSE

The Ellipse tool is used to draw ellipses and circles. To draw an ellipse, select the Ellipse tool from the Rectangle pop-up menu and drag on the canvas to draw. Release the mouse button when you are finished and modify the ellipse's characteristics as needed in the Property inspector. To draw a perfect circle, hold down the Shift key as you draw.

POLYGON

The Polygon tool is used to draw many-sided shapes and stars (see Figure 3.32). To draw a polygon, select the Polygon tool from the Rectangle pop-up menu and drag on the canvas to draw. Release the mouse button when you are finished and modify the polygon's characteristics as needed in the Property inspector.

Figure 3.32
Polygons and stars created with the Polygon tool.

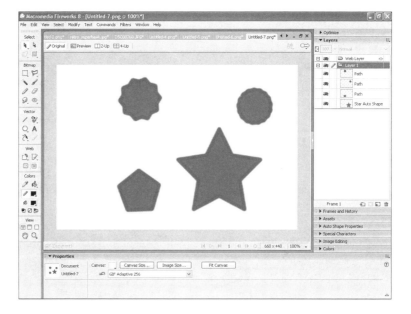

NOTE

One slightly annoying feature of this tool is that you can't change the number or angle of sides after you've drawn the polygon or star. You have to make those decisions before you draw the shape.

To draw a shape, select the Polygon tool (see Figure 3.33). Then, in the Property inspector, select Polygon or Star from the Shape menu, the number of sides or your new shape, and the angle for the sides. Finally, choose the fill and stroke features for the shape. With these options selected, draw the shape on the canvas.

Figure 3.33
Polygon tool options are accessed in the Property inspector and enable you to adjust the attributes of the object.

AUTO SHAPES

A look at the Auto Shapes tools in the toolbar Rectangle menu (see Figure 3.34) reveals a host of shapes that you can use in your designs. Even better, you can modify these shapes by using the control handles, as well as change their stroke and fill properties. Auto Shapes can also be ungrouped and modified as individual objects.

Figure 3.34
Auto Shapes simplifies the process of creating complex shapes by giving you "canned" shapes that can be modified.

Select an Auto Shape from the Shape pop-up menu in the toolbar and click and drag to draw your shape. Use the Property inspector, shown in Figure 3.35, to modify the width, height, position on the stage, fill, and stroke properties. Use the Auto Shape Properties panel to the right to set specific properties for the selected Auto Shape.

Figure 3.35
The Property inspector enables you to modify the various attributes of your shape.

Fireworks comes with the following Auto Shapes:

- **Arrow**—Draws simple arrow shapes of any proportions.
- **Beveled Rectangle**—Draws rectangles with beveled corners.
- **Chamfer Rectangle**—Draws rectangles with corners that are rounded to the inside of the rectangle.
- **Connector Line**—Draws three-segment connector lines like those used in flowcharts.
- **Doughnut**—Draws filled ring shapes.
- **L-Shape**—Draws corner shapes with right angles.
- **Pie**—Draws pie charts.
- **Rounded Rectangle**—Draws rectangles with rounded corners.
- **Smart Polygon**—Draws equilateral polygons with 3 to 25 sides.
- **Spiral**—Draws open spirals.
- **Star**—Draws stars with any number of points from 3 to 7.

The Auto Shapes tab in the Assets panel (see Figure 3.36) also lets you create your own shapes, as well as use shapes from third-party developers.

Figure 3.36
Shapes in the Shapes tab in the Assets panel that are shipped with Fireworks 8.

> **TIP**
>
> You can add also new Auto Shapes by using the Fireworks Exchange website. To add new Auto Shapes, display the Shapes tab in the Assets panel. Click the Options menu and choose Get More Auto Shapes. Fireworks connects to the Fireworks Exchange website. Follow the onscreen instructions to select new Auto Shapes and add them to Fireworks.

FREEFORM

The Freeform tool is one of the more fun tools to play with in Fireworks. This tool enables you to push and pull on various objects to change their curvature. For instance, as shown in Figure 3.37, you can push a segment of a straight line with the tool to create a curved shape. The size and pressure exerted by the tool can be adjusted with the Property inspector.

Figure 3.37
The Freeform tool enables you to push or pull a line segment to create a curve.

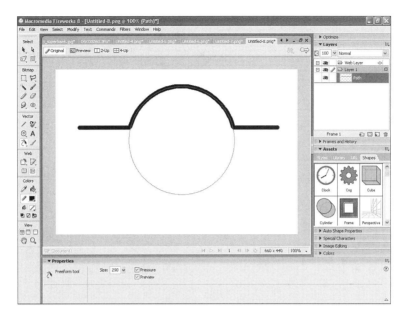

TIP

If you haven't quite gotten the hang of using the Pen tool to create curves, the Freeform tool provides a handy alternative for creating curves.

RESHAPE AREA TOOL

The Reshape Area tool (see Figure 3.38) is a nifty feature that enables you to stretch and mold paths. To use the tool, just select any path and then select the Reshape Area tool. As you roll your cursor over the path, you can see the various handles that are available for each object. Just click and drag any of the handles and you reshape the path as you drag.

PATH SCRUBBER—ADDITIVE AND SUBTRACTIVE

Use the Path Scrubber tools to change the appearance of a path with varying pressure applied to a pressure-sensitive tablet or changing speed if you're using a mouse. Path Scrubber properties, which include stroke size, angle, ink amount, scatter, hue, lightness, and saturation, can be specified in the Property inspector (see Figure 3.39). You can also specify how much pressure and speed affects these properties.

NOTE

Be aware that this feature allows you to adjust only paths that have a pressure-sensitive brush stroke. To adjust the pressure sensitivity of the stroke, select the path and then choose Stroke Options from the Stroke Category drop-down menu in the Property inspector. Click Advanced and choose the Sensitivity menu and the pressure can be adjusted in the Pressure field.

Figure 3.38
Edit and reshape your
vector paths with the
Reshape Area tool.

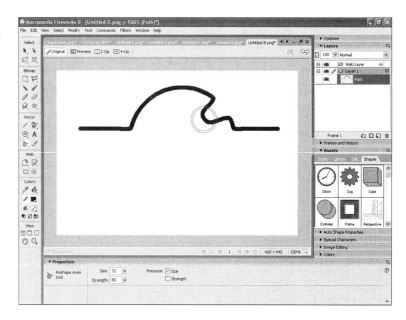

Figure 3.39
Control the pressure
and speed of the Path
Scrubber tools in the
Property inspector.

KNIFE TOOL

As indicated by the name, the Knife tool is used to cut objects apart. Select an object on the canvas, drag the knife across the object, and the plot points are created showing the path that was cut. You can then use the Pointer tool to drag the objects to different locations on the canvas as two separate objects.

NOTE

The Knife tool can split only individual objects. It does not work on AutoShapes or on objects that have been grouped together.

WEB TOOLS

Fireworks is the web designer's best friend when it comes to creating graphics for the online medium. Because many web graphics are used in interactions (links, rollovers, and so on), Fireworks has set aside several dedicated web objects and tools in the Web category of the Tools panel.

HOTSPOT

A hotspot is an area of the canvas that is intended to have user interaction. In Fireworks, this feature comes into play when you export an image as an HTML file and the hotspot becomes an area that provides a function (such as a hyperlink) or changes (such as rollover buttons) when the user rolls the mouse over the area or clicks on it. The Rectangle, Circle, and Polygon Hotspot tools (see Figure 3.40) create hotspots, or image maps, specific to their shape. To create a hotspot, simply drag the Hotspot tool to draw a hotspot over an area of the graphic. Hold down the Alt or Option key to draw from a center point. You can adjust a hotspot's position while you are drawing. While holding down the mouse button, press and hold down the Spacebar; then drag the hotspot to another location on the canvas. Release the Spacebar to continue drawing the hotspot.

Figure 3.40
Use the Polygon Hotspot tool to create an odd-shaped image map.

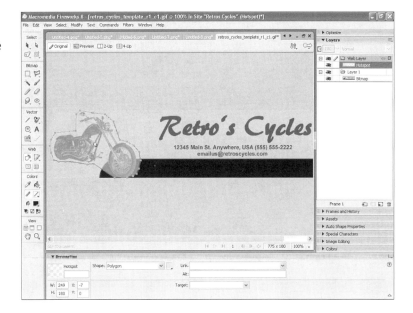

The Polygon Hotspot tool draws a hotspot by connecting a series of points; it's similar to the Pen tool, but without the capability to create curved points.

After you've created the hotspot, use the Property inspector to add the link URL, Alt tag, and Target (None, _blank, _self, _parent, _top) (see Figure 3.41).

Figure 3.41
Modify the hotspot or link settings in the Property inspector.

SLICE AND POLYGON SLICE

A slice is a place in the larger image where you want to create a smaller section that operates differently when the image is exported. Slices are usually areas where you want to create behaviors such as rollover effects or just want to have a larger image divided up into smaller portions.

To create a slice, select the Slice tool and drag to draw the slice object (see Figure 3.42). The slice object appears on the Web Layer, and the slice guides appear in the document.

As with a hotspot, you can use the Property inspector to add a link URL, Alt tag, and target, as well as set a default export compression for each individual slice. This is convenient for those times when you have a top banner for a site that needs some sections to be exported as JPEGs (logo graphics with gradients) and others as GIFs (text navigation).

The options you have for adding behaviors to both hotspots and slices in Fireworks are covered when the Behavior panel is discussed later in this chapter.

Figure 3.42
Create an image slice with the Slice tool or Polygon Slice tool.

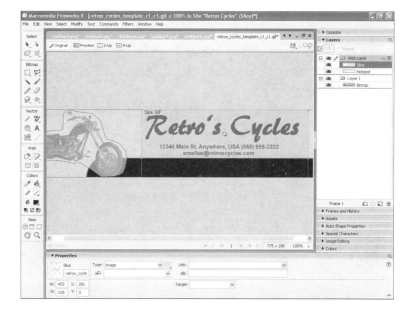

Use the Polygon Slice tool to create a slice by connecting a series of points, similar to the Pen tool.

TIP

Use the Hide and Show Slices buttons below the hotspot and slice tools on the toolbar (see Figure 3.43) to respectively hide or display your slices on the canvas.

Figure 3.43
Hide or show image
slices by using the
Hide or Show Slices
buttons.

PROPERTY INSPECTOR

Similar to the other development applications within the Studio suite, the Property inspector is a context-sensitive panel that changes options as you change your work. Choose a tool from the Tools panel, and the Property inspector displays tool options. Select a vector object, and it displays stroke and fill information. The inspector also displays effects, blending modes, and opacity, saving you tons of time and energy in opening other panels or dialog boxes.

This dynamic panel displays many of the common options for a selected object or tool. When no object or tool is selected, or when the work space is clicked on, the document options appear.

MENU BAR

The menu bar (see Figure 3.44) is chock full of commands that enable you to do everything from opening a file to applying sophisticated effects to your images. Because an encyclopedia could be written on just this topic alone, the following sections simply summarize the important commands in each menu.

Figure 3.44
The menu bar is
home to dozens of
robust commands.

FILE MENU

The File menu in Fireworks is similar to that of just about every other program. As the name suggests, commands in this menu affect whole files or documents. Some special File menu commands include the following:

- **Reconstitute Table**—Used to integrate Fireworks files with web pages in Dreamweaver by allowing you to easily update the table structure used in the HTML pages.

- **Batch Process**—Enables you to automate a series of customizable commands, such as image resizing, on a large group of files, all with the click of a couple buttons.

EDIT MENU

The Edit menu contains a few specialized commands for inserting Fireworks objects. Some unique Fireworks commands include the following:

- **Insert Fireworks Objects**—Enables you to insert objects such as a New Button, Symbol, Hotspot, Slice, Layer, or Frame.
- **Clipboard Variations**—Enables you to Copy HTML Code, Paste Inside, Paste As Mask, and Paste Attributes.
- **Preferences**—Enables you to customize your workspace. Editing Preferences are discussed later in this chapter.

VIEW MENU

The View menu is home to commands that control how you look at your workspace. In addition to the typical magnification, ruler, and guides commands is the Windows/Macintosh Gamma command. Computers that run Windows and Macintosh operating systems use different gamma settings, which typically results in Windows screens being darker than their Mac counterparts. Big whoop, you say. Well, what can happen is that the graphic that looks fine on your Windows monitor appears slightly washed out on the Macintosh monitor. Likewise, the graphic that works on a Macintosh monitor is darker on the Windows screen. Use the Windows/Macintosh Gamma command to toggle between the two gamma settings and see whether there is a difference on your graphics.

SELECT MENU

The Select menu is split into five categories:

- **Vector path and selection tools**—Used to select and edit vector points and paths.
- **Pixel selection tools**—Used to modify pixels of similar colors, feather selections, or invert selections.
- **Pixel region selection tools**—Used to expand, contract, and smooth selected regions of pixels.
- **Convert Marquee to Path command**—Transforms the existing shape of the Marquee into a path that can be edited and reshaped like any other Fireworks object.
- **Save Bitmap Selection tools**—Used to save and restore single bitmap selections.

MODIFY MENU

The Modify menu is the most frequently used menu in Fireworks. This menu contains commands that enable you to alter canvas and object attributes, stacking order, and grouping. Other commands of interest include the following:

- **Pop-Up Menu**—Launches a wizard that enables you to create pop-up menus.
- **Masks**—Provides several masking effects in a submenu.

- **Combine Paths**—Gives you the Join, Split, Union, Intersect, Punch, and Crop commands that allow you to play with ways to combine separate shapes.

TEXT MENU

The Text menu provides common commands for modifying font, style, paragraph settings, alignment, and even spelling. Some unique commands include

- **Attach to Path**—Allows you to attach text to a vector path (see Figure 3.45).

Figure 3.45
Use the Attach to Path command (Text, Attach to Path) to make text follow the contour of a vector path.

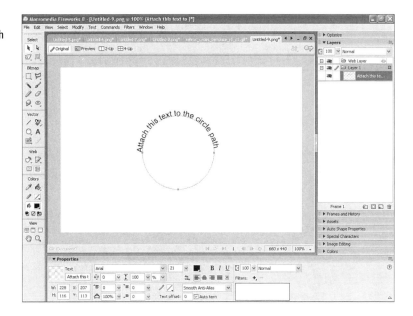

- **Convert to Paths**—Enables you to change text to vector objects so you can modify text as a graphic object.

COMMANDS MENU

The Commands menu is where you can really see the flexibility of Fireworks. Within the Commands menu are several ready-made commands, or macros, that you can use to make your life simpler. You can also create your own commands if you have the programming know-how.

Some interesting commands included in Fireworks are

- **Convert to Grayscale**—Found in the Creative submenu, this is similar to the popular command found in Photoshop.
- **Add Picture Frame**—Found in the Creative submenu, this command adds a textured frame around the canvas.

■ **Resize Selected Objects**—Provides a pop-up window that gives you a graphical interface with which to resize an object (see Figure 3.46). Nothing really special about this, except it looks cool.

Figure 3.46
The Resize Selected Objects command provides a visually slick way of resizing objects.

■ **Twist and Fade**—Also found in the Creative submenu, this third-party command enables you to create a vortex effect with any vector or bitmap graphic (see Figure 3.47). Be careful, though. It's addictive and resource intensive and could lock up the program if you call for too many steps.

Figure 3.47
The Twist and Fade command adds some more special effects to your graphics arsenal.

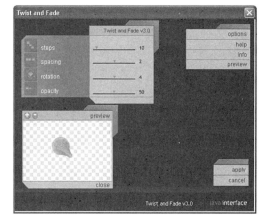

FILTERS MENU

The Filters menu contains all the bitmap filters. Included are filters that handle color adjustment, blurring, levels, curves, the sharpness of a mask, the amount of noise applied to an image, and so on. After it is applied to an image, a filter effect cannot be removed unless you use the Undo command (Edit, Undo Filter Image).

WINDOW MENU

The Window menu provides a list of all the panels and toolbars available in Fireworks. Think of it as your interface repository—just click on any of the selections in this menu and the appropriate panel or pop-up is displayed.

HELP MENU

Learn to appreciate the guidance and wisdom found within the Help menu. Here you can find the entire Fireworks 8 manual in HTML format. You can search for answers to those aching questions about how to draw those pesky Bezier curves with the Pen tool.

You can also access online support from the Fireworks Help Center, as well as exchange ideas on the Macromedia Online Forums. Visiting the forums becomes a daily part of your life if you're interested in expanding your Fireworks capabilities.

FIREWORKS PANELS

At first glance, the panels system used in Fireworks (and the other development applications in the Studio) can be a bit overwhelming. After you get used to the system, however, it's just a matter of finding the right panel and you have all the tools you need grouped together. Let's take a look at some of the most commonly used panels.

OPTIMIZE PANEL

The Optimize panel (see Figure 3.48) enables you to choose from the various compression options that are available for use when your image is exported. From the panel, you can choose between the various file types, color depths, and file quality.

Figure 3.48
The Optimize panel enables you to select from the various compression options.

LAYERS PANEL

The Layers panel (see Figure 3.49) overlays each of the objects that exist within the document. Using the Layers panel, you can adjust the grouping order and choose which layers should be displayed and which should be hidden. You get a more extensive look at the Layers panel in Chapter 4, "Developing Graphics and Animations."

Figure 3.49
The Layers panel enables you to stack objects on the canvas and adjust the order in which they are stacked.

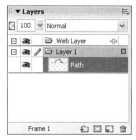

ASSETS PANEL

The Assets panel provides access to reusable objects such as shading styles, recently used URLs, custom objects, and various shapes. Using the elements stored in any of the subpanels is as easy as dragging them into your workspace.

STYLES TAB

The Styles tab (see Figure 3.50) enables you to easily apply custom fills, gradients, and coloring to your Fireworks objects. To apply a style, simply select your object and click the style you would like applied to it.

Figure 3.50
The Styles tab enables you to apply custom shading and gradients.

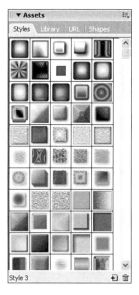

URL TAB

Typing in the same URL over and over can become a tedious task when developing web objects within Fireworks. Luckily, Fireworks 8 remembers the URLs that you have used in the past and stores them in the URL tab (see Figure 3.51). To apply a URL, simply choose a hotspot or slice and select the URL from the drop-down list. You can even create your own custom URL libraries that contain URLs for different uses.

Figure 3.51
The URL tab stores
URLs and enables you
to create custom URL
libraries.

LIBRARY TAB

The Library tab (see Figure 3.52) saves information about symbols that are stored in the current document. Each symbol has a name and a type, and can be reused if you drag it from the panel onto the canvas. The objects in the Library can be sorted by name or by type if you click on the appropriate column header and click the Toggle Sorting button.

Figure 3.52
The Library tab stores
information about
symbols that you
have created.

SHAPES TAB

The Shapes tab (see Figure 3.53) stores the Auto Shapes that supplement those available with the Auto Shape tools. You can download additional Auto Shapes by clicking the menu on the Shapes tab and choosing Get More Auto Shapes.

Figure 3.53
The Shapes tab enables you to easily access any Auto Shapes that you have added to the panel.

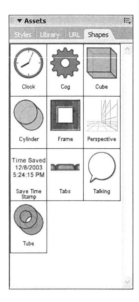

FRAMES AND HISTORY PANEL

The Frames and History panel enables you to track the animation frames that you have created and to also view the actions you have taken in developing your images.

FRAMES TAB

The Frames tab (see Figure 3.54) displays information about the frames you have created toward animating your images. For a complete overview of how frames can be used to develop animations, check out Chapter 7, "Putting It All Together: The Images and Page Layout for Retro's Cycles."

Figure 3.54
The Frames tab shows information about animation frames and enables you to adjust timings.

HISTORY TAB

The History tab (see Figure 3.55) enables you to review the steps you have taken in developing your images. The number of steps that are stored is based on the preferences you set for Fireworks in the Preferences dialog box (Edit, Preferences). By default, Fireworks 8 stores 20 steps, and you can move through the steps and see them replayed by moving the slider on the left side up or down. If you want to replay a set of steps, select them and click the Replay button. You can also save and reuse steps at a later time by selecting the steps and clicking the Save Steps As Command icon.

Figure 3.55
You can easily retrace your steps by moving the slider up or down on the History tab.

CUSTOMIZATION WITH PREFERENCES

It's a fact of life that no two designers are alike. How you like to organize your workspace is different from how I organize mine. The copy of Fireworks 8 you installed on your desktop has preset preferences that the folks at Macromedia thought you'd enjoy. You may like what they've done, and you may be yearning to go in and tailor the program to fit your style.

Most people don't bother messing with customizing their preferences unless they use the program on a daily basis. If you have a hankering to make some changes, read on.

For the most part, the preference settings (accessed by choosing Edit, Preferences) are self-explanatory. I'll review a few key preferences that you may want to consider changing. Note that you need to restart Fireworks for the new preferences to take effect.

GENERAL TAB

The General tab (see Figure 3.56) contains settings that influence the basic aspects of the Fireworks environment. One setting worth changing is the number of Undo Steps. The default setting is 20. The higher the setting, the more RAM is sucked up. The lower the setting, the less RAM is used, but the more hampered you are by your mistakes. It's a balancing act and you will have to determine what's best for you. I like to set my Undo Steps to 10.

Figure 3.56
The General tab enables you to customize basic aspects of the Fireworks environment.

EDITING TAB

The Editing tab settings (see Figure 3.57) affect workflow. You can change cursor styles, hide edges, display striped borders, and so on. Checking the Pen Preview, however, is handy if you're just learning how to use the Pen tool because the next line segment is displayed while you're drawing.

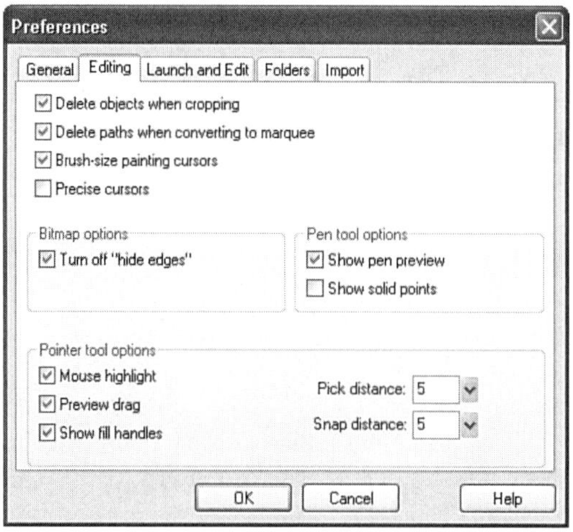

Figure 3.57
The Editing tab enables you to customize workflow settings.

LAUNCH AND EDIT

Launch and Edit settings are used to control how Fireworks integrates with other Macromedia programs such as Dreamweaver. Because most Fireworks graphics comprise an editable graphic (Fireworks PNG) and an exported graphic (JPEG or GIF), the launch and edit settings enable you to select one of the following three options:

- **Always Use Source PNG**—Opens the source PNG file when editing from another application. When you're finished with the file, the original optimization settings are used when it's exported again.

- **Never Use Source PNG**—Opts not to use the source PNG to open the exported JPEG or GIF in Fireworks.

- **Ask When Launching**—Prompts you to decide what to do on a case-by-case basis. Because I believe there are few absolutes in life, I keep the default Ask When Launching setting.

FOLDERS

The Folders tab enables you to designate where plug-ins, textures, and patterns are stored. After restarting Fireworks, the program loads all plug-ins, textures, and patterns in those folders.

IMPORT

The Import tab provides controls on how Photoshop objects are imported into Fireworks:

- **The Layers section**—Dictates how Photoshop layers are brought into Fireworks. They can be imported as Fireworks Objects or as Fireworks Frames. The Share Layer Between Frames option imports the Photoshop layers as Fireworks sublayers and also designates those layers as shared.

- **The Text section**—Enables you to decide whether you want to retain editability or appearance. If you want to preserve the font style from the Photoshop object but don't have the font, select Maintain Appearance. If you want to edit the text, select Editable.

- **The Use Flat Composite Image option**—Flattens and merges all Photoshop layers.

TROUBLESHOOTING

I have used Photoshop in the past and have plug-ins that I would like to use in Fireworks. Is this possible?

Sure. To use Photoshop plug-ins, you need to indicate where the plug-ins are located in your Fireworks 8 preferences. To do this, choose Edit, Preferences and click the Folders tab. Then browse to where your plug-ins are located. You need to close Fireworks and restart it for the settings to take effect.

After I start using the Polygon Lasso tool, is there a way I can go back a step without having to start all over again?

To go back a step, simply release the mouse button. Hold down the Shift key, press Alt or the Option key, and then release the Alt or Option key to temporarily display an arrow cursor. The selection path is reset to wherever you click with the arrow cursor. The cursor then reverts back to the Polygon Lasso tool and you can continue your work.

Is there an easy way to swap the line color and the fill color for an object?

The quickest way to swap colors is to use the Swap Stroke/Fill Colors button on the Tools palette. Just select an object, click the button, and you'll notice that the colors are swapped.

BEST PRACTICES—KNOWING WHEN AND HOW YOUR IMAGES WILL BE VIEWED

Developing graphics and animations is a lot of hard work and a lot of fun. All those cool tools, effects, gradients, and animation tools at your disposal make it easy to get immersed in the process. It's important, however, that throughout the process you consider where and by whom your graphics will be used.

For instance, if you are building a website that will be available to the general public, it's unlikely that every one of your visitors will have a broadband connection. Therefore, adding "heavy" graphics that are large in file size could render some visitors unable to view your site properly. If they have to wait five minutes for a navigation image to load, they probably won't stick around for the rest of the site.

Additionally, it's a very good idea to keep track of who is using your images and in what manner. The last thing you want to have happen is for someone to take an image on which you worked long and hard and stretch it beyond its limitations—resulting in a cruddy-looking image that others think you created. Be prepared to distribute images and logos in a variety of formats, with differently colored (and transparent) backgrounds, and in different sizes. This reduces the risk that someone will do a chop-job on your image to meet some specific need.

Finally, it's good practice to remember that although graphics are a good way to enhance your site, an increasing number of visitors on the web have visual disabilities. To accommodate these users, don't forget to add Alt text to your images within your web pages to allow these visitors to take full advantage of your site.

DEVELOPING GRAPHICS AND ANIMATIONS

In this chapter

GRAPHICS AS OBJECTS

The two types of graphics used in Fireworks are *bitmap graphics* and *vector graphics* (see Figure 4.1). The simplest way to explain the difference between the two is that bitmap graphics are made up of rows and columns of pixels, whereas vector graphics are made up of points in space that are connected by strokes and then colorized with fills. Each of these elements (points, strokes, and fills) are rendered mathematically on the screen as opposed to being displayed physically as pixels are.

Figure 4.1
Notice the difference in selection between the bitmap graphics on the left and the vector graphics on the right. The bitmap graphics are selected by pixel, whereas the vector graphics are selected as individual objects.

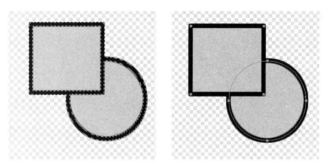

Understanding how Fireworks handles and organizes the elements in your files will help you have a better understanding of how to create graphics for different mediums, as well as increase your productivity.

BITMAP GRAPHICS

If you're familiar with the form of painting called pointillism, where tiny primary-color dots are used to generate secondary colors, then working with bitmap graphics is nothing new. If you've never heard of pointillism, fear not. Simply magnify a bitmap graphic such as a photo to see the individual building blocks, or pixels, that create the graphic, as shown in Figure 4.2.

Each pixel can have only one color. When these pixels are arranged in rows and columns, the human eye blends the individual colors together to create the illusion of an image.

The more dots that are used to define an area of an image, the higher the overall quality of the image will be. Accordingly, bitmap images are quantified by the relationship between the number of pixels and the size of the image. This is known as *resolution* and is usually measured in dots per inch (dpi) for print, or pixels per inch (ppi) for the screen.

If you want to edit a bitmap graphic, you have to modify individual pixels. In addition, because a bitmap graphic is rendered with a finite number of pixels, there is no way to enlarge the image without lowering resolution.

Photographs are bitmap images and you will use Fireworks's bitmap tools to modify photographs, as well as use bitmap effects such as blurring and color replacement.

Figure 4.2
The image on the left is at normal (100%) magnification, whereas the image on the right has been enlarged 800% to show the individual pixels that comprise the image.

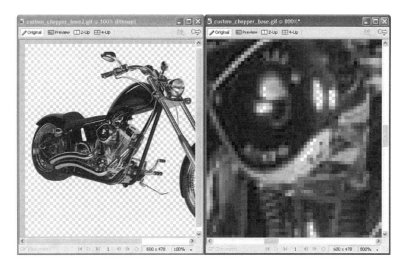

VECTOR GRAPHICS

Vector graphics rely on mathematical instructions that tell the computer how to draw graphics. As an example, a vector might have instructions such as "Draw a circle, starting 100 pixels to the right and 50 pixels down from the top-left corner, with a radius of 200 pixels; draw a red stroke over the circle path that is 2 pixels wide, and fill the circle with a yellow color."

On the other side of the coin, the bitmap version would just describe the pixels that are white (background), red (stroke), and yellow (fill).

Here's where an important concept comes into play. A vector graphic contains instructions for each object it contains. In the circle example, the instructions would create a circle object. The same file could have a line object, a square object, and a text object. Each object would be completely separate from the others.

Because all vector graphics are independent of each other and because a specific set of directions is used to construct them, they are always editable. In addition, because vector objects are independent of the canvas behind them, they are also independent of a graphic's resolution. That's the beauty of vector graphics: They're scalable, whereas bitmap graphics are not.

PATHS VERSUS STROKES

The basic shape or line of a vector graphic is called a *path*. Every vector shape is a path. That path is the representation of a mathematical formula.

Accordingly, each path can have several attributes applied to it. These attributes are what you use to change the path and include stroke and fill color. A path's stroke is the coloring that is painted on the path, whereas the path's fill is the color, or pattern, that covers the area enclosed by the path (see Figure 4.3). Fireworks also enables you to add several more attributes to your paths known as *effects*, such as bevels, glows, drop shadows, and several others.

Figure 4.3
Selecting a polygon helps identify the path, stroke, and fill.

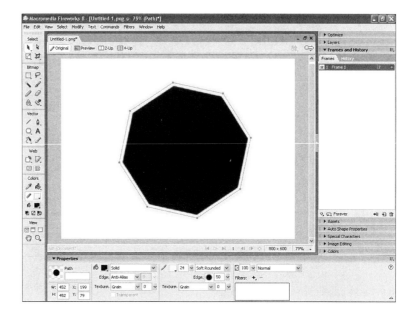

Even if you cannot see a stroke, the path is still there. It's a confusing concept for many, but remember that you can have a path without a visually represented stroke, but you can't have a stroke without a path.

To drive this home another way, modifying paths and modifying strokes are two different things. When you modify a path, you reshape it. When you modify a stroke, you can change its thickness, color, and visual appearance.

LAYERS

The best way to understand layers is to think of each layer as a sheet of acetate like those used with overhead projectors. Layers are independent levels that contain bitmap or vector graphics. The final image is made up of a stack of all the layers within the image, depending on the order in which the layers are laid and the transparency levels that are set for each layer. You can work on each layer as if it were an independent image, without interference from any graphical elements that are on other layers.

It is best to place every new element, or addition to an element, on its own layer. You can always merge (combine) layers, and it is much safer and faster to build each element a layer at a time. After you are satisfied with the look, you can then combine the elements that make up that object.

When you place bitmap graphics on top of each other in the same layer, the pixels of the top object replace the pixels of the object beneath it. After all, only one pixel can occupy a space at a time. To keep the bitmap objects separate, you use layers.

Unlike bitmaps, vector objects can be placed on top of one another on a single layer without affecting one another. They create their own sublayers. So, why use layers with vector objects? Simply put, for organization. Using layers, you can organize your content into logical hierarchies.

Any time you create or import an object, it appears in its own layer in Fireworks. A default name is automatically applied to the layer. I use the default name unless I'm working with files where several layers come into play. At that point, it's handy to know how to organize the layers.

LAYERS PANEL BASICS

As was mentioned briefly in Chapter 3, "Introducing Fireworks 8," the Layers panel enables you to control the object layers in your document. The Layers panel main area (see Figure 4.4) comprises five main columns:

Figure 4.4
The Layers panel for a simple document with a bitmap image, vector graphic, and text. Note that each object appears in its own layer.

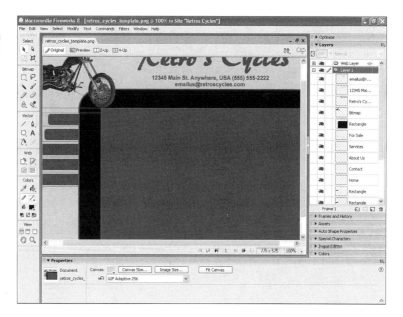

- **Expand/Collapse Layer**—When a collapsed layer contains sublayers, a triangular arrow pointing down (Macintosh) or a + sign (Windows) is shown. Click that arrow or + sign to expand the layer. When the layer is expanded, you see an arrow pointing to the right (Mac) or a – sign (Windows). Click this icon to collapse the layer.

- **Show/Hide Layer**—This column contains the eye icon. When you see the eye, the object on the layer is visible. Click the eyeball to hide the object on the layer. The eyeball icon is also hidden. Hidden layers do not affect the contents of the file, and they are not exported with the file.

- **Lock/Unlock Layer**—The padlock icon indicates that a layer is locked and cannot be edited. Click the icon to lock or unlock the layer. You can lock only full layers, not sublayers.

- **Layer Column**—The layer column contains both the layer name and the thumbnail of the layer's contents.
- **Object in Layer Column**—The last column doesn't have an official name, so we'll just use its function as a name. This column appears beside only full layers, not sublayers. When you select any sublayer, the little blue box (Object in Layer marker) appears for the layer that contains the selected sublayer. If you click the Object in Layer column in any other layer or drag the box to another layer, the selected sublayer is moved to the new layer.

To move layers, or change the stacking order, you can drag the layer or sublayer up or down to a new position in the stack. You can also select a sublayer, and then click in the Object in Layer column of the layer where you want it to move. This option does not work on layers; it works only on sublayers.

To rename layers, double-click the layer and the name can be edited. Type the new name and press Return/Enter to seal the deal.

FRAMES

Whereas layers organize objects in space, frames organize objects based on time and state. Why does an image editing program need to worry about time or state, you might ask? Fireworks is used predominantly to create web graphics, which often include animations and images that change based on events such as the location of the mouse. In these cases, you need to be able to indicate what an image should do and in what state it should be when a certain period of time expires or an event occurs.

To handle how graphics change, Fireworks uses the concept of frames. Fireworks frames work along the same lines as frames in a movie reel, where each frame is the same size and is in the same position, but the visual contents may change to create the illusion of motion. As you roll through the individual frames, an animated effect is created.

FRAMES PANEL BASICS

The Frames panel works much like the Layers panel, except it is divided into three main columns (see Figure 4.5):

- **Skinning**—Onion Skinning is an animation technique that enables you to view multiple frames at the same time.
- **Frame Name and Number**—The main column displays the frame name, which is set to default to Frame X, where X represents the frame number.
- **Frame Delay**—This column contains the value for the frame delay, which is represented in 100ths of second. The frame is displayed for that duration of time before the animation advances to the next frame. This column also contains the Object in Frame marker, which functions the same way as the Object in Layer marker.

Figure 4.5
The Frames panel for a simple animation.

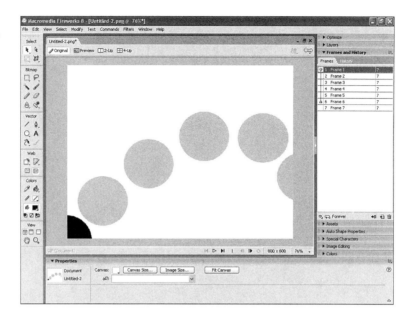

To move frames, drag them up or down in the stack.

To duplicate a frame—an excellent way to distribute positioned content across multiple frames—drag the frame to the New/Duplicate Frame button. When the button appears depressed, release the mouse. The frame and all its layers and sublayers are then copied.

> **TIP**
>
> You can also use the Options menu on the Frames panel to add, delete, or duplicate frames.

To rename a frame, double-click the frame and the name can be edited. Type the new name and press Return/Enter to save the name.

LAYERS AND FRAMES

When you create a new object, it appears on its own sublayer within a layer. As you continue to create your masterpiece, more layers and sublayers are added to the composition.

Let's say you're making an animation and start incorporating frames. Now you have several layers and will be adding several frames. How do layers and frames interact with each other?

SHARED VERSUS UNSHARED LAYERS

The relationship between layers and frames is based on whether or not the layer is shared. Shared layers are the same in every frame. Unshared layers may be different in each frame.

When you add a new frame, Fireworks copies all the unshared layers into the new frame. If you decide to add a new unshared layer in any frame when you're halfway through the project, Fireworks automatically adds that unshared layer to every other frame. Unshared Layers is the default setting for layers. If you want a new layer to be shared, you need to double-click on the layer name in the Layers panel and check the box to indicate that it should be shared.

To share a layer, select the layer. In the Layers panel options menu, select Share This Layer (see Figure 4.6). A check appears beside the option and a Shared Layer icon next to the layer name.

Figure 4.6
You decide whether a layer is shared or unshared.

WEB LAYER

A web layer is always shared. You don't have a say in that. On top of every layer stack in Fireworks is the web layer. You cannot delete it, rename it, or do anything unsavory with it. The web layer is where all web objects, such as slices and hotspots, are stored.

To the right of the web layer's name is the Shared Layer icon. This icon indicates that the web layer's contents are available and identical for all frames in your document.

SIMPLE ROLLOVER

The most basic animation is the Simple Rollover. Rollovers are frequently seen in navigation bars and in buttons on web pages.

The rollover comprises two images: an Up image and an Over image. When a web page is first loaded, the Up image is displayed. When the mouse is moved over or rolls over the Up image, it is replaced with the Over image.

CAUTION

Because both images share the same space, they must be the same size in the overall image. Any variation in size ends up with a "hiccup" during the mouseover and causes the Over image to be distorted.

To create a Simple Rollover button, the first thing you need to do is to create the button's Up and Over states, using Frames 1 and 2. For instance, you could create a piece of black text in Frame 1 for the Up state and then have the same text (same location and size) appear in red in Frame 2.

After you've created two visual arrangements for the button's Up and Over states, use the Slice tool and drag it over the visuals you want to change to create a slice. With the slice still selected, open the Behavior panel Window, Behaviors and click the Behavior (+) button to open the list of behaviors. Select Simple Rollover from the list and Fireworks creates the rollover. The Up state is automatically set as the visual content under the slice in Frame 1, and the visual content in Frame 2 is the Over state.

For ease of use when the rollover graphic is exported to Dreamweaver, you can enter the URL in the Property Inspector's Link field as well as the Alt text in the Alt field. You may also want to delete the default slice name and give each slice a more meaningful name.

You can test simple rollovers in Fireworks' preview mode by clicking the Preview button at the top of the document window (see Figure 4.7).

Figure 4.7
Use the Preview button in the document window to test the Simple Rollover. The left image is the Up state and the right image represents the Over state.

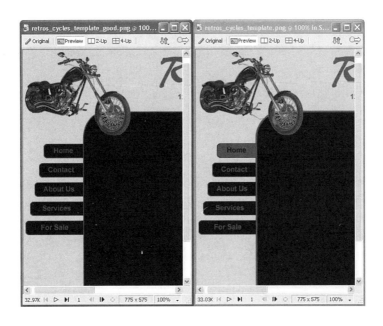

SWAP IMAGE BEHAVIOR

Similar to the Simple Rollover is the Swap Image behavior. The Simple Rollover substitutes the contents of a frame slice with the contents of another frame slice. Although the Swap Image behavior can do that as well, it is mostly used to create disjoint rollovers.

When rolling over one image causes a different image to change, you have a *disjoint rollover*. For example, rolling over Image A causes Image B to change to Image B1 (see Figure 4.8).

Figure 4.8
Rolling over the Home button causes the text below the navigation buttons to appear as well. An image can have both a simple rollover and a disjoint rollover. Using the previous example, rolling over Image A would replace Image A with Image A1 and Image B with Image B1.

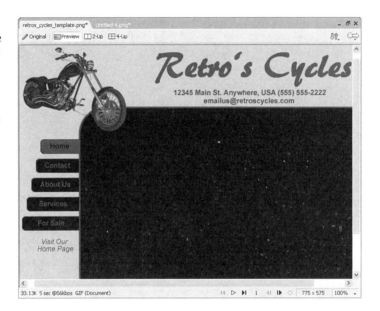

To build a disjoint rollover, follow these steps:

1. Create all assets in their final positions. You need at least two frames and two slices. Use the Slice tool to add a slicing scheme over the affected areas of the document.

2. Select the slice covering the trigger image. The trigger image is the image that users will roll over or click to make the disjoint behavior work. Click the Add Behavior (+) button in the Behaviors panel. Select Swap Image from the menu and the Swap Image dialog box appears (see Figure 4.9).

3. Select the target slice. The target slice is the image that will be affected by the rollover action in the trigger image. You can select the slice in the list or select the slice thumbnail in the slice reconstruction window.

4. Next, select an image to swap from a different frame or an external file. In this example you've already created the image that will be swapped, so select another frame.

Figure 4.9
The Swap Image dialog box enables you to select the target slice for the disjoint rollover.

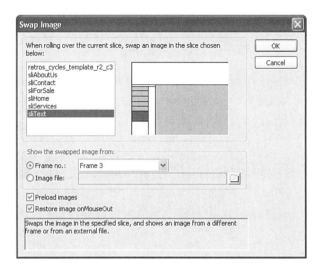

TIP

Preload Images is selected by default to ensure that the swapped image is loaded before the user mouses over the image. I would suggest leaving this option checked to ensure that the swapped image executes quickly, without the new image having to be downloaded at the time of the swap

Restore Image onMouseOut is also the default if you want the original image to be swapped back in after the user rolls out of the trigger image.

5. Click OK to apply the behavior and close the Swap Image dialog box.

NAVIGATION BARS WITH FOUR-STATE BUTTONS

Moving up the complexity ladder is a navigation bar with four-state buttons. The Set Nav Bar Image behavior is used to create this type of navigation bar, where the buttons not only have rollovers, but also communicate to the user which page is currently being browsed.

A navigation bar using this behavior has four states. Each state represents the button's appearance in reaction to a mouse event:

- The Up state is the default or untouched appearance of the button.
- The Over state is the way the button appears when the pointer is moved over it.
- The Down state represents the button after it is clicked.
- The Over While Down state is the appearance when the user moves the pointer over a button that is in the Down state.

To add the Set Nav Bar Image behavior, follow these steps:

1. First, you need to build a navigation bar. Begin by creating a background shape and a piece of text.

2. Next, make those graphics into a Button symbol by choosing Modify, Symbol, Convert to Symbol (F8) and select Button in the dialog box. Make sure you replace the default Symbol name with a more meaningful name.

3. Press OK to convert the text and image into a button symbol.

4. Double-click the new button symbol to launch the Button Symbol Editor. Modify the button attributes in the editor for each of the four states (see Figure 4.10).

5. In the Down and the Over While Down states, make sure that the Include in Nav Bar option (located at the top of the editor) is checked. These options should be checked by default.

Repeat this process for the rest of your navigation bar buttons.

TIP

> To make life easier after you export the navigation bar, take a moment to select each slice and enter a name for the slice, a label for the button, and a URL in the Property inspector.

Figure 4.10
Use the Button Symbol Editor to create four states (Up, Over, Down, and Over While Down) to each button in the navigation bar.

Double-check that everything is going to work by selecting each button and looking in the Behaviors panel. Each slice should now have the Set Nav Bar Image behavior applied to it (see Figure 4.11).

Figure 4.11
Select each slice and use the Behaviors panel to make sure the Set Nav Bar Image behavior is selected.

For the ultimate test, you need to export the file to HTML and view it in your browser. Choose File, Export to get started. In the Export dialog box, make sure that HTML and Images is selected in the Export field.

Click the Options button to launch the HTML Setup dialog box. Click the Document Specific tab. Make sure that the Export Multiple Nav Bar HTML Pages box is checked. Click OK to close the HTML Setup dialog box so Fireworks will export additional pages for each button in the navigation bar. Click Save to complete the export.

Open the page in your browser to see how it works or preview it by clicking the Quick Export button and choosing Preview in Browser from the context menu.

FIREWORKS AND ANIMATION

Creating animations for the web in Fireworks is a lot more fun to think about than to do. The best animation tool is obviously Flash because the program was designed for the job of creating motion.

That being said, however, Fireworks can be used to build simple animations. In fact, there are three different methods you can use to create animations: frame-by-frame, tweened, and animation symbols. Each has its own pros and cons and is discussed later in this chapter. Before you start tweening away to make the next full-feature animation, you should take a look at what's involved in building a good animation.

ANIMATION PLANNING

Motion on the web, or on film, is an illusion. Animation is a series of still images, each with a slight change in appearance from the previous image, that are rapidly presented to the viewer. The human eye processes these images and blends them into a smooth motion. If the images move too slowly, the illusion is gone. This speed is measured as frame rate. Frame rate is measured in frames per second (fps). Most movies and television shows shot on film have a frame rate of 24 fps. Most shows shot on video have a frame rate of 30 fps.

Moving to the web, there is another concern to throw into the mix. The higher the resolution of a pixel-based image, or the more points in a piece of vector artwork, the higher the file size, which results in a longer download time. Increasing the frame rate in an animation also increases the file size.

Bitmap animations have a sequence of bitmap graphics. Each bitmap graphic is added together to complete the animation in terms of file size. Although file compression helps reduce the file size, bitmap graphics can get large quickly. The most common bitmap animation type is the Animated GIF.

Vector animations have vector graphics on each frame. Vector animations just change object parameters from frame to frame and are accordingly smaller in file size than bitmap animations. The most common vector animation type is Macromedia's Flash SWF format.

Before you build an animation, however, there is another issue we need to discuss: What is the output format for the final animation?

An Animated GIF typically has a large file size, but is universally compatible with nearly all browsers. This type of animation is restricted by the GIF file format's limited 256-color palette, and it cannot incorporate sound or any other interactivity. In addition, blends and complex patterns often lose their smooth transitions because of the palette limitations. The Animated GIF is, however, a piece of cake to implement.

The Flash SWF, on the other hand, typically has a small file size, can incorporate both pixel and vector-based artwork, and is compatible with all browsers with the Flash player installed. Currently the player penetration is rated at about 94% of all browsers for the Flash player. The Flash SWF offers the capability to add sound as well as complex interactivity. Mastering Flash, however, takes some expertise that you might wish to acquire by reading the Flash chapters in this book.

BUILDING AN ANIMATION

After you have decided the output format for your animation, you can start building your creative masterpiece of motion. Again, Fireworks enables you to build animations using the frame-by-frame method, the tweened method, or the animation symbols method.

FRAME-BY-FRAME ANIMATION

Frame-by-frame animation is the most basic method of the three types of animation you can do in Fireworks. Each element in each frame is repositioned or modified to create the illusion of motion. Remember the stick figures you drew on your school notebooks and how you flipped through the pages to make them move? Those flip books used frame-by-frame animation.

Frame-by-frame animation requires the artist to create each frame by hand. Tweening and animation symbols use the computer to automate the drawing process required between frames.

The simplest way to create an animation is to create an object, add a new frame, place the object on the new frame, and modify it in some way (change color, reposition, and so on). Repeat each step of this process until the animation is built.

The rub with this method is that you cannot see the previous frame as a point of reference if you're moving the object. If you've ever seen hand animators at work, they're constantly flipping between sheets of tracing paper (also known as onion skin) to gather their reference points for the animation.

Fortunately, Fireworks offers two solutions to this dilemma: Onion Skinning and the Distribute to Frames command.

ONION SKINNING

Onion Skinning pays homage to the traditional animation work process, where animators worked on translucent pieces of paper so they could see several layers of drawings simultaneously. In Fireworks, Onion Skinning simulates that process by displaying nearby frames partially grayed out (see Figure 4.12).

Figure 4.12
Onion Skinning enables you to use surrounding frames to aid in positioning graphics in the animation.

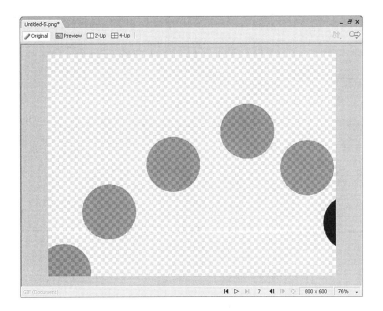

To use Onion Skinning, open the Frames panel. In the lower-left corner is the Onion Skinning button. Click the button to view the Onion Skinning menu (see Figure 4.13). The No Onion Skinning option turns off the feature and shows only the active frame. All other options show a user a selected range of frames. Note that all ranges are relative to the active frame. If you select the Multi-Frame Editing option, all visible objects can be edited, including those on inactive frames.

DISTRIBUTE TO FRAMES

Another option is to use the Distribute to Frames command, which takes a group of selected objects and sends each to its own frame in the order in which it is stacked in the Layers panel.

Figure 4.13
The Onion Skinning
menu provides
several display
options.

To use the Distribute to Frames command, create all the objects in one layer. Notice that there are several sublayers, depending on how many objects you create. Use the Layers panel to make sure your objects are in the proper stacking order for the animation. Because objects are distributed from bottom to top, make sure the graphic that starts your animation is the bottom sublayer and the graphic that ends your animation is the top sublayer.

Select all the objects you want to include in the animation with Edit, Select All, or Shift-click if you want to selectively choose graphics. Click the Distribute to Frames button in the Frames panel and Fireworks automatically inserts each graphic in its own frame, in order (see Figure 4.14).

Figure 4.14
Use the Distribute to
Frames command to
automatically place
each layered object
in its own frame.

PLAYING YOUR ANIMATION

After you've created your animation, you'll want to see whether you've effectively created the illusion of motion. Built right into the document window is a set of playback controls, similar to those found in a VCR (see Figure 4.15).

The animation plays back at a high frame rate and loops continuously. To change the frame delay, which determines how long the active frame is displayed, double-click in the frame delay of any frame. Remember that frame delay is measured in 100ths of a second. The default frame delay of 7 indicates the frame is delayed seven-tenths of a second. To hold the frame for 3 seconds, enter a value of 300.

To control the looping properties of your animation, click the GIF Animation Looping button at the bottom of the Frames panel (see Figure 4.16). Select an option (No Looping, 1–5, 10, 20 and Forever) to set the looping properties.

Figure 4.15
Use the playback controls in the document window to preview your animation.

Figure 4.16
The GIF Animation Looping button controls the looping properties for the animation.

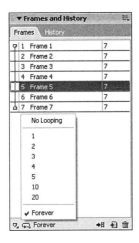

TWEENED ANIMATION

After you've worked with frame-by-frame animations, playing with tweened animations will appear to be a piece of cake. To build a tweened animation, you create a visual beginning and an end point, and then define the number of frames, or steps, in between. Fireworks does the rest. Most tweened animations involve visual changes such a position on the stage, rotation, or scale of the beginning instance and the ending instance.

To create a tweened animation, create a vector object and convert it to a graphic symbol by choosing Modify, Convert to Symbol (F8), and selecting Graphic Symbol in the Symbol Properties dialog box (see Figure 4.17). Drag two instances of the symbol onto the canvas from the Library tab or the Assets panel. Or select the first instance and duplicate it (Edit, Duplicate). They must be instances of the same symbol.

Position and modify each instance as desired. Select both instances and choose Modify, Symbol, Tween Instances (see Figure 4.18). Enter the number of steps in the Tween Instances dialog box. Select the Distribute to Frames option to distribute the symbols across frames. If you want to modify the symbols, leave this option unchecked.

Figure 4.17
After creating the first object in a tweened animation, convert the object to a graphic symbol.

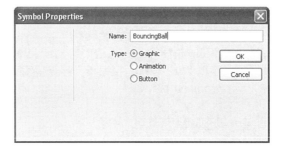

Figure 4.18
Use the Tween Instances command to create the tweened animation.

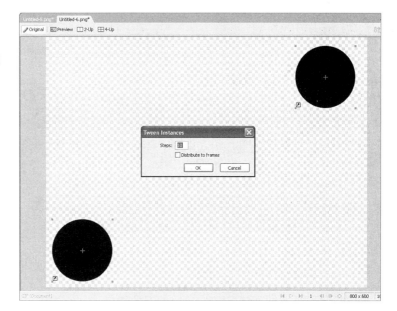

ANIMATION SYMBOLS

Animation symbols are one of the three symbol types in Fireworks (animation, button, and graphic). They are stored in the Fireworks library, and you can use them by simply dragging each symbol onto the canvas. The beauty of using animation symbols is that they hold objects in multi-frame animations together as a single unit. If you move one of the objects, the rest of the visuals inside the symbol are automatically repositioned.

Although animation symbols are similar to tweened animations, there are a few differences. When you use animation symbols, Fireworks sees the entire animation as a single entity. Accordingly, you can make global changes to the entire animation.

Animation symbols are also created from a single object selection and parameters that you control (scaling, positioning, and rotation).

Because animation symbols are treated as a single object, you cannot visually set an endpoint as you could with tweened animations. Instead, you must numerically designate the animation's endpoint along with its other parameters.

CREATING ANIMATION SYMBOLS

The first step in building an animation with animation symbols is to create the symbol. To create the symbol, select one or more objects on the canvas. Choose Modify, Animation, Animate Selection to open the Animate dialog box (see Figure 4.19), where you find the following options:

Figure 4.19
The Animate dialog box enables you to set the parameters of an animation symbol.

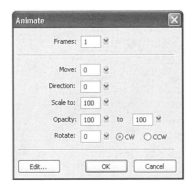

- **Frames**—Sets the number of frames used in the animation.
- **Move**—Controls the number of pixels the object is moved over the course of the animation. You can visually reposition the object later by modifying the motion path.
- **Direction**—Controls the direction, in degrees, the object is moved.
- **Scale To**—Controls the size of the final object compared to the first object. A relative percentage is used to measure this.
- **Opacity**—Changes the object's opacity. The first number represents the opacity of the first object, whereas the second number represents the opacity of the last object.
- **Rotation**—Controls the number of degrees the object is rotated. The CW and CCW radio button options represent clockwise and counter-clockwise rotation, respectively.

MODIFYING ANIMATION SYMBOLS

You can modify animation symbols in several ways, including modifying the visual objects that are animated, editing the animation properties, and modifying the motion path.

To modify the object(s) used in the animation, simply double-click an animated symbol instance and the Symbol Editor window appears (see Figure 4.20). You can then add new objects and modify or replace the existing object used in the animation. When you are finished editing the visuals used in the animation, press the Done button to return to your document stage. Note: All objects in the animation can be modified to add or subtract visuals, but the animation itself is not modified.

The easiest way to edit the animation settings is to select the animation instance on the stage and then make changes in the Property inspector. To make these same changes in the

Animate dialog box, select the animation instance and choose Modify, Animation, Settings to see the Animate dialog box. Make your changes, press OK, and the animation is updated.

After you've created the animation symbol, select an instance and the motion path appears (see Figure 4.21). This path displays the length and direction of the trajectory. To change either setting, drag the first (green) or last (red) point on the path. All intervening frames are updated.

Figure 4.20
Use the Symbol Editor to modify the animated object.

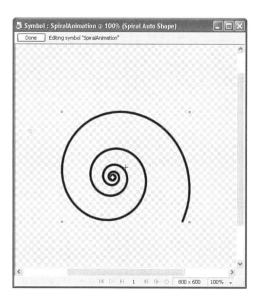

Figure 4.21
Modify the animation symbol's trajectory by dragging the points of the motion path.

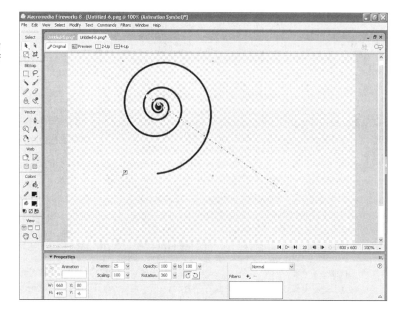

Note that the motion path is a straight line and not a curve. Because you can modify only the first (red) and last (green) points on the motion path, you can change only the length and direction of the trajectory.

You can also change the duration of any part of the animation by going into the Frames tab and double-clicking the Duration column. Enter a new duration in 100ths of seconds and press Return/Enter to accept the change. To view your animation, press the Play button in the bottom of the document window.

OPTIMIZING YOUR ANIMATION FOR EXPORT AS AN ANIMATED GIF

Now that you have created your animations, you need to get them out there for your adoring public to see. You can use the Export tool or the Export command (File, Image Preview) to start the process of creating an Animated GIF.

The Image Preview dialog box appears. Select Animated GIF from the Format pull-down menu under the Options tab.

TIP

> The default export format is GIF. If you forget to choose Animated GIF, the Animation tab remains grayed out.

NOTE

> The Image Preview command and dialog box was named Image Preview in previous versions of Fireworks.

Select the Animation tab to set the compression. A key difference between static exports and animation exports is that animated files require compression across frames.

Fireworks enables you to choose from among three levels of frame-to-frame compression (see Figure 4.22):

- **None**—This yields the largest file size because there is no compression. The Animated GIF describes complete bitmap images for each frame. None is the default setting.

- **Crop Each Frame**—The Animated GIF describes only the rectangular region where the pixels are changed.

- **Save Differences Between Frames**—The Animated GIF describes only the pixels that change within the rectangular region. Note that Crop Each Frame must be checked for Save Difference Between Frames to be enabled. Using Saving Differences Between Frames yields the smallest file size.

When you're finished setting the export options, click the Export button, name the file, choose where to save it, and you've created an Animated GIF.

4

Figure 4.22
Control the frame compression in the Animation tab of the Image Preview dialog box.

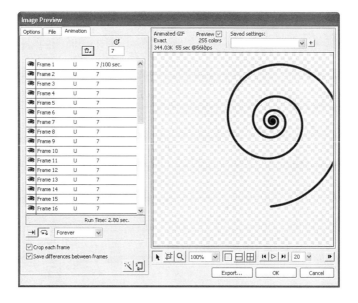

OPTIMIZING YOUR ANIMATION FOR EXPORT TO FLASH

To create a Flash SWF animation file, choose the Quick Export button located at the top right of the document window. Select Macromedia Flash and Export SWF (see Figure 4.23). Enter a filename and press Save and you're finished.

Figure 4.23
Use the Quick Export button to easily send your animation to Flash.

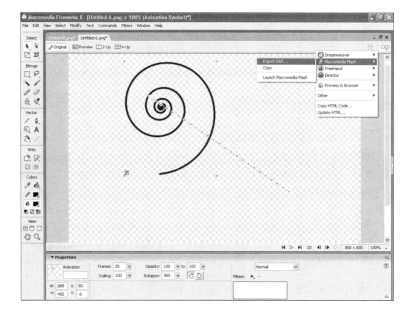

TROUBLESHOOTING

I added a cool pop-up navigation menu to my site that I created in a previous version of Fireworks. Can I update the JavaScript-based menu to the new CSS-based ones created by Fireworks 8?

Sure—as long as you saved the PNG file (the one with all the layers and behaviors intact) for the original menu. You did save that PNG file…right?

Because I'm positive that you saved that PNG file, all you have to do is open it in Fireworks 8 and re-export your navigation menu. After you have done that, just copy and paste the code generated by Fireworks into your web pages and you're good to go.

I have made a few buttons on a black background by using the rectangle tool, black fill, no outer line. I converted those buttons to a symbol and adjusted the up, down, and over graphics. Everything is still black, but only the text changes color on the rollover. But when I view the buttons in a browser, they all have white lines! Help!

Check to make sure you are not working on a transparent canvas. To resolve this issue, change the canvas color to the color of the HTML page on which you'll be putting the buttons and everything should be fine.

BEST PRACTICES—KNOWING WHEN TO CREATE ANIMATIONS WITH FIREWORKS

As you have seen, Fireworks can create some basic animations in a snap. Probably the most common use for animation within Fireworks is to develop different states for rollover buttons and the popular pop-up navigation menus. Beyond that, however, you'll need to consider whether Fireworks is really the best tool for developing your animation.

For instance, if you begin to see your animations creep up in file size, or you find yourself wanting to add functionality such as sound, then you're better off moving on to Flash and developing your animation there.

The trick here is to balance the ease of use but limited functionality found within Fireworks with the complex learning curve and enhanced functionality found in Flash. If you are confident that you can develop your animation in Fireworks without creating an overly large file size, then by all means develop it in Fireworks. If, however, you think that the graphic is complex enough that it might create a pretty hefty file, then you'd be better off creating it in Flash.

OPTIMIZING AND EXPORTING IMAGES

In this chapter

This chapter explores how to prepare graphics for the web. As more Internet users have access to broadband connections, reducing the file size of graphics isn't quite as important as it was a few years ago. However, dial-up connections and their slower counterparts are still quite prevalent and need to be taken into consideration when graphics are prepared for the web.

The process of reducing an image's file size while preserving its quality is known as *optimization*. Several concepts are involved in the optimization process, and a basic understanding of each will help you decide the best method for preparing your graphics for the web.

OPTIMIZATION FUNDAMENTALS

In a nutshell, graphics optimization is the process of reducing the file size of your graphics so they can be downloaded faster when viewed on the web. Graphics optimization is an art where you attempt to balance image quality with file size.

Fireworks has a powerful set of optimization tools that can handle the entire optimization process or let you step in and tinker with settings. Before you begin optimizing graphics, it helps to have a basic understanding of what happens when a file is optimized.

COMPRESSION

Compression is the process of reducing the amount of information used to describe, or render, a digital file. Most types of computer files are fairly redundant in that they have the same information listed over and over again. Rather than list a piece of information repeatedly, a compressed file presents a redundant piece of information once and then refers back to it whenever it appears in the original file.

To better understand compression, look at the following sentence: "I left my heart in San Francisco." Pretend that sentence is a bitmap graphic that Fireworks will compress. The sentence has 7 words, made up of 27 characters and 6 spaces. If each character and space takes up one unit of memory, the total file size is 33 units. To get the file size down, a good place to start is to look for redundancies. To keep this simple, we'll look for redundancies in only the vowels:

- The letter *a* appears 2 times.
- The letter *e* appears 2 times.
- The lowercase *i* appears 2 times.
- The letter *o* appears once.
- The letter *u* is not present.

After the first *a* appears, each consecutive *a* would be replaced with a number ("1" for example). The number would refer to the first *a* and would naturally begin to reduce the file size.

Now, take that line of thought to a real bitmap graphic such as a JPEG or GIF. To the computer, the image comprises X columns and Y rows of pixels and each pixel has a hexadecimal (six-digit) color value. An uncompressed image would describe the image one pixel at a time and specify the hexadecimal color for each pixel.

Lossless Compression

Lossless compression can be found in GIF, PNG, and TIFF file formats and ensures the most accurate representation of the image by not allowing any information to be discarded during the compression process. Lossless compression lists an entire group of the same-colored pixels as single unit, and by doing so, can reduce file size by accounting recurring patterns in a file. Because the patterns are treated as a single unit of data, the file can be reduced to a smaller form for transmission or storage and then put it back together when the file needs to be decompressed.

The term *lossless* indicates that the file size is reduced without any loss of image quality. If an image has only a few colors, such as a screenshot of a computer program or non-gradient "flat" artwork such as you might see in a comic illustration, lossless compression can dramatically reduce the file size. However, if the image is made up of hundreds of unique colors, as a color photograph is, lossless compression has a marginal effect on file size and can even produce a larger file than one that uses another type of compression.

Lossy Compression

Lossy compression takes a completely different approach to reducing file size. This type of compression simply eliminates "unnecessary" bits of information, tailoring the file so that it is smaller. Lossy compression is used for reducing the file size of bitmap pictures, such as photographs and complex drawings, which tend to be fairly bulky. Lossy compression can be found in the JPEG file format.

To see how this works, consider how your computer might compress a scanned photograph. A lossless compression program can't do much with this type of file. Although large parts of the picture may look the same—the lawn is green, for example—most of the individual pixels are different. To make this picture smaller without compromising the resolution, the color value for certain pixels needs to be changed. If the picture had a lot of green grass, Fireworks picks a few colors of green that can be used for every color variation of a green pixel. Then, Fireworks rewrites the file so that the value for every grass pixel refers back to this information. If the compression scheme works well, you won't notice the change in terms of quality, but the file size will be significantly reduced.

Unfortunately, you can't get the original file back after it has been compressed. For this reason, you can't use this sort of compression for anything that needs to be reproduced exactly. In that case, you would need to use lossless compression.

Dithering

Dithering is most often used in GIFs to fake a color that is not in the file's color palette. Two palette colors from the file are alternated one pixel at a time. The hope is that your eye is tricked into seeing a third color. Dithered images tend to increase file size, the effect doesn't always work that well, and you end up with a grainy appearance to the image.

5

TIP

> If you compress a GIF image by reducing the color depth, any gradients that you have created turn into bands of color that don't blend together anymore. To regain the appearance of the blend, try adjusting the dithering settings. Keep in mind, however, that by adding dithering to your image, you are also increasing the file size.

FILE TYPES

Most file types have fairly distinct advantages and disadvantages. This section focuses only on web file formats, thus excluding any discussion on TIFF or BMP.

The top three file formats used on the web today for online graphics are GIF, JPEG, and PNG as a distant third.

USING THE OPTIMIZE PANEL

Fireworks provides you with two ways to control the optimization of your graphics on export: the Image Preview dialog box and the Optimize panel.

Let's take a look at the Optimize panel first. Because the core of image optimization is finding that magical balance between image quality and file size, it's helpful to have a way of comparing images at different optimization settings.

Use the Preview buttons (see Figure 5.1) to preview your images in one, two, or four panes. You can then select each pane and apply a different type of optimization, testing lossless and lossy setting of various levels. Then you compare each pane's results for size and quality.

Figure 5.1
The Preview buttons enable side-by-side comparison of various optimization settings.

When you first view your image in the Preview 4-Up mode of your document window, you see the original image in the top left, and the copies of the original in JPEG or GIF format in other views.

To change optimization settings, begin by opening the Optimize panel on the right. Then select a Preview pane and a black border appears around it. Enter the desired settings in the Optimize panel (see Figure 5.2) and the image preview changes its appearance and its size indication to reflect the settings.

File statistics appear in the bottom of the window (see Figure 5.3).

Figure 5.2
Use the Optimize panel to change optimization settings.

Figure 5.3
File statistics appear in each of the Preview panes to show you how your optimization settings will affect file properties.

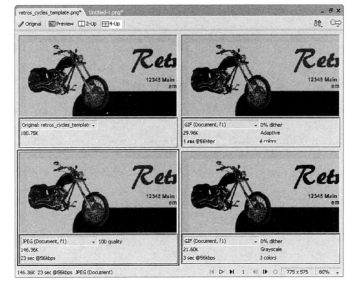

The Optimize panel (see Figure 5.4) has several sections that change, depending on the type of file that is chosen:

- **Title section**—This section comprises three components: the gripper, the panel name, and the Optimize Options menu.

- **Saved Settings section**—This section contains all the saved optimization settings. These settings are presets that are shipped with Fireworks. You can also add or remove your own settings.

■ **File Type/Matte section**—This section contains a drop-down list for the file type, as well as an option that lets you select the matte color. The matte color refers to the background color of the file when it is exported.

■ **File Type Options section**—The contents of this section change based on the file type selected.

■ **Color Palette/Transparency section**—For files with 8-bit or lower color palettes, the entire color palette is displayed here. Also included are tools for adding indexed transparency (GIF and PNG-8 files only) and color palette manipulation.

Figure 5.4
The Optimize panel contains different sections that enable you to adjust the export settings.

5

OPTIMIZE TO SIZE COMMAND

The Options menu in the Options panel contains several options for the optimization process. Many of these options are self-explanatory, or are only in support of specific settings. One option that is worth mentioning is the Optimize to Size command.

This command launches the Optimize to Size dialog box, where you can enter a specific file size for the optimized file (see Figure 5.5). This command is handy if you are restricted to a specific file size, such as those required for banner advertisements.

USING SAVED SETTINGS

Fireworks 8 ships with seven predefined optimization settings. These settings represent common configurations and are often good to use "as is" for nearly every web project. To use one of the settings, simply select one from the Saved Settings drop-down menu at the top of the Optimize panel (see Figure 5.6).

Figure 5.5
The Optimize to Size command enables you to optimize an image to a specific file size.

Figure 5.6
Fireworks 8 comes with seven Saved Settings for image optimization.

The seven settings are summarized as follows:

- **GIF Web 216**—All colors in the image are forced to the GIF 216-color Web Safe palette. Although image quality can be negatively affected, this is a good setting to use if you are concerned about staying within the Web Safe palette.

- **GIF WebSnap 256**—This setting is the same as the GIF Web Snap 128, except there are 256 colors instead of 128.

- **GIF WebSnap 128**—The optimized image contains 128 colors. Colors close to those of the Web Safe palette are changed, whereas colors outside the palette are converted to their closest Web Safe color.

- **GIF Adaptive 256**—The optimized image contains up to 256 colors that are selected to best represent the original colors. It ignores the Web Safe palette.

- **JPEG—Better Quality**—The optimized image is a JPEG with a quality setting of 80 and a Smoothing setting of 0.

- **JPEG—Smaller File**—The optimized image is a JPEG with a quality setting of 60 and a Smoothing setting of 2.

- **Animated GIF Websnap 128**—The optimized image is an Animated GIF that uses the Websnap 128 palette.

For vector art or text, GIF generally provides better compression. Use the Preview button for your document to determine the best of the saved GIF settings to use.

For photographs and gradients, JPEG is typically the best bet. Again, use the Preview button to view your document and test different export settings to select the best of the JPEG settings or even some of the GIF settings such as GIF Adaptive 256.

To create your own custom setting, use the Optimize panel to modify an image. Choose Save Settings from the Options menu (see Figure 5.7). Enter a name in the Preset Name dialog box and click OK. The new setting is now a part of the settings list.

5

Figure 5.7
Create and save your own settings, using the Save Settings command in the Options menu.

| Save Settings... |
| Delete Settings |
| Optimize to Size... |
| Export Wizard... |
| Interlaced |
| Progressive JPEG |
| ✓ Sharpen JPEG Edges |
| Unlock all Colors |
| ✓ Remove Unused Colors |
| Replace Palette Entry... |
| Make Transparent |
| ✓ Show Swatch Feedback |
| Remove Edit |
| Remove All Edits |
| Load Palette... |
| Save Palette... |
| Help |
| Group Optimize with   ▶ |
| Rename Panel Group... |
| Close Panel Group |

TIP

> If you are optimizing the same type of image over and over, you can save yourself time by creating the optimization settings and then saving them as custom settings. Once the settings are saved, you can apply the optimizations to any image by choosing the name of the customization from the drop-down menu.

To remove a setting, make sure it is selected in the Saved Settings drop-down menu. Choose Delete Settings from the Optimize panel's Options menu and click OK in the warning dialog box.

CREATING MANUAL SETTINGS

Although the saved settings are convenient and can be used for most exported web graphics, sometimes you still need to tweak an image's compression settings by hand. Fortunately, Fireworks enables you to manually create custom optimize settings for your images in the Optimize panel.

MANUALLY OPTIMIZING JPEGS

When manipulating JPEG compression settings, use the Quality setting to control the amount of compression applied to the image. Enter a number between 1 and 100 (or use the Quality slider). The higher the number, the better the quality and lower the compression. The lower the number, the more data will be thrown out.

In general, quality settings over 80 are pretty close to the original image. Settings between 60 and 80 are more compressed with generally acceptable quality. Settings below 60 are a gamble as quality begins to degrade quickly because a lot of information has been discarded (see Figure 5.8).

Figure 5.8
Differences in JPEG quality can be seen between the image on the left, set at 80% quality, and the image on the right, set at 40% quality.

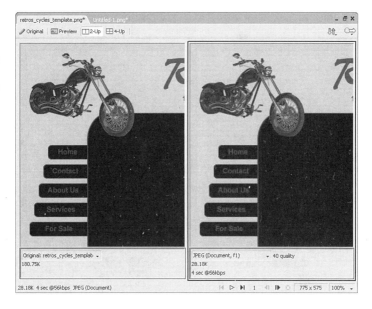

Selective Quality enables you to optimize different regions of the image separately. This control is useful for images with distinct backgrounds and foregrounds. To use selective JPEG compression, identify one region in the image that will use a different compression setting from the rest of the image. Keep in mind that in any image, there can be only one selective JPEG mask.

Use any of the bitmap selection tools (Marquee, Oval Marquee, Lasso, Polygon Lasso, Magic Wand, and so on) to enclose a region (see Figure 5.9).

Figure 5.9
Define a selective JPEG mask, using the bitmap selection tools.

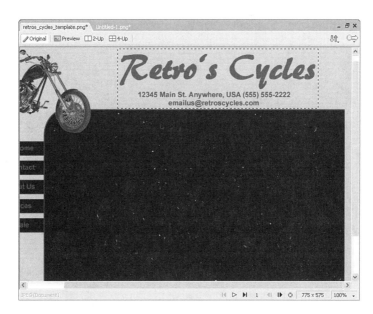

5

While the marquee area is selected, choose Modify, Selective JPEG, Save Selection as JPEG Mask. A translucent pink mask appears over the selected region. In the Optimize panel, double-check that JPEG is the selected file type and use the Quality slider to affect everything outside the mask. In Figure 5.10, everything but the main logo would be affected.

Figure 5.10
Use one of the Preview buttons to see how the Quality setting affects the area outside the selected region of the image.

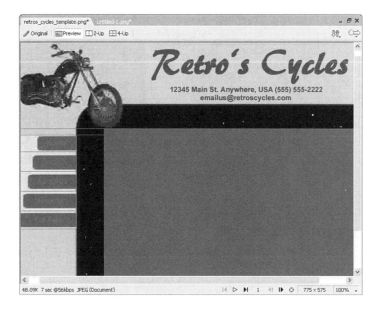

When you have made your adjustments, look at your handiwork by selecting one of the Preview buttons.

Smoothing blurs the transitions between sharp edges in an image. Smoothing makes it easier for an image to be compressed, but also degrades the quality. Smoothing settings below 3 seems to strike the best balance between image quality and file size.

Sharpen Edges has the opposite effect of Smoothing. Edges are sharpened, often resulting in an improved image quality. File size, however, is increased. You cannot control the degree of sharpness. It is either on or off.

The Progressive setting affects the display of the JPEG in the browser, not image quality. There is typically a slight increase in file size, however. When the image is downloaded to the web browser, a low-resolution version appears first. The details are then gradually filled in. The faster the Internet connection, the more seamless this progression appears.

MANUALLY OPTIMIZING GIFS

The GIF format uses 8-bit or lower indexed color, which means that it uses 256 or fewer colors and tracks each color separately. Accordingly, the trick to getting the best optimization with the GIF format lies with the color palette. To modify that palette, choose the palette type and the number of colors in that palette. Other choices include dithering and whether or not to apply lossy compression.

To choose a palette, use the Indexed Palette drop-down menu in the Optimize panel (or the Image Preview dialog box) (see Figure 5.11).

Figure 5.11
Select one of the 10 GIF color palettes from the drop-down menu in the Optimize panel.

Select one of the following choices:

- **Adaptive**—Derived from the actual colors in the document and often produces the highest quality image.
- **Web Adaptive**—Converts colors that are close to the Web Safe palette colors to the appropriate Web Safe color.
- **Web 216**—A palette of the 216 colors common to both Windows and Macintosh computers.
- **Exact**—Contains only the colors used in the original image. If the image contains more than 256 colors, the palette automatically switches to Adaptive.
- **Macintosh**—Contains the 256 colors defined by Macintosh platform standards.
- **Windows**—Contains the 256 colors defined by the Windows platform standards.
- **Grayscale**—Contains a palette of 256 or fewer shades of gray.
- **Black and White**—Converts all pixels to either black or white.
- **Uniform**—Selects colors mathematically, based on RGB pixel values.
- **Custom**—Palettes are loaded from an external palette (ACT file) that you have previously created.

To choose the number of colors, or color depth, select a number from the Maximum Number of Colors drop-down menu. Select a color depth that best represents the color integrity of the original image (see Figure 5.12).

Although the GIF format uses lossless compression, you can still apply lossy compression by using the Lossy GIF Compression slider. To apply lossy compression to the GIF, drag the slider or enter a number in the field. The higher the number, the higher the compression and the lower the image quality.

Interlacing is similar to the Progressive setting for JPEG. When the image is downloaded to the web browser, a low-resolution version appears first. The details are then gradually filled in as the image continues to load and, after the image is completely loaded, the high-resolution version of the image is displayed. If there will be a lot of graphics on the web page, interlacing enables the images to appear onscreen faster, even though they are not the final images. Turn on interlacing by selecting Interlaced from the Options menu.

Figure 5.12
Varying the color depth affects file size and image quality.

As I mentioned earlier, there is a second method for optimizing your images, which uses the Image Preview option. If you want to see what your image will look like and be able to adjust the various optimization settings prior to doing your final export, open the Image Preview dialog box (File, Image Preview). Using the Image Preview, you can make any adjustments to compression, file format, and color options to which you had access in the Optimize dialog box and be able to see what effect the various settings have in real time. After you adjust the preview to the desired settings, you can then export the image directly from the Image Preview dialog box.

TIP

When using the Image Preview dialog box, don't be afraid to play with the various settings and see how they will affect your image. You can always click the Cancel button and any changes you have made are undone and do not adversely affect your base image.

EXPORTING FIREWORKS IMAGES

After you've painstakingly planned, designed, and created your graphics, you need to export the images. There are a number of ways to export Fireworks graphics. You can export a document as a single image in JPEG, GIF, or another graphic file format. You can also export the entire document as an HTML file and associated image files. You can also integrate your Fireworks graphics with Flash and Director.

NOTE

> After you export an image, Fireworks saves the optimization settings for the image within the PNG file. Then, when you go to export the image again, Fireworks automatically recalls those settings so you don't have to reconfigure them.

WEB GRAPHICS

After you have created your web graphic, you need to export it to a web-friendly format such as JPEG or GIF. Up to this point, we've explored the strengths and weaknesses of each file format. We've also covered the optimization process. All that's left is to export the image.

Fireworks provides three ways of exporting a web graphic: the Export command, the Export Area tool, and the Export Wizard.

The Export command exports all the objects on the canvas and excludes objects in the work area. Use the Export command (File, Export) to launch the Export dialog box (see Figure 5.13).

Figure 5.13
The Export dialog box provides options for exporting your document.

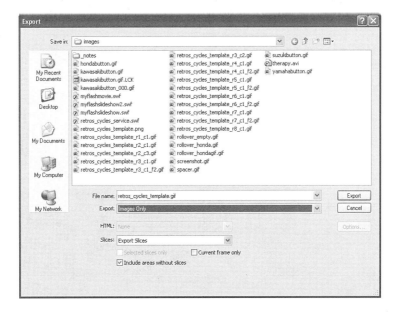

Name the file and be sure that Images Only is selected in the Save As Type drop-down menu. You can choose from several types, depending on how the exported image is to be used. For the web, use Images Only. Press the Save button and you're finished.

After you've optimized your image as a GIF or JPEG, that file format is selected automatically during the export process.

If you want to export only a selected portion of an object or the canvas, use the Export Area tool. Drag the tool to define the area for export (see Figure 5.14).

Press the Return/Enter key to launch the Image Preview dialog box (see Figure 5.15).

Figure 5.14
Use the Export Area tool to define a specific area for export.

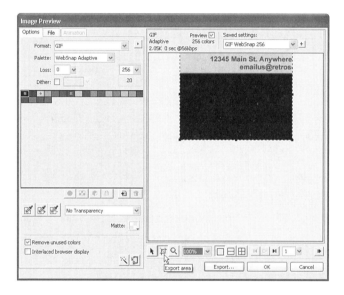

Figure 5.15
The Image Preview dialog box provides the same controls as the Optimize panel and the Preview buttons.

If you've already optimized your image, these controls will look familiar. The Image Preview dialog box enables you to select the export file type and adjust the optimization settings, as well as preview the effect of the optimization settings.

Using the Export Wizard gives you a way to have Fireworks determine the best way to configure the optimization of your graphic for export. To access it, select File, Export Wizard. You are prompted to answer a series of questions (see Figure 5.16). When you're finished, you are presented with a GIF or JPEG (if you chose the web or Dreamweaver as your output preference) or TIFF (if you chose an image editing or desktop publishing application).

Figure 5.16
The Export Wizard offers a simple, but limited, method of viewing export options.

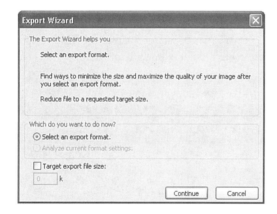

After you exit the wizard, you find yourself in the Image Preview dialog box, where you can once again select GIF or JPEG if you are exporting for the web. If you've read this far, you already know what file format you're going to use, so you can skip the Export Wizard altogether.

WEB PAGES

Fireworks generates HTML that can be read by most web browsers and HTML editors. There are some issues, however, in taking your Fireworks page design and exporting it straight to HTML.

First, HTML is a text-based framework where objects are positioned relative to each other. Fireworks is an object-oriented program where all elements are precisely sized and positioned in pixels relative to the top-left corner of the canvas.

Fireworks elements are constrained to a specific canvas size. HTML is designed to flow to fill browser windows of varying sizes.

In addition, the two major browsers (Internet Explorer and Netscape Navigator) still don't render elements exactly the same. They're getting better about this, but differences that can affect your design still exist.

There are several ways to export Fireworks HTML:

- Export an HTML file, which you can later modify in an HTML editor.
- Copy HTML code to the Fireworks Clipboard, and then paste that code directly into an existing HTML document.
- Export an HTML file, open it in an HTML editor, manually copy sections of code from the file, and paste that code into another HTML document.
- Use the Update HTML command to make changes to an HTML file you've previously created.

To define how HTML is exported in Fireworks, open the HTML Setup dialog box (see Figure 5.17) by choosing File, HTML Setup or clicking the Options button in the Export dialog box. These settings can be document specific or used as your default settings for all HTML that Fireworks exports.

Figure 5.17
Adjust the HTML export settings using the HTML Setup dialog box.

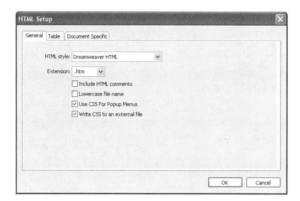

To export an entire page design, your best bet is to use the Slice tool to divide your design in regions (see Figure 5.18).

After the page is sliced up, export the page using the Export command (File, Export). The Export dialog box is launched. Rename the HTML file if necessary and adjust any of the settings to fit your file hierarchy (see Figure 5.19).

Press the Save button and all the HTML code necessary to reassemble sliced images, as well as the sliced images themselves, are created. Fireworks HTML contains links to the exported images and sets the web page background color to the canvas color.

You can then modify the page using an HTML editor of your choice.

INTEGRATING WITH DREAMWEAVER

Dreamweaver and Fireworks are two peas in a pod when it comes to integration. Both programs recognize and share many of the same file commands, including changes to links, rollovers, and table slices. Used together, the two programs provide a streamlined workflow for editing, optimizing, and placing web graphics files in HTML pages.

Figure 5.18
Divide your page design into slices for export.

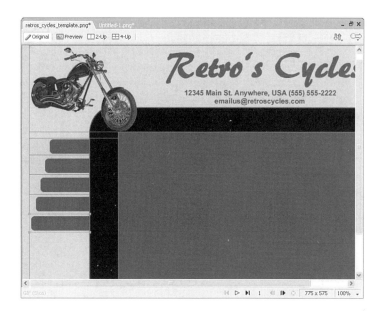

Figure 5.19
The Export dialog box.

The first step in creating an integrated work environment is to define a local site in Dreamweaver and to make sure Design Notes are enabled. Design Notes contain information about the graphic files that Fireworks exports. When you launch and edit a Fireworks image from Dreamweaver, Dreamweaver uses this information to locate the source PNG. For example, suppose you created a graphic called 2002hondashadow.png. You then exported a JPEG image from that PNG document and placed the exported JPEG in your Dreamweaver document. Your source file is 2002hondashadow.png.

In Dreamweaver, select the JPEG image for which you want to edit the original PNG and click the Fireworks icon (see Figure 5.20) in the Property inspector to launch Fireworks. Edit the image, press the Done button, and the changes are automatically applied to the Dreamweaver file.

Figure 5.20
Use the Fireworks icon in the Dreamweaver Property inspector to launch Fireworks for image editing.

If planning is not your strong suit, you can build your page in Dreamweaver and add image placeholders if your graphics are not ready. An image placeholder is a graphic you use in your Dreamweaver document until final artwork is ready to be added to the page. Choose Insert, Image, Image Placeholder to insert it into the HTML document. You can set the placeholder's size, color, and text label.

After the image placeholder is used in Dreamweaver, you can design the graphic at some later point in Fireworks. Then after the graphic is created, save it as a PNG for future editing and export it from the PNG to a web-ready graphic file format (GIF or JPEG). When you return to Dreamweaver, select the placeholder and in the Property inspector choose the source file to replace the placeholder by using the Src field to browse to the appropriate file. The replacement image now appears in the document.

NOTE

> If your image file is located on another server, you can also type the URL to the image in the Src field, rather than browsing to it. Be aware, however, that for remotely hosted images Dreamweaver maintains an image placeholder and does not display images within the page during design.

INTEGRATING WITH FLASH

Although Flash has robust drawing capabilities, you may want to create your complex graphics in Fireworks and export them to Flash. There are two ways to accomplish this.

First, you can copy vector objects from Fireworks and paste them directly into Flash. Select the objects you want to copy and then use the Copy command (Edit, Copy). In Flash, create a new document and then Paste (Edit, Paste). The Fireworks objects are pasted as a group. Ungroup the objects (Modify, Ungroup) and then manipulate as usual in Flash.

You can also import your Fireworks PNG document directly into Flash. For elaborate designs you want to use in Flash, this is often the easiest way to proceed. When you begin importing, a dialog box appears giving you the option to import as an image or to retain vector artwork and text. All frames in your document are retained as keyframes in the Flash document.

To send an animation to Flash, click the Quick Export button located at the top right of the document window. Select Macromedia Flash and Export to SWF (see Figure 5.21). Enter a filename, click Save, and you're finished. Then you can import that SWF file with the animation from Fireworks directly into Flash.

Figure 5.21
Use the Quick Export button to send your animation to Flash easily.

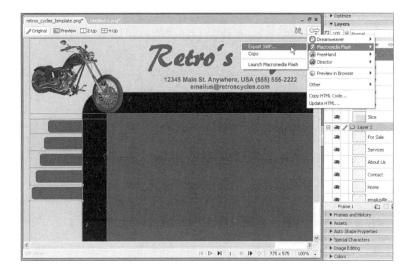

INTEGRATING WITH DIRECTOR

Because Fireworks enables designers to create and export 32-bit PNG file formats, Fireworks is a popular image and vector artwork design tool for Director developers. Director, which is not covered in this book, is a Macromedia application that enables developers to create interactive content that integrates long video streams, photo-quality images, audio, animation, 3D models, text, and Macromedia Flash content. This content is often used in CDs, DVDs, kiosks, and even the web.

Exported layers and slices from Fireworks can be used in Director as individual cast members or as composite user interfaces that can be imported as entire entities onto the stage. Director developers can also use Fireworks to design and script rollovers and navigation interfaces.

Developers can use Fireworks to create cast libraries from a single Fireworks document by using layers in Fireworks and exporting the Fireworks layers to Director. Any Fireworks 8 document that contains layers can be exported as Director HTML with the Source pop-up menu in the Export dialog box set to Fireworks Layers. The 32-bit PNG format supports full Alpha transparency, and transparency in a Fireworks document is retained in the Director movie.

If different graphic elements are arranged in separate layers and the developer does not want to generate separate files for each layer, exporting the entire document as a single file, using the PNG32 setting in the Optimize panel, flattens all the layers.

Fireworks can also be used to create a navigational interface for Director projects. Developers can design the elements in Fireworks, draw slices, add behaviors to the slices, and export the slices to Director. Any Fireworks 8 document that contains slices can be exported as Director HTML with the Source pop-up menu in the Export dialog box set to Fireworks Slices. This setting enables the images as defined by the slices to be imported into the Director movie, along with the behaviors such as Simple Rollovers, Swap Image, Disjoint Rollovers, and Set Navbar Image behaviors.

When exporting an animated GIF from Fireworks for use in Director, you need to disable Auto Crop and Auto Difference in the Animation tab of the Image Preview. For some reason, Director does not correctly display animated GIFs if those settings are enabled.

TROUBLESHOOTING

When I draw vector curves, how come they still look like they're bitmap graphics?

You'll get the best curves in Fireworks if you use a Soft Rounded stroke (Basic, Soft Rounded). The Soft Rounded stroke adds more pixels to smooth the edge of a shape than does the anti-aliasing alone.

I set frame delay and looping settings on an animation I created in Fireworks. Will they be exported to Flash?

No. Frame delay and looping settings apply only if you are exporting your animation as an Animated GIF. These settings are discarded when you export to Flash SWF.

I keep trying to use the Smoothing optimization setting on a masked object, but it doesn't seem to be doing anything.

Certain optimization settings such as Smoothing can be used only outside a masked area. Anything inside the masked area is off limits. Redraw your mask so the area you want to optimize with Smoothing is outside the mask.

BEST PRACTICES—SAVING AND VERSIONING YOUR PNG FILES

One of the most important practices that you can develop when creating graphics in Fireworks (or *any* other program for that matter) is the saving and versioning of your native files (the PNG files you want to go back and edit later). I speak from experience when I tell you that it is immensely frustrating to go back and edit a graphic that you created only to find that you never saved the PNG file. Remember that when you export a file to the GIF or JPEG, your ability to edit those graphics down the road is extremely limited. That's why saving the native PNG file is so important.

You might not save the PNG file for a number of reasons, ranging from computer crashes to just thinking that you'll never have a need for the file again. Trust me when I say that the 30 seconds you take to save files along the way and save when you are finished with them is well worth it.

Just as with any complex document, your Fireworks creations usually involve a lot of steps, and Fireworks stores only so many undo actions along the way. For this reason, as you work on a project, take advantage of the Save As command and save progressive versions of your work. That way, you can always revert back to a previous version if something should go wrong.

Then when the project is complete, and you have that final version and are asked whether you want to save the changes when you close Fireworks, choose to save them.

5

CHAPTER

AUTOMATING AND EXTENDING FIREWORKS

In this chapter

Although Macromedia has done an outstanding job of balancing Fireworks's powerful functionality with its easy-to-use interface, they also recognize that you might want to customize the way Fireworks works to meet your needs. In this chapter, we take a look at how you can use Fireworks to reduce your design time by making repetitive tasks a snap and enhancing the Fireworks interface.

The plain truth is that although a lot of graphic and web design is fun, some repetitive tasks can become mundane. A while back, I designed a website for a client who collected and sold stamps. At any given time, he had several thousand stamps in his collection and the vast majority of them were for sale. He contracted with me to create a website for him and to digitize all the stamps so his customers could view the stamp prior to purchasing it. In addition, he wanted to put a digital watermark on the image with his company logo, so that other philatelists (the fancy name for stamp collectors) wouldn't "borrow" his images for use on their sites. This meant that for each stamp, I would have to

- Scan the stamp.
- Add a digital watermark to the full image.
- Resize the stamp for display on the site.
- Create a thumbnail of the stamp.

For a single stamp, that process would take about 10 minutes to do, which doesn't sound like much until you start getting into the sheer size of the project. At 10 minutes each, 3,000 stamps would take 30,000 minutes or 50 hours. At $50/hour, that's almost $2,500 dollars—a price that my client just wouldn't be able to stomach.

Luckily, automating the process in Fireworks helped me cut the time required to complete the entire process of digitizing the images to less than 15 hours.

AUTOMATING TASKS

The first step in automating any task is to identify what the fundamental steps are. Some steps you can automate, whereas others require a level of detail or attention that might not be suitable for automation. After you identify those tasks that can be automated, Fireworks 8 offers three sets of tools that can assist you:

- **Find and Replace**—Used to search for and replace elements within a file or multiple files. You can specify an asset, such as text, color, URLs, and fonts, and find and replace that asset in a PNG file.
- **Batch Process**—Used to convert entire groups of image files into other formats or to change their color palettes. Batch Process also applies custom optimization settings to groups of files and resizes a group of files.
- **Commands**—Used to create shortcuts for commonly used features or to create a script that can perform a complex series of steps.

FIND AND REPLACE

Find and Replace comes into play when you need to make global changes to elements of source PNG files. Elements that can be modified with Find and Replace include text, fonts, colors, and URLs.

Note that changes made with Find and Replace are undoable. For example, you search your source PNG files for the word "insomnia" and replace it with the word "sleeplessness." If you decide to change the word again, you cannot undo that change. However, you can run another Find and Replace. Run a find for the word "sleeplessness" and replace it with the original word "insomnia."

All Find and Replace commands are handled through the Find panel. Access it by choosing Window, Find or Edit, Find and Replace (see Figure 6.1). You can also use the Ctrl+F keyboard command to open the Find panel.

Figure 6.1
All Find and Replace operations are handled through the Find panel.

From the Search pop-up menu, choose a source for the search:

- **Search Selection**—Finds and replaces elements in the currently selected objects and text.
- **Search Frame**—Finds and replaces elements in only the current frame.
- **Search Document**—Finds and replaces elements in the active document.
- **Search Files**—Finds and replaces elements across multiple files.

From the Find pop-up menu, select an attribute for which to search. The options in the panel change according to your selection.

Next, click one of the following buttons to conduct a Find and Replace operation:

- **Find**—Locates the next instance of the element.
- **Replace**—Changes a found element with the contents of the Change To option.
- **Replace All**—Finds and replaces every instance of a found element in the search range.

6

As long as a file is not open, the act of replacing objects in multiple files automatically saves those changes. Unfortunately, this doesn't allow you to undo any changes that are made to documents that aren't open. To give yourself some extra insurance, you can create backups when you use Find and Replace in multiple files. With the Find panel open, click the Options menu in the top-right corner of the panel. Select Replace Options to launch the Replace Options dialog box (see Figure 6.2).

Select from among the following options:

- **Save and Close Files (if checked)**—This option has Fireworks save and close selected files that are not currently open when the Replace operation is completed.

- **Backup Original Files**—This option has three options to choose from: Select Choose No Backups to have no file backups made; select Overwrite Existing Backups to create one set of backups and overwrite them if multiple operations are performed; and choose Incremental Backups to create a set of backups for every Find and Replace operation completed.

Click OK to save the settings.

Figure 6.2
The Replace Options dialog box specifies how multiple-file Find and Replace operations are handled.

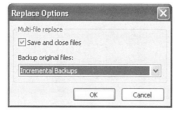

BATCH PROCESSING

Batch Processing is often performed as a series of simultaneous tasks on a group of files. In contrast to Find and Replace, Batch Processing is used on external files that you want to manipulate is some common way. This is usually used to export a series of files to fit a certain size, such as thumbnails and the larger images that they display.

The best way to create a batch process is to use the Batch Wizard by choosing File, Batch Process. The wizard presents three screens, enabling you to accomplish a batch process in a jiffy.

On the first screen (see Figure 6.3) you can add files that will be used to create the batch. Files can be added from more than one directory.

When you have created the batch, click the Next button to continue.

The second screen (see Figure 6.4) is used to add tasks that tell Fireworks what to do to the files in the batch. The following are some of the most commonly used tasks:

- **Export**—This task specifies how the batch will be re-exported. When selected, all the export presets appear.

- **Scale**—This task scales the graphics to a specific size (such as thumbnails) to fit an area, or to a percentage.
- **Find and Replace**—This task opens the Batch Replace dialog box so you can use the Find and Replace operations in PNG files.
- **Rename**—This task enables you to add a prefix or suffix to the files.
- **Commands**—This task displays a list of some of the commands that you may use frequently when manipulating an image for the web.

When you have added your tasks, click the Next button to continue.

Figure 6.3
The first screen in the Batch Process Wizard is where you add files to create the batch.

Figure 6.4
The second screen in the Batch Process Wizard is where you add tasks that are to be applied to the batch.

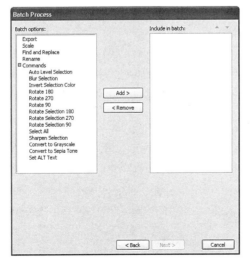

The last screen of the wizard (see Figure 6.5) is where you specify the files' output destination, as well as what should happen to the original files. If the results are satisfactory, you can even save the batch process as a script that you can use again to repeat the exact batch process in the future.

Make your selections and click the Batch button. Fireworks does all the work so you can kick back and take a much deserved break!

Figure 6.5
The third screen in the Batch Process Wizard is where you choose the output destination and specify the fate of the original files.

CREATING CUSTOM COMMANDS WITH THE HISTORY PANEL

Custom commands are similar to batch scripts in that they automate tasks, so you don't have to do all the work. The difference, however, is that whereas batch processes are limited in what functions they can perform, a custom command can be made of nearly any action you can perform in Fireworks.

The simplest way to create a custom command is to use the History panel (Window, History). The History panel is a record of all the steps you have recently taken when working in a document. If you want to automate a sequence of those steps, you can use the History panel to create a custom command.

By default, the History panel shows up to 20 steps. You can increase or decrease this number in the General tab of the Preferences dialog (Edit, Preferences in Windows or Fireworks, Preferences on the Mac).

To create commands with the History panel, execute a series of modifications that are to be used in your command. Using the History panel Options menu, highlight the steps you want to use in the command, and then select Save As Command (see Figure 6.6). The Save Command dialog box appears. Enter a name for your new command. Press OK.

Figure 6.6
Use the Save As
Command option to
save your History
panel options as a
custom command.

Your very own command now has a home in the Commands menu. Use it again and again. If you find yourself becoming a commands junkie and need to get rid of a few outdated commands, you can rename or delete commands in the Manage Saved Commands dialog box (Commands, Manage Saved Commands).

In the case of digitizing the stamps, the custom command feature saved the day. In analyzing the complete set of steps that was required to scan a stamp, I found they looked something like this:

1. Acquire the image into Fireworks with the File > Scan, Twain Acquire command.
2. Add the digital watermark to the image with the text tool.
3. Set the opacity of the watermark to 20% so it doesn't obstruct the view of the stamp.
4. Crop the stamp for display on the site.
5. Export the stamp.
6. Export the stamp a second time as a thumbnail.
7. Save the PNG file.

Fortunately, I was able to create a custom command that took care of the digital watermark and the cropping of the image, so I was able to combine three of the more time-consuming tasks into one automated task that took seconds to run.

EXTENDING FIREWORKS

The last Fireworks tool that can be leveraged to save you time is the Fireworks Extension Manager. The Extension Manager lets you import, install, and delete extensions in Macromedia applications to extend the capabilities of each of the development applications. In other words, you can add more features to the program that weren't included when it was first installed on your computer.

Built into Fireworks is a set of extensibility features. These features are built on an open architecture that enables users and third-party developers to add more goodies to the program.

The most common way to extend Fireworks is through commands. When you save a file, you are using a command. Although this command comes with Fireworks, it was created just like any other custom command script.

Commands are written in a special Fireworks version of JavaScript. If you're a JavaScript ace, the language will come easily to you.

6

EDITING COMMAND SCRIPTS

Commands are usually stored in scripts called *command scripts*. All these scripts are located in the Commands folder on your hard drive. The Commands folder location is specific to settings you used when you installed Fireworks. Each time you create a new custom command, a script is created in the folder so that you can reuse that command over and over.

If you ever need to manually edit one of the scripts (or just want to see what one looks like), simply navigate to the folder that contains the scripts and open it in a text editor such as Notepad. As you can see in Figure 6.7, each command is written in JavaScript and can be easily edited and saved.

Figure 6.7
Any saved command can be edited in a text editor.

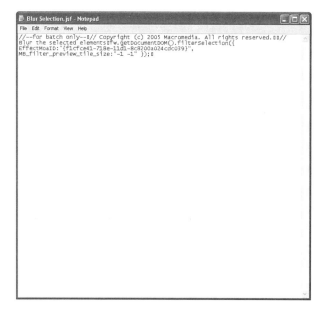

TIP

If you choose to edit your custom commands manually, it's a good idea to make a backup of the original command before you edit it.

INSTALLING EXTENSIONS

Fireworks, along with Dreamweaver and Flash, is part of the Macromedia Exchange, a place where developers who create command scripts can distribute and exchange them. Macromedia tests each script to make sure it works and contains no harmful code (such as viruses) before posting it to the exchange. After it is posted, however, you can download it and easily add the functionality to Fireworks on your workstation. To review the extensions available for Fireworks, click Help, Fireworks Exchange and the exchange opens in your browser.

TIP

> You can also get to the various exchanges by going to www.macromedia.com and choosing Downloads, Exchange from the navigation menu.

Installing extensions is a snap. Simply find the extension that suits your needs, download it to your computer, and then double-click on the extension. After that, the Extension Manager (see Figure 6.8) takes care of the rest.

To view the details of any installed extensions, simply choose which application you want to review and then click on the extension to review its functionality.

Figure 6.8
The Extension Manager can be used to install new Extensions as well as manage your Extensions collection.

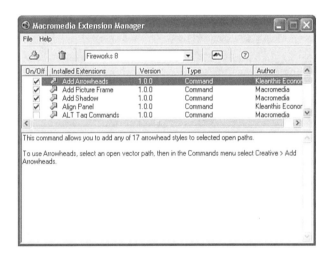

Uninstalling an extension is just as easy as installing it. Simply open the Extension Manager (Help, Manage Extensions), choose the application you want to review, select the extension you would like to delete, and choose File, Remove Extension.

TROUBLESHOOTING

6

I'd like to print my Fireworks graphics but am having resolution problems.

Fireworks is designed for creating web graphics. Although you can use it for print graphics, you need to up the resolution. Set the resolution of your image (Property inspector, Image Size button) so the number of PPI (pixels per inch) is equal to the number of DPI (dots per inch) your printer uses.

I created a custom style and accidentally selected Reset Styles from the Styles panel pop-up menu. Are my styles lost forever?

Most definitely. Your painstakingly created styles have been shuttled off to graphics la-la land. Choosing Reset Styles restores the 97 factory defaults and permanently removes any custom styles you may have created. Unfortunately, this action is not undoable.

BEST PRACTICES—KNOWING WHEN TO USE BATCH PROCESSING

Have you ever started a process and after hours and hours of hard work, realized that you could have made your life a lot easier (and maybe gotten more sleep) if you had known about a tool or feature prior to starting? Trust me, we have all been there—or will be there at some time in our careers.

For this reason, it's a good idea for you to spend some time familiarizing yourself with the Batch Processing tools in Fireworks. Even if you're spending only a couple of hours batch processing made-up steps and applying them to sample graphics, knowing the steps to follow and how long it takes to create and apply a batch process can help you automate redundant tasks in the future.

But knowing *how* to use batch processing isn't enough. You need to also know *when* to use it. Before you begin any long project that will require hours of work, take some time to determine whether or not there are some steps that you could automate. If there are, create a batch process or custom command and save yourself some time.

6

CHAPTER 7

Putting It All Together: The Images and Page Layout for Retro's Cycles

In this chapter

With the site proposal and wireframes in hand, imagine that you successfully proposed the site design and the client liked your ideas. With the green light to move forward, the next step is to begin laying out the actual site template and adding functionality.

In this chapter, you'll use Fireworks to create some stylized artwork for Retro's Cycles and then use that artwork to develop a web page template that you can export for use later on in the Dreamweaver section.

CREATING THE BASE DOCUMENT

The first step in creating the site template is to build a base document with the appropriate size and background color. This base document serves as the canvas and, after it is created, you can begin adding the elements that define your web page.

1. Open Fireworks.

2. Choose File, New from the menu bar to create a new document. Choose to create a canvas that has a width of **775** pixels and a height of **575** pixels and set the canvas color to gray by clicking the Custom radio button, clicking the Color Picker, and choosing the gray value of #CCCCCC (see Figure 7.1).

Figure 7.1
Create a new document and adjust the canvas color.

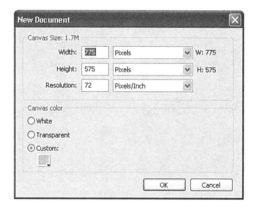

NOTE

When designing a web page in Fireworks, you need to have a pretty good idea what page size you're going to be using. When you export the images to HTML, Fireworks creates a set of tables and these tables have fixed widths. This means that your tables do not grow or shrink to fit the monitor resolution of each individual visitor. If you want your site to do this, you have to take some extra steps while working with the HTML pages in Dreamweaver to convert the pixel-based table sizes to percentage-based.

3. Next, select the Rectangle tool and draw a rectangle on the canvas. It doesn't matter how big or small or where it is positioned, because you'll adjust those aspects in the following steps.

4. With the rectangle selected, set the fill color to black by selecting the Color Picker and choosing a black box or by typing **#000000** in the upper field.

5. Set the stroke color of the rectangle to **#0000FF** by selecting the stroke Color Picker and typing the value. As shown in Figure 7.2, you should now have a rectangle with a blue outline on your canvas.

Figure 7.2
The rectangle has been added to your page.

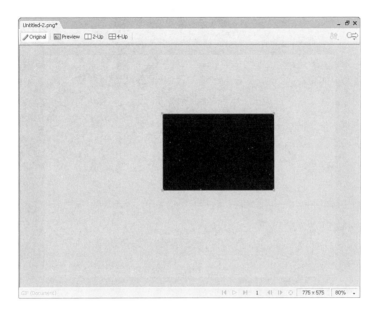

6. Adjust the X and Y positions of the rectangle to **0** and **0** by typing those values in the Property inspector.

> **NOTE**
>
> When adjusting the values of a rectangle numerically, be sure to position X and Y values of the rectangle at 0 and 0 before adjusting the height and width properties. If you don't position the rectangle at 0 and 0, Fireworks automatically adjusts the height and width to be the height and width of the canvas.

7. Set the Rectangle width to **700** and the height to **550** by typing those values in the W and H fields in the Property inspector.

8. Adjust the X and Y positions to **130** and **130** by typing those values and set the rectangle roundness to **20** by adjusting the slider on the Property inspector.

9. Finally, set the stroke width of the rectangle to **2** and adjust the stroke category to Soft Rounded in the Basic set. You should now have a rounded, blue divider on your page that looks like Figure 7.3.

7

Figure 7.3
The page now has a divider.

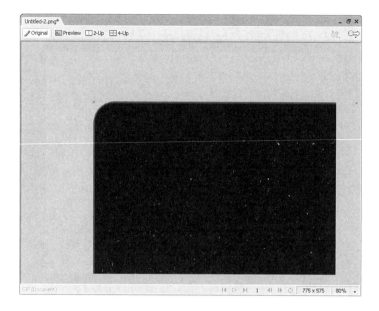

10. Save the page to your local hard drive and name the file `retros_cycle_template.png`.

CREATING A STYLIZED IMAGE

The next step in developing your web template is creating a custom graphic that will be located on each page of the site and adding some custom filters to modify the image colors.

1. Download and extract the Fireworks files from the companion website. Browse to the Fireworks folder and open `custom_chopper_base.gif` in Fireworks. This file contains the image of a motorcycle with a transparent background (see Figure 7.4).

2. Select the motorcycle by clicking anywhere on it and choose Filters, Adjust Color, Hue/Saturation from the menu bar.

3. In the Hue/Saturation box, set the Hue to **225**, the Saturation to **100**, and the Lightness to **0**. Check the Colorize check box and click OK. This changes the motorcycle color from black to blue (see Figure 7.5).

4. Select the motorcycle and choose Edit, Copy (Ctrl+C or Cmd-C) from the menu bar.

5. Switch over to the `retros_cycle_template.png` file by clicking the tab for the document. From the menu bar, choose Edit, Paste and the blue motorcycle is added to your page (see Figure 7.6). Don't worry that the image looks a little rough.

6. To smooth out the edges of the image, select the motorcycle and choose Filters, Blur, Blur from the menu. Fireworks blurs the images slightly by blending the pixel colors together.

7. Next, resize the motorcycle by selecting it and typing **225** in the W: field and **174** in the H: field. Reposition the image by typing **5** in the X: field and **5** in the Y: field. As you can see in Figure 7.7, the motorcycle has been properly placed in the page.

Figure 7.4
Open the `custom_chopper_base.gif` file.

Figure 7.5
By adjusting the hue and saturation, you can change the color of the entire motorcycle.

7

Figure 7.6
The motorcycle has been added to the template page.

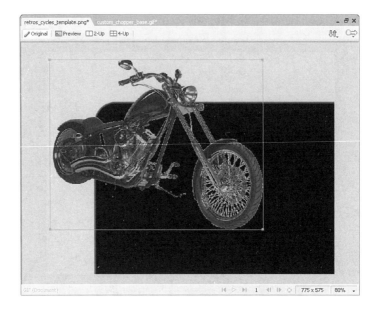

Figure 7.7
The rough edges of the motorcycle have been refined and the image is in its final location.

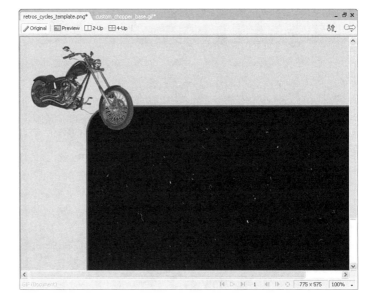

ADDING TEXT TO THE TEMPLATE

Although most of the copy text for the web pages will be added later, when you edit the site in Dreamweaver, there are some text elements that you should add in Fireworks. Because text added via HTML is displayed with the system fonts, you can't be absolutely positive that any fonts beyond those that come with the operating system will display properly. If you use a font in your pages that isn't available to a visitor, the visitor's system adjusts and uses a font that is similar. This means that you can't control how your site is displayed on every machine.

To avoid this, you can use Fireworks to embed the text in an image. Because the text in the image doesn't rely on the font being present on the user's machine, you can be confident that it will display correctly every time. In the case of this client, we'll add the company name, location, and contact information at the top of the site.

1. In the `retros_cycles_template` file, select the Text tool and draw a text block above the blue dividing line and to the right of the motorcycle. Again, it doesn't matter how big it is or where it is located because you can adjust those properties later.

2. In the text block, type **Retro's Cycles**. Create a second text box and type **12345 Main St Anywhere, USA (555)555-2222**.

3. Create a third text block and type **emailus@retroscycles.com**.

4. Select the first text block that you created. Click on the resize handle in any corner of the text block and adjust the height and width of the text block so that the width is 508 and the height is 79.

> **TIP**
>
> As you drag the resize handle around, watch the W: and H: fields in the Property inspector. They change as you move your mouse.

> **CAUTION**
>
> Do not try to manually enter values into the W: and H: fields of the Property inspector to adjust the height and width of your text block. Doing this results in skewed text.

5. Next, adjust the positioning of the text block by typing **247** in the X: field in the Property inspector and **5** in the Y: field.

6. Following the same procedures, select the second text block and set the width to **508**, the height to **79**, the X: position to **247**, and the Y: position to **90**.

7. Do the same for the third text block and set the width to **494**, the height to **19**, the X: position to **246**, and the Y: position to **107**. You should now have three text blocks positioned in the page's header section (see Figure 7.8).

> **NOTE**
>
> Don't worry if your workspace doesn't look exactly like the figure. Depending on the font you use, your fonts might be significantly larger or smaller than the ones in the image. Just adjust your fonts accordingly so they fit on the screen and are similar to the image.

7

Figure 7.8
The header text has been placed.

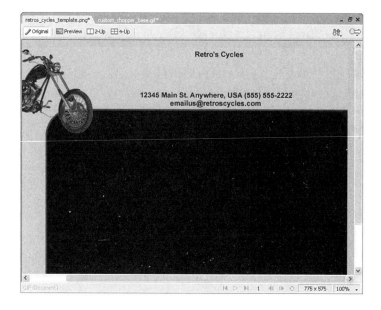

8. Next, select the text in the first text box and set the font size to a size that fits well on the page. Adjust the font style to bold and choose any font type that you would like. Change the color of the font to **#0000FF**. The font in Figure 7.9 is Brush Flash.

Figure 7.9
Adjust the font attributes and choose a custom font.

7

To apply the changes to the font, you have to first select the text you want to change within the text block. If you want to adjust the font of the entire text block, you can do so by selecting the text block and then choosing the desired font from the Property inspector.

9. Select the text in the second text block and adjust the font so that it is Arial, 15, bold, and has a color of **#000FF**. Do the same for the third text block (see Figure 7.10).

Figure 7.10
Adjust the font properties for the second and third text blocks.

10. Save the file.

CREATING THE WEB ELEMENTS

At this point, the document is starting to *look* like a web page, but with the exception of the text reference to an email address, there isn't any functionality that would actually allow this document to *perform* as a web page. To change that, you need to establish those regions of the page that will contain copy text/images and those that will contain navigation elements.

ESTABLISHING THE TEXT/IMAGE REGION

If you review the wireframe you created to present to the client, you'll see that the left side of the blue dividing line is supposed to contain navigation buttons, and the large section below and to the right of the dividing line will contain the copy and images for the site.

7

Creating the region that will contain the copy and images is simply a matter of creating a placeholder region. You can do this by slicing out the region in which you want to be able to add text in Dreamweaver.

1. In the `retros_cycles_template` document, choose the Slice tool from the toolbar and draw a square in the area to the right and below the blue divider. Again, don't worry about the size or location of the slice.

2. Using the Property inspector, set the X position to **190**, the Y position to **180**, the width of the slice to **585**, and the height to **395**. You should now see a slice area that marks the text/images region (see Figure 7.11).

Figure 7.11
Create a slice that represents the area where copy and images will be placed.

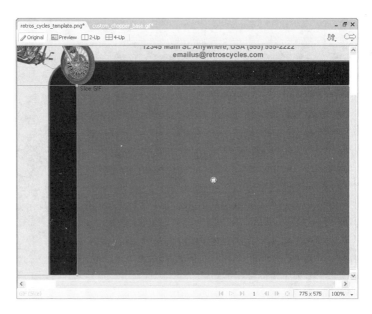

After you export the page to HTML and open it in Fireworks, this region will be represented by a large, black image. All you have to do is delete the image from your web page and the area that is left will be usable for text and images.

ADDING NAVIGATION BUTTONS

The next step to adding web elements to the document is adding navigation buttons. The five navigation buttons that the client has requested are Home, Contact, About Us, Services, and For Sale. Not only can you add these to the page, but you can use Fireworks to make them rollover buttons that change when the visitor rolls a mouse over them.

1. In the `retros_cycles_template` document, choose the Rectangle tool and draw a rectangle in the area to the left of the blue divider. Set the rectangle width to **132**, the height to **30**, the X position at **45**, and the Y position at **196**.

2. Next, set the fill color of the rectangle to **#000000** and the stroke color to **#0000FF**.

3. Set the Rectangle roundness to **50**. You should now have a blue, rounded rectangle on the page (see Figure 7.12).

Figure 7.12
A rectangle has been placed on the page.

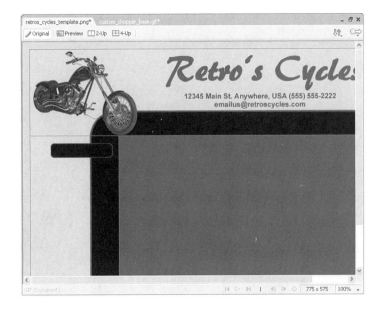

4. With the rectangle selected, choose Edit, Copy (Ctrl+C or Cmd-C) and Edit, Paste (Ctrl+C or Cmd-V) to create a duplicate of the rectangle. The duplicate is selected automatically after it is pasted onto the canvas.

> **TIP**
>
> You can also duplicate the rectangle by choosing Edit, Duplicate from the menu bar or by holding the Alt or Opt key and dragging the object to a new location on the canvas.

5. Adjust the location properties of the new rectangle so that the X position is **35** and the Y position is **236**.

6. Create three additional duplicates with the first having an X position of **25** and a Y position of **276**, the second having an X position of **15** and a Y position of **316**, and the third having an X position of **5** and a Y position of **356**.

7. Select each of the rectangles by holding the Shift key and clicking on each one. From the menu bar, choose Modify, Arrange, Send To Back or using the Ctrl+Shift+Down Arrow keyboard command. This moves the rectangles behind the blue divider and gives the illusion that they are attached (see Figure 7.13).

8. The next step to creating your navigation buttons is to add text. Select the Text tool and draw a text block that stretches across the full width of the top button. In the text

7

block, type **Home** and adjust the text so that it is Arial, 15, and has a color of **#0000FF**. Center the text in the rectangle by clicking the Center Alignment button on the Property inspector.

9. Repeat this step to create the Contact, About Us, Services, and For Sale buttons, as shown in Figure 7.14.

Figure 7.13
Five navigation rectangles have been added to the page.

Figure 7.14
Add text to the buttons.

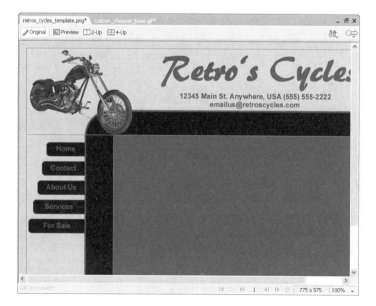

10. Next, you need to create the rollover states for your buttons. Open the Frames panel (Window, Frames) and open the upper-right Options menu. Choose Duplicate Frame from the menu.

11. In the Duplicate Frame dialog box (see Figure 7.15), choose 1 frame, After Current Frame, and click OK.

Figure 7.15
Duplicate the existing frame.

In the Frames panel, there are now two frames. Frame 1 shows what the page will look like normally and Frame 2 displays what the page will look like while a mouse is rolled over specific areas. Because you haven't made any changes to Frame 2, they both are identical. To create the over state for each button, you need to modify it in Frame 2.

12. In the Frames panel, select Frame 2. Select all the navigation buttons on the stage by holding the Shift key and clicking on each of them. Change their fill color to **#0000FF** and their stroke to **#000000**.

13. Next, select each of the text blocks and change the text color to **#000000**. This creates the buttons' rollover state (see Figure 7.16).

Figure 7.16
Create the rollover states in Frame 2.

7

With the rollover states in place, the last step is to create slices that indicate what aspects of the page should change and then to apply the rollover behavior.

14. Select the Slice tool from the toolbar and draw a slice around the Home button. In the Property inspector, set the width of the slice to **130**, the height to **35**, the X position to **0**, and the Y position to **193**. Name the slice sliHome by typing the value in the upper-left field of the Property inspector.

15. Create a second slice for the Contact button with a width of **130**, height of **41**, X position of **0**, and the Y position of **228**. Name the slice sliContact by typing the value in the upper-left field of the Property inspector.

16. Create a third slice for the About Us button with a width of **130**, height of **41**, X position of **0**, and the Y position of **269**. Name the slice sliAboutUs by typing the value in the upper-left field of the Property inspector.

17. Create a fourth slice for the Services button with a width of **130**, height of **41**, X position of **0**, and the Y position of **310**. Name the slice sliServices by typing the value in the upper-left field of the Property inspector.

18. Create a fifth slice for the For Sale button with a width of **130**, height of **38**, X position of **0**, and the Y position of **351**. Name the slice sliForSale by typing the value in the upper-left field of the Property inspector.

As shown in Figure 7.17, you now have five slices that indicate that these areas should be treated differently when the document is exported to HTML.

Figure 7.17
Each of the navigation buttons has been sliced.

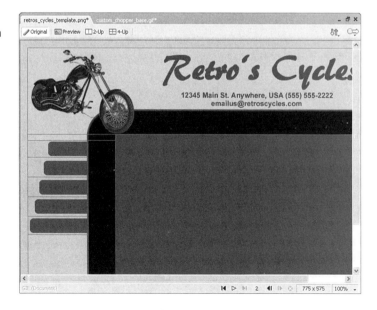

19. Open the Behaviors panel by choosing Window, Behaviors.

20. Choose the Pointer tool from the menu bar and select the slice for the Home button. On the Behaviors panel, click the plus sign and choose Simple Rollover from the menu.

The Behaviors panel now indicates that there is a rollover behavior assigned to the slice (see Figure 7.18).

Figure 7.18
The rollover behavior has been applied.

21. In the Property inspector, type **index.cfm** in the Link field. When the document is exported to HTML, a hyperlink is created automatically to the index.cfm page.

22. Following the same steps, apply the Simple Rollover behavior to each of the other buttons and link them to contact.cfm, aboutus.cfm, services.cfm, and forsale.cfm.

EXPORTING THE IMAGES

With all the navigation links in place, you're ready to export the document to an HTML format that you can edit in Dreamweaver.

1. From the menu bar, choose File, Image Preview.

2. In the Image Preview dialog box, be sure that GIF is the selected format and click Export (see Figure 7.19).

Figure 7.19
Choose to export the image as a GIF.

7

3. In the Export dialog box, choose to Export HTML and Images. In the warning box that pops up, click OK.

4. Name the file `retros_cycles_template.htm` and choose Export Slices from the Slices drop-down (see Figure 7.20).

Figure 7.20
Choose to export slices.

5. Check the box that allows you to place images in a subfolder. By default the folder is named `images`, and that's what we'll keep.

6. In the Save In drop-down, navigate to a folder where you can store the images and HTML files. If you have IIS set up on your machine, the easiest place would be `c:\Inetpub\wwwroot\retroscycles`. If the folder doesn't exist, create one.

7. Click the Export button.

8. To view the resulting HTML page, open your browser and navigate to the page. If you put your files in the `retroscycles` folder, navigate to `http://localhost/retrocycles/retros_cycles_template.htm`. You should be able to roll your mouse over any of the navigation buttons and they should change state.

NOTE

> As I mentioned earlier in the introductory chapters, the localhost path is used for Windows machines using IIS as the web server application. If you are a Mac user or are using an alternative web server application, you need to adjust the path to your file accordingly.

7

See how easy that was? You just created a simple template for a website using just a few of the many tools available to you in Fireworks. The next step is to take a look at Flash and the tools available for creating rich media elements that can be included in the site.

TROUBLESHOOTING

One or more of my rollovers don't work. What did I do wrong?

A couple things might have gone wrong. First, be sure that you created the second frame and that it has the modified navigation images for the over state. Second, check that you applied the Simple Rollover behavior to each of the navigation images.

My rollovers work in reverse. What did I do?

When you created the second set of images for the navigation buttons, you did it in Frame 1 instead of Frame 2. To fix this, open the Frames panel and drag Frame 2 so it is above Frame 1. Re-export the document using the same settings and everything should work correctly.

Everything works fine, but I noticed that my images and HTML page were dumped in the same directory. Is this right?

Nope. Go back through the export process and check the check box that places images in a subfolder.

BEST PRACTICES—CREATING WEB PAGES IN FIREWORKS VERSUS DREAMWEAVER

If you have used Dreamweaver previously or have heard anything about Dreamweaver, you might be wondering why on Earth anyone would create web pages in Fireworks, as opposed to Dreamweaver. Believe me, I used to think the same thing.

That was until I was challenged with developing my first "graphics-heavy" website. Each page on the site had a photograph of a car, and when you rolled over specific areas of the car, various images and text blocks around the site changed. I originally started out in Dreamweaver and developed each individual graphic, but creating the correct table sizes and getting the images to match up perfectly in Dreamweaver was extremely time consuming. Then a colleague showed me how to use the slice tools in Fireworks, and I realized that in minutes I could accomplish in Fireworks what I had spent hours doing in Dreamweaver.

Now when the development of a site involves a lot of graphic manipulation and JavaScript rollovers, I seriously consider whether it would be better to first lay out the site in Fireworks and then move into Dreamweaver. Sometimes it is…sometimes it isn't. In the end, it will be a decision you will have to make, but knowing what Fireworks can do should aid you in your decision.

7

PART III

FLASH 8

Introducing Flash 8

In this chapter

8

WHAT IS FLASH?

Flash is a powerful tool for creating anything from simple animations to interactive applications and simulations. It is also well suited for creating user interfaces for external data and streaming media. Its support for creative expression and practical programming, with a strong developer base, makes Flash an appealing tool to work with. The Flash authoring environment is the program in which you work to create Flash projects. You can use it to create several file types. The first is an editable document that contains your graphics and code for Flash. You create a Flash document by choosing File, Save from the menu bar. When you first save the file, giving it a name avoids the default filename of `untitled-#`. The `.fla` suffix is automatically added to the filename of the new document. You should keep this document in case you need it at a later time, as you most assuredly will. It's known as a *source file*, and is pronounced "eff el ay" or sometimes as "flah."

The published, compressed, ready-for-the-Web document that you produce from your `.fla` document is called a `.swf` file (pronounced "swiff"). This document wraps the contents of your Flash document into a single package that can be played either by a standalone Flash player or by any browser that has the Flash Player plug-in installed. Create it from the saved `.fla` file by choosing File, Publish Settings to open the Publish Settings dialog box, choosing `.swf` from the Format tab, and then clicking the Publish button. The `.swf` is automatically published to the same directory as the `.fla` file.

For a more advanced project, you might use an ActionScript document (`.as`), which is an external (to the `.fla` document) text file that holds a set of ActionScript code that can be included for use in the final published product. An `.as` document is also known as a *source file*. Both `.fla` and `.as` files are known as source files because they can be edited and are not part of the published result.

Before you dive into the details of everything Flash has to offer, you need to know a few more common terms that you will see throughout this section of the book. When a Flash file is being used in the authoring environment, it's called *author-time*. When the published `.swf` file is running in a player, it is called *run-time*. Whenever I discuss file size or the importance of creating small files, I'm always discussing the `.swf` file and not the `.fla` document. The `.swf` is the final compressed file that will actually be downloaded and processed on the end user's computer.

Now that you understand the basic areas of the program, it's time to start exploring the many ways Flash can help you turn out a powerful and dazzling product.

WHAT'S NEW IN FLASH

This section is aimed at readers who are already familiar with Flash. If you are new to Flash, you might want to skip ahead to the next section.

This release includes a lot of really great stuff. Whereas the last release was said to have been mostly aimed at developers, this one should make both designers and developers very

8

happy. Improvements and access to the "expressive" capabilities have been made throughout the interface as well as with ActionScript.

FILTERS AND THE FILTER PANEL

You can now apply graphic effects filters to text, movie clips, or buttons on the stage. These effects include glow, bevel, and drop shadow. Figure 8.1 shows a movie clip before and after the bevel filter has been applied to it. You can apply the filters with the Filters menu, which is grouped with the Property inspector whenever an object that can have filters applied to it is selected (see Figure 8.2).

Figure 8.1
Movie clip with a filter applied to it.

Figure 8.2
Filters panel, with Bevel filter selected.

BLEND MODES (WITH DEVICE TEXT SUPPORT)

The new blend modes let you blend the colors in overlapping movie clips to create composite images. Modes include multiply, lighten, darken, add, subtract, difference, alpha, and invert. Figure 8.3 shows a movie clip without a blend mode next to two overlapping movie clips with the invert blend mode applied to one of them.

If no movie clips or images are located below the blended movie clip, it blends with the stage color.

Figure 8.3
Movie clip with invert blend applied to it.

Blend modes can be applied to a movie clip with the Property inspector (see Figure 8.4).

RADIAL GRADIENT IMPROVEMENTS

The radial gradients have been improved and now enable you to move the focal point of a gradient on the shape to which it's applied to. You can also have more stops (colors) in the gradient, and you have a choice of spreading methods (pad, reflect, and repeat).

The Fill Transform tool has been replaced and expanded with the Gradient Transform tool (see Figure 8.5). It gives you much more control over how gradients are applied to shapes. Additionally, gradients and bitmap fills can now be applied to lines, which are also known as strokes, without requiring that they be converted to fills.

8

Figure 8.4
Accessing the blend
modes with the
Property inspector.

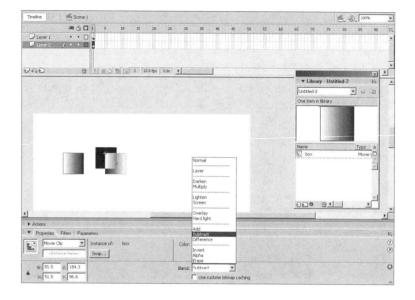

Figure 8.5
Using the Gradient
Transform tool han-
dles to modify a
gradient.

STROKE ENHANCEMENTS

In Flash 8, you have more control over the strokes you draw than ever before. In previous releases, strokes were limited to a maximum size of 10 pixels. This maximum size has now been increased to 200 pixels, which is plenty of room to take advantage of the new feature just mentioned: the capability to color strokes with a gradient fill.

You can now also choose how lines are joined (miter, round, or bevel, as shown in Figure 8.6). Caps, which are the end points of lines that are not joined, also have new settings available (none, round, and square, as shown in Figure 8.7). All of these settings enable you to draw more cleanly and precisely, and can be set in the Property inspector.

Figure 8.6
Line joins: miter,
round, and bevel.

Figure 8.7
Line end caps: none, round, and square.

8

OBJECT DRAWING MODEL

Normally in Flash, when you draw a shape and then another that overlaps the first shape in the same layer, the two shapes meld into one. This is considered normal behavior that helps keep the file size down by not accounting for additional points when shapes overlap. However, Flash 8 gives you a new option for drawing shapes on the stage. When the new Object Drawing model is turned on, which you can do with the button at the bottom of the Tools panel, it creates new objects that don't meld with other objects when you draw on the stage (see Figure 8.8). This new option is found in the Line, Oval, Rectangle, Pen, and Pencil tool options. I like to think of it as a kind of "auto-grouping" mode.

Figure 8.8
Turning on the Object Drawing model in the toolbox options.

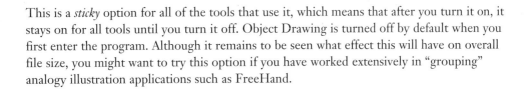

This is a *sticky* option for all of the tools that use it, which means that after you turn it on, it stays on for all tools until you turn it off. Object Drawing is turned off by default when you first enter the program. Although it remains to be seen what effect this will have on overall file size, you might want to try this option if you have worked extensively in "grouping" analogy illustration applications such as FreeHand.

8

Be aware that you need to double-click the drawing object on the stage to enter into edit mode for that object so that you can edit the actual shape, color, or other properties of the vectors that make up a drawing object created while in Object Drawing mode. Shapes drawn in normal mode are editable without double-clicking. To return a Drawing Object to behaving like a regular shape (with no need to double-click and edit), select it and choose Modify, Break Apart. The shapes will now be merged.

OBJECT-LEVEL UNDO IS BACK

In MX 2004, the Undo feature was locked at the Document level, which meant that you had to work back through the history of every step in the document no matter on what timeline they occurred. In this version, to the joy of many, Object-Level Undo is back. With Object-Level Undo mode, each object on the Stage and in the library has its own undo list. As a result, you can once again undo changes to one object without affecting any other object.

However, the default setting for undo remains at the Document level and follows the History document changes. To turn on Object-Level Undo, go to Edit, Preferences (on a PC) or Flash, Preferences (on a Mac). In the General Preferences tab, select Object-Level Undo from the Undo options.

CAUTION

Switching between Undo modes deletes your current Undo history. If you plan to use Object-Level Undo during production, be sure you're in Object-Level Undo mode before making any changes that you might want to undo.

TEXT

Flash 8 offers better text rendering with FlashType, which integrates subpixel rendering technology. This makes text, especially at smaller fonts, much more readable than it has been before now. Another improvement to text in this release is the addition of Bitmap Text Scrolling, which uses the bitmap surfaces capability to provide high-speed text scrolling.

In addition, improvements in the WYSIWYG text display enable you to have a more uniform experience of your text as it appears in the authoring environment versus how it appears when the .swf file is played in the Flash Player. In other words, what you see in the authoring environment is much more like what you get in the published .swf.

BITMAP CACHING

Macromedia has made a number of significant improvements to Flash's performance with this release. Movie clips and vector images are now represented as cached bitmaps to improve rendering performance. When complex vector images or multiple instances of the same image with different effects applied are cached as a bitmap, every frame doesn't have to be redrawn from the vector data. Chapter 9, "Working with Vector Artwork, Bitmaps, and Static Text," explores the difference between vector and bitmap images in more depth.

SCRIPTING AND RUN-TIME ACCESS

Flash 8 introduces features for code development and run-time access to expressive features with ActionScript. These include the following features:

- For those less experienced with coding, there is a new Script Assist mode in the Action panel.

- Previously, you could dynamically load external JPEG files during run-time. Now you can also load external PNG and GIF files.

- ActionScript 2.0 now has the capability to handle file uploads and downloads with user intervention.

- The BitmapData API lets you manipulate images at run-time at the pixel level. This means that new filters and blend modes can be applied with ActionScript.

MEDIA AND COMPONENTS

New features for media and components include an all new video codec and the new FLVPlayback component.

- The new On2 Video Codec (VP6) offers huge improvements for web-based video. It features better control of video quality and data rates.

- The FLVPlayback component makes it easy to import and integrate video into your Flash project.

- The new Video Exporter enables you to convert video files to FLV (Flash Video format) files through the use of a special external application that is installed along with Flash. The Video Exporter also allows batch processing, which speeds the workflow enormously for large projects.

WORKSPACE LAYOUT

Now that you've gotten an overview of what's new in Flash 8, it's time to dig into the details and learn how to make the most of Flash.

The Flash authoring environment comes with a great number of tools for both creative and coding tasks. These tools are grouped into panels. You can customize the way these panels are arranged and even hide or reveal them to suit your needs.

Why have more than one panel set? Most people who work with Flash are involved in both design and coding. A developer might want different panels open when coding than when designing to limit the clutter of tool menus and icons on the desktop.

In previous releases, the task of saving and managing the workspace layout was handled with Panel Sets. These have been improved and are now found at Window, Workspace Layout, which provides options to open a saved layout, save the current layout, and manage the layouts.

When you get a panel layout that you like, you can save and name it. In the Manage Workspace Layouts interface (see Figure 8.9), you have the option to rename or delete a layout you've already saved. Figure 8.10 shows the default layout of the Flash Workspace.

Figure 8.9
Manage Workspace Layouts interface.

Figure 8.10
The Flash Workspace with default layout.

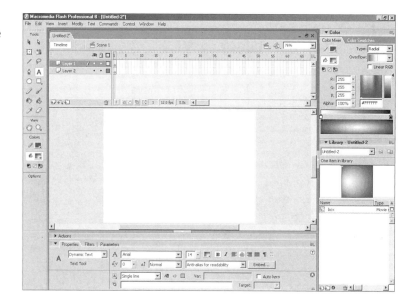

PROPERTY INSPECTOR

The Property inspector is located at the bottom of the Workspace and is used to control the properties of the tools and objects in Flash. The Property inspector is *context dependent*, which means that at any given time, it displays only the properties available to the element you've selected. For example, as shown in Figure 8.11, if you draw a shape with the Oval tool, the Property inspector gives you access to the fill color, stroke color, stroke thickness, stroke style, and custom settings for the stroke.

Figure 8.11
The Property inspector in the Oval tool context.

However, if you select a movie clip symbol instance on the stage, you get access to the symbol type (behavior), the instance name, and color effects that can be applied to the instance (see Figure 8.12). If you expand the movie clip Property inspector, you also get access to the width and height of the clip as well as its x and y positions relative to the registration point of the parent timeline.

Figure 8.12
Properties of the movie clip instance.

When the tool selected does not have specific properties available, the Property inspector defaults to the document properties. For example, the Eraser tool does not have any properties that are listed in the Property inspector, so when it is selected, the Property inspector shows the document's properties.

PANELS

You have a lot of freedom to position panels, as suits your work habits. Panels can be docked or free-floating, and can even be moved from one docked location to another.

Panels can be dragged with the handle in the panel's upper-left corner. To collapse a panel, click on the collapse arrow/button at the top-left corner of the panel or the arrow/button centered above the panel group in the horizontal splitter.

The panels in Flash work the same as they do in all Studio applications, although a few panels are unique to Flash and are covered here.

COLOR MIXER PANEL

The Color Mixer panel offers many tools for selecting colors for fills and lines (see Figure 8.13). Color types include solid color, linear gradient, radial gradient, and imported bitmaps. In previous versions, these types could be applied only to fills. In Flash 8, you can now apply these color types to lines as well.

Figure 8.13
Color Mixer.

You can select your color from the color mixer in different ways:

- From a palette of web-safe colors
- By numerically setting RGB and Alpha values
- By using the color picker with accompanying saturation level selector

You get experience with the color mixer in the coming chapters, especially Chapters 9 and 10, "Animation Basics."

FILTERS PANEL

Filters are special effects or design shortcuts. They can be applied to objects from the Filters panel, which is grouped with the Property inspector at the bottom of the workspace.

Filters can be applied to text fields, movie clips, and buttons, either alone or in combination with other filters. They can be added to or removed from an existing object at any time in the development and design process. The available filters include the following:

- Drop shadow
- Blur
- Glow
- Bevel
- Gradient glow
- Gradient bevel
- Adjust color

Combinations of filters can be saved as presets, which can be renamed or deleted.

THE ACTIONS PANEL

When working in the Flash authoring environment, you write and edit ActionScript in the Actions panel. To open the Actions panel (see Figure 8.14), go to Window, Development Panels, Action, or use the F9 keyboard shortcut.

Figure 8.14
The Actions panel.

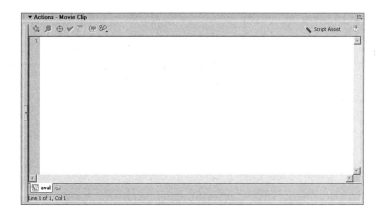

SETTING DOCUMENT ATTRIBUTES

Flash documents have various properties that you can set with the Document Properties panel. You can open this panel by choosing Modify, Document from the top menu bar or by clicking the Size button in the Property inspector while it is in its document context (click in the gray work area or an unoccupied stage area to get it to switch). The Property inspector is in document context by default. When tools or objects are selected, the context of the inspector shifts to the selected tool or object.

The Document Properties panel offers several properties that you can set:

- **Title** is new to this version. Its value is embedded as metadata in the published .swf file. This metadata is designed for use by search engines.

- **Description** is also new and embedded in the .swf file as metadata that will eventually be used to help with content indexing for search engines.

- **Dimensions** are the width and height of your Flash movie/application. They determine the size of the stage for your project.

- **Background Color** is the color of your Flash document's stage.

- **Frame Rate** sets the number of frames for the player to play per second. Frame rate impacts the quality of animation and the size of the published file. The greater the frame rate, the better the quality, but the larger the file size.

- **Ruler Units** are part of the Dimensions property of the document. If you start out with Dimensions in pixels and then change the Ruler unit to inches, Flash converts the pixel value to inches value automatically. Although pixels are the standard measurement unit for web documents, the available Ruler Units options include Inches, Inches (decimal), Points, Centimeters, Millimeters, and Pixels.

8

THE TIMELINE

The *timeline*, shown in Figure 8.15, is basically a visual navigation tool and storage device that provides access to all the elements in your Flash project. It is basically a graph in two dimensions. Time (expressed in frames running from left to right) is placed along one axis, and content (stored in layers stacked on top of each other) is placed along another axis. You can access any particular point in time and space of your movie by clicking on that point in the timeline.

Figure 8.15
The timeline.

To understand the timeline, a basic understanding of animation is helpful. Animation works by showing a series of visuals that change over time. Slight differences in each image can make it appear as though the drawn object is moving. In Flash, each change in the visual information occurs at a certain time that is referred to on the timeline as the *frame number*. The visual change that occurs on that frame number can occur on one or many different layers in the document in a storage device called a *keyframe*.

So, much like a music score, the change over time is graphed on the horizontal scale with frame numbers, and the visual (or code) elements in the document are stored on the vertical axis as keyframes. Every keyframe in every layer at a certain frame number is *played* simultaneously. This is discussed more in Chapter 10, which covers animation and the basic elements of Flash.

As important as the timeline is to organizing the overall project, it can consume precious screen real estate that can often be dedicated better to creating the content of each keyframe during author-time. In previous versions of Flash, you could collapse the timeline. In Flash 8, you can now completely hide the timeline in the authoring environment with a button interface under the tab with the filename at top of the document panel (see Figure 8.16).

Figure 8.16
Button for collapsing the timeline.

LAYERS AND LAYER FOLDERS

You can think of a movie as a stack of transparent sheets that you have painted with the elements of your animation (see Figure 8.17). If you were to look through the stack of sheets,

8

you would see the painted areas of the sheets below, as long as they were not covered by an area where the sheet above it is painted. In Flash, rather than use sheets of transparent paper, you use *layers*.

Figure 8.17
A stack of transparent sheets with artwork.

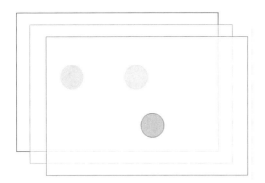

One thing that often confuses new Flash authors is the stacking order of layers in a Flash movie. In a Flash movie, the stacking order matches the spatial order—in other words, the closer the layer is to the top, the more above the stage it will be. The bottom layer on the timeline is always the closest layer to the stage visually. You can think of the stage as a desk on which the stack of sheets is sitting. The sheet on top of the stack is the farthest from the surface of the desk.

Dragging one layer above another changes the stacking order of layers. You can also select several layers and drag them at once.

To add a new layer, click on the Add Layer button at the bottom-left corner of the timeline. You can also add a new layer by right clicking on the name of an existing layer, and selecting the Insert layer from the context menu. To delete a layer, you can click on the Delete button or right-click on the layer's name and select Delete Layer.

Layer folders can help keep layers organized when a project gets big or complex. You can use them to group related layers into a folder that can be expanded or collapsed as you work (see Figure 8.18). You can drag any layer into or out of any folder after the folder has been created. If you select multiple layers into a folder, their order before being moved is maintained in the folder.

FRAMES AND KEYFRAMES

Sometimes the references to *frames* in Flash can get a bit confusing. As mentioned previously, frame numbers on the timeline tell you where you are in terms of time in an animation. Frames are represented visually on the timeline as rectangular boxes with nothing in them. Frames add time for the content of a keyframe to play. Their only function is to play whatever the previous keyframe (to their left) contains.

Figure 8.18
Timeline with folders, open and closed.

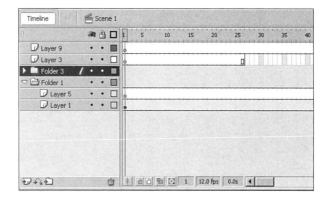

A *keyframe* is a frame that stores a reference to content on the stage that occurs at that frame number and on that layer. Keyframes that include graphic content are represented by a filled circle on the timeline.

A blank keyframe is represented by an open circle in a frame (see Figure 8.19). This is a keyframe without any visual content. Blank keyframes also serve as a place for code to be attached so that it runs when the playback reaches that particular frame. A blank keyframe therefore is a good place to store your frame-based code. Keyframes with code attached always have a small letter *a* above them to let you know they contain code.

Figure 8.19
Frames and keyframes (filled and empty) on the timeline.

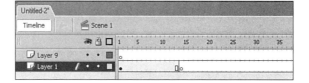

ONION SKINNING AND MULTIPLE FRAME EDITING

Onion skinning is a viewing mode that lets you see the previous frame while drawing in a new frame. The term comes from traditional animation techniques, which used "onion skin" paper that was thin, like the layers of skin on an onion. The paper allowed the animator to see through the layers of drawings as they worked on them.

This sounds a lot like working with layers, so what's the difference between layers and onion skinning? With layers, you see everything that is on all the layers at a certain point in time as if looking through a single stack of transparent sheets. With onion skinning, you view the visuals in keyframes for more than one frame at a time.

Onion skinning is not visible when you publish your .swf file; it's just an author-time tool. You can toggle any of the onion skinning options on and off at any time in the authoring environment with buttons on the bottom of the timeline. Figure 8.20 shows onion skinning turned on for a short animation. The position of the circle at each frame is visible on the stage at once. If you use the outline option for onion skinning, just the outlines of the visual elements for each frame are visible, except for the frame currently being edited. If you'd like to have more than one frame available for editing at once, set the Edit Multiple Frames option, which makes all keyframes within the onion markers. To set the onion markers (the brackets on the number line of the timeline) drag the brackets along the timeline.

Figure 8.20
Onion skinning toggle buttons.

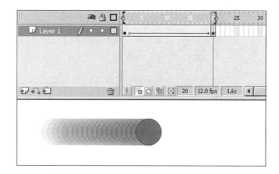

TOOLS

The Tools panel contains the basic visual creation tools that come with Flash (see Figure 8.21). Each tool has its own properties, which can be accessed with the Property inspector panel.

Figure 8.21
The Tools panel.

Below the tools is a small interface that enables you to quickly change the color of the stroke or fill of any tool you select. You can select the colors before using the tool. Many tools offer additional options in the bottom section of the toolbox when you select the tool.

The following sections describe each tool as well as give keyboard shortcuts (capitalized letters in parentheses) that you can use. Keyboard shortcuts can help you save time and develop a smooth workflow when you get comfortable with them. If you are accustomed to the keyboard shortcuts of other applications, you can customize your keyboard shortcuts in Flash to match those shortcuts. To view the default setting, go to Edit, Keyboard Shortcuts (on a PC) or Flash, Keyboard Shortcuts (on a Mac). This brings up the Keyboard Shortcuts dialog box, where you can select the shortcuts of another application and apply them to Flash or define your own custom set of shortcuts.

THE ARROW TOOLS: SELECTION TOOL AND SUBSELECTION TOOL

At the top of the tool panel, you'll find the Arrow tools: the Selection tool (V) and the Subselection tool (A) (see Figure 8.22).

Figure 8.22
The Arrow tools.

The Selection tool (V) is the black arrow, and it lets you directly grab, select, and move any element on the stage. To select an object, just click on it. Double-clicking selects any contiguous parts of a shape. To add to a selection, hold the Shift key down while you select. To remove elements from your selection, hold the (Option) [Alt] key while you select. After a selection has been made, simply hold the mouse down and drag the selection to a new place to move the elements.

You can also drag in any blank area of the stage to create a selection marquee to include an entire shape. However, be aware that when you are using the normal drawing mode in Flash, if you miss a portion of a shape when you are using this method of selection, you cut the shape.

Approaching any deselected vector shape with the mouse cursor enables you to manually edit that shape by dragging and pushing the unselected outlines and fills. It's as if you are selecting the space around the shape, and pushing that space into the shape, like pushing on a water balloon. The indicator for the tool changes depending on whether you are over a corner or a curve point. To move a corner point, drag to a new location. Hold the (Option) [Alt] key while dragging to place a new corner point. Pull in the middle of any line portion to create a curve point. This is covered in more detail in Chapter 9.

The Subselection tool is the white arrow with black outline (A). It enables you to view and manipulate the points of any vector object. Select any line and drag the corner points or change the selected curve points by manipulating the *Bezier handles* (see Figure 8.23). Vector objects and Bezier handles are discussed in later chapters.

8

Figure 8.23
Manipulating a
curve's handles with
the Subselection tool.

Free Transform Tool (Q)

With the Free Transform tool, you can change the dimensions of a selected object by dragging the handles at its sides or corners (see Figure 8.24). In addition, you can rotate the object by positioning the mouse a little outside the corner handle of the shape or object. The rotation usually occurs around the center of the selection, but you can adjust the center of rotation by dragging the white dot in the middle of the selection to another position.

Figure 8.24
The Free Transform
tool applied to a line.

You can manipulate the horizontal or vertical skew of a selected object by dragging from somewhere between any of the rotation and scale points. Drag in the direction you want the shape to skew (lean).

When a shape is selected while the Free Transform tool is in use, the Envelope and Distort options become available in the lower options. These options give you additional control points that you can use to distort the shape. Use curve points for both the Distort option and the Envelope option. Figure 8.25 shows the Free Transform tool applied to a line, with the Envelope option turned on. One of the control points has been used to create a curve in the previously straight line.

Gradient Transform Tool (F)

As mentioned in the "What's New in Flash" section, in Flash 8 the Fill Transform tool has been expanded into the new Gradient Transform tool. It can be used for both gradient transformations and to manipulate bitmap fills. Note that a gradient or bitmap fill must be present on the stage and selected before you can use the Gradient Transform tool on it.

Flash offers two types of gradients: *Linear* and *Radial*. You can choose which type of gradient you want to use, as well as the colors for them, in the Color Mixer panel and add them with the Paint Bucket tool. (Both the color mixer and the Paint Bucket tool are discussed later in this chapter.) A linear gradient transitions from one color to another in one direction. A radial gradient transitions from the center of one color out to another color. When

8

you have your gradient fill, you can transform the scale, location, and rotation of the gradient with this tool (see Figure 8.26). In addition, the focal point of radial gradients can now be adjusted.

Figure 8.25
Using a control point in the envelope of the Free Transform tool to create a curved line.

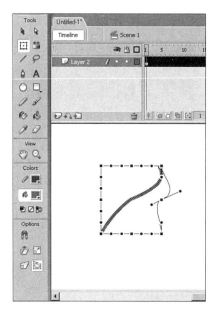

Figure 8.26
Rotating the linear gradient in a selected fill.

The Gradient Transform tool also enables you to manipulate a bitmap fill's size and rotation. Flash 8 also enables you to manipulate the tiling skew of bitmap fills.

LINE TOOL (N)

The Line tool lets you draw by clicking on a start point and then dragging to the endpoint of the line you want to draw (see Figure 8.27). Turn on the Snap to Objects option to see a circle indicator appear when you approach other objects and want to easily and precisely connect the line to that object. In Flash 8, you can also turn on an additional cue called Stroke Hinting in the Property inspector to give you a preview of where your line will interact with other lines.

8

Figure 8.27
Drawing with the Line tool.

Lasso Tool (L)

The Lasso tool (see Figure 8.28) lets you define and select an odd-shaped area by drawing the selection. This is especially useful when working with bitmaps that are broken apart or traced, which is discussed in more detail in Chapter 9. The Lasso tool has a Magic Wand option that selects areas of like colors in broken-apart bitmaps. It does not function for any vector shape.

Figure 8.28
The Lasso tool.

Pen Tool (P)

The Pen tool enables you to draw complex illustrations by manually creating corner points and curve controls that make up your drawing (see Figure 8.29). To begin your drawing, create corner points by clicking on the stage and create curve points by clicking and dragging in the direction you want the curve to grow. To complete your drawing, double-click at the last point in the drawing, or close the shape by clicking on the beginning point.

Figure 8.29
Drawing with the Pen tool.

Text Tool (T)

The Text tool lets you place text fields on the stage (see Figure 8.30). After a new field has been placed, you can modify its properties with the Property inspector. You can set an alpha value (the transparency level) for the text with the Text (Fill) Color property. You can also add any of the filter effects discussed earlier in the chapter by selecting the field and choosing the Filters tab in the Property inspector group.

Figure 8.30
Using the Text tool to place a text field on the stage.

Oval, Rectangle, and Polystar Tools (O and R)

After the Oval or Rectangle shape tool is selected, you can draw the shape by clicking and dragging on the stage. Features of the shape, such as line thickness and color, can be preset with the Property inspector before you draw your shape on the stage.

A PolyStar tool is also available to create a more complex shape. You can access it by clicking on the little black triangle in the bottom-right corner of the Rectangle Tool button (see Figure 8.31). In the Property inspector, you can find additional options for the PolyStar Tool, including an option to create a polygon or a star, the number of sides, and the angle at the points.

Figure 8.31
The Polystar tool is accessed through the Rectangle Tool button.

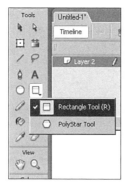

Pencil Tool (Y)

The Pencil tool is a freeform drawing tool that lets you draw lines and curves that follow the movement of the mouse as you drag it across the stage. The accuracy of your drawing is controlled by the Smoothing option in the lower part of the toolbox. You can choose from the following options:

- **Straighten**—Straight lines only
- **Smooth**—Smooth lines that hide small inaccuracies created during drawing
- **Ink**—Exactly what you draw

Usually you will want to use the Smooth option to keep the number of points you draw down and with that the file size. In Flash, keeping the file size small is a concern because larger sizes take longer for the end user to download. Figure 8.32 shows a line drawn in the Ink mode next to a line drawn in the Smooth mode of the Pencil tool. Drawing in Flash is discussed in more detail in Chapter 9.

Figure 8.32
The line on the left was drawn with the Pencil tool in Ink mode. The line on the right was drawn in Smooth mode.

BRUSH TOOL (B)

Although the Brush tool (see Figure 8.33) is similar to the Pencil tool in how it draws, it is different in that the Brush tool draws fills (shapes without outlines). The Pencil tool draws lines. The *Brush mode*, which is set in the toolbox options, enables you to set how your brush stroke fills in the space when other graphic elements are already present. For example, you can set it to Paint Behind to have your stroke visible only where there are no existing lines or shapes. The strokes are there, and are visible if you later move the covering objects. This is discussed in more detail in Chapter 9.

Figure 8.33
A stroke made with the Brush tool, with a linear gradient selected as the fill color.

PAINT BUCKET AND INK BOTTLE TOOLS (K AND S)

You can use the Paint Bucket and Ink Bottle tools (see Figure 8.34) to change the colors of graphic elements that you've already drawn. The Paint Bucket tool adds a fill to a closed shape. A closed shape is a shape that has an outline with no breaks.

The Ink Bottle tool enables you to change the properties of strokes (outlines) instead of fills. You can also use the Ink Bottle tool to add an outline to an existing shape that does not currently have an outline.

EYEDROPPER TOOL (I)

The Eyedropper tool enables you to sample the color of a fill or line and then apply it to another object with the Ink Pot or Paint Bucket tools. When dealing with a stroke, the Eyedropper tool also collects the line width and stroke type information to be added to the new line.

ERASER TOOL (E)

The Eraser tool can come in handy because it lets you erase previously drawn graphic elements. The tool has several settings in its options, which are available on the lower toolbox when it is selected:

- **Erase Normal** erases both fills and outlines.
- **Erase Fills** erases only the fills and leaves outlines untouched. The eraser stroke can start at any point.
- **Erase Lines** erases the lines but leaves fill areas untouched.
- **Erase Selected Fills** lets you select a fill to which you want to apply the eraser before you begin erasing. Only the selected fill is affected; adjacent fills are left intact.

- **Erase Inside** lets you start the erase from inside an outlined shape. Then you can proceed as if with Erase Fills, but this time, it leaves fill areas outside of the outline intact. It's sort of a manual knock-out. Unlike the Erase Fills option, for a fill to be erased in this option the eraser stroke must start inside of the fill shape that is being erased.

The Eraser tool also has a Faucet option, which lets you select and delete a single element (based on color selection) at once (see Figure 8.34). This can save a lot of time when cleaning up traced bitmaps.

Figure 8.34
Eraser tool Faucet
option.

THE LIBRARY

The Library is one of the most important features in Flash. As you will learn in Chapter 10, the Library stores and organizes all the assets in your project that can be reused.

Whenever a symbol is created or imported, it's automatically added to the Library (see Figure 8.35). Even if you later delete that symbol from the stage, it remains in the Library. Symbols in the Library can also be accessed with ActionScript and attached to the stage at run-time.

Figure 8.35
The Library panel.

TROUBLESHOOTING

Why won't the Paint Bucket fill in the shape I drew with the Pencil tool?

Check to see whether there are any gaps in the outline of the shape you are attempting to fill. When the gaps are closed and the shape is completely enclosed, you should be able to apply a fill.

Why doesn't the Gradient Transform tool do anything when I click on a shape with it?

Make sure there is a gradient or bitmap fill in the shape. The Gradient Transform tool can be applied to only existing gradient or bitmap fills.

Why doesn't my .swf file show up when I publish or test my movie?

Make sure that you have saved your .fla document before you publish or use Control, Test Movie to create your .swf file. You have to save the .fla first so Flash knows where to save the .swf file and what its name should be.

BEST PRACTICES—PRACTICE MAKES PERFECT

When you start learning Flash, it can be frustrating and sometimes overwhelming. Be patient. Take your time, keep practicing, and be sure to play. Explore the tools without a project deadline; just experiment with what you can do with Flash.

To experiment without danger of losing what you've already created, get in the habit of implementing simple version control for your projects by using Save As with a new filename, rather than using Save whenever you make changes to a file. This way, you can revert to an earlier version if you make a mistake. If you're working as part of a team that uses a formal version control system, you can still follow the naming convention in your shop while adding suffixes for your own local file versions.

CHAPTER **9**

WORKING WITH VECTOR ARTWORK, BITMAPS, AND STATIC TEXT

In this chapter

9

UNDERSTANDING BITMAP AND VECTOR GRAPHICS

Did you ever play with a Lite-Brite as a child? If so, that may have been your first experience with creating bitmap graphics, albeit at very low resolution. Resolution refers to the number of dots of color, or pixels, that are squeezed into a display screen. With a Lite-Brite, the resolution is about 20 dots per square inch. On the other hand, the resolution on a typical high-resolution desktop monitor is 1024 by 768. That's 768 lines of dots, with 1024 dots in each line. Obviously, the resolution on a computer screen is much greater than that of the colored pegs on a Lite-Brite board; however, the concept is much the same. Individual dots of color are arranged on a grid to form an image. On a computer screen, the image is rendered for display as an array of pixels.

There are two main phases in the life of a digital image: how it is displayed and how it is stored. Both vector and bitmap graphics are displayed in the same way on the monitor with the resulting physical screen image rendered pixel by pixel. The difference between "bitmap" and "vector" refers to how the data describing the image is stored. In a bitmap format, the data is saved as a grid of dots, whereas a vector format saves the data as patches of color defined by geometrical formulas.

Each format has its strengths and weaknesses. Bitmap graphics format the information needed to display an image pixel by pixel. As a result, the files can take up a lot of space, but they don't require much processing before output to the monitor's screen. Vector graphics files, on the other hand, are considerably smaller, but can be processing intensive because they have to be converted from a math formula into the grid of colored dots displayed on the screen.

To better understand the difference between bitmaps and vectors, consider an example. Figure 9.1 shows a blue square that is 30 pixels by 30 pixels. Saving that image as a bitmap would require data for each one of the 900 (30×30) pixels that make up the blue square.

Figure 9.1
Diagram of the pixels in a 30×30 square.

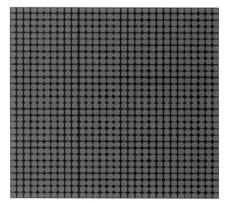

On the other hand, vector graphics use lines and curves to describe the areas on the screen where particular colors should be. The only data you need to save for a square is its size and position in the document (as x and y coordinates) and the function that describes it as a square. The graphics rendering program can evaluate the function describing that square and fill in the appropriate pixels. More complex shapes can be described by more complex functions.

In Figure 9.2, the dark blue dots represent how many points of data are required to save the same blue square in bitmap format and in vector format. As you can see, for simple shapes, vector graphics require less memory, so they are ideal where file size is an issue, as in when you have limited disk space or file transfer speed limitations.

Figure 9.2
Bitmap graphics require more information to describe a simple shape than vector graphics require to describe the same shape.

However, as the graphics get more complex, vector formats can take up even more memory than a bitmap version of the same image. More complex vector graphics require more anchor (or key) points to define areas of color (see Figure 9.3), and the more anchor points used to describe a shape, the larger its file size becomes. One of the benefits of the vector graphics file format is that it's a description of a shape rather than a list of all the pixels that fit into that shape; therefore, it takes up less file space. If you add more anchor points to your description of the square, not only does it increase the number of points saved, but it also increases the number of times a formula is used to draw the shape.

Figure 9.3
A simple vector shape uses fewer key points than a complex vector shape.

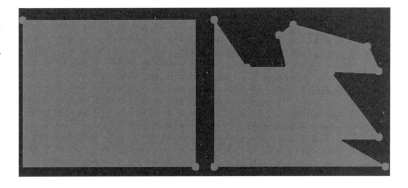

Why care about file size? The bigger the file, the longer it takes for the end user to download it. Even though Internet download speeds continue to increase, remember that Flash is

9

also used on mobile devices with smaller memory capacity and slower processing speeds than desktop and laptop computers.

In addition to file size, vector graphics have the advantage of scaling well. Bitmaps do not. Bitmapped data describes the image as fixed to a grid of a particular size. In vector graphics, the key anchor points are relative, so the functions can accommodate scaling without losing image clarity. Figure 9.4 shows an enlarged bitmap and an enlarged vector graphic.

Figure 9.4
A bitmap image doesn't scale well, but a vector image enlarges without losing clarity.

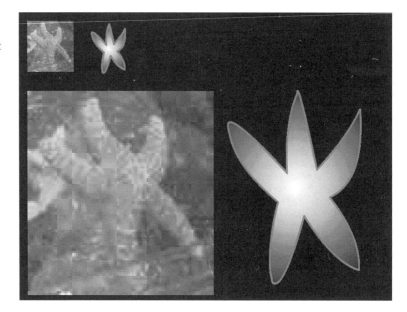

WORKING WITH BITMAPS

Bitmaps can add visual depth and texture to your Flash project. Used in moderation, they can make all the difference in your visual design. They can also be the focus of an application, as in a slide show or picture gallery. Flash supports several bitmap file types, including JPEG, GIF, and PNG. If you have Quicktime installed, you can also import PSD, TIFF, and SGI files.

IMPORTING BITMAPS

There are a couple of ways to bring bitmaps into your Flash project: Import them to the library or directly to the stage. To import to the stage choose File, Import, Import to Stage and select the file you want. You can also open an external library and drag the image to the stage.

TIP
When you import a bitmap directly to the stage, you might find that the image is much bigger than the stage. Before resizing the image, position it so that the upper-left corner is on the stage. Otherwise, you might have to do quite a bit of scrolling to find the reduced image.

COMPRESSING BITMAPS

When authoring with Flash, you should be concerned about file size. Bitmaps can bloat your project, but you can shave off some of that file size within the Flash authoring environment.

In the library, right-click on the bitmap name and select Properties, or click on the Properties icon (the white *i* with a blue circle around it) at the bottom of the library panel. This brings up the Bitmap Properties panel (see Figure 9.5).

Figure 9.5
Bitmap Properties panel.

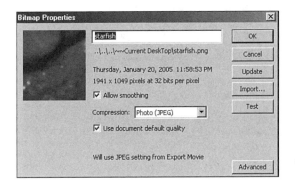

To compress the bitmap with the Bitmap Properties panel, uncheck the Use Document Default Quality option. Then select a compression type, check the Allow Smoothing option, and choose either Test or Update. The Photo (JPEG) compression setting results in lost pixels, so be sure to save a version you can revert to before proceeding. The Lossless PNG/GIF compression setting is best for traced bitmaps (see the next section) or bitmaps with simple shapes and few colors. You can achieve significant file size improvements with this technique. If your imported bitmap has already been compressed, you might want to go with the PNG/GIF option. If you've got a JPEG without any previous compression, you might want to go with double compression. This is something with which you need to experiment. There's a delicate balance between file compression and artistic integrity. If you overcompress your bitmap images, they will look terrible.

TRACING BITMAPS

There may be times when you need to work with a logo or flat artwork in a Flash project. You might receive this artwork as bitmap files that are smaller than you need for your project. As discussed previously, you can end up with ugly pixilated images if you resize them larger than the originals. Figure 9.6 shows a bitmap image that's been enlarged and looks pixilated.

Figure 9.6
Enlarging a bitmap
can result in a dis-
torted pixilation effect.

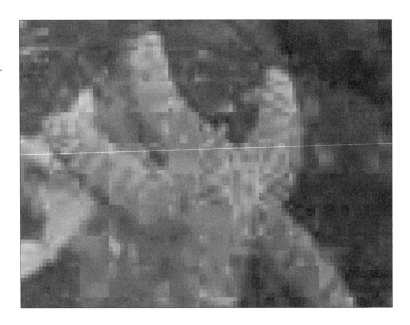

In such a case, it might be best to trace the bitmap. By using the Trace Bitmap command, you can convert a bitmap into a vector image. To trace a bitmap, Select its instance on the stage and then, from the main menu, go to Modify, Bitmap, Trace Bitmap to open the Trace Bitmap panel (see Figure 9.7).

Figure 9.7
Trace Bitmap panel.

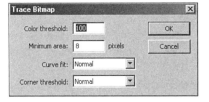

When tracing bitmaps, there are several parameters to set. Each of these options enables you to control the quality of the resulting image and optimize for file size:

- **Color Threshold**—This setting determines how much color detail is preserved. The lower the threshold (from 1 to 500), the more colors are used.

- **Minimum Area**—This setting determines how many pixels should be included in the area for normalization. During a trace, the continuous range of colors in a bitmap is replaced with discrete areas of colors. The lower the minimum area, the more detailed the traced image will be.

- **Curve Fit**—This setting determines how closely the traced curves follow the original image.

- **Corner Threshold**—Much like curve fit, the corner threshold determines how precisely the traced image follows the original image.

If you set your resolution high with these four parameters, be prepared to wait a while. It's very processor intensive.

OPTIMIZING TRACED BITMAPS

Recall how the data is organized in a bitmap image: as a grid of colored dots (or pixels). When Flash traces a bitmap, it converts the data, pixel by pixel, and simplifies it into shapes of color bounded by lines and curves, essentially converting the bitmap into a vector graphic (see Figure 9.8).

Figure 9.8
Tracing a bitmap to a vector graphic.

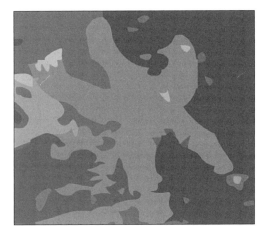

Because tracing a bitmap results in complex shapes, it is important to reduce the complexity and smooth out the curves of these shapes when working with traced bitmaps. Smoothing the curves reduces the number of anchor points needed to describe the shapes in the image. This process is called *optimization*.

To optimize the curves of a traced bitmap, select the image or a portion of the image, and use the Optimize Curves panel by choosing Modify, Shape, Optimize. In this panel, you can set the level of smoothness desired, determine whether you want multiple passes to execute (which slows down the process, but can result in less distortion of the image), and indicate whether you want a report after the optimization is completed. If you've set the main toolbar to be visible in your workspace, you can click directly on the Smooth or Straighten buttons.

NOTE

I'm always looking for ways to keep the file size down, but sometimes traced images just look great! However, you've got to keep the end user in mind. Optimize those traces! A traced bitmap that hasn't been optimized can result in an even larger file than the original bitmap.

Can you further optimize a traced bitmap without losing too much image quality? Of course! One technique to try is to use the selection tool to select a rectangular or oval area on the edge of the image. Then smooth the curves of the selected area. Large shapes can be selected individually and smoothed. This can be tedious work, but selective optimization can pay off with a much smaller file size.

BREAKING APART BITMAPS

Breaking apart bitmaps makes the pixels available to be edited in the Flash authoring environment while preserving the clarity of the bitmap image. You might find this useful if you want to change the color of certain parts of the image. After the bitmap has been broken apart, you can manipulate it with tools such as the Eraser and the Paint Bucket. To change the color of part of the image, select the original with the Lasso or Magic Wand tools, and fill the area with the new color.

Another use for breaking apart a bitmap is to knock out the background of a figure or object. Zoom in on the image to gain more precise control over what pixels are masked with the eraser tool. The process doesn't actually get rid of the pixels and therefore doesn't reduce the file size, so you may want to do your knock-out processing before bringing the image into Flash.

WORKING WITH VECTOR GRAPHICS

You can create original vector graphics with the drawing tools included in the Flash authoring environment. Remember that vector graphics use lines and curves to define areas of color? Well, in the Flash authoring environment, you can draw those lines and curves directly on the stage. The drawing tools let you set the properties of the lines (strokes) and the color areas (fills).

DRAWING LINES

If you haven't done so already, open Flash and create a new Flash document. Start drawing on the stage with the Pencil tool, which enables you to draw free-form lines. The pencil tool has three options that control how many line segments and curves your line has:

- **Straighten**—Use this option if you want to draw a straight line.
- **Smooth**—Use this option if you want to draw a curving line.
- **Ink**—Use this option if you want to draw a curving line, but keep in mind that the Ink option follows the movement of your mouse more exactly than the Smooth option and produces more segments and curves. This leads to a larger file size.

Figure 9.9 compares lines drawn with each of the three options selected.

Figure 9.9
Comparing lines drawn with Straighten, Smooth, and Ink options.

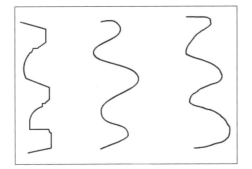

Notice that when you draw an oval with the Pencil tool with the Straighten option selected, the shape snaps into a smooth oval when you complete the oval. This can help you quickly draw ovals. When the pencil options are set to Smooth or Ink, this snapping does not occur (see Figure 9.10).

Figure 9.10
Ovals drawn with Straighten, Smooth, and Ink options.

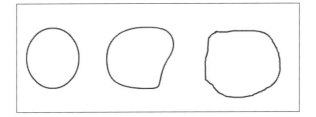

In Flash, lines are often called strokes. You can control certain properties of the lines you draw with Flash such as stroke thickness and color. Flash gives you many options for drawing strokes, whether they are drawn with the Pencil tool or as an outline with a Shape tool (oval or square).

Depending on what stroke style you select, you get access to different properties with the Stroke Style Panel, which you can access by clicking on the Custom button in the Property inspector when using a tool with strokes (see Figures 9.11 and 9.12).

Figure 9.11
Property inspector with Stroke properties.

Figure 9.12
Custom stroke styles.

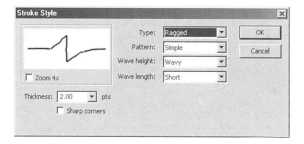

Although stroke styles can enhance the look of your design and save you time, be sure to use them carefully because they can increase the file size. A complex stroke style requires more information to describe the line to which it's applied. In addition to stroke styles, lines also have options for line color and thickness, as well as cap and miter styles. You can set all of these options with the Property inspector.

NOTE

> This is where terminology could be a little confusing: When you draw with the Paintbrush tool, you are drawing a *shape*, not a *stroke*. In the Flash authoring environment, the terms *line* and *stroke* are used interchangeably. For example, the Modify, Shape menu has an option to convert a Line to Fill, and yet there is a Stroke Style panel.

DRAWING FILLS

You can create a fill with the Paint Bucket tool by selecting the tool and a fill color and then clicking on the area you want to fill. For the Paint Bucket tool to work, the area must be a closed shape. Figure 9.13 shows a closed shape as well as a shape that is not closed.

Figure 9.13
Only closed shapes
can have fills applied
to them.

When you draw a shape freehand with one of the drawing tools, you might accidentally leave a gap between curves. If you want to apply a fill with the Paint Bucket tool, you need to close the shape by drawing or stretching a line connecting the two ends on either side of the gap. If you still cannot fill the shape, look for additional gaps. You can use the drawing tool you started with, such as the Pencil tool, or another drawing tool.

When the shapes you are drawing are simple, you can avoid problems with open shapes by using the Shape Tools (Oval, Rectangle, and Polygon). To use these tools, click and drag the mouse across the stage. The point where you initially click becomes the registration point for the bounding box of the shape. The farther you drag the mouse, the larger the shape becomes. The shape tools combine lines and fills, but you can set either the line or fill color to be empty. For example, the oval in Figure 9.14 was set to have the fill color be empty.

Figure 9.14
Oval drawn with the Oval Shape tool and with an empty fill specified.

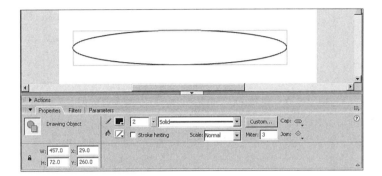

Try out the Brush tool. Whereas drawing with the Pencil tool creates lines, drawing with the Brush tool creates a fill (a shape). You need to use the Fill Color option to set the fill's color. In addition to color, the Brush tool has Fill options and additional tool-specific options, including brush size and shape (see Figure 9.15). Brush shapes range from round and oval to square and slanted.

Figure 9.15
Available brush shapes.

The Fill options let you paint inside of previously drawn shapes without worrying about precision. For example, if you want to fill a shape without going outside its outline, you can select the Paint Inside option. Begin drawing inside the shape, and your strokes will fill only the inside of the shape. If your mouse goes outside the shape, that area is not rendered on the screen when you release your mouse. Figure 9.16 shows a shape being filled with the Paint Inside Option selected. Note that while you are drawing, the color does show up outside the shape's outlines, but when the mouse button is released, only the color inside of the shape remains on the stage. This technique can be used when you want to fill a shape with gaps.

Figure 9.16
The Paint Inside
option allows precise
filling of a shape with
the brush tool.

The Paint Behind option lets you color outside of existing lines and shapes without covering them. You can start at any point on the stage, and the color is rendered automatically behind everything else already on the stage. Figure 9.17 shows an example of painting behind another shape.

Figure 9.17
The Paint Behind
option lets you apply
color behind an exist-
ing shape without
overwriting it.

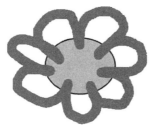

OBJECT DRAWING MODEL

In Flash, overlapping shapes and outlines merge and overwrite each other. This can be very useful when you want to chop up parts of an image or you want to sculpt a shape.

New to Flash 8 is the Object Drawing Model. When the Object Drawing option is turned on, the shape outlines do not affect each other. The main benefit of this is that you can select and move shapes and lines around without them getting chopped up in the process. Flash enables you to toggle Object Drawing mode on and off in the Options for a drawing tool (as shown in Figure 9.18) so you can go back and forth between the default and the Object Drawing mode. The button for toggling Object Drawing mode is located at the bottom left of the Tools panel.

GRADIENTS AND BITMAP FILLS

A fill doesn't have to be a solid color. It can be a gradient or even a bitmap. The Color Mixer panel gives you access to several methods of selecting a fill, as described in Chapter 8, "Introducing Flash 8."

A gradient is a fill that transitions from one color to another, or through several colors, and can be either linear or radial. A linear gradient transitions from color to color in a single direction, whereas a radial gradient transitions out from a central point in all directions.

Figure 9.18
You can toggle the Object Drawing mode on and off in the Options of drawing tools.

The Gradient Transform tool enables you to edit gradients. To access the Gradient Transform tool, select it from the Tools panel and then click on a shape or line filled with a gradient. Figure 9.19 shows the points of manipulation for a gradient. By dragging the manipulation points, you can control the center, focal point, width, size, and rotation of a gradient fill.

Figure 9.19
Gradient Transform tool.

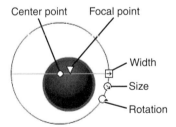

Bitmap fills are used to fill shapes with a bitmap image. The image can be used once, or tiled repeatedly inside of the shape. Used sparingly, bitmap fills can add depth and texture to your projects. To set a bitmap for a fill, select the Bitmap option for Fill Type in the Color Mixer panel, as shown in Figure 9.20, where the bitmap option is selected and highlighted in blue in the drop-down menu. A dialog box opens up where you can select a bitmap to import. Another method for setting a bitmap as fill is to select the Paint Bucket tool, click on a bitmap in your library, and then fill the shape with the selected bitmap.

Figure 9.20
Setting fill type to
Bitmap in the Color
Mixer panel.

In previous versions of Flash, lines had to be converted to fills before they could have gradients or bitmaps applied to them. In Version 8, you can apply a gradient or bitmap to a line and still have access to its stroke properties.

IMPORTING VECTOR GRAPHICS

In addition to creating new vector graphics from scratch in Flash, you can import .swf and other vector graphics file formats that have been prepared in another program. For example, you can import a Freehand file and continue manipulating the curves in the Flash environment. To import an external image file, go to File, Import and select either Import to Stage or Import to Library. If you import a Fireworks PNG file that contains vector graphics, the Fireworks PNG Import Settings dialog box opens and enables you to select settings for how much information the file will bring into Flash about its vector shapes and layers (see Figure 9.21). Be sure to preserve layers and not flatten the image on import.

Figure 9.21
Import Settings
dialog box.

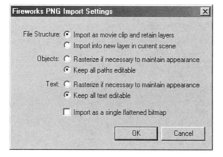

CAUTION

You should avoid importing vector graphics with gradients. Instead, add the gradients within Flash. This helps reduce the file size.

EDITING AND ADJUSTING VECTOR SHAPES

If you're accustomed to drawing with tangible art supplies, drawing with a mouse can be a challenge. It's not the same as the direct control you have with pen and ink or a paint brush. Fortunately, the Flash toolbox comes with handy tools for editing and adjusting shapes and lines.

Rather than try to draw a shape precisely with a mouse, try using the Smooth option or a shape tool (oval, rectangle, or polystar) and then modify it with either the Selection or Subselection tools. You can move the end points of lines and the corners of shapes. You can also drag a line at any point between its endpoints and alter the shape of its curve. If you think of drawing with Flash as something more like sculpting than sketching, you might find yourself warming up to the tool set. The idea is to start with a rough draft and then use the tools to continually fine tune your project until it's the work of art you set out to create.

USING THE SELECTION AND SUBSELECTION TOOLS

The Selection and the Subselection tools give you different ways to manipulate the curves of your drawing. The Selection tool (the black arrow) gives you direct access to the curve or endpoint of a line. To change a line's curve, move your mouse toward the line until a curve icon appears beside your cursor, as shown in Figure 9.22. You can now click and drag the line, stretching it into a new shape. Go ahead and have fun playing with it.

Figure 9.22
Approaching a curve.

As you move your mouse toward the endpoint, a corner icon appears beside the cursor, as shown in Figure 9.23. When the corner icon appears, you can click and drag the endpoint to a new position on the stage.

Figure 9.23
Approaching the endpoint of a line or the corner of a shape.

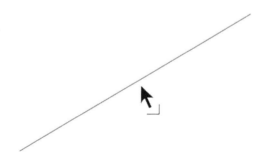

The Selection tool also enables you to select or "pick up" a line or shape and move it. To move the entire line, first select it by clicking on it. When selected, a tight grid of dots overlays it as shown in Figure 9.24.

Figure 9.24
An unselected line and fill and a selected line and fill.

The Subselection tool (the white-filled arrow) is located to the right of the selection tool in the Tools panel. It gives you access to the Bezier handles and anchor points of the curve. By dragging a handle or anchor point with the Subselection tool, you can precisely control a curve's shape.

OPTIMIZING CURVES

The Straightening and Smoothing tools can help you improve the look of your image while greatly reducing its file size. Because vector graphics depend on defining shapes with formulas, and more complex shapes require more formulas, reducing the complexity of a shape reduces its memory space. Therefore, you can shave off a lot of space by straightening and smoothing lines and fills.

When you select a line or shape with the Selection tool, the Straightening and Smoothing tools become available in the options at the bottom of the Tools panel. To apply these tools, first select a line or shape and then click on either the Straightening or Smoothing tool. The Straightening tool simplifies selected lines by converting arcs into straight lines and corners. The Smoothing tool simplifies lines by reducing the number of anchor points in the curve.

TIP

> After tracing a bitmap to vector format, use straightening and smoothing extensively. In fact, you can repeat each process until the image becomes too distorted and then undo it one or two times. This is best done in subsections of the image to avoid too much distortion of the overall image.

The more curves used to define a shape, the more complicated the vector formulas become and the larger the file size. By reducing the number of curves needed to define a shape, you're optimizing the curves of that shape. As an alternative to the Smoothing and Straightening tools, you can optimize curves with the Optimize Curves dialog box (Modify, Shape, Optimize).

WORKING WITH TEXT

There are three text field types in Flash: static, dynamic, and input. *Static* text fields, and the text they contain, are created at author-time. *Dynamic* and *input* text fields and their contents can be created at author-time or at run-time with ActionScript. This section focuses on static text fields. The other types are discussed in detail in Chapter 16, "Putting It All Together: Creating an XML-Based Photo Slide Show."

To create a static text field, click on the Text tool and then on the stage. This places a new text field on the stage, with a cursor ready to accept the input you type from your keyboard. You can set formatting options for text fields with the Properties inspector. These options include font, font size, color, and alignment. Additional options for text fields include changing the direction of text from horizontal to vertical. You can set the spacing between characters. By selecting individual characters in a static text field, you can also create superscript and subscript formatting (see Figure 9.25).

Figure 9.25
Superscript and subscript in a static text field.

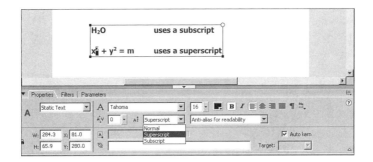

Static text fields can be given a URL link and target attributes, making the text object analogous to an embedded link in an HTML document. When a text field has a URL link, the background for the text is part of the hit area, which is the area that responds to the user's mouse.

EMBEDDED AND DEVICE FONTS

In the Flash authoring environment, you have access to all the fonts that are currently installed on your system. In an HTML document, only the name of the font is stored in that document. The fonts themselves are not included in the HTML file. For those fonts to appear on a user's screen, the specified font must be on the user's system. If it isn't, the browser uses its default font instead. There are two options in Flash for ensuring that your text appears as you designed it, or at least close: embedding and device fonts. They both have advantages and weaknesses.

For static text, embedding is automatic. When a font is embedded, the outlines of the font are saved as vector shapes in the Flash file. Although this assures that the font you chose will always be the font that is displayed, each character adds to your project's file size.

The other option is to use device fonts, which let you set a category of fonts for a text field, such as serif or sans serif fonts. The player then displays a font from the user's system from that category. A sans serif font might be rendered as Helvetica on a Mac or rendered as Arial on a PC. The advantage of using device fonts is that you can keep your file size small while maintaining loose control over font types in your project. It's a good idea to use device fonts when displaying large amounts of text.

BREAKING TEXT APART

To break apart text, select a text field on the stage and then go to Modify, Break Apart. Breaking apart text is different from breaking apart bitmaps. Flash breaks text apart in two steps. The first time, it breaks the text field into individual text fields for each character from the original field. This can add significant size to your file (more than doubling the size of the same text in a single text field). So why would you do this? Because the individual characters are then available to animate or apply individual effects to. This can produce some nice effects, but use it sparingly because it can bloat file size.

The second step of breaking apart text is to break apart a text field containing a single character and convert it into a vector shape that can be manipulated just as any other vector shape. You can create some unique font effects this way (see Figure 9.26).

Figure 9.26
A unique font effect created by breaking apart a letter into a vector shape and modifying its curves.

USING SNAP TO PIXELS TO AUTOMATICALLY ALIGN TEXT

The placement of text on the stage affects how legible that text is in the published .swf file. If a text field is not aligned exactly on a whole pixel, the text appears blurry when rendered. For text to be clearly legible in Flash, modify the snapping settings to Snap to Pixels. You can change this setting by choosing View, Snapping, Snap to Pixel. You must turn off all other snapping options by selecting them in the same menu.

In previous versions of Flash, you had to open the menu repeatedly for each snapping option you wanted to change. Now there is a panel where you can edit all snapping options at once. Stage borders settings, object spacing, and center alignment are available through the Advanced button on the Edit Snapping interface, which you can open by choosing View, Snapping, Edit Snapping (see Figure 9.27).

Figure 9.27
Edit Snapping
interface.

If you place a text field on the stage without using the Snap to Pixel option, you can still make sure that it is positioned on a whole pixel. Select your text field and go to the Property inspector. You can then round off the X and Y coordinates of your text field by directly changing their numerical values (see Figure 9.28). For example, if the X value is 362.9, you can round that up to 363.0. Even a change that small makes your text display more clearly.

Figure 9.28
X and Y coordinates
in the Property
inspector.

Alignment and Justification

In Flash, as with most word processors, you can control how the text is aligned in the text field. The text can be aligned to the left, center, or right, or justified across the entire field. Justified alignment spaces the text so that it is flush to the right and to the left, although there are irregular spaces between individual characters.

Left or right alignment gives you the clearest text. Center alignment and justified text can result in blurry characters because these formats can position characters off-pixel.

Turning Anti-Aliasing Off

Anti-aliasing smoothes the outlines of text so that the edges look less jagged when rendered on the screen. However, when using smaller font sizes, some fonts appear clearer with anti-aliasing turned off (see Figure 9.27). To control the anti-aliasing setting for an individual text field, select the text-field on the stage and then turn anti-aliasing on or off in the Property inspector.

Using Layout Aids

You don't have to position everything by simply eyeballing it. Flash includes many aides to help you precisely position and size objects. These aides include snapping, grids, guides, guide layers, and the align tool.

SNAPPING

Snapping helps position objects relative to each other and to the stage. When the Snapping option is turned on (see Figure 9.29), your object snaps into place when you position it close to its desired location. To set how objects snap, open the Edit Snapping interface by choosing View, Snapping, Edit Snapping, and select the snapping options you want (see Figure 9.29).

Figure 9.29
Quickly turn snapping on and off in the Tools Panel Options.

— Snap control

You can also adjust the Object spacing (how close the objects must be to a snapping guide for snapping to occur) and both the horizontal and vertical distance between objects in the Advanced area of the Edit Snapping interface (View, Snapping, Edit Snapping, Advanced), as shown in Figure 9.30. In previous versions of Flash, this was called *snap tolerance*.

Remember that snapping is especially important for text fields because this affects readability. Flash renders text more clearly when it is aligned on a pixel. If the text is aligned on a half pixel, it appears blurry.

GRIDS, GUIDES, AND GUIDE LAYERS

The grid consists of uniformly arranged vertical and horizontal lines. It sits behind all drawn elements on the stage, and is not rendered at publishing time. From the View menu, you can hide or show the grid. You can customize the spacing of grid lines by going to View, Grid, Edit Grid. You can also set the color of the grid lines in the same panel.

In addition to the grid, you can use a guide to show an element with which you'd like your object to interact at a later frame, or to mark the position of where the two will meet. You can convert any element on the stage into a guide by placing it into a guide layer or setting its existing layer as a guide. Just like the grid, guides and guide layers are not rendered at publishing time. Guide layers can be restored easily to a normal layer.

Figure 9.30
Open the advanced Snap Align options by clicking on the Advanced button in the Edit Snapping interface.

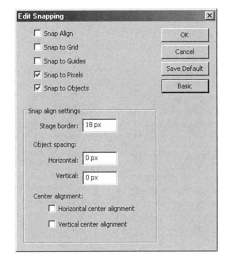

9

TIP

If you're not sure an element will make it to final production, but don't want to delete it yet, set its layer as a guide layer and then make it a hidden layer. It will be there if you want it, but won't get in the way of what you're currently working on.

SIZING SHAPES PRECISELY

You can numerically set the height, width, and position of a selected design element in the Property inspector. For example, imagine that you draw an oval on the stage that is roughly 40 pixels high and 70 pixels wide, and draw another oval that is roughly 30 by 50 pixels. What if you want both ovals to be precisely 34 pixels wide? When you select an oval, its properties become accessible in the Property inspector and you can set its width to exactly 34 pixels. The shape on the stage resizes accordingly.

You can also select Window, Transform to set the scale as a percentage (see Figure 9.31). Check the Constrain box to set the scale for both dimensions (height and width) at the same time by an equal percentage. For example, if you want to reduce a shape by 50%, turn on Constrain and set the width scale to 50%. The height scale resets automatically to 50% as well.

Figure 9.31
Resetting scale with
the Transform panel.

9

THE ALIGN PANEL

The Align panel (see Figure 9.32) enables you to perform several positioning and sizing tasks, including Align, Distribute, Match Size, and Space. It can be your best friend, but be sure to pay attention to whether it's set relative to selected symbols or to the stage. To apply the alignment options to objects on the stage, select the objects you want to align, open the Align panel by selecting Window, Align, and then click on one of the options in the Align panel. Shapes and symbols can be aligned on the left, right, top, or bottom edges, and can be centered vertically or horizontally.

The Match Size options set the smaller objects to the same size as the largest object selected. Be careful, though: If you set this to be relative to the stage, you'll have some very large objects. This is where the Undo button comes in handy.

Figure 9.32
Align panel.

CREATING A MASK

In Flash, using a mask is often called *spotlighting*. A *mask* is a shape in a layer that covers whatever is below it except for your defined area(s), functioning as the window through which the underlying image is seen. To help understand the concept, imagine that you have a photograph for which you want to make a quirky frame. You can take some fancy paper, cut an odd-shaped hole in it, and use this as a frame. When you place the paper on top of the photo, part of the photo shows through the hole in the paper.

To create a mask in Flash, first place an image on the stage (see Figure 9.33) and name its layer. It can be a vector graphic or an imported bitmap (see the previous section on importing bitmaps).

Next add a new layer above the photo layer and name it. Making sure that this new layer is selected, draw a shape over the image (see Figure 9.34).

Figure 9.33
Photo on the stage.

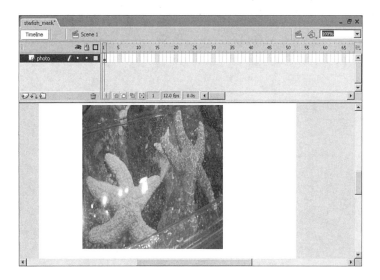

Figure 9.34
Shape that will be the mask.

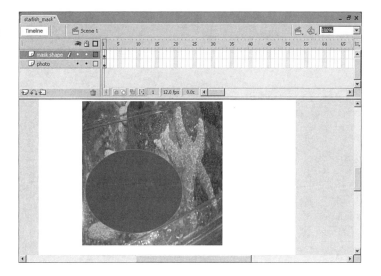

Now you're ready to turn the new layer into a mask. Right-click on the layer you want to use as a mask and select Mask from the menu that opens. Your timeline layers should now be arranged as shown in Figure 9.35. Notice that the image is now hidden, except for the area covered by the shape.

You can also use text as a mask (see Figure 9.36). The process is the same as with any other mask, except that you use a text field in the mask layer instead of a shape.

You might be wondering whether you can animate the shape in the mask layer. Yes you can! More on that in Chapter 10, "Animation Basics."

Figure 9.35
Masked image.

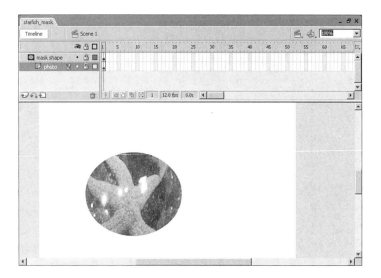

Figure 9.36
Text masking a bitmap.

Starfish

TROUBLESHOOTING

Why does my bitmap image look blurry?

If you enlarge a bitmap to a size greater than the dimensions of its size at import, it ends up with a pixilated effect. To avoid this, try to import the bitmap at the size at which you intend the image to be presented. If it's a simple bitmap, such as a logo, try tracing the bitmap before you resize it. By converting the bitmap to a vector format, you make it better equipped for enlarging.

Why is my shape not accepting a fill?

Check to see whether your shape is closed. The Paint Bucket tool works in closed shapes only.

I selected my shape, but when I moved it, an outline was left behind.

When a shape has both a fill and an outline, both must be selected if they are to be moved together.

BEST PRACTICES—GETTING TO KNOW THE TOOLS

Once you become comfortable with the Tools in Flash, you may find that Flash is a great environment for quickly sketching out ideas. Whether you're a designer, a coder, or a combination of the two, the ability to quickly draft the visual elements of a Flash application will serve you well.

The best way to get to know the tools in Flash is to practice. Try each tool, and see what you can do with it. Then try to accomplish a specific drawing task. If it's not going well, set the project aside for a while and come back to it later.

If you're accustomed to other graphics programs, try to suspend your expectations as you learn the Flash tools. One of the things I have come to treasure in Flash is the ability to directly select and interact with the visual elements in any layer that is visible on the stage.

Compared to other graphics programs I've used, Flash is more sculptural in terms of the artistic process. In fact, the only other applications I've worked with that have had more of a sculptural process have been 3D authoring tools. By sculptural, I mean that you can push and pull the parts. The parts can be nested within each other. They can also have mechanics inside of them (in the form of ActionScript).

While the possibilities of what you envision may outpace your skills for a while, be patient. With practice, your skills can indeed catch up to your visions in Flash.

9

CHAPTER 10

ANIMATION BASICS

In this chapter

Preparing Your Content for Animation

Previous chapters have covered the Flash interface and all the building blocks that you can use in Flash. Now it's time to look at one of the most fundamental skills you need to work in Flash: animating on the timeline.

Before jumping into the specifics of animating, this chapter explores ways that you can prepare your content so that when you start animating you'll create small files and clean animations. The file size that matters is that of the .swf file you will publish, rather than the .fla document in which you work. To work effectively in Flash, you need to use symbols to organize your visual content.

Understanding Symbols

You can think of a symbol in Flash as a container that holds your visual content. What makes symbols different than other visual content—such as shapes on the stage and even groups of shapes that you have created—is that they can be given a name and stored in the library for future use. They can be reused. You can even nest one symbol inside another symbol. The library itself is simply a list of all of the available reusable content in your movie: symbols.

So, making something you can reuse is pretty interesting, but there's more: When you reuse the symbols in the library, you don't increase the file size of your exported .swf. Okay, you do increase the file size by approximately .0012 bytes each time you reuse a library symbol in your movie, but that's not significant, so really go after using them as often as you can.

To understand how this works is pretty simple when you know that the symbols stored in the library are called *master* symbols. When you use those symbols out on the stage in your Flash document, they are called symbol *instances*. The instances on the stage are actually just copies of the original master symbol in your document's library. That's why using multiple copies of the same symbol doesn't increase the file size.

In the overall sense of how a Flash document functions, it's also helpful to realize that the main timeline of your Flash document is the biggest container of all because it holds references for all the symbols, other internal assets, animations, and programming for your entire Flash movie. I like to think of the Flash document main timeline (and the .swf it creates) as the mother ship of all symbols.

While you're thinking of symbols as containers, one more concept will be useful as you explore using symbols in Flash documents: You can open up that container and make changes to what's inside. This is called *editing a master symbol* and all changes that are done while editing the symbol are reflected out to the instances of that symbol that you have on the stage. There are different types of symbols in Flash, and they each have different things happening on the inside. The following sections explore the different types of symbols you can create.

SYMBOL TYPES

Creating a symbol is fairly simple, but you need to understand all your options. With this understanding of when and why to use different symbol types, you'll make better choices as you prepare your Flash documents for animation.

GRAPHIC SYMBOLS

Graphic symbols are the most basic type of symbol used to store the visual elements that are reused in illustrations and animations. Their functionality, beyond grouping shapes or animations with a name, is limited. For instance, you cannot access a graphic symbol instance with ActionScript, nor can you apply the new filters available in Flash 8 to a graphic symbol. This makes graphic symbols most useful for storing pieces of your illustrations so that you can animate them on the timeline.

When you go inside your graphic master symbol you can see a timeline that looks exactly like the regular timeline. It is, however, a different timeline. Above the timeline, you can see the name of your symbol listed. This indicates which timeline is open for editing, on the stage (see Figure 10.1). Any animations that you put on this timeline are always "slaved" to the main timeline. This means that although you've created the animation inside the symbol, it plays on the main timeline as if it was built there. This enables you to compress many layered animations into a single symbol, which helps keep things tidy. It also enables you to store not only static symbols inside a graphic but also animations that you might want to reuse as well. This will become an exciting concept as you explore how to animate later in this chapter.

Figure 10.1
The symbol currently open for editing is indicated above the timeline.

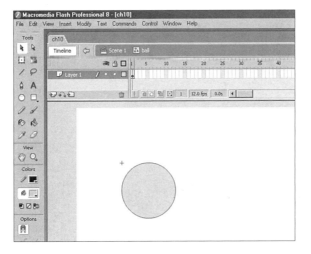

Graphic symbols can be nested inside other graphic symbols, and also in any of the other types of symbols. For example, you may have a background of trees for your animation. Creating a single leaf symbol, and arranging many copies of it within a tree symbol, will save considerable file size in the final project.

10

MOVIE CLIP SYMBOLS

Movie clip symbols are also useful for storing your visual elements. But, unlike graphic symbols, they can be controlled with ActionScript. Each instance on the stage can be given its own name. This instance name is different from the master symbol name in the library and enables ActionScript to talk directly to that particular instance. The ability to be controlled by ActionScript is also the reason that things like the new filter effects work with this type of symbol.

Inside a movie clip master symbol is a timeline like the one on the main timeline. What makes this timeline different from the graphic symbol's timeline is that any animation you place in this timeline plays independently of the main timeline. This means that if the main timeline were stopped, any animation on this timeline would continue playing independently of what is happening on that main timeline. You control a movie clip timeline the same way you would a main timeline animation. You also can set up the movieclip to respond to user input, such as a mouse click.

Movie clips can be nested inside each other or in any of the other symbol types. They can contain timeline elements of their own that operate independently of the main timeline. Figure 10.2 shows the timeline of a movie clip on the stage. Above the timeline, there is a special icon to indicate that this is a movie clip symbol's timeline.

Figure 10.2
A movie clip symbol is indicated with an icon above the timeline.

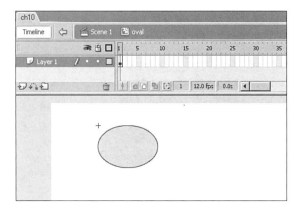

BUTTON SYMBOLS

Button symbols are made specifically to let the user interact with your Flash movie. They have a specialized internal timeline consisting of four frames: Up, Over, Down, and Hit. The first three frames (Up, Over, and Down) hold the visual elements that appear when the user's mouse interacts with the button. These frames are called *button states*. So, although this is still a timeline inside the button symbol, it changes visuals only when the particular type of interaction takes place rather than playing in a linear way as the main timeline and other symbols do.

The Hit frame always contains a shape that indicates the "hot spot" for the button. Any filled shape in this frame is used to tell the button when to display the Over and Down frame visual elements. It's crucial that you always use a filled shape in this frame so that the button can be easily selected. If you have an unfilled shape, such as some text, the button is going to appear to flicker as the user moves the mouse across the filled and unfilled portions of the text. The solution is to simply place a filled rectangle that is larger than the text in the Hit frame. The rectangle is not displayed on the stage, but is available for the user's mouse to interact with.

Button timelines can have layers and contain instances of graphic and movie clip symbols. Figure 10.3 shows the timeline of a simple button.

Figure 10.3
The timeline of a button symbol has four frames.

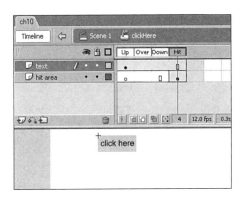

CREATING MASTER SYMBOLS

Now that you've had a primer on symbols, you can begin converting shapes and text into symbols that you will reuse. Planning ahead is the key to being efficient. It's easiest to look at your illustrations carefully, and plan your animations and symbols in advance. You can follow a few simple rules when choosing what to make into a symbol.

First, look at any visual elements that you want as unique objects and might want to store in the library. Having named elements stored in the library is convenient when you start to place and arrange your content on the stage. If you accidentally delete one instance on the stage, you can pull another one out of the library. Also look for elements that can be reused. For instance, one window on a house could become a symbol that gets reused several times to create other windows.

NOTE

With some repeating elements you may want to use a few different elements in a single symbol. Imagine you wanted a night sky with about 50–60 stars in it. Although you're going to save on size by using your star symbol, you will slow the processor down because it has that many individual elements to display each time it draws the screen. So, to get the best of both worlds—small file size and faster redraw on the screen—try putting five or six stars of different sizes and shapes inside a symbol and reuse that.

Another rule of thumb for deciding what to make into a symbol relates to animation. When you animate, typically you should separate out any element that will be animated individually. So if one element is going to be moving across the screen and another is going to bounce, each of those visual elements should be a separate symbol.

So how do you create these amazingly helpful symbols? There are two methods for creating a master symbol. The first method of creating a symbol enables you to convert any visual element already on the stage to a symbol. This process creates a master symbol in the library and automatically converts the selected elements into your first instance of that symbol.

The second way to create a symbol is simply to create a blank symbol, which takes you immediately into editing mode where you can fill the symbol with content. To use this master symbol you then need to go into the library, where it is stored, and pull it out onto the stage. The methods for creating symbols are covered in the following sections.

NOTE

> Be sure to have a naming convention for all your master symbols so you can find them easily in the library. Usually you view your library in alphabetical order, so indicating whether the element belongs with some particular animation or illustration is helpful. Names such as "arm_left" and "arm_right" are much more helpful as you work than relying on the default Symbol # naming.
>
> You can also use folders to keep your library assets well organized (see Figure 10.4).

Figure 10.4
Folders can help you keep your library organized.

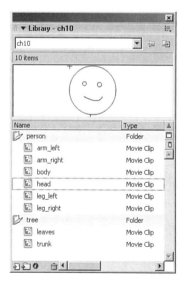

CONVERTING ILLUSTRATIONS INTO SYMBOLS

You've created an illustration and decided which elements to convert into symbols. To convert shapes and lines on the stage into symbols, follow these steps:

1. Select everything on the stage you want to include in your symbol.

2. Choose Modify, Convert to Symbol, or press the F8 key on your keyboard. This brings up the Convert to Symbol dialog box (see Figure 10.5).

Figure 10.5
The Convert to Symbol dialog box.

NOTE

Another method for bringing up the Convert to Symbol dialog box is to use the contextual menu by (Ctrl-clicking) [right-clicking] on the selected elements and choosing Convert to Symbol.

3. Give the symbol a name in the Name field and choose the type of symbol you want to create.

4. Set the symbol type.

5. Choose a registration point. The default registration point is in the upper-left corner.

6. Press the OK button to create the symbol.

NOTE

The registration point is the point inside the symbol in which all your selected content is aligned after it lands inside. Because the registration point for your symbol is what is used when you align your symbol instances on the stage, the real difference this makes is when you're working out on the stage. The registration point is also used to define a rotation pivot point. For example, if the symbol contains the shape of an arm, placing the registration point at the corner with the shoulder would facilitate animating movement for that arm.

You can see that there is now an instance on the stage. You can tell it is a symbol instance because when you select it, the Property inspector changes to show you the symbol name and type (see Figure 10.6). You can also see the crosshair of a selected symbol. The crosshair represents the registration point inside the symbol.

Now open your library (if you haven't already) by choosing Window, Library. Each type of symbol has its own type of icon so you can quickly distinguish them in the library listing (see Figure 10.7). If you select the new symbol you just created, it should show you that the content you selected is now enclosed inside the symbol.

Figure 10.6
Property inspector for
a selected symbol.

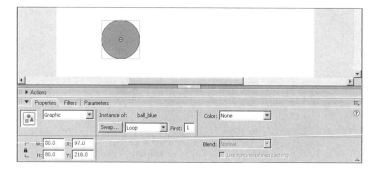

Figure 10.7
Library containing a
graphic symbol, a but-
ton symbol, and a
movie clip symbol.

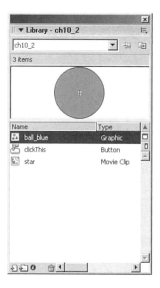

CREATING NEW SYMBOLS

Occasionally, you might want to create the symbol first and then draw visual elements into
it, rather than convert an existing visual element that you have on the stage. To create a
blank symbol choose Insert, New Symbol, or press (Cmd-F8) [Ctrl+F8]. Give the symbol a
name, type, and registration point in the New Symbol dialog box that pops up (see Figure
10.8), and then press OK.

Figure 10.8
Create New Symbol
dialog box.

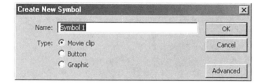

Unlike converting a visual element to a symbol, when you create a new symbol you are
immediately taken into Edit mode, where you can add content as if you were on the main

timeline. Remember, though, that you are actually *inside* the symbol now. To get back out of the symbol press the back arrow or the Scene 1 link at the top of the page. This takes you out of symbol editing mode and back to the main timeline.

To use your symbol, you need to open the library and pull out a new instance to place on the stage.

EDITING MASTER SYMBOLS

It should be clear at this point that the master symbol controls what you see when you use instances on the stage. All the fun that you can have with changing some aspects of individual instances is discussed in the next sections, but first you need to be clear on how to change the content inside of a master symbol.

There are several ways to get into the editing mode of a symbol where you can play with the content inside. If your symbol has an instance on the stage, the easiest thing to do is to double-click the instance, which takes you into Edit in Place mode. In this mode, while you edit your symbol, you can see the stage itself and other elements on it, which are slightly grayed out (so you know you can't affect them). This is particularly useful for making visual changes that will affect your overall layout. In Figure 10.9, a symbol named person1 is in Edit in Place mode, and the trees are in the background (slightly grayed out).

Figure 10.9
Edit in Place mode.

You can also double-click the icon for the symbol you want to edit, in the library. This takes you into Edit mode. This mode gives no reference to the stage and is the mode you see when you create a new, blank symbol.

Finally, you can use the contextual menu. (Ctrl-click) [right-click] to select Edit (no reference to stage), Edit in Place or Edit in New Window (see Figure 10.10).

10

10

Figure 10.10
Contextual menu of a
selected symbol on
the stage.

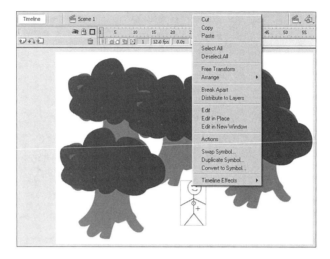

When you are in an editing mode, you can make changes just as you would if the visual elements were shapes on the stage. You can add layers and elements, as you wish, always remembering that you are changing the visuals for every instance of this symbol on the stage at once. You are editing the master symbol.

To exit any editing mode you can use the keyboard command (Cmd-E) [Ctrl+E] or click the Scene 1 link or Back button above the timeline (see Figure 10.11). From the Edit in Place mode you can also double-click on any blank area on the screen to return to the main timeline.

Figure 10.11
Contextual menu of a
selected symbol on
the stage.

NOTE

It's easy to forget that you're editing in a symbol timeline rather than working on the main timeline. The only way you know for sure is to look at the icons above the timeline. Be sure to return to the main timeline as soon as you're finished editing. It might be a good habit to get into to lock layers as you finish with them so you are forced to really look at the top of the document and see where you are when you want to make changes.

SYMBOL INSTANCES

Master symbols are the stored templates in the library. The copies of the symbol out on the stage are the instances. You know that symbol instances are crucial for keeping file size down. This next section covers the specifics of how to work with instances on the stage.

For the most part, you work with symbol instances just as you do any other visual element on the stage. You can change their x and y locations by typing them in the Property inspector or by dragging them around the stage. All symbols are aligned to x and y on the main timeline by their upper-left corner, regardless of where the registration point is set inside the symbol. You can copy and paste them across layers, duplicate them, and if there is more than one symbol in a layer then you can even arrange them so that they fall in front of or behind the other instances on the same layer (Modify, Arrange). The true power of instances comes into play when you start changing some of their surface qualities (their properties) to make each instance somewhat unique.

You can change the behavior of individual instances, such as a movie clip to a button or a graphic to a movie clip, essentially changing the type of symbol it is. To change the type of symbol of a single instance, first select it. In the Property inspector, pull down the menu that shows the current symbol type of your instance (see Figure 10.12). Changing the type makes the instance behave according to the rules already established in the earlier sections. Button symbols enable the user to click and have a four-frame timeline. Movie clips have independent timelines and can contain buttons, actions, and complete interactive timelines of their own. Graphic symbols are slaved to the timeline and have behaviors such as loop and single frame that are helpful in animation.

Figure 10.12
Menu for changing symbol type in the Property inspector.

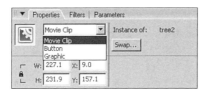

Another helpful way to change your symbol instance as you work is to swap the master symbol link for any instance with a different master symbol. Imagine you discover that instead of a blue flower in an animation, what you really need is that red flower you created a couple of hours ago. So you select the symbol instance of the blue flower, choose the Swap button in the Property inspector, and then select the red flower master symbol in the Swap Symbol dialog box (see Figure 10.13). Press the OK button and your symbol is now changed to the new symbol, retaining all the changes you made to your old instance but using another master symbol.

Figure 10.13
Swap Symbol dialog box.

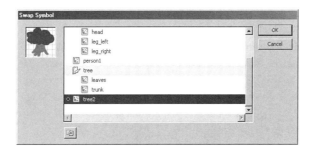

10

INSTANCE TRANSFORMATIONS

Although you can't break the association with the visuals that live inside of the master symbol, you can make some physical changes to the instance on the stage by scaling, skewing, and rotating the instance without affecting the master symbol. This is when symbols really become useful as you create illustrations and animations that reuse symbols over and over, with slight variations to each instance.

For example, imagine you created a tree. You made the tree a symbol and then duplicated the instance on the stage. Now you can arrange those instances in front or in back of each other by using Modify, Arrange, Bring Forward, or Send Back. You can move one tree to the other side of the stage and choose Modify, Transform, Flip Horizontal and have it look like a very different tree. You can select the Free Transform tool and rotate the tree slightly or squash it down so that it can be used as a bush (see Figure 10.14).

Figure 10.14
Using the Free-Transform tool to squash an instance of a tree symbol so that it looks like a bush.

Beyond those transformations you can also affect the overall color of the instance by applying a color effect to an individual instance. Select the instance and choose Brightness, Tint, Alpha, or Advanced from the Color menu in the Property inspector. Brightness gives a highlight or shadow affect. With Tint you can apply an overall color to the instance by choosing from the color picker and then changing how much it affects the color with a percentage slider. The Alpha effect enables you to change the transparency of the instance (see Figure 10.15). Be aware that this can be processor intensive if applied to many instances. And finally, the Advanced option enables you to work with individual color sliders to produce more complex color transformations.

Figure 10.15
Using the Color menu to set the Alpha value and change the transparency of an instance.

Finally, with movie clip symbols you can apply a new effect called a *blend*. Blend modes enable your instance to interact with other elements on the stage in varying ways. For instance, if you select one instance that lies on top of another instance and choose Multiply from the Blend menu in the Property inspector, you can see both shapes with the overlap multiplying the combined colors and transparencies. Figure 10.16 shows the Invert Blend mode applied to a movie clip symbol.

Figure 10.16
Applying the Invert Blend mode to a movie clip symbol.

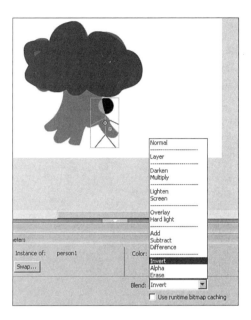

One of the big concerns in Flash when using Blend effects is that, as with Alpha effects, using too many of them can slow down playback of your movie because of how long it takes to redraw each frame. One of the ways that Flash 8 helps with this issue is by enabling you to select Use Runtime Bitmap Caching (below the Blend menu in the Property inspector). This uses a sophisticated method of converting the vector graphics in your movie clip into a bitmap at run-time. It also eliminates the need for the Flash player to repeatedly convert vector descriptions of the shapes in the movie clip before redrawing them in a new position on the screen. An entire processing step is eliminated. This is particularly helpful for large and complex static vector illustrations that might slow down your animation. Make them into a single movie clip and turn on Use Cache As Bitmap. This improves the performance of the entire movie.

REMOVING TRANSFORMATIONS

To remove any of these transformations and return to your symbol as it was originally, you can always select the instance and choose Modify, Transform, Remove Transform. This snaps the shape and alignment to their original specifications. This does not, however, remove any effects that you added. You must do this manually by setting each menu to None in the Property inspector.

BREAKING A SYMBOL APART FROM THE MASTER

Sometimes, as you work with instances, you might want to break your association with a master symbol and manipulate the shape directly. To do so you can simply choose Modify, Break Apart or press (Cmd-B) [Ctrl+B]. This breaks the link with the symbol and returns the internal contents to the stage as they were when you created them. You can then manipulate them as usual and reconvert them into another symbol if you wish.

ANIMATING IN FLASH

Chapter 8, "Introducing Flash 8," introduced the idea of the timeline in Flash being an amazing storage tool for information about changes over time (frames) and the visuals that appear at a particular time on the timeline (keyframes stacked in layers). Recall that a keyframe is a storage location on the timeline, telling the playback head what content to play when it reaches that frame. A keyframe is always a point on a layer where something changes. Frames just add time for a keyframe's content to be displayed. A blank keyframe, following a frame with content, is used to indicate where something disappears from a layer.

NOTE

> When you begin to copy and paste blocks of animation, it is helpful to have every layer in the animation be the same length. This means that all layers in your animation have the same total number of frames, even if they need to use a blank keyframe to have the content disappear before the end of the animation. This way when you copy and paste you're sure that all the content comes across without strange keyframes being added and breaking your previous arrangement.

Now you can put all that knowledge to work as you read about animation in Flash. Much of the terminology of animation has come from the original hand-drawn animation techniques. You'll see that many computer techniques borrow heavily from those early methods of creating the visual illusion of movement over time on a two-dimensional surface.

There are four types of animation in Flash: Static, Keyframe-by-Keyframe, Motion Tweening, and Shape Tweening. When you know how each functions you can start planning your own animations and choose the method that enables you to keep your file size small and reduce the amount of work you have to do.

LAYERS WITH STATIC CONTENT

Much of your content in an animation simply stands still. It's basically a backdrop to the action. To achieve this on the timeline you need a filled keyframe where the content appears and then frames to the end of the animation, which you place by selecting the final frame and choosing Insert, Frame (F5). If you want the static content on a layer to disappear, choose Insert, Blank Keyframe (F7) in the correct frame of that layer. Do not place a keyframe at the end of the layer. Add a keyframe to a layer only when something changes on that layer because each keyframe adds to file size.

KEYFRAME-BY-KEYFRAME ANIMATION

Keyframe animation exactly replicates, in the computer, the methods that early animators used to combine static backgrounds with moving elements to create the illusion of movement over time. In the hand-drawn process, each cell of drawn animation is photographed and then strung together to form the full animation. In Flash each keyframe of content is created and then played by the playback head.

The process is very simple. Draw a shape on the stage. This gives you your first filled keyframe on the layer. Select a frame farther down the timeline and choose Insert, Keyframe (F6). This makes an exact copy of the preceding keyframe. After you make sure the playback head is over the new keyframe, you can make changes to the content on the stage by moving the shape or deforming it in some way. Any time you want to give a keyframe on a layer more time to play you add more frames before the next keyframe on the layer.

The real skill to develop with keyframe-by-keyframe animations involves keeping the file size small. Use symbols for the content in each keyframe whenever possible, and put content that changes independently on different layers.

For instance, in an animation of a face while talking, perhaps only the mouth and eyes change and the rest of the facial features stay still. The eyes may move independently of the mouth. So you would put the content for the eyes on one layer, the mouth on another, and the face (particularly if it's static) on a third layer. This allows you to animate each facial feature independently, with changes occurring more frequently on some layers than on others.

Keyframe animation is typically used for changes that need to move organically, such as smoke or a flower growing. It can also be used for fine control over what changes in every keyframe of your animation. Be aware that this takes more time than some of your other options and so may not always be the most efficient choice.

MOTION TWEENING

With motion tweening, you can have Flash create all the changes in the frames between two keyframes, each of which contains a single symbol instance. We can think of a motion tween as autoanimation for instances.

> **NOTE**
>
> The word *tween* comes from the traditional animation term *in-between*. In traditional animation a key animator is responsible for drawing each keyframe or major moment in the animation sequence. Then, in-betweeners (this is actually the name of the job) go in and create all the frames between those major keyframes. Flash uses exactly the same logic.

So, what is it that you can change about the symbol instance between one keyframe and the next? You can change the position, rotation, skew, scale, and color effect of the instance on stage for each keyframe. The difference between the symbol instances in each keyframe is what Flash is tweening for you. You can even make all these changes (transformations) at one time, although this may slow down the redraw if you have all those things happening on multiple layers at the same time.

The number of frames between the first keyframe and the second tells Flash how many steps to take for each change. If you have 20 frames, there will be 20 intermediate steps from one instance appearance to the other. To speed up or slow down the transition, remove or add frames.

Always be sure to use a single instance in each keyframe of your motion tween. This includes text fields, bitmaps, groups, shapes, and multiple objects that you want to motion tween together on the same layer. Simply select them and choose Insert, Convert to Symbol (F8). If you attempt to make a motion tween without first creating a single symbol instance, Flash silently "helps" you by automatically creating a symbol in your library. Any time you see Tween 1, Tween 2, and so on in your library, it means that you forgot to make a symbol before you created your tween. I usually rename the symbol immediately or swap it for another one.

To prepare your motion tween, begin with a single instance on a layer. Place the symbol instance on the stage, where you would like it to begin, and make any transformations needed. Then move down the timeline, select a frame where you would like the tween to end, and choose Insert, Keyframe (F6). This makes an exact duplicate of your symbol instance. Go onto the stage and make your changes to the instance's position, transformation, or effect.

Now you are ready to create the motion tween. Select the first keyframe and then choose Motion from the Tween menu of the Property inspector. Alternatively, you can (Ctrl-click) [right-click] on the first keyframe. This brings up a contextual menu from which you can choose Create Motion Tween. The keyframe and frames between the two keyframes in your motion tween now turn blue and have an arrow between them, indicating the motion tween has been created (see Figure 10.17). Try pulling the playback head back and forth to see the animation you've created.

Figure 10.17
An arrow and blue background on the timeline indicates a motion tween.

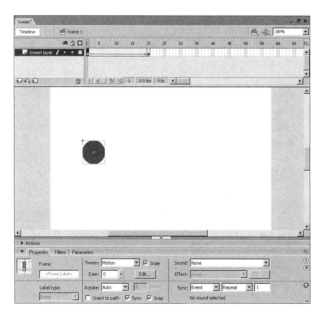

To gain more control over the changes, add additional keyframes into the middle of the tween. This gives you more instances to modify for position or transformations.

To remove a motion tween, either select the first keyframe and choose None from the Tween menu in the Property inspector, or use the frame's contextual menu and choose Remove Tween (see Figure 10.18).

Figure 10.18
Contextual menu of a frame.

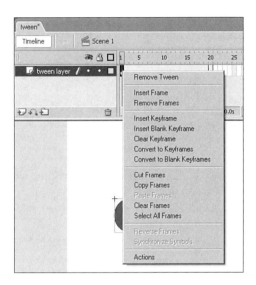

CUSTOM EASING

In Flash 8, you have more control over a feature of motion tweening called *easing*. The easing setting indicates to Flash how fast the changes between keyframes should occur, and whether to weight the changes to earlier in the cycle or later. Easing is one of the techniques used to create a feeling of motion or gravity as your objects move through your scene. The interface for setting easing is just below the Tween options in the Property inspector.

To ease in, starting slowly and speeding up toward the end, you would select the first keyframe in our tween and in the Property inspector choose a number from the slider below 0. To ease out, starting faster and slowing down as you approach the next keyframe, you would choose a positive number.

You can also gain more control by setting up a custom easing pattern. Select the first keyframe in your motion tween and choose the Edit button to the right of the Ease slider in the Property inspector. What appears in the Custom Ease In/Ease Out dialog box, shown in Figure 10.19, is a grid with a rubber band element. Click anywhere on the line to add a point and move it so it is positive or negative to speed or slow the transition at that point in the animation. Use the curve handles to change how the speed changes are distributed. Being able to ease in *and* out of the same motion tween is a very powerful addition to your animation toolbox.

Figure 10.19
Custom Ease In/Ease
Out dialog box.

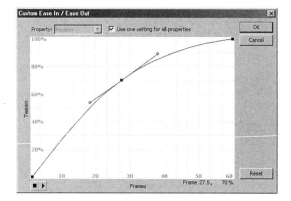

If you'd like to gain even more control, try deselecting the Use One Setting for All
Properties check box at the top of the dialog box. Then you have a different graph for position, rotation, scale, color, and filters (if you have a movie clip instance). You can make some
stunning effects with these new features.

MOTION GUIDES

Now that you've created some linear changes to the positions of your instances, perhaps
you'd like to be able to create a more organic path for them to follow. For instance, you
might want to create a bumblebee and make it meander up and down and around as it
crosses the stage.

To create a motion guide, follow these steps:

1. Create a motion tween with an instance starting in one position and ending in another.

2. After you have the motion tween created, create a new layer above it.

3. Double-click the icon to the left of the layer's name and choose the Guide option.
   Rename the layer "motion guide."

4. In the layer you first created, with the motion tween, double-click the icon to the left of
   its name. Choose the Guided radio button (see Figure 10.20). Press OK and you can see
   the icons change so that now the guide layer is linked to your motion tween layer.

5. Select the motion guide layer so it is active. This is crucial because if you draw on your
   motion guide layer the effect doesn't work.

6. Choose the Pencil tool, setting the options to Smooth in the lower toolbar, and then
   draw a path with loops and ups and downs (see Figure 10.21). If you don't like it, use
   Edit, Undo and redraw the path. The only rule is to have a single continuous path.

Figure 10.20
Layer Properties dialog box, with Guided option selected.

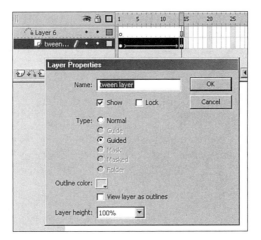

Figure 10.21
Guide layer with a path drawn with the Pencil tool.

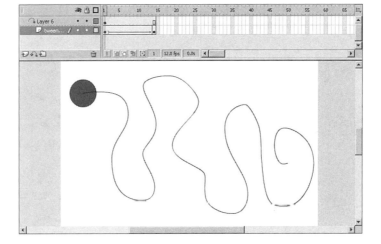

7. Now you just need to attach each instance in your motion tween to the path. Select the first keyframe in the motion guide layer and then click and drag your object by the transformation circle so that it snaps to the point on the line you want the object to start moving along the path. You can tell when it snaps because the circle indicator becomes larger. To edit the location of the transformation point of your instance, choose the Free Transform tool (Q) and move the circle. Return to the Move tool (V) and then resnap your instance to the path.

8. Select the second keyframe and drag the second instance to snap into the end point of your drawn path.

Try dragging your playback head back and forth to see how the instance now follows the path.

You can attach other objects to the same path by making a motion tween, placing them below the motion guide layer, and changing their layer property to Guided. Then snap the objects to the guide as you did with the first.

SHAPE TWEENING

Shape tweening uses the same principle of filling in the in-between frames as motion tweening does. However, it works only with shapes. This means that the content of each keyframe in your motion tween needs to contain only shapes. If you have a piece of text, a bitmap, a group, or a symbol in a keyframe, you cannot use this type of tweening unless you first use the Modify, Break Apart command to break those groupings back into shapes on the stage.

Begin by creating or placing a shape in your first keyframe on your layer:

1. For this example, break apart a static text field with the text "Flash" in it. This makes it into a shape.
2. Insert a blank keyframe down the timeline.
3. Turn on onion skinning (first blue button below the timeline) and set the framing so you can see the text shapes.
4. On the last frame of the tween, draw five circles that are approximately the same size as the text (see Figure 10.22).

Figure 10.22
When onion skinning is turned on, you can see the content in previous frames. They appear faded.

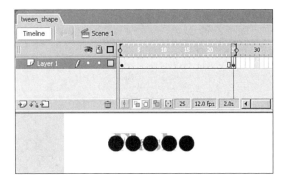

5. Select the first keyframe, and in the Property inspector Tween menu, choose Shape.
6. Now move the playback head back and forth to see the changes.

Be aware that if the vector shapes you transform are very complex, it can slow down the playback. Shape tweening of very complex shapes requires a lot of calculations.

NESTED ANIMATIONS

To place an animation inside a symbol nesting the animation, enter the editing mode for the master symbol and create your animation as you would on the main timeline. You can use layers, frames, and keyframes just as you learned previously.

Any time you want to have multiple types of animations happening at the same time, put some of the animation into a symbol and then use it. For instance, if you created a person walking with a keyframe-by-keyframe animation and then wanted to have that figure follow a motion guide path, you couldn't do it on the main timeline. You could put a walking animation inside a symbol, though, and then motion tween that animated symbol and then add a motion guide for that symbol. The same thing applies to animations that you would like to mask. Put the animation inside a symbol and then mask the playback of the symbol on the main timeline. You'd be amazed at how this enables you to create incredibly complex visual combinations.

Most animations that are stored inside a symbol need to be used in as many ways as possible to be efficient. To change the playback behavior of an animated graphic symbol, place the symbol instance on the stage and then give the keyframe that references the instance some frames to play on the timeline. With the instance selected, look at the Property inspector where you'll notice the menu that currently holds the Loop selection. This is the menu that controls the playback options for your graphic instance. Here you can set the graphic to play a single frame of the animation, play once, or loop continuously as long as it has frames on the timeline. This is extremely useful if you're using animated graphics for sync with sound or other timed animations where certain parts of the sequence need to freeze occasionally.

Usually you put animations into a movie clip and use them in your animations if you want them to loop independently of what is happening on the main timeline. This is helpful any time you have simultaneous movements. For instance, if you have a car driving from right to left on screen, you want the wheels to keep turning the entire time the car is driving. Stars that need to twinkle even when the main timeline is stopped is another good example.

TIMELINE EFFECTS

Timeline effects are automated versions of some of the animation types created manually in the previous sections. You might wonder why they weren't discussed first. Now, though, you can appreciate what they do because you understand the mechanics behind them. You are also more likely to understand that with timeline effects, you are sacrificing customization and increasing file size for ease of creation.

A timeline effect can be applied to any piece of text, graphic symbols, groups, and even shapes. Select the object to which you would like to apply the effect and choose Modify, Timeline Effect. Most of the time you will want to use animation effects such as Transform (position, rotation, scale, and color effect changes) or Transition (fading up and/or wiping the object selected), Blur, Expand, Drop Shadow, or Explode. Many of these effects are made to be used specifically with a text field, but can make interesting effects when applied to other objects.

When the timeline effect is applied to the object, a new layer is created with a newly created symbol on it and the specified number of frames in the layer. In the library there is a new folder called the Effects folder that contains your new symbol with all the applied effects built in. Then, follow these steps:

1. Create text on a new layer.

2. Select the text and use the contextual menu or choose Insert, Timeline Effects, Transform/Transition, Transition from the top menu bar.

3. In the Transition dialog box remove the Wipe feature by deselecting the checkbox and choose the Direction as Out.

4. Then press the Update Preview button to see the effect and press OK to create the effect.

You can now see that when you move the playback head, the effect has been created. To remove the transition or edit it, choose Modify, Timeline Effects, Edit Effect or Remove Effect. The contextual menu provides a nice shortcut if you (Ctrl-click) [right-click] on the object and choose Timeline Effect, Edit Effect or Remove Effect from the menu.

There are a few limitations as you begin playing with these effects: First, you can only apply one effect to any object. You also cannot simply pull the symbol with the effect attached from the library to create a new object. In addition, you need to remember the settings from one transition to the next. Because of these limitations, timeline effects are most useful for creating on-the-fly presentations and slide transitions, but not for production work.

TROUBLESHOOTING

I created a symbol but when I look at it in the library there isn't anything in it. What happened to my symbol?

There could be one of two issues. First, check to make sure that the object inside the symbol isn't the same color as the background. You can do this by changing the background color of the movie, which automatically changes the color behind the symbols in your Library panel, or by double-clicking the symbol and then choosing Edit, Select All to see whether there is any content in the symbol.

If there really isn't any content, it's likely you simply didn't have anything selected on the stage when you chose Convert to Symbol. Delete the symbol from the library and try the process again.

I keep getting symbols in my library named things like Tween 1, Tween 2, and so on. What are those and why do they appear?

These are symbols that Flash is creating to "help" you create a motion tween. Remember, the rule is that you have to create a single symbol for each layer on which you have a motion tween. If you forget or have multiple objects, Flash begins to create these automatic symbols in the library.

Be sure you create a symbol first when you use motion tweening. If you've forgotten, simply rename the symbol in the library so you know what it is for future use. Or if you already had a symbol made, but just forgot to use it, try selecting each instance in the tween and using the Swap button to reassign the master symbol. Then you can delete the Tween 1 reference from the library.

BEST PRACTICES—PLANNING YOUR CONTENT AND ANIMATION

One of the most powerful ways to be efficient when creating animations and layout schemes for your Flash projects is to storyboard. Although it takes some time to actually sit down and do your planning, it saves enormous amounts of time later because you can simply go in and produce or experiment in certain directions based on those plans.

An animation storyboard does not need to be complex. Sit down and on a pad of paper write out in simple sentences what you would like to have happen.

1. The sun rises over the hill.
2. The barn door opens.
3. The pig walks out.

Now draw three rectangles and give some visual indication of where you would like everything to be placed on the stage. This can be as simple as circles and squares if you can't draw very well. Then write the line beside it and show how you want things to move or a particular point where things change. One might show the sun low with an arrow indicating where it should come up. In another the barn door opens. In a third the pig is halfway out the door, with an arrow indicating where he will walk.

Now you can hand that off to someone else to produce, or produce it yourself. If you are creating it yourself, you can begin to write what animation types you need to accomplish those tasks and what symbols you need. For example, you would know that you could use a motion tween for the sun, so the sun needs to be a symbol on its own layer. The barn door should be its own symbol, and you would likely need to create a keyframe animation to give it the feel of a door opening. This might mean that you need three or four door symbols at different stages.

At this point, you're ready to start collecting and creating your visual assets, and composing the movie and its layers.

10

CHAPTER 11

INTRODUCING ACTIONSCRIPT

In this chapter

What Is ActionScript?

ActionScript takes Flash beyond vector graphics and simple animations. With ActionScript you can create user interfaces for rich applications, program multiuser Internet games, or even explore creative possibilities with computational art. One of the great things about ActionScript is that people with different skill levels can use it. You can start with some simple code right away and progress to more advanced coding approaches, such as class-based programming.

Up until now, everything we have discussed about Flash has concerned author-time development. For example, you can use a timeline motion tween to animate the movement of a circle across the stage. With ActionScript, you can program the same animation by writing code that will be executed during runtime while a published SWF file is running. In this chapter, you will learn the basics of coding with ActionScript in Flash.

Code Preparation

One of the biggest questions people have when they begin working in Flash is where to place their code. With Flash, you have a lot of options on where you can place the code. Although technically you can attach ActionScript to the timeline of any frame or to the outside of any button or movie clip symbol instance in your project, it's a good idea to keep your code centralized. All code should be on the main timeline, preferably in the first or second frame. When placing code on the main timeline in the Flash authoring environment, most professional Flash developers place it on its own layer in a blank keyframe. Why? Because it's easy to find. I use the top layer and name it "actions," which is a common practice.

Another step that you can take to make your ActionScripting more easily read and organized is to use comments in your code. Comments are used to explain the code clearly and briefly. They are helpful to you when you return to a project months later. In addition, they are helpful to other people who need to work with your code.

There are two ways to write comments in ActionScript. One option is to place two forward slashes at the beginning of a line of text. This signals to the compiler that the rest of the line is to be ignored and not compiled, and to skip to the next line.

```
// double slashes indicate that this line is a comment
```

The second method enables you to mark a multiline block of text as a comment, with /* and */ characters framing the commented text. Anything between the slash-astrix bookends is skipped over by the compiler. This can be used to quickly "comment out" multiline portions of your code and help you pin down the source of a bug in your project.

```
/*
Anything between these slash-astrix bookends
is ignored by the compiler, no matter
how many lines you type in.
*/
```

CONTROLLING THE TIMELINE WITH ACTIONSCRIPT

One of the simplest things to do with ActionScript is to control the timeline. With ActionScript, you can send the playback head to any frame in the timeline. You can choose a numbered frame, or give that frame a label; however, using frame labels is more flexible than using numbered frames to control the timeline with ActionScript. With frame labels, you don't have to rewrite all your coding every time you reorganize the timeline.

To create a labeled frame, make a new top layer in your project. Place it above your actions layer so that you can easily spot your frame labels. Then insert a blank keyframe. Give the frame a name in the in the <Frame Label> field of the Property inspector. Figure 11.1 shows a frame on the timeline labeled as start.

Figure 11.1
A frame label attached to a blank keyframe in its own layer.

To control the timeline you can use one of the global functions that are built in to Flash. These functions are all commonly used commands that are listed in the actions listings from the upper-left corner of the Actions panel (see Figure 11.2).

Figure 11.2
Accessing the list of global functions for controlling the timeline.

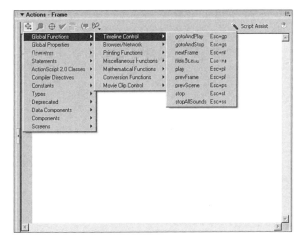

To stop the playback head on a frame, you can use the stop() action attached to a blank keyframe at the location on the timeline where you want to stop.

```
stop();
```

The playback head reads the action on this frame and then stops.

To send the play head to a specific frame, you can use the `gotoAndPlay()` function. For example, use the `gotoAndPlay()` function to send the playhead back to the start frame label in the first frame, creating an animation that loops continuously.

```
gotoAndPlay("start");
```

The entry inside the parentheses of this method is the data that the playback head uses to know where to jump on the timeline. This can be either a frame number or a frame label name. The word `"start"` is in quotes to tell the playback head to go to a frame label with that name.

WORKING WITH VARIABLES

If you're creating an animation that changes the color of the sky at certain times of the day, you need some basic information: What is the current time of day, and what color is the sky at different times? You can create a container in your Flash projects to hold that information. In programming, these containers are called *variables*.

Before you put something into a container, you need the container itself. In Flash, this process is called *declaring a variable*. When you first declare a variable, you typically use the keyword var and then follow it with a name for the variable. To say "I have a variable named myVariable" in ActionScript, you would enter the following code:

```
var myVariable;
```

Now you can give the named container something to hold: the value of your variable. In the following line, write the name of the newly created variable. The equal sign, also called the *assignment operator*, tells the compiler that you're about to tell it the value of the variable. Then you write the value. Afterward, use a semicolon to indicate that this instruction is done. Just as a period ends a sentence, a semicolon ends a statement in ActionScript. This is the syntax for assigning a value to a variable.

```
variableName = variable_value;
```

> **NOTE**
>
> You'll notice that the variable name is written with the first letter of the first word in lowercase and the second letter in uppercase. This is the most common convention for naming variables—lowercaseUppercase. It's a habit I would suggest you acquire, so that others reading your code can quickly recognize variables.

USING THE `trace()` STATEMENT

Imagine there's a container on a shelf in your fridge with take-out from a restaurant. You might want to say, "Hey container! Whatcha got?" I don't know about the containers in your fridge, but mine generally don't answer questions. I have to open them up and look.

The engineers at Macromedia have given us a simple but wonderful tool for looking at the contents of variables while developing and testing ActionScript projects. You can ask your variables what they hold if you use the built-in `trace()` function. Here's an example in

ActionScript where the variable `timeOfDay` is assigned the value of `"dawn"`. The value of `timeOfDay` is then traced to the Output window:

```
var timeOfDay = "dawn";
trace(timeOfDay);
//returns dawn
```

`Trace` is a great tool for developing in ActionScript because you can test whether certain parts of your code are performing as you expect. In other words, it can help you track down bugs and avoid creating them altogether. The `trace` function tries to find, in memory, the argument it's given, and then the results are traced to the Output window. These results are not visible to the end user when the published .swf file is played. In this case, the argument is the variable `timeOfDay`. When you test your movie (Control, Test Movie) in a Flash document with the previous code, `dawn` comes up in the Output window.

> **TIP**
>
> You can exclude `trace` commands from the compiled `.swf` file if you change the preferences in the Publish settings of your project. Go to File, Publishing Settings, and select the Flash tab (see Figure 11.3). Click on the check box next to Omit Trace Actions in the options.

Figure 11.3
Publish Settings Flash options, with Omit Trace Actions selected.

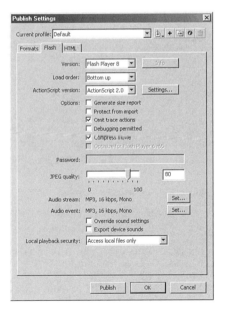

11

DATATYPES

When you begin working with variables, Flash has a powerful way to help you prevent bugs in your projects. To help make sure that the variables you create are holding the correct type of data, you can add some information to your variables called *strict typing*. When a variable uses strict typing, it means it is assigned a datatype so that the debugger then gives you a specific error message if you try to assign a value of another datatype. For example, if you give the variable timeOfDay a datatype of String, you get an error if you assign it the number value of 78.5 (see Figure 11.4).

```
var timeOfDay:String;
timeOfDay = 78.5;
// gives an error message during testing
```

Datatypes are basically ways to store information with different formats. Flash has several basic datatypes, including string, number, Boolean (true/false), array, object, and date. Different datatypes can have different operations performed on them. For example, a number can be multiplied, but a string of characters cannot.

Figure 11.4
Error message in
Output panel.

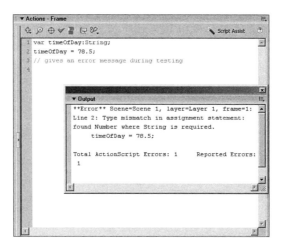

- **String**—A string datatype can hold a string of characters that is read as text. The characters can be letters, numerals, and other characters. String values are declared between double quotation marks.
  ```
  var greeting:String = "Hi There!";
  ```
- **Number**—A number datatype consists of numerical digits.
  ```
  var myAverage:Number = 54;
  ```
- **Boolean**—A Boolean datatype has two possible values: true or false.
  ```
  var myTest:Boolean = true;
  ```
- **Array**—An array datatype is a list of data values. Elements in an array are indexed by numbers, starting at zero.
  ```
  var fruitInBasket:Array = ["apples", "oranges", "bananas"];
  ```
- **Object**—An object is a complex datatype and can hold properties and methods. Properties are variables that are attached to an object. Both an object and its properties have names. Properties can also be other datatypes, such as arrays and even other objects.

In the following code, a new object is created and two properties of that object are declared and assigned values.

```
var myObject:Object = new Object();
myObject.prop1:String = "happy";
myObject.prop2:Number = 42;
```

MAKING DECISIONS WITH CONDITIONALS AND switch

During the course of the day, you make countless decisions. Everything you do depends on decisions large and small. Just eating a meal involves decisions, from what to eat to whether to use a fork or spoon.

With code, complex behaviors can be broken down into a series of simple decisions. These are called *conditionals*, or tests. A test is run, and depending on the result, an action is taken. For example, you may want to check whether the user entered the correct password before running more of the program.

Before jumping into conditionals, I want to briefly mention operators. Operators are the "glue" of ActionScripting. They are symbols that tell the code to do something specific. For instance, when you work with conditionals you'll often see the ==, &&, and || operators. The == operator compares two elements of a statement, and requires that the elements be equivalent before another section of code can run. The && operator requires multiple conditional statements to be true. The || operator requires one or another conditional statement to be true. This is why it is called the or operator.

There are two main formats for independent conditionals in Flash: 1) if, if-else, and if-else-if, and 2) switch.

USING THE if STATEMENT

When the Flash compiler encounters an if statement, it looks at the condition within the parentheses. If the condition is true, the code within the curly braces is executed. A general if statement looks like this:

```
if(condition){
    //do something
}
```

A simple condition compares two expressions, and returns true if the condition is met. Several types of comparisons can be made between expressions. For example, you may want to know whether two expressions are equal or different. Or you may want to know whether one expression is greater than another.

Let's say that you have a project where you have a movie clip instance for the sky in the background of an animation. What if you want to change the color of that instance to blue, when timeOfDay is "dawn"? Before changing the color of the movie clip instance, you first need to determine what color to change it to. In ActionScript, you might write the following, which compares the value of `timeOfDay` to `"dawn"`. If they are equal, the code between the curly braces is run and the variable `skyColor` is assigned the value of `"blue"`.

```
if(timeOfDay == "dawn"){
    skyColor:String = "blue";
}
```

Although this will work, you might want to change the color at various times of the day. An `else` after the first closing curly bracket, followed by a second set of curly brackets enclosing another line of code, presents an alternative code to execute if the condition is not true. In this case, if `timeOfDay` is `"dawn"`, `skyColor` is `"blue"`. If not, `skyColor` is `"black"`. This is called an `if-else` conditional.

```
if(timeOfDay == "dawn"){
    skyColor:String = "blue";
} else {
    skyColor:String = "black";
}
```

You can set another conditional after an `else`. In fact, you can write a whole sequence of `if-else-if` statements. In the following example, the variable `daytime` has a range of numeric values. Notice that the conditional statements are more complex. By using the `&&` logical operator, you can test for two or more conditions at once. Here, it tests whether the value is between specific number ranges:

```
if(daytime > 0500 && daytime 1130)
    skyColor:String = "blue";
} else if (daytime >1130 && daytime <= 1230)
    sky Color:String = "bright_blue;
} else if (daytime > 1230 && daytime <= 1900){
    skyColor:String = "blue";
} else {
    sky Color:String =" black";
}
```

USING THE `switch` STATEMENT

The `switch` style of conditionals can be used when you have a list of specific values that you are testing for equality. It works just like an `if-else` statement, but the code is formatted differently. First, you state that this is a `switch` conditional, with the variable to be tested in parentheses. Then you list each case that you want to test. The syntax for each case is as follows. Note the colon after the case value, which serves as shorthand for the curly braces.

```
case "value":
    //code to execute goes here;
```

The following example shows a series of cases to compare values for the variable `daytime`. Remember that the keyword `case` tells the compiler to test whether the next expression is equal to the variable in parentheses.

```
switch(daytime){

    case "dawn":
        skyColor:String = "dark_blue";
        break;
    case "morning":
```

```
        skyColor:String = "blue";
        break;
    case "noon":
        skyColor:String = "light_blue";
        break;
    case "afternoon":
        skyColor:String = "blue";
        break;
    case "evening":
        skyColor:String = "dark_blue";
        break;
    case "night":
        skyColor:String = "black";
}
```

Switch statements are sometimes easier to read, and are better suited to specific cases than to a range of possible values.

USING LOOPS TO REPEAT ACTIONS

Loops are a type of ActionScript that allow sections of code to execute repeatedly. They usually have a counter to keep track of how many times they have looped. When the counter equals a maximum number, the loop stops running.

Having a counter helps avoid infinite loops, which can cause serious problems in the execution of code, including causing a warning box to pop up. The warning indicates that your code is taking up processor resources and asks you whether you would like to stop running the application. Although this doesn't crash your computer, it is a serious error in your application. Other ways to avoid infinite loops is to be sure you have a break, or escape, from the loop when the condition for stopping is met.

As with conditionals, it would be helpful to be familiar with some operators used for creating loops before you start using them. These operators are used to keep track of how many times the loop has been repeated. The ++ operator increments the value of your variable by 1. The += is a shorthand operator that says to add the value to the right of the = sign and return a value. So count+=3 adds 3 and returns the value to be used. The -= operator simply subtracts and returns the value.

NOTE

It makes a difference whether the ++ appears before the variable (pre-increment) or after it (post-increment). Pre-incrementing says to add 1 now and use that value in the code. Post-incrementing says add 1 the next time it is encountered, and to use its current value for now.

for

The most common type of loop in Flash is the for loop. It enables you to efficiently set up the initial state of a counter, the maximum number of loops, and the amount to increase your loop each time the loop runs. Several other types of loops are available, but this is the one that's used most of the time.

In a `for` loop, parentheses wrap the initialization, condition, and increment statements all in one compact line. In this example, `i` is initialized at zero. The loop runs as long as `i` is less than 20, and `i` is incremented by one each time the loop is repeated. That leaves the space between the curly braces free to concentrate on the business at hand: the action that is to be repeated. In this case, it traces the value of `i` to the output window.

The syntax is as follows:

```
for (initialization; condition; update){
    statement1;
    statement2;
}
```

For example,

```
var i:Number;   // declare the counter
for(i=0; i<20; i++){
    trace(i);
}
```

This is all it takes to make repetitive actions easily accessible in our projects.

COMBINING STATEMENTS INTO FUNCTIONS

Functions enable you to reuse the same set of statements without having to rewrite the code in several places. They make your code more readable and easier to update. You saw global functions that are built in to Flash when you learned to control the timeline. Now you can create your own.

You can use the `function` keyword before the function name to create the block of code you are grouping together. Then all the code inside the curly brackets are run when the function is called.

```
function functionName(arguments) {
    statement1;
    statement2;
}
```

In this example, the function is named `setSkyColor`. In the parentheses, the value for `timeOfDay` is passed to the function.

```
function setSkyColor(timeOfDay) {
    trace(timeOfDay);
}
```

When you write a function, it just sits there until you do something with it. To execute the code in a function, you have to call it, passing any arguments it needs to run, and then all the functionality you wrapped inside the function is performed automatically. Here, the value `"dawn"` is passed to the `setSkycolor` function already created, which causes `"dawn"` to be traced to the Output window.

```
setSkyColor("dawn");
```

With this syntax for defining a function, you don't have to worry about placing the function definition higher in the code than where you call it from. In fact, it can be at the end of the code or even in a class.

You can also use another syntax format called a *function literal*. This syntax places the function name first, and then applies the function to that name after the assignment operator. This way of defining a function enables you to change the scope of the function easily and is the most common way to create a global function that can be accessed from any timeline. However, in this format, the definition of the function must be made before you can call the function.

The syntax is as follows:

```
functionName = function(arguments) {
    statement1;
    statement2;
};
```

For example,

```
this.setSkyColor = function(timeOfDay){
    trace(timeOfDay);
}
```

PASSING INFORMATION TO FUNCTIONS IN ARGUMENTS

One reason to use functions is to make your code more generalized and reusable. Rather than have a lot of different functions that do the same task but with different information, you can write one function to which you pass information and that runs differently depending on that information.

Imagine that you need to get the result of 2×10. You can write this in code as

```
var doubleTen:Number = 2*10;
```

Later on, you may need to multiply 2×6. You could write it as `doubleSix:Number = 2*6`, or you could see that a pattern is emerging. You could save some effort and keep your code more organized by writing a function to handle all cases where you need to double a number. Such a function would need to know what number to double. You give the function this information by passing an argument to it as in the following example:

```
function doubleNum(myNum){
    return myNum * 2;
}
```

You would call this function and pass the value you want to double in the same statement:

```
doubleNum(6);
//output
12
```

11

Remember the switch statement that sets a color for the sky? You can encapsulate it into a function called setSkyColor, with an argument named timeOfDay.

```
function setSkyColor(timeOfDay){
    switch(timeOfDay){
        case "dawn":
            skyColor= "dark_blue";
            break;
        case "morning":
            skyColor= "blue";
            break;
        case "noon":
            skyColor= "light_blue";
            break;
        case "afternoon":
            skyColor= "blue";
            break;
        case "evening":
            skyColor= "dark_blue";
            break;
        case "night":
            skyColor = "black";
    }
}
```

This function could then be called when timeOfDay = "morning", like this:

```
setSkyColor("morning");
```

When this function runs, "morning" becomes the value for timeOfDay and is used in the comparisons of the switch statement.

A function can have several parameters or arguments, but if you find yourself passing a long list of arguments to a function, it may be a sign that you need to simplify your code and break it up into smaller parts. You can do this by creating a series of functions that each contain a single task and then call them from within other functions as you need them. It is with this type of interrelated system that most function-based programming is carried out.

USING RETURN VALUES TO RETRIEVE RESULTS

When you use built-in functions, like Math.sin(), Flash returns a value. You can save this value in a variable for later use. Here, the variable x is declared, and it is assigned the value of 5. Next, another variable (myNumber) is declared, and it is assigned the value of the result of passing x to Math.sin().

```
var x:Number = 5;
var myNumber:Number = Math.sin(x);
trace(myNumber);                 // outputs -0.958924274663138
```

You can write your own functions that return values by using the return keyword.

```
function squareNumber(myNum){
    // return square of argument
    return myNum * myNum;
}
```

Using the result of this function is just like using the result of a built-in function:

```
var x = 5;
var myNumber:Number = squareNumber(x);
trace(myNumber); // outputs 25
```

A function terminates after a line with return in it. Any code following a return line does not execute.

SCOPE

Scope is a term that has to do with where your variable is declared and where it can be accessed from.

A local variable has a small scope, limited to the function in which it was created. To create a local variable, use the var keyword before you set a name and value for your variable. In the following code, the variable myVeg exists only within the function getVeg.

```
function getVegi(){
    var myVeg:String = "potato";
    return myVeg;
}
```

A timeline variable, such as the variable name in a text field on the stage, has a specific timeline scope. To change the value for a variable from a different timeline, you need to use dot syntax to target the specific timeline. Dot syntax gives you access to those other timelines. For example, you might have a movie clip with an instance name of mc2, which lives inside of a movie clip called mc1, which lives on the main timeline. When you want to access mc2, you simply call each child clip in turn.

```
mc1.mc2
```

Movie clips have independent timelines, meaning they can have their own variables and actions just as the main timeline does. When you refer to the main timeline you can use _root to set and/or control that timeline from anywhere in the timeline structure. To address the timeline inside a movie clip instance, simply use the instance name. To back out of a movie clip to a parent timeline you can use the relative addressing of _parent. All this addressing is strung together with dot syntax:

```
//addressing a movie clip from the main timeline
mc1.mcVariable = "mc1 timeline variable"
//addressing the main timeline from inside a movie clip timeline
parent.myVariable = 20;
```

For example, you could have a variable on the stage with the name myText. You can access that variable and modify its value from anywhere in the code by using dot syntax addressing to target the variable. This function assigns a value to a variable on the main timeline:

```
function sayHello(){
    root.myText = "Hi There!";
}
sayHello();
```

11

The _global keyword makes a variable or a function accessible from anywhere in the project. The _global keyword is used only when declaring the variable. You can declare a global variable with or without assigning a value at the same time:

```
_global.myGlobal;
_global.myOtherGlobal:Number = 42;
_global.myFunction = function(){
    //some code
}
```

This function sets a variable on the main timeline (_root) as the value of the global variable. Notice that you don't need to use any dot syntax addressing when you ask for the value of a global variable.

```
function getMeaningOfLife(){
    root.meaning = myOtherGlobal;
}
```

When dealing with scope, the keyword this comes in handy. When used within a function, this refers to the timeline to which the function is applied. For example, if you want to call the function moveButton when the user clicks on a button, you would type in the following:

```
// move a movie clip 10 pixels to the right
function moveClip(){
    this._x +=10;
}
// attach moveButton function to the circle
circle_btn.onRelease = moveClip;
```

The keyword this refers to the movie clip to which the function is attached. In this case, it's circle_btn, not the main timeline.

WORKING WITH BUTTONS

Chapter 10, "Animation Basics," discussed the three types of symbols in Flash: graphic, button, and movie clip. Buttons and movie clips are special. They are objects, and you can create instances of them. They can accept user input from external devices, such as the mouse, send this event to ActionScript, and accept instructions from ActionScript. This all requires that the instance have a unique instance name. If the instance is on the stage, you can give it an instance name in the Property inspector.

A button is a specialized movie clip, with four unique frames. Three frames respond to different mouse states (up, over, and down) and one defines the area that responds to the mouse (hit).

Button objects have built-in methods and properties, and you can use these to control a button instance if you attach a function to an instance's button event. In this example, a function is first defined, and then this function is attached to the button's onRelease method. Now, when the user releases the mouse after clicking on the button, the button is redrawn 10 pixels to the right of its current position.

```
// move a movie clip 10 pixels to the right
function moveClip(){
    this._x +=10;
}
// attach moveButton function to the circle
circle_btn.onRelease = moveClip;
```

Another way to attach a function to a button event is to use a shorthand notation that combines the function definition and the function attachment. In this example, the function is defined inside the onRelease method:

```
circle_btn.onRelease(){
    this._x +=10;
}
```

This can be a quick way to attach code to a button event, but it's not as reusable as attaching a previously defined function to the event. It's fine for when you want to attach unique code that will not be applied to other instances.

There are many button event methods available in Flash. Button event methods are also called event handlers. I've listed a few of them here.

- onPress—An onPress event handler is invoked when the mouse is pressed while its pointer is over the hit area of the movie clip to which the event is attached.

- onRelease—The onRelease event handler is invoked when the mouse is released, while its pointer is over the hit area of the movie clip.

- onReleaseOutside—Like onRelease, onReleaseOutside is invoked when the mouse is released. The difference is that onReleaseOutside is invoked when the mouse pointer is outside the hit area of the movie clip.

- onRollOut—The onRollOut handler is invoked when the mouse pointer rolls out of the hit area of the movie clip. This is often paired with the onRollOver event to trigger events based on the user moving the mouse over a movie clip and then out again.

- onRollOver—The onRollOver event is triggered when the mouse pointer enters the hit area of the movie clip. A common effect is to change the color or alpha value of the clip to indicate to users that they have encountered an element of the user interface.

WORKING WITH MOVIE CLIPS

The MovieClip object is one of Flash's most powerful and useful features. As an object, it's a blueprint from which many instances can be created. After an instance of the object is named, you can access that object's properties (variables) and methods (functions with tasks specific to the movie clip instance), thereby manipulating each instance separately.

Be sure to name each instance as you create it so you can access it with ActionScripting and dot syntax addressing. Then you can also use the Insert Target Path button in the Actions panel, which lets you select named instances that are on the stage. When selected, its target path is inserted into the text in the Actions panel.

11

To see any of your code in action and any change in properties, you need to test or publish the movie. You see how your code works after it's compiled into a `.swf`. For example, if you change the position (`_x` and `_y` properties) and transparency (`_alpha` property) of a movie clip on the stage with ActionScript, the movie clip appears unchanged until you test the movie.

TIP

> If you name your instances with suffixes, code hinting becomes available. For example, if you name an instance `ball_mc`, code hinting will show you all the methods available for a movie clip.

MOVIE CLIP PROPERTIES

Each movie clip instance you create has several properties that you can access with ActionScript. Some properties are read-only, which means that you can get the value, but not change it. An example of a read-only property is `MovieClip._target`, which returns the target path of a movie clip instance as a string. You cannot, however, set the value for `_target`, which is what makes it a read-only property. See Table 11.1 for descriptions of some of the movie clip properties.

TABLE 11.1 MOVIE CLIP PROPERTY DESCRIPTIONS

Property	Datatype	Description
`_alpha`	Number	The alpha transparency of the movieclip.
`enabled`	Boolean	If false, any button events attached to the movieclip are not invoked.
`_rotation`	Number	Specifies the rotation of the movieclip in degrees.
`_visible`	Boolean	If false, the movieclip is not rendered on the screen.
`_x` and `_y`	Number	Specify the x and y coordinates of the movieclip relative to the local coordinates of the parent clip.
`blendMode`	Object	Affects how a movieclip appears when it is in a layer above another object.
`cacheAsBitmap`	Boolean	When set to true, the Flash Player caches an internal bitmap representation of the movie clip.
`filters`	Array	An array containing each filter currently applied to the movieclip. This property requires a little preparation code to use. We'll cover this in Chapter 16, "Putting It All Together: Creating an XML-Based Photo Slide Show."

WORKING WITH MOVIE CLIP PROPERTIES

This example changes the `blendMode` property of a movie clip when the user clicks on it. To do so, follow these steps:

1. On the stage, draw a rectangle and fill it with a gradient.

2. Convert the shape into a movie clip symbol and name it `box`.

3. With the Your New Movie Clip instance selected, open the Property inspector and give the instance an instance name of `box_mc`.

4. Create a new layer and add this code to the first keyframe.

```
function blendEffect(){
    // set blendMode to "hard light"
    this.blendMode = 14;
}
// attach function to event
box_mc.onRelease = specialEffect;
```

When you test this, the colors in the `box_mc` movie clip should change when you click on the box.

What if you want to revert to the original color when you click on the box next time? Adding some simple logic can take care of that. Test whether the `blendMode` is `normal`. If it's already `normal`, you can change it to `hard light` mode with the integer 14. If `blendMode` is not already set to `normal`, you reset it to `normal` mode with the integer 1.

```
function blendEffect(){
    // test whether already normal
    if(this.blendMode == "normal"){
        //if normal, set to "hard light"
        this.blendMode = 14;
    } else {
        // revert to normal blend mode
        this.blendMode = 1;
    }
}

// attach specialEffect to box event.
box_mc.onRelease = specialEffect;
```

That's all there is to it. You've created a movie clip that changes its color on the first click and then reverts to its normal coloring on the second.

MOVIE CLIP EVENTS

Movie clips can have button events attached to them, including all the events listed in the "Working with Buttons" section of this chapter. With no specific hit area determined on the timeline for a movie clip, any filled area in the clip is considered the hotspot for that particular clip. For example, you may want a movie clip to move when the user clicks on it. The following code makes a movie clip move 20 pixels to the right when clicked in your `.swf`. The filled shape drawn in the movie clip is the hit area for button events.

11

```
function moveClip(){
    this._x +=20;
}
moveRight_mc.onRelease = moveClip;
```

TIP

> You can make your movie clip behave exactly like a button and have an up, over, and down visual associated with it. The button timeline is automatically set up to have only four keyframes. To make a movie clip that responds like a button, you must set up the frames yourself.
>
> Create _up, _over, and _down frame labels. This is the only time you ever want to use underscores for a frame label name. Add `stop()` actions below each frame label. Create a graphic below each frame label as in a regular button.
>
> Any filled shape can serve as your hit area, or you can assign one to a movie clip instance inside your movie clip button by double-clicking the instance and adding the following code to the timeline inside:
>
> ```
> this._visible=false;
> _parent.hitArea=this;
> ```
>
> You cannot see the movie clip button function until you assign a button event (for example, `onRelease`) to tell the Flash Player to see it as a button.

Movie clip events other than the button events, which you saw being used in the earlier code, can be viewed as "big picture" events. They tend to handle events triggered by data loading or the progress of the playhead from frame to frame. Following is a list of some of these events:

- onData—This event handler is invoked when all the data is loaded into a movie clip.

- onEnterFrame—Code handled by onEnterFrame is executed continually at the frame rate of the .swf file. onEnterFrame actions are processed before any other code for that frame.

- onKillFocus—The onKillFocus event is invoked when focus is removed from a movie clip.

- onLoad—When the movie clip is instantiated and appears in the Timeline, the onLoad event handler is invoked.

- onUnLoad—The onUnLoad event handler is invoked in the first frame after the movie clip is removed from the Timeline. The code in the handler is executed before any other code associated with the frame.

ADDING AND REMOVING MOVIE CLIP INSTANCES

There might be times when you want to create multiple copies of the same symbol, all of which are acting independently on the stage at runtime. There are three ways to place a movie clip on the stage with ActionScript: duplicate an instance already on the stage, attach a clip from the library at runtime, and create an empty clip on the fly. Each method requires that you give the newly created instance a position by setting the _x and _y properties of the movie clip after it's been created.

duplicateMovieClip

The duplicateMovieClip method copies an instance that was placed on the stage at author time.

The syntax is as follows:

```
name_mc.duplicateMovieClip(newname, depth)
```

For example,

```
// create a copy of box1_mc, named box2_mc, with depth at 30;
box1_mc.duplicateMovieClip("box2_mc", 30);

// position the new clip on the stage
box2_mc._x = 20;
box2_mc._y = 40;
```

attachMovie

The attachMovie method copies instances onto the stage from symbols in the library. This can be especially useful when you want to keep your graphic assets off the stage. When you use the attachMovie method, you are creating an instance directly from the library. Rather than copy an instance onto the stage while authoring your project, you are using code to do the same thing while the movie plays.

To use the attachMovie method, you must create a linkage ID for the symbol in the library. Open the library for your project and right-click on the symbol you want to copy from the library during runtime, and then select Linkage from the options. In the Linkage properties box, select Export for ActionScript. The field for the Identifier is now ready for you to give your symbol a linkage idName. This is the name the compiler will use when looking for the symbol to attach.

The syntax is as follows:

```
name_mc.attachMovie(idName, newName, depth)
```

For example,

```
// place an instance of a library symbol on the stage
this.attachMovie("newClip", "newClip1", 10);

//position the new instance relative to its parent clip
this.newClip1._x = 0;
this.newClip1._y = 0;
```

createEmptyClip

The createEmptyClip method creates a new, empty movie clip. The registration point is set automatically in the upper-left corner.

11

The syntax is as follows:

```
name_mc.createEmptyMovieClip(instanceName, depth)
```

For example,

```
// create a new movieclip
this.createEmptyMovieClip("myEmptyClip_mc", 100);

// position it relative to parent clip
this.myEmptyClip_mc._x = 30;
this.myEmptyClip_mc._y = 40;
```

Creating a new movie clip at the same depth as an existing movie clip results in the new movie clip replacing the old one. If you don't know what the highest occupied depth is in your Flash document, you can use the getNextHighestDepth() method to have Flash determine at what depth to put your new movie clip instance.

```
this.createEmptyMovieClip("myPhoto_mc", this.getNextHighestDepth());
```

REMOVING A MOVIE CLIP

To remove a movie clip, you can use the aptly named removeMovieClip() method with the following syntax:

```
name_mc.removeMovieClip()
```

DRAGGING AND DROPPING MOVIE CLIPS

One way to add interactivity to your Flash projects is to create drag-and-drop objects in your user interface. You can make your movie clips dragable as long as the user has the mouse held down by using the onPress button function.

To let the user pick up a movie clip, enable drag in a movie clip's onPress method:

```
ball1_mc.onPress = function() {
    startDrag(this);
};
```

If you want the movie clip to drop when the user releases the mouse, use the onRelease event and the method for stopping the drag or the movie clip.

```
ball1_mc.onRelease = function() {
    stopDrag();
};
```

WORKING WITH DYNAMIC MASKS

Complex interactive effects can be created with dynamically generated masks. Just like a mask created in the authoring environment, dynamic masks have a content layer and a mask layer. To create a masking relationship between two objects, use the following syntax, where myImage_mc is the instance name of the movie clip to be masked, and myMask_mc is the instance name of the movie clip that will be the mask:

```
myImage_mc.setMask(myMask_mc);
```

To cancel the mask without affecting the mask layer in the timeline, pass `null` to the `setMask` method:

```
MyImage_mc.setMask(null);
```

If you have two movie clips on the stage and you want one of them to mask the other until the user clicks on it with the mouse, use the following code:

```
// assign a movieclip as mask
circle1_mc.setMask(circle2_mc);

// define function to turn off mask
function removeMask(){
    this.setMask(null);
}
// attach removeMask function to onRelease
circle1_mc.onRelease = removeMask;
```

TROUBLESHOOTING

I've used the /* comment */ notation, and I'm getting a weird result. Why is some of the text commented out, and some isn't?

`/*` style comments cannot be nested. If you've already used them in your code, you cannot enclose them in another set. As soon as a closing `*/` is encountered, the comment is considered closed.

My conditional statement doesn't seem to be working. Why doesn't it catch when my variable equals the test?

Check to make sure you've used the correct operator for the conditional statement. An equivalence conditional requires two equal signs (==), whereas a value assignment requires one equal sign (=). Also check for typos in the variable name and the condition.

I've written a function that is called when the user clicks on a button on the stage. Why doesn't anything happen when I click on it while testing?

There are two main things to check for. First, make sure that the instance has an instance name in the Property inspector. Second, make sure that you've used the correct path and that it's spelled the same way as it is in the Property inspector when you attach the function to the button. To make sure that the function is actually being called, put a trace command at the beginning. If the test message is traced when you click on the button, you know that the problem is internal to the function and not with the calling of the function.

BEST PRACTICES—KEEPING YOUR CODE ORGANIZED WITH COMMENTS

Before writing any code for a big project, I usually start out with pen and paper and sketch out the code requirements of the project. This "sketch" usually consists of diagrams, equations, and an outline of what functions will be needed. At this point, my functions have

11

names that describe what they do. For example, if a function will be getting images, I'll name it getImages.

When I finally open Flash, I start by creating an outline of the code with comments. This helps to give an organized structure to the code, much like the headings in a book chapter. As I fill in the outline with code, I continue to comment as I go. This helps me quickly understand what the code is supposed to do, both as I work and when I come back to it later.

11

CHAPTER 12

ActionScripting for Motion Graphics

In this chapter

DRAWING API

Flash comes with a drawing API (application programming interface). The drawing API is simply a set of movie clip methods that enable you to draw lines, curves, and shapes with fills programmatically with ActionScript.

When Flash saves images in a vector graphics file format, information about the vector shapes in the document is saved as areas of color that are defined by lines and curves. In the authoring environment, you define these lines and shapes with the drawing tools directly on the stage. With ActionScript, you can define the lines and fills of vector graphics dynamically. The images are then drawn, based on your code, when you export to your `.swf` document and while the `.swf` is running (run-time).

When drawing "by hand" on the stage of the authoring environment, you can start drawing first and then later convert the lines and shapes into a symbol. However, when drawing with ActionScript, you must create a movie clip symbol *instance* first, and then draw inside of it. You can think of this movie clip as the paper on which you draw with your ActionScript.

If you're going to draw with ActionScript, you need to understand how to position your work on the stage. The Flash coordinate system starts with (0,0) in the upper-left corner. The numbers are positive and increase from left to right and from top to bottom of the stage (see Figure 12.1). This differs from the Cartesian grid you might be familiar with. Figure 12.1 shows the two grid systems side by side. Understanding this difference becomes especially important when working with trigonometric functions and you need to covert the Cartesian coordinates to Flash coordinates before applying the result of the function to a movie clip.

Figure 12.1
Cartesian grid versus a Flash grid, with coordinates plotted on each grid.

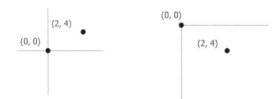

All coordinates passed to the movie clip methods related to drawing are relative to the registration point of the parent clip (the clip inside of which you are drawing). If a line is drawn into a clip, the line's position is relative to the parent clip. If the parent clip is on the stage, its registration point is relative to the stage. The registration point of a movie clip is in the upper-left corner by default. When using the drawing API, you use these coordinates to tell Flash what and where to draw.

DRAWING API METHODS

The Drawing API methods can be applied to any movie clip instance, including the main timeline. The methods work together and some are dependent on others. For example, a `lineStyle()` method must define the style of a line before you can draw the line with the `moveTo()`, `lineTo()`, or `curveTo()` methods. The following section describes the movie clip methods available with the Flash Drawing API.

lineStyle()

Before you can draw a line or curve with your script, you first need to define its line style. Think of it as picking up a certain style of pen before drawing on a piece of paper. The `lineStyle()` statement applies to the `lineTo()` and `curveTo()` statements that follow it. When you draw several lines sequentially, you can change the look of any segment by redefining the line style before drawing the segment.

The syntax is as follows:

```
draw_mc.lineStyle(thickness , rgb , alpha)
```

For example,

```
myLine.lineStyle(5, 0x333366, 80);
```

The `thickness` parameter must have a value between 0 and 255. Any value less than 0 is evaluated as 0 by Flash. Also, any value greater than 255 is evaluated as 255. If no value is specified, the `lineStyle` is undefined and the line is not drawn.

The `rgb` parameter is the hex color value for the line. Its default value is black (0x000000).

The `alpha` parameter sets the transparency level of the line's color. It can range between 0 and 100. The default value is 100, which represents a completely solid color. Just as with thickness, numbers above the maximum are evaluated at the maximum level and numbers below the minimum are evaluated at the minimum. For example, if you accidentally set the alpha value at -90, it is drawn as 0.

moveTo()

The `moveTo` method gives your line a starting coordinate. This is rather like putting your pen down on a specific point on the paper and getting ready to draw. In the flow of your code, it should follow the `lineStyle` statement.

The syntax is as follows:

```
draw_mc.moveTo(x, y)
```

For example,

```
myLine.moveTo(100, 200);
```

The x and y parameters set the coordinates of the starting point for this drawing path. It's important to remember that these coordinates are relative to the parent clip, much like the position of a patch of paint is relative to the canvas it's painted on. In this example, the coordinate (100, 200) is positioned 100 pixels down from, and 200 pixels to the right of, the registration point (0,0) of the `myLine` movie clip.

lineTo()

The `lineTo` method sets the endpoint of a straight line.

The syntax is as follows:

```
draw_mc.lineTo(x, y)
```

For example,

```
myLine.lineTo(200, 200);
```

The x and y coordinates are relative to the registration point of the parent movie clip (the crosshair inside the movie clip). A straight line is drawn from the previous drawing position to the coordinate set with lineTo().

If you use a lineTo method without first using moveTo, the starting point defaults to (0,0). So, if you plan to start at (0,0), you do not need the moveTo line.

curveTo()

The curveTo method draws a line from a starting point to an endpoint with a curve toward a *control point*. The starting and end points are called *anchor points*. It might help to think of this process as drawing a regular straight line and then pulling the middle of it so that it stretches and curves toward a control point but never reaches it (see Figure 12.2).

Figure 12.2
Diagram of curveTo anchor points (squares) and control point (circle).

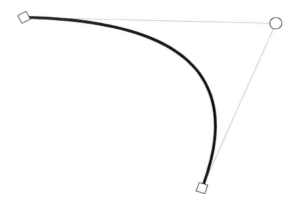

The syntax is as follows:

```
draw_mc.curveTo(controlX, controlY, anchorX, anchorY)
```

For example,

```
myCurve.curveTo(300, 100, 200, 200);
```

The controlX and controlY parameters set the coordinates for the curve's control point.

The anchorX and anchorY parameters set the coordinates for the end point of this curve segment.

clear()

The clear method removes all programmatically drawn elements from the drawing movie clip. It does not affect elements that were drawn in a movie clip during author-time. The MovieClip.clear() statement also resets lineStyle back to undefined.

12

The syntax is as follows:

```
draw_mc.clear()
```

For example,

```
myCurve.clear();
```

beginFill()

The beginFill() method enables you to define the fill color and transparency level of a closed shape. It precedes the methods used to draw the outline of the shape and is closed by calling the endFill() method.

The syntax is as follows:

draw_mc.beginFill(*rgb*, *alpha*)

For example,

```
myshape.beginFill(0x003366, 80);
```

The rgb parameter is the hex color value for the fill. This is the value of the color as you would see it in the Swatch panel, with a 0x proceeding the numeric value.

The alpha parameter sets the fill's transparency level. It defaults to 100 (solid color).

beginGradientFill()

Whereas the beginFill() method lets you define a single fill color and is simple to use, the beginGradientFill() method enables you to define a gradient and is a little more complicated to use. Figure 12.3 shows a gradient filled shape.

The syntax is as follows:

draw_mc.beginGradientFill(*fillType*, *colors*, *alphas*, *ratios*, *matrix*)

For example,

```
this.createEmptyMovieClip("gradient_mc", 1);
with (gradient_mc) {
    colors = [0xFF0000, 0xFF9933];
    alphas = [100, 80];
    ratios = [0, 0xFF];
    matrix = {matrixType:"box", x:100, y:100, w:200, h:200, r:(45/180)*Math.PI};
    beginGradientFill("radial", colors, alphas, ratios, matrix);
    moveTo(100, 100);
    lineTo(100, 300);
    lineTo(300, 300);
    lineTo(300, 100);
    lineTo(100, 100);
    endFill();
}
```

12

Figure 12.3
Radial gradient fill.

The `fillType` can be set to either linear or radial. These gradients are just like the gradients you can create with the tools in the authoring environment. A linear gradient transitions from one color to another in one direction, and a radial gradient transitions out from a central point.

The `colors` parameter holds an array (a list of values) of RGB hex color values for the gradient. You can use several different colors in one gradient fill.

The `alphas` parameter is also an array. This one holds the alpha values for the corresponding colors in the colors array. As with other alpha properties, each value can range from 0 to 100. There must be an alpha setting for each color in your `colors` array. For example, if you have three color elements, you must have three alpha elements.

The `ratios` parameter is an array that holds color distribution ratios for each color in the `colors` array. It sets the width of color that is rendered as a solid color before the transition to the next color begins. For example, you may want a span of solid red before the gradient starts to transition into orange. Values for these widths can range from 0 to 255. There must be a ratio value for each color in the *colors* array.

The `matrix` parameter is an object (like ratios is an array). It holds the `matrixType`, x, y, w, h, and r properties.

- `matrixType` must be set as "box" for this format of the matrix object.
- x and y are the coordinates for the position of the gradient's upper-left corner.
- w is the width of the gradient.
- h is the height of the gradient.
- r is the rotation, in radians, of the gradient.

endFill()

The `endFill()` method closes the `fill` command for either `beginFill()` or `beginGradientFill()`. If you are drawing several shapes into a single movie clip, be sure to use the `endFill()` method before using another `beginFill()` or `beginGradientFill()` to change the fill color. Although it is not required, it is good practice to close every fill with the `endFill()` method.

The syntax is as follows:

```
myshape.endFill();
```

DRAWING A LINE

Now that you have been introduced to the methods of the Flash Drawing API, you can see how to put them together to draw a line. For each step of the process, an analogy to drawing with pen and paper is provided.

Here are the steps to draw a line:

1. Create an empty movie clip (get a piece of paper):
   ```
   this.createEmptyMovieClip("myline", 100);
   ```
2. Create a style for the line (pick up a pen):
   ```
   myline.lineStyle(2,0x333366, 100);
   ```
3. Set the starting point for the line (set the pen down on the paper):
   ```
   myline.moveTo(0,0);
   ```
4. Set the end point for the line (drag the pen across the paper and stop):
   ```
   myline.lineTo(30,30);
   ```
5. Add as many lineTo statements as you want.

DRAWING A CURVED LINE

Now that you've mastered drawing a straight line with the drawing API, it's time to throw you a curve. The process is much the same except that you use the curveTo() method instead of the lineTo() method.

Here are the steps to draw a curved line:

1. Create an empty movie clip:
   ```
   this.createEmptyMovieClip("mycurve", 100);
   ```
2. Create a style for the curved line:
   ```
   mycurve.lineStyle(2,0x333366, 100);
   ```
3. Set a starting point for the curved line:
   ```
   mycurve.moveTo(100,100);
   ```
4. Set the end point (the curve's anchor point) and control point for the curve:
   ```
   mycurve.curveTo(200, 30, 300, 300);
   ```
5. Add as many curveTo statements as you want.

DRAWING A SHAPE

Drawing a shape involves drawing a series of straight or curved lines with the last line ending at the same coordinates where the first line began (closing the shape).

Here are the steps to draw a shape:

1. Create an empty movie clip:
   ```
   this.createEmptyMovieClip("myshape", 100);
   ```

2. Create a style for the line and begin the fill:

```
myshape.lineStyle(2,0x333366, 100);
myshape.begingFill(0x003366, 80);
```

3. Set the starting point:

```
myshape.moveTo(2,2);
```

4. Sequentially set the end points for each line or curve in the shape's line path:

```
myshape.lineTo(88,2);
myshape.lineTo(88,88);
myshape.lineTo(2,88);
```

5. Return to starting point to close the shape:

```
myshape.lineTo(2,2);
```

6. End the fill if there is one:

```
myshape.endFill();
```

TIP

> If you want a shape without a visible outline, omit the `lineStyle`.

PROGRAMMATIC MOVEMENT (ANIMATING WITH ACTIONSCRIPT)

Flash offers two ways to create animations: by drawing the keyframe content "by hand" in the authoring environment or by drawing the frame contents with ActionScript. Even better, you can combine the two approaches as best suits your project needs.

Chapter 10 covered Flash animation basics. Recall that with tweens, you can set the starting point and destination of a symbol instance, and then have Flash "tween" the intermediate frames. You can do much the same thing with ActionScript with the help of the `onEnterFrame` method of the `movieClip` object. Anything within an `onEnterFrame` method executes on every frame. It's a continuous loop.

The syntax is as follows:

```
my_mc.onEnterFrame = function() {
    // your statements here
}
```

To stop an `onEnterFrame` loop, you must remove the `onEnterFrame` with the `delete` operator.

For example,

```
//An onEnterFrame loop, that counts to 20 and stops
this.i = 0;
this.onEnterFrame = function(){
    i++;
    trace(i);
    if(i>=20){
        delete this.onEnterFrame;
    }
}
```

With this approach, you can also move the movie clip holding your shape across the stage and stop it when it reaches a certain position.

```
// move myShape, until it's x-coordinate >= 600
myShape.onEnterFrame = function(){
    this._x += 10;
    if(this._x >= 600){
        delete this.onEnterFrame;
    }
}
```

As you've seen in the previous example, you can essentially program your own motion tweens with ActionScript. You can also program your own shape tweens with the drawing API. Rather than draw in your clip, and then move the clip, you can redraw the line into a new shape and position repeatedly with an onEnterFrame loop. The object stays in one place, but its shape changes. This is analogous to shape tweening.

You can think of your movie clip as a sticky note with your drawing on it. Programming a motion tween is like asking an assistant to move that sticky paper to a specific point at regular time intervals. Programming a shape tween is like asking the same assistant to leave the sticky note where it is while erasing and redrawing the picture a little differently at regular time intervals.

The following code draws a slowly growing shape. When new lines are drawn, the previously drawn lines remain visible. To create a line that slowly stretches, insert a this.clear() statement just above the lineStyle() statement. This way, instead of adding additional lines, you replace the previous line.

```
this.createEmptyMovieClip("mycurve", 100);
// save starting x-coordinate for curve control point
mycurve.controlX:Number = 200;
// stretch curve toward new control point
mycurve.onEnterFrame = function(){
    var x:Number = this.controlX++
    if(this.controlX <=400){
        this.lineStyle(2,0x333366, 100);
        this.moveTo(100,100);
        this.curveTo(x, 30, 300, 300);
    } else {
        delete this.onEnterFrame;
    }
}
```

You can modify this code so that the line stretches when the user moves the mouse. Now the curve is redrawn when the mouse is moved and stops when the mouse is still.

```
// save starting x-coordinate for curve control point
mycurve.controlX:Number = 200;
// stretch curve toward new control point
mycurve.onMouseMove = function(){
    var x:Number = this.controlX++
    this.clear();
    this.lineStyle(2,0x333366, 100);
    this.moveTo(100,100);
    this.curveTo(x, 30, 300, 300);
}
```

12

TROUBLESHOOTING

Why doesn't my line show up at run-time?

Make sure that you define the `lineStyle` before starting your drawing. Until you define a linestyle, it is undefined and the subsequent lines will not be drawn.

Why is my symbol moving in the wrong direction?

Check the sign of the coordinates you're using. The Flash stage coordinate system has the y-axes positive in the downward direction. A negative _y is located above the stage, and a negative _x is located to the left of the stage.

Why is my fill color not working?

Check to make sure you closed the shape by returning to your starting point when drawing the lines of your shape.

Why does my line start from the upper-left corner?

Make sure to start with a `moveTo()` statement before using `lineTo()` or `curveTo()`. The starting point of a line or curve defaults to (0,0) if you don't use `moveTo()` to set another starting point.

Why is my `gradientFill` not showing up?

Make sure you have all parameters of `beginGradientFill()` set properly. Any missing properties of the matrix object can cause the method to not function. Check to make sure that you have the same number of elements in the `colors`, `alphas`, and `ratios` arrays. Make sure that you have set the `fillType` parameter to `linear` or `radial`.

BEST PRACTICES—WHEN TO USE with

Normally it's best to avoid the `with` statement. However, it can help make your code more readable when you use the drawing API. For example, consider the following:

```
this.attachMovie("myBox", "box", 1);
myBox.lineStyle(1, 0x669999, 100);
myBox.beginFill(0x336666, 80);
myBox.moveTo(0,0);
myBox.lineTo(100,0);
myBox.lineTo(100,100);
myBox.lineTo(0,100);
myBox.lineTo(0,0);
myBox.endFill();
```

Contrast that with the following:

```
this.attachMovie("myBox", "box", 1);
with (myBox){
    lineStyle(1, 0x669999, 100);
    beginFill(0x336666, 80);
    moveTo(0,0);
    lineTo(100,0);
    lineTo(100,100);
    lineTo(0,100);
```

```
    lineTo(0,0);
    endFill();
}
```

Another option for making this code more readable is to use a local variable (a variable whose scope is available only in the parent timeline) to refer to the new movie clip. Consider the following example:

```
var b:MovieClip = this.attachMovie("myBox", "box", 1);
b.lineStyle(1, 0x669999, 100);
b.beginFill(0x336666, 80);
b.moveTo(0,0);
b.lineTo(100,0);
b.lineTo(100,100);
b.lineTo(0,100);
b.lineTo(0,0);
b.endFill();
```

12

CHAPTER 13

INTRODUCTION TO CLASS-BASED PROGRAMMING IN FLASH

In this chapter

BRIEF INTRODUCTION TO OOP

Object-oriented programming (OOP) is sometimes shrouded in mystery and mysticism. You might have encountered phrases such as "the zen of OOP." But when you get right down to it, OOP is just a way of organizing code. I'd even go so far as to say that it's the best way to organize complex or large projects.

Chapter 11, "Introducing ActionScript," covered simple datatypes in Flash. Variables are containers, and datatypes are a way to say what kind of data can be stored in that container. A variable with a number datatype holds a number, a string holds a string of characters, and an array holds a list of strings, numbers, or objects.

Each datatype has certain properties and methods unique to its type. For example, a number can hold numerical values and have mathematical methods applied to it. A class defines a datatype.

When we start discussing objects, things start getting more interesting. An object can hold properties, which are simply variables of a datatype (the object container holds the variable container). Objects can also hold another complex datatype called *functions*. In Chapter 11, functions were defined as encapsulated segments of code with a single set of functionality. They are "run" when called by name in another section of code. When functions are stored in an object, they are called *methods*.

CLASSES

So how do you organize code differently when you work with ActionScript 2.0 and object-oriented programming in Flash? When Chapter 11 introduced ActionScripting, you learned to look at variables and functions as ways to organize your code. Now you're ready to move to a more sophisticated organizational structure where all of your code is stored in objects, which are simply containers of containers.

However, before you can create an instance of an object, you must have a class. A *class* describes an object as well as what properties and methods belong to that object. It can be one of the built-in classes, such as Math, or a custom class that you write yourself. In either case, a class is a datatype that describes all the properties and methods that are available to be applied to an object created from the class description.

You can think of a class as the blueprint for an object. Just as many buildings can be constructed from the same set of blueprints, multiple objects can be described by a single class. It is important to understand that *all* datatypes and objects in Flash are class-based. The `MovieClip` object, `Date` object, `Array` object, `Math` object, and even the `Object` object are all based on classes that are built into Flash. For a complete list of all built-in datatypes (classes) available to you in Flash, go to the Action panel and choose Types from the left Action listing.

USING THE BUILT-IN CLASSES IN FLASH

To continue the blueprint metaphor, a class in and of itself isn't a very useful thing until you begin creating object instances of that class. There are several ways to create an object instance of a particular class. For example, instances of the built-in `MovieClip` class can be created at author-time if a shape is converted into a movie clip symbol on the stage. They can also be dynamically created during run-time. There are methods designed specifically for this purpose.

As mentioned, you can create a new instance of a `MovieClip` object either manually (on the stage or in the library) or programmatically. You can use the following `MovieClip` methods to create a `MovieClip` instance with ActionScript:

- `this.attachMovie()`—Grabs a movie clip from the Library.
- `this.createEmptyMovieClip()`—Creates a new blank movie clip.
- `this.duplicateMovieClip()`—Duplicates a movie clip instance already on Stage.

There might be times when you want to access a class property or run a method without going through an instance of its class. Examples of built-in classes that you might want to access in this way include the `Math`, `Date`, and `Mouse` classes. You're not creating multiple instances of `Mouse`, but directly communicating with a single `Mouse` object.

For example, imagine you want to position a movie clip named dot_mc at a specific distance from the center of a circle. In the following code, the `cos` and `sin` `Math` methods are used with the `PI` `Math` property in a formula to determine the position of the dot:

```
dot_mc._x = 100 * Math.cos(45 * Math.PI/180) + 200;
dot_mc._y = 100 * Math.sin(45 * Math.PI/180) + 200;
```

The `Math` object has many other useful methods that you can access directly, without having to create an instance of the `Math` class. These include `Math.random()`, `Math.cos()`, and `Math.pow()`.

The `Mouse` object also has methods that you can access directly without creating an instance. These deal with making the mouse pointer visible in the Flash movie. By default, the mouse pointer is always visible in a Flash movie. To hide the mouse pointer, call

```
Mouse.hide();
```

To show the pointer again, call

```
Mouse.show();
```

Most of the time, you use a constructor function to create a new instance of a built-in class. To instantiate these classes, use a constructor function that consists of the instance name, the new keyword, and the name of the class from which you are creating an object. In the following syntax statement, `Datatype` is the same as the `Class`.

```
var instanceName:Datatype = new Class();
```

13

This should become clearer as you look at the following examples:

```
// create an instance of the Array object
var myList:Array = new Array();

//create an instance of the  loadVars object
var partyData:LoadVars = new LoadVars();

// create an instance of the  Number object
var oneHundred:Number = new Number(100);
```

Now that you have an idea of how the constructor function works you can explore an example more fully. Imagine you're building an application that helps people organize parties. One of the many details the host needs to keep track of is the guest list. Each guest has individual information. You can create an instance of the `Object` datatype to hold that information.

```
var guest:Object = new Object();
```

After you create your instance, you can then use the dot syntax to start adding properties with values to be stored by the object instance.

```
var guest:Object = new Object();

guest.name = "Julie Smith";
guest.address = "123 Anystreet";
guest.age = 6;
guest.favoriteFood = "pasta";
guest.likesMushrooms = False;
```

You can also create object instances for `Array` and `Object` objects by using a shortcut called *literals*. In the following examples, you can see that an `Array` object uses square brackets to enclose its elements. The `Object` object uses the names of the properties, followed by a colon, to organize its data.

```
var my_menu:Array = new Array(); //uses the constructor function
var my_menu:Array = ["eggs", "ham", "beans"]; //use the array literal syntax

var guest:Object = {
        name:"Julie Smith",
        address:"123 Any Street"
}//object literal
```

Learning how to use the built-in classes that ship with ActionScript can help you understand classes in Flash, but you're not limited to them. You can also create your own custom classes.

CREATING YOUR OWN CUSTOM CLASSES

Until this point, you've been saving your projects as `.fla` files and going back and forth between the timeline, the stage, the Actions panel, and other panels in the Flash authoring environment. Now you'll see a different kind of document—the ActionScript (`.as`) file. An `.as` file is a text file that has a specific organized structure and holds only ActionScript code. It can be created either in the Flash authoring environment or in an external editing program.

Custom classes are saved in their own .as files. You can then use your custom classes just as you use the built-in classes. You can save custom classes in any location on your hard drive you wish, but for Flash to find these files when they're referenced from another file, you need to set the classpath. The *classpath* is a list of folders where Flash looks for external .as files.

CREATING A NEW ACTIONSCRIPT FILE

To create a new .as file, go to File, New. This brings up the New Document dialog box. Select the General tab if it is not already selected to see a list of options. Select the ActionScript file option and click the OK button to create an .as file. You can now save this file to a location in your project directory for easy access.

SETTING A CLASSPATH

Flash doesn't automatically know where you keep your .as files. Because they are external files, much like external image files, you have to tell the compiler where to look for them. Use the following steps to set a classpath:

1. Select File, Publish Settings to open the Publish Settings dialog box.
2. Click the Flash tab (see Figure 13.1).

Figure 13.1
The Flash tab of the Publish Settings panel.

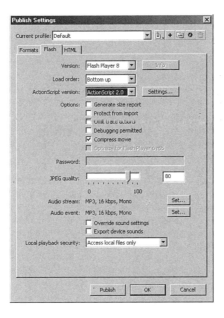

3. Make sure that ActionScript 2.0 is selected in the ActionScript Version pop-up menu.
4. Click on the Settings button. This brings up a panel for ActionScript 2.0 settings (see Figure 13.2).

Figure 13.2
The ActionScript
Settings panel show-
ing the Classpath list.

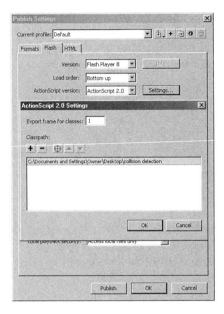

5. Set the Export Frame for classes in this file. The default is the first frame.

6. Select (or create) a folder on your system as a classpath.

To delete a folder from the classpath, select the path in the Classpath list and click the Remove from Path button.

TIP

> As you work on more projects in Flash, you might develop an extensive library of custom classes and their .as files. You can keep them organized by project, by common classes, or any other way that works well for you. You might find it useful to keep them in a place that is easy to find on your system. I keep my .as files, organized by project, in a directory that is easy for me to find and frequently save a backup copy of it.

CLASS STRUCTURE

The ActionScript code in a class is organized into a specific structure. Each class file has a filename (which is the same as its class declaration), and consists of a class declaration, variable declarations, a class constructor, and class methods.

It's good practice to begin your class file with a comment block that gives the class name and purpose, author name and contact information, initial authoring time, and revision notes and dates, as shown in the following example:

```
/*
Class Name
Author Name/Contact
```

```
Initial Author date/Revision date
Notes:
*/
```

The class declaration is simply the `class` keyword followed by the class name:

```
class myClass{ . . . }
```

The first elements to add inside the class declaration are the variable declarations (note that new code has been shaded):

```
class myClass {

    // declare class variables
    var my_var1:Number;
    var my_var2:Srting;

    . . .
}
```

Next, add the class constructor. This defines what properties an instance of your class will have when it's created. If the constructor is empty, no initial properties are defined for the class:

```
class myClass {
    // declare class variables
    var my_var1:Number;
    var my_var2:String;

    //class constructor
    function myClass(){
    }
. . .
}
```

Finally, write the methods for the class:

```
class myClass {
    // declare class variables
    var my_var1:Number;
    var my_var2:Srting;

    //class constructor
    function myClass(){
    }

    //methods
    function myMethod(){
        //do something here
    }

}
```

13

Earlier in this chapter you saw the creation of an instance of the `Object` class named `guest`. We can also create your own custom class for that project.

First, declare the class. When you create a new class, it is usually a good idea to use comments to outline the code you'll be writing. That is what is also done here, as shown in the following example:

```
class Guest{
    // declare variables
    //class constructor
    // define methods
}
```

Earlier in this chapter, an instance of the Object class was created and given an instance name of guest. In the same statement, properties of that instance were simultaneously declared and assigned values. Now that you are creating a custom class, you must first declare the properties, separately from assigning values to them:

```
class Guest{
    // declare variables
    var name:String;
    var address:Object;
    var age:Number;
    var favFood:String;
    var likesMushrooms:Boolean;

    //class constructor

    // define methods
}
```

Next, add the class constructor to the comment outline. The class constructor is similar to the functions you've seen in other chapters except that only properties are defined inside the curly braces. These properties are applied to each instance of your class at initialization (when the instance is created). When you create an instance of your class, you can pass values for its properties, as arguments, to the class constructor.

Take a look at the following code—specifically, the code below the //class constructor comment. First, the function keyword is used, followed by the name of the class, to signal to the compiler that this is the class constructor. Then, the parameters (property values) are listed between the parentheses. These are similar to the variables that you can pass to a function. Within the curly braces of the constructor you can assign the values of the variables you passed to the constructor as values for the properties of the class.

```
class Guest{
    // declare variables
    var name:String;
    var address:Object;
    var age:Number;
    var favFood:String;
    var likesMushrooms:Boolean;

    // class constructor
```

```
function Guest(cNname, cAddress, cAge, cFavFood, cMush){
    name = cName;
    address = cAddress;
    age = cAge;
    favFood = cFavFood;
    likesMushrooms = cMush;
}

// define methods
}
```

Finally, define methods for the class. People can be fickle, and favorite foods can change. The getFavFood method can be used to return the favorite food of a guest by returning the current value of the instance's favFood property. The setFavFood method enables you to change the value of the guest's favFood property by passing a new value for it through the function argument (between the parentheses).

```
class Guest{
    // declare variables
    var name:String;
    var address:Object;
    var age:Number;
    var fav_food:String;
    var likesMushrooms:Boolean;

    // class constructor
    function Guest(g_name, g_address, g_age, g_fav_food, g_mush){
        name = g_name;
        address = g_address;
        age = g_age;
        fav_food = g_fav_food;
        likesMushrooms = g_mush;
    }

    // define methods
    function setFavFood(food){
        favFood = food;
    }

    function getFavFood(){
        return favFood;
    }

}
```

CREATING AN INSTANCE FROM YOUR CLASS

After you create a custom class, you always use a class constructor statement to create an instance of the class. The syntax for creating an instance of a class is as follows:

```
// create a new Dinner instance
var myDinner:Dinner = new Dinner();
```

You can use the class in any ActionScript, including an `.fla` file or another `.as` file. To make a custom class accessible from another file, you must use the `import` statement at the top of the code in that file. For example, to use the `Guest` class in an `.fla` file, type the following code into the first line of the Actions panel:

```
import Guest;
```

Defined classpaths tell the compiler where to look for the class, but if you create folders within that destination and place the class file inside a subdirectory, you must specify the name of that subdirectory in the `import` statement. For example, if you have a common classpath to all your `.as` files, and within that folder you have a folder for a project named DinnerParty, you would use the following import statement:

```
import DinnerParty.Guest;
```

Continuing with the custom `Guest` class just created, the following is an example of creating a `Guest` instance. To make the code easier to read, assign the values to local variables, and then pass these through to the class constructor.

```
// set up local vars to hold the values we'll pass to the class constructor
var cName = "Jill Smith";
var cAddress = new Object;
    cAddress.street = "123 anystreet";
    cAddress.city = "anytown";
    cAddress.state = "home state";
    cAddress.zip = 22222;
var cAge = 3;
var cFaveFood = "mac and cheese";
var cMush = false;

// create a new instance of the Guest object
var guest1:Guest = new Guest(cName, cAddress, cAge, cFavFood, cMush);
```

When you have an instance, you can invoke a method from its class. For example, you can now reset a guest's favorite food to risotto. To use the class in another class, or an `.fla`, you must use the `import` command. If the `Guest` class was saved in a folder named dinnerParty, you'd use the following line to import it:

```
import dinnerParty.Guest
```

From anywhere in the file into which the class has been imported, including from an `.fla`, you can now use the following code:

```
//change guest's favorite food to risotto
guest1.setFavFood("risotto");
```

Now, although you're not likely to edit code to change a dinner guest's favorite food, you could use a class like this along with database management classes as part of an event-planning application. This isn't a tutorial section, but I hope that this concrete example makes it easier for you to understand how to construct your own classes.

STATIC, PUBLIC, AND PRIVATE PROPERTIES AND METHODS

When working with class-based programming, you will most often use classes to define objects of which you will later create instances. Their properties and methods cannot be called directly, like a function, but must be accessed through an instance of the class.

However, you may want to use a method or property without creating an instance of its class. When working with your own custom classes, use the `static` keyword to declare a property or method that you want to use outside of a class's instance. ActionScript has several built-in static methods, such as `Math.random` and `Math.cos`. To use these methods, you don't create an instance of the `Math` object. You just call them directly. For example, the following code sets a variable to be equal to the cosine of 20:

```
var cosTwenty:Number = Math.cos(20);
```

By default, class methods and properties are public. *Public* properties and methods can be accessed from outside the class that defines it. For example, after an instance of `Guest` is created, you can call the `setFavFood` method for that instance:

```
guest1.setFavFood("pizza");
```

Private properties and methods, which are defined with the `private` keyword, can be accessed only from within the class. For example, you might use a private property when using Flash as the user interface to a database application. If you store the data for your guests in a database, each guest's record has a unique ID number. This isn't relevant information for the user interface, but it is important for passing information to the database.

```
private var guestID:Number;
```

Although you might not use the `static` and `private` keywords often, they will come in handy as you continue to develop applications with class-based ActionScript.

SUPERCLASSES AND SUBCLASSES

Superclasses and subclasses come into play only when you borrow code from one class to run in another related class. The terminology can be confusing, so take a look at an example.

Imagine that you want to generate a random pair of numbers. You can create a class for this purpose, and then when you create an instance of it, you can invoke a method that generates a pair of random numbers.

```
class RandomPair{
    // declare variables
    var num1:Number;
    var num2:Number;

    // class constructor
    function RandomPair(){
    }
```

13

```
    // define methods
    function getRandomPair(){
        num1 = Math.random();
        num2 = Math.random();
        var pair:Array = [num1, num2];
        return pair;
    }
}
```

What if you need a pair of random numbers within a narrow range? You can create a subclass (RangeRandomPair) that extends the methods of the RandomPair class. The
RangeRandomPair subclass has a method that calls the method from the superclass and tests
the results to see whether the numbers are within the range you need. If the numbers don't
meet the requirements, the internal superclass method is called again.

```
class RangeRandomPair extends RandomPair{

    // declare variables
    var upperLimit:Number;
    var lowerLimit:Number;

    // class constructor
    function RangeRandomPair(upperLim, lowerLim){
        upperLimit = upperLim;
        lowerLimit = lowerLim;
    }

    // define methods
    function getPair(){
        var n1 = super.getRandomPair();
        var n2 = super.getRandomPair();
        if(n1 <= upperLimit && n1 >= lowerLimit
                && n2 <= upperLimit && n2 >= lowerLimit){
            // numbers are both within range, return them
            var pair:Array = [n1, n2];
            return pair;
        } else {
            // numbers are not within range, try again
            this.getPair();
        }
    }
}
```

Although this case can be handled within a single class, this example should help illustrate
the superclass and subclass relationships. Any class can be a superclass, and you can have a
chain of superclass-subclass relationships. A subclass extends the code of a superclass to create a more specialized object.

To create a subclass of another class, use the extend keyword with the following syntax:

```
class SubClass extends SuperClass{
    . . .
}
```

Now that you've started to create relationships between classes and build structures of code, it's time to move on from class-based systems to explore the use of OOP logic to control events in movies.

ADVANCED EVENT HANDLING

When you press a mouse button, that's an event. When an image finishes loading onto the stage, that's an event. An *event handler* triggers actions the programmer wants to occur when an event occurs during run-time. Chapter 11 explored simple event handlers for Button and MovieClip objects. Now, as you explore class-based logic, it's a good idea to look at object listeners and ways to extend the functionality of the built-in event handlers for MovieClip objects.

SYSTEM EVENTS AND USER INPUT EVENTS

You will normally encounter two main types of events in Flash: system events and user input events. *System events* are generated by the Flash movie and include events such as when data finishes loading or when the movie playhead reaches a particular frame. *User input events* are generated by the user, such as when the user releases the mouse or a key.

User input events can be "listened" to and acted upon in ActionScript. Several objects can have listeners: Key, Mouse, MovieClipLoader, Selection, Stage, and TextField. An advantage to using listeners is that you can add multiple listeners to the same event.

To use a listener, you must first define a method that will be called when the listener object detects an event. Next, you assign the method to the event handler for that object. And finally, you add the listener to an object that has listener event handlers. What this does is extend the types of events to which a particular object can respond.

For example, imagine that you want the user to use the keyboard to control the movement of a spaceship in your movie. The spaceship instance, which is an instance of the MovieClip class, needs to "listen" to the keyboard and respond to an event generated by the user with the keyboard. To do this, you need to register the spaceship movie clip as a listener for the Key class, as shown in the following example:

```
function myOnKeyUp(){
    trace("key up");
}
function myOnKeyDown(){
    trace("key down");
}

spaceship.onKeyUp = myOnKeyUp;
spaceship.onKeyDown = myOnKeyDown;

Key.addListener(spaceship);
```

13

SCOPING AND THE this KEYWORD WITH EVENT HANDLERS

You can make your code more general and reusable by using the this keyword. It refers to the object or movie clip instance that contains it. When a method containing this is called, a reference to the object that contains the method is saved in this.

It's especially useful when dynamically attaching functions to a movie clip. Imagine that you want to make your spaceship move 10 pixels per frame while a key on the keyboard is pressed. Because the myOnKeyDown function has been attached to the spaceship movie clip, myOnKeyDown is a method of the spaceship object and this refers to the spaceship. You can add this._x +=10; to that function to have it execute when the user holds the key down, as shown in the following example:

```
function myOnKeyUp(){
    trace("key up");

}

function myOnKeyDown(){
    trace("key down");
    this._x +=10;
}

spaceship.onKeyUp = myOnKeyUp;
spaceship.onKeyDown = myOnKeyDown;
Key.addListener(spaceship);
```

DISABLING AND DELETING EVENT HANDLERS

If you want the spaceship to stop moving when it reaches a certain position on the stage, you can add a conditional to the myOnKeyDown function that tests whether the spaceship movie clip's x position is less than or equal to 300. If the condition is met, the spaceship keeps moving while the key is pressed. However, if the spaceship reaches its destination, its onKeyDown method is deleted and it no longer responds to the keyboard and stops moving.

```
function myOnKeyUp(){
    trace("key up");

}

function myOnKeyDown(){
    trace("key down");

    if(this._x <= 300){
        this._x +=10;
    } else {
        delete this.onKeyDown;
    }

}

spaceship.onKeyUp = myOnKeyUp;
spaceship.onKeyDown = myOnKeyDown;
Key.addListener(spaceship);
```

Another way to stop the spaceship from moving is to remove its listener, as shown in this example:

```
function myOnKeyDown(){
    trace("key down");
    if(this._x <= 300){
        this._x +=10;
    } else {
        Key.removeListener(this);
    }
}
```

TROUBLESHOOTING

Why is my date off by a month?

The Date object parameters start counting at zero, so January is represented by 0 and December by 11. Check that the number you used to represent the month is set correctly.

I'm trying to set a classpath, but the Settings button is faded and it doesn't respond.

Make sure you have the ActionScript version set as 1.0 or as 2.0. To set a classpath, you must be using ActionScript 2.0.

I get an error when I test my class, which defines a static property in the class constructor.

The class constructor is for setting up the properties that an instance of your class will have. Because a static property is called without an instance of its class, it cannot be defined in the class constructor. Instead, declare a static property where you declare all the variables in your class, but use the `static` keyword. You can also assign it a value in the same statement.

I called a method from the superclass of my subclass, but it's not executing.

Check that you placed an `import` statement at the beginning of your subclass and that you included the `extends` keyword in your class declaration. Additionally, make sure that you use the `super` keyword when calling the method from your subclass.

BEST PRACTICES—ORGANIZING YOUR CODE

13

Well-organized code is especially important when working with class-based programming. Be sure to use comments to give visual structure to your document as well as to explain the code.

Just as you organize lines of code into logical groups as functions, you should organize your classes into logical groups of methods and properties. If you find yourself scrolling through pages of code for a single class, this could be an indication that you should rethink your code organization. Look for ways to encapsulate the code into smaller classes that you can use together.

CHAPTER 14

WORKING WITH EXTERNAL DATA IN YOUR FLASH PROJECTS

In this chapter

A Flash application can communicate with its local environment and pass data back and forth to a remote server. You might be wondering, "Application? Isn't Flash usually a movie?" Flash is probably best known for its animation capabilities as well as interactive media, but Flash is also well suited for working with external data and interactive data visualization. In this chapter you will learn some of the basics of working with external data in Flash, including XML formatted data, so that you can build your own Flash applications.

COMMUNICATING LOCALLY

Your published .swf file exists in various contexts. For example, a .swf can be embedded in an HTML document and viewed in a browser window or as a standalone document in a Flash Projector. This section discusses how your .swf file can communicate with these environments.

NOTE

> Flash can be published in various formats, including as a .swf file displayed by an HTML document, a standalone executable file for Windows or Macintosh (called a Projector), or even as a QuickTime movie.

CONTROLLING BROWSER WINDOWS

One of the common uses of Flash is to provide dynamic and interactive navigational elements for an HTML website. You might do this when you want the navigation to have more interaction (like animated roll-over effects) than a list of HTML links. Although you can create similar effects with JavaScript, Flash has the advantage of cross-platform performance. A Flash navigation element runs essentially the same in any browser that has a Flash Player installed.

To create "links" analogous to the <A HREF > tag in HTML, use the getURL() function. For example, a symbol named "home" in the navigation menu could have the following code attached to it programmatically:

```
home_btn.onRelease() = function{
    getURL("home.html");
}
```

Now, when the user clicks on that button, Flash passes the URL parameter in parentheses to the browser, which then loads a new page into the browser window.

You can also use the getURL command to pass URL-encoded data or a database query, as shown in the following example:

```
image_10.onRelease() = function{
    getURL("images.html?id=10");
}
```

Just as with HTML <A HREF> tags, you can specify the target by adding a second parameter to be passed to the getURL() command. For example, to open a new window with the target attribute, you can use code similar to this:

```
image_10.onRelease() = function{
    getURL("images.html?id=10", "_blank");
}
```

Now you know how to communicate with the browser using the getURL command in Flash. The next section briefly discusses another way to communicate with the browser: using JavaScript.

JAVASCRIPT

JavaScript is a scripting language that is used to communicate with a browser. ActionScript is based on the same code standard and is a close relative of JavaScript. You can use JavaScript in your Flash projects to help you communicate with the browser, although JavaScript itself has some cross-browser and platform issues that you have to stay aware of because they can limit what can be accomplished with a simple script. For example, JavaScript code that works in one browser may not function at all in another.

CONTROLLING A FLASH PROJECTOR

You can use the fscommand() command to control certain aspects of the performance of the standalone Flash projector. When a .swf is presented in a standalone projector, instead of as an embedded file in an HTML document, it exists in the context of the projector that plays the .swf.

To enlarge the projector display window to fill the user's entire screen, use the fullscreen attribute of the fscommand statement. When fullscreen is set to true, the projector fills the screen, as shown in the following example:

```
fscommand("fullscreen", true);
```

When at full screen, the movie fills the entire window and no borders are visible. Although this can be a nice visual effect, be sure to give the end user control over how the movie is displayed.

When fullscreen is set to false, the projector opens at the size you set in the Document settings, as shown in the following example:

```
fscommand("fullscreen", false);
```

> **TIP**
>
> It is generally considered best practice to begin with a non full screen SWF and then provide a button to expand to full screen and one to reduce the display to original size.

Another useful command controls the scaling of the movie. The allowscale parameter of the fscommand enables you to control whether the SWF file stays the same size even when the browser window is expanded and contracted by the user. When the parameter is set to

14

true, it allows the SWF movie to expand and contract with the browser window. To turn off scaling use the following command:

```
fscommand("allowscale", false);
```

Be aware that if you have a lot of bitmap artwork that has been optimized for file size in your movie, it might be a good idea to set the allowscale parameter to false. Otherwise, the images might appear pixilated when enlarged.

LOADING TEXT DATA

In general, data is a collection of facts. When you see the word *data* in a programming book, it usually refers to a formatted set of numbers and letters.

With Flash, you have many options for visualizing data to help the end user gain meaning from that data. You can use a dynamic text field to display data that is as simple as a single string, such as "The cat is brown." You can also visualize a large and complex set of data points with an interactive graph that's been dynamically generated.

THE LoadVars() OBJECT

Previous chapters talked about using event handlers to execute specific code when an event occurs. The LoadVars object has a useful event handler called onLoad(), which is invoked when data completes loading into the LoadVars object.

You might use LoadVars when you are passing simple data, such as a short list of guests, to the .swf. This is very useful when you want to update information displayed in the published .swf, without changing the source .fla and republishing. You could keep a list of guests in an external file and edit it at a later time.

You can use the LoadVars() object to load data from an external text file in a variable/value pair format. The data in the external text file must be formatted as follows:

```
&guest1="Jill Smith"
```

The & symbol signals to the Flash Player that a variable/value pair follows that needs to be passed into a LoadVars object of the .swf file. There must be no spaces between the variable name, the = operator, and the first character in the value.

To use the LoadVars object, first create a new instance of the LoadVars object and give it a name. Next, assign a function to execute when the data has completed loading. Finally, load your external data file.

In the following example, a text file is loaded into a new LoadVars object (guestList). The onLoad function traces the value of the variable name1 to the Output window. Because the function is attached to the guestList instance, the this keyword refers to the guestList instance of LoadVars, which is holding the newly loaded data. Variable names in the original data become property names of the guestList instance and can be accessed as you would access a property of any instance.

```
// create new LoadVars object
guestList = new LoadVars();

// function to execute when data completes loading
guestList.onLoad = function(){
    //trace guest name
    trace(this.guest1);
}

// load data into my LoadVars
guestList.load("guest_list_data.txt");
```

You can also pass data from your movie with the LoadVars object. Instead of a .txt file, you might want to load a .cfm file instead and pass variable/value pairs to a query. In this case, format your URL address much as you would with the getURL example.

```
myLoadVars.load("loadVarsData.cfm?a=22&b=12");
```

You can also send data with the send() method of the LoadVars object:

```
myLoadVars = new LoadVars();
myLoadVars.a = 22;
myLoadVars.b = 12;
myLoadVars.send("loadVarsData.cfm", "_self", "GET");
```

As you can see, the LoadVars object is very useful for loading and handling simple external data. The next section introduces you to how this external data should be formatted.

EMBEDDING DATA IN A TEXT DOCUMENT

The LoadVars example used a .txt source file with the data formatted as follows:

```
&a=22&b=12&c="this is a string, and can have whitespace"
```

Whitespace can interfere with the data parsing process in this format, so be careful about leaving spaces between elements in your data unless they are between quotes, in which case you can leave spaces that will be read and formatted when they go into a text field.

You can also embed data in the Embed and Object tags used to embed the .swf file into an HTML document. This can be used to pass data needed to initialize your application. The following is a simple example of this technique. Note that the variable is created just after the source name.

```
<OBJECT>
<PARAM NAME="movie"
        ➥VALUE= "movie.swf?title=Gallery&imageFiles=images/image1.jpg">
<EMBED src="/support/flash/ts/documents/movie.swf?
➥title=Gallery&imageFiles=images/image1.jpg">
</EMBED>
</OBJECT>
```

What this code does is tell the .swf file embedded in this HTML document that the value of title is Gallery, and that the value of imageFiles is images/image1.jpg. These variable/value pairs can now be used by the .swf.

14

XML DATA

If the data you are using in Flash becomes complicated, it can be cumbersome to format it in a text file or embed it in an HTML document. This is where XML comes in handy.

INTRODUCTION TO XML

XML, which stands for Extensible markup language, is a tag-based markup language for structuring data files, especially for passing data between applications. For example, a server-side database application can pass data to a client-side Flash application formatted as an XML file. XML looks similar to HTML because they are both tag-based markup languages. However, XML is more loosely defined. HTML has several predefined tags such as <p> and <h1>. Although specific applications of XML have predefined tags (as in CML for Chemistry), you can create your own tag definitions in generic XML.

An XML document consists of nested elements called *nodes*. Each pair of beginning tags and closing tags is a node. The elements between an opening tag and its closing tag also make up a node. The *nested nodes* (the element nodes inside the outer pair of tag nodes) have a parent/child relationship with the outermost node, which is called the *base node*. A base node is simply the outermost node in an XML structure. The sets of nodes within the parent node are *siblings*.

The following is an example of a simple XML data structure that uses the same data used in the previous LoadVars example. This is the same data and variable/value pairs, but in a different format. The tags are user-defined, and I designed this particular XML data structure. As you practice with XML, you'll design your own user-defined XML tags.

```
<myData>
    <a>22</a>
    <b>12</b>
</myData>
```

Although this example may seem more involved than the LoadVars version, it illustrates how the same data would be formatted. If you wanted to expand this example and add several more data points, the embedded data of the LoadVars version can become unwieldy, whereas the XML format makes the same data easier to read.

XML nodes can have attributes similar to HTML tag attributes, which are variable name/value pairs included inside the brackets. Each node can have several attributes. Nodes must have a closing tag, but a syntax shorthand for empty nodes is to combine the opening and closing tags into a single tag. This is advised when using attributes with no text element for a pair of tags to enclose. In the following, this single tag syntax is used for information on each image. Each node represents a single image. In this shorthand form, the closing slash is what serves as the closing tag, and closes the img node.

```
<images>
    <img title="photo1" url="photo1.jpg" />
    <img title="photo2" url="photo2.jpg" />
```

This XML structure tells Flash that there are two objects in this list of images, and what the title and URL of each object is.

Designing a well-formed XML data structure requires attention to the character of the data itself. If each node has the same set of variables, you might want to use attributes instead of nested nodes because attributes can be parsed quickly by Flash. On the other hand, if your data is more globular in structure and each node has its own internal data structure with unique variables, a nested node structure might be more appropriate.

Now that you have a basic understanding of how to structure data with XML, you are ready to learn how to use it in Flash.

IMPORTING XML DOCUMENTS

Importing XML documents into your Flash project is a fairly simple process that makes use of the XML() object in Flash. Just as with the LoadVars object, the XML object includes an onLoad event handler that executes when data finishes loading.

You should note that it is important to tell the XML object to ignore the whitespace in the document. *Whitespace* includes all extra returns or tabs in the document that don't actually contain any data. This way, the XML object works only with nodes and ignores the whitespace formatting, which makes the XML document much easier to read. You do this by setting the ingoreWhite property of the XML object to true, as shown in the following example.

```
// create a new XML object for the XML formatted data
myXML = new XML();

// make sure that whitespace is ignored during parsing
myXML.ignoreWhite = true;

// function to execute when XML done loading
myXML.onLoad = function(){
    // do something with data
}

// load external xml file
myXML.load("myData.xml");
```

> **TIP**
>
> If you use the following code in the myXML.onLoad function, your XML data is traced to the output panel when you run a test:
>
> ```
> trace( myXML.toString() );
> ```
>
> This is a quick and easy way to test and make sure that your XML data is loading.

Flash's XML object enables you to load XML-formatted data and use its onLoad event handler. The next section discusses some of the other methods of the XML object.

14

USING XML DATA

You can now get your XML-formatted data into Flash. Now what? The XML object has several properties that give you access to the nodes.

- firstChild returns the first child of a node.
- hasChildNodes returns true if the node has children.
- lastChild returns the last child of a node.
- nextSibling returns the next node from the same generation.
- nodeName returns the name (in the tag) of a node. If the node is a text node, it returns a 3.
- nodeType returns 1 if it is a tag node or a 3 if it is a text node.
- nodeValue returns the content of a text node or null if it is a tag node.
- parentNode returns the parent node of a node.
- previousSibling returns the previous node from the same generation.
- attributes returns the attributes of a tag node, if they have been defined.
- childNodes returns a list of child nodes. childNodes.length returns the number of elements in the list of child nodes.

After the XML-formatted data is loaded into an XML object in Flash, that's where it lives and you can access it from that object. One way to see that data in the authoring environment is to trace the entire contents of your XML object instance (myXML) to the output window, as in the following example:

```
trace(myXML.toString() );
```

Test the movie and you can see all your lovely XML in the output window.

You can also explore your XML object with the debugger's Variables panel. When you play your movie, it presents the information for each node in your XML object (see Figure 14.1).

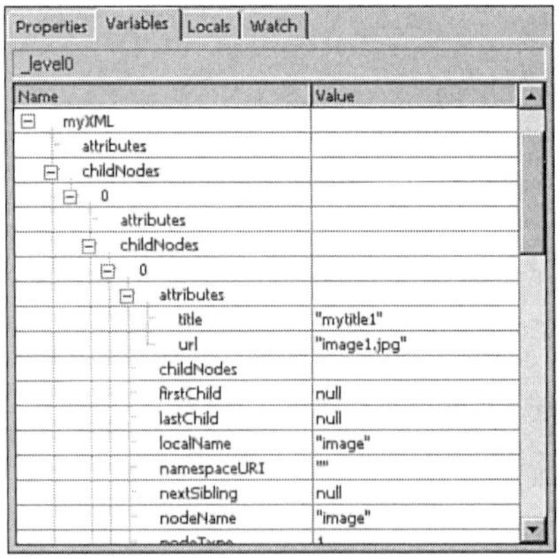

Figure 14.1
View of node information in the Variables panel of the debugger.

Now would be a good time to look at an example of how to use these properties of the XML object to get access to XML-formatted data. First, however, take another look at the simple XML data structure we created earlier. In the following example, two variable-value data pairs are formatted in XML.

```
<myData>
    <a>22</a>
    <b>12</b>
</myData>
```

As you can see, the first node is `<myData>`. You can get some interesting information about it with ActionScript. For example, you can get its name, even if you didn't know it ahead of time:

```
// show the name of the XML's first node
trace(myXML.firstChild.nodeName);
```

That's all well and good, but what you really need is a variable name/value pair equivalent to a=22 that you can then use elsewhere in the application. How do you get that? Well, you know that the node named a has a child node, which is a text node with a value of 22. So, in ActionScript, you can write the following:

```
var a_name:String = myXML.firstChild.childNodes[0].nodeName;
trace(a_name);
```

This should return an output of a. This creates a local variable that holds the name of the node in which you're interested. Next, you could run a conditional to test whether the local variable name is the same as the node name before proceeding:

```
if(a_name == "a"){
    // this is the node we want, continue
}
```

This is not a requirement, but it gives you more ways to manipulate your data after you've gotten it into Flash. I mention it now mainly to illustrate the relationships between the nodes, as well as how to access their data with ActionScript.

Next, you can get the value of the a node's child node and assign it to a local variable (which is also called a):

```
var a:Number = myXML.firstChild.childNodes[0].firstChild.nodeValue;
trace("a = " + a);
```

When you test this, you should see a = 22 in the output panel.

Look at another simple example, this time with attributes. This time, the goal is to package information about image files, such as the title and URL address of each image in the list. You've seen this example earlier in the chapter:

```
<images>
    <img title="photo1" url="photo1.jpg" />
    <img title="photo2" url="photo2.jpg" />
</images>
```

To keep the code shorter and easier to read, you can give your node paths a name. For example, you can give the `myXML.firstChild` path the name `path`. This turns this code

```
img_0.title = myXML.firstChild.childNodes[0].firstChild.attributes.title;
```

into the following code:

```
// save root XML path as local variable
var myPath:String = myXML.firstChild;

img_0.title = myPath.childNodes[0].firstChild.attributes.title;
```

This technique is especially helpful when the data structure gets more complicated, with many levels of nested nodes.

To get the image title for the second node, you can use the following:

```
img_1.title = myPath.childNodes[1].firstChild.attributes.title;
```

This gives you the next node in the list of images. You can keep track of which node you're on, much as with an array. Both XML nodes and array elements are numbered. The count starts at zero, so the first node is at `childNodes[0]`, the second at `childNodes[1]`, and so on. If you have several images described in an XML file, it would be a good idea to loop through them rather than write out line after line of complicated XML navigation. By using the node count, you can keep track of how many times you need to run a loop that does something with all the nodes describing the images. The following is an example of such a loop:

```
// get number of images to process
var i_max:Number = myXML.firstChild.childNodes.length;

// save root path as local variable
var path = myXML.firstChild;

for(var i=0; i<=i_max; i++){
    // save dynamic name as local variable
    var img:Object = ["image_" + i];

    // save title for this image
    img.title = path.childNodes[i].attributes.title;

    // save url for this image
    img.title = path.childNodes[i].attributes.url;
}
```

Working with XML data in Flash can be a challenge, but the XML object gives you a lot of methods for accessing that data. In the next section, you learn some of the basics of building XML data with Flash.

BUILDING XML DATA

If you want to send data out of your Flash file to the server you can build XML data at run-time. In this section, you learn how to build XML data with ActionScript. One of the benefits of this is that you can use XML to format data passed to Flash from a database, create a user interface that enables the end user to edit the data content during run-time, and send the edited data in XML format back to the database.

Imagine you want to build an XML file to hold information for the guest list for a dinner party. Starting simply, you need some basic information for each guest, including his or her name. The XML structure for this data might look something like this:

```
<guestlist>
    <guest>Joe Smith</guest>
    <guest>Sally Jones</guest>
</guestlist>
```

To build this XML-formatted data structure from ActionScript, you must first create a new XML object to hold your data as shown in the following example:

```
guestXML = new XML();
```

Next, you create a node for your guest list and then attach it to an existing node as follows:

```
newList = guestXML.createElement("guestlist");
guestXML.appendChild(newList);
```

To add a node for a guest, you must first create the new node. This new node is the parent node; you can think of it as a wrapper for all the nodes that will contain information about the guest. Next, create a text node for the guest's name. Finally, append the text node to the guest node, which nests the node containing the guest's name inside of the wrapper for the guest's information, as shown in the following example:

```
// create and append node for guest
newGuest = guestXML.createElement("guest");
newText = guestXML.createTextNode("Joe Smith");
newGuest.appendChild(newText);
```

At this point, the guest node is just hanging out in the XML object and is not yet part of the XML structure. To add the new guest node to the list node, do the following:

```
newList.appendChild(newGuest);
```

This process must be done for each guest that you want to add to the XML data.

What if you want to add an attribute to the guest node? For example, imagine you want to include the phone numbers of your guests. No problem. Before appending the newGuest node, add a line similar to the following:

```
newGuest.attributes.phone = "555-5555"
```

After your data is in XML format, you can send it back to the server, where it can be stored for future use.

SENDING XML DOCUMENTS TO THE SERVER

To send XML-formatted data back to the server, use the send() method of the XML object as shown in the following example:

```
myXML.send("getxml.cgi");
```

This sends your XML object to the server. As you can see, XML-formatted data can be passed back and forth from your user interface (built with Flash) and a server-side database.

14

LOADING EXTERNAL IMAGES AND MOVIES

Flash is wonderful. Not only can you load data that is mostly numeric or text, but you can also load assets such as images and even other `.swf` files.

GLOBAL `loadMovie()`

The global `loadMovie` method enables you to load an image (JPG, GIF, or PNG) or `.swf` file into any target movie clip, and requires the name of the file that will be loaded and a path to the target clip into which the file will be loaded. The image or `.swf` file replaces any contents of the movie clip and is aligned by its upper-left corner at the registration point (crosshairs) inside the clip. This technique could be useful when you want to load images into different targets.

> **TIP**
>
> It is usually easiest to create a movie clip with a placeholder rectangle the same size as the `.swf` or image that you are trying to load. This enables you to visually place it and know where your loaded content will be landing.

In the following code, the `image.jpg` image file is loaded into the `target_mc` movie clip:

```
loadMovie("image.jpg", target_mc);
```

This code can be used with a button event handler to provide a user interface to a selection of images:

```
myButton.onRelease = function(){
    loadMovie("image1.jpg", logo_mc);
};
```

With the global `loadMovie` method, you can load images and other `.swf` assets into any target clip in your project. However, the global `loadMovie` method is just one way to approach loading external assets. The next two sections discuss approaches that are preferred over the global `loadMovie` method.

MovieClip.loadMovie()

The `loadMovie` method of the `MovieClip` class permits you to dynamically load external assets into a target clip that has been created at run-time. This is useful because it can reduce your project's initial file size and allow for more flexibility in your code. In fact, this method for loading external images and `.swf` files is preferred over the `global loadMovie` method.

First, create an empty movie clip as the target clip:

```
this.createEmptyMovieClip("target_mc", 100);
```

After you have a target movie clip, you can load an external `.swf` or image file into it:

```
target_mc.loadMovie(image.jpg);
```

The major drawback of using the loadMovie method is that there is no built-in method to handle the loading progress of external files.

MovieClipLoader()

The MovieClipLoader class is used to load external resources (such as .swf, .jpeg, .gif, and .png files) and utilize the built-in event handlers of a MovieClipLoader object. It works much like the event handlers in the LoadVars and XML objects. You can either create a new MovieClipLoader object for each file you will be loading or use a single MovieClipLoader object to handle the loading of several files. If you're loading only a few assets into the .swf, you might want to create a new MovieClipLoader for each asset. On the other hand, if you are loading many assets, a single MovieClipLoader can manage them all without stressing the user's processor.

In the following example, an empty movie clip is created to hold the incoming image file. Then a new object is created to be a listener for the MovieClipLoader (which is created soon). In the listener function, called mclListener.onLoadInit, the code to be applied to the holder clip is applied after it holds the external image file.

Why do this? When an external file is loaded into a movie clip, it overwrites any existing code on that clip (just as it replaces any visuals). So any changes to the clip must be done after the external image or .swf is loaded.

When the listener functions are defined, you can create the MovieClipLoader object instance and register the listener. After all this preparation, you can finally load the external image into the holder clip with the MovieClipLoader.

```
// create an empty clip into which the image is loaded
this.createEmptyMovieClip("image_mc", this.getNextHighestDepth());

// create an object to use as a listener
var mclListener:Object = new Object();

//define a function for the onLoadInit event handler
mclListener.onLoadInit = function(target_mc:MovieClip) {
    // position target clip on stage
    target_mc._x = Stage.width/2-target_mc._width/2;
    target_mc._y = Stage.height/2-target_mc._width/2;

    // resize image to 40%
    target_mc._xscale = 40;
    target_mc._yscale = 40;
};

// create a new MovieClipLoader
var image1_mc:MovieClipLoader = new MovieClipLoader();

//register the listener to the MovieClipLoader
image1_mc.addListener(mclListener);

// load an image into the target movie clip
image1_mc.loadClip("image_url.jpg", image_mc);
```

14

The advantage of the `movieClipLoader` is that it can respond to more events related to loading of the data than the other approaches to loading external assets.

MovieClipLoader EVENTS

With the `MovieClipLoader`, you can listen for various events during the loading process, including the following:

- `onLoadStart`—Invoked when the first bytes of the downloaded file have been written to disk.

- `onLoadProgress`—Invoked during the loading process. `MovieClipLoader.getProgress()` can be called at any time during the load process.

- `onLoadComplete`—Invoked when the entire downloaded file has been written to disk.

- `onLoadInit`—Invoked after the downloaded file's first frame actions have executed. When invoked, you can set the properties, use methods, and interact with the loaded file.

- `onLoadError`—Invoked if the file fails to load completely.

When these events are invoked, you can run code specific to that event. For example, you can use the `onLoadProgress` event handler to give your end user feedback on how the download is progressing.

MovieClipLoader METHODS

There are several methods in the `MovieClipLoader` class, and they involve the loading and unloading of external assets. Following is a list of methods that can be applied to an instance of the `MovieClipLoader`.

- `addListener()`—Registers an object to receive notification when a `MovieClipLoader` event handler is invoked.

- `getProgress()`—Returns the number of bytes loaded and the total number of bytes for a file that is being loaded using `MovieClipLoader.loadClip()`.

- `loadClip()`—Loads a `.swf` or image file into a movie clip in the Flash Player while the original movie is playing (in other words, it loads an external file during run-time).

- `removeListener()`—Deletes an object that was registered as a listener.

- `unloadClip()`—Removes a movie clip that was loaded with `MovieClipLoader.loadClip()`.

Now that you know how to load external resources into your Flash application, you need to know something about the security issues involved.

SECURITY FEATURES ADDED SINCE FLASH PLAYER 7

Back with version 7 of the Flash Player, Macromedia introduced new features that improve security, including those discussed in the following sections.

CROSS-DOMAIN POLICY FILE

If you are planning to load data from a domain (such as www.macromedia.com) or subdomain (such as store.macromedia.com) other than the one in which your Flash .swf file resides, you need to set up a cross-domain policy file. Without it, the Flash player pops up a warning box from the browser asking users whether they want to download data from a second domain.

Domains must be an exact match. For example, if you have a Flash .swf file on the www.mydomain.com domain, data on the data.mydomain.com subdomain is seen as belonging to a different domain and requires a cross-domain policy file.

A *cross-domain policy file* is a small XML-structured file on the domain server root, as shown in the following example. It contains a list of domains that are allowed to access those files. This tightens up the security of Flash, and offers some protection to end users because only files from domains listed in the policy file can be loaded into the host .swf without triggering an alert box. The file must be named crossdomain.xml and saved in the document root directory of the server from which your movie is accessing a file:

```
<cross-domain-policy>
    <allow-access-from domain="www.domain_to_allow_here.com" />
</cross-domain-policy>
```

You can list more than one domain. You can also use * to permit subdomains in one line.

```
<cross-domain-policy>
    <allow-access-from domain="www.mydomain.com" />
    <allow-access-from domain="*.anotherdomain.com" />
</cross-domain-policy>
```

With the cross-domain policy file, you can control from which domains external content can be loaded into your projects. The Flash Player automatically looks for this file in the domain server root of the file to be loaded. The next section discusses situations when you may need to tell Flash to look for a policy file in a specific location.

System.security.loadPolicyFile()

You need to use System.security.loadPolicyFile() to tell Flash where to look for your policy file in the following situations:

- The server in question serves through a port other than a standard port.
- You want to store your policy file in a location other than the root directory.
- You want to name the policy file something other than crossdomain.xml.

14

In the following example, the policy file is named `myPolicy.xml` and is located in the `flash` directory.

```
System.security.loadPolicyFile("http://www.mysite.com/flash/myPolicy.xml");
```

This code collects the list of allowed domains listed in the policy file in the specified location.

For more information on the security enhancements, see the Macromedia Developer Center article, "Security Changes in Macromedia Flash Player 7," which can be found online at http://www.macromedia.com/devnet/mx/flash/articles/fplayer_security.html. For information on the security enhancements introduced in Flash 8, see the article "Security Changes in Flash Player 8," which can be found at http://www.macromedia.com/devnet/flash/articles/fplayer8_security.html.

DETECTION OF THE FLASH PLAYER

To set up detection of the Flash Player, go to File, Publish Settings in the Flash authoring environment and choose the HTML tab. Check the Detect Flash Version option to turn on Flash detection. The version to check for is automatically set to 8, but you can specify from which dot release you want to update. For example, if Macromedia makes a minor change to the player, it might be released as version 8.0.1.

Although it is true that over 94% of the web browsers include the Flash 7 Player plug-in, it still a good idea to provide non-Flash versions of any critical content for audiences that have older machines or browsers. For example, if you're using Flash for navigation of an HTML website, you might also want to include an HTML version of that navigation at the bottom of the page. Another option is to create two side-by-side sites, one HTML and one Flash-based, and send users to the correct version after detecting whether or not they have the Flash Player. In addition, offer a link on your page to the Flash Player download page to give users a non-automatic option to acquire the most recent player version.

The Macromedia website has a great resource for learning about Flash Player detection, including the new Express Install options, at http://www.macromedia.com/software/flashplayer/download/detection_kit/.

As you can see, Flash has a lot of options for bringing in external data and resources. Although this chapter has focused mainly on data and images, the next chapter focuses on sound and video.

TROUBLESHOOTING

I've formatted my data in a text file, but when I pull it into Flash it doesn't all show up.

Whitespace can affect how text file data is parsed by Flash. Check for any spaces between important characters in your data file.

When I test loading my data with loadVars()*, instead of the traced value in the output box,* undefined *is displayed in the output box.*

There are several possible causes to check for. Check that the variable name is spelled the same in your ActionScript as it is in the external data file. Also, check that you have the correct path to the data file itself.

When I try to get the name of a text node, I get an error in the output panel.

Text nodes in XML don't have names. If you've named a node for a variable, and its child node contains the value of that variable, you need to get the name of the parent node and the value of the child node.

I've written a function that uses the MovieClipLoader *method and resizes an image after the image finishes loading, but when I run a test the image never resizes.*

Check to be sure that you registered the function as a listener to the MovieClipLoader and that the function is packaged as one of the MovieClipLoader event handlers.

BEST PRACTICES—WHICH METHOD TO USE WHEN LOADING DATA

If your images are the same physical size that you want them to be on the stage and they are optimized for small download file size, you can use the MovieClip.loadMovie method. However, if you need to do anything to the external file after it's loaded, you're much better off using the MovieClipLoader approach. This way, you can resize the files or execute other modifications when they're loaded into a target clip.

When you use loadXML versus loadVars depends on the format in which the incoming data will be and how much processing of that data you want to perform. When using loadVars, the external data file is not designed to be easy for you to read, but the variable name/value pairs transfer directly into property name/value pairs of the object instance into which it's loaded. On the other hand, the XML data format has the advantage of being easier to read and edit. However, you must take the extra step of extracting the data from the XML object if you want to use it as the property of an object instance.

14

Enhancing Projects with Sound and Video

15

INTEGRATING VIDEO

One of the most popular things to do with Flash is to add video to websites. Because of the high penetration of the Flash Player in browsers, you can include video in your site without necessarily having to use sophisticated server technology to deliver it. Flash's video tools make adding video to your projects an amazingly easy thing to do. This chapter covers your options for importing, creating FLV content, and playback in Flash.

There are two main ways to add video to your Flash projects: either embed video into your Flash file during author-time, or dynamically load external video files in a special media playback component during run-time. The following sections discuss each of these options in more detail.

EMBEDDED VIDEO

Embedding video in a Flash document involves importing it into the file and actually placing it either on your main timeline or in a movie clip timeline. This imported video file must be prepared in advance: its length and content edited and saved in its final form. In addition, the frame rate of the video you import and the Flash document frame rate must be the same.

The most common video file types you will encounter when working on Flash video projects are .avi, .mov, and .flv. AVI is a Windows format, but is supported on Macs if QuickTime is installed. MOV is a QuickTime format, and FLV is the Flash video format, which has quickly become popular because of its stunning file compression size combined with higher quality video. You will find that in most cases, other file formats are converted to the FLV format for use on the Web.

The list of supported video file formats grows depending on what other software is installed on your system. If you have QuickTime 7 (or later) installed (Windows or Mac), the following video file formats can be imported into Flash: .avi, .dv, .mpg, .mpeg, and .mov. If DirectX 9 (or later) is installed on a Windows system, you can also import video files with the .wmv and .asf Windows media file formats.

When you import a video file and embed it into your Flash project, it becomes a part of the published document. You can actually see the individual frames of the video on the Flash timeline. This gives you a lot of control over the individual frames of the video; however, it can greatly increase the file size of your project. Therefore, if the playback time is more than 10 seconds, you should consider using progressively downloaded video or streaming video with the Flash Communication Server, as discussed later in this chapter.

To import video into Flash, go to File, Import, Import Video. This brings up the Video Import Wizard (see Figure 15.1). When you are in the Video Import Wizard, you have the option to browse for the video file you want to import. Select the file and click on the Next button.

TIP

> At this point, if you don't have either DirectShow 9 (Windows) or QuickTime 7 or higher (Mac or Windows) installed on your system, you will get an error message. If this happens, take some time to download and install either program.

Figure 15.1
The Video Import Wizard.

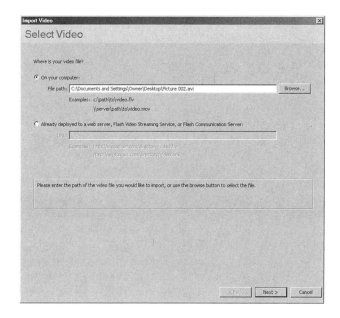

Next, you are asked how you would like to deploy the video. If you're embedding a small video clip, select the Embed Video in SWF and Play in Timeline option and then click on the Next button. We discuss other options later in this chapter.

At the next screen (shown in Figure 15.2), you can select what type of symbol you want to embed your video from the following options:

- **Embedded video**—The video is integrated into the timeline selected when you import your video. This could be useful when you want to work with the frames of a video on the main timeline, especially if the resulting .swf contains just the video.

- **Movie clip**—This option gives you the most control over playback of the video because movie clips can be accessed and controlled with ActionScript.

- **Graphic**—This option encloses the video in a symbol that belongs to the main timeline. This gives you fewer options for controlling the video because a graphic symbol is not accessible to ActionScript.

15

Figure 15.2
The Embedding
Options panel.

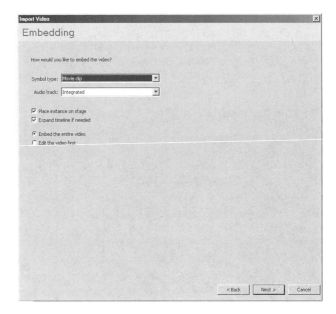

You can select the option to place an instance of the symbol containing the embedded video on the stage. You can also expand the timeline, if needed, to fit all the frames in the video automatically. You usually should have this option checked for embedded projects, so that your timeline is long enough to hold all of the frames needed for the embedded video. You can select the Edit option to trim the clip's start or end point before you embed the file into Flash. If you choose to edit, a new panel comes up that enables you to trim the video by resetting the start and/or end frames. This does not change the file size, but changes how many frames are visible on the timeline.

The final step is to select the video encoding profile for your video. The *video encoding profile* determines what level of compression is applied to your video, which is based on the version of the player for which you want to publish. The level of compression is determined by which codec you select. A *codec* is an algorithm that controls how video files are compressed during encoding and then decompressed during playback. If you're publishing for the Flash 8 Player, your end users will benefit from the use of the On2 VP6 video codec because it optimally combines video quality and small file size. If you're publishing for the Flash 7 Player, you should choose the Sorenson Spark video codec. This is also a great compression strategy, just not as small as the On2 codec.

After you select the video encoding profile, click the Finish button, wait for the Flash Video Encoding Process to complete, and you're finished. Flash has now encoded your video into the `.flv` format and embedded the video into the FLA file.

If you embed the video as a movie clip, you have access to some interesting properties. You can change the alpha and color properties for the movie clip instance, and by definition, the video inside the movie clip. You can also use the Blend modes that are available for movie clip symbols. However, applying these effects to video is processor intensive, and can cause problems for end users with slower systems.

You can also use ActionScript to control the playback of video embedded as a movie clip. For example, to stop the video from playing more than once in a continual loop, you can open the video instance, add an actions layer, and put a `stop();` action in a blank keyframe on the last frame of the video's timeline. If you wanted the video to restart after the user clicks on the video itself, you could use the following code in the main timeline:

```
myVideo_mc.onRelease = function(){
    this.gotoAndPlay(1);
}
```

If you wanted the video to restart when the user clicks a rewind button, you could use the following code on the main timeline. This code is programmatically attached to your rewind button instance.

```
rewind_mc.onRelease = function(){
    myVideo_mc.gotoAndPlay(1);
}
```

You need to pay close attention to scope in a situation like this. Although using the keyword `this` is correct, you can also address the video movie clip directly because it is assumed you are talking to the timeline on which the `rewind_mc` button lives.

As with other movie clips, a video embedded in a movie clip can respond to most traditional button or movie clip event handlers and can use all the same timeline control methods to stop, rewind, pause, and play the video embedded on the timeline. The next section explores other simple ways to accomplish these tasks with video.

PROGRESSIVE DOWNLOAD VIDEO

Now that you know something about how to create videos in FLV format, and balance video quality versus file size, you can move into a more sophisticated way of working with video in Flash. Projects with progressive video download enable users to download the video only when they want to and to watch the movie almost instantly. Users don't have to wait for the entire video to download before they can start watching it. Although this may sound like streaming video, it's not. Streaming video is covered in a later section of this chapter.

The *progressive download* process buffers a little bit of video into the end user's computer and then starts to play the video while the rest continues to download. One big advantage of progressive video downloading is that you can keep your video assets external to the Flash file. This is much more convenient for the end user because it greatly reduces the wait, while the SWF file is downloading.

The progressive video process is also convenient for you as you develop your project. Imagine that you're almost finished integrating video into a mid-size to large project. Suddenly, the client (or project manager) drops a bomb and says that all the video has to be replaced with new versions, and more clips need to be added. If you've built the project with embedded video, this could be a problem. But because progressively downloaded video files are external, the changes are as simple as swapping the existing video files with newly edited video that has the same filenames and then adding the extra files into your directory and project architecture. This is all possible because the video file isn't modified by Flash. Instead, you're using Flash to store information on which frames of the video you want to play for the end user. The other frames are there; you're just not playing them.

VIDEO IMPORT WIZARD

To create a Flash document that progressively downloads a single FLV movie in a special video display component, open the Import Video Wizard by selecting File, Import, Import Video, as shown in Figure 15.3. Yes, you read correctly, you need to go to go to the Import Video screen even though the video will ultimately be an external file. This import process is more of a preparation for the display of the video than it is about actually importing the video itself. When you have the wizard open, you can set the path to the video you are going to import just as you would for importing video to embed.

You are next asked how you would like to deploy the video. Select the Progressive Download from a Web Server option.

Figure 15.3
Selecting the Progressive Download deployment method.

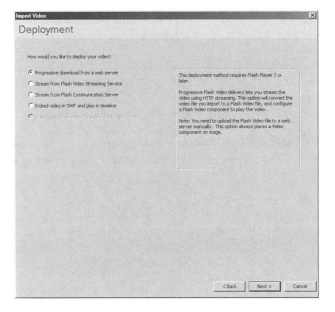

In the next step, you can select the video encoding profile and preview the quality your setting will produce. As you did earlier in the chapter, choose the On2 VP6 codec for Flash Player 8 or the Sorensen Spark codec for Flash Player 7.

In the Skinning step, you select how the user interface for the Flash Video Playback component will appear and function. Many skins are provided with Flash. These skins provide the look of the video player, but also include interactive elements that enable the end user to

15

control the playback of the video. If you want to use a custom skin, select Custom Skin URL from the Skin drop-down menu and enter the relative directory path of the skin's .swf file that you want to use into the URL field. This path is relative to the directory of the .swf into which the video will be loaded. If you want to just play the video without giving the end user control over the player (such as stop, start, rewind, and the loading indicator), select None from the skin menu. Figure 15.4 shows some of the different skins that come with Flash.

Figure 15.4
Several skins for the Video Playback Component are available in Flash.

The last screen of the wizard displays some useful information including the current location of the video you selected for encoding and the relative path where your Flash file will find the encoded video file (.flv). To complete the process, click on the Finish button.

After the video file is encoded, notice that a new file has been created in the directory where the original video file resides. This is the newly encoded .flv version of the video. In addition, you can see that the FLVPlayback component is now on the stage of your Flash file, all set to load the .flv movie file at run-time.

Now all you need to do to play the file on your web server is publish an HTML display document that includes the SWF and upload the FLV, SWF, and HTML documents to your server.

TIP

When you are ready to publish your project on a web server, you need to upload the external video files, the SWFs that play the video, and all the HTML files that display the SWFs to the server to see your video display in the HTML document. Be aware that you cannot see the video display when you test your HTML documents locally in a browser. You can see them only after you have uploaded them to your web server. However, you can view the video by playing the SWF locally.

FLVPLAYBACK COMPONENT

In addition to automatically creating an FLVPlayback component as a part of the Video Import Wizard as described in the previous section, you can also manually insert it into your projects and set it up to play any external FLV files that you want to include. This manual method is helpful when you create your FLV content in Sorensen Squeeze or with the Flash 8 Video Encoder, which is covered later in this chapter. Figure 15.5 shows the Playback component in the Components panel.

15

Figure 15.5
FLVPlayback compo-
nent in the
Components panel.

In the Components panel, (Window, Components), open the FLV Playback Player 8 menu
item. Drag the FLVPlayback component from the menu to the stage. When you place it on
the stage, it automatically adds the component to your document's library, so from now on
you can go to your library to pull out a new instance of the component. Figure 15.6 shows
an instance of the FLVPlayback component on the stage.

Figure 15.6
The FLVPlayback com-
ponent on the stage,
with component and
library panels open.

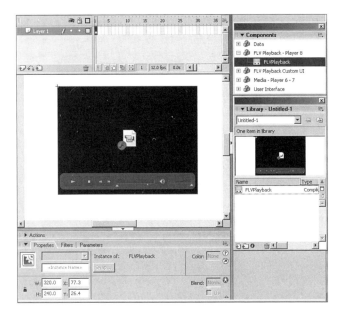

After you have an instance on the stage, you're ready to set the parameters for the component, including the video source file and skin. Select the component instance on the stage
and open the Component Inspector panel (see Figure 15.7).

Setting the parameters for the FLVPlayback component is easy. Double-click on one of the
parameters and either a drop-down menu or a dialog box opens to set that parameter. For
instance, to tell the component what FLV to play, set the content path. Double-click the
Content Path item in the Component Inspector and a dialog box opens that you can use to
browse your system and select the FLV file to load into the component (see Figure 15.8).

Figure 15.7
The Component
Inspector panel.

Figure 15.8
The Content Path
dialog box for the
FLVPlayback
component.

As with the Video Import Wizard, the FLVPlayback component enables you to choose from a selection of skins with different styles and functions. Double-click the Skin parameter to bring up the Select Skin interface, which has a drop-down menu of skins to choose from and a preview window so that you can see what you've selected before clicking on the OK button.

If you give the component an instance name, you can access it with ActionScript. You can use ActionScript to set the value for the contentPath parameter dynamically, rather than with the Component Inspector. You can use the following code, placed on a keyframe of the main timeline, to load an .flv into an instance of the FLVPlayback component.

```
family_vid1.contentPath = "family_vid1.flv";
```

The FLVPlayback component combines flexibility with ease of use. The capability to use ActionScript to dynamically set parameter values is a powerful feature. In my own work, I don't use components, but this one is working its way into my projects. Although you can use the Import Video Wizard to prepare a single .flv and the component that plays it, you can also use the standalone Flash 8 Video Encoder to batch process many video files at once.

15

FLASH 8 VIDEO ENCODER

The Import Video Wizard is great for importing a single video file, but if you're working with several video files, you should get familiar with the Flash 8 Video Encoder, which is automatically installed when Flash 8 Professional installs on your computer. To open it directly, use the Windows Start menu to navigate to All Programs, Macromedia. You can also locate the applications folder in which Flash 8 was installed and open Macromedia Flash 8 Video Encoder directly and/or create a shortcut (alias) on the desktop for future use. Figure 15.9 shows the Flash 8 Video Encoder.

Figure 15.9
The Flash 8 Video Encoder.

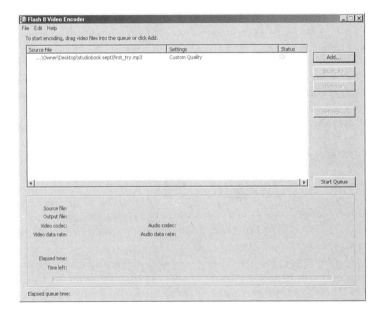

Whereas the wizard steps you through the process, you can control all the settings directly when creating multiple FLV files with the Video Encoder. With the Flash 8 Video Encoder you can build a list (queue) of one or more files to be processed all in one batch.

To add a file to the batch processing queue, click the Add button and browse for the file on your system. You can delete files in the queue list by selecting them and clicking the Remove button.

When added to the queue, a file can be duplicated and then configured with its own settings. This way, you can process one original video file and create multiple compiled files with different compression levels at once. For example, one might be set for end users with broadband access and another might be set for slower connections. This is incredibly helpful when creating web projects.

To configure a file's settings, highlight the file in the list and click on the Settings button, which brings up the Flash Video Encoding Settings dialog box (see Figure 15.10). Here you can select a compression profile and assign an output filename.

Figure 15.10
The Flash Video
Encoding Settings
panel.

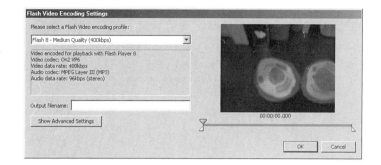

You can also configure advanced settings such as custom encoding options, cue points, and crop and trim options (see Figure 15.11). Note that when you crop the video area and trim the ends of the video, you are marking only the part of the video that Flash plays, so this does not change its file size. To optimize the file size, you should make these changes in an external video editor before associating the file with Flash.

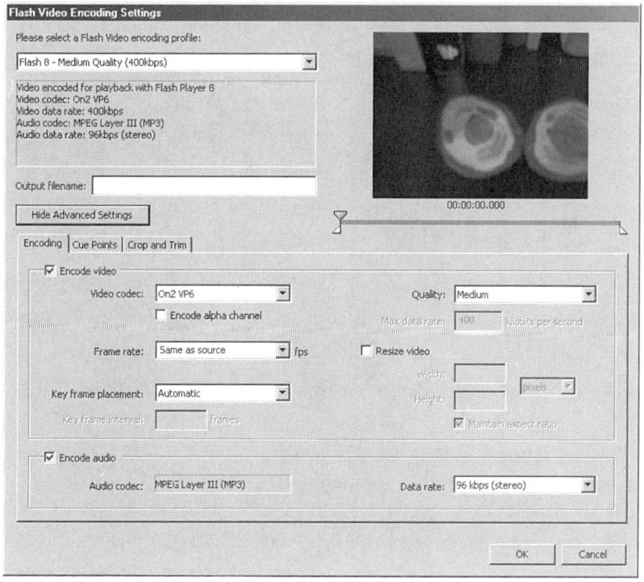

Figure 15.11
Advanced Flash Video
Encoding Settings.

When you're ready to begin the batch process of your video files, click the Start Queue button. The Encoder shows you a preview of each video as it's being encoded, along with the settings for that file. If you don't like what you see, you can stop the encoding and reset the file's settings.

15

STREAMING VIDEO

True streaming video is never cached in your browser as a progressive download is. It is streamed by special server-side software and really is played on-demand. In this case, the special software is the Flash Communications Server. With streaming, a persistent connection is established between the Flash Player (the client) and the Flash Communications Server. As a result, streaming video has far more controls over buffer time and adjustments to accommodate different user connection speeds. If you're working with video that is more than 20–30 seconds long, or anticipate high traffic, you should consider using streaming video.

NOTE

> Flash Communications Server provides not only streaming video for your projects, but live multiuser streaming for video chat and video conferencing applications. For more information on the Flash Communication Server, check out the Macromedia Flash Communication Developer Center at http://www.macromedia.com/devnet/mx/flashcom/.

USING SOUND

There are many uses for sound in Flash. Sound can include a voiceover to a presentation, sound effects for an animation, user interaction cues, jukebox lineups, and any kind of ambient soundtrack for your site. Although Flash doesn't provide any sound-editing tools, it does give you a wide variety of options for embedding and playing external sound files for any type of project you are working on.

Flash has two types of playback sound. The first is event sound, which must be completely downloaded into the user's system before it begins playing. These types of sounds continue playing until stopped, when they either run to the end of their cycle or receive a command from ActionScript. Event sounds are used for short sound effects or other sounds that play over and over. The second type is streaming sound. Streaming sounds are synchronized to the timeline and begin playing as soon as enough data is downloaded for a few frames to play. They are used whenever the sound needs to be synced to an animation or when you want it to end at a specific moment on the timeline.

IMPORTING SOUNDS

By default, both Windows and Mac systems can import MP3 files into Flash. In addition to MP3, which is a compressed file format, Macs can import AIFF files and Windows can import WAV files into Flash. Additional audio file formats can be imported if QuickTime 4 or later is installed on your system. When you add multimedia to your Flash projects, always start with high-quality, uncompressed content whenever possible, which means 16-bit WAV or AIFF audio and `.mov` or `.avi` content for video. These files can then be compressed in Flash and encoded in the `.flv` format.

To import a sound file go to File, Import, Import to Library and select the file you want to import from your system files. Another way to import sound files into a Flash project is to drag them from a common library (Windows, Common Libraries, Sounds) to the library or onto the stage of your current Flash project.

ADDING SOUND TO YOUR TIMELINE

To add sound to any timeline you must first import the sound file as described in the previous section. Then create a new layer in the timeline for the sound, make sure this layer is selected, and create or select a blank keyframe on the new layer where you want the sound to begin. In the Property inspector, choose the name of the sound from the Sound menu. Choose your settings and add frames to the layer as needed for correct playback. See Figure 15.12 for an illustration of how to add sound to the timeline.

Figure 15.12
Adding sound to the timeline.

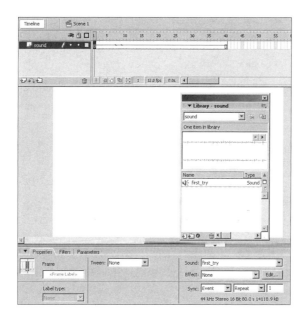

Adding sound to a button symbol instance is an easy way to learn this process. To start from scratch, draw a simple shape on the stage. Next, select the drawing and convert it to a symbol (Modify, Convert to Symbol), choose Button as the type, and give it a name. Go into symbol edit mode by double-clicking the symbol and you should see the four frames of a button timeline, as shown in Figure 15.13.

Figure 15.13
The four frames of a button symbol's timeline.

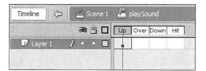

15

Begin by adding a new layer called *sound*. If you want to have the sound play when the user clicks on the button symbol, select the frame labeled "Down" and insert a blank keyframe (F7) on the new sound layer. With the blank keyframe selected, drag one of the sounds from the Window, Common Libraries, Sounds library to the stage. That's it! You've added sound to your button. Use Test Movie, (Cmd-Return) [Ctrl+Enter] to export the SWF, and the sound plays when you click on the button.

This is the same process you would use to add sound to any frame in the movie, changing the sync setting to fit the particular sound. The sound file plays at the same rate as any animation on the stage. To create an animated mini-music video, you could have your animation elements on their own layers of the timeline, and the music sound file on a separate layer.

CHANGING IMPORTED SOUND PROPERTIES

Although you can't really edit sounds within Flash, you can modify properties of those sounds and apply a number of effects to them. For example, you can change the envelope of the sound and add effects such as fade out. The envelope is basically the wrapping that Flash puts around the sound file, which tells Flash how to play back the file.

To edit a sound's properties in Flash, first select the frame in which the sound starts and then view the options in the Property inspector, as shown in Figure 15.14.

Figure 15.14
Property inspector for a sound.

In the Property inspector you can apply effects to your sound by selecting options from the Effect drop-down. These include Fade Out (the sound fades from its current volume to silence) and Fade Left to Right (the sound fades from the left speaker to the right speaker). To edit an existing effect or create a custom effect, click the Edit button next to the Effect drop-down menu. This brings up the Sound Edit Envelope panel (see Figure 15.15), where you can edit how the effects are applied to your sound. The upper view shows the left channel and the lower view shows the right channel. The ruler in the middle is the timeline for the sound, which enables you to trim the sound with the time-in and time-out handles on the left and right sides.

To change the effect, you can select one of the preset options (such as fade in or fade out) in the drop-down menu. To create your own custom effect, click anywhere on the upper or lower view to add a new point on the envelope rubber band. This point can be dragged up or down to raise the volume or lower it. Remember that just as with video, trimming a sound file doesn't decrease the file size. If you need to edit the sound for length, you should use a sound-editing program and then update the sound file in the project's library.

Figure 15.15
The Sound Edit Envelope panel enables you to edit how effects are applied to your sound track.

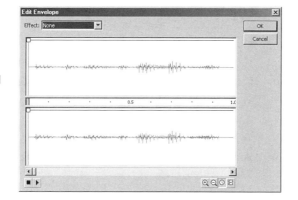

15

You can also choose from the following Sync properties with the Property inspector:

- **Event sync sounds** need to download before playing and play to the end of the sound, creating new iterations of the sound each time the starting keyframe is reached on the timeline.

- **Start sync sounds** are the same as Event sounds, but do not start a new iteration of the sound if the playback head returns to the keyframe until the previous sound has ended. This is useful for looping sounds on your timeline.

- **Stop sync sounds** enable you to stop the sound at the chosen keyframe to which the sync is added.

- **Stream sync sounds** are tied to the timeline on which they occur and play as fast as they are downloaded. You can also set how many times the sound repeats, either by setting a specific number of repetitions or directing the sound to loop continually.

Now that you have an understanding of how to bring sound files into Flash, you are ready for some more advanced topics such as compression and loading external MP3 files.

SWF SOUND EXPORT COMPRESSION

MP3 files that are imported and embedded use the settings with which they were imported with, whereas AIFF and WAV files have compression performed on them as the SWF file is created.

Different types of sounds can be compressed with different methods that are uniquely suited to provide high sound quality and compression for that type of sound. It's a good idea to find the balance between compression and quality, because although you want to minimize the file size as much as possible, there is little point in having an overcompressed file that sounds terrible. The following list shows which compression setting should be used with different sound types:

- **ADPCM compression**—Short event sounds such as button clicks
- **MP3 compression**—Longer stream sounds such as music sound tracks

- **Speech compression**—Compression that is adapted to speech
- **Raw**—No compression is applied

There are two different scopes for setting sound compression: globally for the entire document and all of the sound files in it, or individually for each sound file used in the document.

The global setting is applied to all sounds, both event and streaming. You can find this by going to File, Publish Settings and choosing the Flash tab. Near the bottom of the dialog box, the compression settings for Streaming and Event audio are displayed. To change them, click the Set button. The default setting for the global compression settings is the MP3 option.

Individual settings for a sound file override the global settings configured in the Publish settings. If you've embedded a number of AIFF and WAV files into your document, this is the best route to getting the tightest compression with the highest sound quality. To create individual settings, open the Library and double-click the individual sound file icon. In the Sound Properties dialog box, you can select and test the compression settings for that sound. These include Sample rate for Speech, and Bit rate and Quality for MP3.

LOADING EXTERNAL MP3 FILES

If you're working with large sound files, especially if they are not tightly tied to animation on the timeline, you should consider loading external MP3 files. The benefit to this is that it decreases the file size of the published .swf file, and allows flexibility similar to that of using external video files. You can more easily change and stream the content, and allow the user to initiate download of sound files without having to wait for the application and all its assets to download.

You can control the loading and playback of external MP3 files with ActionScript. As shown in the following code, you must first create a new Sound object. Then you can load the external .mp3 file into your Sound object instance. After it is loaded, you can play the sound:

```
mySound = new Sound();
mySound.loadSound(myfile.mp3);
mySound.start();
```

Use the following code to stop the sound at any point:

```
mySound.stop();
```

You can also add some simple buttons to let the user stop and start the .mp3 file after it is loaded. If you name your buttons soundPlay_mc and soundStop_mc, you could use this code:

```
soundStart_mc.onRelease = function(){
    mySound.start();
}
soundStop_mc.onRelease = function(){
    mySound.stop();
}
```

The sound object gives you control over how you load and use external sound files in your applications. Working with external MP3 files and ActionScript, you can create some sophisticated applications, including a Flash jukebox.

TROUBLESHOOTING

I imported a video file, but there is no sound when I run a test.

Check to see that the original video file is in a format that your system supports and that you have QuickTime 7 installed. If you have QuickTime 4 installed, MPG/MPEG files do not have their audio portion imported into Flash. The video imports, but not the audio portion. Also, make sure that your speakers are turned on and that the sound channel is not muted.

The playback of my embedded video is inconsistent.

Make sure that the frame rate of the embedded video is the same as the `.fla` document file in which it's embedded. A difference in frame rates can result in inconsistent playback. Embedded video is automatically set to the same frame rate as the `.fla`. If you have changed the video frame rate during the import process, be sure that you changed the `.fla` frame rate as well.

My embedded video doesn't restart when the user clicks on a rewind button I've created.

Make sure that you have the correct path and scope when you reference the video clip from another symbol.

I dragged a sound to the stage. Why don't I see it in the timeline?

When any symbol, including a sound, is dragged from the library to the stage, it's added to the currently selected layer. Check the other layers to see whether your sound is on one of them.

I'm having trouble getting the playback of FLV video from my server. What could be causing this?

To avoid any problems with playback, your HTML document, SWF, FLV, and MP3 files should all be in the same directory. Also, be sure to check that your ISP is set up to play and receive the FLV video mime type (`x-flv`). The mime type needs to be set to octect-stream, particularly on Windows 2003 servers.

BEST PRACTICES—FILE PREPARATION AND BANDWIDTH CONCERNS

Although it's possible to do some minor editing in Flash, such as trimming and cropping, you should do your sound and video editing in an external application. This way you can make sure that there is no fat in your project because trimming in Flash controls only what portion of the file is shown to the end user, not the actual file. By preparing your files ahead of time, you can keep bandwidth concerns in the project plans from the beginning.

15

Bandwidth concerns should be primary in every project plan. If you're publishing large sound or video files, be sure to offer end users the chance to choose a download option best suited to their connection speeds.

Finally, if your project has several sound files, set the compression for each sound individually. Some sounds might be compressed more tightly than others and every little optimization lightens the whole load.

CHAPTER 16

PUTTING IT ALL TOGETHER: CREATING AN XML-BASED PHOTO SLIDE SHOW

In this chapter

The quickest way to create a photo slide show with Flash is to use one of the templates that comes with Flash. However, you can also take advantage of the power of Flash to create highly customized presentations from scratch. This chapter goes over the steps involved in building a photo slide show with XML-formatted data and external image files. If you like to build things yourself or if you're using this as a learning experience, this project presents an opportunity to apply many of the concepts covered in previous chapters. Be sure to check out this book's web page for the images and source code you'll need, as well as the finished slide show.

GETTING STARTED

So, you've got this collection of images. What kind of information about them would be useful in your project? At the bare minimum, you need to know the image's filename so that you can tell Flash from where to load the image. Another useful bit of information is the image's title. You might also want to add more and more information about the image, such as the photographer's name and a description of the image.

If you're using only the title and URL (filename and path) of each image, a simple XML data structure such as the following would work well:

```
<images>
    <image title="Slide 1" url="images/slide01.jpg" />
    <image title="Slide 2" url="images/slide02.jpg" />
</images>
```

In this case, you're using the XML node attributes to format the information that is unique to each image. This format is easy to use with ActionScript.

NOTE

One misconception I've encountered as people start working with XML and media is that the photos are stored in the XML document itself. This is not true. All that actually is stored by the XML document is the file path to the photos used in the slide show. The photos themselves reside in individual files on the server.

CREATING THE XML DOCUMENT

In this section, you will create an XML file that describes the information needed to load your images into the slide show.

1. Create a new text document in a text editor. Save it as `images.xml` in a folder on your desktop called slideshow.

2. Enter the following XML structure into the document:

```
<images>
    <image title="Orange 1970 Honda sl175" url="1970_honda_sl175_orange.jpg" />
</images>
```

3. Edit the structure so that there is an image node for each external image file that you will be loading into the slide show.

4. Save the document.

CREATING THE FLASH SLIDE SHOW DOCUMENT

Okay, it's time to start working with Flash. All the ActionScript will be on the first frame of the movie in the actions layer. This will keep the code centralized and easy to find.

1. Open Flash and create a new document. Save it as `slideshow.fla` in the slideshow folder on the desktop.

2. Set the background to white, or another light color, and set the stage size to 500×400.

3. Create three layers named `text`, `image mc`, and `actions`, with `actions` as the top layer.

4. Select the text layer, choose the Text tool, and draw a text field that stretches almost all the way across your stage. With the text field still selected, go to the Property inspector (see Figure 16.1) and format the text field as Dynamic, Arial, 14 point, white, and bold. In the upper-left instance name field, name the instance `title_txt`.

Figure 16.1
Properties of the
`title_txt`
text field.

5. In the `image_mc` layer, create a 400×300 grey rectangle with no outline. Select the rectangle and choose Modify, Convert to Symbol (or press F8). Select Movie Clip as the symbol option and click the upper-left dot on the registration widget to set the upper-left corner as the registration point. Name the new symbol `mc_holder`. This is the name of the master symbol that resides in your library. In the Property inspector, name the instance that resides on the stage `holder_mc` (see Figure 16.2).

Figure 16.2
Properties of the
movie clip instance on
the stage.

LOADING THE XML DATA AND IMAGES

Now you're ready to start writing the code that gets the XML-formatted data and loads the images into the basic structure you set up for your slideshow.

Select the first frame, which should be a blank keyframe, in the actions layer of the timeline. With this new keyframe selected, add the following code to the Actions panel. This will pull the XML document information into Flash:

```
myXML = new XML();
myXML.ignoreWhite = true;
myXML.onLoad = handleLoad;
myXML.load("images.xml");
function handleLoad(success){
    //process XML
    if(success) {
        //trace( "xml loaded" );
        displayXML();
    } else {
        trace ( "xml loading failed" );
    }
}
```

This code first creates a new XML object and names it myXML. Next, it tells myXML to ignore the whitespace in the external XML file and tells myXML what function to call when the XML-formatted data is loaded from an external source. Then it tells myXML that it's time to load the data and where to get it. This example uses a relative path to the images.xml file so you can save all the files for this project in the same directory folder.

To test the success of your loading process, uncomment (remove the // at the start of the line) the trace statement inside the success if statement. Then save the file and choose Control, Test Movie. If the XML document successfully loads, you'll see the output window display xml loaded. If you do not see that statement, check your typing and syntax carefully. Re-comment the trace statement before you move on to the next step.

EXPLORING THE XML DATA

Next, you need to add the code that will use the XML-formatted data you just loaded. You can explore the XML by tracing it out first, and use this technique to discover the code you need to load and display the image (and its title) into your Flash document.

```
displayXML= function(){
    trace(myXML.toString());
}
```

When you run this code, you can see that there are no spaces between the nodes in the output panel. Flash ignores the whitespace from the XML document. Remember whitespace? It's the tabs, blank spaces, and lines that visually organize the text characters for human eyes. Although these spaces make it easier for humans to read XML, it complicates things for the computer, so Flash ignores it. Figure 16.3 shows the results of trace(myXML.toString()) in the Output panel, which is "floating" over the Actions panel containing the code producing the output.

How do you get Flash to display your data? The first step is to get the information in one node, and then you can figure out a general method later.

Figure 16.3
The output of the results of trace (myXML.toString());.

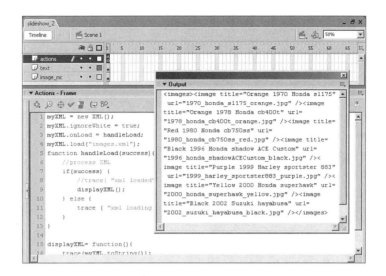

Looking at the XML structure, you can see that you've got a node named images with three child nodes that are each named image. These child nodes each have attributes named title and url.

```
<images>
    <image title="Orange 1970 Honda sl175" url="1970_honda_sl175_orange.jpg" />
    <image title="Orange 1978 Honda cb400t" url="1978_honda_cb400t_orange.jpg" />
    <image title="Red 1980 Honda cb750ss" url="1980_honda_cb750ss_red.jpg" />
</images>
```

You know that you can get the entire structure if you trace out myXML.toString(), but how do you get to a specific node? Try tracing out myXML.firstChild.toString(). This returns the same thing as myXML.toString(). Why? Because the images node is the first child node of the document. To get at the inner nodes that contain the information about the individual images, you need to go deeper into the structure of the document:

```
trace(myXML.firstChild.childNodes[0].toString());
```

This traces the first image node in the output window, as shown in Figure 16.4.

Figure 16.4
A single node is traced to the output window.

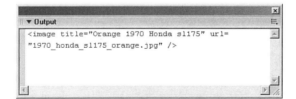

Great! Now, how do you get the rest of the nodes? Recall that in Chapter 14, you learned that XML structures are indexed similar to array indexes. That is, they start counting at 0. So, if childNodes[0] is the first node in its generation, you can get the next node with childNodes[1], and so on.

If you know that there are only three images, you can just write a new line of code for every image for which you want to access the information in the XML document. But it would be more efficient, and less prone to error, to write a looping function to collect the information in sequence. Because the index number is the part that changes for each node, it sets you up to use the following loop:

```
var i_max = myXML.firstChild.childNodes.length;
for(var i=0; i<i_max; i++){
    trace( myXML.firstChild.childNodes[i].toString() );
}
```

In this code example, you first get the number of child nodes through which you need to loop. Because you start the count at zero, you want to stop looping when the index counter is one less than the number of child nodes. Rather than make Flash do a calculation, you set the condition that i must be less than the node count for it to continue.

Now that you know how to get the node you want, how do you get the information from that node? You access its attributes. With a slight modification to the code you just wrote, you can trace out the title and url values for each image node. The results of this script can be seen in the output window shown in Figure 16.5.

```
var i_max = myXML.firstChild.childNodes.length;
for(var i=0; i<i_max; i++){
    trace(myXML.firstChild.childNodes[i].attributes.title);
    trace(myXML.firstChild.childNodes[i].attributes.url);
}
```

Figure 16.5
Tracing node attributes to the output window.

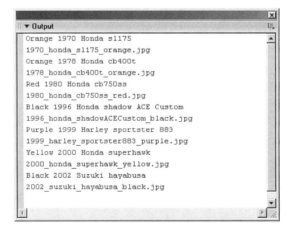

```
Orange 1970 Honda sl175
1970_honda_sl175_orange.jpg
Orange 1978 Honda cb400t
1978_honda_cb400t_orange.jpg
Red 1980 Honda cb750ss
1980_honda_cb750ss_red.jpg
Black 1996 Honda shadow ACE Custom
1996_honda_shadowACECustom_black.jpg
Purple 1999 Harley sportster 883
1999_harley_sportster883_purple.jpg
Yellow 2000 Honda superhawk
2000_honda_superhawk_yellow.jpg
Black 2002 Suzuki hayabusa
2002_suzuki_hayabusa_black.jpg
```

CREATING THE SLIDE DISPLAY CODE

Now you're ready to create the code that loops through the images in your XML file, creates an empty movie clip for each image, and saves the title and URL for that image as properties of that movie clip.

1. Modify the code used to loop through the nodes of the XML file. The following addition creates an empty movie clip to store each image. The image will be loaded into this clip later on:

```
var i_max = myXML.firstChild.childNodes.length;
for(var i=0; i<i_max; i++){

        // create an empty clip to load the image into
    var targ:MovieClip = this.createEmptyMovieClip("image" + i, 100 + i);

}
```

2. Create a new object and name it `imageListener`. Add this code below the existing code inside the for loop in the `displayXML` function.

```
// create an object to use as a listener
var imageListener:Object = new Object();
```

This gets the listener object ready to load the image with a `MovieClipLoader` object (which you'll create later). At this stage, you're still getting everything ready to load the image.

3. Define a function for the `onLoadInit` event handler to call. This is where you put all the code that needs to run after the image is loaded into the target movie clip, such as resizing the image and displaying the title. This goes immediately after the previous code inside the for loop in the `displayXML` function. Use `temp.slice(5)` to get the index number because i does not scope to the loop inside of which the function is defined when it is inside the `onLoadInit` function.

```
//define a function for the onLoadInit event handler
imageListener.onLoadInit = function(targ) {
    // get the index number for this image
    var temp = targ._name;
    targ.i = temp.slice(5);

    // set position as the manually created clip
    targ._x = holder_mc._x;
    targ._y = holder_mc._y;

    // save title
    targ.myTitle = myXML.firstChild.childNodes[targ.i].attributes.title
};
```

4. Next, create the movie clip loader, register the listener with the loader, and then use the listener to load the image into the holder movie clip:

```
// create a new MovieClipLoader
var myLoader = new MovieClipLoader();
```

5. Finally, register the listener to the `MovieClipLoader`:

```
//register the listener to the MovieClipLoader
myLoader.addListener(imageListener);
// load an image into the target movie clip
myLoader.loadClip(myXML.firstChild.childNodes[i].attributes.url, targ);
```

That's it. Save and test the document. Be sure to save the `.fla` in the same folder as the external images. When you test the code at this point, only the last image is visible. All the movie clips are on the stage with external images loaded into them, but they are stacked on top of each other so only the top image is visible (see Figure 16.6).

Figure 16.6
The last image listed in the XML file is the only visible image in the published .swf.

TIP

> One of the simplest things you can do is bring an image to the top of the display stack when the user clicks on part of it. If you arrange your images to have at least some portion visible at all times, this can be an intuitive interface that takes very little code. Just place this code in the `listener.onLoadInit` function after you change the assignment of coordinates so each image has a unique position on the stage:
>
> ```
> //bring this image to top if clicked
> target.onRelease = function(){
>     this.swapDepths(this._parent.getNextHighestDepth());
> }
> ```

SHOWING THE IMAGES IN SEQUENCE

At this point, you have a skeletal application that loads a series of external images into a Flash application and is ready to display their titles. Now you need to show the images sequentially.

A slide show can be a fairly simple application to code. In the simplest version, you turn on and off the visibility of the images, one at a time, over a set interval of time. To do this, you need a function to cycle through the images and control their visibility.

1. First, you need to get the reference to all movie clip holders that have images successfully loaded into them. Add a line to create a new array to the top of the code on the first frame of the actions layer:

   ```
   var loadedImages = new Array();
   ```

2. Now skip to the `displayXML` function on the first frame of the actions layer, just after the empty movie clip is created, and add the following shaded line of code to save the new movie clip to the array for later use:

   ```
   var i_max = myXML.firstChild.childNodes.length;
   for(i=0; i<i_max; i++){
       // create an empty clip to load the image into
       var targ:MovieClip = this.createEmptyMovieClip("image" + i, 100 + i);
   ```

```
                //define a function for the onLoadInit event handler
                imageListener.onLoadInit = function(targ) {

                    // save image holder clip to an array
                    loadedImages.push(targ);

                    // get the index number for this image
                    var temp = targ._name;
                    targ.i = temp.slice(5);

                    // set position as the manually created clip
                    targ._x = holder_mc._x;
                    targ._y = holder_mc._y;

                    // save title
                    targ.myTitle = myXML.firstChild.childNodes[targ.i].attributes.title
                };

            }
```

3. You want to show a different image after every increment of a specified interval of time. ActionScript has a method to call a function at set intervals called setInterval(). You use this to control the display of your loaded images. Place the following code at the top of the Actions panel, above all other code. It enables you to call a function named cycleImages() every 1000 milliseconds (which equals one call per second). By saving a value for myTime and using the myTime variable in the setInterval function, you can easily reset the time interval either by hand or by programming additional code later in the application.

```
var myTime = 1000;
var myInterval = setInterval( cycleImages, myTime);
```

4. Next, add the cycleImages function, which has two main jobs to accomplish: show the next image and hide the previous image. This code goes at the bottom of the existing code.

```
function cycleImages(){
    nextImage._visible = true;
    lastImage._visible = false;
}
```

5. Now you need to tell Flash which is the next image and which is the last image. If you know what the index number is for the current image, you can get the path to the movie clip from the loadedImages array and save it as the next image. Add the following lines of code, which create the variables that track what the next and current images are in the cycle of images.

```
cycleImages(){

    var nextImage:MovieClip = loadedImages[iNext];
    var lastImage:MovieClip = loadedImages[iLast];

    nextImage._visible = true;
    lastImage._visible = false;
}
```

6. Next, you need to create a new object to keep track of what index you're currently using in the array. Naming the object `control` will help you remember what the data it's holding is to be used for. You can give your `control` object a property named `slideNum` to hold the current index number for the images array. This is how Flash knows which image target clip to display next. Add the following lines just after the close of the `cycleImages` function code. Initializing at 0 when you first declare the property sets up the image count as the first in the array:

```
var control:Object = new Object();
control.slideNum = 0;
```

7. Next, insert a counter-incrementer into the `cycleImages` function so that it moves on to the next image in the array the next time it's called by `setInterval`.

```
cycleImages(){
    // get the holder clips for the next image and the last
    var nextImage:MovieClip = loadedImages[iNext];
    var lastImage:MovieClip = loadedImages[iLast];

    // show the next image and hide the last image
    nextImage._visible = true;
    lastImage._visible = false;

    // increment index counter of the images array
    control.slideNum++;
}
```

8. Now set the values for `iNext` and `iLast`, which are dependent on the current value of `control.slideNum`:

```
cycleImages(){
    // get the next index and the last index
    var iNext = control.slideNum;
    var iLast = control.slideNum - 1;

    // get the holder clips for the next image and the last
    var nextImage = loadedImages[iNext];
    var lastImage = loadedImages[iLast];

    // show the next image and hide the last image
    nextImage._visible = true;
    lastImage._visible = false;

    // increment index counter of the images array
    control.slideNum++;
}
```

9. This is great, but after it goes through the array of images once, the counter just keeps going and no more images are displayed. You need a way to loop back to the beginning of the image series again.

First, loop through by getting the length of the `loadImages` array to get the total number of images. Then use this result to test whether the `slideNum` counter is less than the total. If it's less, then Flash gets the next image in the array. If it's greater than or equal to the total, it's time to go back to the beginning of the array again. The next image will be at index 0 and the last will be at the end of the array, which is the total minus one. (Recall that the arrays start counting at zero; so, for example, the last element in an array with 10 elements in it has an index of 9.) You need to reset the `control.slideNum` to zero as well.

```
cycleImages(){
    var iTotal = loadedImages.length;

    if(control.slideNum < iTotal){
        var iNext = control.slideNum;
        var iLast = control.slideNum - 1;
    } else if (control.slideNum >= iTotal){
        control.slideNum = 0;
        var iNext = 0;
        var iLast = iTotal-1;
    }
    // get the holder clips for the next image and the last
    var nextImage = loadedImages[iNext];
    var lastImage = loadedImages[iLast];

    // show the next image and hide the last image
    nextImage._visible = true;
    lastImage._visible = false;

    // increment index counter of the images array
    control.slideNum++;
}
```

10. You also need to change the title, which is displayed in the text field you manually created earlier in Step 4 of the "Creating the Flash Slide Show Document" section. This can be accomplished with one line of code. When the `cycleImages` function is called by `setInterval`, the image title is changed to the title for the currently displayed image:

```
cycleImages(){
    var iTotal = loadedImages.length;

    if(control.slideNum < iTotal){
        var iNext = control.slideNum;
        var iLast = control.slideNum - 1;
    } else if (control.slideNum >= iTotal){
        control.slideNum = 0;
        var iNext = 0;
        var iLast = iTotal-1;
    }

    // get the holder clips for the next image and the last
    var nextImage = loadedImages[iNext];
    var lastImage = loadedImages[iLast];

    // show the next image and hide the last image
    nextImage._visible = true;
    lastImage._visible = false;
```

16

```
    // show title for this image
    title_txt.text = nextImage.myTitle;

    // increment index counter of the images array
    control.slideNum++;
}
```

Before you move on, take a step back and take a look at the entire code set on the first keyframe in the actions layer. It's always a good idea to keep the big picture in mind as you progress in your project.

If you haven't already, save and test the file.

ADDING USER-FRIENDLY FEATURES

Now that you have a nice little slide show as a base, you can add a few additional features using your code knowledge from previous chapters. Many of these features either inform users of what is happening, allow them control, or simply add some fun visual effects to give the user feedback.

"DATA LOADING" MESSAGE

It can take a few seconds for the images to load and for the slide show to start. You don't have to keep end-users in the dark and risk that they'll give up on your slide show while they wait for the images to download to their systems. You can give users a message saying that data is loading. A simple way to handle this is to place a text field on the stage where the images will be displayed. When loaded in, the images cover it up.

USER CONTROLS: PAUSE, START, SLOW DOWN

While the slide show is running, users might want to pause the show and later restart it to get a longer look at one of the images. They might also like to speed up or slow down the playback.

CREATING THE MOVIE CLIP BUTTONS

First, create the movie clip symbols that become the interactive elements that enable the end-user to control the slide show.

1. Set up the movie clip buttons. To keep all the control interface elements organized, create one movie clip to hold them all and call it `controls_mc`. Create the `controls_mc` clip directly on the stage by drawing with the rectangle tool and then converting the shape to a symbol with upper-left registration and the Movie Clip behavior.

2. Select the new symbol instance on the stage and give it an instance name of `controls_mc` in the Property inspector (see Figure 16.7).

Figure 16.7
Give an instance
name to the instance
of the `controls_mc`
symbol on the stage.

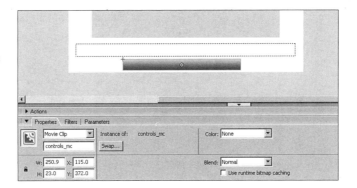

3. Double click the `controls_mc` instance to edit it and add a new layer for the `stop_mc` movie clip. To create this clip, draw a button shape, convert it to a symbol, again as a movie clip type, and name it `stop_mc`. Give the instance that is on the stage the same name (`stop_mc`) (see Figure 16.8) and return to the main timeline.

Figure 16.8
Create a `stop_mc`
instance on a new
layer inside the
`controls_mc`
symbol.

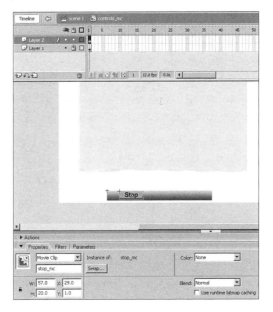

ATTACHING BUTTON CODE

Now you're ready to attach some code to the `stop_mc` clip.

1. Open the Actions panel and go to the end of our existing code on the first frame of the main timeline. Create a comment header so that you can easily find this segment of code later on.

```
//---------------
// user control interface
//---------------
```

2. Above the code area of the Actions panel, you can select from a number of buttons. For now, select the Insert Target Path button. A nifty panel comes up with all the named instances that are currently on the stage. You should see controls_mc with a plus sign next to it. If you click on the plus sign, you should see stop_mc listed. Select stop_mc and then click the OK button in the panel. Now take a look at the Actions panel, as shown in Figure 16.9. You now have the path to the stop_mc instance in the code.

Figure 16.9
You can use the Insert Target Path panel to insert the target path of the stop_mc instance into the Actions panel.

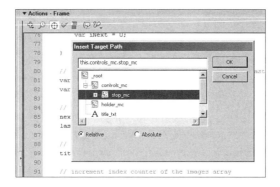

TIP

When working with movie clips that are on the stage at author-time, and you want to attach code to them programmatically, the Insert Target Path panel is a very useful tool and can help you avoid typo and path errors.

3. Now that you have the target path for the stop_mc movie clip, it's time to attach to it a function that will be called when the user clicks in it:

```
this.controls_mc.stop_mc.onRelease = function(){
    trace("stop slideshow");
}
```

4. Test this out. You should see stop slideshow in the output panel every time you click on the stop_mc symbol (see Figure 16.10).

Figure 16.10
The output panel displays stop slideshow when the stop_mc instance is clicked.

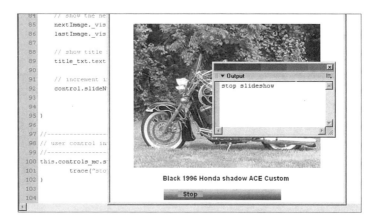

5. Create another movie clip in the controls movie clip, this time for the `start` function. Be sure to give the movie clip an instance name or it won't be available to ActionScript. Add the following code, which is similar that of to the `stop_mc` clip:

```
//--------------------.
// user control
//----------------------
this.controls_mc.stop_mc.onRelease = function(){
    trace("stop slideshow");
}
this.controls_mc.start_mc.onRelease = function(){
    trace("start slideshow");
}
```

6. Test this out. You should now get `stop slideshow` in the output panel when you click on `stop_mc` and `start slideshow` when you click on `start_mc`.

DEFINING ACTIONS FOR THE EVENT HANDLERS

Now that you know your event handlers are working for the basic user interface you're creating, you can start giving them some work to do.

1. To stop the cycle of images displayed, you need to clear the `setInterval` function. Because the function is defined on the main timeline, you need to go up the hierarchy of symbols from the `stop_mc` clip for the path to `myInterval`:

```
this.controls_mc.stop_mc.onRelease = function(){
    trace("stop slideshow");
    clearInterval(this._parent._parent.myInterval);
}
```

2. To restart the slide show, use the following code:

```
this.controls_mc.start_mc.onRelease = function(){
    trace("start slideshow");
    var myPath = this._parent._parent;
    myPath.myInterval = setInterval( myPath.cycleImages, myPath.my_time);
}
```

3. Now, if you just leave these functions as they are, the user could run into some very buggy behavior. You need to have only one button active at a time. You can accomplish this by adding a little code to each `onRelease` function.

```
this.controls_mc.stop_mc.onRelease = function(){
    trace("stop button");
    clearInterval(this._parent._parent.myInterval);

    //disable this
    this.enabled = false;

    var myPath = this._parent._parent;
    //enable the start_mc clip
    myPath.controls_mc.start_mc.enabled = true;
```

```
}

this.controls_mc.start_mc.onRelease = function(){
    trace("start slideshow");
    var myPath = this._parent._parent;
    myPath.myInterval = setInterval( myPath.cycleImages, myPath.my_time);

    //disable this
    this.enabled = false;

    //enable the start_mc clip
    myPath.controls_mc.stop_mc.enabled = true;

}
```

Adding Visual Indicators to Interactive Elements

4. This works great, but it can use a little polish. The user would benefit from a visual indication that the interface element is either active or inactive. You can accomplish this by changing the alpha, or *transparency*, value of the clips. The following bolded code sets the value to 100% alpha when they are active and 40% alpha when they are inactive:

```
this.controls_mc.stop_mc.onRelease = function(){
    trace("stop button");
    clearInterval(this._parent._parent.myInterval);

    //disable this
    this.enabled = false;

    this._alpha = 40;

    var myPath = this._parent._parent;
    //enable the start_mc clip
    myPath.controls_mc.start_mc.enabled = true;

    myPath.controls_mc.start_mc._alpha = 100;

}

this.controls_mc.start_mc.onRelease = function(){
    trace("start slideshow");
    var myPath = this._parent._parent;
    myPath.myInterval = setInterval( myPath.cycleImages, myPath.my_time);

    //disable this
    this.enabled = false;

    this._alpha = 40;

    //enable the stop_mc clip
    myPath.controls_mc.stop_mc.enabled = true;

    myPath.controls_mc.stop_mc._alpha = 100;

}
```

5. Now you need to set the initial state for the start_mc clip as disabled and with alpha set to 40%. Where you place this bit of code is up to you. I personally prefer to put all initialization-related code at the top of the ActionScript.

```
// initialize start_mc control element as disabled
this.controls_mc.start_mc.enabled = false;
this.controls_mc.start_mc._alpha = 40;
```

At this point, you have a slide show with some basic user control elements. Check out the book's web page and compare your source code with `slideshow_4.fla`. The next thing to examine is how you can apply one of the new filter effects.

APPLYING A DYNAMIC DROP SHADOW

One of the new filters included in Flash 8 is `dropShadow`. You can apply it to individual movie clips on the authoring environment's stage. You can also apply it programmatically to externally loaded images with ActionScript. This is handy because the application dynamically loads and displays external bitmap images.

APPLYING A FILTER WITH ACTIONSCRIPT

Let's start with a simple example, and when you have that working, you can integrate it into the code you developed for the slide show application.

1. Open a new Flash document and make sure that its publishing settings are set for Flash 8 and not an earlier version. On the stage, draw a shape, convert it into a movie clip, and give it an instance name of `myShape_mc`.

2. Create an actions layer above the layer with the movie clip, select the first frame in the layer, and open the Actions panel. Next, import the class for the `DropShadowFilter`. At the top of the page, add the following code:

   ```
   import flash.filters.DropShadowFilter;
   ```

3. Before you can apply the filter, you have to set up some parameters for it. The following code not only assigns values to the parameters of the filter, it does so in a way that is easy to read and modify:

   ```
   // set dropshodow properties
   var shadowDistance:Number = 20;
   var shadowAngleInDegrees:Number = 45;
   var shadowColor:Number = 0x000000;
   var shadowAlpha:Number = .6;
   var shadowBlurX:Number = 16;
   var shadowBlurY:Number = 16;
   var shadowStrength:Number = 1;
   var shadowQuality:Number = 3;
   var shadowInner:Boolean = false;
   var shadowKnockout:Boolean = false;
   var shadowHideObject:Boolean = false;
   ```

4. Next, create a new `DropShadowFilter` object (datatype), passing the parameter values through local variables:

   ```
   var myFilter:DropShadowFilter = new DropShadowFilter(shadowDistance,
   ➥ shadowAngleInDegrees, shadowColor, shadowAlpha,
   ➥ shadowBlurX, shadowBlurY, shadowStrength, shadowQuality,
   ➥ shadowInner, shadowKnockout, shadowHideObject);
   ```

Although this might not seem easy to read, it is more meaningful than entering the values into the definition as it is created, which would look like this:

```
var myFilter:DropShadowFilter =
➥new DropShadowFilter(20, 45, 0x000000, .6, 16, 16, 1, 3, false, false,
➥false);
```

5. Now you need to create a new array to hold the filters you will apply to this movie clip. The movie clip object has an array property that holds the filters applied to it. If the array is empty, no filters are applied. This means you can apply more than one filter to a movie clip and you can specify in which order they are applied.

6. Create an array for the filters applied to this movie clip and then push the filter you just created (the DropShadowFilter) into the array. Finally, save the array as the filters array of the myShape instance of the movie clip:

```
var filterArray:Array = new Array();
filterArray.push(myFilter);
myShape.filters = filterArray;
```

All together, the code now looks like this:

```
import flash.filters.DropShadowFilter;
// set dropshodow properties
var shadowDistance:Number = 20;
var shadowAngleInDegrees:Number = 45;
var shadowColor:Number = 0x000000;
var shadowAlpha:Number = .6;
var shadowBlurX:Number = 16;
var shadowBlurY:Number = 16;
var shadowStrength:Number = 1;
var shadowQuality:Number = 3;
var shadowInner:Boolean = false;
var shadowKnockout:Boolean = false;
var shadowHideObject:Boolean = false;

// create new filter object with the parameters from above
var myFilter:DropShadowFilter =
➥ new DropShadowFilter(shadowDistance, shadowAngleInDegrees, shadowColor,
➥   shadowAlpha, shadowBlurX, shadowBlurY, shadowStrength, shadowQuality,
➥   shadowInner,shadowKnockout, shadowHideObject);

// create array to save filters for this movie clip
var filterArray:Array = new Array();
filterArray.push(myFilter);
myShape.filters = filterArray;
```

Doublecheck that the publishing settings are set for Flash 8 and test it out. Figure 16.11 shows a black rectangle that has a DropShadowFilter applied to it by the previous code. When it's working, you can move on to integrating this into your project.

Figure 16.11
Application of the new DropShadow Filter.

ADDING A DROP SHADOW TO YOUR SLIDE SHOW

Now you can incorporate this into your project by adding code to the `cycleImages` function.

1. As mentioned earlier in the chapter, it's best to put the `import` statement at the top of your existing code to keep all `import` statements at the beginning of all code.

```
import flash.filters.DropShadowFilter;
```

2. Apply the filter to the movie clips holding the loaded images. You could put the filter code in the `onLoadInit` function, but then the filters would be prepared before they're visible. This is generally not the best use of the end-user's system resources.

   An alternative, and better option, is to put the filter code in the `cycleImages` function, which is called when the application is scheduled (with `setInterval`) to transition from one image to the next in the gallery. With the added code, the `cycleImages` function looks like this:

```
function cycleImages(){

    var iTotal = loadedImages.length;v

    if(control.slideNum < iTotal){
        var iNext = control.slideNum;
        var iLast = control.slideNum - 1;
    } else if (control.slideNum >= iTotal){
        control.slideNum = 0;
        var iNext = 0;
        var iLast = iTotal-1;
    }

    var nextImage = loadedImages[iNext];
    var lastImage = loadedImages[iLast];

    nextImage._visible = true;
    lastImage._visible = false;

    // set dropshodow properties
    var shadowDistance:Number = 20;
    var shadowAngleInDegrees:Number = 45;
    var shadowColor:Number = 0x000000;
    var shadowAlpha:Number = .6;
    var shadowBlurX:Number = 16;
    var shadowBlurY:Number = 16;
    var shadowStrength:Number = 1;
    var shadowQuality:Number = 3;
    var shadowInner:Boolean = false;
    var shadowKnockout:Boolean = false;
    var shadowHideObject:Boolean = false;

    var myFilter:DropShadowFilter =
 ➥ new DropShadowFilter(shadowDistance, shadowAngleInDegrees, shadowColor,
 ➥ shadowAlpha, shadowBlurX, shadowBlurY, shadowStrength,
 ➥ shadowQuality, shadowInner, shadowKnockout, shadowHideObject);
    var filterArray:Array = new Array();
```

16

```
        filterArray.push(myFilter);
        nextImage.filters = filterArray;

        control.slideNum++;

    }
```

3. To free up memory, you can also remove the filter from the filter array of the lastImage. This way, you don't have an accumulation of filters as Flash cycles through the images in the slide show:

```
function cycleImages(){

    var iTotal = loadedImages.length;v

    if(control.slideNum < iTotal){
        var iNext = control.slideNum;
        var iLast = control.slideNum - 1;
    } else if (control.slideNum >= iTotal){
        control.slideNum = 0;
        var iNext = 0;
        var iLast = iTotal-1;
    }

    var nextImage = loadedImages[iNext];
    var lastImage = loadedImages[iLast];

    nextImage._visible = true;
    lastImage._visible = false;

    // set dropshodow properties
    var shadowDistance:Number = 20;
    var shadowAngleInDegrees:Number = 45;
    var shadowColor:Number = 0x000000;
    var shadowAlpha:Number = .6;
    var shadowBlurX:Number = 16;
    var shadowBlurY:Number = 16;
    var shadowStrength:Number = 1;
    var shadowQuality:Number = 3;
    var shadowInner:Boolean = false;
    var shadowKnockout:Boolean = false;
    var shadowHideObject:Boolean = false;

    var myFilter:DropShadowFilter =
 ➥ new DropShadowFilter(shadowDistance, shadowAngleInDegrees, shadowColor,
 ➥   shadowAlpha, shadowBlurX, shadowBlurY, shadowStrength, shadowQuality,
 ➥   shadowInner, shadowKnockout, shadowHideObject);
    var filterArray:Array = new Array();
    filterArray.push(myFilter);
    nextImage.filters = filterArray;

    // remove filter from image movieclip to conserve memory allocation
    // this is optional, but might be good to use if you have
    // a large collection of images
    lastImage.filters.pop();

    control.slideNum++;
}
```

So, there you go: a slideshow with several additional features that make for some pretty sophisticated Flash magic. Take the code (as well as the principles behind it) and apply it to your own projects. That is the easiest way to become a really great Flash coder.

TROUBLESHOOTING

When I trace myXML, *I get* [type Function] *in the output window instead of the xml data.*

Make sure that you called toString() correctly. If you leave out the (), you get the object type instead of the result of the function call. To get the string output of an XML object, write **myXML.toString()**.

I've got the cycleImages *function working now, but the titles are out of synch with the images.*

Make sure that you push the target clip into the loadedImages array inside of the onLoadInit function. If you push the target clip (targ) before the image loads, the image information becomes available to the cycleImages function too early.

When I test my code, I get the following error message: The class or interface 'flash. filters.DropShadowFilter' could not be loaded.

Check the document's publishing settings. This can result from using Flash 8 classes when the player version is set to Flash 7.

It's taking a very long time for the images to show up, and when I test this on my server it takes even longer.

Check the file sizes of your images. The bigger the file size, the longer it takes to process the images in Flash. To speed up things, try to optimize your file sizes for faster download and rendering.

I'm trying to load images from another server, but a warning box comes up.

This is the result of cross-domain security issues. For more information, visit the Macromedia website at http://www.macromedia.com/devnet/mx/flash/articles/ fplayer_security.html. For information on the security enhancements introduced in Flash 8, see the article, "Security Changes in Flash Player 8," which can be found at http://www.macromedia.com/devnet/flash/articles/fplayer8_security.html.

BEST PRACTICES: AN APPROACH TO PROJECT DEVELOPMENT

Before starting a project of this size, it's a good idea to plan it out before creating it. I'm a coder, so I usually start with the data. When I have an idea of how the data is "shaped," I can start designing the XML's data structure. Then I start sketching out the user interface and determine what has to be accomplished with code.

In general, when I'm developing an application, I start out with a lot of trace commands. I don't add the "guts" of a method until I know it's called and is responding correctly. This helps me pin down the source of bugs during development.

It's important to constantly test as you are developing. I usually test after adding each functional element of code. I also Save As with a new version number in the filename whenever adding anything that could potentially break the existing code. This way, I can revert to a previous version if I really mess things up.

16

PART IV

COLDFUSION MX 7

CHAPTER **17**

INTRODUCING COLDFUSION MX 7

In this chapter

INTRODUCING COLDFUSION MX 7

The term *ColdFusion* has definitely become a popular buzzword in the web community over the last five years or so. If you haven't ever heard of ColdFusion, you might be wondering whether Macromedia has discovered a way to derive incredible amounts of power from a single glass of salt water and has, somehow, done it using the web. Although Macromedia's version of ColdFusion doesn't have anything to do with salt water, it has a *lot* to do with power and the web.

ColdFusion is one of several dynamic server infrastructures (or "platforms") that enables you to extract data from a database and display it in your web pages. Other dynamic platforms include Active Server Pages (ASP), ASP.NET, Java Server Pages (JSP), and Hypertext PreProcessor (PHP). What sets ColdFusion apart from these other platforms is that it is extremely easy to learn, easy to use, and as powerful as any of the other platforms.

The developer version of ColdFusion, included with Studio 8, enables you to develop ColdFusion applications and run them strictly on your development machine. This limitation is enforced by the fact that the server can be accessed by only one additional IP address—just enough for testing.

You need a production ColdFusion server to make your applications available on the web. You can either buy and manage your own production ColdFusion server or pay a monthly fee for a hosting service—the same options you have for an ordinary website. You may also be able to find free ColdFusion hosting, which may be appropriate for testing or for non-critical uses that don't put much stress on the server or demand a lot of bandwidth.

In addition, the developer version of ColdFusion can be used as a versatile personal automation tool for tasks. Consider a few examples:

- For repetitive find-and-replace operations, ColdFusion offers powerful find-and-replace functions that use regular expressions.

> **NOTE**
>
> Regular expressions use special placeholder characters such as * and ? to represent unknown characters. Windows Explorer supports regular expressions that use * and ? in searching for filenames.

- If you regularly gather the same information from the same web page, or from a number of web pages, you may find that ColdFusion's screen scraping capabilities can automate the whole process. This enables you to gather content easily from other websites that you can use for analysis or (if authorized by the other site owner) for inclusion in your site.

- To automate emailing with ColdFusion, you can use a database to store and retrieve names, email addresses, and perhaps other information to personalize the messages.

After ColdFusion is installed, there are a few things you need to do before you can start working with it:

- Take some time to familiarize yourself with the functionality of the ColdFusion Administrator. This tool enables you to configure the various ColdFusion settings and even establish data sources that allow your applications to communicate with databases.

- Configure a web server to work with ColdFusion. There is a built-in web server that requires no configuration, but it limited to development and doesn't function as a full production web server.

- Create or obtain a database file, created by a program such as Microsoft Access, Microsoft SQL Server, or MySQL. (On the CD accompanying this book, there is a Microsoft Access database, `retroscycles.mdb`, that you can use for testing.) Typically, you install the database on the ColdFusion server or the development machine on which you are working.

- Create a System DSN (Data Source Name) so that Windows applications can access the database. You can create the System DSN with the ColdFusion Administrator.

- If you are not developing on the same machine as that on which ColdFusion is running, you may also need an RDS (Remote Development Services) password to log on to the ColdFusion server.

- A final, optional step is to configure debugging options by using the ColdFusion Administrator so that you get adequate information when an error occurs to help you in identifying and resolving the issue.

WHAT'S NEW IN COLDFUSION MX 7

Several new features have been introduced in ColdFusion MX 7, including the following:

- **A brand new, Java-based engine and compiler**—This new feature allows all code to be precompiled, which means that pages load faster and more consistently.

- **Enhanced reporting tools**—Coldfusion MX 7 introduces the new CFR (ColdFusion Report) file format that allows you to create professional-looking reports and embed them in your web pages.

- **Printer-friendly web content**—Gone are the days of having to create secondary pages that enable you to display your pages in a printable format. Now ColdFusion does it all for you in either the Adobe PDF or Macromedia FlashPaper format.

- **Enhanced input forms**—ColdFusion now fully supports Flash-based forms and enables you to easily perform both client-side and server-side form validation to ensure that your visitors are completing forms properly.

- **Improved charting and graphic features**—Using the charts and graph features within ColdFusion, you can now draw data from a database and display the results in a graphical format. As your data updates, so do your charts.

17

- **Verity text searching**—A new, more powerful version of the Verity search engine is included in ColdFusion MX 7 and allows for more accurate text searching within documents.

- **Mobile device communication integration using Event Gateways**—ColdFusion now enables your web applications to communicate beyond the browser to devices that use the Simple Message Service (SMS) or Instant Messenger protocols. This means that when certain events occur on your site (for example, you receive a new order), you can be notified via your wireless phone or Instant Messenger application.

UNDERSTANDING THE COLDFUSION ARCHITECTURE

ColdFusion has three basic components: the server, the administrator interface, and ColdFusion Markup Language (CFML). The server is the central element because without the capability to serve pages, the other two elements are useless.

The ColdFusion server runs side by side with a web server. As the web server displays pages, the ColdFusion server watches for ColdFusion pages (pages with the `.cfm` extension). ColdFusion pages contain a mixture of standard HTML and CFML. If the web server receives a request for a page with a `.cfm` extension, it hands that request off to the ColdFusion server. The ColdFusion server then retrieves the appropriate page, processes it (a process known as *preprocessing*), retrieves any data that it requests from a database, and then turns all the resulting data into pure HTML. It then hands that HTML back to the web server and the web server sends the data to the client for display in the client's browser (see Figure 17.1.).

Figure 17.1
The ColdFusion server preprocesses any CFM pages and then sends the resulting HTML back to the web server.

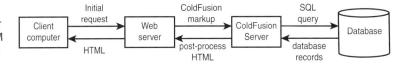

During the preprocessing task, the ColdFusion server can do several things beyond just processing HTML, including

- Database operations, such as retrieving, inserting, updating, and deleting data in databases stored on the server.

- File operations, such as reading, writing, and appending to text files.

- Server-to-server communications, in which the ColdFusion server exchanges data with other servers, including other ColdFusion servers, servers running Flash Remoting software, and directory servers that use Lightweight Directory Access Protocol (LDAP).

- Page processing such as text formatting, search and replace, and building tables, forms, and charts.

- Messaging with protocols such as SMS and Instant Messaging.

CONFIGURING COLDFUSION

Macromedia has made it relatively easy to configure and administer ColdFusion. Before you can begin coding pages and viewing them in your browser, though, you need to configure your local web server to handle ColdFusion requests and configure a data source that draws data from your database.

USING THE BUILT-IN WEB SERVER

When you first set up ColdFusion on your local workstation, you may have configured the web server on your machine to handle ColdFusion requests. If you didn't, or don't know whether you did, you can take a few minutes to ensure that your machine is configured properly for serving web pages.

ColdFusion MX 7 comes with a built-in web server, but its use is limited to development purposes because it can be accessed only via the IP address 127.0.0.1, or if you use the server name localhost. In addition, the only port that the built-in server can use is port 8500.

Therefore, if you wanted to access the ColdFusion Administrator, you would have to use one of the following addresses:

> http://127.0.0.1:8500/CFIDE/administrator/index.cfm
>
> http://localhost:8500/CFIDE/administrator/index.cfm

Because of these limitations, the built-in web server isn't very effective in a real-world environment. Therefore, if you are going to be working with ColdFusion beyond your workstation, you need a more powerful server than the server included with ColdFusion. Luckily, ColdFusion can be easily configured to work with other popular web servers such as Microsoft's Internet Information Server (IIS) or Apache's HTTP Server.

CONFIGURING COLDFUSION FOR USE WITH AN ALTERNATIVE WEB SERVER

Configuring ColdFusion for use with Apache or IIS is an easy process. The basic steps for configuring ColdFusion to work with IIS or Apache Server are

1. Open the Web Server Configuration Tool by choosing Start, Programs, Macromedia, ColdFusion MX 7, Web Server Configuration Tool.

TIP

> If you already have the web server application installed, you can also open the ColdFusion administrator by typing either of the following addresses in your browser:
>
> http://127.0.0.1:8500/CFIDE/administrator/index.cfm
>
> http://localhost:8500/CFIDE/administrator/index.cfm
>
> Note that the reference to port 8500 is required in the URL.

17

17

2. Add a new configuration and select the hostname and server.

3. Choose either IIS or Apache.

4. Choose to configure the server for ColdFusion MX applications and click OK.

> **TIP**
>
> For complete instructions on configuring other web server applications for use with ColdFusion, check out the document at the following address:
>
> http://livedocs.macromedia.com/coldfusion/7/htmldocs/wwhelp/wwhimpl/common/html/wwhelp.htm?context=ColdFusion_Documentation&file=00000049.htm

CONFIGURING DATA SOURCES

After you have ColdFusion working with a web server, the next step is to create a conduit that enables you to draw information from a database and display it on your web pages. A data source is essentially a translator that extracts data from the appropriate database and then feeds the data back to the ColdFusion server. Because each database speaks a different "language," it's important to use the correct conduit for your database.

Creating a data source is actually an easy process. The basic steps for creating one are as follows:

1. Open the ColdFusion Administrator by choosing Start, Programs, ColdFusion Administrator, or by typing `http://localhost/CFIDE/administrator` in your web browser.

2. Under Data & Services, click Data Sources (see Figure 17.2).

Figure 17.2
The ColdFusion Administrator's browser-based interface.

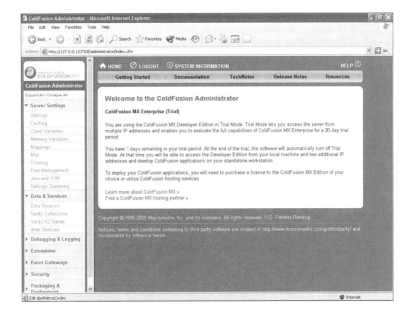

3. In the Data Source Name dialog (see Figure 17.3), provide a name for the System DSN, choose a database driver type from the drop-down menu, and click the Add button.

CAUTION

Do not use spaces or special characters in your DSN names. If you do, you receive an error when you submit the form.

Figure 17.3
The Add New Data Source dialog.

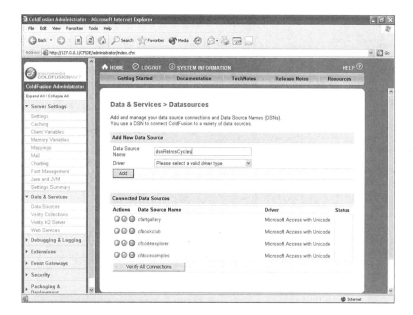

4. In the Data Source dialog box, provide the full path to the database file on the ColdFusion server hard disk, or browse to the database file. Figure 17.4 refers to a folder path based on the IIS folder structure. The Database file field displays the path to the database file (only partially visible in the box), which is C:\InetPub\wwwroot\retroscycles\rcdb9984048\retros_cycles_99300d2.mdb.

NOTE

If you are using a web server other that IIS, the path to your database may be different. Most web server applications use a root folder of wwwroot to indicate the location where web pages should be placed to be accessed by the public. Be sure that you enter the correct path to your database file when creating your data source.

CAUTION

Be careful not to name the location and database something that someone could guess. The last thing you want is some clever person downloading your database file—especially if you store user information (for example, usernames and passwords) or order information such as credit card numbers.

Figure 17.4
Type the data source
name and the path to
your database file.

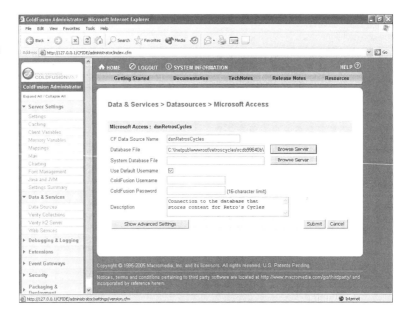

5. Click Submit. The ColdFusion Administrator verifies that the data source was created successfully. When the connection is verified, OK appears in the status column for the connection.

In the Administrator, you can use the three Action buttons in this column to edit, verify, or delete the DSN. These actions do not affect the database file itself, but only the DSN.

After you have your web server configured to handle ColdFusion requests and a connection to your database, you're almost ready to open Dreamweaver and begin developing web pages that can display dynamic data. If, however, you are going to use Flash to display dynamic data, there a few other things to consider.

USING FLASH TO ACCESS THE COLDFUSION SERVER

Flash can be used to implement the client side of ColdFusion applications. A Flash client typically interacts with a ColdFusion server in one of two ways: using web services or using Flash Remoting. Figure 17.5 shows the architecture and protocols associated with each approach.

WEB SERVICES

The web services architecture enables the client to get dynamic data from servers by making requests with Simple Object Access Protocol (SOAP) and by receiving XML replies. By using standard, open protocols, web services enable any-to-any communication. For example, you can create web services that run on the ColdFusion server, and they can be accessed by clients using PHP, JSP, ASP.NET, or any other technology that supports web services standards.

Figure 17.5
The Flash Player (lower left) can access the ColdFusion server with either the WebServiceConnector component or Flash Remoting.

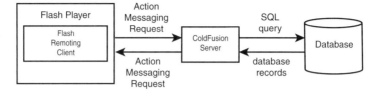

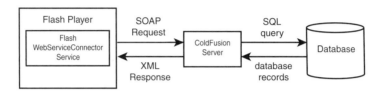

Note, however, that the Flash Player's prohibition on cross-domain data transfers without a cross-domain policy file puts a serious restriction on this potential for universal communication.

Web services are best accessed from the Flash Player through the WebServiceConnector component in Flash MX 2004 Professional. The WebServiceConnector makes it easy to get the basic web services connection going.

The web services architecture requires the client to communicate with the server via a proxy, which replicates server behaviors on a local server, such as the ColdFusion server.

Dreamweaver has tools for creating ColdFusion server behaviors for use as web services. Dreamweaver also makes it easy to create the proxy for the client on the ColdFusion server. Finally, Dreamweaver makes it easy to create simple client interactions with web services.

FLASH REMOTING

To use Flash Remoting, you have to download the Flash Remoting components from www.macromedia.com. With the components installed, your Flash applications can communicate directly with the ColdFusion server and interact with a database.

Flash Remoting clients communicate via the Flash Remoting Gateway, a standard feature of the ColdFusion server. The Flash Remoting client invokes a function, created by the ColdFusion developer and often contained in a ColdFusion component (CFC) on the ColdFusion server. The function returns a value to the Flash Remoting client.

Flash Remoting is the most efficient way to communicate with the ColdFusion server. The ColdFusion server and the Flash client store data in the same format, eliminating the need

17

for time-consuming translation required with technologies like XML. In addition, the proprietary Action Message Format (AFM) used for communication between client and server is efficient and compact.

TROUBLESHOOTING

I'm getting a `Connection verification failed` *error. What's going on?*

If you get a message such as `Connection verification failed for data source: retroscycles`, look at what comes after it. A lot of it may not be very helpful, but somewhere in there, there should be a solid clue as to what is wrong. For instance, `Could not find file` tells you there is something wrong with the filename or path that you entered in the Database box.

If the file is on your local machine, and the error message says `Please check your username, password, URL, and other connectivity info`, the database file may be protected by a username and password. Two options are to uncheck Use Default Username and provide the correct username and password in the appropriate boxes (ColdFusion Username and ColdFusion Password), or to un-protect the database by using the database management system.

If all else fails, you might try using the Windows interface for working with DSNs (Start, Settings, Control Panel, Administrative Tools, Data Sources [ODBC], System DSN tab) to create the System DSN.

BEST PRACTICES—WHEN IS COLDFUSION THE RIGHT PLATFORM?

One of the few drawbacks of ColdFusion over other platforms such as ASP, ASP.NET, JSP, and PHP is that ColdFusion is relatively expensive compared to the others. ASP functionality is native to IIS, so no additional downloads or configuration is required. JSP, PHP, and ASP.NET are free downloads that can be downloaded and installed easily. ColdFusion, on the other hand, can cost up to $6,000 for the Enterprise Edition. So why use a product that costs that much, when you can get others for free? There are several reasons.

First, the $6,000 Enterprise Edition is really for companies that are going to run multiple sites and applications from more than one server. So if your company is looking to develop a web presence, an intranet, and a host of dynamic applications, it would make sense to spend the money on a server platform that will not only enable you to leverage database content, but has search functionality, reporting capabilities, and a wide variety of messaging functionality built in. That way, you're not having to look around at third-party applications that might affect the way your applications perform.

The Standard Edition, weighing in at $1,300, is also oriented toward an environment where multiple applications and sites will be developed, but everything will be stored on a single server. This is an ideal option for small- to medium-sized businesses who need their own web servers (as opposed to a hosted site).

But what if your company or organization doesn't have the budget for $1,300 plus the cost of a server and someone to maintain it? The answer is to find a hosting company that offers access to the ColdFusion platform to its clients. There are quite a few reasonably priced companies out there that offer ColdFusion in their packages, and because ColdFusion has a web-based configuration utility, they often allow you to create DSN entries on the fly via your browser.

So if you aren't part of a Fortune 500 company or don't have a budget that allows you to purchase the necessary equipment and licenses to run ColdFusion...fear not! Options are available that will allow you to leverage all that ColdFusion has to offer without breaking the bank.

17

USING COLDFUSION MARKUP LANGUAGE (CFML)

Introducing CFML

When ColdFusion was introduced in the last chapter, I mentioned that one of the elements was the ColdFusion Markup Language, frequently referred to as CFML. CFML is a tag-based programming language, very similar to HTML in that the functionality that the ColdFusion server is expected to perform is indicated by a start tag like <CFOUTPUT> and an end tag like </CFOUTPUT>. Anything inside those tags is processed by the ColdFusion engine and everything else is left up to the web server application. This means that in the following snippet of code

```
<B><CFOUTPUT>Hello World!</CFOUTPUT><B>
```

the ColdFusion engine would output the text Hello World! and the web server would bold the text. This might seem a little silly at this point because the web server could just as easily handle the output of the text, but as you'll see later in the chapter, the power of ColdFusion goes way beyond creating simple text.

NOTE

You'll notice throughout this book that when I refer to tags, I type them in all caps. This is not a requirement because ColdFusion is not case sensitive (for example, <cfoutput> is the same as <CFOUTPUT>), but is merely a coding style that I use. By doing this, I am able to easily distinguish my CF tags from other non-ColdFusion text.

TIP

If you're not into writing your own code, don't worry. Dreamweaver is an excellent development tool for the ColdFusion platform and it writes the code for you.

Understanding the Language

The CFML language consists of about 100 tags, each enclosed in angle brackets like HTML tags, and all the CFML tag names start with CF. Each of these tags indicates what function the ColdFusion server should perform on the content that falls between the tags.

ColdFusion also contains quite a few functions that enable you to perform operational comparisons, check for certain conditions, and even perform simple file-based operations. These functions are also invoked by a set of tags and many of them are capable of accepting arguments.

Table 18.1 lists some commonly used ColdFusion tags and functions, and later in the chapter we'll take a look at how they operate.

TABLE 18.1   SOME COMMONLY USED COLDFUSION TAGS

Tag	Purpose
CFAPPLICATION	Defines various client behaviors associated with an application, such as whether the client can log information in a cookie, and whether the client session will time out.
CFARGUMENT	Within a function, defines a parameter (data passed to the function).
CFBREAK	See CFLOOP.
CFCALENDAR	New in ColdFusion MX 7, this tag allows you to invoke interactive Flash-based calendars.
CFCATCH	See CFTRY.
CFCOMPONENT	Creates a ColdFusion component (CFC), an object encapsulating procedures (functions, referred to as methods), and data (variables and parameters).
CFDIRECTORY	Returns a list of files in a directory. Can also create, delete, and rename directories.
CFDOCUMENT	New in ColdFusion MX 7, this tag creates a PDF or FlashPaper output of the content that falls between the tags.
CFDUMP	Displays the contents of variables, objects, components, user-defined functions, and other elements. Useful for debugging.
CFELSE	See CFIF.
CFFILE	Performs operations such as reading, writing, and appending to files on the ColdFusion server.
CFFORM	Creates an instance of a form that can be validated on the server side.
CFFORMITEM	New for ColdFusion MX 7, this tag enables you to create a container that specifies controls for multiple forms.
CFFUNCTION	Defines a ColdFusion function (an object encapsulating a procedure).
CFHTTP	Generates an HTTP request and handles the response from the server.
CFIF	Executes enclosed code if a condition is true. Can be used with CFELSE to define an action to perform if the condition is not true.
CFIMPORT	Imports all ColdFusion pages in a directory into the calling page as a custom tag library.
CFINCLUDE	Adds the contents of the included ColdFusion page to the page containing the CFINCLUDE tag, as if the code on the included page were part of the page containing the CFINCLUDE tag.
CFINVOKE	Invokes (runs or executes) either a function (method) in a component or a web service.
CFLOCK	Locks (prevents simultaneous access to) a single section of code, two or more different sections of code, or a scope. Locks prevent simultaneous change of the same variable to two different values.

18

TABLE 18.1   CONTINUED

Tag	Purpose
CFLOOP	Loops through the tag body zero or more times, based on a condition specified by the tag attributes. The CFBREAK tag exits a CFLOOP tag.
CFMAIL	Sends SMTP mail messages with application variables, query results, or server files. (See also CFPOP, for getting mail.)
CFMODULE	Invokes a custom tag, providing a workaround for custom tag name conflicts.
CFNTAUTHENTICATE	New for ColdFusion MX 7, this tag enables you to authenticate user credentials against a Windows NT domain.
CFOBJECT	Loads an object into a variable. Can load a CFC or an object written in other programming languages, including COM (Component Object Model) components, Java objects such as Enterprise JavaBeans, or CORBA (Common Object Request Broker Architecture) objects.
CFOUTPUT	Displays output that can contain the results of processing ColdFusion functions, variables, and expressions.
CFPARAM	Creates a variable if it doesn't already exist. Optionally, sets the variable to a default value. If the variable already exists, CFPARAM does not change its value.
CFPOP	Retrieves and/or deletes email messages from a POP mail server.
CFQUERY	Establishes a connection to a database (if a connection does not exist), executes a query operation such as insert, retrieve, update, or delete, and returns results.
CFRETURN	Returns a result from a function.
CFSET	Sets or resets the value of a ColdFusion variable. If the variable doesn't already exist, CFSET creates the variable and sets the value. If the variable does exist, CFSET sets the value.
CFTIMER	New in ColdFusion MX 7, this function displays a timer indicating how long it took a section of CFML code to execute.
CFTRY	Used with one or more CFCATCH tags to catch and process exceptions (events such as failed database operations that disrupt normal program flow).

Many of ColdFusion's functions are able to accept arguments that further refine how the function behaves. When learning the tags, pay close attention to what types of data the functions can accept.

In addition to tags and functions, ColdFusion enables you to create variables. Think of a variable as a data container that contains a unique name. Using CFML, you can not only name the container, but fill it with data as well. For instance, take a look at the following code:

```
<CFSET myName = "Sean">
```

This code defines a variable called `"myName"`. It also specifies that the initial value of the variable is Sean. Because the data being inserted into the variable is surrounded by quotes, ColdFusion recognizes it as a string—or data that can contain both numeric and alphanumeric data. After the variable is established, you can display it by using the `cfoutput` tag like this:

```
<CFOUTPUT>#myName#</CFOUTPUT>
```

NOTE

> When calling variables, surround the variable name with pound signs so that the ColdFusion engine knows that it shouldn't simply output the text between the tags.

TIP

> When creating variables in ColdFusion, remember these tips:
> - Variable names must begin with a letter, underscore, or Unicode currency symbol. You cannot begin variable names with a number.
> - Variable names cannot contain spaces.
> - Variable names are not case sensitive.

Now that you've created your variable, you aren't limited to simply displaying the variable. Depending on the type of data stored in the variable, you can use it in calculations or even run comparisons against it.

When you create your variable, you also need to consider its scope. The scope of a variable defines how long the variable should exist and what portions of the page code can use the variable. Because it's important to know when it's okay to use your variable, it's important to define the scope of each variable. ColdFusion has a variety of predefined scope types, so the easiest way to define the scope of a new variable is simply to assign it to one of these types.

You can specify a scope explicitly by putting it before the variable and separating the two with a period. For instance, if you wanted to define the myName variable scope as `"session"` so that it lasted for the duration of the user's browser session, you would define it by typing

```
<CFSET Session.myName = "Sean">
```

This would define the variable, set the initial value, and define the scope of the variable as existing until the session expires.

Table 18.2 lists some commonly used variable types that are available in CFML.

TABLE 18.2 COMMONLY USED VARIABLE TYPES AVAILABLE IN CFML

Data Type	Data Stored
String	Text data wrapped in quotes such as `"Hello World"` or `"Sean"`.
Number	Numeric values. Unlike other languages, CFML does not require that you specify whether or not the number contains decimal points.

18

Data Type	Data Stored
Boolean Value	"Yes", "No", "True", "False", 0, or 1.
Date/Time	Date and time values in formats such as 08/05/2005, 2005-08-05, or 08/05/2005 02:30:00 pm.

TABLE 18.2 CONTINUED

CUSTOM TAGS

In the previous section, you saw how simple it was to call some of the built-in tags such as the CFOUTPUT and CFSET tags. Because the behaviors of these tags are predefined, adding a built-in CFML tag to your code is as easy as adding a standard HTML tag. One of the greatest features of ColdFusion, however, is its extensibility. This means that you can extend CFML beyond the capabilities of the built-in tags by creating your own custom tags, which work just like standard CFML tags. This means that you can create your own tags that contain functionality that can be reused over and over in any ColdFusion pages.

If you're not up to authoring your own custom tags yet, literally thousands of custom tags are available through the ColdFusion Exchange at www.macromedia.com, many of them freeware or shareware. Before you go and spend a lot of time creating a custom tag, it's usually a good idea to browse the Exchange to see whether someone else has already done the work for you. No need to reinvent the wheel!

CUSTOM TAG BASICS

When you create a custom CFML tag, it is stored in its own separate file. Although there are several ways of invoking a custom tag, the easiest is simply to use a tag with the name of the file, with `cf_` in front of it. For example, if the custom tag is contained in a file named `lastmodified.cfm`, you would invoke the custom tag by typing **`cf_lastmodified.cfm`**. You can also invoke a custom tag with the `cfmodule` and `cfimport` functions. They are often favored for managing a large number of custom tags because they are capable of handling any custom tag name conflicts that might arise.

> **N O T E**
>
> There are two kinds of custom tags: CFML and CFX. CFX tags are written in C++ or Java. Only CFML tags are covered in this book.

ColdFusion looks for custom tags first in the same directory as the calling page, then in the `CFusionMX\CustomTags` directory, then in subdirectories of the `CFusionMX\CustomTags` directory, and finally in directories that you can specify in the ColdFusion MX Administrator.

CREATING A CUSTOM TAG

Creating your own custom tag might sound like a daunting task, but keep in mind that custom tags usually consist of code that you might be writing over and over again (hence the need for a custom tag). So if you're going to build the same code block over and over, you might as well create a custom tag instead and save yourself some time.

The first step in creating a custom tag is to determine what it is you want to accomplish. For instance, suppose you wanted every page to display a "last updated on" text block that also included the date when the page was last updated. You could open a text editor and build the following code block:

```
<CFPARAM name="attributes.lastmodified" default="">
<CFOUTPUT>
<I>This page was last updated on #attributes.lastmodified#</I>
</CFOUTPUT>
```

Essentially, this code block takes a date that is passed by the calling page and displays the code block and the date. To invoke the custom tag, you would call it in a CFML page by using code similar to the following:

```
<HTML>
<HEAD>
<TITLE>My Page</TITLE>
</HEAD>
<BODY>
Type your content here.
<CFLastModified LastModified="June 6, 2005">
</BODY>
</HTML>
```

This page now passes the date on which the page was last modified and it is then displayed, along with the text block, on the page. Although this example may seem a bit remedial, it does demonstrate that each custom tag requires two fundamental things:

- The defined custom tag code
- A page that calls that tag and passes any parameters to it.

Truly, the best way to fully understand how custom tags work is to build a few remedial tags yourself, and then spend time on the Macromedia Exchange downloading, reviewing, and looking at the code involved in each of the custom tags on the Exchange.

USING COLDFUSION FOR DATABASE OPERATIONS

Although defining and displaying custom variables might enhance the functionality of your website, the more powerful tool that ColdFusion offers is the capability to communicate with databases and display and interact with content stored within them.

Imagine if your client, Retro's Cycles, had 100 motorcycles in inventory for sale. It wouldn't be reasonable to consider creating an individual web page for each of the 100 motorcycles. It would, however, be a better idea to store the information about the motorcycles in a database and then create a small set of pages that interacts with the database to display information about what is in inventory. Imagine being able to build a search page, a results page, and a details page that enable you to display the content details for each of the 100 motorcycles. That's 3 pages that now have taken the place of 102 pages. Talk about a timesaver!

ColdFusion is able to interact with a database in several different ways. It can retrieve data, update data currently stored in the database, insert new data, or delete existing data.

RETRIEVING DATA

The most common database interaction is simply drawing data out of the database for display on a page. To do this, however, you need to have established a connection to the database and then create a recordset. Think of a recordset as a container that holds all the database records that you have requested. For instance, if you asked the database to retrieve all records where the Make field is equal to "Honda", the recordset would contain only the records for Honda bikes.

To request this data, you need to combine the <CFQUERY> tag with a SQL query that contains the proper syntax for returning the correct records. The <CFQUERY> tag specifies the database from which to retrieve data. The SELECT statement specifies the table(s) within the database, and which records in the tables to get.

The simplest SELECT statement looks like this:

```
SELECT * FROM Inventory
```

This statement says, "Retrieve all columns (fields) of all rows (records) from the Inventory table." The asterisk is a wildcard meaning "all columns." All rows are retrieved, because the statement contains no limiting clause for selecting only a subset of rows. In this case, each row is a different product, and the columns are the attributes of the product, such as the item's unique ID, make, model, year, list price, and so on.

If you want to limit the records your recordset contains, you can use a WHERE clause to select only specified rows. For instance, the following statement retrieves only records where the Make is equal to "Honda":

```
SELECT *
FROM Inventory
WHERE Make = 'Honda'
```

To use this SQL statement in ColdFusion, enclose it in a <CFQUERY> tag. In the following example, the <CFQUERY> tag specifies the retroscycle database, and assigns the name rsHondas to the recordset that is created:

```
<CFQUERY name="rsHondas" datasource="retroscycles">
SELECT *
FROM Inventory
WHERE Make = 'Honda'
</CFQUERY>
```

INSERTING RECORDS

Adding content to your database is almost as simple as retrieving data. Inserting a record usually requires completion of a form and form fields: You enter the data into the form and have it added after you submit it. The form then passes the data to a page (or code on the same page) that processes a SQL command similar to this:

```
INSERT INTO Inventory (Year, Make, Model)
VALUES (#FORM.Year#, #FORM.Make#, #FORM.Model#)
```

Basically, this SQL query takes the contents of the Year, Make, and Model form fields and adds them to the Year, Make, and Model fields in a new record in the database.

Therefore, when you create your full CFML code, it would look something like this:

```
<CFQUERY name="rsHondas" datasource="retroscycles">
INSERT INTO Inventory (Year, Make, Model)
VALUES (#FORM.Year#, #FORM.Make#, #FORM.Model#)
</CFQUERY>
```

UPDATING RECORDS

Another common database interaction is updating a record that already exists in the database. Like the Insert process, this requires two different elements: a form that displays the existing data and allows you to change it, and an action that replaces the existing data with the updated information after the form is submitted.

The form is created with a standard HTML form, or you can use a form created in CMFL by using the <CFFORM> tag. The update action uses the <CFQUERY> tag, along with the SQL update statement that looks something like this:

```
UPDATE Inventory
SET Make='Kawasaki'
WHERE Make='Honda'
```

This update statement modifies all records in the database where the Make is currently Honda and changes the Make field to Kawasaki. Although this is a global change to the entire table, you can limit the update to a single record by further refining the WHERE clause to look something like this:

```
UPDATE Inventory
SET Make='Kawasaki'
WHERE Make='Honda' AND InventoryID = '00011'
```

This update statement would affect only the record that has an InventoryID of 00011.

Because it's likely you'll be making the updates via a form, the form variables that are submitted can also be used in the SQL statement. For example, look at the following:

```
UPDATE Inventory
SET Make=#FORM.Make#
WHERE Make='Honda' AND InventoryID = #FORM.InventoryID#
```

18

This grabs whatever value is stored in the Make form field and enters it into the Make field in the database. Note that this affects only the record that is passed in the `InventoryID` form field.

> **NOTE**
>
> Fields present in the database but not in the UPDATE statement remain unchanged.

DELETING RECORDS

Although deleting records is certainly an important part of database maintenance, it is important to remember that deleting permanently and irrevocably removes records from the database. There is no Edit, Undo command, and you can't restore the data without resorting to a known, good backup such as a tape backup or SQL backup file. So use the command deletion process wisely and cautiously.

When deleting records, the more detail about which record to delete, the better. For instance, consider this simple statement:

```
DELETE * FROM Inventory
```

Because it puts no limits on what to delete, it totally wipes out all the records in the Inventory database. Gone…wiped…kaput.

Therefore, it's a wise idea to restrict your delete commands so that they affect only the record you want. For instance, consider the following command:

```
DELETE FROM Inventory
WHERE InventoryID = '00001'
```

If the `InventoryID` field is a primary key that increments automatically, you can be sure that there will only ever be one record with an `InventoryID` of `000001`. This means that you have deleted only one record and you hope it's the correct one.

Keep in mind that relationships between tables can cause delete operations to fail. For example, if you had a `Sold` table that depended on the `Inventory` table and you tried to execute a `DELETE FROM Sold` (delete all records in the `Sold` table), you would receive an error stating `The record cannot be deleted or changed because table 'Inventory' includes related records`.

TROUBLESHOOTING

I tried connecting to my database, but I got an error that connection could not be established. What happened?

There are a couple things you can check. First, ensure that you spelled the data source name correctly in your code. If it is correct, check that the path specified in the ColdFusion Administrator is still the correct path to the database.

I am receiving a syntax error that I just can't seem to figure out. Where should I look to resolve the issue?

First off, pay close attention to the line number that is being indicated in the error. Look at that line and determine whether you forgot to add an end tag or close a quote or add a pound sign at the beginning or end of your variables. These three things cause a lot of syntax errors and are usually easy to track down after you know what to look for.

BEST PRACTICES—PROPERLY DOCUMENTING CODE

As you begin developing CFML code, I can't stress to you how important it is to document your code as you go along. Just like HTML, CFML provides special character combinations that indicate when a comment tag begins and when it ends. To start a comment, the <!- combination is used, whereas the --> combination is used to indicate that a comment has ended. For instance, suppose you write a block of code that draws two values from the database and averages them. Something as simple as adding a comment line such as the following

```
<!--This function draws the number of motorcycles in the database and
the prices of all the motorcycles and creates an average price-->
```

can save you a lot of time when you have to revisit your code down the road. In addition, if someone else comes along and has to interpret your code, these helpers go a long way in helping them to understand what you were trying to accomplish.

Start developing your documentation skills now and you will reap the benefits of clear, understandable code for the rest of your career.

18

USING COLDFUSION TO GENERATE REPORTS

Although developing database-driven web applications is great, it's likely that at some point you will want to do something with the data other than just display it on a web page. Whether it's understanding how many customers you have, how many orders you have processed, how many posts have been added to your forum, or a host of other data-related questions, you can often answer them by generating a report. Tools such as Crystal Reports and Active Reports generate nicely formatted reports complete with charts and graphs.

The difficulty, however, is creating dynamic reports that are easily incorporated into a web page. Luckily, Macromedia has addressed that point of pain in the new version of ColdFusion and has added a wealth of reporting capabilities to the application.

RICH MEDIA FLASH FORMS

One of the most important aspects of developing reports is the form that specifies what criteria should be retrieved from the database. In the past, web developers have had to rely on HTML forms to create an interface that enables the user to select report criteria. The problem with HTML forms, however, is that they are very limited in their capabilities and aren't really suited for selections that require multiple steps.

For instance, suppose that Retro's Cycles decided to add eCommerce to their website and that they want their customers to be able to create a profile that stores their shipping information and payment information so that they don't have to fill in their information every time they return to the site. Using traditional HTML forms to accomplish this, several forms would be necessary. The first, shown in Figure 19.1, enables the user to input user information and shipping information.

Figure 19.1
A traditional HTML form that collects customer information.

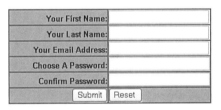

Next, a second form would be necessary to collect information about payment information, similar to the one shown in Figure 19.2.

Finally, a third form would be necessary that enables the customer to enter details about the current order, such as the one in Figure 19.3.

As a result, there are now three forms on three different pages, which increases the possibility that something could go wrong on one of the pages.

Figure 19.2
This form collects payment information.

Please review your shipping and credit card information and complete any required fields. When you are ready to complete your order, please click the Complete Transaction button and your order will be processed.

First Name:	Sean
Last Name:	Nicholson
Address 1:	12345 My Place
Address 2:	Room 202
City:	Kansas City
State:	MO
Zip:	64114
EMail:	annicholson@myemail.com
Telephone:	816-555-5555
Credit Card Type:	VISA
Credit Card Number:	1111111111111112
Credit Card Expiration Month:	01
Credit Card Expiration Year:	07
Any Special Order Instructions:	

Confirm & Checkout

Figure 19.3
This form collects order information.

Your Shopping Cart

Currently, your shopping cart contains the following items:

Scott Number	Price	Quantity	Total
715 - FEATURED	$54.95	1	$54.95
1895(m)	$2.39	1	$2.39
WS0002	$7.98	1	$7.98
WS0007	$6.95	1	$0.95
WS0008	$9.49	1	$9.49

Update Cart   Empty Cart   CheckOut

19

NOTE

Although you could group all these form fields into one long form, this makes the interface difficult to use for your visitors. Think of what would happen if they completed all the information and then, while completing the last field, something happened such as a browser crash. All the time they spent filling in the long form is now wasted because they have to start over from scratch.

For this reason, it's a wise idea to create forms that are short and save segments of data prior to moving on to the next step. That way, if something happens, customers can return and pick up where they left off, having only lost a small portion of their data.

So what's the solution to the problems presented with traditional HTML forms? Flash forms! ColdFusion now allows you to develop forms in the Flash format that enable you to create tabbed views of forms, enable your visitors to save their progress while filling out a form, and give you much more flexibility in controlling how your forms look to your customers.

Using the <CFFORM> tag and the Flash format, you can create a single rich media form that provides the same functionality as the HTML forms I previously mentioned, using a tabbed layout. These forms can be created within Dreamweaver's code view or with a simple text editor. As shown in Figure 19.4, the first tab of the form allows the visitor to enter personal information.

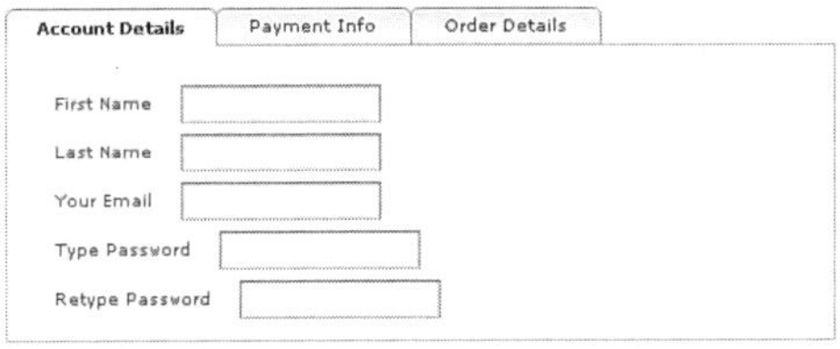

Figure 19.4
This rich media tab collects personal information.

Notice that the form allows users to save their customer information before moving on to the next tab if they choose. The second tab (see Figure 19.5) allows customers to enter their payment information and again, allows them to save their information.

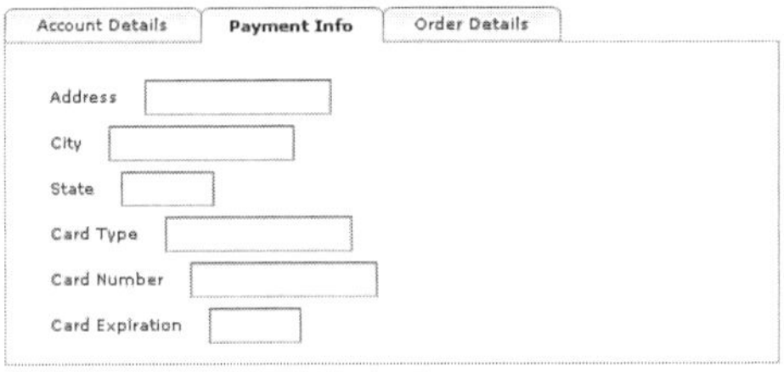

Figure 19.5
This tab collects payment information.

Finally, the third tab (see Figure 19.6) enables them to review any orders they have submitted and the status of those orders.

Figure 19.6
This tab displays orders and their status.

As you can see, the Flash-formatted form offers a wider variety of options and functionality over the traditional HTML forms. So how do you create Flash forms in ColdFusion? It's easy because the Flash content is generated automatically, without requiring you to write complex code.

CREATING A BASIC FLASH FORM

The first step in creating a Flash form is to use the `<CFFORM>` tag to create a ColdFusion form, as shown in Figure 19.7.

Figure 19.7
Use the `<CFFORM>` tag to create a form.

Next, add any input types that you want, such as first name, last name, address, and so on, using the `<CFINPUT>` tag. The fields in Figure 19.8 are all text fields and are named tfFirstName, tfLastName, tfAddress, tfCity, tfState, and tfZip. There is also a single input button.

Figure 19.8
Add text fields and assign types and names.

Next, change the format of the form to the Flash format, as shown in Figure 19.9 and presto! you have a Flash form.

Figure 19.9
A simple Flash form
has been created.

```
1  <!DOCTYPE html PUBLIC "-//W3C//DTD XHTML 1.0 Transitional//EN"
   "http://www.w3.org/TR/xhtml1/DTD/xhtml1-transitional.dtd">
2  <html xmlns="http://www.w3.org/1999/xhtml">
3  <head>
4  <meta http-equiv="Content-Type" content="text/html; charset=iso-8859-1" />
5  <title>Untitled Document</title>
6  </head>
7  <CFFORM format="flash">
8  <CFINPUT name="tfFirstName" type="text" label="First Name" width="120" />
9  <CFINPUT name="tfLastName" type="text" label="Last Name" width="120" />
10 <CFINPUT name="tfAddress" type="text" label="Address" width="120" />
11 <CFINPUT name="tfCity" type="text" label="City" width="120" />
12 <CFINPUT name="tfState" type="text" label="State" width="60" />
13 <CFINPUT name="tfZip" type="text" label="Zip" width="60" />
14 <CFINPUT type="submit" name="submit" value="Submit" />
15 </CFFORM>
16 <body>
17 </body>
18 </html>
19
```

ADDING TABS TO A FLASH FORM

Suppose that you wanted to follow the example discussed earlier and provide additional functionality with tabs. Adding a tab to your form is as simple as adding the form fields you want to display on the second tab, creating a `tabNavigator` group, and then creating form groups with the `<cfformgroup>` tag.

As shown in Figure 19.10, ColdFusion MX 7 enables you to group form elements into groups. The first group you need to establish is the `tabNavigator` group. This group type establishes that you are going to use multiple tabs in your form.

Figure 19.10
The `tabNavigator`
group type specifies
that your form will be
tabbed.

```
1  <!DOCTYPE html PUBLIC "-//W3C//DTD XHTML 1.0 Transitional//EN"
   "http://www.w3.org/TR/xhtml1/DTD/xhtml1-transitional.dtd">
2  <html xmlns="http://www.w3.org/1999/xhtml">
3  <head>
4  <meta http-equiv="Content-Type" content="text/html; charset=iso-8859-1" />
5  <title>Untitled Document</title>
6  </head>
7  <CFFORM format="flash">
8  <CFFORMGROUP type="tabnavigator">
9  <CFINPUT name="tfFirstName" type="text" label="First Name" width="120" />
10 <CFINPUT name="tfLastName" type="text" label="Last Name" width="120" />
11 <CFINPUT name="tfAddress" type="text" label="Address" width="120" />
12 <CFINPUT name="tfCity" type="text" label="City" width="120" />
13 <CFINPUT name="tfState" type="text" label="State" width="60" />
14 <CFINPUT name="tfZip" type="text" label="Zip" width="60" />
15 <CFINPUT type="submit" name="submit" value="Submit" />
16 </CFFORMGROUP>
17 </CFFORM>
18 <body>
19 </body>
20 </html>
21
```

Next, you need to create additional groups that contain the specific inputs for each tab (see Figure 19.11). For each group you create with the `<cfformgroup>` tag, a new tab is created. In addition, the label assigned to the group is what is displayed in the tab.

TIP

Remember to add an input button on any tab that you want to allow the user to submit.

Figure 19.11
The different groups define the various tabs.

```
3   <head>
4   <meta http-equiv="Content-Type" content="text/html; charset=iso-8859-1" />
5   <title>Untitled Document</title>
6   </head>
7   <CFFORM format="flash">
8   <CFFORMGROUP type="tabnavigator">
9   <CFFORMGROUP type="page" label="Name">
10  <CFFORMGROUP type="horizontal">
11  <CFINPUT name="tfFirstName" type="text" label="First Name" width="120" />
12  <CFINPUT name="tfLastName" type="text" label="Last Name" width="120" />
13  </CFFORMGROUP>
14  </CFFORMGROUP>
15  <CFFORMGROUP type="page" label="Address">
16  <CFFORMGROUP type="horizontal">
17  <CFINPUT name="tfAddress" type="text" label="Address" width="120" />
18  <CFINPUT name="tfCity" type="text" label="City" width="120" />
19  <CFINPUT name="tfState" type="text" label="State" width="60" />
20  <CFINPUT name="tfZip" type="text" label="Zip" width="60" />
21  <CFINPUT type="submit" name="submit" value="Submit" />
22  </CFFORMGROUP>
23  </CFFORMGROUP>
24  </CFFORMGROUP>
25  </CFFORM>
26  <body>
27  </body>
28  </html>
```

With the basic form in place, you can then add functionality such as adding the information to a database, sending emails to administrators or staff, or retrieving and displaying content in a report format.

COLDFUSION REPORT BUILDER

Now that your visitors can use Flash forms to submit limiting criteria, they should be able to choose what data they would like to retrieve from your database. You can represent the results of their data requests either numerically or graphically by using the ColdFusion MX 7 Report Engine. Before your visitors can see the report, however, you need to develop a report template that contains a header, footer, and the appropriate data labels and data placeholders.

The tool that Macromedia has developed for building reports is called the ColdFusion Report Builder (see Figure 19.12). This tool doesn't come installed with ColdFusion, but is available on the Macromedia website at http://www.macromedia.com/software/coldfusion/reporting/.

NOTE

At the time of publishing, the Report Builder was available for only the Windows operating system.

CONFIGURING THE REPORT BUILDER

Before you can begin building your new reports, you need to configure the Report Builder. After you run the Report Builder for the first time, you are asked to indicate what you want your default measurement for page layout to be (see Figure 19.13). Choose the measurement with which you're most comfortable for tasks such as page layout.

Figure 19.12
The Macromedia
ColdFusion Report
Builder interface.

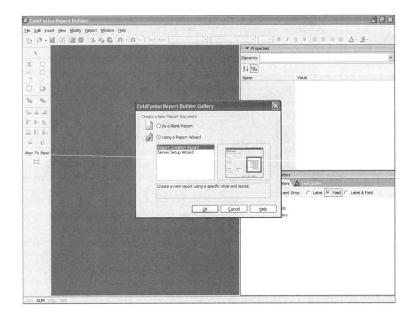

Figure 19.13
Select a default mea-
surement.

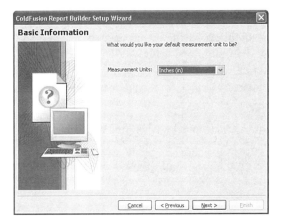

Next, you need to add a CF Server and indicate where your local web pages are stored (see Figure 19.14).

To add a CF server, simply click the plus sign and complete the details for the server to which you want to connect. Be sure to type the correct RDS username and password to avoid authentication issues (see Figure 19.15).

Figure 19.14
Establishing
connectivity.

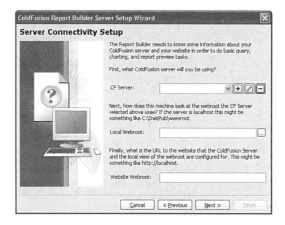

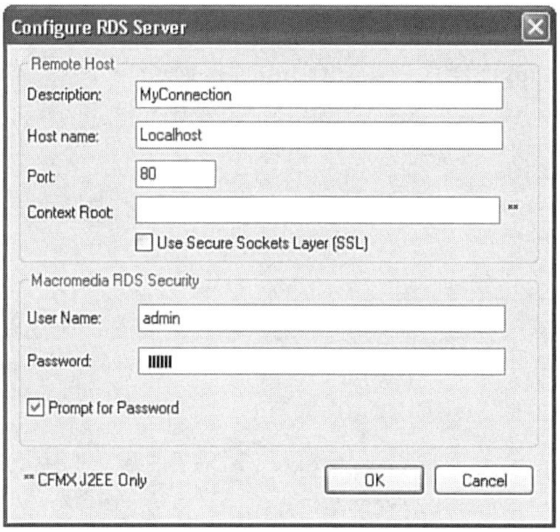

Figure 19.15
Enter the details for
your RDS server.

TIP

To use the Report Builder, you need the ColdFusion server to be running the RDS Security service. If you installed ColdFusion on your local machine, but did not configure RDS, you need to configure it via the ColdFusion Administrator before you can work with the Report Builder application.

Next, type or browse to the local web root and ensure that the website web root field is correct (see Figure 19.16). When the values are correct, move on to the next step and complete the setup wizard.

19

Figure 19.16
Complete all the fields to establish a connection to your ColdFusion server.

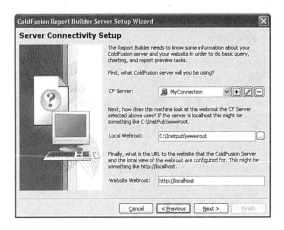

UNDERSTANDING THE REPORT LAYOUT

After downloading and configuring the Report Builder, you can easily create reports and subreports by using the two wizards that are included in the application:

- Report Creation Wizard
- Server Setup Wizard

As you become more and more adept at creating reports, you can skip the wizards and create completely custom reports based on the blank report, your data, and input submitted by the visitor. To give you an introduction to the application, we give you a look at the Report Creation Wizard and its functionality.

The first step in using the wizard to create a report is to develop a SQL query that draws the correct data from the database, creating a recordset that you can use to display in the report. Click the Query Builder button and choose a database, table, and selection criteria for the data that is to be used in the report. The SQL query in Figure 19.17 would retrieve all the records in the Inventory database.

You can refine your data by using conditional variables to limit the results. For instance, if you had developed a form that allowed visitors to choose the make of a motorcycle they wanted to view, the contents of that form field might be passed as a form value called "Make." The query in Figure 19.18 shows how the SQL query can be limited with this variable.

Figure 19.17
Choose a SQL query to retrieve your data.

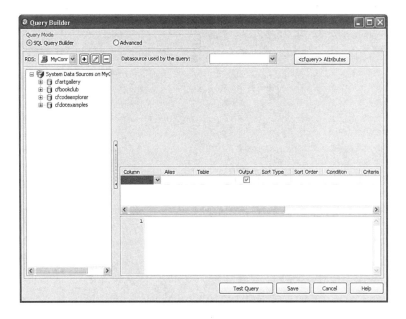

Figure 19.18
You can further limit the SQL query by using variables.

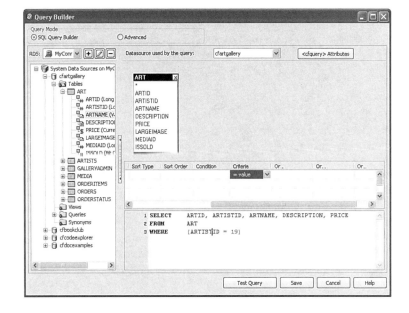

After you have developed your query, click the Save button to return to the Report Creation Wizard. The wizard now displays the columns you chose to retrieve from the database (see Figure 19.19) and enables you to choose which will actually be visible in the report.

Figure 19.19
Your fields are now
available for display in
the report.

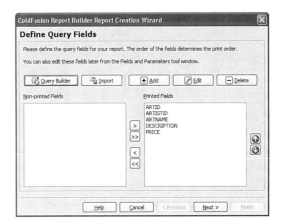

In the next dialog within the wizard, you can choose how to group the records retrieved by
your SQL query (see Figure 19.20). Groupings generally help the reader of the report easily
compare the data that is being displayed. For instance, if Retro's Cycles had four Honda
Super Hawk motorcycles for sale, you could group the data by Model and the person
reviewing the report could easily compare the attributes of the four Super Hawks.

Figure 19.20
Choose how to group
the data that is
retrieved.

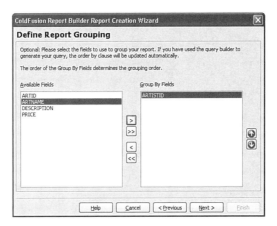

Following through the rest of the wizard, you can customize your report's layout (see
Figure 19.21), style (see Figure 19.22), theme (see Figure 19.23), and name (see
Figure 19.24).

Figure 19.21
Select a layout for
your report.

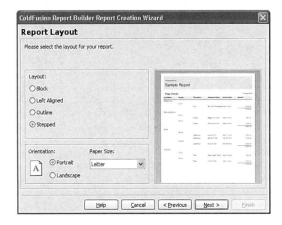

Figure 19.22
Select a style for your
report.

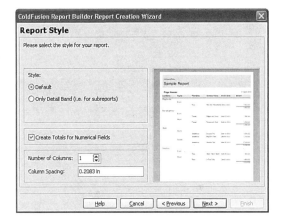

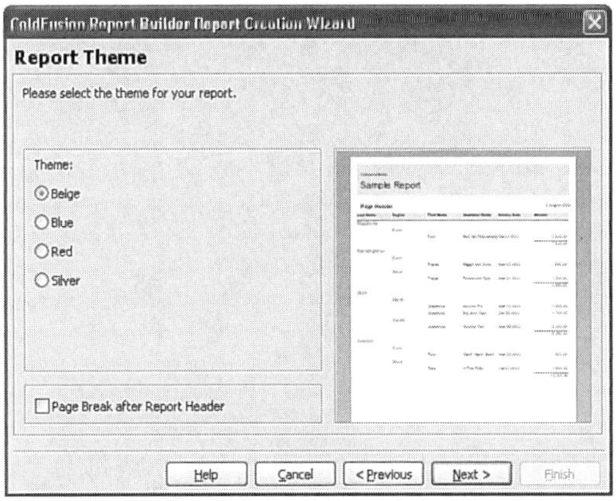

Figure 19.23
Select a theme for
your report.

19

Figure 19.24
Customize the name
of your report.

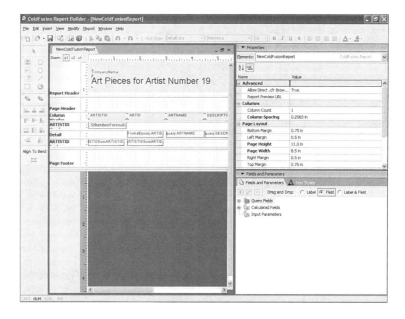

With those elements in place you can now build the report. As shown in Figure 19.25, the complete report enables you to further customize any of the report elements, data placeholders, and layout options within the report.

Figure 19.25
The report template
has been created.

The last step to creating your custom report is to save the report file. Each report is saved with a `.cfr` extension that the ColdFusion server can interpret. As you'll see in a minute, this single CFR page can then be displayed in a variety of different formats.

TIP

For a great walkthrough on using custom input parameters in reports, check out Ben Forta's tutorial at http://macromedia.breezecentral.com/p99229136/.

REPORTING FORMATS

ColdFusion MX 7 not only enables you to create stunning, dynamic reports based on your database content, but it also enables you to provide these reports to your users in a variety of formats. In fact, you can display the same report in multiple formats in a snap. After you create a report, just add the appropriate tag to your web page and ColdFusion does the rest.

PDF REPORTS

One of the most popular formats for displaying reports via a web browser is the Adobe Portable Document Format (PDF). This file format enables you to package a document in a single file that can be emailed, stored on disk, or displayed on your website with the free Adobe Acrobat Reader application that is available via Adobe's website.

To create a report that uses the PDF format, all you need to do is add the `<cfreport>` tag to your page and set the format to PDF. For instance, the following code would call a report named `retros_customers.cfr`:

```
<cfreport template = "artist_19.cfr" format = "PDF"></cfreport>
```

NOTE

When you specify the template location for your report, the filename is relative to your site's web root.

That's it! Just save your page and view it in your browser (see Figure 19.26).

Figure 19.26
A report created in the PDF format, using the ColdFusion Report Generator.

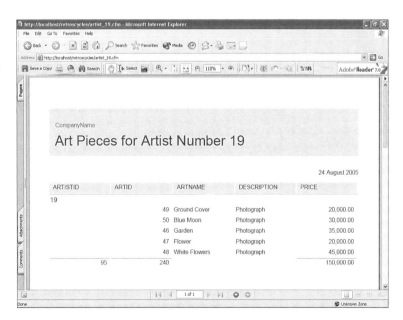

Before we move on to the next format, it would probably be good to mention the various attributes that you can add to the `cfreport` tag when generating reports:

- `Name`—Enables you to specify the name of a ColdFusion variable that holds report output.
- `Filename`—Used instead of the Name attribute, it enables you to specify a filename that will contain the report after it is generated.
- `Query`—Enables you to specify a SQL query if one has not been embedded in the report.
- `Overwrite`—Specifies whether or not files that already exist can be overwritten.
- `Encryption`—Used for PDF reports only, this attribute can be set to 128-bit, 40-bit, or none.
- `Ownerpassword`—Enables you to set a password for owners on a PDF report.
- `Userpassword`—Enables you to set a password for users on a PDF report.
- `Permissions`—Specifies eight different permission levels for PDF reports (`AllowPrinting`, `AllowModifyContents`, `AllowCopy`, `AllowModifyAnnotations`, `AllowFillIn`, `AllowScreenReaders`, `AllowAssembly`, and `AllowDegradedPrinting`).

FLASHPAPER REPORTS

Another option for creating reports in ColdFusion is the FlashPaper format developed by Macromedia. This format converts your document into a Flash movie that can be viewed with the Macromedia Flash Player. Creating a FlashPaper report is just as easy as creating one in the PDF format. Just use exactly the same code you used for the PDF format and adjust the format attribute:

```
<cfreport template = "retros_customers.cfr" format = "FlashPaper"></cfreport>
```

Again, view the document in your browser and the Flash Player renders the report (see Figure 19.27).

MICROSOFT EXCEL REPORTS

The final format that the ColdFusion Report Generator is able to create is the Microsoft Excel format (see Figure 19.28). Where the PDF and FlashPaper reports are generally read-only, the Excel format offers access to data, and reports can be saved and edited offline. As with FlashPaper and PDF, generating an Excel report is as simple as adjusting the format attribute:

```
<cfreport template = "retros_customers.cfr" format = "Excel"></cfreport>
```

Be aware, however, that there are some limitations as to how well your formatting will be retained in the Excel format. Objects such as images and charts may not render properly, and numeric data that contains special characters such as commas, percent signs, and dollar signs might cause issues in the generation of the report.

Figure 19.27
A report created in the FlashPaper format, using the ColdFusion Report Generator.

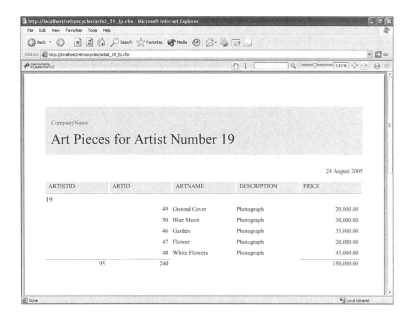

Figure 19.28
A report created in the Excel format, using the ColdFusion Report Generator.

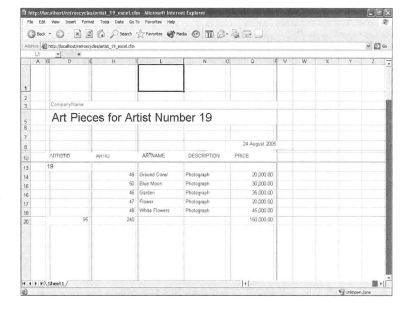

CREATING PRINTABLE WEB PAGES

Printing web pages has been a problem since the beginning of the web itself. Because a computer monitor is wider than it is tall, developing pages for the screen often results in pages that print off the edge of standard paper because it is taller than it is wide. To address the issue, web developers have come up with scripts that parse text, secondary printable page templates, and a host of other tricks, but most of them take quite a bit of time and energy to create.

With the new ColdFusion MX 7, Macromedia has created a quick, easy way to make any web page printable with the introduction of the new <cfdocument> tag. This tag renders any text or images located inside the tag in the PDF or FlashPaper formats and enables you to control page aspects such as orientation, page size, headers, footers, and formatting options.

So with the addition of one simple tag, you can now avoid the hassle of making printable pages, and ensure that your pages will be just as readable offline as they are online. You can implement application of the <cfdocument> tag by using it like this:

```
<cfdocument format = "PDF">
Hello World!
<img src="my_image.gif">
</cfreport>
```

To adjust the properties of the resulting document, you can use the following attributes:

- Format—Determines whether the output will be PDF or FlashPaper format.
- MarginTop—Sets the top margin for the output document. Default is .5 inches.
- MarginBottom—Sets the bottom margin for the output document. Default is .5 inches.
- MarginLeft—Sets the left margin for the output document. Default is .5 inches.
- MarginRight—Sets the right margin for the output document. Default is .5 inches.
- BackgroundVisible—Determines whether the web page's background color or image is printed.
- Orientation—Specifies landscape or portrait. Default is portrait.
- PageType—Specifies one of nine different output file types: letter, legal, A4, A5, B4, B5, B4-JIS, B5-JIS, and custom.
- PageWidth—Used with the custom page type, enables you to set a custom page width.
- PageHeight—Used with the custom page type, enables you to set a custom page height.
- Encryption—In the PDF format, this attribute enables you to choose from 128-bit, 40-bit, or no encryption.
- OwnerPassword—When encryption is enabled, this tag sets an owner password.
- UserPassword—When encryption is enabled, this tag sets a user password.
- Permissions—Sets various permission types.
- Unit—Determines whether your numeric attributes are measured in inches or centimeters.
- FontEmbed—Embeds the fonts within the document for accurate rendering.
- Filename—Specifies where to save the output file.
- Overwrite—Determines whether existing files with the same name can be overwritten.

- Name—Saves the result content to a ColdFusion variable that can be used later in the document.

- Scale—Specifies the zoom factor for the document.

After you have the tag in place and the attributes set, implementing the printable document is easy. Use code similar to this:

```
<cfhttp url="http://www.yahoo.com" method="get" resolveURL="true">
<cfdocument format="PDF">
    <cfoutput>#cfhttp.filecontent#</cfoutput>
</cfdocument>
```

The `<cfhttp>` tag specifies the URL to obtain and the `<cfoutput>` tag renders the page content to a PDF document (see Figure 19.29).

Figure 19.29
A web page that would have printed off the page is now easily printable.

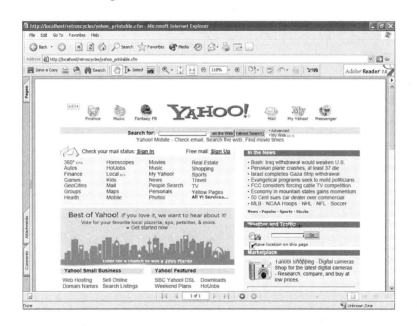

As you can see, ColdFusion continues to grow in its capabilities. Being able to generate stunning reports and printer-friendly web pages is certainly one of the application's biggest steps in continuing to establish the ColdFusion platform as the most user-friendly and adaptable platforms on the market.

TROUBLESHOOTING

I can't seem to find the Report Builder functionality you mention in the ColdFusion Administrator. Am I missing something?

The ColdFusion Report Generator is not included with ColdFusion MX 7 and must be downloaded and installed separately. You can download the executable at http://www.macromedia.com/software/coldfusion/reporting/.

I don't see the Mac version of the Report Builder executable. Is there a place to download it?

No. At this point Macromedia has released the Report Builder for only the Windows platform.

My report is extremely slow to load. What can I do to speed up the report's build time?

The first step is to limit your SQL query to only those fields that are absolutely necessary to the report. Adding fields to the recordset that will not be used in the report is a waste of server resources and a waste of time waiting for the report to load.

BEST PRACTICES—LIMITING SQL QUERIES

When generating reports, the ColdFusion Report Builder enables you to select as many fields into your SQL query as you would like. It then enables you to choose which of those fields you would actually like to display in the report. You therefore might be tempted to simply select every field from the database into your query and then filter out what you don't want to see with the Report Builder.

Be cautious in this approach. Remember that each time your page or report loads, the recordset is built. This means that if your database has 50 fields and 5,000 records, your SQL query will have to draw 25,000 pieces of data from the database. If, however, you determined that you wanted to display only 5 of those fields, your SQL query has to return only 2,500 pieces of data—which decreases the amount of time it takes for your report to load.

So before you ever begin developing your SQL query, take some time to determine which fields you really need and which can be left alone to conserve load times.

CHAPTER 20

USING THE INTEGRATED VERITY SEARCH ENGINE

In this chapter

So you have planned out your next site, given a lot of time to the database backend, identified thousands of products for your visitors to buy, and you're ready to roll…right? Well, maybe not quite yet. Sure, you might have tons of stuff to buy, but how are your visitors going to find the item they're looking for in your mega-catalog? The answer is usually a search application for your site.

Companies such as Google, AltaVista, and Yahoo! have made a pretty penny developing search engine technology, but don't be fooled into thinking that search engines are only for the big boys. Any site that initially has a large volume of data or even those that start small and grow over time can be benefited by the addition of searching capabilities.

UNDERSTANDING THE BASICS OF SEARCHING

Searching is searching is searching. It doesn't matter whether you're referring to the process of finding your keys in the morning or finding your favorite library book in an online catalog, the process usually works the same (assuming you have had your coffee in the morning).

Every logical search that we perform relies on a set of reference points. These reference points enable you to filter out unnecessary data and focus on the data that is pertinent to your search. For instance, when you begin your search for your car keys in the morning, is India in the search criteria? Probably not, unless you live in India. I know the example might seem a little silly, but it demonstrates that there are lots of possible options (no matter how improbable) that we automatically filter out when performing simple searches.

So suppose I were searching for my keys. I have pretty much filtered out India and all countries outside of the U.S. In addition, I filter out all states except Kansas, and all cities except Olathe. I'm pretty sure I had them when I came home (because I drove), so I filter out all other houses in Olathe.

Next, I can start filtering out rooms within the house. I could search every nook and cranny within each room, but by understanding some criteria about the keys and my habits, I can further limit the number of places I have to look. For instance, if I think back to yesterday, I know I had them when I walked in the door, and I tend to put them on the kitchen table, on the dresser, or leave them in my work pants. So after a check of these usual places, the majority of the time I end up with my keys.

Although I'm sure it's absolutely fascinating for you to review the whereabouts of my car keys, the exercise has a point. It demonstrates how important filters are in finding data. Each of the filters I applied to the search for my keys significantly narrowed the number of places I had left to look.

The same concept applies to search applications within websites. Think of the search criteria that your visitors type into form fields as filters on all the data stored in your web pages. For instance, if a visitor to the Retro's Cycles site typed "Honda" into the search field, it's likely that he or she is not interested in seeing any information other than that relating to Honda motorcycles, and the results that you provide should be tailored to those needs.

Major search engines take this concept one step further by expanding their searchable data through the proactive searching of other websites—a process commonly referred to as *spidering*. For instance, Google (see Figure 20.1) has a search program called GoogleBot that visits thousands of websites each day and reads the content on the site.

Figure 20.1
The simple, yet effective Google search interface.

If GoogleBot determines the information to be new and useful, it copies portions of the site content into its database (or index) and adds additional information (called metadata) such as the time the site was last indexed, keywords that might be useful in retrieving the data, and title of the page where the data is located. Then, when you visit Google and type search criteria into the form, Google searches the index and returns only those results that apply to your search term.

Adding search capabilities to your site, however, doesn't necessarily require complex tools such as a spider or a metadata index. You can also accomplish a very similar result by allowing your visitors to run SQL queries against your database without them ever having to understand what a SQL query is.

USING SQL QUERIES TO RETURN SEARCH RESULTS

For sites that use data stored in a database, one of the most common methods of implementing search capabilities is to simply allow your visitors to query certain fields within your database. For instance, suppose you have a database table named `tbInventory` that contains the following fields:

- `InventoryID`
- `Year`
- `Make`

20

- Model
- Color
- Size
- Condition
- Description

With this table structure, you could allow your visitors to easily narrow their searches by providing them with a search form on which they could choose from the available years, makes, and models, like the one shown in Figure 20.2.

Figure 20.2
A search form like this enables visitors to easily limit their results.

For instance, suppose a visitor selected "2000" from the year field, selected "Honda" from the Make field, and selected "VT1100" from the Model field. When the Submit button was clicked, the visitor would effectively be submitting a query that says "Show me all the records in the `tbInventory` table where the Year field is equal to `2000`, the Make field is equal to `Honda`, and the Model field is equal to `VT1100`." Luckily, we can translate this request into a SQL query that the ColdFusion application understands, and it would look something like this:

```
SELECT *
FROM tbInventory
WHERE Year = "2000" AND Make = "Honda" AND Model = "VT1100"
```

If there were any records that met all these criteria, those would be displayed for the visitor to review (see Figure 20.3).

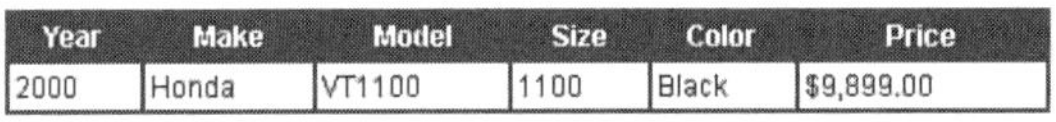

Figure 20.3
Results from a simple SQL query search.

Year	Make	Model	Size	Color	Price
2000	Honda	VT1100	1100	Black	$9,899.00

If no matching data was found, the visitor would be informed and might have the opportunity to refine the search (see Figure 20.4).

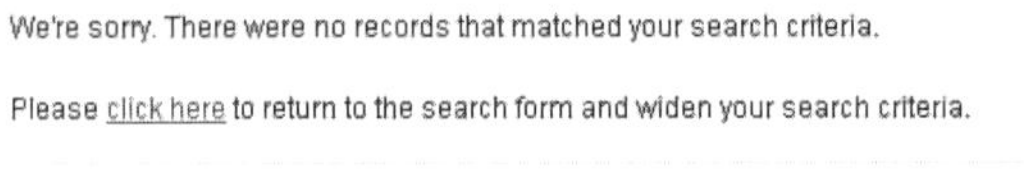

Figure 20.4
No data is returned by the query and the user has the opportunity to modify the search.

We're sorry. There were no records that matched your search criteria.

Please click here to return to the search form and widen your search criteria.

Creating this type of search application is quick and easy and requires no further configuration of the ColdFusion engine. Instead, it requires an understanding of developing web forms, database connections, recordsets, and results pages that we explore further in the Dreamweaver section of this book. For now, just be aware that through the use of web forms and database connectivity, ColdFusion is capable of allowing your visitors to easily search your database content.

A second type of query is one that searches the results of a search engine index or collection. This type of search is extremely useful when your site contains a large number of pages with static content or a large number of documents.

COLDFUSION'S VERITY SEARCH ENGINE ARCHITECTURE

ColdFusion MX 7 comes with its own search server, called the Verity Search Server. The Verity application runs separately from ColdFusion and stores the page metadata in indexes called *collections*. When a search request is presented to ColdFusion with the `<cfsearch>` tag along with a collection attribute, it hands off the search criteria to the Verity Search Server. Verity then searches the collections for the site and returns any corresponding metadata back to ColdFusion. ColdFusion then builds the results page based on that metadata for the visitor to review (see Figure 20.5).

Figure 20.5
The search request and results delivery process using Verity.

Search Retro's Cycles Web Site
Search Results

No	Score	File	Title
1	.9950	aboutus.cfm	About Retro's Cycles
2	.9115	contactus.cfm	Contact Retro's Cycles
3	.8657	forsale.cfm	Motorcycles currently for sale
4	.8169	index.cfm	Retro's Cycles Home
5	.7967	2002_vt1100_1.cfm	Honda Shadow VT1100
6	.7967	2000_vtr1000_1.cfm	Honda Super Hawk VTR1000
7	.6952	2000_gsxr1000_1.cfm	Suzuki GSX-R 1000

For the collections to be searchable, however, there must first be data stored in them. Populating this data is done in one of two ways. The easiest method is via the ColdFusion Administrator, which handles the indexing of any collections created with the Administrator.

The second option is to use the command-line interface to create the collection and to index the site. Verity comes with its own search spider, called vspider, that can scan all the pages and files within your website, including Microsoft Office documents, WordPerfect, text, and PDF documents, and include their contents in the collections. The only drawback, however, is that by default the vspider is not capable of indexing collections created within the ColdFusion Administrator. You can, however, make modifications to ColdFusion and Verity that allow vspider to index these collections.

20

TIP

> For instructions on configuring vspider to search collections created within the
> ColdFusion Administrator, check out the ColdFusion TechNote located at
> http://www.macromedia.com/cfusion/knowledgebase/index.cfm?id=50f419a.

CONFIGURING VERITY AND CREATING A COLLECTION

Before you can begin using Verity as your search engine, you need to create a collection for
your site. To create a new collection, open the ColdFusion MX 7 Administrator by typing
`http://localhost/CFIDE/administrator` in your browser's address bar. Log in to the administrator and choose Verity Collections from the left navigation menu.

As shown in Figure 20.6, the form for creating a new Verity collection is very simple.

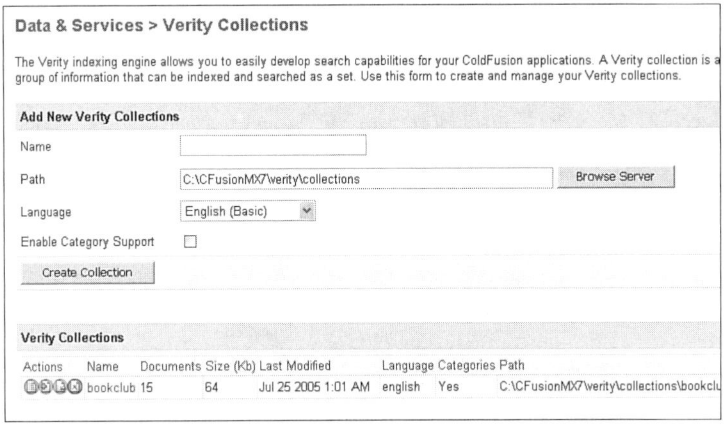

Figure 20.6
You can create a new
Verity collection via
the ColdFusion
Administrator.

Simply type the name for your new collection and designate a path where that collection
will be stored. Next, choose a language for your collection and choose whether or not you
want to enable category support. Category support enables you to easily group your pages
into logical categories that can be used to further assist your visitors in their searches. For
instance, in the results page, you could add a link that says "View similar pages," which links
to the other pages in the same category.

CAUTION

> You can choose whether or not to enable category support only at the time of collection
> creation. You cannot go back and turn the feature on after the collection has been cre-
> ated, so consider whether you think you want to use this feature before you click the
> Create Collection button.

After you have completed the form, click the Create Collection button and the collection is created and added to the list of collections (see Figure 20.7).

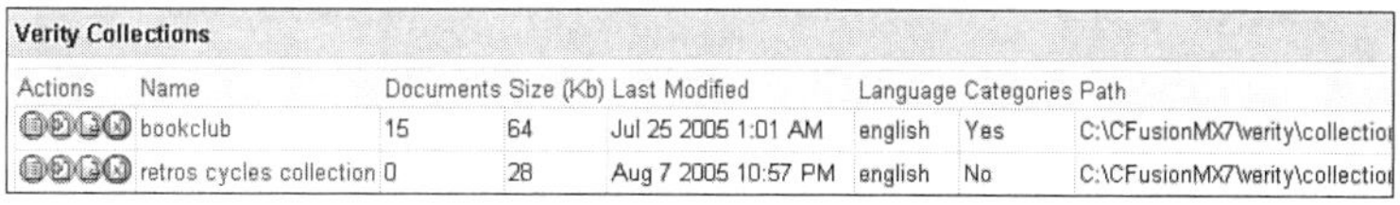

Figure 20.7
Existing collections are listed in the ColdFusion Administrator.

The Verity Search Server application does not necessarily have to be installed on the same server as ColdFusion. If you choose to install Verity on a different server, you need to indicate where the application is located for ColdFusion to be able to access the collections. To modify this setting, click the Verity K2 Server link in the ColdFusion Administrator, type the name of the server in the Verity Host Name field, and click Submit Changes (see Figure 20.8).

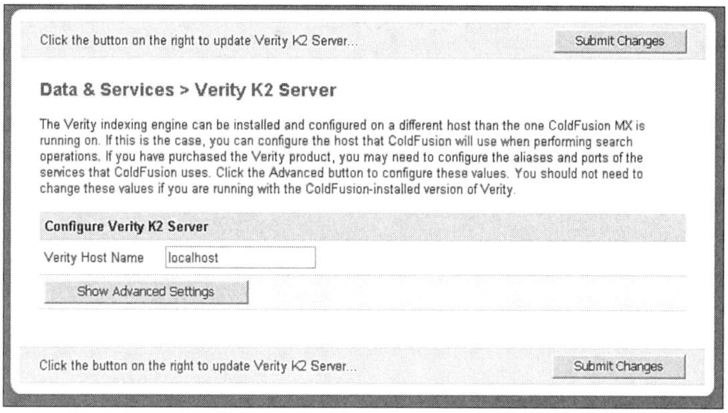

Figure 20.8
The ColdFusion Administrator enables you to indicate where Verity is installed if it is not on the same server as ColdFusion.

After you have created your collection and specified the location of the Verity Search Server, you can use the Action buttons next to the collection to index, optimize, purge, and delete the collections. When you choose to index a collection (see Figure 20.9), you can indicate which file types and directories should be indexed.

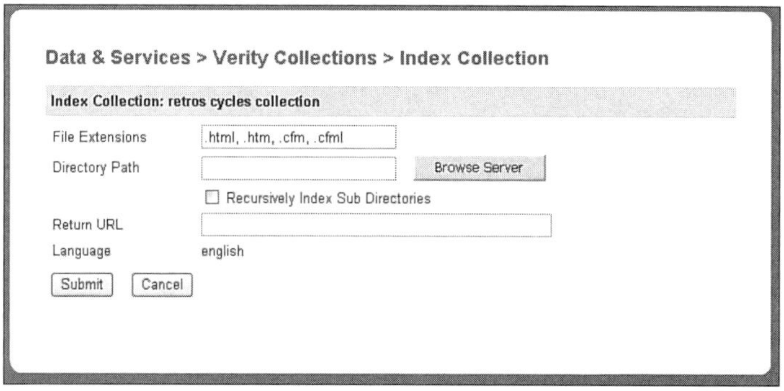

Figure 20.9
Indexing a collection is easy to do from within the ColdFusion Administrator.

SUBMITTING QUERIES TO THE VERITY SEARCH SERVER

After you have your collection in place and your site indexed, you should create a search interface that enables your visitors to submit their queries to the Verity server for comparison against the collection. A simple form such as the one in Figure 20.10 enables the visitor to enter a search term and submit it to a page that displays the results.

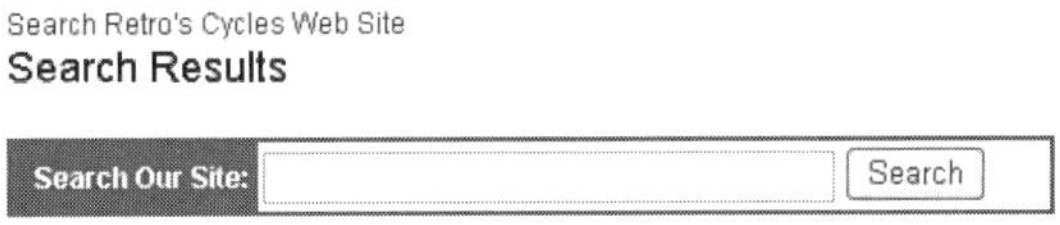

Figure 20.10
A simple search form that submits a query to Verity.

The results page is where the real search magic takes place. For instance, suppose that the text field in the search form was named `tfSearchTerm`. The results page needs a snippet of code like the following to begin the search:

```
<CFSEARCH NAME="searchMyCollection"
➥COLLECTION="myCollection" CRITERIA="#FORM.tfSearchTerm#">
```

This tag compares the content of the `tfSearchTerm` text field with the data stored in the `myCollection` Verity collection.

> **NOTE**
>
> The value of the COLLECTION attribute must match the name of the collection that you created in the ColdFusion Administrator.

To output the search results on the page, add the following code:

```
<CFOUTPUT QUERY="searchMyCollection">
    <a href="#URL#">#Title#</a>
</CFOUTPUT>
```

This code outputs the results of the `searchMyCollection` search and displays the Title as a clickable hyperlink. The `#URL#` and `#Title#` variables are built-in variables that are returned by the `<cfsearch>` tag. Some additional variables that you can use include the following:

- `score`—Displays the relevancy score of the result based on the frequency with which the search term occurs in the page.
- `summary`—Displays a brief summary of the document.
- `recordCount`—Displays the number of results returned by the query.
- `recordsSearched`—Displays the number of records searched within the collection.
- `author`—New in ColdFusion MX 7, this variable displays the name of the document author.
- `category`—New in ColdFusion MX 7, this variable displays the category of the document if the collection allows for categorization.

- `size`— New in ColdFusion MX 7, this variable displays the size of the document in bytes.
- `type`—New in ColdFusion MX 7, this variable displays the MIME type of the document.

Using these basic concepts, you should understand how the Verity Search Server can assist you in providing search capabilities to your site visitors. When coupled with SQL queries against the database, this powerful search engine application can assist you in ensuring that your visitors are able to find the information they are looking for.

TROUBLESHOOTING

When I view the results of my search, I see no results. Where should I look to figure out what's happening?

The first place I would look is the ColdFusion Administrator. Be sure that you have indexed your collection or it will contain no metadata to search. Next, take a look at your `<cfsearch>` tag and ensure that the collection attribute is spelled exactly as it is in the ColdFusion Administrator.

I have made significant changes to the content on my site. Do I have to delete and re-create my collection to ensure that the information stored in the collection is correct?

No. Just purge the data stored in the collection via the ColdFusion Administrator and then rebuild the index. All your new data will be included in the new index.

BEST PRACTICES—DESIGNING A USER INTERFACE FOR YOUR SEARCH APPLICATION

Almost as powerful as the database backend or the search engine application you use, your search interface can determine whether your users are successful in retrieving the search results they are seeking. Sometimes, the most effective search forms are as simple as possible, allowing the hard work of parsing out the search term to be done on the back end without the user ever knowing that the query is being sliced and diced. For instance, when designing a search interface, you might consider some of the following:

- Do your search form and results page accommodate for multiple search terms? For instance, does the search term "sticky wicket" return only those pages with the full phrase "sticky wicket," or does it also return pages that contain "sticky" or "wicket"?
- Is your search form accessible to those with disabilities? For tips on making your forms accessible, check out http://www.netmechanic.com/news/vol5/accessibility_no19.htm.
- Is your search form easy to find? Is it visible on every page in your site so that visitors can use it if they get stuck in the navigation process?

20

- Can your search form handle and parse out Boolean functions such as "and" and "or"?
- Does your simple search form include a link to a more advanced search form that provides more functionality?

Addressing some of these concerns may help you in your search form development and may produce a stronger search form that helps your users in their search activities.

CHAPTER 21

PUTTING IT ALL TOGETHER: CONFIGURING COLDFUSION FOR DATABASE CONNECTIVITY

In this chapter

With the site design in place and the template created, the next step is to choose a platform for your pages and decide whether the site will be dynamic or static. In the case of Retro's Cycles, they would like to be able to make updates to their own site, without having to rely on a web developer whenever a change is necessary. In this situation, there are two primary options. The first is to provide the client with a copy of an HTML editor or WYSISYW web page editor and give them basic instruction as to its use. The second option is to create a database-driven website that has an administrative section that enables clients to make updates to content stored in the database via their browsers. This second option is the one that the client has chosen.

This means that the web pages can't be static HTML pages. Instead, they need to be created on one of the dynamic platforms such as ASP, JSP, PHP, or ColdFusion. Because we have covered just the fundamentals of ColdFusion and because ColdFusion is part of the Macromedia Studio, we'll stick with the ColdFusion platform.

The second element that you need is a database that contains the data for the pages. Although a variety of databases is out there, one of the most common is a Microsoft Access database. Access databases are ideal for small sites because they are easy to build, perform relatively well on the web, and can be updated easily by someone with a basic understanding of Access.

UNDERSTANDING THE DATABASE STRUCTURE

The database that has been built for Retro's Cycles is a very simple one. If you have Microsoft Access installed on your workstation, download the `retros_cycles_99300d2.mdb` database from the ColdFusion section of the companion website and familiarize yourself with the structure. If you don't have Access installed, the figures should give you a pretty good understanding of how the database is structured. To examine the structure of the database, follow these steps:

1. Open `retros_cycles_99300d2.mdb` in Microsoft Access. In the Database window, notice that the database consists of three tables named `tbCustomers`, `tbInventory`, and `tbPageData` (see Figure 21.1).

Figure 21.1
The three tables that are located within the database.

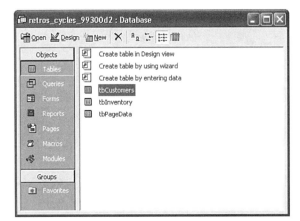

NOTE

Depending on what version of Access you have installed, you might have to convert the Access database to your version. All the functionality that is discussed in this section applies to any version of Access.

2. Select the `tbPageData` table and click the Design button. This table, shown in Figure 21.2, contains the content that is displayed on each of the web pages and information relating to its status, an image URL that is associated with the page, and a unique page ID that also serves as the primary key for the table. The page ID field is an autonumber field, which ensures that each record has a unique page ID.

Figure 21.2
The `tbPageData` table structure.

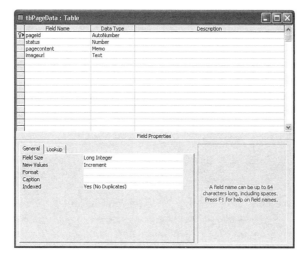

3. Close the `tbPageData` table. In the Database window, double-click on the `tbPageData` table to open it in the data view. As you can see in Figure 21.3, several records in the database contain page content. Each of the records has a numeric page ID that is incremental in nature.

Figure 21.3
The `tbPageData` table data.

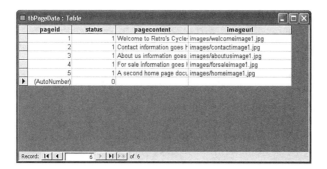

21

4. Close the `tbPageData` table.

5. In the Database window, select the `tbCustomers` table and click the Design button. This table, shown in Figure 21.4, contains information about Retro's Cycles customers. Again, the table has a primary key called `customerid` that is an autonumber field. The staff at Retro's Cycles can use this table to track customer information and purchases and to create mailing labels for periodic mailings.

Figure 21.4
The `tbCustomers` table structure.

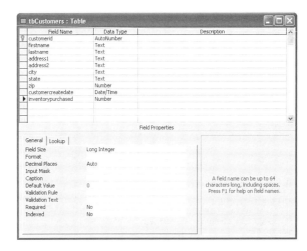

6. Close the `tbCustomers` table. In the Database window, double-click on the `tbCustomers` table to open it in the data view. As you can see in Figure 21.5, this table contains customer information. Again, each of the records has a numeric `customerid` that ensures it is unique.

Figure 21.5
The `tbCustomers` table data.

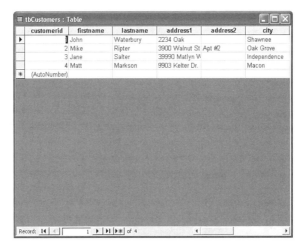

7. Close the `tbCustomers` table.

8. In the Database window, select the `tbInventory` table and click the Design button. This table, shown in Figure 21.6, contains information about the various motorcycles that are in stock. The primary key for this table is `inventoryid`.

Figure 21.6

The `tbInventory` table structure.

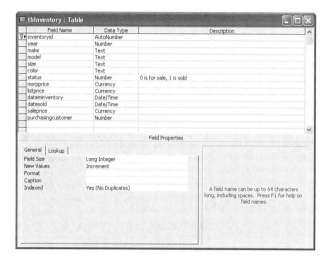

TIP

When developing a database for the web, primary keys are very important. A primary key ensures that the record you request via a web page is the only record that is returned. For instance, suppose you didn't have a primary key that identified each record as unique. If you created a query that said "Show me the record in the database where the last name is Smith," you might encounter problems if there is more than one Smith in the database. If, however, you assign a primary key to each record and you ask "Show me the record in the database where the customerid is 1223," then you know you're going to get the correct record because there will never be more than one record in the database with a customer ID of 1223.

9. Close the `tbInventory` table. In the Database window, double-click on the `tbInventory` table to open it in the data view. As you can see in Figure 21.7, this table stores information relating to the motorcycles that are in inventory and their status.

10. Close the `tbCustomers` table and close the database.

As you can see, this database structure is relatively simple and straightforward. Just because a database will be used on the web doesn't mean it has to be complex.

21

Figure 21.7
The `tbInventory` table data.

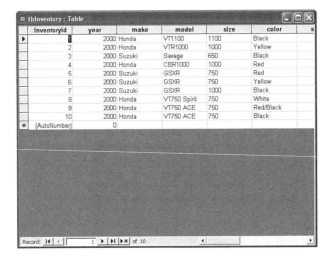

DATABASE NAMING AND LOCATION

When you use an Access database to store information that will be available via the web, you need to address a few security issues. Microsoft Access creates file-based databases, which means that all the data is stored in a single, portable file that can be copied to a floppy, burned to a CD, or downloaded from a website. Although this is great because it makes it easy to transport your database from one place to another, it is also a security concern because you don't want anyone downloading your database and having access to your customer information. A few things, however, will significantly decrease the chance of your database being stolen.

The first step you can take is to place the database in a directory with a unique name. Naming the directory something highly unique diminishes the chance that some clever hacker can to go to your site, guess the name of the directory, and be that much closer to downloading your database.

Create a new folder in your web root called `rcdb99840b` and save the `retros_cycles_99300d2.mdb` to that folder. If you are using IIS and chose the default settings when setting it up, the path to your database would be `c:\InetPub\wwwroot\rcdb99840b\retros_cycles_99300d2.mdb`, as shown in Figure 21.8.

NOTE

Remember that the location of the root folder for your website is going to be different if you are using a web server other than IIS in Windows. If you are using a web server such as Apache, adjust the path to the database accordingly.

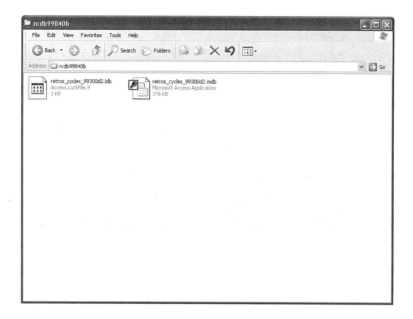

The second step you can take to protect your Access database is to simply name it something very unique. If you accept the default name of db1.mdb that Access tries to assign to your database, it's likely that someone with an understanding of Access will be able to guess that name. In addition, it wouldn't be safe enough to name the database for Retro's Cycles something like retros_cycles_database.mdb because this name is still one that is easy to guess. Instead, name it something that you will be able to recognize and append a string of totally random letters and numbers, so that it's highly unlikely that someone could just guess the name of the database. As you saw in the previous section, the database that was created for Retro's Cycles is named retros_cycles_99300d2.mdb. The next step you can take is to disable directory browsing in your web server application. As shown in Figure 21.9, IIS and other popular browsers allow you to determine whether browsing to the root of a site that does not contain a home page displays the contents of that directory. To disable directory browsing in IIS, follow these steps:

21

1. Open the Computer Management console by right-clicking on My Computer and choosing Manage. In the Computer Management console (see Figure 21.10), click the plus sign next to Service and then click the plus sign next to Internet Information Services.

Figure 21.10
The Computer Management console.

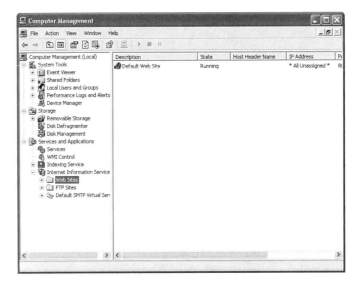

NOTE

If you don't see IIS in the list of services, you probably don't have IIS installed. If you have Windows 2000 or XP Professional, refer back to Chapter 17, "Introducing ColdFusion MX 7," for additional information on installing IIS. If you have Windows Me or XP Home Edition, you're going to need to consider upgrading because neither of these operating systems support IIS. Mac users can use Apache as their web server.

TIP

If you are using Apache as your web server application, you can disable directory browsing by creating a text file in your root directory named .htaccess. In that file, add the following line of code and save it:

```
Options All - Indexes
```

With this .htaccess file in place, directory browsing is disabled for all folders within the site.

21

2. Click the plus sign next to Web Sites. Right-click on the Default Web Site and choose Properties.

3. In the Default Web Site Properties dialog box (see Figure 21.11), choose the Home Directory tab and uncheck the Directory Browsing check box.

Figure 21.11
Disable Directory
browsing via the Web
Site Properties.

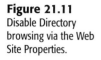

4. Click OK to apply the changes and close the dialog box.

One additional note should be mentioned when it comes to securing your database directory. If you are familiar with Microsoft Windows directory permissions, you may know
that in the Windows operating system, the typical default permission level is to allow the
Everyone group access to your folder. This means that any user accessing the machine has
access to that directory. To reduce the possibility of inappropriate access, consider removing
the Everyone group's access and further restricting access to the database directory to those
accounts that need to access it. Before you rush in and remove all the permissions, however,
be aware that certain accounts need to have read and write access to the database directory
or your web applications may not function correctly. For complete details on the minimum
permission levels that are required on your database directory, check out the Technote from
Macromedia that can be found at the following URL:

http://www.macromedia.com/cfusion/knowledgebase/index.cfm?id=tn_18802

CREATING A CONNECTION TO THE DATABASE

The final step you need to take to prepare for using the ColdFusion platform for your web
pages is to create a connection to the database by using the ColdFusion Administrator. This
connection enables the web server to access the contents of the database and tells the web
server what driver should be used to "talk" to the database.

1. Open the ColdFusion Administrator by typing `http://127.0.0.1/CFIDE/`
   `administrator/index.cfm` into your browser's address bar. In the login screen
   (see Figure 21.12), type your administrator password.

21

Figure 21.12
Log on to the
ColdFusion
Administrator.

2. In the left navigation frame, click Data Sources. The Data Sources page in the right frame (see Figure 21.13) displays all the existing ColdFusion data source names and enables you to create new entries.

Figure 21.13
The Data Sources
page enables you to
manage your DSNs.

> **Data & Services > Datasources**
>
> Add and manage your data source connections and Data Source Names (DSNs).
> You use a DSN to connect ColdFusion to a variety of data sources.
>
> **Add New Data Source**
>
> Data Source Name
>
> Driver — Please select a valid driver type.
>
> Add
>
> **Connected Data Sources**
>
> | Actions | Data Source Name | Driver | Status |
> |---------|------------------|--------|--------|
> | | cfartgallery | Microsoft Access with Unicode | |
> | | cfbookclub | Microsoft Access with Unicode | |
> | | cfcodeexplorer | Microsoft Access with Unicode | |
> | | cfdocexamples | Microsoft Access with Unicode | |
>
> Verify All Connections

3. Type `dsnRetrosCycles` in the Data Source Name field, choose Microsoft Access from the Driver dropdown (see Figure 21.14), and click Add.

4. In the Microsoft Access page (see Figure 21.15), click the Browser Server button next to Database File.

5. In the next page (see Figure 21.16), browse to your database's location. If you are using Windows and used the default path referred to earlier, the path would be `c:\InetPub\ wwwroot\rcdb99840b\ retros_cycles_99300d2.mdb`.

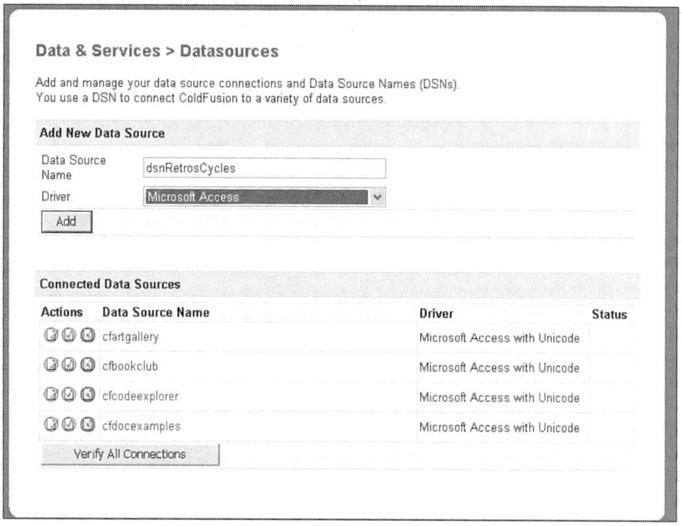

Figure 21.14
Type the name of your new DSN and choose its type.

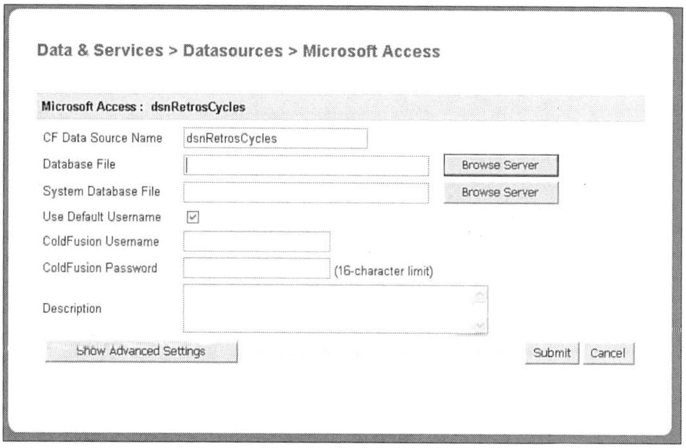

Figure 21.15
Click to Browse to your database file.

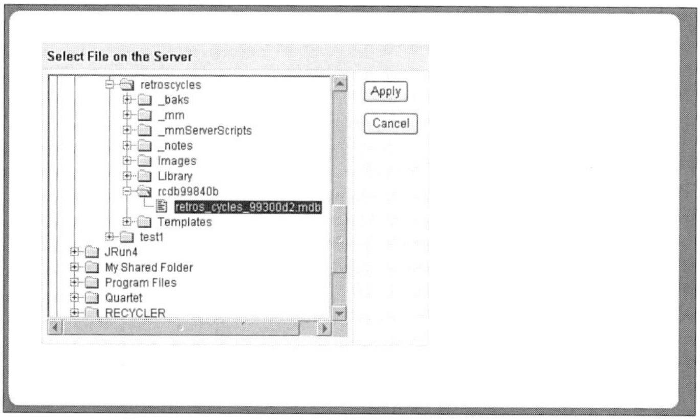

Figure 21.16
Browse to your database.

6. Click Apply.

7. Back in the Microsoft Access Page, type a description for your DSN and then click Submit. After your DSN has been created, you will see it in the list of Connected Data Sources at the bottom of the page (see Figure 21.17), along with its status.

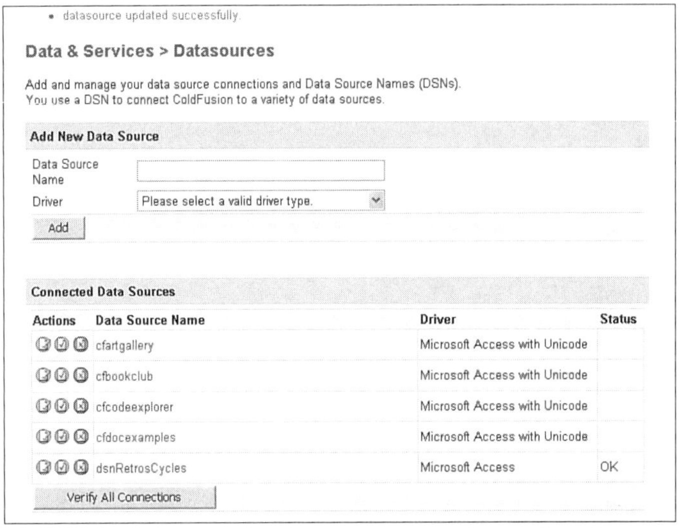

Figure 21.17
The DSN has been added and your database is connected to the ColdFusion server.

8. Log out of the ColdFusion Administrator.

With your database in place and your connection created, you're ready to begin creating your pages and adding dynamic content to them. For this task, there is no better tool than Dreamweaver, which is covered in depth in Part V, "Dreamweaver 8."

TROUBLESHOOTING

When I tried to create a DSN, I received an error that the data source name is invalid. What did I do wrong?

More than likely, you entered an invalid character in the name of your DSN. Make sure that your name contains only numbers and letters with no special characters such as ~ or _. In addition, the DSN cannot contain any spaces.

My DSN used to say OK *in the status field, but now nothing is displayed there. Is there a way to check the connection?*

Yes. Log in to the ColdFusion Administrator and choose Data Sources. In the Data Sources page, click the Verify All Connections button at the very bottom of the page. The status of the connections should return.

BEST PRACTICES—PERIODIC MAINTENANCE OF YOUR ACCESS DATABASE

When using an Access database as the backend for your website, it's often easy to forget about the database's health. Because you're accessing it through a web browser, it's easy to focus more on web functionality and any coding errors and forget that your database might not be performing at its optimal level.

For this reason, it's a good idea to create a periodic maintenance schedule for your Access database. This maintenance schedule might include the following elements:

- Routine backups of the database and moving those backups to a secure location.
- Archiving of the database on the local machine so that a copy is readily available in case of database corruption.
- Periodic usage of the Compact and Repair tool from within Microsoft Access to reduce the size of your database.
- Periodic defragmentation of the disk where the database is stored to ensure optimal performance.
- Periodic review of the database size to ensure that size limitations are not being reached.

Adding these tasks to your database maintenance will move you in the right direction toward a worry-free database backend for your website.

21

PART V

DREAMWEAVER 8

CHAPTER **22**

INTRODUCING DREAMWEAVER 8

In this chapter

22

WHAT'S NEW IN DREAMWEAVER 8

In developing Dreamweaver 8, Macromedia has worked hard to integrate more tools that allow web developers to work smarter in Dreamweaver. New toolbar additions, the capability to paste structure and formatting as well as content, and a broader range of support for more dynamic platforms enable you to develop your applications more efficiently. Some of the most prominent features in Dreamweaver 8 include

- **Enhanced CSS Support**—Features such as a newly reorganized CSS panel and enhanced functionality for elements such as border styles, inline boxes, horizontal rules, and CSS positioning make the use of style sheets even easier and more effective in your pages.

- **New Paste Special Command**—When pasting text into a document, the Edit, Paste Special command now enables you to decide whether you want to paste just the text or the text and certain structural elements.

- **Zoom Tool**—Dreamweaver's new Zoom tool enables developers to zoom in on specific areas of their sites to analyze images and design pages of varying sizes.

- **Flash Video Integration**—This feature enables you to easily add Flash Video files to your web pages.

- **New Code View Toolbar**—When working in the Code view, the new Code View toolbar provides quick access to common tasks such as indenting/outdenting code, adding and removing comments, and expanding or collapsing code blocks.

- **Improved Site Synchronization and WebDAV functionality**—The enhanced functionality improves the reliability of the site synchronization feature to ensure that the comparison between local and remote files is correct. In addition, WebDAV support has been enhanced to support the latest versions of the application.

- **File Comparison Integration**—Offers the capability to compare local and remote files to determine differences in the documents.

- **Capability to Save Panel Configurations**—When adjusting the position and visibility of the various panels with Dreamweaver, you can now save your custom layouts and restore them when necessary.

THE DREAMWEAVER 8 INTERFACE, IN DEPTH

Dreamweaver has so many tools and features it's unlikely that you'll use all of them for every site. However, knowing what's available in Dreamweaver will help you customize your workspace to put frequently used tools within easy reach and hide toolbars and panels that may not be as frequently used. After you know what features are available and how they work, you can customize your workspace and begin adding content to pages by putting those tools to work for you.

WORKSPACE LAYOUTS

If you're using Windows, your first decision in setting up your workspace is choosing a layout. When you installed Dreamweaver, you were prompted to select an initial Workspace Setup (see Figure 22.1). Regardless of whether you chose the Designer or Coder workspace, Dreamweaver enables you to change your workspace at any time to meet the development style of the project you are working on.

Figure 22.1
The Workspace Setup dialog box appears when you first install Dreamweaver on a Windows system. You can also access Workspace Setup from the Preferences dialog box.

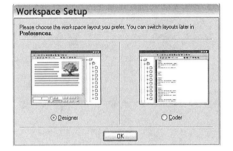

You can change your workspace by selecting Window, Workspace Layout from the menu bar and selecting the layout you'd like. In addition, you can save specific layouts and restore them whenever necessary.

The workspace layouts that Dreamweaver 8 offers are

- **Designer Workspace**—All windows, panels, and inspectors are contained within one application window, in the same manner as in Fireworks and other Macromedia applications (see Figure 22.2). All panels are docked on the right side of the application window. Documents are opened in Design view by default, and multiple documents are tabbed at the top of the Document window.

- **Coder Workspace**—All panels are docked on the left in the same manner as in HomeSite and ColdFusion Studio (see Figure 22.3). This workspace opens all documents in Code view by default.

- **Dual Screen Left/Right**—The workspace can be stretched onto dual screens with the document window stretched to fill either the full left or full right screen.

> **NOTE**
> Mac users have only the floating layout available.

Regardless of which workspace you choose, you can customize it beyond the standard layout by moving and changing Dreamweaver's various panels. Panels that are regrouped or undocked from the panel group remain in that new state even in future Dreamweaver sessions. The Property inspector is initially collapsed, showing only the most common options. If you expand the Property inspector, it remains expanded in future sessions unless you manually collapse it.

Figure 22.2
The Designer work-space contains all documents, panels, and inspectors in one application window.

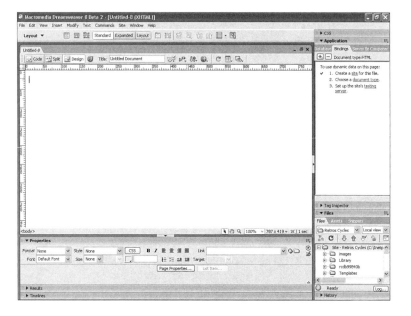

Figure 22.3
The Coder workspace is similar to that of the Designer workspace, but the panel groups are positioned on the left side of the window.

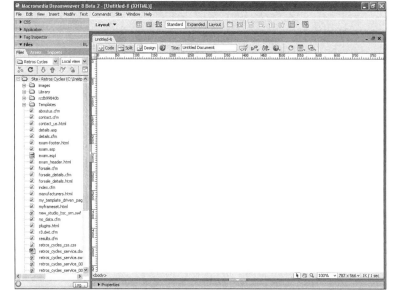

EXPLORING THE DOCUMENT WINDOW

The Document window represents the development view of the document that you are working on and is where you'll be adding content and applying the tools offered with Dreamweaver's various panels and inspectors. The Document window contains a title bar, menus, toolbars, and a status bar. All the other panels, inspectors, and toolbars exist to add to or modify the contents of the Document window. The Document window is capable of displaying a visual representation of the site in Design view (see Figure 22.4), the HTML and scripting code for the site in Code view (see Figure 22.5), or a split window containing both the design and the code (see Figure 22.6).

Figure 22.4
Design view enables you to work in a what-you-see-is-what-you-get (WYSIWYG) atmosphere.

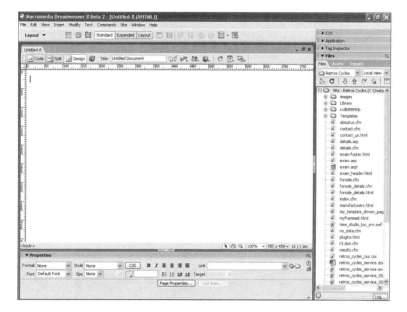

Figure 22.5
Code view enables you to develop or edit the code directly.

22

Figure 22.6
Split view enables you to make changes to either pane and see how changes in one affect the other.

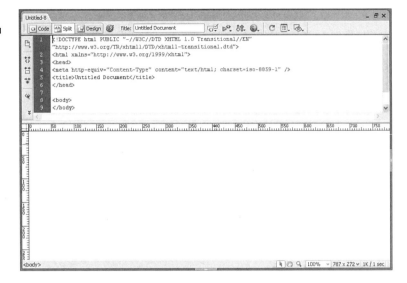

Regardless of your preference, it's likely that you will use all three views at some point in development. Even with the advancements of WYSIWYG development environments, it's still good to understand and be able to modify and write code by hand.

TIP

> In Code and Design view, changes you make to the code aren't reflected in the Design pane unless you refresh the view. You can do this by clicking the Refresh button on either the Property inspector or the Document toolbar, or simply by pressing F5.

TITLE BAR

The Title bar displays the title and filename of the open document. Aside from being a reminder of the name of the page on which you're currently working, it can also serve as a reminder of the path to which you have saved the file and whether or not you have given the page a title. If the title bar shows the page to be unnamed, you need to save the page for any changes to be preserved. As you work in the document, an asterisk is appended to the filename, signifying that you've made unsaved changes to the document. Use the Save keyboard shortcut (Command+S) [Ctrl+S] or select File, Save to save your file.

MENU BAR

The Menu bar contains nearly all the commands and features of Dreamweaver. Most of these commands are also accessible from panels or the Property inspector, as well as context menus that pop up when you (Control-click) [right-click] your mouse.

TOOLBARS

Four toolbars are available from within the Document window. To toggle these toolbars from view, select View, Toolbars, and select from the three options. All the toolbars can be visible at the same time, but they cut down on your workspace.

The Standard toolbar contains the usual File, Save, Copy/Cut, and Paste commands (see Figure 22.7). If you already know the keyboard shortcuts for these common commands, they're the same as those for most Windows or Mac applications.

Figure 22.7
The Standard toolbar is useful for novices, but it takes up valuable development real estate.

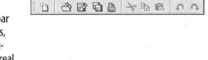

The Document toolbar, shown in Figure 22.8, also contains options available elsewhere in Dreamweaver, such as switching views or titling the document. In addition, this toolbar enables you to easily monitor potential browser and markup errors as well as toggle visual aids on and off.

Figure 22.8
The Document toolbar makes it easy to switch views, title the page, and preview the document in a browser.

The Insert toolbar, shown in Figure 22.9, enables you to easily insert elements into your pages such as images, code snippets, and hyperlinks. The available elements are divided into logical categories, which can be selected from the drop-down menu at the far left of the Insert bar. When selected, each category displays a unique set of buttons that enable you to add any specific element to your page with the click of your mouse.

Figure 22.9
The Insert toolbar enables you to easily add elements to your pages.

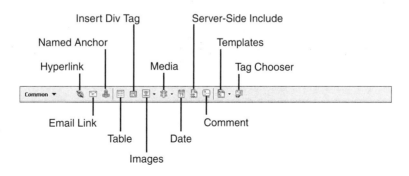

22

The Insert bar contains eight categories, each containing icons for the most frequently used options in that category (see Table 22.1).

TABLE 22.1   INSERT BAR CATEGORIES

Category	Function
Common	Contains image, table, link, layer, comment, and other commonly used objects.
Layout	Enables toggling of standard, expanded, and layout views for creating tables and provides the tools to use Layout view to draw tables and cells.
Forms	Inserts form containers and elements.
Text	Adds text formatting, such as bold and italic, and paragraph formatting, such as headings and lists. It can also be used to access the Font Tag Editor to set multiple attributes at once.
HTML	Adds HTML elements, such as horizontal rules, tables, or frames to your page.
Application	Enables you to build recordsets containing data from your database connections and display content from those recordsets on your pages.
Flash Elements	Enables you to control Flash elements stored within your pages.
Favorites	Enables you to create your own toolbar with buttons for your favorite elements.

To insert an element from one of the Insert bar categories, position the cursor in the page where you want the object to be inserted and then click the Object button in the Insert bar (or drag the Object button to the insertion point). In the case of inserting images or creating links, among others, a dialog box appears to help you complete the insertion, in which you can perform such actions as selecting an image file or defining the link parameters. To insert placeholders for these elements, when available (such as for images), press the (Option) [Ctrl] key while clicking the Object button. You can then select a final image or fill in other required attributes later in the development process.

STATUS BAR

The Status bar is located at the bottom of the Document window (see Figure 22.10). It provides information about the file size and estimated download time for the document. Dreamweaver calculates an approximate download time based on the Connection Speed setting in the Status Bar category of the Preferences dialog box (Edit, Preferences). By default, Dreamweaver calculates page load times at 56 kilobits per second, but you can change these settings to calculate download time for faster or slower connections.

Figure 22.10
The Status bar displays the Tag selector, Window Size selector, and Download Size/Speed indicator.

WINDOW SIZE SELECTOR   You can change the dimensions of your default screen size to match those of your typical site visitor. This enables you to design for a wide range of browser dimensions or to test the general appearance of the document in a specific configuration.

Choosing the Right Viewing Size

More and more web visitors are using upgraded monitors, enabling them to view pages in a broader array of colors and at a higher resolution. As a result, many designers are now developing for an 800×600 screen size or higher. MSNTV (previously known as WebTV) users have a display size of only 560×384 (and an equally limited range of colors and other limitations). In addition, if you are developing for PDAs or browser-capable mobile devices, you need to take into account the maximum display size for your targeted device.

TAG SELECTOR   The Tag Selector combines the best of working in Design view with the need to occasionally make changes to the underlying code by hand. The Tag Selector shows the HTML tags (see Figure 22.11) relative to the position of the cursor in Design view.

Figure 22.11
The Tag Selector gives you quick access to tags used in your document.

This feature is often overlooked because there are so many methods for accessing and editing code. But when you're working on nested tables or have multiple layers on the page, the Tag Selector can help you find your place in the code. Just click a tag in the Tag Selector to highlight the contents of the tag in Design view. You can then make modifications to that element in the Property inspector or by using the menus and panels. You can also select a tag from the Tag Selector, switch to Code view, and the element and its contents will be highlighted.

The Tag Selector also makes deleting blocks of content easy. You can delete tables or blocks of text easily by right-clicking on the container tag in the Tag Selector and then pressing the Backspace or Delete key on the keyboard.

In addition, the Tag Selector also can be used to edit existing tags. To edit a tag, (Control-click) [right-click] on the tag in the Tag Selector, which activates the context menu. The context menu provides one of many methods for setting the class of a tag, used extensively with Cascading Style Sheets. You can also use the context menu to access the Quick Tag Editor by choosing Edit Tag.

USING THE PROPERTY INSPECTOR

The Property inspector (see Figure 22.12) is one of the most important tools in Dreamweaver because it enables you to adjust the editable properties of any text or objects located within your pages. The context of the Property inspector and the elements that are visible within it change depending on the element that is selected within the Document window. As with all panels, the Property inspector can be moved. It can be docked either above or below the Document window or undocked to become a floating panel.

Figure 22.12
The Property inspector changes with the context of the selection.

The Property inspector is initially in a maximized state, displaying all the editable properties for the selected object. If you want to maximize your workspace, you can minimize the Property inspector by clicking the arrow in the bottom-right corner. The minimized view then displays only the most commonly edited attributes for the object.

In addition to the standard text fields and buttons, the Property inspector also contains several other features. Color pickers are used to select a color for text, table borders, and other objects. The Point-to-File and Folder icons are used to locate files to insert images or links; the Quick Tag Editor, signified by a pencil-and-paper icon on the right side of the Property inspector, enables you to add element attributes not found on the Inspector. Selecting the question mark icon launches the Using Dreamweaver help system. In addition, the Property inspector in Dreamweaver 8 now contains a CSS button that opens the CSS Styles pane, which enables you to easily format text based on styles embedded within the document or available from an attached style sheet.

WORKING WITH PANELS

Unless you've already started to change the default workspace by removing from view or resizing the panels and inspectors, you'll see that the Document window is surrounded by groupings of additional options and site information. Some of these panels are critical to Dreamweaver's ease of use, whereas others can be minimized or hidden without worry.

Panels are grouped by default in logical panel groups. Of course, this logic might or might not be applicable to your style of work, so the arrangement of panels and their groupings can be modified to meet your working style.

To expand a panel group, click the arrow to the left of the panel group name or click the panel group name itself (see Figure 22.13).

Figure 22.13
Click the arrow next to panel groups to open and close panels. Here, you see the Databases, Bindings, Server Behaviors, Components, Files, Assets, and Snippets panels, with the Application and Files panel groups open.

ARRANGING PANEL GROUPS

Each panel group has several controls (see Figure 22.14). The icon to the right of the panel group name activates a drop-down options menu containing several commands within the context of the panels contained in the group. The menu for each panel group is unique and contains commands that apply to that panel group.

Figure 22.14
The panel group controls include a gripper and a drop-down menu with group commands.

Gripper

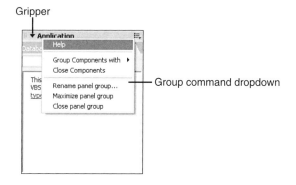

Group command dropdown

To the left of the group name is an area called the *gripper*. Clicking and dragging the gripper for a group enables you to undock that panel group. These floating panels can then be moved around the workspace. To dock a floating panel group, drag it by its gripper until the insert indicator is positioned where you want in the panel dock.

If you would like to move an existing panel into another panel group, you can do this by opening the panel group where the panel is located and clicking the options menu. From the options menu, choose the Group [*panel name*] With command and select the target group.

The moved panel immediately appears in its new group. If you choose to create a new panel group, open the Options menu in the new group and select Rename Panel Group to give it an appropriate name. You can then add other panels to the new group.

Panel groups can also be resized to take up more or less space in the panel dock. When you position the mouse between panel groups, the cursor changes into a double-headed arrow, which can be clicked and dragged up or down to modify the size of expanded panel groups. To maximize a panel group to take up as much space in the panel dock as possible, select Maximize Panel Group from the Panel menu. This minimizes other open panel groups to give the select group full use of the vertical space.

Some panels, such as those located in the Results panel group, benefit from the additional horizontal space they get when they are placed below the Property inspector. Position the mouse cursor between the panel dock and the Document window until it becomes a double-headed arrow; then click and drag horizontally to give additional space to the panel dock. Keep in mind, however, that this decreases the size of the Document window.

If you're not using a panel group at all, you can close it by selecting Close Panel Group from the Options menu for that group. To reopen a closed panel group, select it from the Window menu on the menu bar.

CSS PANEL GROUP

The CSS panel group contains panels that control the styles and layers of the elements on the page. The two panels in this group are CSS Styles (see Figure 22.15) and Layers (see Figure 22.16).

Figure 22.15
The CSS Styles panel is used to define and modify Cascading Style Sheets.

Figure 22.16
The Layers panel is used to control any CSS layers that exist within the document.

APPLICATION PANELS

When you're using databases and advanced server technologies to generate content for your pages, the tools used most frequently are found in the Application panel. Initially, each of the panels in this group prompts you to configure the site, document type, and testing server (if you haven't already done so in the Site Definition).

Using the Databases panel (see Figure 22.17), you can then create a connection to a database containing content for your site.

Figure 22.17
The Databases panel controls database connections.

The Bindings panel, shown in Figure 22.18, is used to create recordsets or datasets (depending on your platform) and displays the field names stored in those recordsets. After you have created the recordsets you need, the Bindings panel enables you to drag and drop dynamic content into your pages and select formatting options for the dynamic data placeholders.

The Server Behaviors panel (see Figure 22.19) gives you access to a broad range of dynamic server behaviors ranging from restricting access to your pages to repeating regions.

Finally, the Components panel (see Figure 22.20) enables you to easily add web services or ColdFusion components to your page.

22

Figure 22.18
The Bindings panel enables you to add dynamic text and elements to your pages.

Figure 22.19
The Server Behaviors panel provides access to database-driven server behaviors.

Figure 22.20
The Components panel provides access to ColdFusion components and web services.

NOTE

If you don't plan on designing dynamic pages, you can close this panel group entirely to save space.

TAG PANEL GROUP

The Tag panel enables you to visualize how tags are nested within other tags within your document and what attributes are associated with each tag. By selecting an element within the page or choosing a tag from the Tag Selector and then choosing the Attributes panel (see Figure 22.21), you can view information about the tag, such general attributes, any styles that are associated with it, the language in which the code is styled, and any uncategorized attributes associated with the tag.

Figure 22.21
The Attributes panel enables you to visualize attributes of specific code tags.

The Behaviors panel, shown in Figure 22.22, provides you with access to commonly used JavaScript behaviors that can be associated with tags within your document. For instance, after you create a hyperlink from text and select the <a> tag, the Behaviors panel provides access to numerous behaviors that are unavailable to nonlinked text.

Figure 22.22
The Behaviors panel gives you access to JavaScript behaviors that can be applied to specific elements.

FILES PANEL GROUP

The Files panel, shown in Figure 22.23, enables you to view and manipulate the files and folders located within your local site. The Files panel also enables you to create, edit, and delete Dreamweaver sites.

With the Assets panel you can easily organize elements located within your site, such as images, movies, rich content, and hyperlinks. It can save you time because you simply drag and drop elements right into your page (see Figure 22.24).

Figure 22.23
The Files panel enables you to manage the files and folders contained within your site.

Figure 22.24
The Assets panel organizes many of the elements contained within your site.

The Snippets panel (see Figure 22.25) provides a place for you to organize and manage predefined blocks of code known as "snippets." These reusable code snippets can easily be dragged into your code and customized for the individual application.

FRAMES PANEL

The Frames panel is used to design and manage any frames used within your page layout. From within the Frames panel, you can also select a specific frame.

Figure 22.25
The Snippets panel enables you to store reusable code for reuse in pages.

HISTORY PANEL

The History panel maintains a list of the steps you take in creating the current document (see Figure 22.26). You can then use this list to create new commands for repetitive, time-consuming actions. You can also use the History panel to undo multiple steps at once or to replay steps to see their effect on the page design.

Figure 22.26
The History panel tracks the steps you take in creating a document.

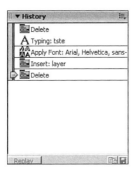

When you look at the items in the History panel, the last item on the list is the most recent, and the panel scrolls upward. To undo the last several actions, drag the slider that's to the left of the steps upward to select the steps you want to undo. After you've made your selection, continue editing. The selected steps are not undone until you take another action that overwrites those steps in the history.

To repeat steps, use the slider to select them and then click the Copy Steps button.

NOTE

> After you've undone multiple items and overwritten them with other steps, you cannot redo the original steps.

To create a command that completes multiple steps, select a series of steps with the slider and then click the Save Selected Steps As a Command button. You are prompted to give the command a name, and the new command appears on the Commands menu.

NOTE

> The History panel tracks only a limited number of steps per session. You can increase or decrease this number in the Maximum Number of History Steps field of the General Preferences settings.

RESULTS PANEL GROUP

The Results panel automatically appears to display the results of searches, validation checks, and various reports. It's one of two panels that are docked horizontally below the Property inspector because the content displayed in the various panels is much easier to read and review horizontally.

SEARCH PANEL   The Search panel is displayed at the bottom of the workspace whenever you issue a Find command (see Figure 22.27) that reaches beyond the active document (such as if you're conducting a site-wide search). This panel displays the results of your search and enables you to click the results to edit them in the Document window. Buttons on the left side of the panel enable you to initiate, cancel, or save Find commands.

Figure 22.27
The Search panel lists the results of searches in a document or site.

REFERENCE PANEL   The Reference panel, shown in Figure 22.28, provides access to reference material for HTML, CSS, JavaScript, and quite a few of the dynamic platforms and scripting languages.

Figure 22.28
The Reference panel provides you quick access to helpful reference materials.

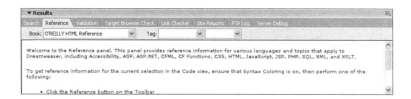

VALIDATION PANEL   The Validation panel, shown in Figure 22.29, lists any coding errors in the site or document when you validate the site (by selecting File, Check Page, Validate Markup/Validate As XML). This validation can also be initiated directly from the panel, and corrections can be located from it.

Figure 22.29
The Validation panel lists coding errors.

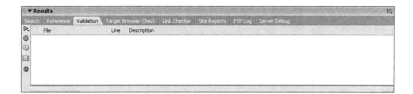

TARGET BROWSER CHECK PANEL The Target Browser Check panel, shown in Figure 22.30, lists browser compatibility issues that have emerged in a running of the Check Target Browsers report (File, Check Page, Check Target Browsers, or use the Target Browser Check button on the left side of the Target Browser Check panel). The panel also provides options to save the report for future reference. By highlighting an item in the report and clicking the More Info button, you can view a dialog box explaining exactly why an item is marked. If you double-click an entry, it opens in the Document window in Code and Design view with the offending code highlighted.

Figure 22.30
The Target Browser Check panel lists elements that can't be viewed properly in the target browser.

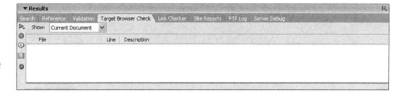

LINK CHECKER PANEL The Link Checker panel, shown in Figure 22.31, lists the results of the Check Links report (File, Check Page, Check Links, or run from within the Link Checker panel). This report lists broken links, orphaned files within the site, and all external links.

Figure 22.31
The Link Checker panel enables you to fix broken links, eliminate orphaned files, and manually validate external links.

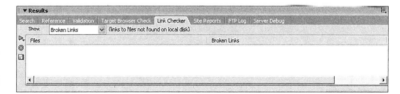

SITE REPORTS PANEL The Site Reports panel, shown in Figure 22.32, displays the results of the Site Report (activated by choosing Site, Reports from the menu bar or by clicking the Reports button on the Site Report panel). The Site Report can be quite extensive, depending on the options you choose when initiating the report. As with the other Results panels, you can use this report to get more information on the items listed and use the items to locate the specific code in question to make modifications.

Figure 22.32
The Site Reports panel lists problems found with accessibility, incomplete tags, or missing `alt` attributes.

FTP LOG PANEL   The FTP Log tracks communication with the remote server. You can also enter commands directly to the server from this panel, which is useful to experienced developers.

SERVER DEBUG PANEL   The Server Debug panel is used with dynamic pages to locate errors in the code. To use this feature, select View, Server Debug from the menu. The Server Debug panel displays the results of this command, including the server variables and values, execution time, and SQL queries on the page. If you didn't configure your testing server correctly, this panel prompts you through the required steps.

TIMELINES PANEL

After being removed from Dreamweaver MX 2004, the Timelines panel has now returned to Dreamweaver 8 (see Figure 22.33). This panel enables you to time interactions on your site such as the moving of layers or the hiding/displaying of objects.

By dragging an image into the timeline frame, you can control the image's source URL and, if the image is stored in a layer, its location.

Figure 22.33
The Timelines panel enables you to relocate images and other objects over a period of time.

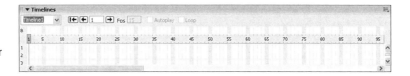

CODE INSPECTOR

The Code Inspector contains all the same features as the Code view, but is located on a floating panel (see Figure 22.34). The Code view is where you generally want to work if you plan on doing major code review or revisions. If, however, you're interested in taking a quick look at your code, you can activate the Code Inspector either by choosing Window, Code Inspector or by pressing the F10 key. If you're using dual screens, the Code Inspector is especially handy because you can keep the Design view open and move the floating Code Inspector window to your other screen.

Figure 22.34
The Code Inspector duplicates the functionality of the Code view in the Document window.

WORKING WITH TEXT IN THE DESIGN VIEW

Now that you know what tools are available for your use, it's time to start putting them to use. Probably the most common element of all web pages is text that conveys information. You enter text into Dreamweaver by either typing directly in the Document window or cutting/copying and pasting text from another source. You can select text for editing or cut and paste within the document, using many of the same menu commands and keyboard shortcuts available in most word processors.

After the text is entered into the Document window, you have many options for formatting it. Because text itself may not necessarily convey emphasis or emotion, a variety of styles, fonts, sizes, and colors can be used to tailor the message to the audience.

PARAGRAPHS

Most of the text you'll be adding to your web pages is probably going to be formatted into standard paragraphs. To create a paragraph break, simply press (Return) [Enter] and a blank line of whitespace is inserted below the paragraph. You can then begin typing your new paragraph and the two blocks of text will be separated by whitespace.

NOTE

From a markup standpoint, Dreamweaver assumes your text is in paragraph format by default until you apply formatting to the contrary. All text within the <p>...</p> tag pair is formatted as one paragraph.

LINE BREAKS

Whitespace is important for control of design and readability. In most HTML editors, including Dreamweaver 8, when you press the (Return) [Enter] key, a new <p> tag is inserted. Dreamweaver also automatically inserts a new HTML paragraph with a nonbreaking space   entity between the opening and closing tags. If you then type on this new line, the nonbreaking space is replaced with your content. If you leave the paragraph blank, however, the paragraph tags remain with a non-breaking space. Because the tag is not empty, browsers correctly interpret this paragraph as a blank line.

22

Conversely, you might want to start a new line of text without that blank line inserted by the paragraph tags. To do this, use a line break. A *line break* inserts a carriage return in the text without closing the paragraph tags and, thus, without inserting extra space between the two lines. If you view the line break in the code view, you'll see that a single <br> tag is inserted instead of the <p> </p> tags.

To add a line break to your text, place the cursor in the appropriate location and press the Shift+Enter key combination. You can also insert a line break from the menu bar by choosing Insert, HTML, Special Characters, Line Break.

With the line break inserted, the text is forced to a new line without additional whitespace between lines. Line breaks can also be used to force more whitespace within a paragraph if you add multiple breaks consecutively.

STYLING TEXT

Styling the text used to present your content is usually one of the easiest ways to personalize the presentation of your information. Until the last few years, however, the use of the font element as the preferred method of styling left web developers with a very limited selection of "safe" fonts and attributes from which to choose. With the announcement of new HTML 4.0 standards, the font element has now been deprecated (meaning it's not recommended anymore) by the World Wide Web Consortium (W3C) and Macromedia has shifted the way that Dreamweaver 8 applies font styling to pages from the use of <font> tags to Cascading Style Sheets (CSS).

NOTE

Dreamweaver 8 has not abandoned the use of the font element completely. If you have existing projects that already use the font element, you can continue applying font styling in that manner by choosing Edit, Preferences, and in the General category remove the check in the box next to Use CSS Instead of HTML Tags.

The nice thing about using CSSs in Dreamweaver is you can have as much or as little control over them as you wish. If you're accustomed to using the standard fonts that have traditionally been "safe" for web use, the Font drop-down in the Property inspector enables you to apply a font and never have to touch a style sheet. Instead, Dreamweaver embeds the style into your document and you are able to reuse it over and over.

If, however, you would like to work with new fonts and styles that are available with the adoption of CSS, you can create custom style sheets that can easily be applied on a page-by-page basis or linked throughout your entire site. CSS is covered in depth a little later.

When applying a style to your text, you can modify several attributes easily via the Property inspector (see Figure 22.35).

Figure 22.35
The Property inspector puts the most common text style attributes within easy reach.

SETTING THE FONT FACE

In Dreamweaver, fonts are chosen from one of the predefined font groups available in the Font drop-down in the Property inspector. To apply a font to a block of text, simply select a range of text, and then choose from one of the six fonts.

When you apply the font, Dreamweaver automatically creates a style based on the font face, font size, and any other formatting and embeds it in the page. This makes the style available from the Style drop-down in the Property inspector and you can reapply it throughout your pages.

SETTING THE FONT SIZE

Prior to the adoption of CSS as the preferred styling method, the `font` element used a set of arbitrary font sizes ranging from 1 to 7. The worst part about these sizes is that different browsers interpreted their sizes differently. This meant that text would appear differently in different browsers. Through the use of CSS, however, you can now control the exact pixel size of your fonts, ensuring that they are displayed consistently across every browser. To set the font size for a block of text, select the text and then choose the appropriate size from the Size drop-down in the Property inspector.

Just as it does with font styling, Dreamweaver creates a style for size changes that you make to a block of text. If the selected text already has a style applied to it, Dreamweaver updates that style to include the font size as well.

SETTING THE FONT COLOR

The default text color for the page is set in the Page Properties dialog box. Unless you modified the page properties, the default color for text is black (#000000). To change the color of text from the default, select the text and then use the Color Picker in the Property inspector to select a new color (see Figure 22.36). The Text Color field uses the same Dreamweaver color picker as the Page Properties and other color tools. Alternatively, you can type the hexadecimal code in the text box to the right of the Color Picker.

Figure 22.36
Using the Color Picker to set the font color is a quick, visual way to colorize your fonts.

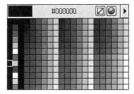

TIP

To return text to the default text color, either delete the hexadecimal value in the field next to the Color Picker or click the Color Picker and then click the white square with the red strikethrough.

Setting Font Styles

A *font style* is formatting such as bold or italic applied to a font. Styles can be used to show emphasis, provide editorial marks, or even differentiate between standard text and computer code.

Although the Property inspector enables you to apply bold and italic to a text block, you can also choose additional font styles by selecting Text, Style from the menu bar (see Table 22.2). If appropriate, you can also apply more than one style for the same text selection, such as when creating bold, italicized text.

TABLE 22.2   FONT FACES AND THEIR USES

Font Style	HTML Element	Used For
Bold	b	Adding bold emphasis
Italic	i	Adding emphasis with italicization
<u>Underline</u>	u	Adding emphasis with underline
~~Strikethrough~~	s or strikethrough	Editorial purposes
Teletype	tt	Monospaced font
Emphasis	em	Usually displayed as italic
Strong	strong	Stronger emphasis than just using the emphasis style; usually displays as bold
Code	code	Text that represents a computer program listing
Variable	var	Text that represents a program variable
Sample	samp	Text that represents sample output from a program
Keyboard	kbd	Text that represents user input
Citation	cite	Source of a quote
Definition	dfn	Text that is a definition
Deleted	del	Text that has been deleted from the page
Insert	ins	Text that has been inserted into the page

If you select a style before typing, the style is applied to all subsequent text.

CAUTION

> Remember to exercise caution when applying the underline style to a web page. Text that is underlined on your pages can be confused with a link.

ALIGNING TEXT

Paragraph alignment is used to position text relative to its confining margins, whether those margins are the page margins, a table cell, or a layer. To change the alignment of text, select the appropriate text and then click the Align Left, Align Center, Align Right, or Justify buttons on the Property inspector.

You can also align text by selecting Alignment from the Text menu or by using the appropriate keyboard shortcut.

INDENTING TEXT

Text can be indented or outdented in several ways. Select the desired text and use one of the following methods to indent or outdent the text:

- Use the Property inspector and click the Text Indent or Text Outdent button.
- From the menu bar, select Text, Indent or Text, Outdent.
- If the text you highlight is a list, you can right-click it and select List, Indent or List, Outdent from the context menu.

Indents and outdents can be applied multiple times until the text is positioned where you want. Although this is easy to do, it's not the preferred method for positioning text. A better solution is to use a table or CSS.

CREATING LISTS IN DOCUMENTS

Lists bring order and structure to text on the web. Large blocks of text are difficult to read onscreen, so lists tend to break things into manageable blocks of text that are much easier to read.

In HTML, you create list items by placing each item inside the `<li>`...`</li>` tag pairs. The list in its entirety also needs to be defined. The manner in which this is done depends on the type of list.

UNORDERED (BULLETED) LISTS

An unordered list is used when the sequence of the items isn't important. Bulleted lists can be created from text you've already entered, or the list can be created as you type the text. To create a list, select the text you want to include in the list and click the Unordered List button on the Property inspector. If you want to create a new list, place your cursor in the

22

appropriate place in the page and then click the Unordered List button. Any text you type after that is preceded by a bullet. To end a list, either press (Return) [Enter] twice or click the Unordered List button again.

List items are spaced more closely together than paragraphs (see Figure 22.37). If you look at the Code view, the unordered list is contained within a <ul>...</ul> tag pair.

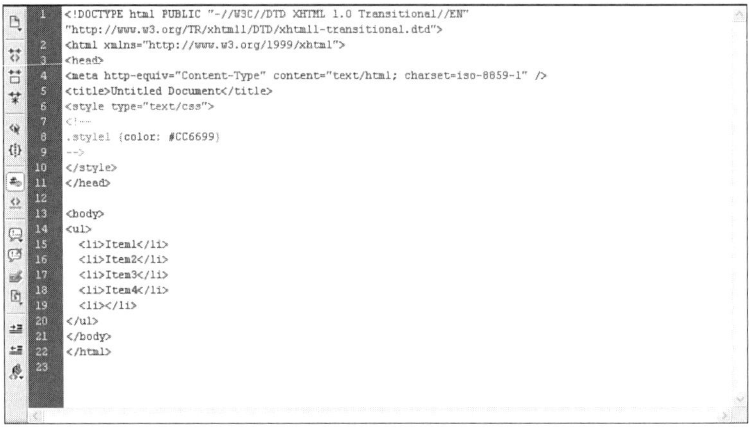

Figure 22.37
An unordered list is used for items that don't need to appear in a specific order.

```
1    <!DOCTYPE html PUBLIC "-//W3C//DTD XHTML 1.0 Transitional//EN"
     "http://www.w3.org/TR/xhtml1/DTD/xhtml1-transitional.dtd">
2    <html xmlns="http://www.w3.org/1999/xhtml">
3    <head>
4    <meta http-equiv="Content-Type" content="text/html; charset=iso-8859-1" />
5    <title>Untitled Document</title>
6    <style type="text/css">
7    <!--
8    .style1 {color: #CC6699}
9    -->
10   </style>
11   </head>
12
13   <body>
14   <ul>
15     <li>Item1</li>
16     <li>Item2</li>
17     <li>Item3</li>
18     <li>Item4</li>
19     <li></li>
20   </ul>
21   </body>
22   </html>
23
```

Font faces, colors, sizes, and styles can be applied to lists. Paragraph formatting, however, is likely to destroy the list layout, so it should be avoided. To remove list formatting, select the entire list and then click the Unordered List button in the Property inspector. The text itself remains, but the formatting of the list is deleted, as is the markup that created the list.

ORDERED (NUMBERED) LISTS

Ordered lists are used when items follow one another sequentially. Create these lists in the same manner as unordered lists, but click the Ordered List button instead. Examining the code, you can see that ordered lists are defined by the <ol>...</ol> tag pair.

One of the best features of an ordered list is its capability to renumber itself as items are added, deleted, or moved. To add an item to the list, position the insertion point at the end of the list item above which you want the addition to appear. Press (Return) [Enter] to add a new line; then type in the new item. To move an item in the list, either use the cut-and-paste method or highlight the list item and then drag it to its new location.

GENERATING CONTENT IN THE CODE VIEW

Although Dreamweaver makes it extremely easy to create and format new content with the Design view, you can also use the Code view to easily manipulate your exiting code or create new code. In addition, Dreamweaver incorporates some nice features that make it easy to work in the Code view.

COLLAPSIBLE CODE BLOCKS

A new feature in Dreamweaver 8 that definitely makes coding a bit easier is the capability to hide blocks of code that you may not be working on. That way, you can focus on a specific section of code without having to wade through the entire document's code. To hide a code block, select the code that you want to hide and click the minus sign next to the line number. With the code block hidden, the line numbering jumps and a code block placeholder is displayed (shown in Figure 22.38).

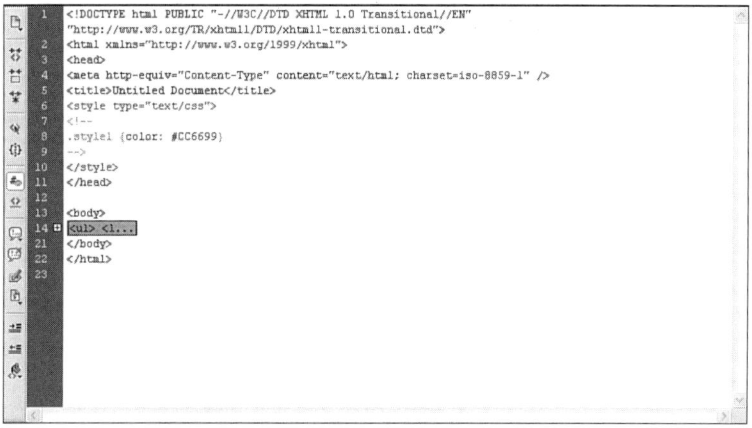

Figure 22.38
A block of code has been collapsed and hidden from view.

INDENTING CODE BLOCKS

When developing complex code, proper indenting can make a tremendous difference in understanding the workflow of what is happening in the code. Statements such as `if/then` or `While` loops tend to be much easier to read and understand if they are indented properly. Rather than making you go through your code line by line and set up your indention, Dreamweaver makes it easy for you to follow an indention convention by selecting entire blocks of code and allowing you to indent the entire block.

To set the indention for a block of code, select the code and press the Tab key to indent to the right or the Shift+Tab key combination to indent to the left.

TAG HINTS

As you type code in Dreamweaver, the application works to help you. One handy feature is the code hint drop-down that appears when you type code that Dreamweaver recognizes. For instance, if you type `<%Response.` in the Code view, Dreamweaver recognizes that you are going to use one of the VBScript Response functions and displays a drop-down with the available functions. From there you can click the down arrow to move through the list (see Figure 22.39) and select the appropriate function, or use the mouse to click on the correct one.

Figure 22.39
The code hint drop-down helps you choose the appropriate code.

AUTO TAG COMPLETION

Many HTML tags require both an opening and a closing tag. To save you time and typing, Dreamweaver includes an auto tag completion feature that automatically adds the closing tag after the opening tag has been completed and the closing tag has been started. For instance, if you place your cursor in the code view, and type **<div>** and then type </, Dreamweaver automatically closes the tag for you by adding the div> to the end of the tag.

If you would prefer to have Dreamweaver create the entire close tag after you type the opening tag, you can set this preference by choosing Edit, Preferences from the menu bar and clicking the Code Hints category. You can also turn off the auto completion feature in this category.

CODE COLORS

Another Dreamweaver feature that comes in handy when authoring code is Code Coloring. This feature modifies the color of the code depending on what type of code Dreamweaver perceives it to be. Depending on what type of document you are working in, you can customize the colors of the various types of code you are working with.

For instance, if you are developing an ASP page that contains HTML, VBScript, and JavaScript, you can adjust the colors of each type of code (and their subtypes). To adjust the default code coloring, open the Code Color category in the Preferences dialog box (Edit, Preferences) and double-click on any document type. From there you can adjust the various subtypes within that document and their code colors.

TROUBLESHOOTING

I selected a tag and deleted it, only to find that all my content had disappeared. What happened?

You likely selected the body tag and pressed Delete while attempting to delete another tag or some portion of your content. When you use the Tag Selector for deletion, select the body tag, and then press Delete, the head content remains but the body tag returns to a completely empty state. Of course, this also means you should use this feature with care when selecting the body or other large containers on a page. If you do make a mistake, remember that you can use the Undo command (Edit, Undo) to fix the error.

I want to use the font *element and still have valid documents. Is that possible?*

You can do so by DTDs:

- HTML 4.0 transitional
- HTML 4.01 transitional
- XHTML 1.0

You can't use the font element in any strict HTML or XHTML document or with the XHTML 1.1 public DTD. As you are already aware, the use of the font element is highly discouraged in favor of CSS.

BEST PRACTICES—PROPERLY COMMENTING AND INDENTING CODE

If you are new to web development or have been working with HTML for a while, you probably haven't had to delve into the world of custom-generated code too much. However, as you progress in your web development skills, you will be required to create more complex web applications that will, in turn, require more complex code. This means that down the road, you'll have to get your hands a bit more dirty when it comes to writing custom code.

One of the best practices you can get into when you start writing code is to add the appropriate comments and indentation to your code. Appropriate comments will help you, and others who review your code, understand what the code is doing. In addition, by adding comments that document the purpose of a code block, you help yourself when it comes time to troubleshoot issues with the code.

On the same note, proper indentation makes code much easier to read. With properly indented code, you can follow the workflow much more easily by seeing that certain indented lines of code are dependent on those that are outdented.

So, before you are called on to write that next web application that uses a ton of custom code, consider developing a coding style of your own that includes proper documentation through comments and correct indentation.

CHAPTER **23**

CREATING A DREAMWEAVER SITE

In this chapter

23

ESTABLISHING A DREAMWEAVER SITE

Before you can begin developing your pages in Dreamweaver, you need to set some parameters regarding the location of your files, the primary file platform in which you will be working, and the location of the testing server (if any). This process, known as defining your Dreamweaver site, helps Dreamweaver ensure that your hyperlinks function properly and that code generated by the application is created in the correct language.

Dreamweaver uses the concept of the *site* to organize the files in your website into a logical structure so that it can understand the relationships between the files as well as the objects that are contained within those files. For instance, to ensure that you don't have any broken images in your pages, Dreamweaver needs to know where you will be locating your images so it can ensure that that a proper path is created to an image when it is inserted into your page. Other functionality, such as database connections and cascading style sheets, also rely on the site structure.

In addition, defining your Dreamweaver site enables you to more easily manage the pages, assets, and objects that make up your site. Then, as the number of sites you manage grows, you can easily switch between the sites and Dreamweaver will automatically adjust its configuration based on the settings for each specific site.

NOTE

> To develop in Dreamweaver, you don't necessarily have to have a remote host or even a web server set up. While you are developing, you can use your local workstation as a testing machine. The only exception is users with the Windows XP Home Edition operating system. This version of the software does not contain built-in web services and, therefore, cannot serve web pages.

DEFINING THE SITE LOCALLY

The first step in creating your local Dreamweaver site is to create the folder structure that will store your files, images, media files, and supporting documents such as PDF files. Depending on the operating system you are using, you need to create a new folder in the root directory of your web server. If you have already worked through the Fireworks section of this book, you probably have already created a folder called retroscycles in the WWWRoot folder on your hard drive. If you skipped ahead to the Dreamweaver section, now would be a good time to create the retroscycles folder.

After your directory structure is in place, the next step is to define your Dreamweaver site. To define a site, open Dreamweaver and choose Site, New Site from the menu bar. Through the Site Definition dialog box, as shown in Figure 23.1, Dreamweaver offers a basic option and an advanced option for creating a site.

The basic option is a simple wizard that asks you to complete questions that provide the bare essentials of information needed to create a Dreamweaver site. In the majority of cases, the information collected by the basic view is enough to begin development work. If you find yourself needing to configure additional features such as cloaking (discussed later in this chapter) or Design Notes, you can use the advanced feature to customize additional site settings.

Figure 23.1
The Site Definition dialog box offers a basic and advanced option for defining your site.

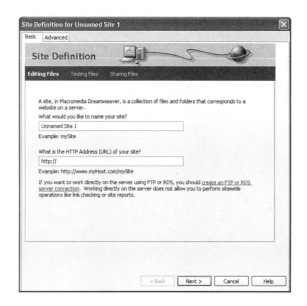

Using the Basic tab, type **Retros Cycles** as the name for your new site and then type **http://localhost/retroscycles** as the HTTP address for the site if you are using IIS as your web server or **http://localhost/retroscycles:8500** if you are using Coldfusion as your web server. Using the localhost address enables you to test your pages on your local workstation. After you name your site, click the Next button. The next step in defining your site is to choose whether or not you intend to use a server technology to create database-driven pages. This example leverages the ColdFusion platform, so choose the Yes, I Want to Use a Server Technology radio button and then select ColdFusion from the drop-down menu that appears (see Figure 23.2). Click the Next button to continue.

The next step is to determine whether you will be developing and testing your pages on the local workstation, testing them locally and uploading them to a server, or creating and testing the pages directly on a server. In this case, the pages are created locally and tested on the local workstation, so select the first radio button and type the path (or browse) to the retroscycles folder you created on your local workstation (see Figure 23.3). Click the Next button.

23

Figure 23.2
Choose to develop the site with the ColdFusion platform.

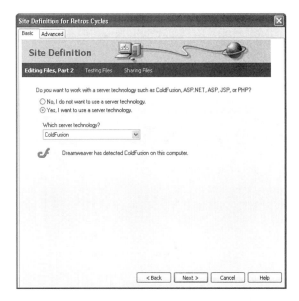

Figure 23.3
Choose to create the pages and test them locally.

As shown in Figure 23.4, Dreamweaver asks you to confirm and test the URL that will be used to test your pages. Click the Test URL button. If you typed your URL correctly, you receive a confirmation that the URL test was successful. Click the Next button.

Figure 23.4
Enter the URL that will enable you to test your pages.

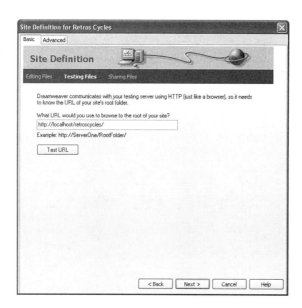

If you plan on copying your files to another server for production, the next step is to identify how Dreamweaver should access that server. Dreamweaver is capable of transferring files via FTP, across a local area network, via WebDAV, via RDS, and through Microsoft's Visual SourceSafe. The remote connectivity options are covered a little later. For now, choose the No radio button to indicate that you won't be using a remote server (see Figure 23.5). Click the Next button.

Figure 23.5
Choose not to use a remote server.

With the necessary settings established, Dreamweaver next supplies the basic summary of the site that you have created (see Figure 23.6). If any of the settings do not appear correct, you can click the Back button to progress backward through the steps to make corrections. To complete the site, click Done.

NOTE

You can always go back and edit the site in either basic or advanced mode if you find that you need to adjust fields or preferences. To access the site, choose Site, Manage Sites from the main menu.

Figure 23.6
The summary displays the settings for your new site.

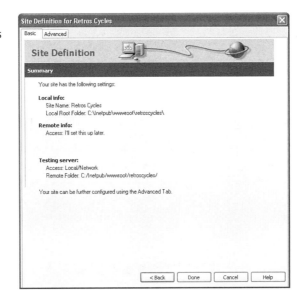

When the Dreamweaver site is completed, you can access the site files, images, and objects via the Files panel shown in Figure 23.7.

Creating the Best File Structure

With simple sites comprised of just a few pages and images, file structure isn't an area of extreme concern. However, when sites grow to contain hundreds, thousands, or even greater numbers of files, it becomes imperative to design a good file structure system to accommodate them.

The use of a local root folder is a good beginning. This area should contain top-level files such as the index page, as well as the main pages for the site. But if your site contains a great number of articles and resources, you might have to break this down into much greater detail. Let's say you publish an e-zine that regularly includes articles, columns, comics, and classifieds. It is in your best interest to create subfolders for each of these areas and keep things organized by topic.

Similarly, if you are using media other than images on your site, you might want to create subfolders for each type of media, such as images, audio, video, and so on.

The one potential problem that can arise out of creating too many subdirectories is that the resulting URLs can be very long, which makes them difficult to remember and bookmark and, depending on the way they are fashioned, even likely to cause problems with page validation.

A good exercise is to sketch out the file structure ahead of time. This gives you a blueprint from which to work as you proceed in the building of your site. Although it's not always easy to anticipate the future, keep in mind that the site, if successful, will grow in size and that the growth will need to be accommodated.

Figure 23.7
You can now manage the content of your new site.

SETTING THE REMOTE INFORMATION

Now that you have your local site established, you might need to set up a connection to your remote server that enables you to transfer files between your local workstation and the server where your site is hosted. For instance, if Retro's Cycles has a web host that allows FTP transfers, you can configure Dreamweaver to easily update the pages stored on the web server with the changes made on your local workstation. Some details about the various remote connectivity types are available in Table 23.1.

TABLE 23.1   REMOTE INFORMATION OPTIONS

Option	What It Does
None	Select this if you want to build your site on just your local computer. You can always consider transfer options later.
FTP	This is the File Transfer Protocol, which is a widely used method of transferring files between a local machine and a remote machine.
Local/Network	If you are working on a network or running web server software locally, select this option.

23

TABLE 23.1 CONTINUED

Option	What It Does
WebDAV	Certain servers use the web-based Distributed Authoring and Versioning tools. If you are using a WebDAV system, select this option.
RDS	This is Remote Development Services, which is used by people working with dynamic content in ColdFusion.
SourceSafe Database	This is a special Microsoft database that enables powerful management features for teams working on sites. SourceSafe must be installed and in use if you want to use this option.

To demonstrate how these types of connections are configured, let's take a look at the FTP protocol because it is one of the most popular. To set up FTP, you need to obtain the following information:

- FTP hostname
- Login name (this is your user ID information)
- Password (this is a password selected or provided to you by your service provider)
- Any additional information provided by your service provider regarding required settings

Typically, your service provider configures your login to default to the remote root folder. This folder corresponds to the local root folder because it is the folder where the top-level documents and the subdirectories can be found.

With your FTP information in hand, you can add FTP functionality to your site by choosing Site, Manage Sites from the menu bar. In the Manage Sites dialog box (see Figure 23.8), select the site to which you want to add FTP functionality and click the Edit button.

Figure 23.8
Highlight the appropriate site in the Manage Sites dialog box and click Edit.

Next, click the Advanced tab and choose the Remote Info category, shown in Figure 23.9. Change the Access drop-down to FTP and enter the appropriate host information, login ID, and password. If your host requires additional settings, you can configure them via this dialog box as well.

Figure 23.9
Enter the appropriate
FTP information
required to access
your site.

Two other options on the dialog box are worth mentioning:

- **Automatically Upload Files to Server on Save**—If you check this option,
  Dreamweaver automatically transfers the site to the remote server whenever you save
  the site. Because this can actually upload files that are in the process of being edited, I
  don't recommend choosing this option unless you are using an external versioning system such as SourceSafe.

- **Enable File Check-in and Check-out**—If you want to enable this feature, click once
  in the check box. The advantage of enabling this feature is that if multiple people are
  working on the site, Dreamweaver helps manage team files to prevent overwriting and
  the need for additional edits.

To complete the addition of FTP connectivity, click the OK button and Dreamweaver is
configured for FTP access. However, because you probably don't have an extra FTP host
handy at this time, click Cancel.

You can connect to and manage the files on your remote site by opening the Files panel
(Window, Files), selecting your site from the list, and clicking the Connect button shown in
Figure 23.10.

Figure 23.10
Clicking this icon con-
nects you to a remote
site. When you are
connected, clicking it
again disconnects
you.

Connect/Disconnect

CLOAKING SPECIFIC FILE EXTENSIONS

The cloaking feature is another site feature that can make managing your files easier in Dreamweaver. Cloaking enables you to choose which files are displayed in the Files panel and hide files that you wouldn't necessarily use in Dreamweaver. For instance, when the site images for Retro's Cycles were created in the Fireworks section, all the PNG files were also saved. Although it's great to keep the PNG files for future editing of those images, they won't be used in the Dreamweaver site, so it's not necessary to display them in the Files panel.

TIP

> If you are managing a team of developers, the cloaking feature is a handy tool to hide specific file types from the team members to prevent tampering.

To hide them, cloak them from view by opening the Manage Sites dialog box (Site, Manage Sites), selecting the Retro's Cycles site, and choosing Edit. Switch to the Advanced view and select the Cloaking category shown in Figure 23.11.

Figure 23.11
Open the Cloaking category in the Site Definition dialog box.

To cloak a specific type of file, check the Enable Cloaking check box and then check the Cloak Files Ending With check box. Type **.png** in the text box to hide all PNG files and click OK. Dreamweaver re-creates the site cache and excludes all images ending with the .png extension.

MANAGING DOCUMENTS

After you have created a Dreamweaver site, you're ready to begin adding pages to your site, editing their content, and (when necessary) deleting or renaming them. For the most part, Dreamweaver follows the same methods of managing documents as most of the popular word processors.

CREATING A NEW DOCUMENT

Creating a new document in Dreamweaver can be done in a variety of ways. When you open Dreamweaver, the welcome page (shown in Figure 23.12) offers you a quick way to create pages in some of the most popular formats with a single click.

Figure 23.12
The Dreamweaver welcome screen provides you with links to create a variety of new documents.

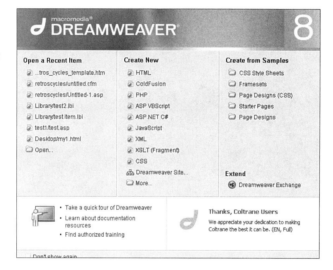

If you have disabled the welcome screen, you can create a new document by choosing File, New from the menu bar. In the New Document dialog box, shown in Figure 23.13, you can choose from the entire range of document platforms that Dreamweaver supports.

A third method of creating a new file is to click the menu button in the Files panel and choose File, New File. Rather than opening a new file, Dreamweaver simply adds a new untitled file to the list of pages in your site (as shown in Figure 23.14) using the default extension for the page (in this case .cfm). You can then open the file by double-clicking on it.

SAVING FILES

Whenever you modify a page, you'll want to save the file. Dreamweaver enables you to save a file by choosing File, Save or File, Save As and selecting the appropriate location.

If you have multiple pages open in the Design view, you can also right-click on the page title tab and choose Save, Save As, or Save All to save all the active, unsaved documents.

Figure 23.13
The New Document dialog box enables you to choose your page type.

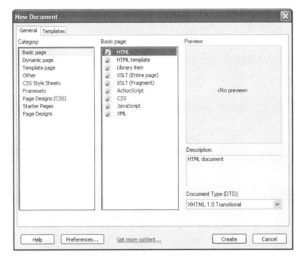

Figure 23.14
A new document is added to the Files panel with the default extension.

Tips for Saving Data

File management is easy, but it can also be risky. You can overwrite files, lose data, and save files to the wrong area of your computer. You also can run the risk of saving files improperly. Dreamweaver's management tools help you a great deal with this, but it's still a good idea to adhere to the following guidelines for general saving and file management:

- **Save your work regularly**—Whenever you begin a new file, immediately name it properly and save it to the correct location in your directory structure.

- **Be careful when using existing pages as templates**—If you want to create a new page based on an existing page with the Save As command, be sure that you save the new document with a new filename before making changes. Otherwise, you risk unintentionally editing the existing document and saving over its content.

- **Back up your work**—Whether you make a copy of the file to floppy disk, Zip disk, or CD doesn't matter—just make sure you keep a copy! Few things feel worse than losing your hard work with no chance of recovering it.

- **Create your directory structure first and then save files to that area**—Use Dreamweaver's Site Definitions dialog box to ensure you set up your directory structure before trying to manage a project. This way you'll know where your files are as you set up a logical structure upon which to form the linking of pages and page assets within a given document. Although Dreamweaver tracks changes in the locations of documents and site assets and can make some adjustments automatically, it's a very good idea for you to understand the structure of your site as well as any possible adverse effects that might result if you move files around.

Another problem with file management has to do with saving files to the wrong format. Let's say you're in Fireworks MX and want to save a file as a JPEG, but you mistakenly select another format. If you give the file an incorrect extension, the program saves the file improperly.

This problem holds true when saving HTML, XHTML, and Cascading Style Sheets (CSS) files and related documents. It's important to remember that HTML, XHTML, and CSS are saved in ASCII, or *text*, format. If you save a file as a binary file or transfer it as a binary file, the file becomes corrupt. The same is true with binary formats: You can't save or transfer a GIF or JPEG file in ASCII, for example, because you will destroy the file's integrity.

DELETING, DUPLICATING, AND RENAMING DOCUMENTS

As you are developing your site or reworking an existing site, you'll find it necessary at times to duplicate a document to create a new document with similar content, rename an existing document, or delete documents that you no longer need. To do this, simply (Control-click) [right-click] the document in the Files window, choose the Edit submenu, and select the option to fit your needs (see Figure 23.15).

Figure 23.15
With the Site window open and a file selected, you can access a context menu with a variety of options, including Delete, Duplicate, and Rename.

To delete a file, select the Delete option from the context menu. A pop-up window asks whether you really want to delete the selected file. Click OK. The file is now deleted.

CAUTION

> Be sure to always double check your files before you delete them. It's frustrating to accidentally delete the fruits of your labor just because you didn't open the file and check it first.

NOTE

> When managing the documents in your site, consider archiving files rather than deleting them. A corollary to Murphy's Law states that any time you delete a document, it's likely you'll need a block of code from it later. If you archive instead of delete, you maintain a copy that you can use down the road.

Duplicating files is particularly handy when you want to use most of the information in a given page but modify some content. You can duplicate the page you want, make modifications to the copy, and then rename the copy.

To duplicate a file, highlight the file to be duplicated in the Site panel. Then bring up the context menu and select Edit, Duplicate. A copy of the file immediately appears with the words copy of in front of the original filename.

To rename a file, bring up the context menu, select Rename, and enter the new name for the file.

CAUTION

> When renaming files, be sure to provide the proper file extension. If you rename a file with a different extension (or without one altogether), the file opens improperly or does not open at all.

OPENING AN EXISTING DOCUMENT

To open an existing document located on your hard drive, begin by selecting File, Open. The Open dialog box appears. Browse for your file, highlight the file you want to open, and then click the Open button.

The file now opens and is available for your modifications.

You can also open documents from the Site panel by simply double-clicking the document you want to open.

NOTE

> Files open in the view in which you're working. So, if you're in Design view, the file opens in Design view.

USING DESIGN NOTES TO TRACK CHANGES TO A DOCUMENT

As you work, you'll occasionally find that you want to jot down information about the pages with which you're working to remember later or to tell a co-worker about. Dreamweaver provides a handy tool called Design Notes that enables you to make notes for a page and save them to a separate file. You can also attach Design Notes to objects such as Flash files or applets, and you can use Design Notes in other programs such as Fireworks. Here, the focus is on attaching a Design Note to a new or an existing document. To add a Design Note to your page, be sure to save your page; then choose File, Design Notes from the menu bar.

NOTE

You must save your page before you can add any Design Notes to it.

In the Design Notes dialog box, shown in Figure 23.16, choose a status and type the corresponding note. If you want the note to be displayed whenever the file is opened, check the appropriate check box. If you choose not to check the box, each team member has to review the notes manually.

Figure 23.16
The Design Notes dialog box enables you to add notes to your pages to track changes or convey other information.

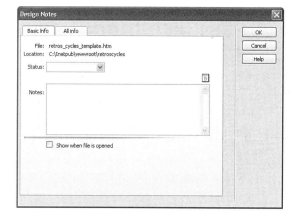

The file's status can be marked as follows:

- Draft
- Revision 1
- Revision 2
- Revision 3
- Alpha
- Beta
- Final
- Needs Attention

If you want the date to appear with your Design Note, click the Date icon above the Notes text box and Dreamweaver inserts a datestamp. You can also use the All Info tab within the Design Notes dialog box to add name and value pairs to the notes. So if you want to show that the author of the document is Harry, you can do so by clicking the plus symbol in the All Info tab and adding the name of author and the value of Harry (see Figure 23.17).

When you click OK, the Design Note is saved with the page.

Figure 23.17
The All Info tab enables you to add your own custom matched pairs to the Design Note.

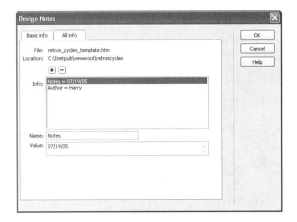

You can view and edit your Design Note at any time by selecting File, Design Notes. When the Design Note appears, make modifications by using the Basic and All Info tabs. For example, if you want to remove a name-value pair entry, highlight it in the All Info tab and click the minus symbol.

PREDESIGN PAGE SETUP

Before you begin with the layout and content of your page, it's a good idea to set up the foundation of your page, including elements such as the page title, style preferences, page margins, and backgrounds. Dreamweaver makes it easy to set these preferences through the Document toolbar and the Preferences dialog box.

ADDING A PAGE TITLE

Titling each page in your site is essential for several reasons. The page title is displayed in the browser window's title bar and is used to do the following:

- Denote bookmarks when a visitor bookmarks that page.

- Provide a marker for a browser's history feature.

- Promote better accessibility by assisting site visitors with orientation—your page title helps visitors know where on the web they are, and specifically, where on your site they might be.

- Label the page, should it be printed out.

The title is ASCII text that resides in the title container in the head of a web page. It can contain letters, numbers, and character entities as well as spaces.

NOTE

> Although you can use character entities (such as   and so on) in the title, you *cannot* use any HTML or XHTML itself. So, if you want to add quotation marks or a copyright symbol to your title, you can do so by using an entity. However, you can't use any formatting such as bold or italic.

23

Whenever you create a new web page in Macromedia Dreamweaver, it has the default title of Untitled Document.

To change the page's title, type the new name in the Title field in the Document toolbar, as shown in Figure 23.18.

Figure 23.18
Type the new title for your page into the Title Field of the Document toolbar.

ESTABLISHING PAGE PROPERTIES

In addition to setting a page title, Dreamweaver enables you to easily customize other page properties. Through the Page Properties dialog box, you can establish elements such as text properties, link colors, page encoding, and much more.

SELECTING A BACKGROUND COLOR

Selecting the right background is important to the design process. You want to select a color that contrasts with the text (foreground) color so that reading is easier. If you decide to use a background image, use one that promotes readability, unless you are going for a completely visual effect.

New Dreamweaver documents have a white background by default. You can set the background of the page by choosing Modify, Page Properties from the menu bar to open the Page Properties dialog (see Figure 23.19). In the dialog box, you can either type the hexadecimal color value for the background into the Background Color text field or use the color picker to select from the palette.

SETTING BACKGROUND IMAGES

Using a background image can enhance the page both aesthetically and functionally, such as when using an image with a heavy transparency as a watermark for your page. However, selecting an inappropriate background can be distracting and cause eyestrain, especially if the site has a lot of text to read.

Figure 23.19
Type the color value in directly or select a color using the color picker.

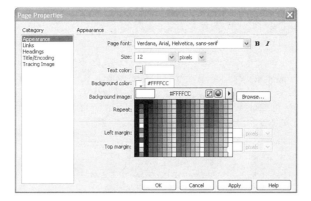

Image Formats for Page Backgrounds

Background images can be any type of image that browsers can display.

Generally, the image format you choose should be the one that compresses your image the most with the least loss of visual quality (the GIF format for graphics with large areas of solid color and the JPEG format for more complex images and photographs).

You can use a PNG graphic in the background. However, older browsers either do not support PNG or support it poorly. This makes the format a bad choice in general unless you know without a doubt that your audience is using browsers that have correct PNG support for your needs.

You can also use GIF animations as background graphics, but use background animations with extreme care and only in special cases in which the visual or motion design of the page is more important than its readability.

All background graphics tile by default (see Figure 23.20), which means that the background graphic, no matter how large or small in dimension, repeats horizontally and vertically across the page. So when you create it, consider how it will look when placed end-on-end in two dimensions.

Figure 23.20
The background image is automatically tiled.

To add a background to your page, open the Page Properties dialog box and click the Browse button next to the Background Image field. Locate the image that you would like to use and click OK. Click Apply and a link to the image is embedded in your code and the background displays in the page.

CAUTION

If the image file you selected is not within the current website's local root folder, you are prompted as to whether you want to move a copy of the image file into the website. This is usually a good idea because it avoids the risk of forgetting to transfer the image when you upload the site.

If the image specified in the background URL does not exist, no image is displayed—not even a broken image icon—and the background color is used instead.

WORKING WITH PAGE MARGINS

Page margins are considered to be the distance between the edge of the viewable area of the browser window and the HTML content within it. You can control the top, bottom, and both side margins by opening the Page Properties dialog box (see Figure 23.21) and typing the appropriate value in the margin field. Be sure that when you type the value, you also select the appropriate unit of measurement.

Figure 23.21
Use the Page Properties dialog box to set margins.

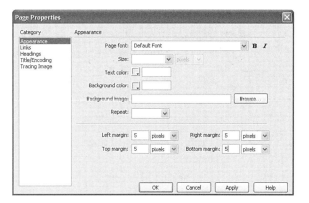

CHANGING THE DEFAULT TEXT COLOR

Although the color of your page text is entirely up to the design you choose and how it integrates with the color scheme of your site, text color is traditionally black for any text running longer than a few sentences. Black text on a white background provides the highest contrast possible and, arguably, is the easiest to read on screen and paper alike.

Tips for Choosing a Color Scheme for Your Pages

Selecting a color scheme for your pages can often be as difficult as creating the page layout. If you are designing a site for an organization that has already chosen the colors to use in their logo, stationery, or media materials, it's a little easier to integrate those colors into your site. If, however, the organization has left it up to you to determine the color scheme, keep these tips in mind:

- Stick with the web-safe palette, which is available when you choose any color picker within Dreamweaver. Although most home and business computers can see beyond the 216-color palette, an increasing number of people are browsing web pages on their cell phones and PDA devices, and these devices might not be capable of rendering colors properly beyond the web-safe palette.

- Choose three or four colors that complement one another and stick with them. Don't try to add too much color to your pages, which can overload the look and feel.

- Keep in mind that certain colors can invoke a specific mood from your visitors. Loud colors such as bright red or yellow can convey excitement or agitation whereas mellow colors such as pastels can have a calming effect. Choose colors that match the feel of your site.

- Be certain that your text is readable when placed on any background color.

- Keep in mind that unless controlled by a style or the document, the color of hyperlinked text is controlled by the browser. If you need your hyperlinks to be a specific color, be sure to create a style that controls them.

- Be sure to accommodate users who have visual disabilities. Reds and greens are colors that commonly can't be seen by those with visual disabilities, so avoid using those colors for your text.

After you select your color scheme, be sure to test it out in a number of different browsers, at different screen resolutions, and at different color depths. This ensures that all your visitors can enjoy your site to the fullest.

Of course, to create compelling designs, you might want to use other colors from your palette for the general text color. But remember that the higher the contrast between the text and the background, the more readability is enhanced. What's more, visitors who are visually impaired (such as those who are color blind) might not be able to see certain colors or combinations of colors. Therefore, your knowledge of the potential audience as well as the intent of the site should help dictate your color choices.

To change the text color with the Page Properties window, adjust the Text color field by typing a hexadecimal value or using the color picker to choose a color.

MANAGING LINK COLORS

The Page Properties dialog box also allows you to set colors for various different hyperlink states. These states include

- **Link**—This is the color of the link in its normal state prior to being clicked, and is expressed with the attribute name `link`.

- **Visited link**—When a link had been visited by a site visitor, the `vlink` attribute setting changes that link's color to denote that it has already been followed.

- **Rollover link**—When a hover style is selected, the `rlink` attribute changes a link to this color by default whenever the mouse pointer is placed over the link.

- **Active link**—This is the link color that displays as the visitor clicks on the link. Its attribute name is `alink`.

When a new document is opened in Dreamweaver, no default link colors are set. If left unset, each visitor's browser controls the link colors according to its default settings or the custom settings that have been set by the visitor. Generally, the browser's default link colors are blue for unvisited links, red for active links, and purple for visited links.

As with other page properties, link colors can be set easily in the Page Properties dialog box. The link colors are located in the Links category of the dialog box, as shown in Figure 23.22. To adjust the values, type the hexadecimal value into the field or use the color picker to choose the desired color.

Figure 23.22
Select a color for the hypertext links on the page.

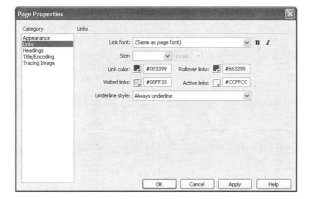

TIP

Hypertext links need to stand apart from other text on the screen so that users can recognize them as links. To that end, the colors you choose should contrast sharply with the text color. Generally, it is best to select a more vibrant color for unvisited than for visited links.

PREPUBLISHING CHECKS

After you have established your page properties and added content to your page, it is wise to follow a few more steps before you unleash your newest web creation on the world. Taking a close look at how quickly your site loads, conducting a spell check, and checking for browser compatibility will go a long way toward ensuring that your visitors enjoy your site.

ESTIMATING DOWNLOAD SPEED

Even with the advent of broadband, download speed is still an issue for many web surfers. If anything, faster Internet access has made visitors even more impatient as they wait sites to load. The web is fraught with websites that have become "bandwidth-heavy." Developers using fast T1 connections tend to forget that just because a page loads quickly in their browsers doesn't mean that users on DSL, cable, or even 56K connections will tolerate the slowness that they can experience. To avoid creating a site that takes too long to load, you can estimate the speed at which a page will download by looking at the Download indicator at the bottom of the Document window (see Figure 23.23).

Download indicator

Figure 23.23
The Download indicator displays the file size of the page and all its components and approximates the download time at a preselected connection speed.

`<body> <table> <tr> <td> <img>`   100%   787 x 427   37K / 6 sec

The Download indicator settings are controlled by the Status Bar category of the Preferences dialog box (accessed by selecting Edit, Preferences, and then clicking the Status Bar category). The indicator speed is set to 56.0 kilobits by default. As you work, set this option to match that of the expected average visitor of your site. However, when your page is complete, you should set this preference at various connection speeds to get an estimate of the download times on both extremely fast and very slow connections.

If the download time appears significant, you can use the Clean Up HTML/XHTML command to remove any extraneous tags and comments. In addition, be sure that you have optimized all images to their fullest without sacrificing too much quality.

NOTE

Remember, the Download indicator provides only an approximation of download speed. Dreamweaver can't assess factors such as network traffic and server speed.

SPELL CHECKING

There are very few truly great spellers on the planet, and even the best spellers make mistakes. Dreamweaver's spell-check feature helps both the best and the worst spellers hide their flaws from public view. To run the spell checker, place your cursor anywhere in the page and choose Text, Check Spelling from the menu bar. The spell checker (see Figure 23.24) stops at the first word in the document that is not in its dictionary and highlights the word. From there, you can choose to update the word manually, choose a word from the suggested list, ignore the word, or add it to your personal dictionary.

CAUTION

As with all spell checkers, Dreamweaver can't catch misuse of homonyms (by, bye) or commonly misused words (affect, effect).

Figure 23.24
The spell checker highlights the misspelled word so you can see it in context. The dialog box makes suggestions as to the proper spelling or allows you to manually type the correct word.

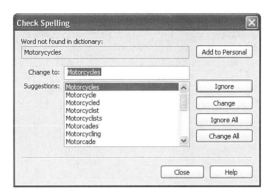

CHECKING PAGES FOR CROSS-BROWSER COMPATIBILITY

One of the biggest pitfalls for web developers is forgetting to check how their sites are rendered by different browsers. There's nothing worse than rolling out a great web application and then having someone ask you why the pages don't load properly, the tables are out of alignment, or elements of the application don't function properly. By checking to be sure that your application works in both Internet Explorer and Netscape, you save yourself the hassle of having to fix problems after the site is released to the public. If you really want to go a step further, test your application in Opera and Firefox as well. Although not currently as popular as IE and Netscape, they are both rapidly gaining popularity.

NOTE

> Checking for cross-browser compatibility means more than just opening the pages in the most recent version of the browser. If you really want to ensure that most visitors can use your site, check the site with several versions of each browser to ensure that the pages are not browser compatible in just one version or another.

To help you create pages that are cross-browser compatible, Dreamweaver has a handy utility called Check Target Browser. By choosing File, Check Page, Check Target Browser from the menu bar, you can run a report that displays each of the browser errors that the page would generate (see Figure 23.25). This command checks the page for specific browsers and versions and looks for page errors that might be generated by those browsers. When the check is complete, you can double-click on any error discovered to display the problematic code in the code view.

Figure 23.25
The Target Browser Check displays each error that might be encountered and the browser that would cause the error.

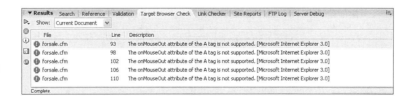

23

TIP

> You can edit the browsers that are included in the target browser check by clicking the Target Browser Check menu drop-down in the Results panel. From the menu, choose Settings and select the minimum browser levels you want included in the report.

In addition, if the Document bar is visible, Dreamweaver maintains a running tally of potential browser errors, which can be accessed with a simple click of the Target Browser Check button. Click on the button, which is located next to the Title field, to check your page against the specified target browsers.

A FINAL MANUAL REVIEW

The Dreamweaver tools mentioned in this chapter all help you prepare your site for its final journey to the remote server. Nothing, however, beats a good eye. After you've cleaned up your HTML, spell checked the site, and ensured that everything is optimized, it's worth taking one last look at each and every page of the site. Be especially on the alert for the following:

- Table layouts that have gone awry as you inserted images and text
- Missing page titles, descriptions, and keywords
- Commonly misused words that wouldn't be picked up by the spell checker
- Images that don't suit the final content
- Placeholder images that weren't replaced with final graphics
- Cross-browser compatibility and design integrity

Remember that organizations often rely on their website to be the first point of contact with potential customers or clients. Therefore, a site that contains errors, broken links, or problematic code probably won't project the image the organization is looking for. For this reason, it's imperative that you take the extra time necessary to ensure that your pages function as expected and are error free. Although Dreamweaver offers some great tools that can help you check for issues, the final check should always be a manual one performed by you.

TROUBLESHOOTING

How can I make sure my site files are always up to date?

To ensure that all files are automatically refreshed, be certain to select the Auto Refresh feature. This is a helpful feature because it updates new files as you add them to the site.

I'm not really sure what the title of my page should be. Is it really necessary?

If you leave title information out of your page, the title publishes as Dreamweaver's default `Untitled Document`. This gives your page visitors absolutely no help when trying to orient themselves to the page, figure out its purpose, and/or bookmark the page for further reference. Plus, the `title` element is required in HTML 4.0 and 4.01, as well as in XHTML 1.0

and 1.1. Using a clear title is an important part of setting page properties, so be careful not to overlook it!

Are there any hard and fast rules for what color links should be? I'd like to make them match my site, but someone said that they have to be a certain color.

Many usability pundits—including Jakob Nielssen—have expressed that the use of colored links other than browser defaults cause usability problems with navigation. Although this might be true for people who are very new to using the web (and nowadays, newcomers see so many different link colors, the point is almost moot), it's highly unlikely that any experienced user will fail to recognize a link. Unless you are expressly asked by a client or superior to follow defaults, you should feel free to color links as you see fit.

BEST PRACTICES—FOLLOWING THE DEVELOPMENT, TESTING, AND PRODUCTION MODEL

One of the most common—and dangerous—mistakes I see novice web developers engage in is the editing of web pages or applications on their production servers. Usually, these changes are made after an urgent request, and when the change or changes seem relatively harmless. The danger of doing this, however, is magnified when you start making live changes to complex applications such as those that are database-driven. A single slip of the keyboard in the code view and you can delete a single character such as a % in VBScript or a ! in JavaScript. This missing character can either break the application or change its entire functionality. For example, a function that is supposed to check for form fields that are not empty with the != "" command might now check for fields that are empty with the ="" command.

Because of the possibility of making these simple mistakes, it is important to create a development machine where you can test your changes prior to migrating them to your production server. Each change that is made on the development machine shouldn't just be tested to see whether the page loads, but also tested to ensure that the entire page functions as expected. Only after you are positive that your changes are valid should you move it into production and even then, it's a good idea not to replace the previous file, but rename it and archive it in case you need to step back a version.

This process might seem tedious and time-consuming, but I speak from experience in saying that it can ensure that the changes you make do not adversely affect your web application.

WORKING EFFICIENTLY IN DREAMWEAVER

In this chapter

REUSING PAGE ELEMENTS AND CODE

Although two projects are never exactly alike, similar page elements or objects often can be applied to multiple sites. For instance, if you develop a script that verifies that the user has completed the required fields of a form, it's likely that you could reuse that same code (with slight modifications, of course) down the road on another project. With that in mind, Macromedia has built several features into Dreamweaver that enable you to save objects and code that can be reused within the same site or on other projects.

In addition, several tools within Dreamweaver help you keep track of your ever-increasing assortment of HTML pages, images, links, color schemes, templates, Flash, and multimedia. As the number of sites that you manage grows, it becomes harder and harder to keep everything organized. Even if you organize your sites well with folders for images, multimedia, and style sheets, you'll soon find the need to add folders for navigational images, movies, or articles relating to a particular section of your site. Navigating to these separate folders time after time during the development process can become tedious and fraught with opportunities for mistakes—which can lead to broken links.

Links and color schemes present different challenges, of course. These items aren't stored in files, so you can't just navigate the folders of your site to find the link you used on one page or that exact color of blue you used on another. If the same color scheme isn't used from page to page, site consistency is lost. Templates can solve the color consistency issue to some extent, as can Cascading Style Sheets (CSS), but they certainly don't completely solve the problem.

Enter Dreamweaver's Assets panel (see Figure 24.1). Dreamweaver stores every major element of a site in a cache and makes those elements available to every page in the site. The Assets panel is a complement to the Files panel, and therefore they're both docked in the

Figure 24.1
The Assets panel breaks the site cache into nine categories, each of which can be viewed as a site-wide list or a user-generated favorites list of often-used assets.

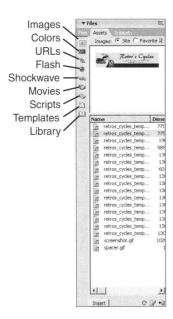

same Files panel group. The Files panel lists the tangible files for the site. The Assets panel lists the intangibles—the colors, URLs, templates, images, and multimedia used on the site's pages.

WORKING WITH ASSETS

The Assets panel might not recognize every asset type, but it does recognize many of the most common ones. The left side of the Assets panel has a column of buttons that let you choose the category of assets to display—Images, Colors, URLs, Flash, Shockwave, Movies, Scripts, Templates, and Library. The right side of the panel lists the assets within the selected category. A preview version of a selected asset is displayed above the list.

Unfortunately, Dreamweaver doesn't track assets such as audio files, Adobe Acrobat PDFs, or Java applets. Also, be aware that although the Movies category might recognize and include assets such as Windows Media movies, you can't preview them in the Assets panel.

TIP

> You can expand the preview area by dragging the splitter bar between the preview and list areas.

CREATING A FAVORITES LIST AND FAVORITES FOLDER

The Assets panel has two different views, which you can toggle between by using the two radio buttons at the top of the panel. The Site list provides a complete list of all the assets in every folder and page of the site. The Favorites list displays only the assets you choose to put there (see Figure 24.2). If you create a well-planned Favorites list for your site, you'll have the colors, URLs, and other elements that you use frequently readily available, while still having convenient access to the less-used assets from the Site list.

Figure 24.2
The Favorites list contains only assets you select, creating a specialized list of your most frequently used assets.

ADDING AN ASSET TO THE FAVORITES LIST

To add an asset to the Favorites list, choose the asset from the Site list and then click the Add to Favorites icon at the bottom of the panel.

You can also add images and media files to the Favorites list by right-clicking on the object in the Site view and then choosing Add to Favorites from the context menu.

Assets added to the Favorites list remain on the list unless you manually remove them. Even if you delete the item from your computer and refresh or re-create the site cache to update the Assets panel, the Favorites list remains the same. Therefore, you need to keep a close eye on your Favorites list and periodically go through and remove assets that no longer exist. To remove an asset from this list, select it and then click the Remove from Favorites button.

> **NOTE**
>
> Removing an asset from the Favorites list doesn't delete the asset from the site. It's still accessible from the Site list.

CREATING A NEW FAVORITES FOLDER

Even when you're using the Favorites list, it's easy to become overwhelmed with assets, particularly on a large site. An advantage the Favorites list has over the Site list is that it enables you to organize assets into groups called Favorites folders.

Favorites folders can be useful for organizing and quickly locating images you want to use together on your pages. For example, when developing the site for Retro's Cycles, you might have images of the various motorcycles for use within the site. If you group these into Favorites folders, you'll know exactly where to look to find the images you seek. If you really want to keep your favorites organized, you can even nest Favorites folders.

To create a Favorites folder, switch to the Favorites view in the Assets panel and then click the New Favorites Folder button at the bottom of the panel. Give the folder a name and you're ready to begin adding assets to the folder by either dragging and dropping them from your pages or creating them directly in the folders.

ASSET TYPES

When adding assets to your site, you need to be aware of some of the specific purposes and limitations that go along with the various asset types that Dreamweaver tracks.

IMAGES

The Images category lists every image file that you've placed within your local site, even if you've not yet used them on a page. Whenever you refresh or re-create the site list, Dreamweaver searches the root site folder as well as all subfolders and adds the GIF, JPEG, and PNG formatted files it finds to the list of available assets.

COLORS

The Colors category lists all colors that have been used for text, backgrounds, or links on any page within the site. Again, when you rebuild the asset cache, all colors that have been used are added to the site for future reference and reuse. Dreamweaver does not include colors from images or media files, so the colors used in your Flash SWF or Fireworks PNG files are not included in the Assets list. If you have a color that you have not used in a page, but want to include as an asset in your site, you can manually add it to the panel by switching to the Favorites view, clicking the New Color button, and using the color picker to select the color from either the swatch (see Figure 24.3) or an area of the page.

NOTE

After a color is added to a page within the site, it remains in the Colors category even if the color is completely removed from every page in the site.

Figure 24.3
The color picker enables you to select colors from the palette or type a hexadecimal number for the color.

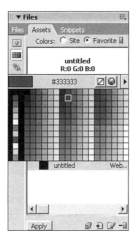

URLS

Just as Dreamweaver tracks the colors and images that you use in your pages, it also tracks the links you create to pages outside of your site. It scans your documents for hyperlinks and includes all references to HTTP, FTP, Gopher, HTTPS, JavaScript, and email. Keep in mind, however, that links to documents within your own site are not included in the URLs section of the Asset panel.

As with colors, you can create new URLs directly in the Favorites list by choosing the Favorites view, selecting the URLs category, and clicking the New URL button at the bottom of the panel. In the Add URL dialog box (see Figure 24.4), type the full URL, give it a nickname, and click the OK button.

The URL's nickname simply provides an easy reference for where the URL points. For instance, if you create a link to http://www.macromedia.com/cfusion/knowledgebase/ index.cfm?id=tn_16563, you might create a nickname called Dreamweaver Sessions to help you remember that the URL links to a tech tip article that discusses how to create a session variable.

Figure 24.4
Enter a URL and nick-
name for the new
asset. The nickname
can be used as the
source text for the
link when inserted
into a document.

FLASH MOVIES

If your site contains Macromedia Flash (SWF) files, they'll be listed in the Flash category of the Assets panel. This list also includes Flash buttons or text objects that you create in Dreamweaver. The Assets panel also enables you to preview your Flash content. When one of these assets is selected, a small Play button appears in the upper-right corner of the pre-view area. Most likely, you will need to resize the Assets panel to view the entire Flash movie. Another way to preview the movie is to double-click the file in the Assets list, which opens and plays the Flash Movie in a new browser window.

TIP

The preview area is useful for movies that are small enough to fit in the preview area. Large movies are not easily displayed in this area, so it's best to double-click on them in the Assets list to view them in a new browser window.

NOTE

The Assets panel does not list Flash source (FLA) files.

SHOCKWAVE MOVIES

This category shows all movies created in the Macromedia Shockwave format. As with Flash movies, Shockwave files can be previewed in the preview area or with a standalone QuickTime player.

MOVIES

If your site has any movies in the MPEG or QuickTime format, they are displayed in the Movies category. As with Flash and Shockwave movies, you can preview them in the Assets panel or the standalone QuickTime player. Movies created in the Windows Video (WMV) and RealMedia formats are also included in the Assets panel, but they cannot be previewed.

SCRIPTS

JavaScript and VBScript files are listed in the Scripts category—as long as they are named with the proper extension. The Assets panel contains only scripts in files with JS or VBS extensions. Scripts contained within HTML files aren't listed. For quick preview reference, the text of the script file is displayed in the preview pane when you select the asset.

When a script asset is inserted into a document, a `<script src="file://...>` tag is created with the `src` attribute containing a link to the script file.

TEMPLATES

This category lists Dreamweaver template (DWT) files. A *template* is a document you can use to provide a standardized layout for your pages. Templates are among the few assets you can create from the Site list. The creation and use of templates is covered in more detail later in the book.

LIBRARY ITEMS

Library assets are elements you want to use in multiple pages. A Library item is created from an object such as an image or even a full navigation bar. After it is created, you can include the Library item, rather than the original object, in your pages. The reason for doing this is evident when it comes time to update the object. Rather than having to make the update on every page that includes the object, you can simply update the Library item and the changes replicate automatically throughout every page that contains that Library reference.

REUSING ASSETS

Of course, the real power of the Assets panel is in its capability to streamline your development time. You can insert most types of assets directly into a document by dragging them from the Assets panel to the Design view of the Document window or by using the Insert button at the bottom of the panel. In the Colors and Templates categories, the Insert button changes to the Apply button.

Keep in mind that the asset is added to the page at the insertion point. In the case of colors, text typed after the insertion point appears in the selected color. When you insert a URL asset, the destination path of the URL appears as the source for the link; the source text can, of course, be modified if you would rather display alternate text.

For assets such as URLs and colors, you can also apply them to selected text in Design view by highlighting the appropriate text, selecting the asset in the Assets panel, and clicking the Apply button.

To apply scripts to the head of the page, select View, Head Content; then drag the script from the Assets panel into the Head Content area of the Document window.

MAINTAINING THE ASSETS PANEL

The Assets panel requires regular maintenance to retain its value. As the site evolves, so do the assets, but the Assets panel lacks the capability to automatically keep up with its listings. Assets themselves might need to be updated. And, finally, it might be useful to for a site to share assets already listed on another site. In addition, as mentioned previously, you need to update your Favorites lists manually because Dreamweaver does not automatically remove assets that have been relocated or deleted from your workstation.

EDITING ASSETS IN OTHER PROGRAMS

Because Dreamweaver integrates so easily with Fireworks and Flash, with the click of a button you can start editing objects that were initially created outside of Dreamweaver. To edit an asset, either double-click it in the Assets panel or select the asset and click the Edit button. If the asset was created within Dreamweaver (such as a script), you can edit it directly in Dreamweaver. Otherwise, the application to use is determined by the settings in the Dreamweaver Preferences tool. If you want to use a different application than the default, select Edit, Preferences and select the File Types/Editors category. Then add the application you want to use to edit that file type. Keep in mind, however, that because Fireworks and Flash are so tightly integrated with Dreamweaver, keeping them as your default editors for graphics and rich media is generally the fastest and easiest way to work.

Assets that don't reside in physical files, but are scanned from your documents instead—such as URLs and colors—can be edited only in the Favorites list.

USING THE ASSETS PANEL BETWEEN SITES

Often assets are useful across multiple sites. However, for an asset to be available, it must first be copied to the Favorites list of the new site. To make an asset available to another site, right-click on the asset in the Assets panel of the site that currently has the asset, choose Copy to Site, and select the name of the site to which you want to copy it.

WORKING WITH CODE SNIPPETS

The process of developing and maintaining websites often consists of reusing the same code elements again and again. Rather than retyping that code for each page, you can store the code in a snippet and then reuse and customize it when you need to use it again. For those Dreamweaver users who are used to writing their own scripts and functions, this is a very useful feature that can be leveraged to create your own personal code library.

Snippets are managed via the Snippets panel in the Files panel group. By default, Dreamweaver ships with a number of snippets that might be useful. For instance, if you want to add a drop-down menu to a form that contains the months of the year, simply expand the Form Elements folder in the Snippets panel and then expand the Dropdown Menus subfolder. You can then drag the Months, 1–12 snippet into any form on your page (see Figure 24.5) without writing a single line of code or building a drop-down menu with the Dreamweaver interface.

You can create new folders and subfolders for organizing your own snippets by clicking the New Snippet Folder button at the bottom of the Snippets panel.

Figure 24.5
Predefined snippets can make it easy to add content to your web pages.

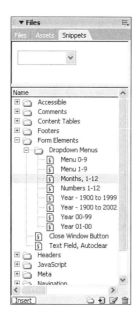

24

CREATING A CODE SNIPPET

Creating a snippet is a relatively easy process. However, creating a snippet the *right* way takes a little more effort, but is worth the extra energy in the long run. When I speak about the "right way" to create a snippet, I mean you should take into account that you might not be the only person to ever view your snippet, so the snippet should include detailed commenting that describes what the snippet is supposed to do.

For instance, suppose that you want to create a new JavaScript snippet that validates that two form fields are not left blank. Start the process by clicking the New Snippet button on the Snippets panel. In the Snippet dialog box (see Figure 24.6), type the name of the snippet and be sure the name is something that clearly defines the nature of the code and the language in which it was developed. For instance, JS-FormValidation would be a good name for this form validation code.

The next step in defining the snippet is to type a description of how the code works. Remember, the more detailed you are in the description, the more easily someone else can understand what the code is intended to do. So, instead of typing a short description such as "performs form validation," you might try typing a description such as: "This JavaScript snippet checks the values entered into form fields. If the value of the form is null, then the script pops a notice to the end user to complete the field and returns a false value to the form function that calls the snippet."

The next step in creating the snippet is to choose how the snippet code will be inserted into your overall code. If you choose Insert Block, the entire code block that you type is inserted into your page code when you apply the snippet. If, however, you choose Wrap Selection, Dreamweaver can apply the code before the insertion point and after the insertion point if necessary. For instance, if you select an image, Dreamweaver can place <a href="http://www.mysite.com"> before the object and </a> after the object, creating an effective hyperlink.

Figure 24.6
The Snippet dialog box enables you to store the details and description of your code.

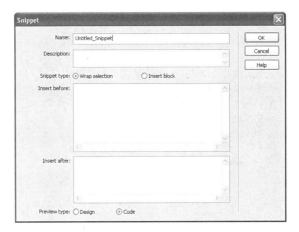

The third step is to actually type the code. If you have not already typed the code into a page, you can enter the code in the appropriate field or fields (in the case of a wrapped snippet). Otherwise, select the code in the Code view prior to clicking the New Snippet button and Dreamweaver automatically assumes that you want to create a snippet based on the selected code and populates this field with the selected code.

When creating your snippets, be sure to include comments that detail who created the snippet, what the snippet does, any variables that need to be assigned, and so on. This is where creating a snippet the correct way comes into play. The more documentation your snippet has, the more likely someone else will be able to understand easily what the code does, and the more portable the code becomes. This becomes important when colleagues ask you whether you have authored any code that could help them out with a project. If you properly document your snippets, you can send them the snippet and the comments will help them understand how to apply the code and how it is expected to function. For instance, using the previous example to create a snippet that adds a hyperlink to an image, the code inserted before the image would be

```
<a href="http://www.mysite.com">
```

However, the following code adds a comment to further explain how the snippet works:

```
<!-- The following line of code adds the preliminary
HREF tag and URL to add a hyerlink to an object. -->
<a href="http://www.mysite.com">
```

In addition, a comment should also be included with the code that follows the image, such as:

```
<!-- The following line of code closes the HREF tag -->
</a>
```

The final step in creating a snippet is to choose in which format the snippet will be displayed when it is previewed. Code that produces a visible object in the Design view (such as a drop-down menu or an image) can be set to Design so that the object rather than the code can be previewed. Code that performs strictly behind the scenes (such as form validation or complex calculations) should be set to Code so that the preview pane displays only the code.

ORGANIZING SNIPPETS

As mentioned previously, Dreamweaver comes with several folders containing useful snippets. For organizational purposes, feel free to reorganize the entire snippets folder to make it easy for you to find snippets quickly and easily. You can drag and drop folders from within the Snippets folder just as you do in the Windows or Mac operating systems. You can also create new snippets folders by clicking the New Snippets Folder button at the bottom of the Snippets panel.

REUSING SNIPPETS

After you have created a snippet, reusing it is as simple as dragging it and dropping it into the design or code view. You can also place your cursor at the appropriate insertion point and click the Insert button at the bottom of the Snippets panel. Another helpful feature that is worth mentioning is that Dreamweaver stores a record of the most recent snippets that you have used. You can access this feature and insert recently used snippets by choosing Insert, Recent Snippets from the menu bar.

USING LIBRARY ITEMS

Although snippets enable you to reuse code over and over, and assets provide you with easy access to the various objects within your site, Dreamweaver contains an additional tool that enables you to reuse entire portions of a page that you have created. This tool, known as the Library, provides a place to store commonly used page elements for reuse throughout your entire site. For instance, you can store the entire header for your site in the Library and have each page reference that single Library item. Then, when you make a change to the Library item, all instances of that object within your site are automatically updated. This makes it extremely easy to make site-wide updates.

Just think—you can create a Library item that adds a copyright notice to the bottom of each page in your site. Then, you can update the single Library instance of the notice once a year and the entire site is updated.

When you create your first Library item, Dreamweaver generates a Library folder in your local site. This folder contains all the Library items for the site, each of which is identifiable by its .lbi extension.

Although you can edit Library files directly in this folder, the best place to work with Library items is in the Library category of the Assets panel (see Figure 24.7). In this panel, you can create and edit Library items, insert them into pages, and even copy them to another site's library. You can use the horizontal slider to view additional information about the Library item such as size and the path to the Library file.

Figure 24.7
The Library category of the Assets panel displays a preview of the Library items.

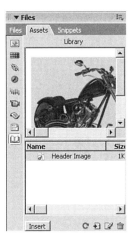

CREATING LIBRARY ITEMS

Creating a Library item in Dreamweaver is extremely easy. Simply add any object or element to the Design view of a page and select it. Next, choose the Library category in the Assets panel and click the New Library Item button (see Figure 24.8). Dreamweaver then creates a Library item based on the selected object and allows you to name it accordingly.

Figure 24.8
The New Library Item button allows you to create a new item.

USING LIBRARY ITEMS

After the Library item is created, you can apply it to any page by dragging and dropping it into the Design view or by placing your cursor at the appropriate insertion point and clicking the Insert button at the bottom of the Assets panel. When the Library item is inserted, the item is surrounded by markup code (see Figure 24.9) that indicates the path to the Library file, much like a server-side include.

EDITING LIBRARY ITEMS

As mentioned earlier, the main advantage of the Library is that modifications made to an item are updated site-wide. To edit an existing Library item, select the item in the Assets panel and click the Edit button at the bottom of the panel. Make the appropriate changes to the `.lbi` file that is opened and click the Save button. When you save the `.lbi` file, you are prompted to update all pages in the site that contain an instance of the item (see Figure 24.10). If you Click the Update button, Dreamweaver automatically updates the dependent pages.

Figure 24.9
When you insert a Library item, the markup for the elements is inserted and surrounded by comment tags. The item appears highlighted in Design view to distinguish it from regular, editable content.

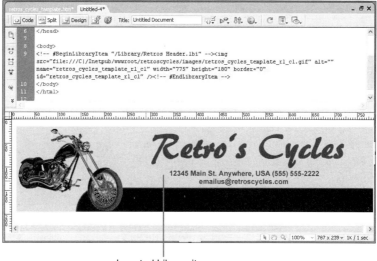

Inserted Library item

Figure 24.10
When you save changes to a Library item, you're prompted to update all instances of the item throughout the site.

If you don't update pages at this point, later you can use Modify, Library, Update Current Page or Update Pages. If you choose to update, the Update Pages dialog box appears (see Figure 24.11). You can also use this opportunity to update the remainder of the site's Library and template instances by choosing Update Site from the Assets panel's menu.

Figure 24.11
The Update Pages dialog box is used to update both Library items and templates used in the site.

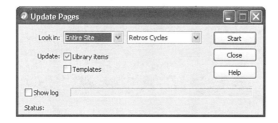

CAUTION

When editing Library items, you can't use Cascading Style Sheets (CSS) or timelines. These features insert code into the head section of the page. Library items can insert a consecutive block of code into only the *body* of the document.

24

NOTE

You can't include style rules in a Library item; however, you can include class attributes. When a Library item is inserted, it assumes the styles set for that class in the attached internal or external style sheet, thus assuming the appearance of the rest of the site. Be sure, however, that the style sheet is attached or referenced, or the Library item cannot take on the correct styles.

When a Library item is updated, all markup between the comment tags is modified to reflect the changes. In templates, certain regions can be locked so you don't inadvertently modify pieces of the template.

Library items, however, have no such constraints. Changing the content of the inserted Library item doesn't break the link to the Library. However, if you manually modify the content of the Library item within the document—for example, adding content to a table that was inserted as a Library item—those changes are lost if and when the Library item is updated. If you don't want your changes to be overridden, you need to detach the inserted Library item from the source, as described in the following section.

DETACHING FROM THE ORIGINAL

If you have an instance of a Library item that you don't want to be updated when the original item is updated, you can detach it from the original and preserve it in its current state. To detach an instance of a Library item from the Library, you need to break the link between the document and the item by selecting the instance of the item and clicking the Detach from Original button in the Property inspector (see Figure 24.12).

Figure 24.12
When the Library item is detached, the reference code that pointed to the Library item is removed from the page and the actual page code is inserted.

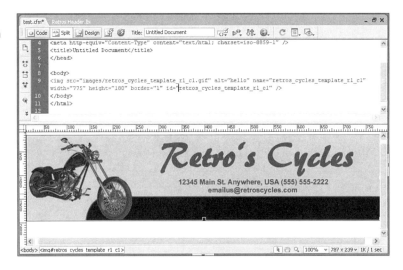

Before Dreamweaver detaches the item, a confirmation dialog box informs you that any future updates to the Library item won't be reflected in this instance (see Figure 24.13). If you Click the OK button, the item is detached and the corresponding markup removed in the code.

Figure 24.13
This dialog box confirms that you understand that after this instance is detached, it cannot be updated when the original Library item is edited.

Deleting Library Items

Deleting Library items is even easier than creating them. To delete a Library item, select the Library item to be deleted and click the Delete button at the bottom of the Assets panel. Although the item is deleted from the Library, the instances of the item in your site are not removed. Instead, they are detached from the original and remain intact in your web pages.

CAUTION

The delete process is irreversible. After a Library item is deleted, it is removed from the hard drive. Even though the original image that was used as a basis for the Library item may remain within the site and can still be referenced in your pages, the specific Library code that Dreamweaver created to reference the Library object is deleted.

Behaviors in Library Items

When you create a Library item out of content that contains Dreamweaver behaviors, the elements and event handlers are copied, but the associated JavaScript is not. Remember: The Library item can't update content that resides in the HTML head tag.

Fortunately, though, when you insert a Library item into a document, Dreamweaver is smart enough to know to add the appropriate JavaScript functions. If those functions are already in the head, Dreamweaver knows not to duplicate them.

TIP

Library items can be copied to another site in the same manner as any other asset on the Assets panel. Select the Library item (Command-click) [right-click] and select Copy to Site from the context menu. A pop-out menu lists all the defined sites to which you can copy the Library item. If this is the first Library item being added to the other site, Dreamweaver creates a Library folder in the local site.

TROUBLESHOOTING

I'm getting so much stuff in my Assets panel that I can no longer remember what's what. Is there an easy way to keep things straight?

One of the more useful features of the Favorites list is the capability it gives you to nickname your assets. Rather than have an asset appear in the list as "http://www.scooterpuzzles.com," you can nickname the asset as "Lu's Custom Paint for Motorcycles," which should jog your memory more easily.

To change an asset's nickname, be certain you're in the Favorites view, select the asset, and then select Edit Nickname from the context menu. You can also edit the Nickname by single-clicking the current nickname twice. After entering the nickname, press (Return) [Enter] or click elsewhere in the Assets panel. The actual filename, color, or URL still appears in the Value column of the Favorites list, and the preview display remains unchanged.

I deleted a Library item and then realized I need it again. What can I do?

If you accidentally delete a Library item, your only recourse is to re-create it from one of its instances in a document. To do this, select an instance of the Library item and click the Recreate button in the Property inspector.

If there aren't any instances of the Library item in your site—which could occur if you made the original instance editable and either didn't create any other instances or made all those instances editable as well—you must create a new Library item from scratch.

If I want to edit a photo in my favorite photo editor instead of the default editor, can I do that?

Certainly. The easiest way is to right-click on the image and then choose Edit With, Browse from the context menu. You can then browse to the executable for your editing software. When you use another photo editor, Dreamweaver remembers it and stores it in the Edit With submenu so you can easily reference it at a later time.

BEST PRACTICES—CREATING CODE SNIPPETS FROM CUSTOM CODE

It's happened to the best of us. You write a complex piece of code to perform a special function and it works beautifully. A while down the road, you find yourself needing the same functionality and you can't seem to remember which page it was that performed the function, so you spend valuable development time racking your brain to find the code. This scenario is the exact reason why it's so important to take advantage of the snippets functionality of Dreamweaver. By adding the custom code you create to the snippets library, you end up creating your own customized code library that is organized to fit your needs.

I spent a half hour a few weeks ago searching for a chunk of VBScript code that I had created to convert MS SQL Timestamp fields into epoch numbers (the number of seconds since 01/01/1970). I needed the function to interface one of my web applications with a help desk application and couldn't seem to remember where and when I used the function. After spending quite a bit of time searching (and wishing that I had created a snippet), I finally found the code and immediately placed it into my code library.

No matter how obscure the code, no matter how tied to a specific client or website it might seem to be, it's still a great idea to add *all* your custom code to the snippets panel for future reference.

TIP

Don't worry that your code library will be limited to use on a single computer. With Dreamweaver, you can export your site settings and the snippets that go with it by choosing Site, Export from the main menu. After you export the site to a single file, you can transport that file to a new computer and import the site by choosing Site, Manage Sites from the main menu and then clicking the Import button.

24

CHAPTER **25**

ADDING STYLE TO YOUR SITE USING CSS

In this chapter

INTRODUCING STYLES

Style is all about the way something is presented. Whether it's the style used by a runway model strutting down the catwalk or the style used by the latest Hollywood heartthrob in the latest blockbuster film, it's all about presentation—and styles in web design are no different. The web would be a pretty drab place if every website was restricted to a white background, black text, and the Courier font. In fact, I dare predict that were the web that boring, it would be significantly less popular than it is today.

Fortunately, developing for the web goes far beyond black and white, and you have a wealth of tools at your disposal to ensure that each website is relatively unique from the others. Whether it's colored text, stylized forms, rollover hyperlinks, or a host of other elements, each and every customization that you make to a site gives it its own style.

Today's browsers operate according to a set of rules that set the guidelines for defining a site's style. For instance, when you create a hyperlink, browsers underline them by default. In addition, the use of the `<p></p>` HTML tags defines that the text placed between the tags be formatted normally and that the browser should include a blank line after the text. These rules, and a host of others, establish the default framework that defines how a browser renders a web page, but they also provide options for customizations beyond that basic framework.

When you look at stepping beyond that default framework to add some zing to your site, you have a couple of choices. HTML provides tags that enable you to modify the appearance of your page, such as the `<font>` tag or the `<body>` tag. These tags, however, are relatively limited and focus more on rendering the site's basic structure than on the presentation aspect. That's where cascading style sheets (CSS) enter the picture.

Because the purpose of CSS is less focused on the layout of a page and more on the presentation, the language contains significantly more options for customizing the look and feel of a single web page or an entire site. In other words, HTML tags take care of the structural rendering of the site while CSS can supplement HTML by making the site more visually appealing.

INDIVIDUAL STYLES

The tool used to alter the presentation of the site is called a *style*. Styles can apply to specific instances of an object such as a single word or an image, or they can be applied to a group of objects. For instance, when you apply a style to a table column, each of the cells in that column is affected by the style.

Styles can be embedded individually into a web page, but more frequently they are grouped together and stored in an external *style sheet*. This is covered more deeply in a moment. First, it's a good idea to take a look at the structure of an individual style.

The following style is named `.bodyblueText`. When applied, it modifies the text that is applied to use the Arial font, 12-point size, a bold style, and the color of blue.

```
.bodyblueText {
    font-family: Arial, Helvetica, sans-serif;
    font-size:12px;
    font-weight:bold;
    color: blue;
}
```

The .bodyblueText style consists of a single *style rule*, which in turn is made up of sets of matched pairs of properties and values that define elements such as the font face, size, weight, and color. Table 25.1 provides a list of the available matched pairs that can be modified when you create styles for text.

NOTE

When creating your style, be aware that you don't have to set a value for every attribute. You can pick and choose those attributes that are necessary and set only those.

TABLE 25.1   TEXT PROPERTIES CONTROLLED BY STYLES

Name	What It Does
color	Sets the text's color.
font-family	Sets the font face and the default font family.
font-size	Sets the font size in absolute or relative sizes.
font-style	Sets the text italic or oblique.
font-variant	Sets the text to small capital letters instead of lowercase letters.
font-weight	Sets the text to bold, light, bolder, lighter, or a numeric value.
line-height	Sets the text's line spacing.
text-transforms	Sets the text's case.
text-decoration	Applies effects to the text such as underline or blinking text.

Although customizing the text within a web page is one of the most common uses of styles, it isn't the only application for this useful tool. In fact, styles can be applied to the page as a whole as well as to tables, images, and just about any object that can be placed within a web page. So does that mean that you have to buy another book on how to write CSS styles? Absolutely not! One of the really nice things about Dreamweaver 8 is that you can build, modify, and apply styles without ever having to write a single line of code. Dreamweaver's CSS panel provides an easy-to-use interface that lets you take care of your CSS needs from within the Dreamweaver environment.

STYLE SHEETS

Individual styles can be either embedded into a web page or grouped together and stored in an external text file called a *style sheet*. A style sheet can then be referenced by any web page via a link to the file. With the style sheet attached to the page, any of the styles that are part of the style sheet can then be applied to the referencing HTML page. Because the styles are stored in a single file, this makes site-wide updates extremely easy. If you want to change one property of a style, simply open the style sheet, make the adjustment, and save the sheet. When the save is applied, every reference to that style in each HTML page in the site automatically reflects the change.

NOTE

> The *cascade* in Cascading Style Sheets comes from the fact that multiple styles can be applied to the same element within a page. The browser applies the most specific style to that element. For instance, imagine a piece of text located inside a cell within a table. You can apply one style to the row that contains the cell and yet another to the cell itself. When rendering the text, the browser applies the highest level style first and then replaces it with more specific styles if available. So in this case, the style that would take precedence and be displayed in the browser would be the style applied to the cell.

When working with style sheets, three specific tags control the style sheet functionality. The `<link>` tag is embedded in the head section of the web page and specifies the location of the external style sheet in relation to this HTML document. This tag essentially creates a connection between the referencing page and the style sheet so that the referencing page can apply the styles to its page objects. The link tag generally looks something like this:

```
<link href="mystylesheet.css" rel="stylesheet" type="text/css">
```

NOTE

> If the location or spelling of the link to the style sheet is incorrect, it doesn't break your web page. In that case, the browser just applies the default text styles to the page until the issue is resolved.

The `<class>` tag is used within a web page to apply a style to an HTML tag. For instance, you can apply the `.blueText` class to an entire paragraph of text by using the following code:

```
<p class="blueText">The rain from Spain falls mainly on the plains</p>
```

NOTE

> When you define an individual style, be aware that each style must start with a period, such as `.blueText`. However, when applying the style within the page, the period is not used.

The third tag that is used to apply styles is the `<span>` tag, which applies style to a subelement of an HTML object. For instance, suppose that you wanted to italicize the word *Spain* in the previous example. You would do so by applying a span in the following manner:

```
<p class="blueText">The rain from <span class="bodyitalicText">Spain</span>
falls mainly on the plains</p>
```

Obviously, you would need to define a style called `.bodyitalicText` that would set the text to italic.

As you can see, styles and style sheets aren't as complex as they might appear at first glance. And although they are relatively easy to create and manage, Dreamweaver makes the process even easier by providing a graphical interface to adjust the CSS code.

ADDING STYLES TO YOUR SITE

If your goal is to make the presentation of your site easy to manage, Dreamweaver's Styles panel (see Figure 25.1) is your new best friend. From within the Styles panel you can create and manage style sheets, adjust the properties for individual styles, and easily apply styles to page content with a few clicks of your mouse.

Figure 25.1
The CSS Styles panel is used to manage all your styles and style sheets.

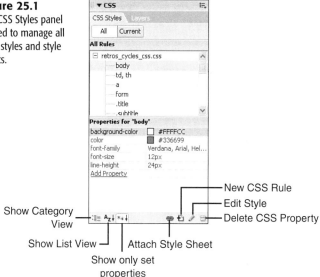

CREATING A NEW STYLE SHEET

The first step in managing your styles is to create an external style sheet. The style sheet can be stored in any location in your site and linked to by any of your HTML pages. When linked to, the styles included in the style sheet are available for application to objects within the page.

> **TIP**
>
> As you begin developing your site, you'll likely use only one style sheet that contains all the styles for your entire site. It's a good idea to keep that single style sheet in the root folder of your site. As the site grows, you might find a need to develop custom styles that

apply to only certain sections of your site. In these cases, you can store these style sheets in the folder that corresponds to the specific section of the site, or you can create a folder named styles to store them—similar to the way you store images in the site's images folder.

There are several ways to create a new style sheet from within Dreamweaver 8. If you're new to creating styles, the easiest way is to start with the predefined style sheet templates that come with Dreamweaver. To access these templates, choose File, New from the menu bar and choose the CSS Style Sheets category in the New Document dialog box (see Figure 25.2).

Figure 25.2
The CSS Style Sheets category provides access to predefined style sheets.

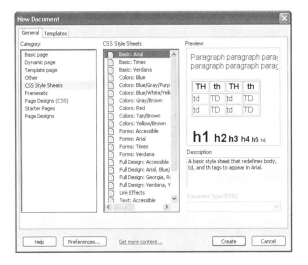

Each of the style sheet templates contains a variety of different font styles and colors for you to choose from. The templates are divided into categories ranging from Basic, which contains simple font styles, to Full Design, which includes styles for text, tables, and navigation bars.

NOTE

Remember that your pages can link to as many style sheets as you would like, so you aren't limited to just one style sheet for your website.

When you select a style sheet that you think will fit with your web page design, click OK and a new instance of the style sheet is created in the code view (see Figure 25.3). This new page must be saved within your site before you can apply any of the style rules to your documents.

After you have saved the page to your site, you can access the styles contained in the style sheet by selecting the All button on the CSS Styles panel (see Figure 25.4).

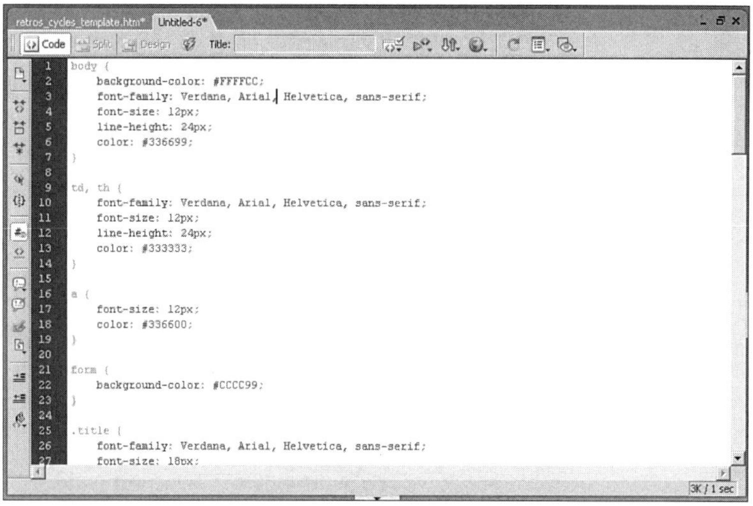

Figure 25.3
A new style sheet has been created based on the template that you chose.

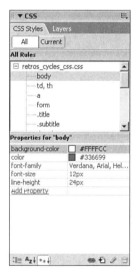

Figure 25.4
The styles are now accessible via the CSS Styles panel.

If you don't want to use the predefined styles, you can generate your own style sheet by simply defining a new individual style rule.

DEFINING NEW INDIVIDUAL STYLES

To start the process of creating a new style rule in Dreamweaver, click the New CSS Rule button at the bottom of the CSS Styles panel or click the CSS Styles panel menu and choose New. Regardless of which way you choose, the New CSS Rule dialog box, shown in Figure 25.5, enables you to choose what type of style rule you want to create, designate a name for the rule, and choose whether you want to create a new style sheet, add the rule to an existing style sheet, or embed the style in the current document.

Figure 25.5
The New CSS Rule
dialog box starts you
in the process of cre-
ating a new rule.

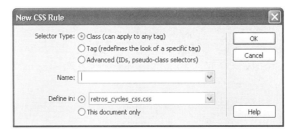

Generally, the rules you will be creating are the Class rules because these rules can be applied to any tag placed in a web page. Tag rules can be used to define the presentation of a specific tag when it is added to your page. Advanced rules further define existing rules by enabling you to add additional properties to them. To create an advanced rule, you need to select the existing style that you want to enhance from the Name drop-down menu.

If you choose to create a class rule, the next step is to create a name for it. Each class name must start with a period, so an appropriate name for a style that sets text to green, Arial, 10pt might be `.bodygreenTextA10`.

> **TIP**
>
> Keep in mind that when naming a style, it's a good idea to name it something that will remind you what the style is supposed to do. Generic names such as Style1 and Style2 are used by Dreamweaver when creating embedded styles, but good to get into the habit of providing custom names for your style rules.

Next, you need to define whether the rule will be embedded in the current document or stored in an external style sheet. Style rules that are embedded in the document are available to only that document, so if you plan on using the style in any other page in your site, be sure to either create a new external style sheet or embed the new style rule in an existing style sheet. When you have selected where Dreamweaver should define the rule, click OK.

With the type and location of the rule determined, the next step is to set the rule parameters. Elements such as font face, size, style, and a host of other properties can be selected via the CSS Rule Definition dialog box, as shown in Figure 25.6.

Figure 25.6
The CSS Rule
Definition dialog box
enables you to cus-
tomize how the rule
will modify the object
to which it is applied.

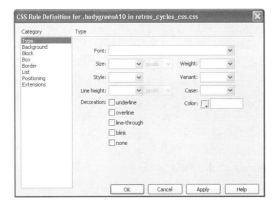

Each category provides access to a list of parameters that define how the object will be presented when the style is applied. Table 25.2 provides some basic information about the various categories and the functionality they control.

TABLE 25.2   STYLE PROPERTY CATEGORIES

Category	What It Controls
Type	Defines the appearance of text, using properties such as font, size, and style.
Background	Controls background colors and images for the page.
Block	Provides control over the spacing and alignment of text blocks.
Box	Sets the positioning and spacing of objects within the page as opposed to positioning them with tables.
Border	Controls the style, width, and color of any border that surrounds an object.
List	Provides control over ordered and unordered lists, including the use of custom bullets.
Positioning	Sets the exact location and size of an object within the page.
Extensions	Enables you to control special page properties such as custom cursors and page breaks.

After you set the definitions for your new style, click OK and the style rule is either added to your style sheet or embedded within the page, depending on what you instructed Dreamweaver to do.

> **TIP**
>
> If your style sheet is open and you add a new style to it, you need to save the style sheet before the additions are applied to your pages.

APPLYING STYLES THROUGHOUT YOUR PAGES

So far, so good...right? Now you know that creating style sheets and style rules in Dreamweaver is a pretty easy process. Just about the only thing easier than creating the styles, however, is applying them. In most cases, you can simply attach your style sheet to the HTML page, select the object to which you want to apply the style, and then select the style you want from either the Property inspector or the CSS Styles panel.

ATTACHING A STYLE SHEET TO A PAGE

Attaching a style sheet to a page is done by clicking the Attach Style Sheet button at the bottom of the CSS Styles panel. When you click the button, the Attach External Style Sheet dialog box, shown in Figure 25.7, enables you to specify the location of the file, whether you want to link to the file or import the style rules into the current document, and to what type of media the style sheet is to be applied.

25

Figure 25.7
The Attach External Style Sheet dialog box enables you to link to or import an existing style sheet.

Although the file location and URL property is relatively straightforward, the link versus import option and the media type might be a little confusing. If you choose to link to the style sheet, a line of code is added to the header of your page, instructing the page to include the contents of the external style sheet. This ensures that when the page is rendered, the style rules are included so that they can be applied. Importing the style sheet, on the other hand, makes the style rules a permanent part of the code for the page. This option is generally used when you want to combine two style sheets into a single sheet. It is not recommended that you import styles on a regular basis because the capability to make updates to a style and have it applied site-wide is lost when the style is imported.

The capability to select a target media type is new within Dreamweaver 8. It enables you to specify to what types of media the styles should be applied. For instance, you can create two different style sheets and specify that one set of style rules should be applied when the page is rendered on the screen and another set of rules applies when the page is sent to a printer.

When you complete the information about the external style sheet, click OK and the rules located within the style sheet become available to you in the All category of the CSS Styles panel.

USING STYLES TO SET PAGE PROPERTIES

Using style rules to control the page properties is generally done through the application of style rules to the <body> tag. After attaching or embedding your style sheet, click the <body> tag in the tag selector and click the Current button in the CSS Styles panel. As shown in Figure 25.8, the panel displays a summary of the styles currently applied to the tag and enables you to adjust the existing properties or add a new property to the page.

Modifying the page properties is as simple as clicking in the Value column (the right column) in the Properties section of the panel and selecting or typing a new value. When the value is a color, Dreamweaver provides access to a color picker. When the value is one that can be selected from a list of available options (such as font-family or font-size), the list is made available. If you want to add a new property, click the Add Property icon and choose from the list of available properties. You can then select from the available values for that property in the right column. To delete a property, right-click or Ctrl-click on it and choose Delete from the context menu.

Figure 25.8
The CSS Styles panel displays the summary and properties for the selected <body> tag.

> **NOTE**
>
> Whenever you make changes to any of the properties, the actual style rule is changed. This means that if you make a change to a rule that is in a linked style sheet, the actual style sheet is updated. If you make a mistake and change a color in the properties, you need to switch to the style sheet document that opens automatically when you edit properties and select Edit, Undo to undo the change.

To apply the changes to the page properties, save the style sheet. Note that the changes are applied to every page that links to the style sheet.

> **TIP**
>
> If you want to override a setting such as the background color in a linked style sheet, open the Page Properties dialog box by choosing Modify, Page Properties. All settings that you specify in this dialog box generate embedded styles in the document that override the styles in the linked style sheet.

APPLYING STYLES TO TEXT

Modifying the style of text can be done in a couple of ways. If the style that you want to apply already exists, select the text that you want to modify and then select the desired style from the Style drop-down menu in the Property Inspector. As shown in Figure 25.9, all styles that are embedded in the page or exist in any linked style sheets are visible in the Style drop-down.

25

Figure 25.9
The Style drop-down menu provides easy access to the styles embedded in your page or linked to in an external style sheet.

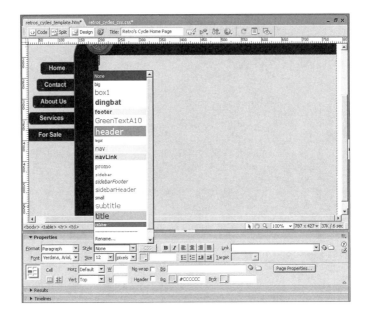

If you want to create a new text style, you can either follow the process outlined in the previous section to add a new style to your style sheet or just highlight the text and apply font, size, and formatting changes. If Dreamweaver does not recognize the combination as one that exists in a style, it generates a new style and embeds it in your page. This style is then reusable throughout the page. It is not, however, accessible to any other pages, which is good justification for adding it to your style sheet.

TIP

It's worth mentioning again that the cascade of styles dictates that the style that will be rendered is the style applied on the most specific level, so a style applied to a specific word overrides a style applied to a paragraph of text. If you run into problems with a style not displaying as you expected, the best place to start figuring it out is by selecting the text or the object and removing the style applied at that level.

APPLYING STYLES TO TABLES

Just as you can apply styles to the page and to text, you can also format tables with styles. The style can adjust more than just the text contained within the cells. Using properties such as background-color and background-image, you can specify the presentation of table rows and columns.

To apply a style to a table, insert the table into your page by choosing Insert, Table from the menu bar. In the Table dialog box, shown in Figure 25.10, select the desired number of columns and rows and then choose a table width, border thickness, cell padding value, and cell spacing value. Click OK to create the table.

Figure 25.10
Add a table to your page so you can apply styles to it.

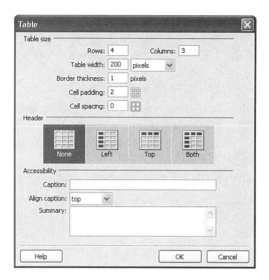

With your table in place, you can apply styles on the row, column, cell, or cell contents level. To apply a style to a row, click on the leftmost border of the row or place your cursor in any cell within the row and click the rightmost <tr> tag in the Tag Selector. With the row selected, choose the appropriate style from the Style drop-down in the Property inspector.

Applying a style to a column is done in exactly the same manner, with the exception that you select the column by clicking on the topmost border of the desired column and then apply the style.

If you want to apply a style to a specific cell, place your cursor inside the cell and click the rightmost <td> tag in the Tag Selector. With the cell selected, apply the style.

Finally, you can apply a style to specific text within a cell by selecting the text and applying the style via the Property inspector.

APPLYING STYLES TO FORMS

HTML forms tend to be one of the more boring aspects of web design because they tend to look like every other form out there. Luckily, using styles, you can get rid of those generic gray buttons, blah text fields, and dull drop-down menus by applying custom styles to them. You can even get rid of that annoying extra space that occurs after a </form> tag is used in HTML by using the margin-bottom style property to set the margin to zero. Table 25.3 highlights some popular style options that can be applied to form elements.

25

TABLE 25.3 FORM PROPERTIES THAT CAN BE CONTROLLED BY STYLES

Style Property	How It Can Be Applied
background-color	Can be applied to form buttons, text fields, text areas, and drop-down lists to change the background color.
font-family	Can be applied to text fields, text areas, buttons, and drop-down lists to change the font displayed.
font-size	Can be applied to text fields, text areas, buttons, and drop-down lists to change the font size.
background-image	Can be applied to text fields and text areas to insert a background image.
margin-top	Can be applied to the form to control the number of pixels in the top margin.
margin-bottom	Can be applied to the form to control the number of pixels in the bottom margin.
margin-left	Can be applied to the form to control the number of pixels in the left margin.
margin-right	Can be applied to the form to control the number of pixels in the right margin.

APPLYING STYLES TO OTHER OBJECTS

As you have seen, it is relatively easy to apply styles to popular page elements such as the background color, text, tables, and forms. The great thing is that the power of CSS doesn't stop there. Styles can be applied to just about any other visual object that you can place in a web page. Want to set the margins of an image or adjust the way text wraps around the image? CSS can do that. Want to ensure that all images displayed in a certain area are scaled to the appropriate size? CSS can do that, too. The process of applying styles to objects is the same as applying them to text, forms, or tables. Simply create the style, choose the attributes you would like to adjust, set values for them, and apply the style to the object. Just as it does with text or forms, Dreamweaver makes applying styles to any object a snap.

ADDING COMMENTS TO CASCADING STYLE SHEETS

Just as other coding languages do, the CSS language enables you to add comments to your style sheets to make them easier to read and understand. Comments in CSS are surrounded by a /* opening tag and a */ closing tag. So the following code would be considered a comment and would not be rendered in the style sheet:

```
/* This is a comment within a style sheet */
```

Again, I cannot stress enough how important it is to fully document your code by using comments. Even if you plan to strictly use the Dreamweaver CSS panel to create and manage your styles, you might consider opening your style sheets and providing the appropriate comments throughout the page to indicate what each style is expected to do.

TROUBLESHOOTING

I adjusted the background color in my style sheet, but one of the pages in my site doesn't seem to be using the style. What could be wrong?

Take a look at the page's properties by choosing Modify, Page Properties. It's likely that the background color for the page has been set, which would override the style rule in your style sheet. To resolve the issue, delete the hexadecimal value in the Background Color field.

I updated my style, but when I preview the pages in my browser, the old styles are still showing.

You need to save the style sheet before the changes propagate out to your pages. When you adjust a style, Dreamweaver opens the style sheet and makes the changes, just as you would with any other HTML page. For the changes to be applied, you need to save the style sheet.

I uploaded my website to my host and viewed it in my browser, but none of the styles are there. What did I do wrong?

Make sure you uploaded your style sheet as well as the HTML pages. If you don't upload the style sheet, the browser will not include the styles in the page when it renders it. Additionally, there will be no error telling you that the browser experienced errors locating the style sheet.

BEST PRACTICES—MIGRATING SITES AND PAGES AWAY FROM THE <FONT> TAG

On a continuing basis, the World Wide Web Consortium (W3C) reviews the standards that are in practice regarding the technical standards used to develop web pages. During these reviews, they work to identify elements that are no longer effective and deprecate them. A good example of a deprecated element is the <font> tag. In the past, applying styles to text required that a <font> tag be applied everywhere in the text that the font changed beyond the default settings. This meant that whenever you changed font face, a <font> tag was applied. When you changed font size, a <font> tag was applied. The end result was <font> tags being heavily used in pages, causing bloated code and slower download times. Luckily, CSS provides a much better method of adding style to text.

If, however, you built sites in the past that relied on the <font> tag rather than style sheets, it might be a good idea to schedule a code review and work toward migrating them to styles instead. Does this mean that your website will not continue to work or that the font styles will suddenly stop working? No. But it does mean that as newer versions of browsers are released, the support for the <font> tag will be removed and your pages might not render predictably.

NOTE

> For more details on working with text in Dreamweaver, take a look at Chapter 22, "Introducing Dreamweaver 8."

SELECTING A PAGE STRUCTURE

In this chapter

CHOOSING A DESIGN FORMAT

When creating web pages, you can choose from among several options to select a design layout. Probably the most popular method currently in use is using tables to design pages. By using tables, you have a good level of control over where and how your content is displayed, and you can use either relative or fixed table, column, and cell widths to adjust for various screen resolutions. The difficulty of tables appears when you start to nest tables on multiple levels. Spacing tables and adjusting relative properties can get difficult as the number of nested tables increases.

Another option that has been losing some popularity is designing with frames. The attractive element of using frames is that content in one frame doesn't have to be reloaded and can stay static while content in another frame changes. This has traditionally been used in situations where the navigation bar was loaded into a static frame while the content frame changed as navigation links were clicked. Frames, however, can be difficult to manage and present additional issues with things such as getting your site correctly listed in search engines.

The third and latest design format involves designing with layers. Layers are tag-driven objects created to give developers complete control over where their content is displayed and how it relates to other objects on the page. The major difference is that layers enable you to think along not only the X and Y axes, but on the Z-axis as well. This means that you can stack layers on top of each other to create the perception of depth. The downside to layers, however, is that they are not fully supported in earlier browsers. This means that if your site might be accessed by a visitor with an older browser, the site may not render properly. If, however, you're developing in an environment where you are sure of the browser being used to access the pages (such as in a corporate intranet setting), layers can offer quite a bit of enhanced functionality beyond what tables offer.

NOTE

> When developing with layers, one thing you need to consider is the possible browser versions your audience might be using. Versions of Internet Explorer and Netscape earlier than version 4.0 can't display layers and 4.0 browsers don't render them consistently. With that in mind, if your target audience might be using older browsers, you should consider a table-based or frame-based design.

DESIGNING WITH TABLES

Using tables is really the tried and true method for giving your pages a solid structure. Table structures are supported by all major browsers, they are relatively straightforward to develop, and Dreamweaver makes it really simple to create and nest tables.

To create a table, open a new document and choose Insert, Table from the menu bar. In the Table dialog box, shown in Figure 26.1, you can choose how many rows and columns you want to include in the basic table. Don't worry if you don't know exactly what your table is going to look like; you can always add more rows and/or columns later.

Figure 26.1
The Table dialog box enables you to set up your new table.

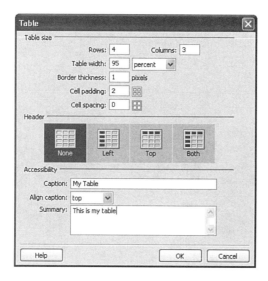

In addition to the number of columns and rows, you can also adjust the table width, border thickness, cell padding, and cell spacing. The table width can be set to a static measurement in pixels or can be a percentage relative to the size of the browser. The border thickness is a simple numeric value, as are the cell padding and cell spacing. The cell padding refers to how much room you want between the content of a cell and the interior wall of that cell. Cell spacing, on the other hand, refers to the distance between the cells themselves.

You can also use the Table dialog to establish whether or not your table will have a header column, header row, both, or none by clicking the appropriate layout.

Finally, you can set accessibility options for your table by providing a caption, caption alignment, and summary of the table and its contents. The accessibility elements are becoming more important as more and more people with disabilities are using the web. By completing these fields, you ensure that everyone can enjoy your content.

After you have finished setting the table properties, click OK and Dreamweaver constructs the table for you and inserts it into your page, as shown in Figure 26.2. You can customize your table and its layout by selecting the element you want to modify and using the Property inspector.

For instance, to modify the properties of the entire table, click just outside the outer border to select it. After it is selected, the Property inspector provides access to similar properties offered by the Table dialog box, along with added features such as border color, background image, and background color (see Figure 26.3).

26

Figure 26.2
A new table has been inserted into the page.

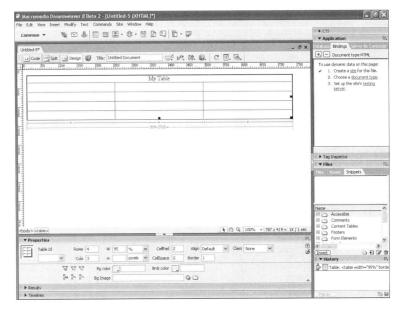

Figure 26.3
The Property inspector enables you to adjust the various properties of the table and its elements.

If you want to adjust an element of the table such as a column, row, or cell, you can do that as well. Select columns by clicking on the topmost border of the column. The entire column is highlighted after it is selected (see Figure 26.4).

Figure 26.4
A table column has been selected.

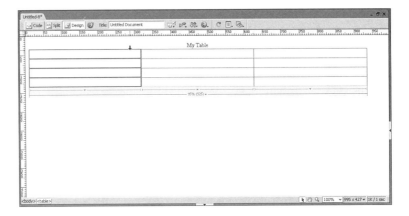

Rows are selected in a similar manner: Click the leftmost border of the row or place your cursor inside any cell within the row and select the leftmost <tr> tag in the tag selector (see Figure 26.5).

Figure 26.5
A table row has been selected.

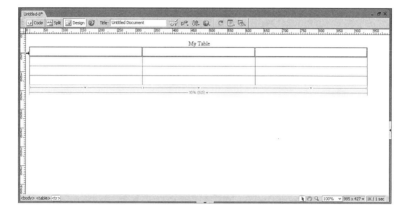

To select cells, place your cursor inside the cell and click the rightmost <td> tag in the tag selector. When the cell is selected, the cell border is darkened (see Figure 26.6).

Figure 26.6
An individual cell has been selected.

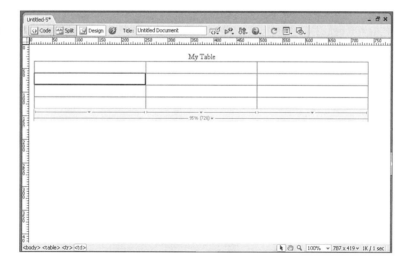

After the element is selected, you can adjust properties such as height, width, alignment, text styles, background color, and several others. You can also join elements together by selecting multiple items and clicking the Merge button on the Property inspector. Merging cells, shown in Figure 26.7, is an easy way to adjust your table layout to meet your design needs.

26

Figure 26.7
The cells in the top row have been merged together.

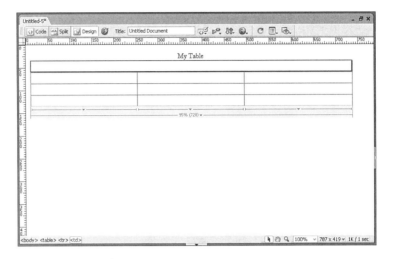

DRAWING TABLE LAYOUTS AND CELLS IN LAYOUT MODE

Dreamweaver also provides developers a second tool for generating tables, known as *Layout mode*. This environment is usually more comfortable for users who have a graphic design or page layout background, because it involves drawing the table as you want it, rather than letting Dreamweaver build it and then adjusting the properties after it is placed in the page.

To switch to the Layout mode, choose View, Table Mode, Layout Mode from the menu bar. As shown in Figure 26.8, Dreamweaver alerts you to some of the tools that are useful in this mode. Click OK to close the box.

Figure 26.8
Dreamweaver alerts you to some of the useful tools in the Layout mode.

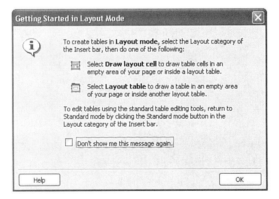

One other thing you might have noticed about Layout mode is that Dreamweaver also activates the Insert toolbar (see Figure 26.9), if it isn't already open. The Insert toolbar gives you access to the tools necessary for using this mode.

Figure 26.9
The Insert toolbar in Layout mode provides access to the tools necessary to create tables.

DRAWING A LAYOUT TABLE

Drawing Layout tables is simple if you have ever used a graphics program. Basically, it's the same action as if you were to draw a rectangle on your page with a mouse. Just click the Layout Table button on the Insert bar and then draw a rectangle on your page that represents the outer borders of your table. The result is a rectangle drawn in your page, as shown in Figure 26.10.

Figure 26.10
A table has been added that has one column, one row, and one cell.

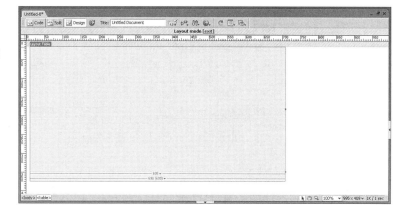

DRAWING A LAYOUT CELL

After your table is in place, the next step is to create the cells that are located within the table. The process of creating cells is almost identical to the process of creating the table, except that you'll be drawing inside the table boundaries.

To draw a cell within your table, just click the Draw Layout Cell button on the Insert bar and then draw your cell inside the table (see Figure 26.11).

Figure 26.11
The cell within the table has been drawn.

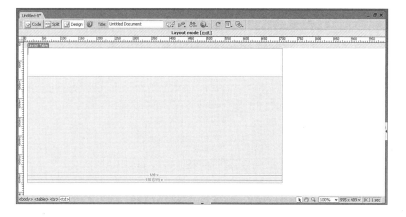

26

Be careful, however, about how many cells you draw and the layout design you choose. What appears to be a straightforward layout of columns and rows can quickly turn into a mess of nested tables, unnecessary spacer images, and tables that don't render properly in older browsers. To help avoid this, draw out a page plan on paper that indicates what the page structure should look like. Next, when creating your tables, be sure to follow the page plan carefully to ensure that your tables are as clean as possible and will render correctly.

NESTING A LAYOUT TABLE

Nesting tables refers to the process of placing a table inside another table, and it is just as easy in Layout mode as simply drawing a new table. As shown in Figure 26.12, you can select the Layout Table button in the Insert bar, place the cursor inside the first table, draw the shape of the second table, and Dreamweaver then nests the second inside the first.

Figure 26.12
The table within the table has been drawn.

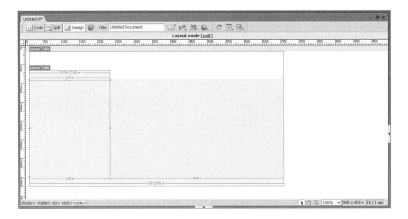

Take care, however, that you don't attempt to draw the second table on top of an existing cell. Dreamweaver does not allow you to draw a second, nested table when it would be placed on top of an existing cell.

> **NOTE**
>
> Nesting cells in Standard mode is just as easy as nesting them in Layout or Expanded mode. Just place your cursor in the cell where you want to nest the table and choose Insert, Table from the menu bar. After you specify the settings for the table and click OK, the second table is nested within the first.

USING THE EXPANDED MODE TO ASSIST WITH TABLE LAYOUT

When using the Layout Mode to create tables, it's sometimes difficult to work with tables that have been drawn close to one another. In addition, the borders between the tables and cells are extremely light, so they are difficult to see. To address this issue, Dreamweaver includes an Expanded mode (see Figure 26.13), which makes it much easier to select tables and table objects and to visualize the relationships between the page objects. To switch to the Expanded mode, click the Expanded button on the Insert toolbar.

Figure 26.13
The Expanded mode provides a view that makes it much easier to select table objects or resize them.

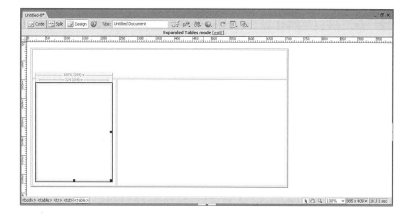

SETTING LAYOUT TABLE AND CELL ATTRIBUTES

Regardless of which mode you use to insert your tables, the common element among all the modes is that the Property inspector allows you complete control over the various attributes of your tables, rows, columns, and cells. For the most part, the Property inspector, shown in Figure 26.14, remains the same for all table objects.

Figure 26.14
The Property inspector allows you full control over your table and table object attributes.

Although most of the elements of controlling table attributes via the Property inspector are straightforward, a couple of items should be pointed out. First are the Merge Cells and Split Cells buttons in the lower-left corner of the inspector. The Merge Cells button takes all selected cells and makes them one cell. This is a really cool tool that can help you avoid having to use nested tables. The Split Cells button does the opposite: It takes a single cell and splits it into as many columns or rows as you indicate.

A second element in the Property inspector that you should be aware of is the No Wrap check box. Usually, when text exceeds the specified width of a cell, column, or table, Dreamweaver wraps the text to the next line and expands the size of the row. When the No Wrap check box is checked, however, Dreamweaver ignores the width limitations set in the W field and expands the table to fit the text—no matter how long it is. Wrapping is on by default.

26

MOVING AND RESIZING CELLS AND TABLES

Just when you have developed that perfect table layout that does exactly what your site needs is usually when you discover that something has to change. For example, a client may suddenly decide to use images that stretch the table design beyond its limitations. Luckily, Dreamweaver makes it relatively easy to go back and adjust your designs, either by selecting the appropriate item or items in the table and using the Property inspector to make numeric adjustments, or by placing your cursor on the gridlines within the table and adjusting the size of your rows vertically or adjusting your columns horizontally. If you choose the latter method, just place your cursor over the gridline that you want to move and Dreamweaver changes the cursor (see Figure 26.15) to show that you can adjust the line by clicking on it and dragging.

Figure 26.15
When you place your cursor over a gridline within a table, it changes to indicate that you can drag the line to adjust the row or column size.

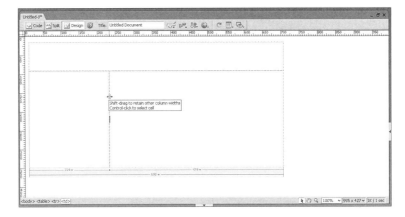

NOTE

If you are adjusting the table, row, or column in Layout mode, click on the item you want to change first, and then change the shape of the object by clicking and dragging any of the object's handles.

TIP

When you make adjustments to rows and columns, the table design does not always automatically update in the design view. To force Dreamweaver to render the changes, simply click the `<body>` tag in the tag selector and Dreamweaver re-renders the page and displays the changes.

ADDING CONTENT

After your table structure has been created and the appropriate sizes set, adding content is a snap. Simply place your cursor in the cell where you want to add the text, image, or media displayed and choose the appropriate command to insert it (or simply type away). Keep in mind, however, that if you insert an image or media object that is larger than the height or width restrictions of a table, row, column, or cell, the table will expand beyond its limitations to accommodate the object. This means you need to carefully consider what sizes and types of images and media you might be inserting into your pages before you complete your table design. Believe me, it is frustrating to have to rebuild your table design when you realize that it won't accommodate an image or media object.

After your content is in place, keep in mind that you can apply styles to entire columns and rows by clicking on them and then choosing the style from the Style drop-down in the Property inspector.

DESIGNING WITH FRAMES

Using frames to create website designs has decreased in popularity over the last few years, especially because early search engine technology had difficulties "seeing" into frames and indexing their content. There are still some very good uses, however, for frames-based sites, so Dreamweaver continues support for them.

I ran into an instance recently that was well suited for the use of frames. It involved the creation of an eLearning module for a client (see Figure 26.16). The client wanted timed exams and wanted each employee to be able to keep an eye on the time left during the exam. The perfect solution was to create a frameset that displayed a timer in the top frame and the eLearning question in the bottom. Because employees were submitting the test answers in the bottom frame, the page visible in the bottom frame could change as needed without the top frame ever having to reload. The solution worked out great and is still in use.

Figure 26.16
An example of a web application that benefits from frames. The top frame displays the timer and never reloads; the bottom frame displays the exam question.

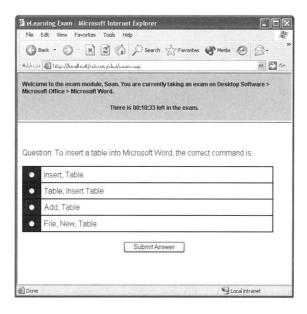

26

CREATING FRAMESETS

The fundamental element of a site design that relies on frames is called the *frameset*. A frameset is an HTML document that contains the information about each individual frame within the site and their positions in the layout. The frameset document itself doesn't contain any actual content, but it plays a key role in determining how the content stored in the frame pages is displayed. For instance, if you were to develop an eLearning application similar to the one in Figure 26.15, you would need a single frameset that consisted of two frames. The code for the frameset might look something like this:

```
<frameset rows="80,*" frameborder="no" border="0" framspacing="0">
    <frame src="timer.asp" name="timerFrame" scrolling="No" ¦
    noresize="noresize" id="timerFrame" title="timerFrame"/>
    <frame src="examp.asp" name="examFrame" id="examFrame" title="examFrame"/>
</frameset>
```

This simple frameset contains a top frame called timerFrame that displays the `timer.asp` page. The frame height is set to 80 pixels. The user cannot resize the top frame and the scrollbars are deactivated. The bottom frame is called examFrame and occupies the rest of the available browser height. It does allow for scrolling when the content extends beyond the limitation of the frame.

So, how would you create this frameset? Begin by choosing File, New from Dreamweaver's main menu. In the New Document dialog box, shown in Figure 26.17, select the Framesets category, choose Fixed Top from the available framesets, and click Create.

Figure 26.17
Create your new frameset by using the New Document dialog box.

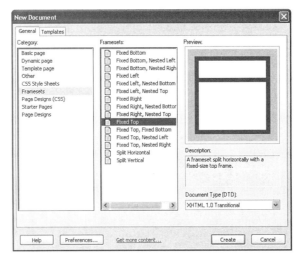

N O T E

Dreamweaver 8 offers a wide range of preconfigured framesets to choose from. These templates can be configured easily to fit any custom needs you might have.

Because each frame in the frameset needs to have a title, Dreamweaver opens the Frame Tag Accessibility Attributes dialog box (see Figure 26.18) and asks you to specify a title. For the mainFrame, type **examFrame** in the Title field.

Figure 26.18
Type a name for the mainFrame.

Next, select topFrame from the Frame drop-down menu and type **timerFrame** for the name. Click OK to create a frameset.

The final step to creating your frameset is to save it. To save the Frameset HTML document, choose File, Save Frameset As from the menu bar. Choose a location and name for the frameset in the Save As dialog box and click Save. Notice that when the frameset is selected, the tab at the top of the document displays the name of the frameset.

Place your cursor in the top frame and you'll note that the tab changes to UntitledFrame. The top frame is treated as an entirely separate HTML page from the frameset itself and needs to be saved. From the menu bar, choose File, Save and save the top frame. Finally, save the bottom frame in the same manner.

TIP

When naming your frame, it's extremely important to use names that tell you what the frame does. Using generic names such as "frame1" or "myframe" doesn't really help when you are trying to determine which frame to link to. More specific names such as "rightnavFrame" or "timerFrame" are much more likely to help you know what the file does.

NOTE

You can also create new frames and insert frames into existing framesets by using the Frames drop-down button on the Insert toolbar.

MANAGING THE FRAMESET WITH THE FRAMES PANEL

With your frameset in place and saved, you're ready to make any customized adjustments to the predefined frameset. The easiest way to do this is via the Frames panel and the Property inspector. To open the Frames panel, choose Window, Frames from the menu bar. The

Frames panel, shown in Figure 26.19, displays your current frame configuration and provides you with an easy way to select the appropriate frame for adjustment.

Figure 26.19
The Frames panel provides a way to view and select the various frames in your frameset.

You may have noticed in the Frames panel that your frames are still named topFrame and mainFrame, even though you specified new names for accessibility reasons. To adjust these values, click on the appropriate frame in the Frames panel and then type a new name in the Frame Name field of the Property inspector. Again, name the top frame timerFrame and the bottom frame examFrame.

Now, suppose that you wanted to increase the size of your top frame from 80 pixels to 100 pixels. Your first instinct might be to select the timerFrame in the Frames panel and make the height adjustment in the Property inspector. Unfortunately, as shown in Figure 26.20, you would be surprised to find that there is no height adjustment in the Property inspector when a single frame is selected.

Figure 26.20
The Property inspector does not display a height value when a single frame is selected.

Instead, the frameset actually controls those values, so you would need to click on the outermost border of the frameset from within the Frames panel. This selects the entire frameset and enables you to adjust the values of the individual frames via the Property inspector (see Figure 26.21).

To adjust the height of the top frame, click on the top frame in the Property inspector and type **100** for the value in the Row field. Press Enter or click anywhere in the page and Dreamweaver updates the design view. Before your change becomes permanent, however, you need to save the changes to the frameset. With the frameset selected in the Frames panel, choose File, Save Frameset from the menu bar.

Figure 26.21
When the frameset is
selected, you can
adjust additional
properties of the indi-
vidual frames.

ADDING CONTENT TO THE FRAMES

With your frame structure in place, adding content just means typing away or adding
images, Flash movies, or any other object that you might add in any other web page. The
biggest difference comes when you want to create images or hyperlinks that, when clicked,
change the contents of a different frame. So, for instance, suppose that you want to create a
link in the top frame that says "Start Exam," and this link is supposed to load the exam page
in the bottom frame.

To create this link, place your cursor in the top frame and type **Start Exam**. Select the text
and type **exam.html** in the Link field of the Property inspector. Pretty straightforward
process of creating a hyperlink, right? The only problem is that if someone clicks this link,
the exam.html page is going to load in the top frame, rather than the bottom frame.

To fix this, you have to tell Dreamweaver to add code that indicates that the page should
open in the bottom frame. To do this, choose examFrame from the Target drop-down menu
(shown in Figure 26.22). That's it! Save the pages and the frameset, and the top link automatically opens the exam.html page in the bottom frame.

Figure 26.22
Select the appropriate
target for the link.

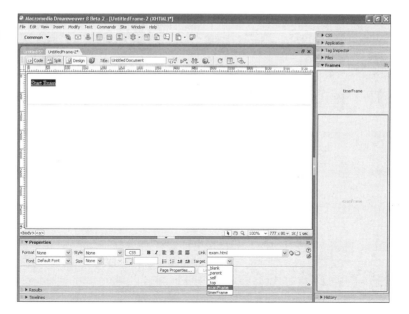

26

Other than that, you can basically create each HTML page in each frame as if it were a normal web page, using tables, layers, and even subframes (although I would really recommend against that unless you *really* need them).

DESIGNING WITH LAYERS

Now that you are comfortable with building a page layout with tables or frames, let's add one more tool to your toolbox. Layers are a third design tool, and they provide you with the most flexibility of any of the three. Using layers, you can "draw" out your design in a manner similar to that you would use in the Table Layout view, except that with layers you can lay objects on top of one another, creating a "layering" effect.

The only downside to the use of layers is that some older browsers (Netscape in particular) aren't capable of rendering layers correctly. When an older browser tries to render layers, it fails miserably and your entire design is compromised. For this reason, layers haven't supplanted tables as the most popular method of page design. As browser support grows, however, layers will play an important role in adding the third dimension of depth to web pages.

CREATING A LAYER

Creating a layer is very easy. Open any page and ensure that the Insert toolbar is visible by choosing Windows, Insert. On the Insert toolbar click the Standard mode and then click the Draw Layer button. Dreamweaver turns the cursor into a crosshair that enables you to click anywhere in the page and drag the cursor to create a square or rectangular layer. After you let go of the mouse button, the layer is created in your page (see Figure 26.23).

Figure 26.23
A layer has been added to the page.

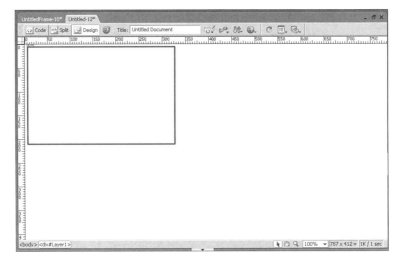

After the layer has been added to the page, you can view and manage that layer via the Layers panel, located in the CSS panel group and shown in Figure 26.24.

Figure 26.24
The Layers panel enables you to manage the layers in your page.

Using the Layers panel, you can select, hide, rename, and even choose the order in which your layers are stacked.

NAMING THE LAYER

To rename a layer, double-click on the layer name in the Layers panel and the layer name becomes an editable text field. Type your new name, press the Enter key, and the new name is applied to the layer.

> **NOTE**
>
> It's a good practice to name your layers something meaningful instead of leaving them set to the default names given to them by Dreamweaver. By giving a layer a name like "myNavBar," you ensure that you can easily identify the code that controls that layer when viewing your page code.

SETTING VISIBILITY

If you are working on your page design and need to work on layers that are stacked on top of one another, a handy tool is the visibility icon in the Layers panel, indicated by an eye. Clicking in the visibility column next to any layer adds an icon that looks like a shut eye and hides the layer (see Figure 26.25). Clicking the icon again changes the icon to an open eye and makes the layer visible again.

> **NOTE**
>
> Visibility doesn't just affect the design view. If you make your layer invisible, it doesn't show up on your web page when viewed in a browser either.

26

Figure 26.25
A shut eye icon indicates that the layer is not visible.

Setting the Stacking Order

If you are going to use layers to create objects that overlap one another, you need to be sure that the stacking order is correct. To adjust the stacking order, go to the Layers panel, click the number in the Z column, and type a new value. Keep in mind that if you make a layer invisible, its stacking order doesn't matter.

Selecting, Moving, and Resizing a Layer

To select a layer, click on it in the Design view or the Layers panel. After the layer is selected, the Property inspector displays the attributes for the layer that can be adjusted, including the left and top positions of the layer and the height and width. With these four attributes, you can fix the layer at any point in the page.

You can also resize or move a layer by using your mouse. To move a layer, click and hold the handle in the top-left corner of the layer and move the layer to its destination. If you want to resize the layer with the mouse, click on any of the handles in the corners or sides of the layer and click and drag. As shown in Figure 26.26, clicking on a corner handle resizes the height and width of the layer proportionally.

Adding Content to a Layer

You can add content to layers just as if you were adding it directly to the page. Text can be typed in layers, images can be inserted, and media such as Flash movies and videos can be added as well. One consideration when designing with layers, however, concerns images. Unlike tables that expand to fit the size of the image, layers give you full control over how the layer behaves when the content is larger than the layer. This is done by setting the value of the Overflow field in the Property inspector. When the Overflow field is set to Visible, a set of scroll bars enables you to scroll to see the rest of the image. If, however, the Overflow field is set to Hidden, then any portion of the image that is not displayed in the layer is inaccessible.

Figure 26.26
Click on the corner handle of a layer to resize the height and width proportionally.

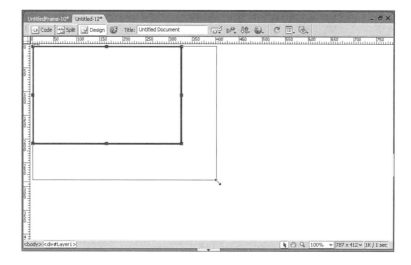

For instance, suppose you place an image in your layer that is larger than the height and width properties of the layer. By default, the layer uses the Visible setting and is resized to fit the size of the object. If, however, you don't want the layer resized, you can use the Hidden value, which makes it appear that the image has been cropped to the size of the layer, as shown in Figure 26.27.

Figure 26.27
The Hidden value hides any part of the image that doesn't fit within the layer.

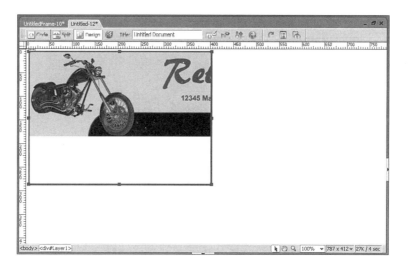

26

TIP

> The Hidden value is particularly useful when you are displaying a series of different images in a layer and the images are all slightly different sizes. To make sure that each image displays correctly, set the size of the placeholder image to be the size of the smallest image in the series. Then the layer displays only the portion of each image that fits in the layer.

The third Overflow setting you can control is Scroll. This setting acts similar to the Hidden value, with the exception that scrollbars are added to the layer so that the user can scroll to see the rest of the image (see Figure 26.28).

Figure 26.28
The Scroll value hides any part of the image that doesn't fit within the layer, but also gives scrollbars so the rest of the image can be viewed.

The final Overflow setting is the Auto setting. Auto behaves like the Scroll setting except that the scrollbars are visible only if they are necessary.

NOTE

> When using the Scroll or Auto settings, the scroll bars are not visible in Dreamweaver. To see what they will look like in your design, you need to preview them in a browser.

CONVERTING LAYERS TO TABLES

This chapter has talked about the pros and cons of using tables, frames, and layers for developing your website layout. If you recall, tables are reliable because all browsers tend to render tables the same. Layers, on the other hand, become problematic when it comes to rendering them in older browsers. For development, though, layers are easy to use and draw, whereas tables can get cumbersome—especially when it comes to nesting tables. So which do you choose? How about both?

Dreamweaver offers a great tool that enables you to convert either your layers to tables or your layers to a table. This enables you to design in whichever layout method you prefer and then convert your pages to the other presentation method later on down the road.

To convert layers to tables, save your page and then choose Modify, Convert, Layers to Table. The Convert Layers to Table dialog box (see Figure 26.29) enables you to decide whether you prefer the most accurate method of conversion or that which creates the smallest file size. If you choose to create the smallest, Dreamweaver removes cells that are empty and are smaller than a specific pixel size, which you can choose.

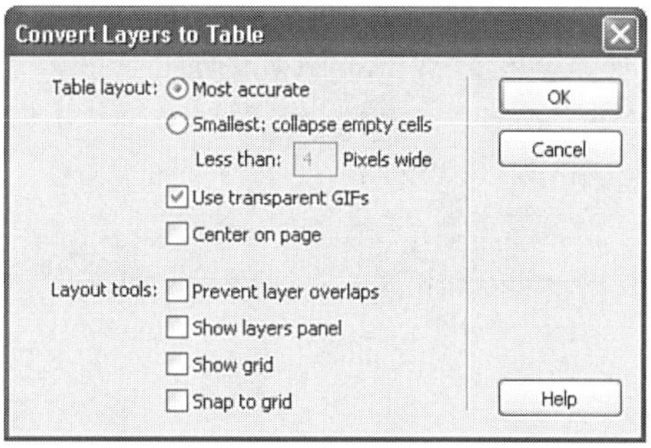

Figure 26.29
The Covert Layers to Table dialog box helps you convert your layers to tables.

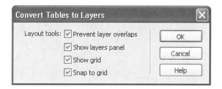

In addition, you can select whether or not to use transparent GIFs, whether you want the resulting table centered on the page, and a host of additional layout options.

The Convert Tables to Layers dialog box (see Figure 26.30) offers the same layout options, which determine whether, during the process, Dreamweaver prevents layers from overlapping, automatically opens the Layers panel, shows the design grid, and snaps the layers to that grid.

Figure 26.30
The Covert Tables to Layers dialog box allows you to configure how the layout will be displayed.

If you opt to use one of these methods, be aware that Dreamweaver does a great job, but it's not always 100% faithful to your original design. In some cases, you need to do some tweaking to the pages to ensure that your design behaves as expected.

TROUBLESHOOTING

Is there a limit to how many levels of nesting I can have in my table structure?

Theoretically, there is no limit to the number of tables you can nest. Realistically, however, you need to really re-examine your page layout if you are nesting tables beyond four levels. As you nest tables, more and more code is added to your pages, causing the size of your final file to grow. This growth affects download speeds and can even cause some older browsers to lock up. For these reasons, keep your table nesting simple and try to keep it to four or fewer levels.

Does the choice of tables versus layers affect my site's chances of being listed in the search engines?

Yes. If search engine placement is of concern to you, you need to be aware of the way that search engine spiders treat tables. Generally, the spiders read the content of your pages from left to right. So if you have a web page that contains a table with three columns, and the text the search engine is looking for is in the middle column, the spider reads the leftmost column and uses that information to index your site. Because spiders don't usually read the entire page, it's possible that the only information on which it will base your page rank is the content in the first column. Obviously, this is a problem because your content is in the middle column. Because spiders read only a limited number of lines of your code, it's possible that the spider will never read your content.

Using layers, however, can increase the chances that the spider will read your content because layers produce significantly less code than nested tables, so the spider gets to read more of your site code.

Speaking of search engines, I am using layers for my design and I'm thinking about placing a hidden layer at the top of my page that contains the indexing information I want the spider to read. Is this a good idea?

No. And not only is it not a good idea, it may get your pages added to the search engine's blacklist. The major search engine companies have made it very clear that they expect the spider to see exactly the same thing that the visitor sees. If the spider is seeing something different, the spider is being tricked and this opens the door to fraud. To keep this from happening, search engines look for sites that have layers hidden or positioned off the screen and, if they determine that the use of these layers is fraudulent, they blacklist the site from being indexed.

BEST PRACTICES—COMBINING LAYERS WITH TABLES TO ENSURE PROPER PAGE LAYOUT

The use of tables and layers has been a hotly contested subject on web development forums over the last few years. Those in the tables camp have rallied around the battle call of "Some browsers don't support layers, so we don't want to alienate visitors." Those in the layers camp have returned fire with "Tables produce bloated code and are meant to display only tabular data." On a rare occasion, however, someone steps in and suggests the use of both in design, leaving the two sides scratching their heads. Why can't we use both in our designs to overcome the weaknesses of both? The answer is...we can.

The trick here is to leverage the consistency of tables while reducing their use to a point that it won't bloat our code. In addition, we can reduce the possibility that older browsers will completely destroy our layers by nesting them inside tables to ensure that even if they are rendered improperly, they will at least be placed in the correct general location and won't leave our visitors wondering what went wrong in the layout.

An excellent example of the combination of tables and layers can be found at http://developer.apple.com/internet/webcontent/bestwebdev.html. This article provides a solid example of how to blend layers and tables to produce a consistently placed footer row, without excess code.

CHAPTER 27

REUSING PAGE DATA WITH TEMPLATES

In this chapter

INTRODUCING TEMPLATES

"Working smart" in web development is usually equated with reusability. As we have talked about in previous chapters, you can save time by reusing library elements, reusing code snippets, and even reusing your workspace layout. This chapter focuses on one of Dreamweaver's strongest features when it comes to reusability—page templates.

Imagine being able to create one single web page that you could then duplicate with a few clicks of your mouse and use over and over and over. You might be thinking, "Hey, I can already do that by creating a page and choosing File, Save As for every page that I need." Although this is true, it doesn't enable you to make site-wide changes by editing a single file, which is what templates offer over the Save As option.

When you create a template in Dreamweaver, the page code that is specified as locked content is stored in a separate Templates folder within your site. Then a child page that is derived from the template links to the single instance of the template. Whenever you make changes to that single template document, the updates are automatically included in every child page that still remains attached to the template. Pretty cool, eh?

BUILDING A TEMPLATE

Creating a new template can be done in either of a couple of ways. You can build a template from scratch by creating the page layout and then saving it as a template, or you can create a template based on a page you have already built, which is a really nice feature. That means that you can go backward through any sites you have created in the past and update the pages so that they are based on a template.

CREATING A TEMPLATE FROM SCRATCH

Creating a template from a brand new page is the easiest way to build a template. To create a template, choose File, New from the menu bar. In the New Document dialog box, shown in Figure 27.1, choose the Template page category and then choose the platform on which you want your base page developed. Click Create to build the blank page.

Although the resulting page may look like any other new page, Dreamweaver has added some code to indicate that this is a template.

Click the Code button on the Document toolbar to switch to the Code view and you can see some additional markup that has been added to the page. As you can see in Figure 27.2, Dreamweaver has added an editable region for the title so that the title of each page can be adjusted to reflect the page's contents. As you'll see in a bit, these editable regions are what make it easy to customize the content stored in templates.

Figure 27.1
The New Document dialog box enables you to create a template.

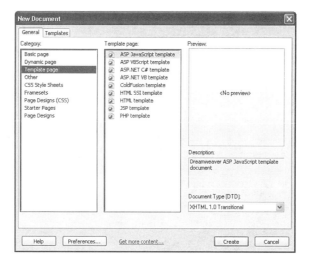

Figure 27.2
This page may look like an ordinary blank page, but there's more going on behind the scenes.

```
1  <!DOCTYPE html PUBLIC "-//W3C//DTD XHTML 1.0 Transitional//EN"
   "http://www.w3.org/TR/xhtml1/DTD/xhtml1-transitional.dtd">
2  <html xmlns="http://www.w3.org/1999/xhtml">
3  <head>
4  <meta http-equiv="Content-Type" content="text/html; charset=iso-8859-1" />
5  <!-- TemplateBeginEditable name="doctitle" -->
6  <title>Untitled Document</title>
7  <!-- TemplateEndEditable -->
8  <!-- TemplateBeginEditable name="head" -->
9  <!-- TemplateEndEditable -->
10 </head>
11
12 <body>
13 </body>
14 </html>
15
```

CREATING A TEMPLATE FROM AN EXISTING PAGE

If you already have a page that you want to convert to a template, doing so is pretty simple. The first thing you need to do is take a look at the page and determine which areas of the page will remain static and which need to be able to be updated. By default, every area of the new template is locked down so items such as navigational elements, logos, and links that are common to each page can be updated easily. Those areas that need be altered on each page such as text content, photos, and so on will need to be specified later as editable regions so that you can customize each child page.

After you know which areas should remain locked and which will become editable regions, open the page and choose File, Save As Template. In the Save As Template dialog box, shown in Figure 27.3, choose the site to which you want the template to be related, type a description of the template, choose a template name, and then click Save.

27

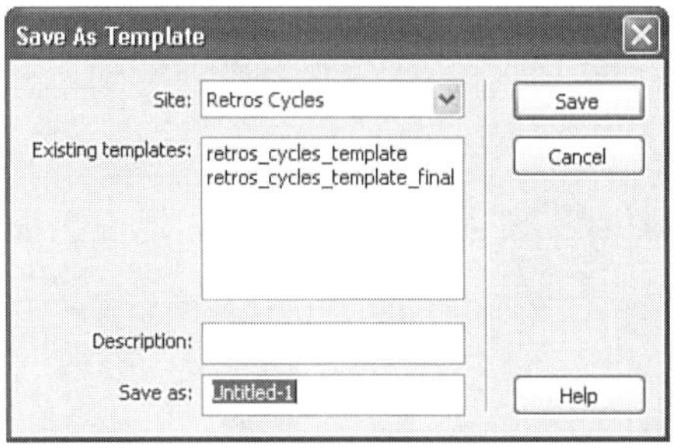

Figure 27.3
Set the settings for
your new template.

Before the save process is completed, Dreamweaver asks whether you want to update the links in the document (see Figure 27.4).

Figure 27.4
Dreamweaver asks
whether you would
like to update the
links located within
the template.

This occurs because Dreamweaver is moving your page out of the root of the site and into a subfolder named Templates. That means that the relative links to graphics and pages need to be updated to reflect the template's new location. Click Yes and Dreamweaver does the rest. After the save is completed, you'll notice that the file is now named with a .dwt extension, which indicates that it is now a Dreamweaver template.

DESIGNATING EDITABLE REGIONS

Regardless of whether you created your template from scratch or by converting an existing page, you now need to designate certain areas of the page as editable. When child pages are created from the template, these are the only areas that can be modified, so be sure you have planned carefully.

To designate an area as an editable region, select the area (usually a cell within a table) and choose Insert, Template Objects, Editable Region from the menu bar. As shown in Figure 27.5, the New Editable Region dialog box asks you to provide a name for the new region. Type a name and click OK.

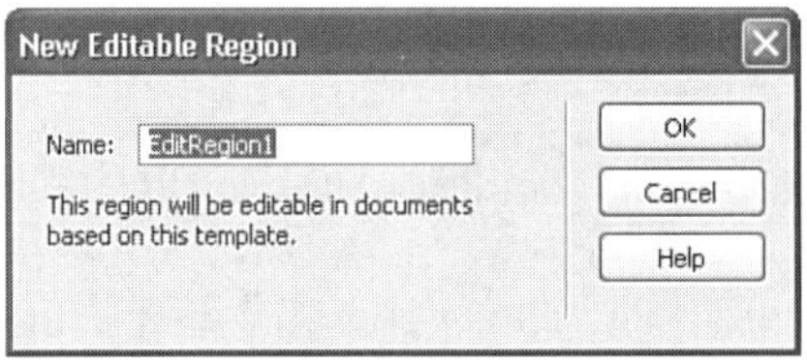

Figure 27.5
Designate a name for
your editable region.

After the editable region has been placed in the page, a placeholder is inserted, marked by the name that you specified. You can enter any text or placeholder content that you'd like in that editable region, and it will be used as the default for any child pages that are created. So if you have a content editor that might add information to your page designs, you might type something like Add your page content here to indicate that this is the area to type information or add images.

CREATING OPTIONAL REGIONS

Another type of template region is called an optional region. These regions hold content that may or may not be visible on every page, depending on whether or not you want to show it. For instance, suppose some of your pages have an image in the main content area. Some pages might not have a corresponding image, so you would want to be able to turn the image on for some pages and off for others. Enter the optional region.

Designating an area as optional is just as easy as creating an editable region. To choose the area, select Insert, Template Objects, Optional Region from the menu bar. In the New Optional Region dialog box, shown in Figure 27.6, type the name for the region and choose whether you want the region visible by default on child pages.

Figure 27.6
Create a name for your optional region.

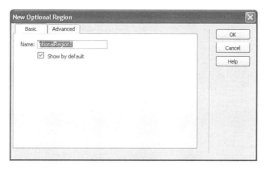

If you want to enhance automation of your optional region's visibility, you can click the Advanced tab and specify an expression that triggers whether or not the region is visible. Click OK to create the new region in your page.

27

CREATING REPEATING REGIONS

Repeating regions are those over which you want to give your content editor control to duplicate. For instance, if you were to create a table with two rows in an editable region, the content editor would be able to type in those two rows, but not add any additional rows. If, however, you made the rows repeating regions, the content editor would be allowed to create new rows because the new rows are exact duplicates of the data that is in the repeating region.

For instance, a blog would be a perfect example where a repeating region might be appropriate. As the web developer, you could create a template for the pages that contain the blog and lock down every aspect of the page except the repeating region where the content editor is to make periodic entries. Because the region is set to repeating, they would be able to create new entries at their convenience without ever worrying about adversely affecting the site design.

To create a repeating region, choose Insert, Template Objects, Repeating Region from the menu bar. Type a name for the repeating region and click OK.

SETTING OBJECT ATTRIBUTES AS EDITABLE

An additional template tool that is available for your use enables you to allow certain objects within a template to have editable attributes. Objects that you can specify as having editable attributes include tables, images, layers, or Flash movies. For instance, if you want to place an image placeholder in your template that requires the URL to be editable on each child page, you could add the placeholder and make only the URL editable.

To set an object's attribute as editable, select the object and then choose Modify, Templates, Make Attribute Editable from the menu bar. In the Editable Tag Attributes dialog box, shown in Figure 27.7, select the attribute that you want to edit and click the Make Attribute Editable check box. Specify the appropriate label, type, and default and click OK.

Figure 27.7
Choose the attribute and values that you want to be editable in your child pages.

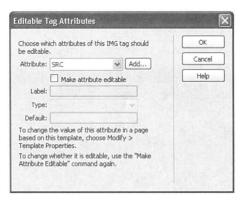

After the attribute has been set to editable, you should be able to view that attribute in the Property Inspector and see that it has been replaced by special code such as @@name@@. This markup indicates to the template that this is an editable attribute in any child pages.

EDITING AN EXISTING TEMPLATE

Editing an existing template is very similar to editing any other document. To open a template for editing, choose File, Open from the menu bar. In the Open dialog box (see Figure 27.8), navigate to the Templates folder in your site root and then open the template that you want to edit.

Figure 27.8
Template files are stored in the Templates subfolder of your site root.

You can also edit a template by selecting the Templates category in the Assets panel, and double-clicking on the template you want to edit (see Figure 27.9).

Figure 27.9
You can also access templates via the Assets panel.

After you have made the necessary changes to the template, choose File, Save from the menu bar. After the page is saved, you need to replicate those changes out to any child pages by either allowing Dreamweaver to do it when you save the changes, or manually initializing the process later by choosing Modify, Templates, Update Pages from the menu bar. In the Update Template Files dialog box, shown in Figure 27.10, choose which pages to update and click the Update button.

Figure 27.10
After changes to a template are made, you should update any child pages.

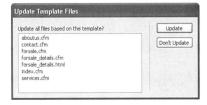

After the updates are completed, all the changes made to the template should be replicated out to your child pages.

APPLYING A TEMPLATE

After you have your template created and saved, you'll probably want to start creating pages based on it. Before you start generating pages, though, you need to know a few things about templates and their child pages.

As I mentioned earlier, the templates created for your site are located in a subfolder of your site root called Templates. It's important that you don't rename or move that folder, or you won't be able to automatically update pages that are reliant on templates.

In addition, when you make changes to the pages and templates within your site, you need to be sure that you not only transfer child pages, but also transfer the template file to the server if it has been modified, so that the child pages can be viewed correctly.

Lastly, you should be aware that creating pages based on templates can add quite a bit of code to your pages and more code means slower load times. If you are building a website that needs to be accessed via dial-up connections and the site has a complex layout, you need to balance the slower load times with the benefits that templates offer for site maintenance.

CREATING NEW PAGES FROM YOUR TEMPLATE

Creating a new child page from a template is similar to creating any other new file and can be done by choosing File, New from the menu bar. In the New Document dialog box, however, select the Templates tab (see Figure 27.11), where Dreamweaver displays all of your different sites and the templates that are stored associated with them.

Figure 27.11
The New from Template dialog box enables you to select from the available templates associated with your site.

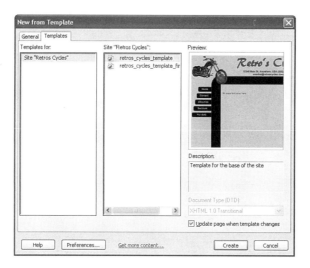

To create a new child page, select the template on which you want to base it and click Create. Dreamweaver creates a new page and indicates that it is based on a template by placing `Template:` and the name of the source template in the upper-right corner of the page (see Figure 27.12).

Figure 27.12
A new child page has been created based on the template.

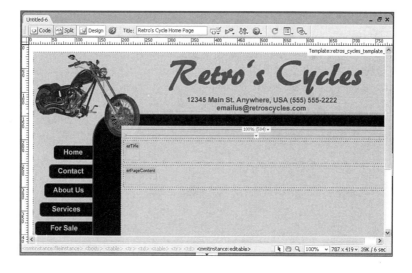

In addition, if you switch to Code view (see Figure 27.13), you'll notice that the majority of the code for the site is grayed out. Because these regions are locked by the template, you can't adjust them in either Design or Code view.

Figure 27.13
The code is locked by
the template.

```
1   <html><!-- InstanceBegin template="/Templates/retros_cycles_template_final.dwt"
    codeOutsideHTMLIsLocked="false" -->
2   <head>
3   <!-- InstanceBeginEditable name="doctitle" -->
4   <title>Retro's Cycle Home Page</title>
5   <!-- InstanceEndEditable -->
6   <meta http-equiv="Content-Type" content="text/html; charset=utf-8">
7   <!-- Fireworks MX Dreamweaver MX target.  Created Tue Jul 19 00:45:32 GMT-0500 (Central Daylight Time)
    2005-->
8   <script language="JavaScript">
9   <!--
10  function MM_findObj(n, d) { //v4.01
11    var p,i,x;  if(!d) d=document; if((p=n.indexOf("?"))>0&&parent.frames.length) {
12      d=parent.frames[n.substring(p+1)].document; n=n.substring(0,p);}
13    if(!(x=d[n])&&d.all) x=d.all[n]; for (i=0;!x&&i<d.forms.length;i++) x=d.forms[i][n];
14    for(i=0;!x&&d.layers&&i<d.layers.length;i++) x=MM_findObj(n,d.layers[i].document);
15    if(!x && d.getElementById) x=d.getElementById(n); return x;
16  }
17  function MM_swapImage() { //v3.0
18    var i,j=0,x,a=MM_swapImage.arguments; document.MM_sr=new Array; for(i=0;i<(a.length-2);i+=3)
19     if ((x=MM_findObj(a[i]))!=null){document.MM_sr[j++]=x; if(!x.oSrc) x.oSrc=x.src; x.src=a[i+2];}
20  }
21  function MM_swapImgRestore() { //v3.0
22    var i,x,a=document.MM_sr; for(i=0;a&&i<a.length&&(x=a[i])&&x.oSrc;i++) x.src=x.oSrc;
23  }
24
```

To make changes to the child page, adjust the content of the editable regions on the template and then save the page.

APPLYING TEMPLATES TO EXISTING PAGES

If you want to bring existing pages into your template/child page structure, Dreamweaver offers a tool to assist with the process. The benefit is that all the pages in your site can be based on a template, which means that your entire site can be updated through template updates.

Be aware, however, that to successfully apply a template to an existing page, you need to do some work to ensure that the existing page already has the same structure as the template. Trying to apply a template to a page that is structurally different really doesn't work. Keep in mind that the goal here isn't to have Dreamweaver modify the structure of your existing pages—things go bad when you ask Dreamweaver to mesh two different pages' structures. The goal, instead, is to ensure that all pages that do have the same page structure can be updated via the template.

To apply a template to an existing page, open the page and choose Modify, Templates, Apply Template to Page from the menu bar. As shown in Figure 27.14, the Select Template dialog box enables you to choose from the available site templates. Choose the appropriate template and check the box indicating that the page should be updated when the template is changed.

Figure 27.14
The Select Template
dialog box enables
you to choose which
template to apply to
the page.

Click Select and Dreamweaver presents you with any content that might not fit into the template schema, and enables you to determine how to deal with the existing content prior to the application of the template (see Figure 27.15).

Figure 27.15
Indicate which editable regions should be used for any existing content.

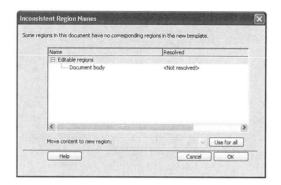

To apply the template, click OK and the template regions and markup code are added to the page.

REMOVING TEMPLATE MARKUP

As I mentioned earlier, when you apply template data to your pages, Dreamweaver adds markup code indicating where template regions should begin and end. Depending on how complex your template is and how many different regions it contains, this markup can be considerable, which affects the download speeds of your pages.

In addition, the template markup does provide information about your site's structure, naming conventions that you use, and the simple fact that the pages were created based on a template.

If you are concerned about bandwidth or you want to conceal the information stored in the template markup, you might consider removing the markup before you publish your pages to the web. Dreamweaver offers several different ways to remove the markup, each having a slightly different effect. Be aware, also, that after your template markup is removed, Dreamweaver no longer can perform automatic updates to the page when the template is updated.

27

CLEAN UP HTML

The Clean Up HTML command, found under Commands, Clean Up HTML, enables you not only to remove your template markup, but to run a check on other aspects of your code as well. Depending on how in-depth you want Dreamweaver to get when analyzing your code, you can check any or all of the options (see Figure 27.16).

Figure 27.16
The Clean Up HTML dialog box enables you to check and remove unnecessary code.

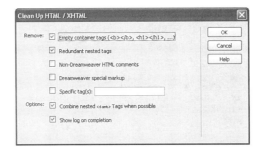

The option that removes template markup is the Dreamweaver Special Markup option. To apply the cleanup, click the OK button and, if you chose to display one, Dreamweaver provides a log of the changes that were made to the page.

EXPORT WITHOUT MARKUP

The second option you have for removing template markup is to use the Export Without Markup command. This command exports the entire site to another folder, removing all the template markup as it goes. The nice thing about this feature is that it ensures that all the pages in your site are as bandwidth-friendly as possible. In addition, when you use this command, your original site is left intact with the markup in place while the copy of the site is created with all template and library references removed. Be aware, however, that this command affects your entire site, so don't use it if you want to remove markup from only a single page.

To export your site without markup, choose Modify, Templates, Export Without Markup from the menu bar. In the Export Site Without Template Markup dialog box, shown in Figure 27.17, choose a folder to receive the export and indicate whether you want to keep the original template data files or extract only changed files. Click OK to export the site.

Figure 27.17
Using this dialog box, you can export your entire site without template markup.

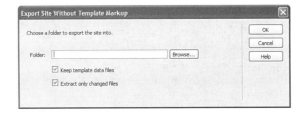

DETACH PAGE FROM TEMPLATE

The third option for removing markup is one that can be used on a page-by-page basis. Suppose you have a page that you need to have a similar look and feel to the rest of your site, but you also need to change some of the elements that would normally be protected by the locked regions in your template. Not a problem. Dreamweaver enables you to create a new page based on the template and then detach it from the template so that your page structure will match that of the template to start, and locked regions won't stop you from making changes to the page. In addition, after the page is detached from the template, all template markup is removed.

To detach a page from a template, choose Modify, Templates, Detach from Template from the menu bar. After they are detached from the template, all template regions are removed and the page becomes fully editable again (see Figure 27.18).

Figure 27.18
The page has been detached and all template regions have been removed.

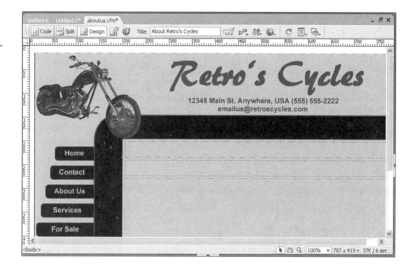

In addition, with the page detached from the template, switch to the code view and you'll notice that the template markup has been removed and the code is now fully editable again (see Figure 27.19).

Figure 27.19
The code has become editable and the template markup has been removed.

NESTING TEMPLATES

One last element of templates that we need to cover is the nesting of templates inside one another. To nest a template, you would create a primary template, and then create a child page based on that template and save it as a secondary template. This secondary template is then nested inside the primary template and any changes that are made to the primary template are not only propagated out to child pages based on the primary template, but also affect the secondary template and any child pages based on the secondary template.

Sound confusing? Let's look at a scenario that might occur in the real world and it should get a little clearer. Suppose that Retro's Cycles asked you to design a set of pages that their administrative assistant could update. They don't want her to be able to change the site layout, but they'd like her to be able update content and maybe add a few photos. Sounds like a good opportunity for a template, right? So, you'd create a template with an editable region that would allow the administrative assistant to edit the content in only that region. Pretty straightforward.

But what happens when the company wants to allow the sales manager to update the details of the various used motorcycles for sale in the "For Sale" section of the site? They want the administrative assistant to update the general copy for the rest of the site, but the sales manager should be the one updating the pages in the For Sale section.

The way to accomplish this is to create a series of child pages from the original template and save them as the pages for the site. The admin can access each of the editable regions for these pages. The second step, however, is to save the For Sale page as a template and then spawn child pages from that secondary template. The service manager can then be sure that his pages retain the look and feel of the For Sale section and he can update the pages as necessary.

As you can see, nested templates can get very complicated, very quickly. For that reason, put some serious thought into whether or not they are something you want to use. Although they can be a good tool for ensuring consistency across your site, they can get very difficult to manage as the number of nested templates you use grows.

TROUBLESHOOTING

I made some changes to my template and when I saved it, no updates were made to my child pages. What gives?

The most likely reason that your child pages were not updated is that the changes made to your template were in the editable regions. Because editable regions do not depend on the template, Dreamweaver does not update child pages when changes to the template's editable regions are made.

In earlier versions of Dreamweaver, I recall there were issues applying behaviors to the editable regions of child pages because the Dreamweaver behaviors needed to write to the <head> section of the page. Do these issues still exist in Dreamweaver 8?

No. You can apply Dreamweaver behaviors to any content within your editable regions and Dreamweaver adds the necessary JavaScript code to the head section of your child page.

Does this mean that I can use the Insert, HTML, *and* Head Tags *commands successfully to add metadata to my pages?*

Yes. This command now inserts the meta tags into the <head> section of your page, even if it is template-driven.

I did some cleanup of my files and folders and now my child pages don't show any of the template items anymore. What did I do and how can I fix it?

More than likely, you moved or renamed the Templates folder. This is not an option because Dreamweaver's template markup relies on the name and location of this folder remaining static. The answer to fixing the issue is to put the Templates folder back where it was or rename it back to Templates.

BEST PRACTICES—EXPORTING PAGES WITHOUT MARKUP FOR PUBLICATION ON THE WEB

You have heard it from me in previous chapters, and you're going to hear about it again: bandwidth, bandwidth, bandwidth!

As I have mentioned throughout this chapter, one of the downsides to using templates is that the additional markup code added by Dreamweaver increases page size, which can slow down your load times. If your goal is to produce the leanest, meanest code possible (which it should be), then using templates doesn't fit with that concept because the markup unnecessarily bloats your file sizes. Does this mean that you can't use templates and still accomplish the most bandwidth-friendly pages possible? Absolutely not! It does mean that you're going to have to take a few extra steps to ensure that your code is as clean as possible.

The best way to accomplish clean code after using templates is to export the entire site without markup before you publish it to the web. This means that on the development side you get to take advantage of all the functionality that templates have to offer, but after you export the pages without markup and publish them, your visitors get to take advantage of the cleanest code and, therefore, the fastest-loading pages possible.

27

ADDING INTERACTIVITY AND MULTIMEDIA

In this chapter

UNDERSTANDING DREAMWEAVER BEHAVIORS

As the development of your web pages continues, it's likely that you'll want to add feature functionality beyond just the simple hyperlinks. The good news is that JavaScript offers you a whole range of new options that supplement those offered by standard HTML. So what if you're not a scripting guru who can create functions and arrays in your sleep? Dreamweaver is going to do most of the work for you and even write the necessary code to add options such as opening external browser windows, validating forms, and even checking to see whether the visitor has a specific browser plug-in installed.

Just sit back and you'll see how easy it is to make Dreamweaver behaviors spice up your web applications!

JAVASCRIPT AND DREAMWEAVER

Oh sure, I said that you wouldn't have to understand any JavaScript and the first subsection I jump into is called "JavaScript and Dreamweaver." Great trick, eh? Actually, before we start exploring the snippets and behaviors that come with Dreamweaver, I thought it would be a good idea to give a brief background on JavaScript because it is the language that Dreamweaver uses to generate behaviors. If the thought of learning anything about a scripting language is completely revolting, go ahead and skip on to the next section. If, however, you want to learn a little more about JavaScript and how it relates to Dreamweaver, read on.

JavaScript is one of the more popular client-side scripting languages in use today. Don't confuse JavaScript with its big brother Java—which is a full-blown object-oriented language. Although they share similar syntax, JavaScript is essentially a stripped-down version of Java that is much easier to write and implement because it doesn't have to be compiled prior to execution. In addition, because it is a client-side language, the machine rendering the code in the browser is the one that does all the work.

Unless you really want to get into developing your own scripts, it's likely that you'll take advantage of the predefined functions that are built into JavaScript. For instance, if you wanted to open a new browser window, you could use the JavaScript function

```
Window.Open()
```

If you want to close that same browser, you could use the function

```
Window.Close()
```

These are just a couple of examples of the many built-in functions that JavaScript offers and, as I mentioned before, Dreamweaver makes it very easy for you to access some of the more common functions through the JavaScript snippets and behaviors.

USING JAVASCRIPT SNIPPETS

Although Chapter 24, "Working Efficiently in Dreamweaver," already covered snippets, it's worth spending a minute to take a closer look at the JavaScript snippets that are included in the Snippets panel. To view the JavaScript snippets, open the Snippets panel by choosing Window, Snippets and then expand the JavaScript folder (see Figure 28.1)

28

Figure 28.1
The Snippets panel
with the JavaScript
folder expanded.

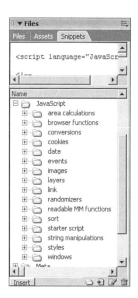

As you can see, Macromedia has provided quite a few JavaScript code snippets that can be used for everything from mathematical calculations to reading cookies.

I highly recommend that you take some time to go through these folders and see what types of scripts are available for use in your pages. Doing so could save you the time and hassle of building your own script, only to discover that Macromedia had already provided you with everything you needed.

> **TIP**
>
> One of the snippets I use most frequently is the Starter Function snippet located in the starter script folder. This snippet places the bare necessities of a JavaScript function in the page and saves me the hassle of typing it every time I need to create a function. It also saves me from typos, to which I am prone.

Just as was discussed in Chapter 24, after you find a snippet that you want to use, it's extremely easy to apply it to your page. Just place your cursor on the code line where you would like the snippet inserted, and then double-click on the appropriate snippet and the code is added to your page. If areas of the code need to be customized, they are indicated as such. Figure 28.2 shows the Starter Function applied to the head section of the page code.

APPLYING BEHAVIORS

If you're still unsure about your ability to add JavaScript functionality to your pages, let's make it even easier. What if I told you that you could add JavaScript to your pages and never have to write a line of code? Sound good? Well, Dreamweaver's behaviors do exactly that.

28

Figure 28.2
The Starter Function snippet has been added to the code.

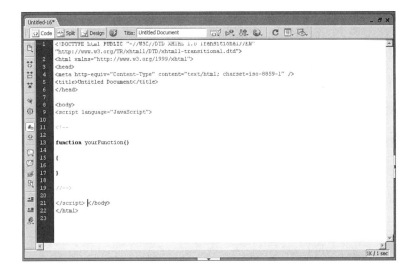

Dreamweaver behaviors are accessed via the Behaviors panel and represent some of the most commonly used scripts applied to web pages. The Behaviors panel (see Figure 28.3) enables you to track and organize those behaviors that are already applied to your pages and apply new behaviors to the page.

Figure 28.3
The Behaviors panel helps you track the behaviors that have been applied to your page.

To apply a behavior to your page, click the plus sign on the panel and choose the appropriate behavior from the menu. Some behaviors require that a specific object be selected before the behavior can be applied, such as the Control Shockwave or Flash behavior. Logically, Dreamweaver applies this behavior only to Shockwave (Director) or Flash movies.

Other behaviors are grouped into categories such as the Set Text behaviors, shown in Figure 28.4, which enable you to choose between setting the text of a frame, layer, text field, or the status bar.

Figure 28.4
Some behaviors are logically grouped by their function.

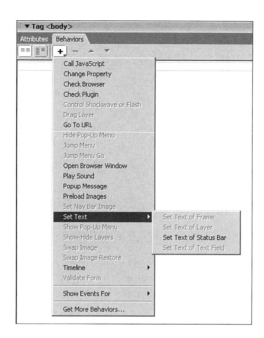

Table 28.1 gives a brief overview of the Dreamweaver behaviors.

TABLE 28.1	DREAMWEAVER BEHAVIORS
Name	**What It Does**
Call JavaScript	Enables you to call a custom JavaScript function such as `Window.Open()` or `Window.Close()`. When using the behavior, you need to know the appropriate placement of the code.
Change Property	Enables you to change the various attributes of layers, forms, text areas, images, and several other objects. When it is applied, you need to select the property to be altered and choose a new value for it.
Check Browser	Enables you to determine what browser and version visitors are using and redirect them appropriately. This is very handy if you build sites that are based on layers and want to redirect visitors with older browsers to a table-based version of your site instead.
Check Plugin	Checks to see whether a specific plug-in is installed on the visitor's machine. Enables you to designate where the visitor should be sent if the plug-in is found and an alternative location if the plug-in is not located. The behavior enables you to check for Flash, Shockwave, LiveAudio, QuickTime, and the Windows Media Player plug-ins.
Control Shockwave or Flash	Enables the visitor to stop or play Shockwave or Flash movies.
Drag Layer	Enables you to add interactivity to your pages by allowing visitors

28

TABLE 28.1   CONTINUED

Name	What It Does
	to drag layers around the page. This behavior is restricted to use on layers.
Go to URL	Opens a new URL in the existing browser window or in a new window. Commonly used with the onLoad behavior to do an auto-redirect for pages that have been moved to a new location.
Hide Pop-Up Menu	Hides a pop-up menu, usually used with the onMouseOut event handler.
Jump Menu	Creates a form-based menu on which visitors can click and access files, documents, and other websites.
Jump Menu Go	Activates the selection within the Jump menu.
Open Browser Window	Opens a new browser window, taking parameters such as the URL that should be displayed in the window, the size of the window, and the name of the new window.
Play Sound	Plays a sound file when the designated event handler occurs.
Pop-up Message	Opens a pop-up dialog box, also referred to as an alert box, and enables you to specify what information is presented in the box.
Preload Images	Enables you to specify that certain images should be preloaded before the visitor can view the page. This behavior slows the load time of the page slightly, but ensures that graphics are correctly loaded and cached before the user interacts with them. This is extremely important in the case of rollover buttons.
Set Nav Bar Image	Enables you to create a navigation image using the up, over, down, and while down states.
Set Text of Frame	Indicates what text should be displayed in a specified frame.
Set Text of Layer	Indicates what text should be displayed in a specified layer.
Set Text of Status Bar	Indicates what text should be displayed in the status bar.
Set Text of Text Field	Indicates what text should be displayed in a specified text field.
Show Pop-Up Menu	Creates a pop-up menu that is primarily used for navigation.
Show-Hide Layers	Makes an existing layer visible or invisible.
Swap Image	Changes the specific image to have a new source value. This behavior is most commonly coupled with the Swap Image Restore behavior to create rollover effects.
Swap Image Restore	Restores the image to its original source.
Go to Timeline Frame	Works in conjunction with JavaScript timelines and moves to a specific frame in the timeline.

28

TABLE 28.1   CONTINUED

Name	What It Does
Play Timeline	Starts a JavaScript timeline.
Stop Timeline	Stops a JavaScript timeline.
Validate Form	Enables you to verify that certain form fields have been completed and, in some cases, are of a particular type.

After they are applied to the page, these behaviors are assigned an event handler that indicates when they should be triggered. If the default handler is not the one that you want, you can adjust it via the drop-down menu in the leftmost column of the Behaviors panel. The states that are available are

- OnBlur—Triggers the event when a form field loses focus, meaning that the cursor is no longer in the field.
- OnClick—Triggers the event when the user clicks on the object.
- OnDblClick—Triggers the event when the user double-clicks on the object.
- OnFocus—Triggers the event when a form field gains focus by being clicked on or tabbed to.
- OnKeyDown—Triggers the event one time when a key on the keyboard is depressed.
- OnKeyPress—Triggers the event continuously when a key on the keyboard is depressed.
- OnKeyUp—Triggers the event when a key on the keyboard is released.
- OnMouseDown—Triggers the event when any mouse button is depressed.
- OnMouseMove—Triggers the event when the mouse is moved in any direction.
- OnMouseOut—Triggers the event when the mouse cursor is moved off of the target object.
- OnMousOver—Triggers the event when the mouse cursor is moved over the target object.
- OnMouseUp—Triggers the event when any mouse button is released.

After you have applied behaviors to your page, you may determine in the future that a behavior is no longer necessary. To remove a behavior from your page, click the minus sign in the Behaviors panel to remove it from the page.

TIP

Using the minus sign is truly the only safe way to fully remove a behavior. Deleting objects that have behaviors assigned to them without first deleting the behavior can result in orphaned code being left in your pages, so be sure to use the minus sign.

28

ROLLOVER IMAGES AND NAVIGATION BARS

Probably the most commonly used Dreamweaver behaviors are the Swap Image and Restore Image behaviors because rollover buttons and interactive navigation bars are extremely popular. Creating rollovers is very easy in Dreamweaver, both for the use of buttons and for altering other images on the page. Let's take a look at some of the different methods that can be used to change the various images on your pages.

CREATING A ROLLOVER IMAGE

The concept of a rollover image is relatively straightforward. When you place your mouse cursor over an image, an image on the page is changed. The changed image most commonly is the image that was rolled over, but other images can be altered as well.

The easiest way to create a rollover image in Dreamweaver is to place your cursor at the place in the page where you want the rollover inserted and choose Insert, Image Objects, Rollover Image from the menu bar. The Insert Rollover Image dialog box, shown in Figure 28.5, enables you to name the image, specify the locations of the original image and rollover image, and choose what alternative text and URL should be assigned to the rollover. If you don't want the rollover to be a button, simply leave the URL field blank.

Figure 28.5
The Insert Rollover Image dialog box helps you create a rollover image.

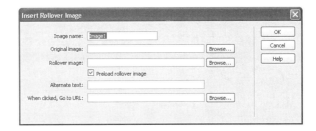

When you create a rollover (or any object, for that matter), it is a very good practice to provide a name for the object that is meaningful to you. Dreamweaver, by default, names objects with generic names such as "Image1" and "Form1." Although it might be easier just to leave these names, it makes it more difficult when you need to interact with the items, as you'll see in a bit. So be sure that you type a meaningful name like "homeButton" for a navigation button that returns your visitors to the home page.

Another important aspect of this dialog box to note is the Preload Rollover Image check box. It is a good idea for you to always leave this box checked for rollovers. If you don't preload the image, the first time a visitor rolls over the image, it will load from the server, and if the server is busy or slow, the visitor might be presented with a broken image. For that reason, preloading rollovers can ensure consistency in the way your site displays. After you have entered the appropriate values, click OK and Dreamweaver places the image in your page (see Figure 28.6).

Figure 28.6
The rollover image has been placed in the page.

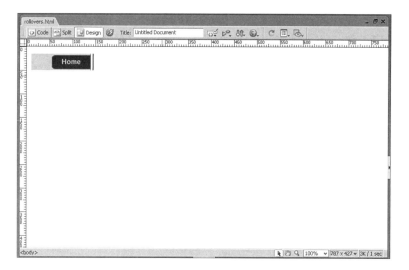

DESIGNING REMOTE ROLLOVERS

If you already have an image placed in your page and want to swap out a different image on the page when the first is rolled over, you can do that by using the Swap Image behavior. This is where uniquely naming your objects comes in handy. For instance, suppose that the Retro's Cycles site has a series of buttons on the page that say "Honda," "Yamaha," "Suzuki," and several other motorcycle manufacturers. The client has asked that when you roll over any of those links, an image below changes to display one of the manufacturer's motorcycles. Basically, the buttons change to a secondary image when rolled over.

To accomplish this, select a button and click the plus sign on the Behaviors panel. Choose Swap Image from the menu and Dreamweaver displays the Swap Image dialog box, shown in Figure 28.7.

Figure 28.7
The Swap Image dialog box enables you to change an image's source.

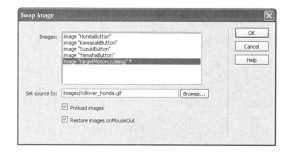

28

In the Swap Image dialog box, choose the image that you want to change. This is where naming your images something logical comes in handy. Because I named the image "targetMotorcycleimg," I can more easily identify it than I could if it were named "Image4." With the target image selected, type or browse to the image to which you want to swap. Leave the check boxes so that the image is preloaded and restored to its original state when the mouse is rolled off the button. Click OK and Dreamweaver adds the Swap Image and Swap Image Restore behaviors to the page. Note also that the Swap Image behavior uses the onMouseOver event handler and the Swap Image Restore behavior uses the onMouseOut event handler (see Figure 28.8).

Figure 28.8
The behaviors have been added to the page and are manageable via the Behaviors panel.

To see the remote rollover in action, preview the page in a browser and roll your mouse over the button to which the behavior was assigned. Figure 28.9 shows the image in its native state, and Figure 28.10 shows what happens when you roll over the button.

Figure 28.9
The image in its native state.

Figure 28.10
The image is changed when the button is rolled over.

CREATING NAVIGATION BARS

Now that you know how to create single instances of rollover buttons, imagine being able to easily create a collection of them that would result in an entire navigation bar for your site. Well, hold on tight, because Dreamweaver can do just that!

To create a navigation bar, place your cursor in the page where you want the navigation bar to be inserted and then choose Insert, Image Objects, Navigation Bar from the menu bar. The Insert Navigation Bar dialog box, shown in Figure 28.11, looks complex, but it's relatively straightforward when you break it down.

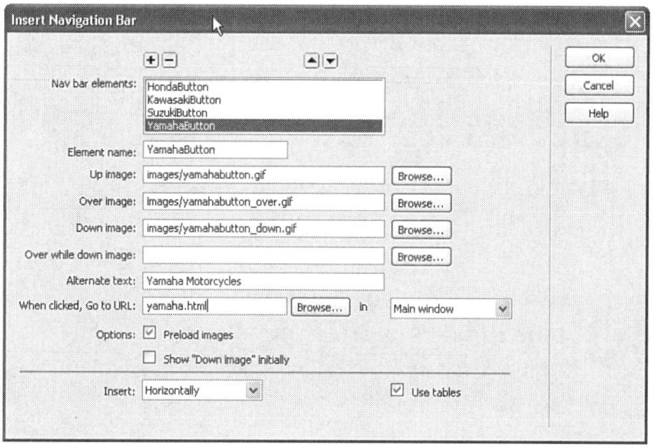

Figure 28.11
The Insert Navigation Bar dialog box helps you create interactive navbars.

28

Table 28.2 provides a look at the various fields in the Insert Navigation Bar dialog box and the function they perform.

TABLE 28.2   INSERT NAVIGATION BAR DIALOG BOX FIELDS

Name	What It Does
Navbar elements	Displays the various images that you have added to the navbar. Each element in the navbar must have at least a unique name and an up image value. The plus sign and minus sign button add and remove elements, respectively.
Element name	Provides a unique identifier for each navbar object. The unique name ensures that the swap image and restore image behaviors are performed on the correct object when interaction occurs.
Up image	Provides the source of the image in its natural state.
Over image	Provides the source of the image when the object is moused over.
Down image	Provides the source of the image when the object is clicked.
Over while down image	Provides the source of the image when the object is clicked and the mouse button is held down.
Alternate text image	Provides alternate text for accessibility.
When clicked, go to URL	Provides the target URL that is opened when the object is clicked.
in	Determines whether the link is opened in the existing window or in a different window (especially useful in framed sites).
Preload images	Determines whether or not images are preloaded before the page is displayed. This check box should generally be left checked.
Show "Down Image" initially	Determines whether the down image is initially displayed before the button is ever rolled over.
Insert	Specifies whether the navbar should be built horizontally or vertically.
Use tables	Specifies whether Dreamweaver should use tables or CSS to build the navbar.

For each button in the navbar, you need to create an element and specify its settings. You can also reorder the objects by using the up and down arrows to place the objects in the correct order. When the final navbar is built, a horizontal bar has the item at the top of the list at the far left and the item on the bottom of the list at the far right. Vertical bars list the objects in the same order that they appear in the elements list. After you have completed the list, click OK and Dreamweaver inserts the navigation bar into your page (see Figure 28.12).

Just as with the rollover buttons, Dreamweaver displays only the initial state of the buttons in the design view; to see the buttons in action, you need to preview them in your browser.

Figure 28.12
Dreamweaver adds a
navigation bar to the
page based on your
criteria.

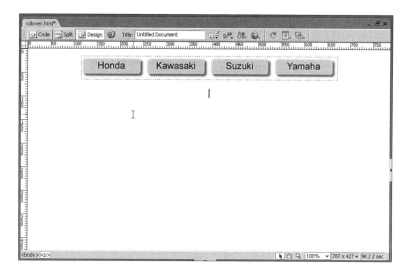

PLUG-INS, APPLETS, AND CONTROLS

As more and more different types of audio, video, and application formats are released on the market, third-party plug-ins, Java Applets, and ActiveX controls have provided additional support beyond the native browser's capability to display certain types of content. Let's take a look at how Dreamweaver can help you manage these custom browser extensions and the content they serve.

PLUG-INS

Browser plug-ins are helper applications that enable you to display a specific type of application. One of the more popular plug-ins on the market today is the Adobe Reader application, which enables you to view PDF documents in your browser. When you link to a PDF document on your site and an end user clicks on that link, one of two things happens. Either the PDF document is sent to the Adobe Reader application installed on the user's machine, which renders the document for display, or if the Acrobat Reader isn't installed, the user is asked whether or not the file can be downloaded.

Because the second option isn't exactly what you had intended for your visitor, Dreamweaver enables you to determine whether or not a plug-in is installed on the user's machine and can redirect the user if the plug-in isn't found. To do so, use the Check Plugin behavior found in the Behaviors panel (see Figure 28.13).

If the plug-in you want to check for isn't included in the Select list, you can also type the exact name of the application in the Enter field and the behavior checks for that plug-in.

If you really want to ensure that your visitors have access to the correct plug-in to view your content, you can also embed the plug-in in your page. To do this, select the Common category of the Insert bar and then click the Media button. You can either select the plug-in from the drop-down or click Plugin to select a custom plug-in (see Figure 28.14).

28

Figure 28.13
The Check Plugin dialog box enables you to specify which plug-in should be located and what to do if it is or isn't found.

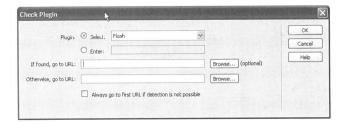

Figure 28.14
Using the Media button, you can embed a plug-in into the page.

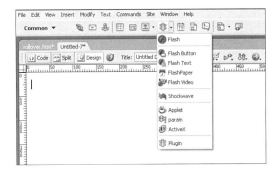

Table 28.3 provides information about some of the common plug-ins and their uses.

TABLE 28.3 COMMON PLUG-INS

Name	What It Does
Adobe Reader	Renders documents created in the Adobe PDF format.
Flash Player	Displays movies created with Macromedia Flash.
Java Runtime Environment	Renders miniprograms called applets created in the Java language.
Apple Quicktime	Displays movies create in a variety of formats and is used primarily to display .mov and .avi files.
RealPlayer	Displays audio and video files created on the Real Network platform, as well as other formats.
Shockwave Player	Renders movies created with Macromedia Director.
Windows Media Player	Displays audio and video files of nearly all types. Primarily used to render .wmv and .wma files.

After you embed a plug-in in your page, you can configure the plug-in parameters by using the Property inspector (see Figure 28.15). Although most of the parameters are common, the Plg URL field deserves an additional note because it enables you to specify the location of the appropriate plug-in to be downloaded if the user doesn't have the plug-in installed on his or her machine.

Figure 28.15
The Property inspector enables you to configure the embedded parameter.

JAVA APPLETS

Java Applets are programs written in the Java language and compiled so they can be run on virtually any platform. Typically, Java applets are stored in archive files known as JAR files (derived from Java Archive). To process the applet, however, the end user's machine must have some version of Java or the Java virtual machine installed. Most of the later browsers come standard with the virtual machine installed, but earlier versions required the application to be installed separately.

Like plug-ins, Java applets can be embedded in your pages if you use the Media drop-down button from the Insert toolbar. To embed an applet, select the Applet icon with the coffee cup symbol and indicate the location of the applet file in the Select File dialog box.

ACTIVEX CONTROLS

ActiveX controls act very similarly to plug-ins and applets in that they provide a way for your web page to display a specific file format by using a helper application. Java applets, however, require the Java virtual machine, whereas ActiveX controls can be developed to run any application stored in the Windows environment. This means that application developers can create an ActiveX control that serves as a conduit to their application, and after the application is installed on the end user's machine, they can view the application from within a web page. A perfect example of this is the Microsoft Excel ActiveX control that enables you to view and interact with Excel worksheets from within Internet Explorer.

NOTE

The fact that ActiveX controls are calling an application in the Windows environment means that these controls are limited to the Windows environment.

Like plug-ins and applets, you can also embed ActiveX controls in your pages by using the Media drop-down button from the Insert toolbar. To embed an ActiveX control, place your cursor in the page where you want to embed the control and select the ActiveX icon. Be aware that for the ActiveX control to function effectively, you need to use the Property inspector to set appropriate attributes and parameters.

AUDIO AND VIDEO FOR THE WEB

As more and more computers are connected to the web via broadband, the demand has risen for high-bandwidth content such as video, audio, and rich media files such as Flash movies. In response, new streaming and compression technologies have improved the

28

delivery methods for these technologies, making them much easier to deliver from within web pages.

Keep in mind, however, that although audio and video may be fun to add to your pages, it needs to be done properly to ensure that the sounds aren't annoying and the videos stream properly, rather than require the end user to download the entire movie before being able to watch it.

No matter how you distribute your audio or video, keep in mind that for the most part, the Web has been muted since its inception. People aren't necessarily prepared for blaring music or plug-ins that talk to them from a web page, so give them the choice as to whether or not the sound should play before you deluge them with the latest sounds of your motorcycle revving or your favorite MIDI file.

ADDING SOUND FILES

Dreamweaver offers a couple of different options when it comes to adding sound to your web pages. The first option is to create a hyperlink to the audio file on your server. This option enables users to choose whether to open the file or save the file to the local machine. If they choose to open it, the workstation decides which application plays the audio, depending on which application is assigned the audio file's particular format. To link to an audio file, add an image or text to your page and select it. Using the Link field in the Property inspector, locate the audio file or type the path to it.

The second option is to simply embed the sound in your page, which requires users to have either an audio plug-in or ActiveX control to play the audio. As with all plug-ins or ActiveX controls, you can determine which application should process the audio, and if the user doesn't already have it installed, you can link to the plug-in or control that can be downloaded. To embed audio into your page, use the Media button on the Insert toolbar to embed the appropriate ActiveX control or plug-in.

The third option is to create a Flash movie, using only the audio track, and embed the Flash movie in your page. This option is becoming more and more popular because most modern browsers have the Flash Player installed and, therefore, no additional software is required to play the audio. In addition, the Flash Player offers controls that can be embedded into your page layout that enable the end user to pause, play, and stop the audio. To add a Flash movie to your page, use the Media button on the Insert toolbar and choose Flash. Select the location of the Flash movie and be sure to upload that movie to your server when you upload your pages.

INSERTING VIDEO

Programmatically, the process of adding video to your pages is virtually identical to that of adding audio. The difference lies in the fact that you'll be selecting a video formatted file, as opposed to an audio file, as the source or target of your link. Although new video formats are always emerging, Dreamweaver can embed a variety of existing formats, including video formatted for the Apple Quicktime player, the Windows Media Player, and the RealMedia Player.

28

One relatively new format, called Flash Video, does deserve some extra detail because support for it is now standard in Dreamweaver 8. Flash Video is a new format created by Macromedia that enables you to capture new video or transfer existing video to the FLV format. Flash Video files are then stored on your server and either linked to or embedded in your web pages. One of the great features about this new format is that it is rendered with the Flash Player, so nearly every browser out there is capable of displaying it. In addition, Flash Video uses a technology called "progressive download," which means that users start downloading the video to their hard drives, but during the course of the download, the video plays. This means that they don't have to wait for the entire video to be downloaded before they can start watching it.

To insert a Flash Video into your page, choose Insert, Media, Flash Video from the menu bar. Using the Insert Flash Video dialog box, shown in Figure 28.16, you can determine whether you want to use the Progressive Download Video for video stored on any web server, or stream the video if you have access to a Flash Communication Server connection. Streaming the video means that you are not caching the video in the browser, but rather are relaying it from a special server directly to the user's browser in real time.

TIP

> For more information on the Flash Communication Server, take a look at Chapter 15, "Enhancing Projects with Sound and Video."

Figure 28.16
The Insert Flash Video dialog box enables you to add video easily to your pages.

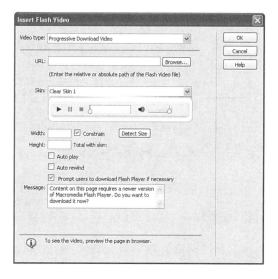

In addition, you can specify the look and feel (the "skin") of the player, the size of the video in the page, and the text of the message displayed to users who don't have the latest version of the Flash Player. After you specify the settings for your video, click OK and Dreamweaver embeds the movie into your page. To view it, you need to preview the HTML page in your browser.

ADDING RICH MEDIA CONTENT

In addition to Flash Video, Dreamweaver 8 also includes support for other rich media formats such as traditional Flash movies, images via the Image Viewer, Flash Text, Flash buttons, and FlashPaper documents.

FLASH MOVIES

Embedding a Flash movie is pretty straightforward in Dreamweaver 8. Choose Insert, Media, Flash from the menu bar, choose the location of the Flash movie by using the Select File dialog box, and click OK.

Next, add the accessibility information via the Object Tag Accessibility Attributes dialog box and click OK. Dreamweaver embeds the Flash movie placeholder in your page and the Property inspector, shown in Figure 28.17, enables you to modify the attributes of the movie.

Figure 28.17
When a Flash movie is selected, the Property inspector provides you with access to the movie's attributes.

IMAGE VIEWER

The Flash Image Viewer was added to Dreamweaver in the MX 2004 version and offers an easy way to add an images slideshow to your pages. To insert the Image Viewer into your page, choose Insert, Media, Image Viewer from the menu bar. Because the resulting slideshow is a Flash file, type a name and choose a location for the file in the Save Flash Element dialog box, shown in Figure 28.18.

Figure 28.18
Select a name and location for the Flash slideshow.

Click OK and Dreamweaver embeds a Flash movie placeholder into your document. As with any other Flash movie, the attributes of the movie are editable via the Property inspector. The next step in creating your slideshow is to indicate the locations of the images that are to be included in the show. To do this, select the Flash placeholder and notice that Dreamweaver opens a special panel called the Flash Element panel (see Figure 28.19). This panel enables you to adjust any of the attributes of the Flash objects in your page.

Figure 28.19
The Flash Element panel displays the attributes for the selected Flash object.

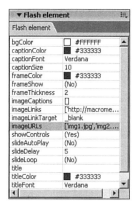

The locations for the images to be displayed in the slideshow are stored in the imgURLs attribute and can be adjusted by selecting the imgURLs attribute and clicking the Edit button that appears. In the Edit 'imgURLs' Array dialog box, shown in Figure 28.20, add or remove as many values as you would like to the list and click OK.

Figure 28.20
Add the URLs to the images that should be included in the slideshow.

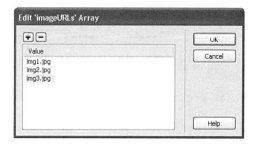

Save the page and preview it in your browser and the slideshow displays the images you included in the array.

FLASH TEXT

One of the biggest issues with placing text in a web page is the fact that if the font of the text is not one that is supported by every browser, you run the risk of your page not displaying as you intended. Flash Text resolves that issue by enabling you to render your text into a Flash movie, using any font present on your current system, style, or color, and then convert the text into a Flash movie that retains all this information for all users to be embedded in your page. To create Flash Text, chose Insert, Media, Flash Text from the menu bar. In the Insert Flash Text dialog box, shown in Figure 28.21, add your text and style it however you would like.

Figure 28.21
Use the Insert Flash Text dialog box to create a text-based Flash movie.

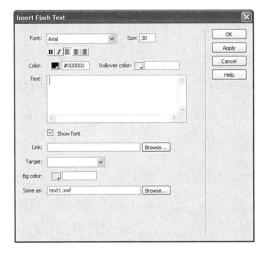

You can also turn the Flash Text movie into a hyperlink by typing the URL to which it should point in the Link field. Be sure to type a name and location for the resulting filename and click OK. Dreamweaver saves the movie and embeds it in your document.

FLASH BUTTONS

Similar to Flash Text, Flash buttons enable you to style your text into a clickable button format that contains different states for when the button is moused over or clicked on. To insert a Flash button, choose Insert, Media, Flash Button from the menu bar. In the Insert Flash Button dialog box (see Figure 28.22), choose a button style, enter the text for the button, style it to your taste, and type the URL to which the browser should go when clicked.

Finally, indicate where the resulting Flash movie should be saved and click OK. Dreamweaver embeds the button in your page and you can view it by previewing the page in your browser.

FLASHPAPER

The last rich media type that I want to cover in this chapter is new to Dreamweaver 8 and is called FlashPaper. FlashPaper is a new format created by Macromedia that enables you to convert documents such as those created in Microsoft Word or Excel into Flash movies. These movies, referred to as FlashPaper, can then be displayed in your pages just like any other Flash movie.

Figure 28.22
Use the Insert Flash button dialog box to create your Flash button.

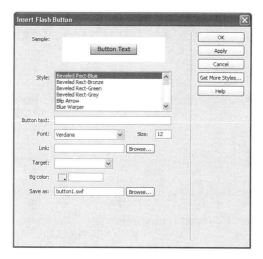

> **NOTE**
>
> The creation process of FlashPaper documents is covered a little later in the book in the "Adding FlashPaper Documents" in Chapter 34, "Putting It All Together: Using Contribute to Manage Site Content."

To insert a FlashPaper movie, choose Insert, Media, FlashPaper from the menu bar. In the Insert FlashPaper dialog box (see Figure 28.23), select the source FlashPaper movie and the size to be displayed.

Figure 28.23
Use the Insert FlashPaper dialog box to add FlashPaper documents to your page.

Click OK and Dreamweaver embeds the button in your page. You can then view it by previewing the page in your browser.

USING TIMELINES TO CREATE MOVING AND INTERACTIVE LAYERS

Have you ever wondered how some web pages move content or images across the screen as though they were being dragged? The likely answer is that movement either took place as part of a Flash movie or through the use of moveable layers. We have already talked in depth about using Flash movies to create motion, so let's take a look at a feature that has returned to Dreamweaver in version 8—Timelines.

28

Timelines enable you to animate the layers in your page by moving them or resizing them. The process of creating and managing these animations is controlled by the Timelines panel, shown in Figure 28.24. You can access this panel by choosing Window, Timelines.

Figure 28.24
The Timelines panel enables you to animate your layers.

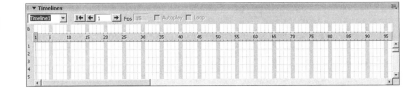

As you can see, the Timelines panel looks a lot like the Flash development environment in that it can accommodate multiple objects and it uses frames and keyframes. To create a timeline, add a layer to your page and insert an image into the layer. Select the layer in the Design view, right-click in the first row of the Timelines panel, and choose Add Object from the menu. This indicates to Dreamweaver that the timeline will be changing the layer in some fashion. Dreamweaver adds the object to the Timelines panel and creates a default 15-frame timeline for the object (see Figure 28.25).

Figure 28.25
The layer has been added to the timeline as an object.

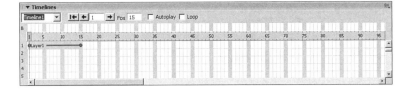

NOTE

By default, the timeline is set to 15 frames per second in the FPS field. This means that the default 15 frames that Dreamweaver establishes play for only one second.

Suppose that you wanted to move your layer across the screen over a 3-second period. The easiest way to do this is to extend the object to 45 frames (3 seconds at 15 frames per second) by clicking on the ending keyframe, indicated by a white circle, and dragging it out to 45 (see Figure 28.26).

Figure 28.26
Extend the number of frames out to 45 by dragging the ending keyframe.

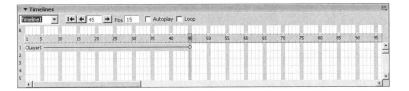

Now you need to indicate where the layer should end up after the timeline is completed. To do this, drag your layer to wherever you want it to end up in the Design view. Notice that Dreamweaver creates a line in the Design view that shows the path the layer will take as it is animated (see Figure 28.27).

Figure 28.27
The path of the layer is indicated by a line in the Design view.

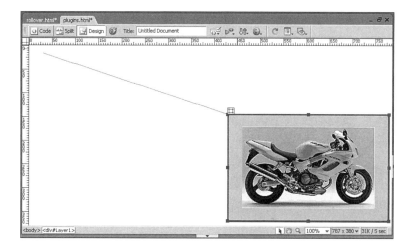

But what if you don't want the layer to proceed to its destination in a straight line? You can accommodate custom paths by using the Record Path command. To see how this works, create a second layer with an image inside it and add it to the Timelines panel. Now select the layer in the Design view and click on the Menu button for the Timelines panel. From the menu, choose Record Path of Layer.

After you click this link, Dreamweaver remembers where you drag the layer and creates a custom path for it. In the design view, drag the layer in a looping manner to a random destination. Notice that Dreamweaver draws the line following the path you indicated. When the layer is at its destination, release the mouse button and Dreamweaver alerts you that only certain aspects of the layer can be controlled (see Figure 28.28).

Figure 28.28
Dreamweaver alerts you that some modifications to layers aren't visible in earlier versions of Netscape.

Click OK to close the alert. In the Timeline panel, click the first frame for this object and then use the right arrow to proceed through the frames. The layer moves according to the path you recorded. To see your animations in action, save the page and preview it in your browser.

NOTE

> Although layer animations and timelines are fun, be aware that they can get annoying after a while. Be cautious in how you apply them and make sure that they serve a true purpose that enhances your website, and that they aren't just used for the wow factor.

TROUBLESHOOTING

I need to delete an object from my page that has behaviors associated with it. What is the best way to remove it?

The best way to ensure that all unnecessary code is removed from your page is to select the object, open the Behaviors panel, remove all the behaviors associated with the object, and then delete the object from the page.

I like the Flash buttons and want to use them in my site, but I would like to modify them. Can I change their colors, gradient, and so on?

No. The Flash button templates are pretty much set in stone. You can, however, use Flash to create your own buttons that use the same states as the Flash buttons. When embedding any custom-created Flash buttons, use the Insert, Media, Flash menu item as opposed to the Insert, Media, Flash Button menu item.

I want to record the path of my layer for a timeline, but when I click the menu button on the Timelines panel, the Record Path of Layer menu item is grayed out. What is the problem?

To see the Record Path of Layer menu item, you need to be sure that the layer is selected in the Design view first.

BEST PRACTICES—BEING AWARE OF BANDWIDTH LIMITATIONS WHEN SERVING VIDEO

The use of video as a training tool and for entertainment is becoming more and more popular as the availability of broadband and high-speed Internet connections grows. Be aware, however, that just because more data can be transferred easily across the Web doesn't mean that you shouldn't use good judgment in determining the best way to provide video to your end users.

For instance, I work in a centralized office that also has several outlying offices in different locations of the country. These offices are significantly smaller than the main office and, therefore, have limited resources. In addition, they use Voice Over IP for their telephone systems, which relies on having available bandwidth.

28

If I were to start streaming large video files to my technicians in these offices, it's possible that these large videos could adversely affect the office's telephone system. In addition, the more bandwidth I consume in pushing the videos, the more my company has to pay for their consumption.

For these reasons, be cautious when providing video to your end users. Be sure you optimize the video for your audience, but take care to keep bandwidth usage and cost considerations in mind as well.

DEVELOPING DYNAMIC APPLICATIONS IN DREAMWEAVER

In this chapter

29

INTRODUCING DYNAMIC APPLICATIONS

Over the last decade, the amount of data being delivered via web applications has grown at a tremendous rate. Every day, the web delivers content ranging from product catalogs to children's sports league schedules to educational training and nearly everything in between. And as the need to manage vast amounts of information has grown, so have the options for storing and delivering it. Although today's web pages are based around the HTML language, they have been paired with additional languages such as the ColdFusion Markup Language (CFML), JavaScript, VBScript, Java, PHP, VB.NET, and C# to supplement what HTML can't do. Through their own syntax and functions, each of these languages provides additional calculation, data validation, and connectivity functionality.

Probably the most important aspect of any of these is the connectivity element. Each of these languages is capable of connecting to a wide variety of database management systems and communicating data requests, updates, edits, and deletions that enable you to leverage the powerful storage capabilities of databases and use them to provide data for your web applications.

Now, that was quite a mouthful, wasn't it? What this all boils down to is that by using a supplemental language, you can allow your web applications to talk to databases and extract data from them. In real terms, this means that you can build a 10-page web, and those 10 pages can serve the same purpose as 1,000 HTML pages could have.

Imagine your company has a product catalog that consists of 500 items. As the web developer, your boss just told you that he needs an online catalog built that showcases each of these products. With only HTML in your toolbox, you would have to develop a catalog site that had at least 501 pages. The first page would be an index of all the products, and the other 500 would be product details pages for each of the individual products. Just think about how long it would take to create 501 HTML pages—even leveraging the template functionality that Dreamweaver offers. If creating each page and adding content took you one hour, you'd be looking at 12 weeks of straight work just to create the pages and fill them with data. And then what happens when it's time to update the information? Ugh!

Now, what if I told you that you could provide exactly the same functionality with only two pages? Sounds much better, right? Just the savings in development time alone would make it worth the effort. And how about the opportunity cost savings of not having you tied up with the mundane task of generating HTML pages for the next three months? Those types of arguments are certainly going to grab your boss's attention. So what is this solution that I'm offering? Database-driven web pages.

When combined with a relational database such as Microsoft SQL Server, MySQL, and even Microsoft Access, Dreamweaver is one of the most powerful web development tools on the market because the application makes it so easy to interact with databases. In this chapter, you're going to see what it takes to develop database-driven (also referred to as "dynamic") applications and how to add dynamic content to your site.

NOTE

Some web developers argue that any web page that changes (for example, via rollover buttons, Flash movies, and so on) is a dynamic web page—which is technically true. The term *dynamic*, however, has become somewhat of a technical term in the web community that typically refers to pages that display dynamic content extracted from databases. Throughout this chapter, I'll be using the terms dynamic and database-driven interchangeably.

29

CREATING A DREAMWEAVER SITE FOR DYNAMIC PAGES

NOTE

The basics of creating a Dreamweaver site were already covered in Chapter 23, "Creating a Dreamweaver Site," so if you haven't read that chapter you might look over it so you have the fundamentals of what's going to be covered here.

Before you can begin developing dynamic web pages, you need to ensure that your Dreamweaver site is configured for a specific platform. Because Dreamweaver will be generating the vast majority of your code, it needs to know in what language to write. To do this, open the Retro's Cycles site that was created in Chapter 23 by choosing Site, Manage Sites from the menu bar. In the Manage Sites dialog box, shown in Figure 29.1, choose the Retro's Cycles site and click Edit.

Figure 29.1
The Manage Sites dialog box enables you to edit your existing sites.

In the Site Definition dialog box, click the Advanced tab and choose the Testing Server category. If you followed the configuration set forth in Chapter 23, the dialog box should look similar to the one in Figure 29.2.

Figure 29.2
The Testing Server information for the Retro's Cycles site.

The ColdFusion section of the book explored the process of configuring ColdFusion on your local workstation so that you could develop and test dynamic applications. Here is where that configuration comes into play. The Site Definition dialog box defines on which server model your pages will be developed, which, in turn, determines in which language Dreamweaver will create code.

If you wanted to develop on the ASP, .NET, or PHP platforms, you could change this setting to reflect that platform and Dreamweaver would write in the appropriate language. Note, however, that you cannot mix platforms when developing with Dreamweaver. If you have a mixed environment and need to work on multiple platforms, you need to create a Dreamweaver site for each of the platforms and store the appropriate pages in separate root folders.

After you have your Dreamweaver site configured for the appropriate platform, click OK to close the Site Definition dialog box and click Done to close the Manage Sites dialog box, and we're ready to talk databases.

DATABASE OPERATIONS

Now that you have chosen a platform on which to develop pages, the next step is to determine what database you want to use for the back-end.

TIP

> The user-facing portion of your website is generally referred to as the *front-end*, whereas the database and code that is processed by the server are generally referred to as the *back-end*.

There are quite a few relational database management systems on the market today, spanning the spectrum when it comes to price, portability, and power. Those databases that are extremely powerful usually (but not always) come with a high price tag. But how much you need to pay and how powerful you need the database to be depend on the expected usage of your web application. Will you be competing with eBay? Then you probably want to fork out the dollars for a high-end database such as SQL Server or Oracle. Are you creating a catalog that will serve your customer base of 500 companies? Then you would probably be better off saving yourself some coin and going with a MySQL database or Microsoft Access database.

TIP

Before I get lambasted with emails telling me that I shouldn't compare MySQL with Access because it far outperforms Access, let me state that my comparison here was one of pricing. For those who aren't familiar with MySQL and are looking for a very powerful database management system that is low cost, definitely look into MySQL. The biggest drawback of MySQL, however, is that there is no commercial support for the application, something that corporate America hasn't quite grown comfortable with.

Regardless of which database you choose, you need to create a communication conduit between your website and the database called a *connection*.

THE DATABASE CONNECTION

The next step in developing a database-driven site is to build a connection to the database. All database connections are managed via the Databases panel, shown in Figure 29.3.

Figure 29.3
The Databases panel is where all connections are stored.

If the proper steps have not been taken to facilitate the creation of a database connection, Dreamweaver lets you know the steps that you need to take before you can proceed. If you have already created the ODBC connection to the database in the ColdFusion Administrator in Chapter 21, "Putting It All Together: Configuring ColdFusion for Database Connectivity," your Databases tab should look like Figure 29.4 and you are ready to build a connection.

Figure 29.4
All the requisite steps have been completed and Dreamweaver can create a connection to the database.

> **N O T E**
>
> When you created a connection to the database in Chapter 21, you created a connection between the database and the ColdFusion server. The second connection that needs to be created within Dreamweaver is a connection between your pages and the ColdFusion server.

Because the Retro's Cycles site is using ColdFusion, Dreamweaver automatically generates a list of data source names (DSNs) that were built with the ColdFusion Administrator. As you can see in Figure 29.4, the dsnRetrosCycles DSN is already in the list, so we would be ready to move on to the next step.

If, however, you are using a server platform such as ASP or PHP, you need to create either an ODBC DSN on your machine or a custom connection string by clicking on the plus sign in the Databases panel and choosing the appropriate connection method.

> **N O T E**
>
> For instructions on setting up a DSN in Windows, check out this Macromedia TechNote:
> http://www.macromedia.com/cfusion/knowledgebase/index.cfm?id=tn_19072
> For instructions on setting up a custom connection string, check out this Article:
> http://livedocs.macromedia.com/dreamweaver/mx2004/using/wwhelp/wwhimpl/common/html/wwhelp.htm?context=Using_Dreamweaver&file=28_con17.htm

THE SEARCH FORM

Although search forms aren't necessarily required for displaying dynamic data, they are frequently used to pass criteria to a Results page, so it's worth taking some time to look over and understand them before you jump into the dynamic pages. Figure 29.5 shows a basic form with a single text field and a Submit button.

By selecting the form and taking a look at the Property inspector (see Figure 29.6), you can see that the form is named fmSearch and, when submitted, passes its content to the search_results.cfm page, using the GET method.

Figure 29.5
A simple search form.

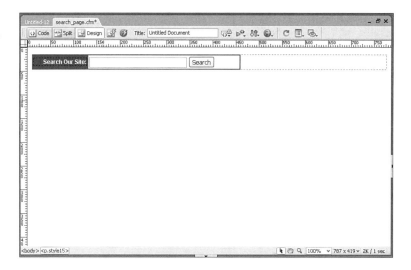

Figure 29.6
The form's properties.

In addition, clicking on the text field and taking a look at the Property inspector tells you that the text field is named tfSearch (see Figure 29.7).

Figure 29.7
The text field's properties.

This means that when the user types **Honda** in the text field and clicks the Search button, the contents of the form are passed to the search_results.cfm page via the querystring (because you are using the GET method). To accomplish this, the search form constructs a URL that contains the form data and looks something like this:

http://www.retroscycles.com/searchresults.cfm?tfSearch=Honda

This URL now presents you with the opportunity to extract data from the database that matches the search criteria and display it on your pages.

NOTE

The difference between the GET and POST methods is the fact that GET passes the contents of the form via the URL to the target page, which means the contents of the form are visible in clear text. POST, on the other hand, passes the data behind the scenes, which means the data is not visible in clear text. Both have their pros and cons, but a good rule of thumb is to use GET unless your data should be protected (as with credit card numbers, for example) or you are passing large amounts of data. In those cases, POST is the better choice.

CONSTRUCTING A RECORDSET

After you have your database connection created and tested, the next step is to learn how to retrieve content from the database. Each relational database uses a derivative of the Structured Query Language (known as SQL and pronounced "see-quel" or "ess-cue-el," depending on who you are talking to).

SQL can be used to specify what data should be retrieved from a database and even perform actions such as inserting, updating, or deleting data.

NOTE

The syntax and use of SQL is beyond the scope of this book, but even without a complete understanding of the SQL language you can still use Dreamweaver to have interactions with databases. If, however, you are planning on developing dynamic applications, I would highly recommend that you spend some time learning about SQL and its applications.

In the case of retrieving data, SQL enables you to specify limitations on the types of data that you want retrieved. For instance, a query that you might perform might ask the application to retrieve all the database fields from the tbInventory table where the Make field is equal to the value that has been submitted via the search form. After the query is executed, all the records that match the criteria are returned in the form of a recordset. Think of a recordset as a subset of the entire database that contains only the specific information that was requested.

Luckily, Dreamweaver makes creating recordsets extremely easy. To build a new recordset, open the Server Behaviors tab on the Application panel by choosing Window, Server Behaviors. Click the plus sign and choose Recordset from the menu. As shown in Figure 29.8, the Recordset dialog box provides an easy-to-use interface for gathering data from the database.

The first step in creating the recordset is to give it a name. As with other page objects that we have discussed, it's a good idea to give your recordsets names that mean something. So a recordset that retrieves all the search results might be named rsSearchResults.

Figure 29.8
The Recordset dialog box enables you to extract data from your database.

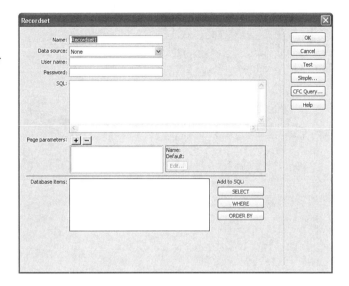

The next step is to choose the data source from which you want to extract data. This drop-down contains all the database connections found in the Databases panel. Because a successful connection was created to the Retro's Cycles database, you could choose the dsnRetrosCycles database. If the database were secured with a username and password, they would need to be entered so that the recordset could access the data.

Next, you need to specify from which table the data should come. Because you want to search the inventory, the tbInventory table would be selected.

Finally, you can apply any filters to ensure that only the data you want is retrieved. In this case you would choose to select all the columns in the table, and set the Filter field so that Make is equal to the URL parameter tfSearch (see Figure 29.9). This tells the recordset to extract the value of tfSearch from the URL (also called the "querystring") and compare it to the data stored in the Make field.

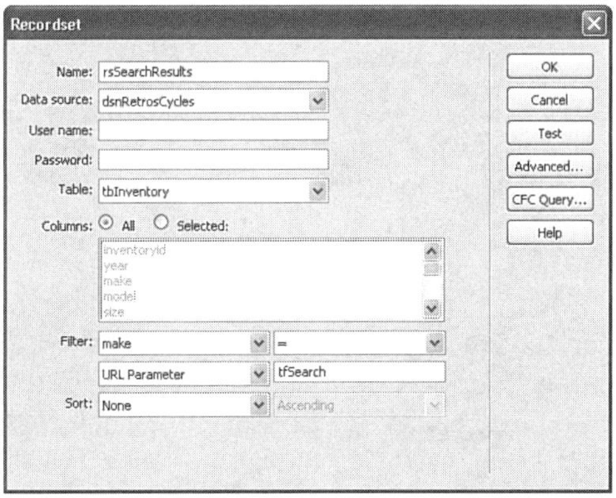

Figure 29.9
The recordset has been created and is ready to test.

To see whether or not the recordset is retrieving only the data that you have asked for, click the Test button and Dreamweaver asks you to enter a test value. If you type **Honda** and click OK, you can see that Dreamweaver displays the first 25 records in the recordset that have the Make field set to Honda. As you can see in Figure 29.10, all the motorcycles in the results are Hondas.

Figure 29.10
The recordset contains the correct data.

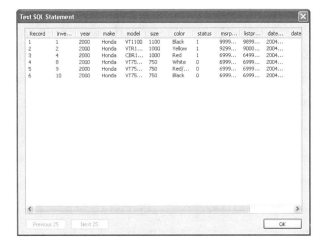

If you are proficient in using SQL and want to expand on your SQL queries or use some of the advanced functions within SQL, you can click the Advanced button and customize the query to meet your needs by using the Advanced view (see Figure 29.11).

Figure 29.11
The Advanced view of the recordset enables you to build your own custom SQL queries.

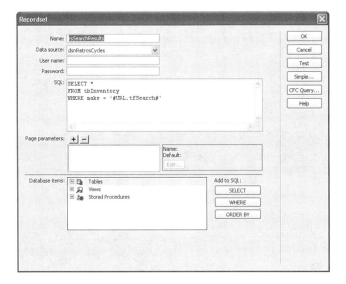

To finish building the recordset, click OK and the recordset is added to the Server Behaviors panel and the Bindings panel.

ADDING DYNAMIC DATA BINDINGS

After you have created a recordset that contains the appropriate results, the next step is to add data bindings to your page. Data bindings are placeholder blocks of code that, when rendered in the browser, are replaced by the actual data from the database. The available data bindings are located in the Bindings panel, shown in Figure 29.12.

Figure 29.12
The Bindings panel shows all the available recordsets and their corresponding data bindings.

To add a data binding to your page, expand the recordset from which you want to choose data by clicking the plus sign and then dragging the placeholder you want from the panel to the page. After the placeholder is in place, Dreamweaver indicates that it is dynamic by highlighting it (see Figure 29.13).

Figure 29.13
The data binding has been added to the page.

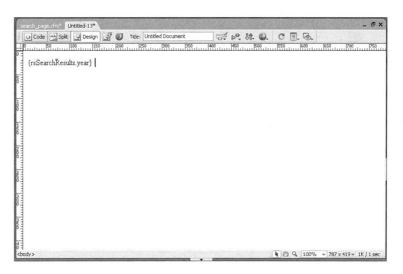

TIP

You can also add data bindings to your page from the Server Behaviors panel. With the panel open, click the plus sign and choose Dynamic Text from the menu. In the Dynamic Text dialog box that is opened, select the binding that you want and click OK.

USING SERVER BEHAVIORS TO AVOID ERRORS

When using dynamic data, one of the most common mistakes developers make is to forget to account for the rare occurrence that a recordset does not contain any records. This might occur because of a typo in the SQL query, or because the type of data requested just doesn't exist in the database.

For instance, suppose you were building an events calendar for your company. The calendar contained hyperlinked dates that, when clicked, displayed all events that were scheduled to occur on that date. Sounds great, right?

But what happens when a user clicks on a date when nothing is scheduled? You might automatically think that nothing would display, right? Unfortunately, that's wrong. What happens, instead, is that the application server tries to display something that doesn't exist and it gets confused. As a result, your browser throws a nasty error like the one shown in Figure 29.14.

Figure 29.14
This browser error occurred because the requested data didn't exist in the database.

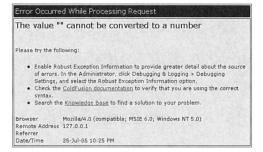

To avoid errors such as this one, the best thing to do is to define two regions in the page. The first region displays the contents of the recordset if it is not empty. The second region displays a block of text that lets the user know that there are no results.

TIP

> A good way to accomplish this is to create a table in the area of your page that displays the content. The table should have one column and two rows. The top row displays the data if the recordset is not empty, and the bottom row displays your text alerting the user that no data matches the request.

The tools used to accomplish this are called *server behaviors* and are found on the Server Behaviors panel, shown in Figure 29.15.

To display a region only when the recordset contains data, highlight the data or table region that you want displayed, and click the plus sign on the Server Behaviors panel. From the menu, choose Show Region, If Recordset Is Not Empty. From the Show Region If Recordset Is Not Empty dialog box (see Figure 29.16), choose the correct recordset and click OK.

Figure 29.15
The Server Behaviors panel.

Figure 29.16
Select the recordset that governs the server behavior.

When the server behavior is applied, Dreamweaver places a border around it and an indicator tab to show which region is affected (see Figure 29.17).

Figure 29.17
The server behavior has been applied to the region.

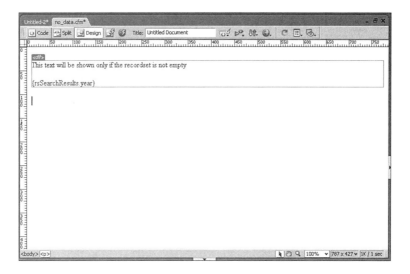

Next, you need to create the area of the page that displays only if the recordset contains no data. To do this, add the appropriate text to the page that lets the user know that no data was found and then select the text or table row. Next, click the plus sign on the Server Behaviors panel and choose Show Region, If Recordset Is Empty from the menu. From the Show Region If Recordset Is Empty dialog box (see Figure 29.18), choose the correct recordset and click OK.

Figure 29.18
Again, select the
recordset that governs
the server behavior.

With these regions in place, you can be sure that your visitors see only your message, as opposed to the messy browser error message.

USING THE LIVEDATA VIEW

After you have added your data bindings to the page, you can see what they would look like when rendered in the browser by clicking the Live Data View button on the Document toolbar (see Figure 29.19).

Figure 29.19
The Live Data View
enables you to see
what your data would
look like when ren-
dered. Because no
search term was
passed to the record-
set, it is empty and
the appropriate data
is visible.

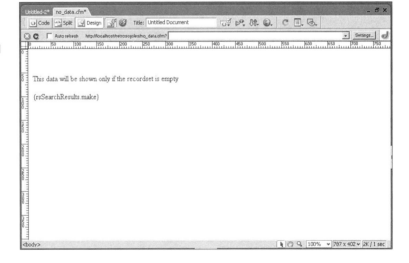

The data displayed in the Live Data View is the first record found in the recordset and is meant to give you an idea as to whether or not your design is functioning as expected. To fully test the page, be sure to preview it in your browser.

CREATING DYNAMIC PAGES

Now that you know how to extract data from the database, you're ready to start building dynamic pages. Although there are endless uses to how you can use dynamic data, five page types are typically used across dynamic web sites:

- **Results Page**—Displays a list of records in the database that match certain criteria and typically links to a Details page.
- **Details Page**—Displays information pertaining to a specific record in the database.

- **Insert Record Page**—Inserts data into a new record in the database.
- **Update Page**—Updates an existing record in the database.
- **Delete Page**—Deletes a record from the database.

RESULTS PAGE

After the recordset has been tested, it's likely that you'll want to display the results somewhere. The easiest way to do this is to create a Results page that displays the contents of the recordset in a table. The easiest way to display the data is to create a dynamic data table that extracts the information from the recordset and displays it on the page.

To create a dynamic data table, click Insert, Application Objects, Dynamic Data from the menu bar. In the Dynamic Table dialog box, shown in Figure 29.20, choose the appropriate recordset and determine how many records should be displayed on the page at a time. For this example, we show 10 records at a time. You can also specify table settings by entering a value for the border, cell padding, and cell spacing.

Figure 29.20
The Dynamic Table dialog box helps you extract data from your recordset to display on your page.

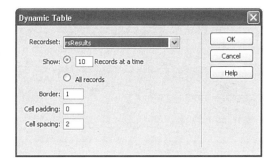

Clicking OK places a table in the page, complete with data bindings (see Figure 29.21). Note that Dreamweaver assumed that you wanted to display all the columns in your recordset, but you can remove any columns that you don't want to display.

Because the user probably doesn't want to review every detail of every record that meets the search criteria, you can delete all the columns from the data table except InventoryID, Year, Make, Model, and Color. This should give users enough information to choose which motorcycle they might want to look into further (see Figure 29.22).

After users determine which motorcycles they want to see more information about, they need to be able to click a link to open the Details page, which then displays the full informational record on that specific motorcycle. To create this link, select the InventoryID data binding and type **details.cfm** in the Link field of the Property inspector.

Next, you need to pass the InventoryID field through the URL so that the Details page will know which record to display. To set this up, click the folder icon next to the Link field in the Property inspector and click the Parameters button. In the Parameters dialog box, shown in Figure 29.23, type **InventoryID** as the name for the parameter.

Figure 29.21
Dreamweaver adds the dynamic data table to your page.

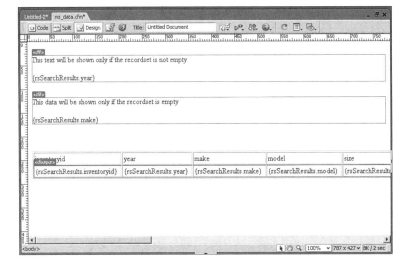

Figure 29.22
Columns have been removed from the table to streamline the user's view.

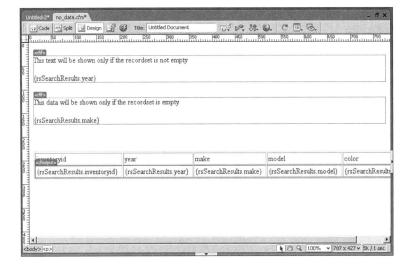

Figure 29.23
The Parameters dialog box enables you to pass custom parameters through the querystring.

Next, click the lightning bolt icon next to the Value field and choose inventoryid from the list of data bindings in the rsInventory recordset (see Figure 29.24).

Figure 29.24
Choose the invento-
ryid to be passed as
the value.

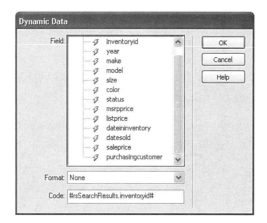

Click OK to close the Dynamic Data dialog box, click OK again to close the Parameters dialog box, and click OK a third time to close the Select File dialog box. After it is created, the inventoryid now becomes a hyperlink that, when clicked, passes the inventoryid of that specific record to the details.cfm page.

DETAILS PAGE

A Details page usually contains the information stored in the database that relates to a specific record. This page enables users to get detailed information about an item after they have determined from the Results page that it might meet their needs.

In the case of Retro's Cycles, clicking the link on the Results page passes an inventoryid to the Details page, so you need to build a Details page that reads that value, extracts the appropriate record from the database, and displays it on the page. To do this, you need to create a new page and save it as details.cfm.

Next, a recordset needs to be built that looks for the URL parameter called inventoryid and finds the record whose inventoryid matches that value. The recordset would look like the one shown in Figure 29.25.

After the details recordset is completed, you can construct the page however you want to display the full details of a specific motorcycle. Figure 29.26 shows a sample configuration of the data bindings.

INSERT RECORD PAGE

Because the database for the Retro's Cycles site already had data stored in it, recordsets and data bindings could be used to extract information from it. But what if the database is empty and you need to populate it with data? Or what if we wanted to add additional records beyond those that are already stored in the database? The answer is to create a page that inserts new records into the database. Dreamweaver makes the creation of an insert page easy through the use of the Record Insertion Form Wizard.

Figure 29.25
The Details page recordset.

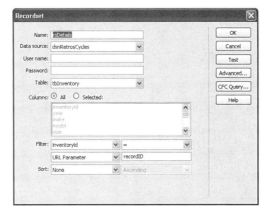

Figure 29.26
A sample Details page.

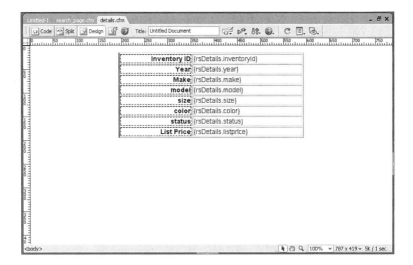

To activate the wizard, choose Insert, Application Objects, Insert Record, Record Insertion Form Wizard. The wizard, shown in Figure 29.27, enables you to specify the data source that connects to the database, any username/password information required, the table to which you want to add, and a page to which the user is redirected after the record is added.

The really nice thing about this wizard is that it lets you set up your form and the form elements in one handy interface. For instance, suppose that you wanted the year field to be a menu instead of a text field. You could select the year field in the Form Fields panel and choose Menu in the Display As field (see Figure 29.28).

To give users values from which to choose in the menu, click the Menu Properties button to add the various years and values (see Figure 29.29).

Figure 29.27
The Record Insertion Form dialog box enables you to add a form to your page that inserts data into the database.

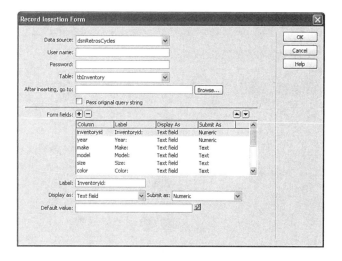

Figure 29.28
The year form field has been changed to a menu item.

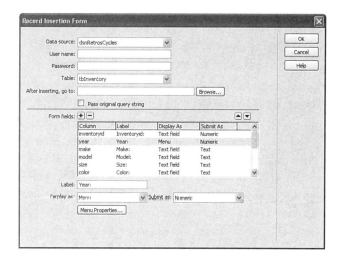

Figure 29.29
Custom values can be added to the menu.

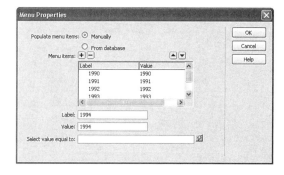

When the OK button is clicked, Dreamweaver does all the work and adds the records insertion form to your page (see Figure 29.30). You can then customize the form and the table layout to match your site's design.

Figure 29.30
The record insertion form is added to the page.

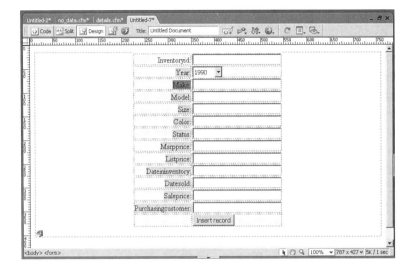

UPDATE RECORD PAGE

Updating information that is stored in the database is nearly as easy as inserting it. To update a record, you can create a page similar to the page that adds a record. The update page, however, requires a recordset that determines which records to update, and the existing data that matches that record is displayed in an editable form. Upon submission of the form, the content stored in the form replaces the content stored in the database record.

NOTE

> The earlier Results page linked to a Details page and passed a URL parameter to indicate which record should be displayed in the Details page. Here, as well, a Results page needs to be created (or some other clickable link) that passes the variable to the update page, which indicates to the recordset which specific records should be edited.

To accommodate the creation of an update page, Dreamweaver has added another handy wizard called the Record Update Form Wizard, which you can access by choosing Insert, Application Objects, Update Record, Record Update Form Wizard from the menu bar.

The wizard, shown in Figure 29.31, is very similar to the Record Insertion Form Wizard and enables you to customize the form to meet your needs. This wizard does, however, have one additional field named Unique Key Column, which indicates which field in the database serves as the primary key and ensures that the record is unique.

Figure 29.31
The Record Update Form Wizard helps you create a page that makes updates to existing records.

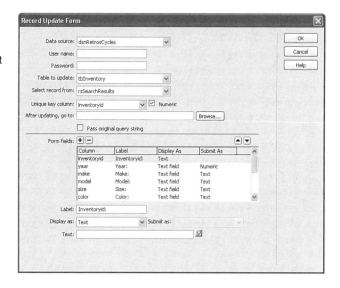

In the case of the tbInventory table, the autonumber inventoryid field serves this purpose, and choosing this field ensures that the form makes the update to the correct field.

After the wizard is completed, the table and editable fields are added to the page and are customizable to meet your page's design.

DELETE RECORD PAGE

The last of the common dynamic page types is the oh-so-dangerous Delete Record page. This page enables you to permanently remove a record from your database. Did I mention that the deletion of the record is permanent? If I didn't mention that, let me state clearly that the deletion of the data done with a Delete Record form is permanent. If it sounds like I'm beating a dead horse, it's because on numerous occasions I have heard the question "Can you get that back for me?" after a user deleted a record from the database. Although the Delete Record page can certainly be a valuable tool in the right hands, it can be just as dangerous in the wrong hands.

Unlike the Update Record page, this page type doesn't rely on a recordset to identify which record should be deleted. Instead, the page traditionally accepts a variable via the URL or from a form that indicates the unique record ID that should be deleted. Then, when the page is loaded, the record with the corresponding record ID is deleted from the database.

To create a Delete Record page, simply create a new dynamic page and then apply the Delete Record Application behavior by choosing Insert, Application Objects, Delete Record from the menu bar. The Delete Record dialog box (see Figure 29.32) then asks you to specify the data source, authentication information, table, primary key column, and the source of the record ID that matches the primary key. In addition, you need to specify where the user should be redirected to after the record is successfully deleted.

Figure 29.32
The Delete Record dialog box helps you create pages that remove data from your database.

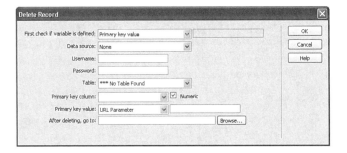

Before you venture out into the world with your new found dynamic tools, let me suggest that you take a moment to read the Best Practices section of this chapter. As you have already probably guessed, I am not a huge proponent of putting delete capabilities into the hands of end users, so I have detailed another option in the Best Practices section.

After you have read that section, go forth, apply your new dynamic data skills, and build powerful, portable, productive websites that knock the socks off your friends and co-workers.

TROUBLESHOOTING

When I try to update my record, I get an error that tells me the operation must use an updateable query. What's going on?

This error is probably the most common error experienced by those new to dynamic pages. The error is usually generated in conjunction with Access databases and the good news is, it's an easy fix. In order for your database to be updated, you need to ensure that the folder where it is located gives the Internet Guest account for your server the rights to write to it. To resolve the issue, walk through the steps set forth by Macromedia in this TechNote:

http://www.macromedia.com/cfusion/knowledgebase/index.cfm?id=tn_14520

Now, when I try to add a record or update a record, I get an error stating that there is a syntax error in my INSERT INTO statement. What's happening now?

Again, another common error that is easily fixed. The reason this usually occurs is because a field in your table is named with a special character like "date&time". This is not an acceptable field name because the & character is a special character that is interpreted by the SQL INSERT INTO statement. This causes the syntax error and stops your page from functioning properly. To fix the problem, adjust your field names so that they all start with alpha characters, contain no special characters or spaces, and don't use words reserved by your database. For additional information on this error, check out this TechNote:

http://www.macromedia.com/cfusion/knowledgebase/index.cfm?id=tn_14622

I uploaded my web pages and my database to my host and now I get an error that the include file Connections/yourfilename was not found. What did I do wrong?

It's likely that you're using a Custom Connection string and simply forgot to upload the Connections folder and its contents to your web server. Try uploading that folder and the error should be resolved.

BEST PRACTICES—USING RECORD UPDATE PAGES TO ARCHIVE DATA RATHER THAN RECORD DELETION PAGES TO DELETE DATA

As you can probably tell, I am not a big fan of deleting data. Because data deletion is permanent, it often poses more problems that if you had simply archived the data and hidden it away from the world. Back when storage was costly and the size of databases was a constant concern, deletion was a necessary evil and part of the cost of doing business. In today's market, however, the cost of storage has dropped significantly and databases have become more efficient in the way they store data to ensure the optimal size of their tables. As a result, the cost of deleting data and losing the information has now outweighed the cost of storing the data and we, as web developers, should be looking at archiving data instead of deleting it.

The most common model I use to accommodate archiving is to create a field in each of my tables called "archived". If this field is set to yes or 1 (depending on the database), I don't ever display the data to anyone. If the field is set to no or 0, the data is visible to the end users. While this method is easy to implement, your tables will eventually become bloated with records that have been archived.

Another common model that alleviates the bloating problem is to set an expiration date for each record, review it prior to that expiration date, and then migrate those records that have expired to a secondary archive table. Following this model minimizes the number of records stored in your table and ensures that your dynamic web pages aren't adversely affected by having to sift through lots of archived data.

These are just two of the common methods used to archive data instead of deleting it. Regardless of whether you choose to implement one of these methods or another archiving method, the value of this type of model becomes evident when you are asked to restore data. Rather than having to perform restore operations from tape backup and risk losing data that may have been written since the backup, you are able to go into the database and reset the archive value or migrate the record from the archive table to the active table and the data is now available again.

PUTTING IT ALL TOGETHER: CREATING A SITE USING DREAMWEAVER

In this chapter

With all the Macromedia Studio tools in your toolbelt, you're ready to get to work. This chapter takes a look at the process of building the core elements of the site for the client, Retro's Cycles. Although you won't build the entire site out, you'll see items such as the site template built in the Fireworks section, create a Dreamweaver template and child pages, and then build out the For Sale section, using database-driven content.

When you finish this chapter, you should have a good understanding of how Dreamweaver can be leveraged to create a database-driven website and should be able to continue building on the site from there.

30

> **NOTE**
>
> Before you start these exercises, you need to create the Retro's Cycles Dreamweaver site. If you haven't done that already, revisit Chapter 23, "Creating a Dreamweaver Site," and learn how to create the site.

EXAMINING THE FIREWORKS TEMPLATE

Earlier in the Fireworks section of the book, you saw how Fireworks can be used to create an HTML template for your site that includes images, hyperlinks, and rollover buttons. Now would be a good time to revisit that template and see how you can use it to begin building out the site for Retro's Cycles.

> **NOTE**
>
> If you haven't worked through the Fireworks section of the book, now would be a good time to look it over. If you're comfortable with using Fireworks to create HTML templates or just want to skip to building in Dreamweaver, you can also download the support files for this chapter from http://www.retroscycles.com/supportfiles.

1. Open Dreamweaver.

2. Open the file named `retros_cycle_template.htm` that you created in the Fireworks section of the book (see Figure 30.1).

3. Click on each of the navigation links on the left side and ensure that the Property inspector (see Figure 30.2) indicates the following links for each of the rollover buttons:

   - **Home**—Links to `default.cfm`
   - **Contact**—Links to `contact.cfm`
   - **About Us**—Links to `aboutus.cfm`
   - **Services**—Links to `services.cfm`
   - **For Sale**—Links to `forsale.cfm`

Figure 30.1
The template for the Retro's Cycles site in Dreamweaver.

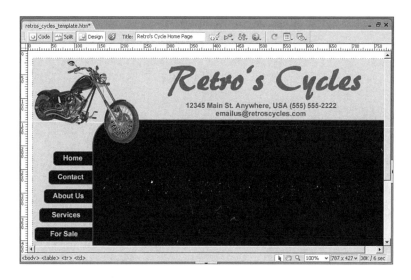

Figure 30.2
The Link field in the Property inspector should indicate the appropriate link for each rollover button.

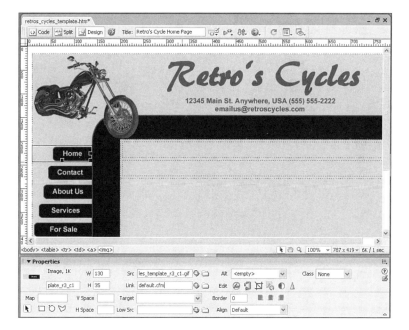

4. For each of the rollover buttons, add the appropriate Alternate text, as shown in the following list, by typing the value in the Alt field in the Property inspector. This assists users with disabilities who might visit the site.

- **Home**—Return to the Home Page
- **Contact**—Contact Us
- **About Us**—About Retro's Cycles

- **Services**—Learn About Our Services
- **For Sale**—Motorcycles We Offer for Sale

5. Click on the black image located in the main content area of the document and press the Delete key. Fireworks placed this image here as a placeholder. You want the background of your content area to match the background of the site, so deleting the image is necessary (see Figure 30.3).

Figure 30.3
The page content area is now gray.

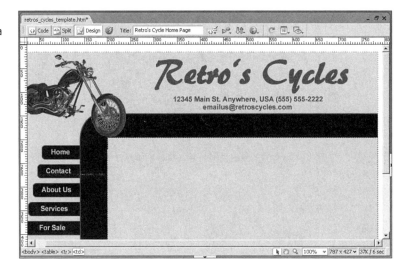

6. Next, you need to ensure that any content placed in the main content area does not run up against the black borders, so you need to add a table to the main content area to provide a buffer. From the menu bar, choose Insert, Table.

7. In the Table dialog box (see Figure 30.4), create a table that has two rows and one column and is 100% in width. Set the border thickness to 0, the cell padding to 5, and the cell spacing to 5, and then click OK.

8. Place your cursor inside the top row of the new table and click the Align Center button on the Property inspector.

9. Next, we need to ensure that the table always stays at the top of the main content area. To do this, select the table and press the left arrow key on your keyboard. This places your cursor inside the `<td>` tag that houses the table. In the Property inspector, select Top from the Vert drop-down options.

10. Save the page.

Figure 30.4
Insert a table into the main content area.

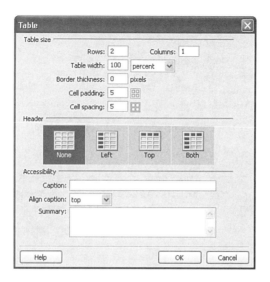

CREATING A DREAMWEAVER TEMPLATE AND CHILD PAGES

Now that you have made the necessary adjustments to the Fireworks template, you can easily turn the page into a Dreamweaver template and spawn child pages from it.

1. From the menu bar, choose File, Save As Template.

2. In the Save As Template dialog box, choose the Retro's Cycles site and save the template as `retros_cycles_template_final` (see Figure 30.5). Click OK to save the template. When asked to update links, click Yes.

Figure 30.5
Save the new Dreamweaver template.

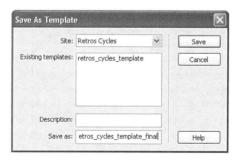

3. With the template saved, you need to add editable regions to the template. Select the top row of the table and choose Insert, Template Objects, Editable Region from the menu bar. In the New Editable Region dialog box, name the editable region `erTitle`, as shown in Figure 30.6. Click OK to close the dialog box.

Figure 30.6
Add a new editable region to the template.

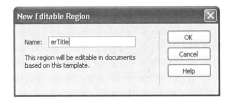

4. Select the bottom row of the table and add an additional editable region named `erPageContent`.

> **NOTE**
>
> Don't worry if the template starts to look a little disjointed. You can always click the `<body>` tag in the Tag Selector to force the template to realign itself.

5. Save the template.

6. Lastly, you need to create the child pages that are based on the template. From the menu bar, choose File, New.

7. In the New Document dialog box (see Figure 30.7), choose the Templates tab and select the Retro's Cycles site. Choose `retros_cycles_template_final` as the base for your new document and click Create.

Figure 30.7
Choose the appropriate template on which to base the page.

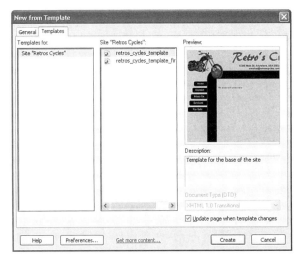

8. Choose File, Save from the menu bar and select ColdFusion Templates from the type menu. Save the page as `index.cfm` in the root of the site folder.

9. Following the same process, spawn a second page based on the template. In the Title field of the Document toolbar, type **Contact Retro's Cycles** (see Figure 30.8), choose ColdFusion templates from the type menu, and save the page as `contact.cfm`.

Figure 30.8
Change the title of
the page before you
save it.

30

10. Follow the same process to create pages saved as `aboutus.cfm`, `services.cfm`, and
    `forsale.cfm`. Set the titles for each page as follows:

    - `aboutus.cfm`—About Retro's Cycles
    - `services.cfm`—Our Services
    - `forsale.cfm`—Motorcyles For Sale

Now that you have the base pages for the site, you can be sure that any changes made to the
template are applied to each of your child pages.

BUILDING THE INVENTORY RECORDSET

One of the dynamic elements that the client has requested is a database-driven section of the
site that displays the motorcycles that are currently for sale. To accommodate this, a field
called `status` has been created in the `tbInventory` table. This field is set to record either a 0
or 1 value, with 0 being for sale and 1 being sold. Before you can display the motorcycles
that are for sale on the site, you need to build a recordset that contains only those motorcycles that are currently for sale.

1. In Dreamweaver, switch to or open the `forsale.cfm` page.

2. On the Server Behaviors panel, click the plus sign and choose Recordset from the
   menu. In the Recordset dialog box, type the name **rsForSale**, choose the
   `dsnRetrosCycles` data source, and choose the `tbInventory` table (see Figure 30.9).

Figure 30.9
Choose a name, con-
nection, and table for
your recordset.

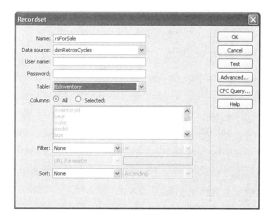

NOTE

Because the original page was developed in an HTML template and then converted to a ColdFusion page, you might need to reconfigure your site so that the test server address is set to http://localhost:8500/retroscycles before you can create your recordset. You can adjust this in the settings for your site.

3. Next, click the Selected radio button to limit the fields that are retrieved from the database. Using the Ctrl key and the mouse, select the `inventoryid`, `year`, `make`, `model`, and `color` fields. Set a filter that retrieves only records where the status is equal to the entered value of 0, as shown in Figure 30.10. Click OK to create the recordset.

Figure 30.10
Choose the appropriate field and set a filter for the recordset.

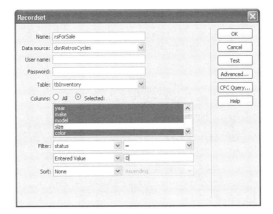

4. Save the page.

CREATING THE FOR SALE SECTION

To build out the For Sale section of the site, you need to have two pages. The first displays all the motorcycles in the `rsForSale` recordset. Each motorcycle listed contains a hyperlink to a second details page that provides the user with additional details about that specific motorcycle.

BUILDING THE FOR SALE DYNAMIC TABLE

Displaying the motorcycles that are for sale can become a difficult task as the inventory grows. Before the advent of dynamic web pages, each entry would have been manually added to a table, which can quickly become a tedious task. Dreamweaver, however, provides an easy way to retrieve the motorcycles that are for sale from the database and display them in a dynamic table. To create a dynamic table, follow these steps:

1. Place your cursor in the `erTitle` editable region. Type **Motorcycles For Sale** in the region. Highlight the text and click the Bold button on the Property inspector.

2. Next, you need to place a dynamic table in the page content section. Delete the `erPageContents` placeholder text and place your cursor in the `erPageContent` editable

region. Next, choose Insert, Application Objects, Dynamic Data, Dynamic Table from the menu bar.

3. In the Dynamic Table dialog box (see Figure 30.11), choose the `rsForSale` recordset and choose to show 10 records at a time. Set a border for the table to 1, the cell padding to 0, and the cell spacing to 2. Click OK to create the table.

Figure 30.11
Add a dynamic table to your page.

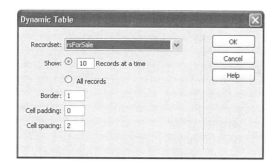

4. Select the table and choose Center in the Align field of the Property inspector. Select the top row in the new dynamic table and click the Align Center button and Bold button on the Property inspector.

5. Lastly, you need to create a hyperlink that enables the user to click on the `inventoryid` and view additional details about the motorcycle. Select the `inventoryid` element in the first cell of the table and type **forsale_details.cfm** in the Link field of the Property inspector. Click the folder icon next to the Link field and then click the Parameters button in the Select File dialog box.

6. In the Parameters dialog box (see Figure 30.12), type **inventoryid** in the Name field and click the lightning bolt icon in the Value field to choose a data binding.

Figure 30.12
Add the necessary parameter to be passed to the details page.

7. In the Dynamic Data dialog box, expand the `rsForSale` recordset and select `inventoryid`. Click OK to close the dialog box and click OK again to close the Parameters dialog box. Click OK one more time to close the Select File dialog box and the hyperlink is created in the page. As shown in Figure 30.13, the `inventoryid` data binding is now a hyperlink to the `forsaledetails` page.

Figure 30.13
The inventoryid data binding is now a hyperlink.

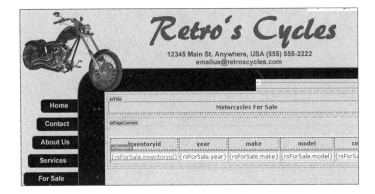

8. Save the page.

9. Click the F12 button on your keyboard to preview the page in your browser. As shown in Figure 30.14, the page now contains a data table that lists the motorcycles that are for sale.

Figure 30.14
The database records are now visible in the page.

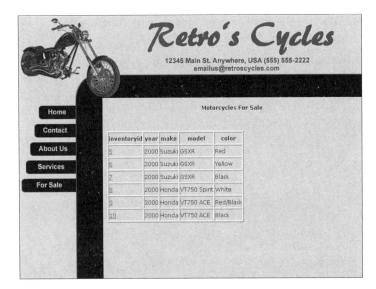

CREATING THE DETAILS PAGE

The last step in creating the For Sale section of the site is to create a details page that shows additional information about the specific motorcycle the user has chosen.

1. Create a new page based on the retros_cycles_template_final template. Change the page title to read "For Sale Details" and save the page as forsale_details.cfm.

2. Place your cursor in the erTitle editable region and type **Product Details**, select the text, and click the Bold button on the Property inspector.

3. Create a new recordset for the page by clicking the plus sign on the Server Behaviors panel and choosing Recordset from the menu. In the Recordset dialog box, shown in

Figure 30.15, name the recordset rsDetails, choose the dsnRetrosCycles data source, and select the tbInventory table.

Figure 30.15
Create a new recordset.

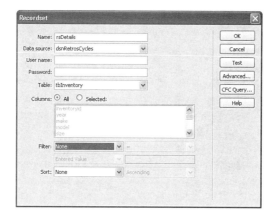

4. Next, select the following fields to be included in the recordset:

- Year
- Make
- Model
- Size
- Color
- ListPrice

5. Set a filter on the recordset that selects only the record where inventoryid equals the URL Parameter inventoryid, as shown in Figure 30.16. Click OK to create the recordset.

Figure 30.16
Choose which fields will be included in the recordset and set the filter to retrieve only the appropriate record.

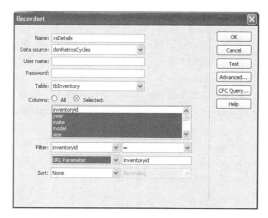

6. Place your cursor in the erPageContent editable region and add a table to the page that contains six rows, two columns, and a width of 450 pixels. Set the border to 1, the cell padding to 2, and the cell spacing to 0. Click OK to insert the table, as shown in Figure 30.17.

Figure 30.17
A new table has been added to the page.

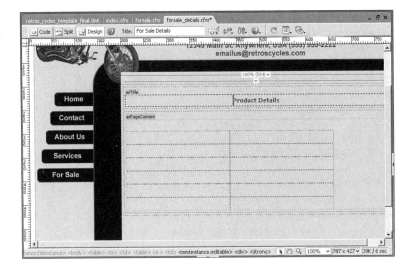

7. In the left column of the table, add the following values in each of the six cells:
   - Year:
   - Make:
   - Model:
   - Size:
   - Color:
   - Price:

8. Select the left column and click the Align Right and Bold buttons on the Property inspector. Set the width of the column to 50% by typing the value in the W field.

9. For each of the labels in the left column, drag the appropriate data binding from the Bindings panel into the corresponding cell in the right column. When completed, your page should look like Figure 30.18.

10. Select the listprice data binding and in the Bindings panel, scroll to the right, and drop down the format menu. From the menu, choose Currency, Dollar Format (see Figure 30.19).

11. Save the page.

12. Switch to the `forsale.cfm` page in Dreamweaver and press the F12 key on your keyboard to preview the page in your browser. Click on any of the inventory IDs and you are directed to the `forsale_details.cfm` page with the corresponding details (see Figure 30.20). Click back to return to the original table and test the other links.

Figure 30.18
Add the data bindings to the table.

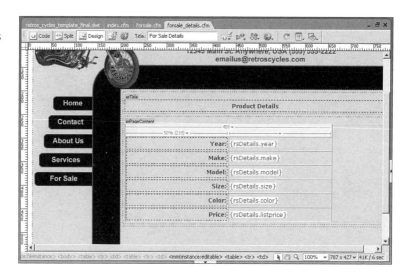

Figure 30.19
Assign the appropriate format for the list price.

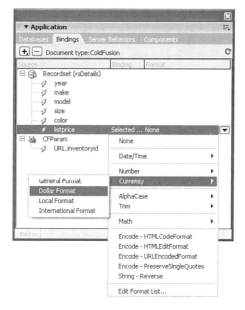

In this chapter, you have seen how to use a template created in Fireworks to create a Dreamweaver template and spawn child pages. In addition, you saw the process of creating recordsets that draw data from a database and created a set of pages that enable you to display items for sale and their corresponding details.

Figure 30.20
The page displays the appropriate details.

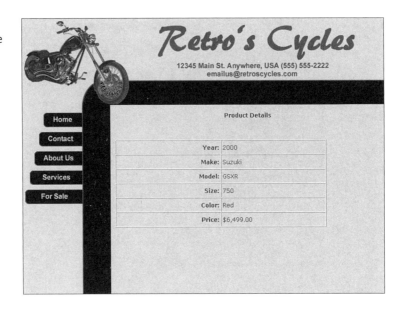

In the final section of the book, we take a look at how Contribute, Macromedia's content management tool, can be used to edit web pages without disrupting the site's structure.

TROUBLESHOOTING

When I view my page in the browser, no data is displayed. What went wrong?

The likely suspect is the recordset. If no data displays, it means that your recordset is empty. Take a look to see that all filters you applied are filtering on the correct field and that the filter is spelled correctly.

If the recordset is correct, check the link that you created on the For Sale page and be sure your parameters are spelled correctly and that the binding you chose is the appropriate binding.

When I make changes to my template and update the child pages, will it affect the dynamic data stored in my editable regions?

No. Dreamweaver templates do a really good job of working around dynamic data. Making updates to your templates should have no adverse effect on your data.

BEST PRACTICES—CREATING MASTER/DETAIL PAGE SETS MORE QUICKLY

In this chapter, you learned how to create two separate pages that display dynamic data. The first displayed a list of products for sale and the second displayed product details based on information passed to the page through the querystring. You walked through the process so you could learn the details of creating each one individually and better understand how each piece works.

Fortunately, creating these types of related pages doesn't have to be this long of a process. Dreamweaver has a built-in application object called a Master Detail Page Set that creates the basics of both pages for you. To use this tool, create a new dynamic page and create a recordset that draws the appropriate records for the master page. Next, choose Insert, Application Objects, Master Detail Page Set from the menu bar. The dialog box for the application object walks you through the process and actually creates both pages for you.

30

CONTRIBUTE 3

CHAPTER **31**

INTRODUCING CONTRIBUTE 3

In this chapter

31

INTRODUCING CONTRIBUTE

The newest application in the Macromedia Studio is Contribute 3.1. Contribute is a content management tool that enables those with little or no understanding of HTML to create and edit content stored in web pages. Using an intuitive browser interface, Contribute makes it easy for just about anyone who understands the basic concepts of a web browser and a word processor to make page updates.

From a web developer's point of view, Contribute can be a huge time saver because it enables you to delegate the content management aspect of website maintenance to others, freeing you up to build web applications.

Take a moment to look at the Contribute environment before getting into the nuts and bolts of connecting to a site, editing content, and managing pages.

THE CONTRIBUTE ENVIRONMENT

The Contribute environment is geared toward nontechnical users, so it is straightforward and simple to use. The environment is based on the web browser concept and enables users to navigate through the pages of their sites by clicking on hyperlinks, as well as using the traditional buttons and toolbars found in the most popular browsers. In addition, Contribute adds a set of panels that provide supplemental information for navigating pages and using Contribute.

THE CONTRIBUTE START PAGE

On startup, Contribute displays the start page shown in Figure 31.1. The start page provides quick links to sites you have configured and to tutorials for assistance in using Contribute.

Figure 31.1
The Contribute start page gives you access to your configured sites.

Just as you can with the start pages in the other Studio applications, you can disable the start page by checking the Don't Show Again check box.

MENU BAR

Similar to the other Studio applications, the Contribute menu bar offers access to all the various tools and functions that can be used to configure Contribute or manage your web pages. In addition to containing some items that are common to the other Studio applications, Contribute's menu bar also includes a couple of items that are unique to Contribute. The menu categories in Contribute 3.1 are as follows:

- **File Menu**—Enables you to perform document-related actions such as save, publish, preview in browser, and print.
- **Edit Menu**—Enables you to perform common editing tasks such as cut, copy, and paste, as well as create connections to Contribute websites and set program preferences.
- **View Menu**—Enables you to choose which page elements are visible in the workspace, as well as perform browser-related functionality such as back and forward.
- **Bookmarks Menu**—Enables you to bookmark pages within your site for quick access and editing.
- **Insert Menu**—Enables you to insert elements such as tables, hyperlinks, images, and rich media content. Also provides access to eCommerce tools via PayPal.
- **Format Menu**—Provides access to editing tools for text, images, and page properties.
- **Table Menu**—Enables you to insert and adjust tables placed in your web pages.
- **Help Menu**—Provides access to common help functionality as well as the Contribute Support Center.

SIDEBAR

The Contribute sidebar, shown in Figure 31.2, provides access to two different panels, each of which can be minimized individually.

The following panels are located in the sidebar:

- **Pages panel**—Provides access to page information as well as one-click access to recently edited pages.
- **How Do I panel**—Provides quick access to help topics and step-by-step instructions for common tasks.

Although the sidebar provides easy access to help topics for novice users, it also takes up valuable real estate. To close the sidebar, choose View, Sidebar from the menu bar. This command toggles the sidebar on and off.

31

Figure 31.2
The sidebar provides access to the Pages and How Do I panels.

BROWSE/EDIT WORKSPACE

The majority of the Contribute environment is dominated by the Browser/Edit workspace (see Figure 31.3), which enables you to navigate the pages in your configured sites and edit their content in a single, easy-to-use interface.

Figure 31.3
The Browser/Edit workspace is where most of the work is done in Contribute.

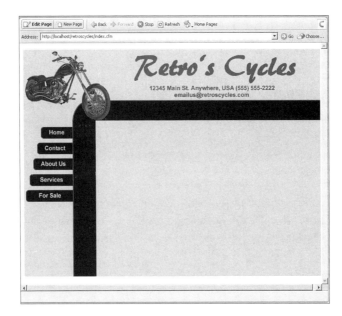

CONTRIBUTE TOOLBAR

The Contribute toolbar, located at the top of the workspace, contains task-oriented buttons that enable you to either browse or edit the pages in the site. When a page is not being edited, the Contribute toolbar displays buttons that focus on the navigation of the pages, such as Back, Forward, Stop, and Refresh. In addition, the address of the current page is displayed in the Address bar (see Figure 31.4).

Figure 31.4
The Contribute toolbar displays browser buttons when in browser mode.

When the Edit Page button is clicked, the Contribute bar changes to display buttons that assist with the various editing and save functions (see Figure 31.5).

Figure 31.5
When a page is being edited, the Contribute toolbar changes to display common editing tasks.

Switching between browsing and editing mode is done with a single click of a button. When in browsing mode, clicking the Edit Page button switches the workspace to editing mode. When in editing mode, clicking the Cancel button switches you back to browsing mode, after first confirming that any changes made to the draft will be lost unless saved.

CONTRIBUTE WORKSPACE

The Contribute workspace serves as both a browser and inline editor to make editing pages as simple as possible. Content editors can use the browser mode to find the page they want to edit and then switch to edit mode to make adjustments to that page. When in browser mode, the workspace renders the page just as the most popular browsers do (see Figure 31.6).

When the content editor switches to edit mode, however, the page becomes an editable document. If the page is based on a Dreamweaver template, the editable regions are indicated and the template regions remain locked, as shown in Figure 31.7.

> **NOTE**
>
> If you open a page that is located in a site that is not configured for use in Contribute, the page is displayed in the workspace and you can make edits to it, but Contribute allows you to save it as only a draft. Until the site is configured for use in Contribute, you cannot publish the changes.

31

31

Figure 31.6
When in browser mode, the workspace renders the web page just as a browser would.

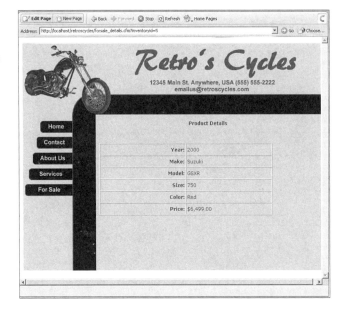

Editable region indicated by blue border

Figure 31.7
The Contribute workspace adjusts based on whether a document is being viewed or edited.

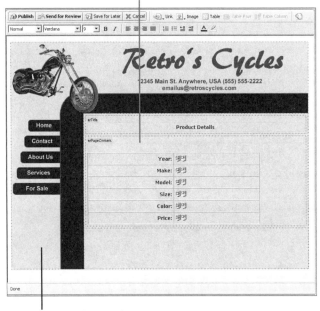

Noneditable region controlled by template

STATUS BAR

Located at the bottom of the workspace, the status bar behaves exactly like a browser status bar. It displays the status of the page loading process, the hyperlink targets when a link is rolled over, and the results of any JavaScript behaviors that modify the status bar.

CREATING A WEBSITE CONNECTION

The first step in configuring Contribute is to connect to an existing website. However, before you create a connection to the site, the administrator of that site has to send you the proper authentication information. The administrator might send this information in the form of a Website Connection Key sent to you via email, or he might give you the user ID, password, and other appropriate connection information required to set up the connection. Without the Connection Key, you can't publish pages to the site from your workstation.

If the administrator sends a connection key, setting up the site is as simple as double-clicking on the key file. When activated, the key file automatically configures the site settings in your copy of Contribute and you are ready to edit pages. If, however, the administrator chooses to just send configuration information, you have to manually create a connection to the site. Keep in mind that you don't need anything other than your copy of Contribute and the connection information to edit pages. When you have these two elements, you're ready to begin editing and publishing.

If you are the site's administrator, the process of creating a connection is started by choosing Edit, My Connections from the menu bar. In the My Connections dialog box, shown in Figure 31.8, click the Create button to start the wizard.

Figure 31.8
The My Connections dialog box enables you to manage your website connections.

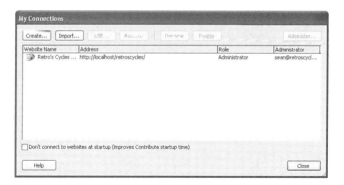

Contribute's Connection Wizard (see Figure 31.9) is a step-by-step guide for entering the appropriate information for connecting to a site. The Connection Wizard's welcome screen reminds you that clicking on a Connection Key accomplishes the same results as stepping through the wizard.

Figure 31.9
Contribute's
Connection Wizard
steps you through
the process of
creating a site.

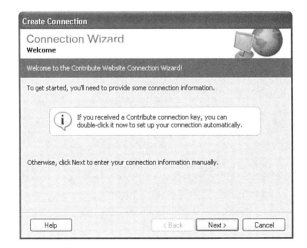

The next step is to input the URL of the root for your website, as shown in Figure 31.10. This enables Contribute to locate the pages of your site and manage new links created via Contribute.

Figure 31.10
Type your site's URL.

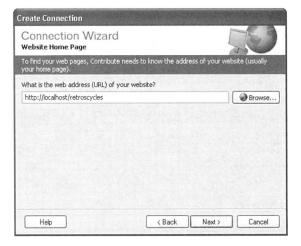

The wizard also enables you to select from a variety of connection options (see Figure 31.11). FTP is the most popular option for sites hosted remotely, whereas Local/Network is the usual option for those working in a networked environment.

Figure 31.11
Contribute offers multiple ways to connect to your site.

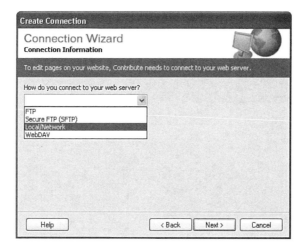

In the next step, you are asked to enter your name and email address to help Contribute identify which changes were made by you (see Figure 31.12). The username and email address are stored for each site user to ensure that all changes to the site can be tracked.

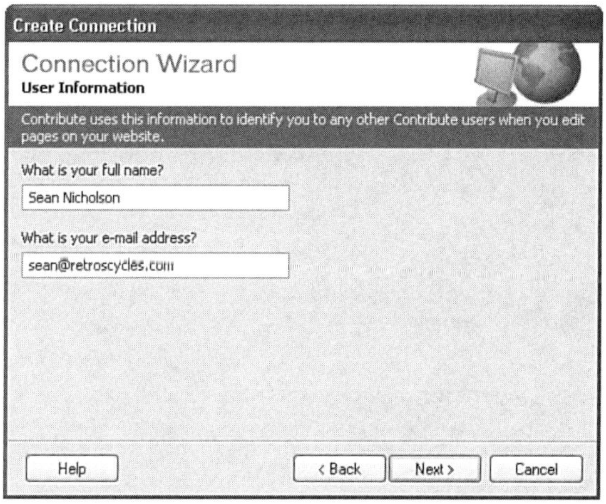

Figure 31.12
By storing the name and email of each user, Contribute attributes site changes to the appropriate user.

After you enter your name and email, you need to choose the role that you will perform in managing the site. By default, Contribute offers the roles of Administrator, Writer, or Publisher (see Figure 31.13). After the site is created, however, Administrators can create and configure additional roles based on their needs.

Figure 31.13
By default, Contribute offers the roles of Administrator, Writer, and Publisher.

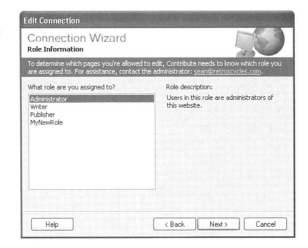

The three default roles offered by Contribute have the following attributes:

- **Administrator**—Able to create new roles, modify existing roles, add users to the site, and send connection information to those users.

- **Publisher**—Able to create, edit, and publish pages to the site.

- **Publisher**—Able to create and edit pages, but does not have the authorization to publish pages.

After you have completed all the necessary information, Contribute enables you to review your entries and either accept them or proceed backward through the steps in the wizard to make any needed adjustments (see Figure 31.14).

Figure 31.14
Contribute summarizes your entries into the wizard for your review.

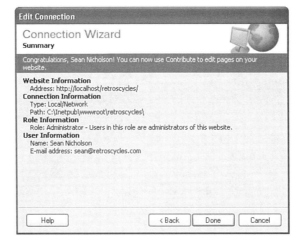

Upon completion of the wizard, the My Connections dialog box displays the site you created. From the My Connections dialog, you can edit, rename, disable, administer, and even delete connections to sites.

MANAGING FILES

Contribute not only enables you to manage the content stored inside your pages, but to add and remove files from your site as well.

LOCATING AN EXISTING PAGE

The easiest way to find a page in your site is to navigate to it with the browser interface. At times, however, you cannot navigate to a page that you have created, so Contribute offers the Choose button located on the Contribute toolbar. Clicking the Choose button brings up the Choose File on Website dialog box, which enables you to browse to a file located in the site (see Figure 31.15). If you know the URL of the page, you can also type it directly into the Address bar.

Figure 31.15
The Choose File on Website dialog box enables you to find files that cannot be linked to.

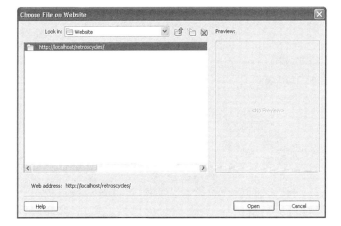

NOTE

The Choose button is available only when in browser mode. When you begin to edit a page, the Choose button disappears and you have to either publish or cancel editing the page to view the button again.

CREATING A NEW PAGE

As your site becomes more popular and/or you identify new content that needs to be included, you'll want to expand by adding new pages. Contribute enables you to not only add blank pages, but also derive pages from an existing layout by either copying an existing page or by building a new page based on a Dreamweaver template. Choose File, New Page from the menu bar or click the New Page button on the Contribute bar to open the New Page dialog box, shown in Figure 31.16, and select from the various options.

Figure 31.16
The New Page dialog box enables you to spawn blank pages, copies of pages, or even pages based on Dreamweaver templates.

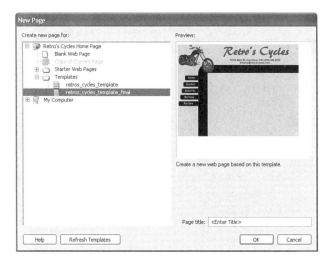

After you add a new title for the page and click OK, Contribute automatically opens the new page in edit mode, allowing you to add new content (see Figure 31.17).

Figure 31.17
The new page is ready for content.

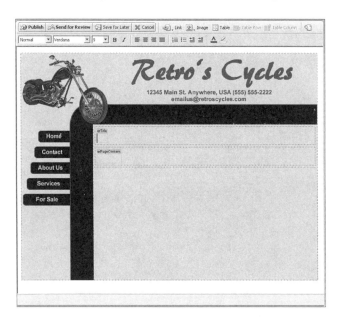

DELETING PAGES

Removing pages from your site is also a relatively simple process in Contribute. The first step is to either navigate to the page or open the page by selecting it with the Choose button. When the page is visible in the browser, select File, Actions, Delete Page. You are prompted to confirm that you want to permanently remove the page from your site (see Figure 31.18).

Figure 31.18
Before deleting a page from the site, Contribute prompts you for a confirmation.

When you click OK, the page is deleted and no longer accessible via your site.

CAUTION

Before deleting a page, double check to be sure that no other pages in the site link to it. This helps you avoid broken links on your site.

TIP

If you want to keep certain users from deleting files, you can restrict their access to times when they're defining the settings for their roles. See Chapter 32, "Administering Contribute 3," for more information about the creation and restriction of different roles.

EDITING CONTENT

Content management is really where Contribute's strengths lie. In developing Contribute, Macromedia has created a simple, easy-to-use application that allows anyone who is comfortable with a word processor to add and edit content without having to understand HTML and other coding languages. The types of content that can be included in Contribute-generated pages include text, images, tables, hyperlinks, and even rich media content such as Flash movies. Best of all, your content editors don't have to worry about causing problems with your page design because you can restrict to which areas of the design they have access by basing your pages on Dreamweaver templates.

WORKING WITHIN DREAMWEAVER TEMPLATES

Using Dreamweaver templates to create your Contribute pages doesn't require any extra steps or configuration. When you create a connection to the site, Contribute scans the folder structure and, if present, recognizes the Templates folder as the location for Dreamweaver templates. All files located in that folder that use the .dwt extension are treated as Dreamweaver templates, and Contribute adheres to the various editable regions that were established when the template was created.

EDITING TEXT

Editing text in Contribute is very similar to editing text in many of today's popular word processor applications. Simply place your cursor in the appropriate region to add content by typing. In addition, the formatting tools available on the Contribute toolbar (see Figure 31.19) enable you to apply styles, select font face, color, and size, and apply bold and italics. In addition, you can apply formatting to paragraphs of text by using the various align and indent buttons, as well as create numbered and bulleted lists.

Figure 31.19
The Contribute toolbar provides access to a variety of text editing tools.

Contribute also enables you to copy and paste text from many of the major word processors while retaining as much of the formatting and text style as possible.

> **NOTE**
> Although Contribute does a great job of formatting text that is copied and pasted from word processors, maintaining font appearance is often a challenge. If the font used in the document is not one of the standard fonts available to web pages (Arial, Courier, Geneva, Times New Roman, and Verdana), then Contribute adjusts the font to the default font for the web page. In addition, custom text effects such as shadows, embossing, or outlining do not display in Contribute.

ADDING IMAGES

Adding images to a page in Contribute is a snap as well. Just click the Insert Image button on the Contribute toolbar and select whether to add the image from your computer or from another website. When adding the image from the images folder of your site, Contribute creates a relative link to the image based on the location of the image compared to the page and the directory structure of the site.

If, however, you choose to insert the image from another website, Contribute creates a copy of the image from the other website and places it in your site's images folder. The link to the image then points to the local copy.

> **NOTE**
> When linking to an image on a website, the site must be one configured within Contribute. Contribute does not accommodate linking to images stored on external websites.

Depending on which option you choose, Contribute presents you with a different dialog box to locate your image. The Select Image dialog box, shown in Figure 31.20, is activated when you choose to insert an image from the images folder of your local site. Using this dialog box, you can navigate to the file, select it, and click Select. The image is then inserted into your page.

Figure 31.20
The Select Image dialog box enables you to navigate to an image located within your site.

Inserting an image from a website, however, activates the Choose Image on Website dialog box (see Figure 31.21), where you can navigate to the images folder of another Contribute site.

Figure 31.21
The Choose Image on Website dialog box enables you to link to an image stored in another website.

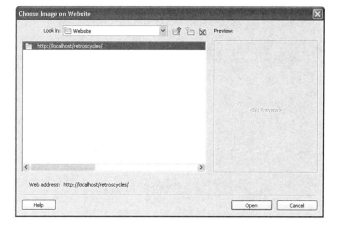

After an image has been added to the page, selecting it activates a new set of tools on the Contribute toolbar, as shown in Figure 31.22. These tools enable you to scale, rotate, and crop the image from within Contribute, as well as sharpen the image and adjust the shading.

Figure 31.22
Contribute adds tools to the Contribute toolbar when an image is selected.

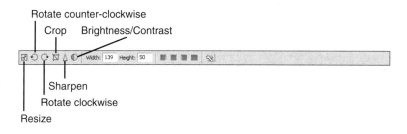

31

In addition, double-clicking on the image opens the Image Properties dialog box, shown in Figure 31.23, which enables you to adjust a variety of attributes.

Figure 31.23
In the Image Properties dialog box you can adjust the display attributes of any image inserted into a page.

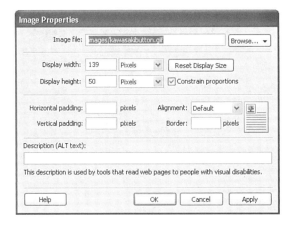

NOTE

Adjusting the attributes of an image does not modify the image itself. Therefore, inserting a large image into your page and changing the attributes so it appears smaller does not affect the image's actual file size. If you need to resize an image, it's best to edit the image with Fireworks first and then insert it into your page.

ADDING TABLES

Using Contribute to add tables to a document is simple as well. A content editor can place the cursor at the desired insertion point and click the Table button on the toolbar to activate the Insert Table dialog box, shown in Figure 31.24, to quickly add a table to a page.

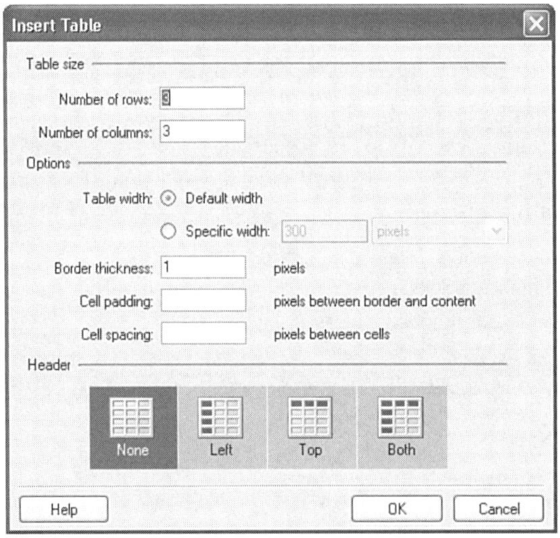

Figure 31.24
Use the Insert Table dialog box to add tables to your pages.

The dialog box enables you to adjust the number of rows and columns in the table, as well as specify the table width, border attributes, and cell padding and spacing. In addition, you can choose whether to indicate a particular row or column as a header by shading it differently from the rest.

CREATING HYPERLINKS

Contribute can help you create a variety of hyperlinks to items such as pages within your site, email addresses, and even files located on your computer. Click the Link button on the Contribute toolbar and choose from the various link types. The Insert Link dialog box helps you locate the resource and apply any attributes that are specific to that type of link (see Figure 31.25).

Figure 31.25
The Insert Link dialog box enables you to create hyperlinks to pages within your site or to external pages in other sites.

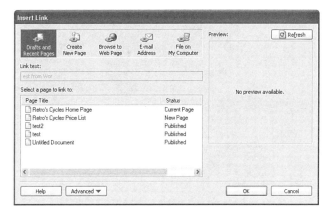

SAVING CHANGES TO PAGES

After your page content has been edited and the appropriate page elements added, Contribute offers a variety of options for saving the changes. Rather than simply save the page changes and have the page become live immediately, you can choose from the following options:

- **Publish**—When you click the Publish button on the Contribute toolbar, the changes are immediately visible to site visitors. When a page has been published successfully, Contribute notifies you that of the success by displaying the notice shown in Figure 31.26.

Figure 31.26
This notice indicates that the page has been successfully published.

- **Send for Review**—Sending the page for review enables you to either send a link to the page to someone via email or send an actual draft of the page to another Contribute user. When you choose this option, the Send for Review dialog box, shown in Figure 31.27, lets you designate the reviewer and add an additional description of the changes to the document for his or her review.

Figure 31.27
The Send for Review dialog box enables you to send a copy of the page or a link to the page to another person.

- **Save for Later**—This creates a draft of the page and enables you to revisit the page later to make additional edits. Saving the page for later has no effect on the actual live version of the page. When a draft is created, an entry for that draft is added to the Draft Console in the Pages panel, as shown in Figure 31.28.

Figure 31.28
The Draft Console displays links to all pages that remain unpublished.

- **Cancel**—This option allows you to cancel all changes and close the page.

As you can see, using Contribute to edit and manage pages is extremely easy. Although the program might not have the complex authoring tools contained in Dreamweaver, it provides quick, easy access to content editing features that make updating a website an easy task for just about anyone.

TROUBLESHOOTING

I am having trouble creating a connection to my server. What can I do to resolve the problems?

If your website is located on a Unix server, be sure that the URL to the site uses the proper case. For instance, ftp://ftp.retroscycles.com/mysite on a Unix server is not the same as ftp://ftp.retroscycles.com/MySite (note the differences in capitalization). To avoid possible issues like this, be sure that the case used in the URL is the same case used in naming the folder.

When installing Contribute, should I use Transition Mode or Compatibility Mode?

This depends on whether or not any of your users will be using earlier versions of Contribute. If you have users who will be using Contribute 1 or 2 to access the site, you should install using Transition Mode because of compatibility issues between Contribute 3.1 and earlier versions. If, however, all of your users are using Contribute 3.1, you should use Compatibility mode.

How can I apply a cascading style sheet in Contribute?

Contribute does not currently support linking to style sheets. Instead, when you create a new style in a document, Contribute embeds that style directly into the document.

If, however, you are using Dreamweaver templates as the base for your site, you can attach the style sheet to that template. All pages based on the template include the style sheet and those styles are available within Contribute.

BEST PRACTICES—CONTENT REVIEWS PRIOR TO PUBLISHING

No matter how long you have been developing websites or how careful you are in creating content, mistakes always occur during the process. Whether it's a simple misspelling or a broken link, mistakes are something that can seriously affect end users, so you should do everything you can to minimize them.

For this reason, it's always a good idea to have someone else review your work prior to publishing it. Contribute makes this process easy by making it possible to send a page to another user for review. As you create your content management system and offer your clients or co-workers the ability to generate their own content, pass this concept on to them and express how important it is that someone else review their work before it goes live on a site.

In addition, a second review of the content should be done after it has been transferred to the production server. Even if it's just clicking through the links to ensure that they all function and reading over the content one last time, the process of checking your work can improve the end-user experience and ensure that your work is functional and accurate.

31

ADMINISTERING CONTRIBUTE 3

In this chapter

ADMINISTERING A CONTRIBUTE WEBSITE

When you are familiar with the Contribute workspace and have created a connection to your website, the next aspect of Contribute you should take a look at is the administration features. Although Contribute is a relatively simple program to use, Macromedia includes powerful administrative functions that enable you to control who has access to what pages via Contribute, what functions they can perform, and whether or not Contribute maintains copies of past pages to accommodate rollbacks. To start a closer look at the administrative features, select Edit, Administer Websites, Website Name from the menu bar.

USERS AND ROLES

The main idea behind Contribute is to distribute the workload of editing and maintaining the content of a website. To accomplish that goal, you need to ensure that other content providers and editors have access to the pages. On the other hand, you want to keep unauthorized users from accessing the pages and ensure that those who are allowed to edit can make changes to the site only when appropriate.

By default, Contribute has three user levels:

■ **Administrator**—Administrators have full control over the site including access to the administrative features. Administrators can make changes to pages and publish those changes immediately.

■ **Publisher**—Publishers do not have access to the administrative features, but can edit and publish changes at will.

■ **Writer**—Writers can make changes to content, but cannot publish them. Instead, writers must send their pages to a Publisher or Administrator to have that person review the changes and publish them if appropriate.

The Users and Roles category in the Administer Website dialog box, shown in Figure 32.1, enables you to view who is currently assigned to the various roles within your site. In addition, this category provides functionality to define custom roles, edit existing roles, and allow other users access to the site.

EDITING ROLE SETTINGS

By selecting an existing role and clicking the Edit Role Settings button in the Administer Website dialog box, you can access the various settings that control what someone assigned to that role can and can't do in the site.

TIP

Adjusting the settings for a user role affects every user who is assigned to that role. Before making changes to the default groups, be sure that everyone in that particular role will be able to continue working as expected after the changes are applied.

Figure 32.1
The Users and Roles category enables you to manage your users and their authority levels.

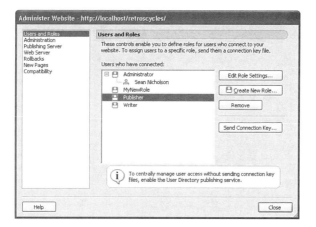

GENERAL SETTINGS

The General category of the Edit Settings dialog box (see Figure 32.2) is where you determine whether or not users in that role can publish files. In addition, you can create a role description to help other administrators when assigning roles. You can also establish the default home page for users assigned to this role.

Figure 32.2
The General settings enable you to determine whether this type of user can publish pages.

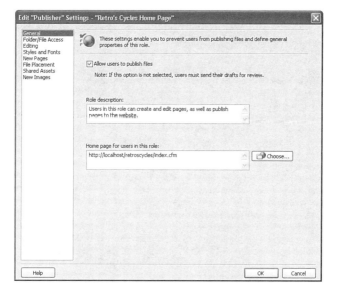

FOLDER/FILE ACCESS

The File/Folder Access category (see Figure 32.3) lets you specify which files and folders can be accessed by users assigned to this role. This is helpful when working with an organization where individual departments edit their own sections of a site. This category also enables you to determine whether users in this role can delete files from the site.

Figure 32.3

The Folder/File Access category lets you restrict access at the folder level.

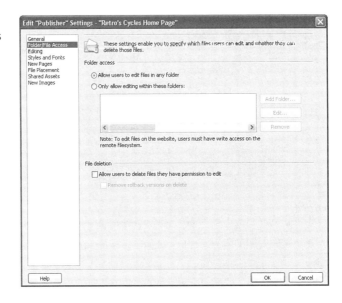

EDITING

In the Editing category, shown in Figure 32.4, you can clearly define what page elements a user is allowed to edit. For instance, by adjusting this category, you can determine whether users can make changes to form elements and custom scripts, decide whether users can insert images, and even implement rules such as requiring <ALT> text for images.

Figure 32.4

The Editing category allows you to clearly define restrictions for each role with regards to editing pages.

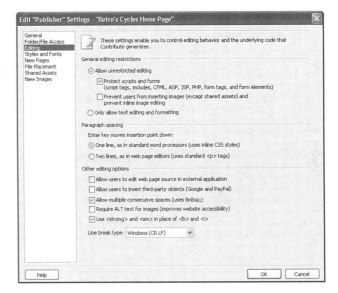

Styles and Fonts

The way that font styles are applied to the pages of the site can be adjusted in the Styles and Fonts category. The Styles and Fonts category, shown in Figure 32.5, enables you to specify whether styles or the <Font> tag is used to assign a font face to text. In addition, you can determine whether or not the various text styling tools such as the Styles and Font and Size drop-down menus, as well as the bold and italic buttons, are available to the user in the Contribute toolbar.

Figure 32.5
The Styles and Fonts category lets you restrict what text styling tools the user group can access.

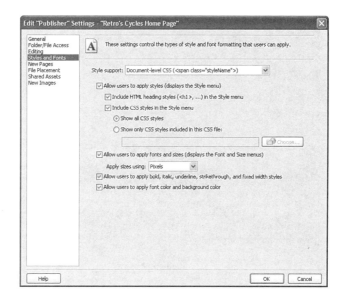

New Pages

The New Pages category, shown in Figure 32.6, is used to determine whether or not the user group is allowed to create new pages within the site and by what means. In addition, you can use this category to maintain the continuity of your page layout by requiring that new pages be based on a copy of a specific page or Dreamweaver template.

File Placement

The File Placement category, shown in Figure 32.7, enables you to specify where certain types of files are to be located within the site. For instance, when a user inserts a file from a website into a page, Contribute makes a copy of that image and places it in the local site. This category specifies where Contribute should place that copy. This category also controls the placement of PDF and FlashPaper files that are generated from within Contribute. In addition, if you want to restrict whether content editors can add files such as PDF documents or Word documents to the site, you can choose to reject linked files that exceed a specific file size.

Figure 32.6
The New Pages dialog box lets you determine whether or not new pages can be created and in what manner.

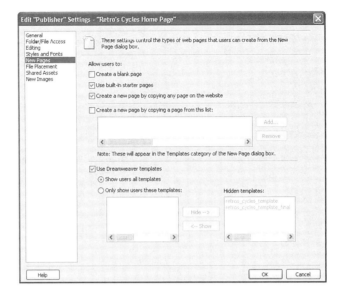

Figure 32.7
The File Placement category specifies where certain types of files should be placed.

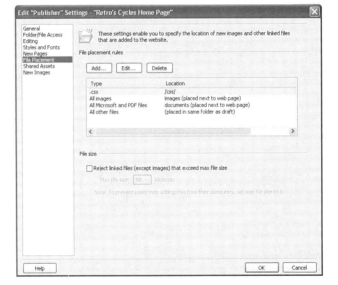

SHARED ASSETS

The Shared Assets category, shown in Figure 32.8, gives users access to objects such as images, Flash movies, and Dreamweaver library items. When items are added to the list, users can quickly access them and add them to their pages by using Contribute's shared assets list.

Figure 32.8
The Shared Assets dialog box enables you to edit the list of images and objects that are available to all users via the shared assets list.

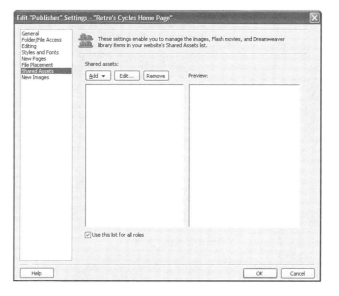

NEW IMAGES

The last category of settings for a specific role is the New Images category, shown in Figure 32.9. In this category, you can enable or disable the built-in image processing tool within Contribute that enables users to easily resize images and adjust for quality levels. In addition, you can maintain controls over bandwidth usage and download times by limiting the size of images that can be placed into a page.

CREATING NEW ROLES

One of the great features of Contribute is the capability to define custom editing roles to fit the needs of your client or organization. To create a new role, copy an existing role and then add or remove restrictions based on the appropriate editing levels of the users who will be members of the group.

Figure 32.9
The New Images category enables you to place restrictions on the images that are placed into pages.

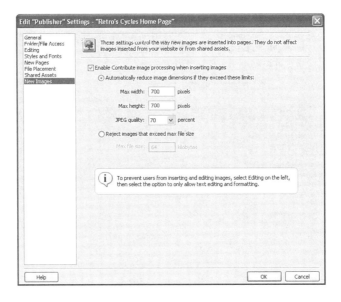

The first step in creating a new role is to click the Create New Role button in the Users and Roles section of the Administer Website dialog. Contribute asks you on which existing role you would like to base the new role and to provide a name for the new role (see Figure 32.10). The new role is then added to the list of roles and you can edit the role settings to meet your needs.

Figure 32.10
The Create New Role dialog box enables you to designate a new role within your website administration schema.

SENDING CONNECTION KEYS

As mentioned in the previous chapter, the easiest way for a user to create a connection to a website is to click on a connection key sent via email. The administrator of the site is in charge of sending these connection keys and does so by clicking the Send Connection Key button in the Users and Roles category of the Administer Website dialog box.

When the button is clicked, Contribute starts the Connection Key Wizard, shown in Figure 32.11, which begins by asking whether the current connection settings are appropriate for the target user. The connection settings that are sent include how the user accesses the site, the path to the site folder, and other necessary connection information such as FTP site and username/password. If everyone in your workgroup accesses the site in the same way (such as via a network drive), the standard connection settings are usually fine. If, however, your workgroup members access the site in different ways (for example, some via a network drive and some via FTP), then you need to customize the connection settings.

Figure 32.11
The Connection Key Wizard helps you send a connection key to a user that grants access to the site.

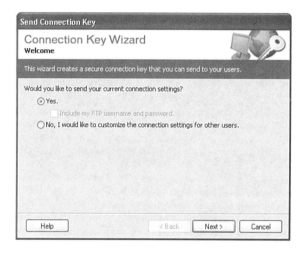

The next step in the wizard asks you to specify what role the user should be assigned. From this dialog, you can choose from the existing roles, including any custom roles that you have created (see Figure 32.12).

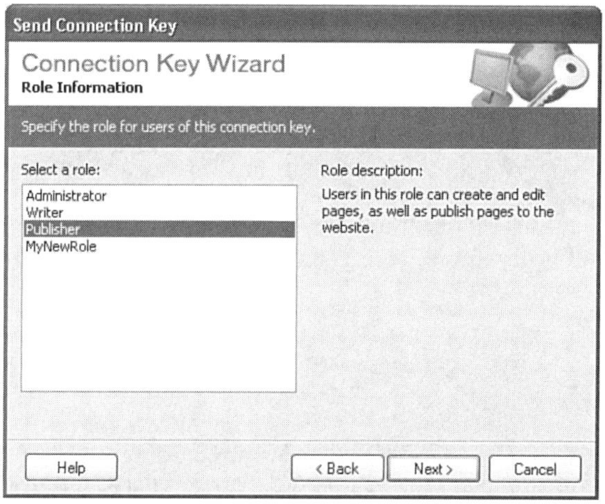

Figure 32.12
Choose a role that the target user will be assigned.

NOTE

> Each connection key that you create is valid for only a specific role. Therefore, you need to send one connection key to your publishers and another to your writers.

When you have chosen a role, the next step is to determine whether the connection key will be sent via email or placed on the local machine (see Figure 32.13). If the user will be making edits on a different machine, emailing the key is the best method.

Figure 32.13
Select a delivery method for the new key.

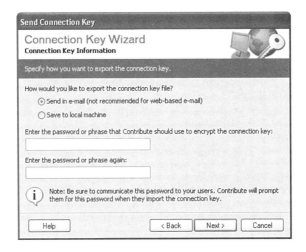

TIP

> Pay close attention to the warning to not send connection keys to web-based email accounts. Some web-based accounts add code to the connection key, rendering it useless. For details on the issue, check out the Macromedia tech note about this topic at http://www.macromedia.com/go/tn_18734.

In addition to choosing the delivery method, you need to type a password or phrase to be used as the base of the key encryption. After the connection key is sent to the user, you need to communicate the password or phrase so that the user can activate the key.

The final step in the wizard is to confirm the information and click Done. When the wizard is completed, an email is generated from your default mail client, which can then be sent to the user.

ADMINISTRATION

The Administration category of the Administer Websites dialog box, shown in Figure 32.14, enables you to select the contact email address for the primary administrator of the site, as well as set an administrative password. If necessary, this category also enables you to remove all administration settings from the site.

Figure 32.14
Add the contact email address and set the Administrator password.

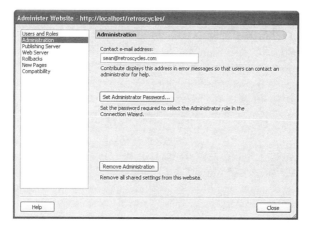

NOTE

Be sure to establish an administrative password for your site. As with the administration of any information, a strong password reduces the possibility of unauthorized access and tampering.

CAUTION

Removing the administration from the site effectively disconnects everyone who has authorization to the site. All previously established keys are voided and all custom user roles are deleted.

UNDERSTANDING PUBLISHING SERVICES

If your client or organization uses a network infrastructure that uses LDAP or Active Directory to manage user accounts, you can leverage either of those services to manage access to Contribute sites as well. Contribute 3.1 offers an optional service called Publishing Services that, when installed, enables you to assign roles to network user accounts. Publishing Services can be enabled via the Publishing Services category of the Administer Website dialog box (see Figure 32.15). If you use this option, you no longer need to create user accounts in Contribute. Instead, you assign roles to users from the LDAP or Active Directory.

To enable Publishing Services, Contribute requires that the services be installed on a Java Application server that is accessible across the network. After the Publishing Services are enabled, Contribute is capable of performing additional services such as logging website errors and emailing administrators and publishers when writers create drafts that require their attention.

Figure 32.15
The Enable Publishing
Server dialog box
allows you to enable
the services and man-
age users from a net-
work user directory.

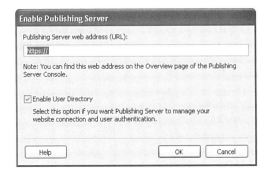

TIP

For complete details on the installation and configuration of Contribute's Publishing
Services, take a look at the Publishing Services home page located at
http://www.macromedia.com/software/webpublishingsystem/cps/.

WEB SERVER CONFIGURATION

The Web Server category of the Administer Website dialog box enables you to configure
Contribute settings that affect how the application interacts with your Web Server application. If you use multiple addresses to access your site, you can add them to the list using the
Web Addresses tab shown in Figure 32.16. Contribute enables your users to edit the pages
using any of the addresses in the list.

Figure 32.16
The Web Addresses
tab lets you add any
additional URLs that
you use to access
the site.

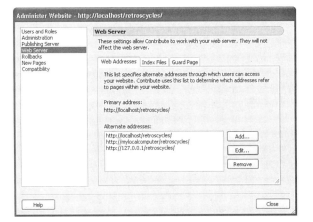

The Index Files tab, shown in Figure 32.17, enables you to indicate which filenames and
extensions should be considered index files to be displayed by the web server as the default
page in a directory.

Figure 32.17
The Index Files tab enables you to indicate what files and extensions should be treated as index pages.

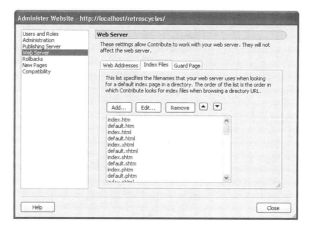

Finally, the Guard Page tab, shown in Figure 32.18, lets you specify a page that restricts access to files placed in administrative folders. This keeps intruders from viewing the contents of folders such as the _mm and MMWIP folders, which store drafts of documents and administrative alerts regarding the status of those drafts. This guard page serves as the index page for a folder, letting visitors know that they are not allowed to view the files contained in a specific folder.

Figure 32.18
The Guard Page tab allows you to specify the filename of the guard page that prevents directory indexing

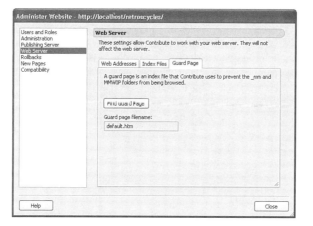

TIP

To ensure that unauthorized users cannot access the _mm and MMWIP folders, be sure to create a `default.htm` page (or whatever you set for your guard file page name) and place a copy of the page in each of these folders. The page can either be blank or contain text that lets the visitor know access is restricted to the contents of the folder.

SETTING UP ROLLBACKS

Rollbacks are saved copies of previous versions of a page that enable you to return a page to a state prior to the last published version. Basically, they serve as backups in case something goes wrong in the publishing process or the content that is published is incorrect. The Rollbacks category of the Administer Website dialog box (see Figure 32.19) enables you to turn rollbacks on or off, as well as indicate how many versions of a page should be maintained if rollbacks are enabled.

Figure 32.19
In the Rollbacks category you can choose whether or not Contribute maintains previous versions of pages that are edited.

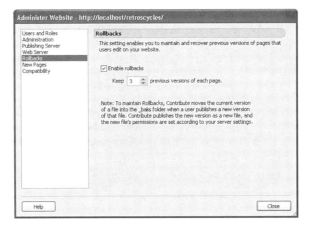

NOTE

About the only drawback to enabling rollbacks is the fact that the backups require storage space. However, setting rollbacks to a reasonable level, such as three levels back, shouldn't require a substantial amount of space unless you work in a large corporate environment where major page changes are made on a frequent basis. If your organization has a comprehensive backup plan, it is probably a good idea for you to discuss the level of rollbacks allowed to ensure that your workgroup can return pages to a previous state if necessary.

NEW PAGE SETTINGS

The New Pages category, shown in Figure 32.20, enables you to establish the default page encoding for your site, as well as the default file extension. Depending on what platform you use to develop your site (such as HTML, ASP, ColdFusion, and so on) you need to adjust the extension so that new pages automatically reflect the correct platform.

NOTE

For more details on document encoding, check out the World Wide Web Consortium (W3C) discussion on the topic at http://www.w3.org/TR/REC-html40/charset.html.

Figure 32.20
The New Pages category enables you to establish the default encoding and file extension for any new pages.

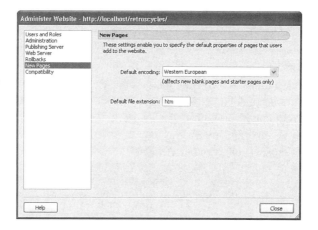

CHOOSING A COMPATIBILITY MODE

The Compatibility category, shown in Figure 32.21, lets you choose between the Transition Mode or the Compatibility Mode.

Figure 32.21
The Compatibility category enables you to choose between Transition Mode and Compatibility Mode.

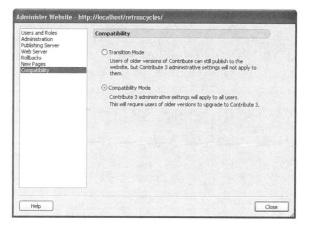

If you have users who will be accessing your site with Contribute 1 or Contribute 2, you need to run in Transition Mode because some features in Contribute 3 are not compatible with the earlier versions. If, however, all your users are running on Contribute 3, you should select Compatibility Mode to take full advantage of all the features available in Contribute 3.

TROUBLESHOOTING

My users are receiving permission errors when they try to publish a page. Where do I adjust their permissions in Contribute?

Read/Write access to a folder is not something that is controlled from within Contribute. A user who wants to publish a document must have the correct authorization level in Contribute to begin the publishing process. However, if an attempt to publish a page results in a permissions-related error, it usually means that the user doesn't have permission to write to the folder on the server. This type of permission must be set on the server at the folder level.

I changed the FTP password for the site and now my users are complaining that they can't access the site. How do I resolve this?

Most likely, what has happened is that the users who can't access the site haven't closed Contribute since the password was changed. Have them close Contribute and open it back up. They should then be able to access the site via FTP once again. If the password to the FTP site is changed while they have a session open, Contribute continues sending the previous password, which results in errors. When they close Contribute, the updated password is transmitted and they can reconnect properly.

I have WebDAV set up on my local network to track versions of files. Can I use it to track changes in Contribute as well?

No. Contribute does not work with versioning software such as Visual SourceSafe and WebDAV. To track versions of pages in Contribute, enable the rollback feature.

BEST PRACTICES—MINIMUM SETTINGS THAT SHOULD BE SET FOR ADMINISTRATORS

A couple of settings in the Administrative section of Contribute should be set up if a connection key is ever sent to a user. First, be sure that you create an administrator password that follows the strong password guidelines. This means that the password should contain a mixture of upper- and lowercase alphabetic characters, numeric characters, and special characters. In addition, try to avoid words that you can find in the dictionary. Instead, find a representation of a phrase that you can easily remember. For instance, a good example is something such as the phrase "My mother loves me today," which can be turned into Mmlmt_352. When changing an administrative password, you need to know what the old password was, so keep track of that information.

Second, be sure that the administrative contact email is set to a valid email address that is monitored. This email address is available to all the Contribute users as the contact for issues regarding the site. Therefore, it needs to be monitored so that someone can address user issues in a timely manner.

Finally, unless you absolutely do not have the space available, consider turning on the rollback feature. This feature is basically the undo feature within Contribute and will save you a lot of grief should something go wrong in the publishing process.

USING FLASHPAPER

In this chapter

INTRODUCING FLASHPAPER

FlashPaper 2 is a plug-in application that is automatically installed with Contribute 3. FlashPaper is a new content management tool that converts an existing document into a Flash movie or PDF that can be inserted into any web page. The nice thing about FlashPaper is that the FlashPaper interface enables you to zoom in and out and even search the document text. In addition, by placing the document inside a Flash movie, you can ensure cross-browser compatibility through the use of the Flash Player plug-in.

CONVERTING A DOCUMENT TO FLASHPAPER

FlashPaper 2 provides several different methods for converting a document to the FlashPaper format. Documents can be converted from within Microsoft Word, from the Windows Explorer environment, or even from within Contribute.

CONVERTING A MICROSOFT WORD DOCUMENT TO FLASHPAPER FROM WITHIN WORD

One easy way to convert your Microsoft Word documents to FlashPaper movies is to use the FlashPaper menu added to Word when FlashPaper was installed. As shown in Figure 33.1, the FlashPaper menu enables you to create a Flash movie or PDF file with the click of your mouse.

Figure 33.1
The FlashPaper menu is added to Microsoft Word when FlashPaper is installed with Contribute.

33

After a document has been converted, it can be inserted into any web page as a Flash object.

TIP

> After FlashPaper is installed, the FlashPaper menu also exists in Microsoft Excel and PowerPoint. Following the same process, you can also publish Excel worksheets and PowerPoint presentations as FlashPaper.

TIP

> Mac users can convert a document to FlashPaper by choosing File, Print and then selecting FlashPaper as the printer option.

CONVERTING DOCUMENTS FROM WITHIN WINDOWS EXPLORER

A second option for converting a document to FlashPaper is to navigate to the document in Windows Explorer and right-click on the document. From the context menu, shown in Figure 33.2, you can choose whether to create a Flash document or PDF document.

Figure 33.2
The context menu from within the Windows Explorer environment.

Just as it does when converting documents from within Word, the FlashPaper application asks you to select an output destination for the new Flash movie and then converts the document to FlashPaper.

INSERTING FLASHPAPER FROM WITHIN CONTRIBUTE

Inserting a FlashPaper document into a web page from within Contribute is a simple process. If you have already created the FlashPaper Flash movie from within Microsoft Word or the Windows Explorer environment, you can add the movie to the page by going to the Contribute menu bar and choosing Insert, Flash, From My Computer. Then browse to the location of the Flash movie and add it to your page. Because the movie was created with the FlashPaper application, it contains the same zoom, search, and print options that all FlashPaper objects have. In addition, the object also has resize handles that enable you to adjust the size of the movie to fit your page design (see Figure 33.3).

If you haven't converted the document to FlashPaper yet, the other option is to insert the FlashPaper document from within Contribute by using the Insert, Document with FlashPaper command. To convert a document, browse to the file's location and select it. Contribute then asks you to specify the attributes of the FlashPaper that will be created (see Figure 33.4).

After the FlashPaper is inserted into the page, it is the exact size that you specified in the FlashPaper Options dialog box. If you need to resize the document to fit your page design, drag the resize handles to make any adjustments.

33

Figure 33.3
The FlashPaper movie has been inserted into your page and is resizable.

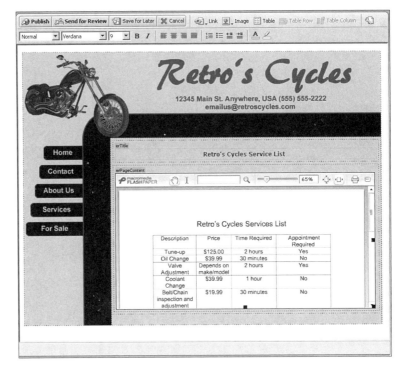

Figure 33.4
Specify the attributes for the resulting FlashPaper document.

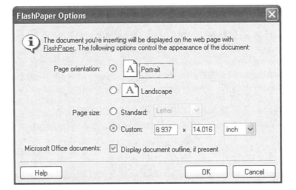

SEARCHING FOR TEXT

Similar to the interface used to search text in PDF documents, the FlashPaper interface provides a search tool that enables you to find text inside your FlashPaper movies (see Figure 33.5).

To search for text, type your search string in the text box and click the magnifying glass icon to conduct the search. If the first result is not the instance of the keyword or phrase you are looking for, click the magnifying glass again until you find the results you want.

Figure 33.5
The FlashPaper search interface.

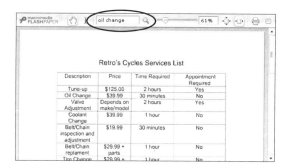

SELECTING TEXT

FlashPaper also enables you to select text stored in a FlashPaper document by using the Select Text tool that looks like an IBeam on the toolbar (see Figure 33.6). Using this tool, you can highlight text and copy and paste it into another document by using the Ctrl+C keyboard command in Windows or Command-C in the Mac OS.

Figure 33.6
The Select Text tool enables you to copy content from a FlashPaper movie.

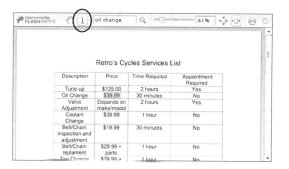

Be aware that there is no copy command on the context menu for the FlashPaper file, so the Ctrl+C command is the only way to copy content from a FlashPaper movie. In addition, because you cannot affect the contents of the FlashPaper without republishing it, you cannot cut content from the movie and the Ctrl+X command does not function.

EDITING FLASHPAPER CONTENT

FlashPaper documents are simply snapshots of what your document looked like at the point when the movie was generated. As a result, updates to the base document that you used to generate the FlashPaper do not automatically propagate to the FlashPaper.

This means that when you want to update your FlashPaper content, you need to update the base document, remove the existing FlashPaper document from your page, and then insert a newly generated FlashPaper object. You can also simply save over the existing FlashPaper object and any pages that contain references to that object display the newly created document.

CREATING HYPERLINKS FOR USE IN FLASHPAPER OBJECTS

When a FlashPaper object is created, any hyperlinks found in the base document are automatically converted to clickable links in the FlashPaper. Therefore, creating hyperlinks inside a FlashPaper is as simple as selecting the appropriate text and choosing Insert, Hyperlink from within the Word, Excel, or PowerPoint document. Using the corresponding dialog box in that application, create the hyperlink, save the page, and then publish your FlashPaper.

CREATING AN OUTLINE

One very handy feature that FlashPaper offers to accommodate long documents is the outline feature. If an outline exists in the base Word document, FlashPaper can create a corresponding outline with clickable links to the various sections based on that outline.

The trick, however, is that you have to use style headings to indicate where the different sections are for the outline to be generated appropriately. So if you have created a particularly long document that could benefit from an outline, be sure that you go through it and assign headings for your different sections.

In addition, in the FlashPaper Options dialog box, be sure to check the Display Document Outline check box, if it is present (see Figure 33.7).

Figure 33.7
Check the box to display the outline if you have created one for your document.

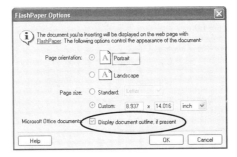

TROUBLESHOOTING

I inserted a FlashPaper document into my page and it was inserted at its native size. This adversely affected my page layout. How can I reduce the size of the FlashPaper object?

There are two ways to resolve this issue. The first is to reconsider the size that you indicated in the FlashPaper attributes. By default, the resulting movie is the same size as the original base document, so decreasing the height and width reduces the object size and probably causes it to fit better into your site design.

The second option is to manually resize the object by clicking on the FlashPaper in Edit mode and resizing it by dragging the resize handles. Following this method enables you to easily control the object's size and determine which size fits best without having to export the object over and over.

I installed FlashPaper, but now when I try to convert a document I get an error stating that the FlashPaper printer was not found. What can I do?

Most likely, the FlashPaper printer driver did not install correctly on your machine during the FlashPaper installation. You can download the FlashPaper driver from the Macromedia site at http://tofu.macromedia.com/fpinstaller/FlashPaperDriverInstall2.zip. Installing the printer driver manually should resolve the issue.

BEST PRACTICES—CHOOSING FLASHPAPER OR PDF FOR YOUR DOCUMENT MANAGEMENT MODEL

You may have noticed that FlashPaper is capable of creating PDF documents as well as Flash movies. This might, in turn, spark the question as to which document platform is better and why. Over the last few years, Adobe has really advanced document management by developing the PDF format to its current state. PDFs are excellent because they are snapshots of a document that can be made non-editable. From personal experience in the legal industry, the PDF format has been very useful because documents can be submitted and there is no question about whether or not they have been altered. Other formats, such as Word or Excel documents, don't offer the same level of security.

The only downside to the PDF format has been the reader required to view the documents. To read a PDF, you have to install the Adobe Reader on your machine, and then, each time you open a PDF document, the Reader application has to open and process the document before either sending it to the browser for rendering or displaying it natively in the Reader application.

FlashPaper is Macromedia's attempt to improve on this document management model by allowing the document to be captured in a static, uneditable format similar to that of a PDF document, while reducing load time for the document significantly. Because the Flash Player is already installed on the vast majority of machines connected to the web, no additional download or installation is required. In addition, the Flash Player always renders Flash movies in the browser, ensuring that the user doesn't have to wait for the helper application to initialize and process the document, as is the case with Acrobat Reader.

On the other hand, your users might be accustomed to PDF documents because they have become the standard for document management on the web over the last few years and switching to the FlashPaper model might cause some confusion. Therefore, I would suggest generating and providing access to documents in both formats while the popularity of FlashPaper grows. Then, as your user base becomes more comfortable with using FlashPaper documents instead of PDF documents, you can slowly phase out the PDF versions.

33

PUTTING IT ALL TOGETHER: USING CONTRIBUTE TO MANAGE SITE CONTENT

In this chapter

The last piece of the puzzle of building a site for Retro's Cycles is enabling the organization to manage certain aspects of their own site. As you saw in the Dreamweaver chapters, one way to do this would be to build the site using strictly database-driven content and then build an administrative section of the site to allow the client to log in and modify their page content.

Although this might make sense for a large company that has to maintain hundreds or thousands of pages, it's probably not worth the time and development cost to create an online content management system in this situation.

In the past, the only other alternative was to turn over the keys to the entire site and then, when an accident happened and an employee compromised the page layout, the page would have to be restored from backup or the site creator would have to be re-engaged to fix the problem.

Contribute provides a happy medium between these two extremes by providing a low-cost solution that enables you to enforce template-based structures to allow content to be updated while avoiding alterations of the page layout.

CREATING A CONTRIBUTE CONNECTION FOR RETRO'S CYCLES

The first step in setting up the content management system with Contribute is to create a site for Retro's Cycles.

NOTE

> Yes, yet another connection. Throughout the book you have seen the creation of several connections, including a ColdFusion connection to the database which, in turn, provided access to a Dreamweaver connection and now a Contribute connection. Be sure that you understand the differences between the connections and why each is important.

1. Open Contribute.
2. From the menu bar, choose Edit, My Connections.
3. In the My Connections dialog box, shown in Figure 34.1, click the Create button.

Figure 34.1
The My Connections dialog box enables you to connect to websites.

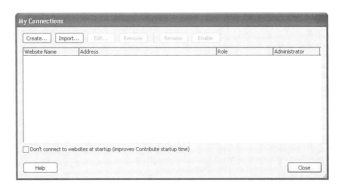

4. In the Create Connection dialog box (see Figure 34.2), click Next because you don't have a connection key.

Figure 34.2
Because you don't have a connection key, you need to create a connection manually.

5. In the URL field for the website, type the URL to the site you have been creating for Retro's Cycles. If you followed the defaults throughout the book, the URL is http://localhost/retroscycles (see Figure 34.3).

Figure 34.3
Add the URL to the site to which you are connecting.

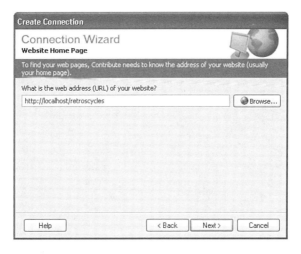

34

6. Because the site is located on your local hard drive, choose to connect to the site via Local/Network (see Figure 34.4). Click the Choose button and browse to the local folder that contains your pages. If you have been following the defaults, the path is c:\InetPub\wwwroot\retroscycles.

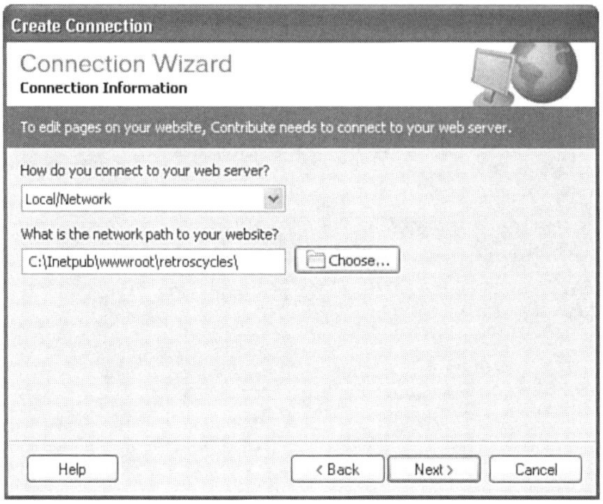

Figure 34.4
Choose the connection type for your site.

7. Next, Type your full name and email address. This information helps to identify who made changes to a page for review purposes (see Figure 34.5).

Figure 34.5
Type your identification information.

8. The last step in creating the connection is to review the information you just entered (see Figure 34.6). If corrections need to be made, click the Back button until you reach the page you want to correct. If the information is correct, click the Done button.

9. When the connection has been created, it is visible in the My Connections dialog box. From this dialog, you can edit the connection settings and administer the website settings.

Figure 34.6
Confirm that the connection information is correct.

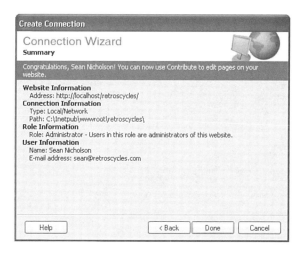

SETTING UP USERS VIA CONNECTION KEYS

Now that you have the connection created, the next step is to invite the appropriate people to become editors of the site. Do this by sending them a connection key, which they will install on their local machines. When clicked, this key automatically adds the site connection to Contribute on their local machines and sets the authorization level for their accounts. In the case of Retro's Cycles, two people will be managing the content of the site. Nancy is the sales manager and has agreed to take responsibility for the website. But because she is busy at times, she has asked that Joe, one of the parts guys who is pretty knowledgeable about computers, be able to create pages that she can review and approve before publishing them to the site.

The roles that Nancy has described for herself and Joe are those of Publisher and Writer. Nancy needs to be able to edit content and publish changes to the site, whereas Joe needs to be able to edit content and save drafts for Nancy to review and publish. To create these permission levels, follow these steps:

1. In the My Connections dialog box, click the Administer button in the upper-right corner. Contribute opens a dialog box indicating that you can choose the environment in which you would like your users to edit.

2. Because the staff of Retro's Cycles are comfortable with using a word processor, choose the standard word processing environment and click Yes to indicate that you want to become the Administrator for the site.

3. In the Administer Website dialog box, shown in Figure 34.7, select the User and Roles category. This dialog shows users who are part of the site and enables you to invite others to have a role in managing content. Click the Send Connection Key button to send a key to Nancy.

34

Figure 34.7
The Administer Website dialog box allows you to configure users and their roles.

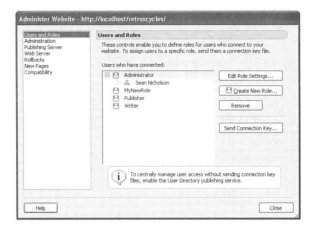

4. In the Send Connection Key dialog box (see Figure 34.8), choose Yes to send the current connection settings. Click Next.

Figure 34.8
Choose to send the current connection settings.

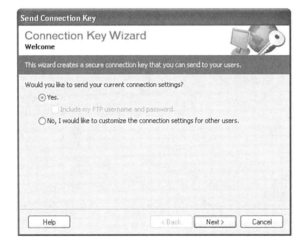

5. Because Nancy will be a Publisher for the site, choose Publisher and click Next.

6. To communicate the connection key, you'll be sending the key to Nancy via email, so choose the Send in Email radio button and then type a unique password for Contribute to use for the base of the encryption key (see Figure 34.9).

Figure 34.9
Type the password that will be used for the base encryption.

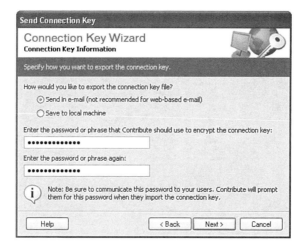

7. Finally, review the connection key settings shown in Figure 34.10 and click OK if everything appears to be correct.

Figure 34.10
Review the encryption key settings.

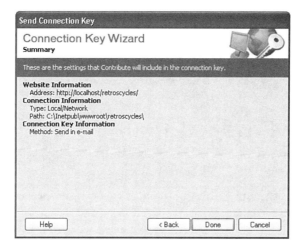

8. With the connection key settings configured, Contribute spawns an email in your default mail client that includes the encryption key as an attachment (see Figure 34.11). The recipient need only click on the attachment to install the key.

NOTE

When Nancy receives her email, she also needs to know the password that you set up for the base of her encryption, so be sure to communicate that password to her in a way other than in the same email that sends the encryption key.

34

Figure 34.11
Send an email to
the user with the
encryption key as
an attachment.

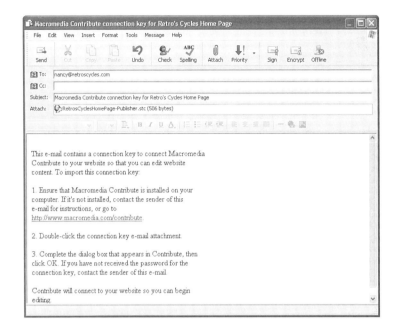

9. Next, follow through the same steps to create an encryption key for Joe, only set him up as a Writer rather than a Publisher.

10. When completed, close the My Connection dialog box by clicking Close.

BROWSING THE EXISTING LAYOUT

Before you start adding content to the pages, you should take a look at how the Contribute browser works and examine the site's current structure.

1. When the site was configured in Contribute, the home page of the site was opened in the Contribute browser (see Figure 34.12). Roll your mouse over the rollover links on the left side of the home page and notice that they change state as expected.

2. Next, click the Contact button and notice that the browser renders the contact.cfm page. Click through the About Us and Services links and they render the appropriate links as well.

3. Click the For Sale button and notice that the database-driven table created in Dreamweaver is displaying correctly (see Figure 34.13).

Figure 34.12
The home page is displayed in the browser and the rollover links function as expected.

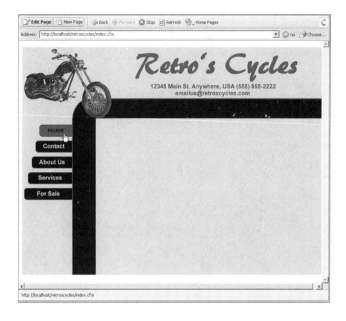

Figure 34.13
The dynamic table displays the correct content.

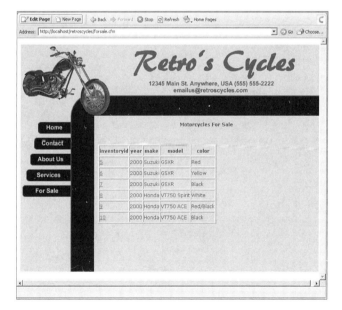

4. Click on any of the links in the inventoryid column and note that the Contribute browser loads the details for that record (see Figure 34.14).

Figure 34.14
The dynamic details are displayed correctly as well.

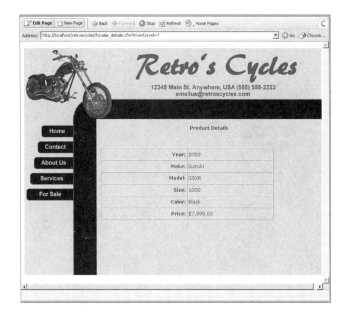

Now that you know that the hyperlinks work as expected, you can start adding content to the blank pages.

ADDING CONTENT TO THE PAGES

With the site connection configured and the user encryption keys sent, the next step is to use Contribute to add the base content that the staff of Retro's Cycles will use to build their site. At this point, you are adding placeholder text that indicates to Nancy and Joe what type of content they should be placing in the site. To create the placeholder text, follow these steps:

1. In the Contribute browser, click the link to the home page.

2. To edit the page, click the Edit Page button in the upper-left corner of the browser. Contribute switches to Edit mode and the Contribute toolbar changes, replacing the navigation buttons with editing buttons (see Figure 34.15).

3. Because these pages are based on a Dreamweaver template, Contribute recognizes the markup and allows you to access only the `erTitle` and `erPageContent` editable regions. Place your cursor in the `erTitle` editable region.

4. In the editable region, type **Welcome to Retro's Cycles**. Highlight the text and click the Bold button on the button bar. Change the font style and size to Arial, 12. Note that Contribute automatically creates a style for you named Style1 that you can reuse throughout the page (see Figure 34.16).

Figure 34.15
Switch Contribute to
Edit mode.

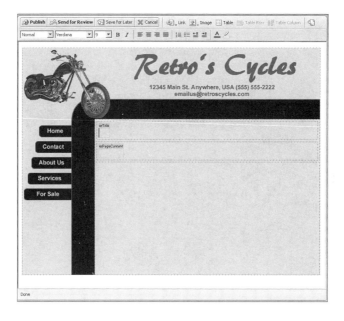

Figure 34.16
Add a title to the page
and create a style
based on the title.

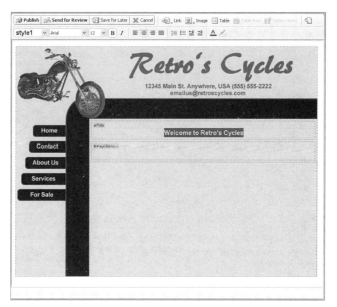

5. Next, place your cursor in the erPageContent editable region and type **Add introductory page content here** (see Figure 34.17).

Figure 34.17
Add the placeholder text to the page.

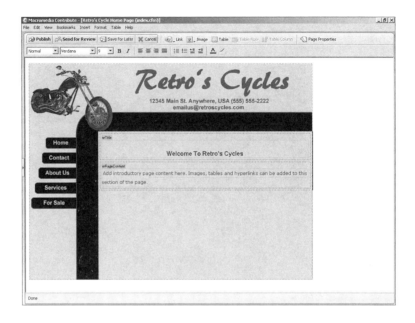

NOTE

Don't worry if the page layout starts to look a little strange when you add new content. As soon as you publish the changes, the layout returns to normal.

6. Note in Figure 34.17 that the default font for the page has automatically been set to a sans serif typeface. In addition, notice that the title of the page—Retro's Cycle Home Page—displays in the application bar of Contribute. You need to update this to read "Retro's Cycles Home Page" instead. To do this, click the Page Properties icon in the browser's upper-right corner.

7. In the Page Properties dialog box, you can select from the various page settings that are editable. Adjust the title so that it reads "Retro's Cycles Home Page," as shown in Figure 34.18. Click OK to close the dialog box.

Figure 34.18
Adjust the page title so it reads correctly.

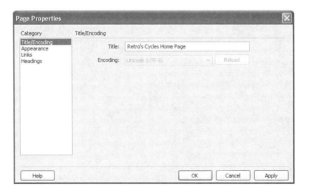

8. To apply the changes to the page, click the Publish button in the Contribute bar. Contribute displays a pop-up box (see Figure 34.19) letting you know that the content was published successfully.

Figure 34.19
The adjusted page content has been published.

9. Click OK to close the message and Contribute renders the new page in the browser.

Following the same steps, you can easily add placeholder text for each empty page in the site. This would provide Nancy and Joe with a starting point to determine what content they need to develop before publicizing the site to their customers.

ADDING FLASHPAPER DOCUMENTS

One additional content element that Retro's Cycles indicated they wanted on their site is a price list of the various services that they offer. They have the price list in a Microsoft Word document and, rather than retyping it into HTML, they want to place it on the site as a FlashPaper document.

1. To add the document to the site in Flashpaper, navigate to the Services page in the Contribute browser.

2. Click the Edit Page button to switch to Edit mode.

3. Place your cursor in the erTitle editable region and click the Align Center button on the Contribute toolbar.

4. In the editable region, type **Retro's Cycles Services**. Highlight the text and click the Bold button on the button bar. Change the font style and size to Arial, 12. Again, Contribute automatically creates a style for you named Style1 that you can reuse throughout the page (see Figure 34.20).

5. Place your cursor in the erPageContent editable region and click the Align Center button on the Contribute bar. In the editable region, type **Click here for a complete list of our services**.

6. Because the Word document does not fit in the template of the site, you must create a link to a new page and insert the FlashPaper object into that file. Highlight the text and click the Link button on the Contribute bar. From the drop-down, choose Create New Page.

34

Figure 34.20
The title has been added to the Services page.

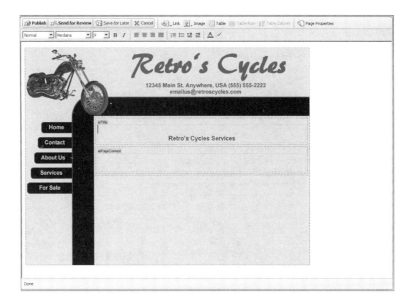

7. In the Insert Link dialog box, choose Blank Web Page and type `Retro's Cycles Price List` in the New Page Title field (see Figure 34.21). Click OK to create the new blank page.

Figure 34.21
The Insert Link dialog box enables you to create a new page and link to it.

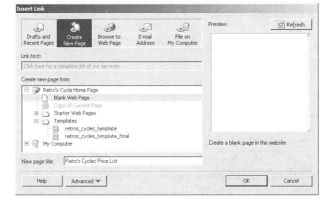

8. Click OK to create the new page.

9. From the menu bar, choose Insert, Document with FlashPaper. Browse to the `retros_cycles_services.doc` document, located in the images folder of the site, and click Open.

10. From the FlashPaper Options dialog box, shown in Figure 34.22, accept the default settings and click OK.

Figure 34.22
Accept the defaults for the new FlashPaper file.

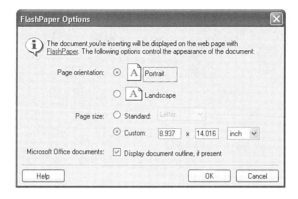

11. Wait a few seconds while FlashPaper converts the document and places it into the page (see Figure 34.23).

Figure 34.23
The FlashPaper document has been placed in the page.

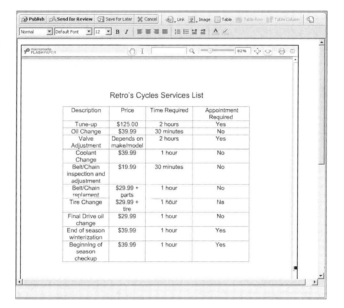

12. Click the Publish button. In the Publish New Page dialog box, shown in Figure 34.24, name the file `service_list.cfm` and click Publish.

Figure 34.24
Publish the new page to your site.

13. To finalize the link to the page, click the Back button in the Contribute bar to switch to the Services page. Click the Edit Page button and then click Publish to apply the changes to the page.

As you can see, using Contribute to manage website content is easy and flexible. The wide range of editing tools offered by Contribute can help you enable clients and coworkers to manage their own content without having to worry about adversely affecting site design.

Troubleshooting

I can't find the retros_cycles_services.doc *document that you reference. Where can I find it?*

If you worked through the Dreamweaver section of the book, the document is located in the images folder of the site that you created earlier. If you haven't worked through that section of the book, you need to download the support files from the companion site.

When testing the rollover links, I don't see where to roll over in the far left of the Contribute interface. Where should I look?

The rollover links are tested in the far left of the page, not in the far left of the Contribute interface.

Best Practices—Contribute Versus Content Management Systems

When developing a website for a client or in an environment where others will be maintaining the content, there is always the question of which content management tool is appropriate. In many cases, Contribute provides the solution. However, a browser-based content management system is more appropriate in others.

When developing a site, one of the first questions you should ask yourself is whether your content will be embedded into the page or drawn from a database. If the answer is in a database, Contribute won't do you much good. Contribute isn't capable of editing database-driven content, so it would be more appropriate to look toward building a browser-based content management system. Browser-based systems usually must be homegrown and therefore take time to develop. In addition, a higher level of training must often be offered to end users before they are comfortable with the process of maintaining content.

Sites that feature static content, on the other hand, benefit from the features that Contribute has to offer. Contribute's low cost and easy-to-use interface offer a quick way to get your end users up to speed quickly. In addition, inexpensive training on Contribute is offered in a variety of formats, ranging from web tutorials to print books.

So, when planning your next web project, be sure to think about the content maintenance aspect and which tool might be more beneficial to your client or your project in the long run. Both options have their pros and cons. Taking the time to perform the analysis prior to the development phase can help you determine which would be appropriate.

INDEX

How can we make this index more useful? Email us at indexes@quepublishing.com

bitmaps (Flash)
 blurry, 206
 breaking apart, 190
 caching, 164
 compressing, 187
 file size, 185
 importing, 186
 optimizing, 189-190
 saving, 184
 tracing, 187-190
 vector fills, 195
 vector graphics,
  compared, 184-185
Contribute, 622-624
exporting (Fireworks)
 as HTML, 121-122
 web graphics,
  119-121
frames (Fireworks),
 88-89
GIFs
 animated, 96, 103
 background images,
  460
 optimizing, 116-118
integrating (Fireworks)
 Director, 125-126
 Dreamweaver, 122
 Flash, 124-125
JPEGs
 background images,
  460
 optimizing, 114-116
layers (Fireworks), 86-87
 expanding/collapsing,
  87
 Layers panel, 87-88
 locking/unlocking, 87
 moving, 88
 naming, 88

shared/unshared,
 89-90
 stacking order, 88
 viewing/hiding, 87
 web, 90
loading (Flash), 294
navigation bars with
 four-state buttons
 (Fireworks), 93-95
optimizing, 108
 compression, 108-109
 dithering, 109
 Optimize panel. See
  Optimize panel
  (Fireworks)
 troubleshooting, 126
resolution, 184
rollovers (Dreamweaver)
 creating, 548
 naming, 548
 preloading, 548
 remote, 549-550
slicing, 152
slide shows (Flash),
 558-559
stylized, 142-143
templates, 147
vector, 85
 animations, 96
 bitmaps, compared,
  184-185, 195
 curves, 126
 editing, 197-198
 file size, 185
 fills, 192-195, 206
 gradients, 194
 importing, 196
 layers, 86
 lines, 190-192
 Object Drawing
  mode, 194

paths, 85
saving, 184
tools (Fireworks). See
 vectors, tools

**Grid, Edit Grid command
(Flash View menu), 202**

grids (Flash), 202

**grippers (Dreamweaver),
424**

groups (Dreamweaver)
 behaviors, 544
 panels, 422
  Application, 425
  arranging, 423-424
  closing, 424
  CSS, 424
  docking/undocking,
   424
  expanding, 422
  Files, 427
  grippers, 424
  maximizing/minimizi
   ng, 424
  Results, 430-432
  sizing, 424
  Tag, 426

**guides (Flash), 202,
226-228**

H

**Head Content command
(Dreamweaver View
menu), 475**

Help menu commands
 Contribute, 611
 Fireworks, 75, 137

**Hide Pop-Up Menu
behavior
(Dreamweaver), 546**

Optimize panel (Fireworks), 75, 110-112
  Optimize to Size command, 112
  settings
    GIF, 116-118
    JPEG, 114-116
    saving, 112-114

Optimize to Size dialog box (Fireworks), 112

optimizing
  bitmaps, 189-190
  curves, 32, 198
  graphics, 108
    compression, 108-109
    dithering, 109
    Optimize panel. *See* Optimize panel (Fireworks)
    troubleshooting, 126

optional regions, 529

Options menu commands (Dreamweaver), 424

or operator, 239

ordered lists (Dreamweaver), 438

organizing snippets (Dreamweaver), 479

Orientation attribute (<cfdocument> tag), 384

Outdent command (Dreamweaver Text menu), 437

outlines (FlashPaper), 650

Oval Marquee tool (Fireworks), 49

Oval tool (Flash), 27, 178

Over states (buttons), 93

Over While Down states (buttons), 93

overflow (Dreamweaver layers), 520

overlapping shapes, 23

Overwrite attribute
  <cfdocument> tag, 384
  <cfreport> tag, 382

OwnerPassword attribute
  <cfdocument> tag, 384
  <cfreport> tag, 382

P

<p> tag, 433

Page Properties dialog box (Dreamweaver), 435
  backgrounds, 459-461
  color
    links, 462-463, 467
    text, 461-462
  margins, 461

PageHeight attribute (<cfdocument> tag), 384

PageType attribute (<cfdocument> tag), 384

PageWidth attribute (<cfdocument> tag), 384

Paint Bucket (Flash), 179, 192

panels, 18-20
  docking/undocking, 20
  Dreamweaver, 422
    Application, 425
    Assets. *See* Assets panel
    Attributes, 427
    Behaviors, 427, 544
    Bindings, 577
    Components, 425
    CSS Styles, 491
    customizing, 414
    Databases, 425
    Files, 427
    Frames, 428, 515-516
    groups, 422-424
    hiding, 37
    History, 429-430
    Property inspector, 422
    Results, 430-432
    Server Behaviors, 425, 578
    Snippets, 428, 542
    Tag, 426
    Timelines, 562
  finding, 37
  Fireworks, 45, 75
    Assets, 76-78
    Frames, 88-89
    Frames and History, 78-79
    History, 134-135
    Layers, 75, 87-88
    Optimize. *See* Optimize panel
    Tools, 18, 22
  Flash, 167
    Actions, 168
    Align, 204
    Bitmap Properties, 187
    Color Mixer, 25, 167, 195
    Component Inspector, 309
    Components, 308
    Document Properties, 169